Autobiography and Independence
Selfhood and Creativity in North African Postcolonial Writing in French

Contemporary French and Francophone Cultures 2

DEBRA KELLY

Autobiography and Independence

Selfhood and Creativity in North African

Postcolonical Writing in French

LIVERPOOL UNIVERSITY PRESS

First published 2005 by
Liverpool University Press
4 Cambridge Street
Liverpool L69 7ZU

British Library Cataloguing-in-Publication data
A British Library CIP record is available

ISBN 0-85323-659-3 hardback

Typeset by XL Publishing Services, Tiverton
Printed and bound in the European Union by
Bell and Bain Ltd, Glasgow

Contents

Acknowledgements

I began research for this book with the encouragement of colleagues at the University of Westminster in what was then called the Maghreb Research Group, and I would especially like to thank Ethel Tolansky and Margaret Majumdar (both, sadly, no longer at Westminster) for stimulating my interest in North African writing in French. I have also been fortunate to work with several scholars in the field who have participated in the work of the former Association for the Study of African and Caribbean Literature in French (ASCALF), regrouped and renamed in 2002 as the Society for Francophone Postcolonial Studies; especially Andy Stafford, who read the manuscript with care and insight and made this a better book. I have had the opportunity to try out various sections of this book at research seminars and conferences in Britain and abroad, and I would like to thank colleagues and students who took the time to listen and comment. Of these events, three were especially useful: the 'Life/Writing' seminar that extended over three years (organised by Michael Sheringham and Johnnie Gratton at Royal Holloway, University of London); and conferences held in Tunisia (the Conseil International d'Etudes Francophones) and Morocco (organised by the British Council and the University of Nottingham). I have also had the pleasure of discussing the work of Assia Djebar particularly over the last three years with the students on the MA in Cultural Memory at the Institute of Romance Studies, School of Advanced Study, University of London, and many elements of those discussions are embedded here. On a practical level, enormous thanks go to Helena Scott, Research Coordinator at the University of Westminster, for help with the preparation of the manuscript at various stages and for her expertise in translation. On a personal level, my husband sustained me throughout a period of research and writing that unexpectedly coincided with a difficult period of our lives. Finally, thank you to Ed Smyth, my series editor, for originally suggesting that I develop work that had begun with the autobiographical discourses of Memmi and Camus, and for his patience.

This book is dedicated to my father, the son of an Irish immigrant, a poor man's son.

Copyright Acknowledgements

The author and publishers are grateful to the following for permission to reproduce copyright material: the Photography and Imaging Department at the British Museum, London, for the Dugga stele on page 303; Albin Michel (Publishers), Paris, for quotations from *L'Amour, La Fantasia* by Assia Djebar; Éditions Arléa (Publishers), Paris, for quotations from *Le Nomade immobile* by Albert Memmi; Gallimard (Publishers), Paris, for quotations from *La Statue de sel* and *Le Scorpion* by Albert Memmi; Éditions Denoël (Publishers), Paris, for quotations from *La Mémoire Tatouée* by Abdelkébir Khatibi; Éditions du Seuil, Paris, for quotations from *Le Fils du pauvre* © Éditions du Seuil, 1954, coll. Points, 1995; *L'Anniversaire* © Éditions du Seuil, 1972, coll. Points, 1989; *Journal (1955–1962)* © Éditions du Seuil, 1958, 1962; and *Lettres à ses amis* © Éditions du Seuil, 1969, all by Mouloud Feraoun.

Introduction:
A Place in the Word

Une vie d'écriture m'a appris à me méfier des mots. Ceux qui paraissent les plus limpides sont souvent les plus traîtres. L'un de ces faux amis est justement 'identité'. Nous croyons tous savoir ce que ce mot veut dire, et nous continuons à lui faire confiance même quand, insidieusement, il se met à dire le contraire.

Amin Maalouf, *Les Identités meutrières*[1]

(A life of writing has taught me to mistrust words. Those which seem the most transparent are often the most treacherous. One of those false friends is precisely 'identity'. We all think we know what that word means, and we continue to trust it even when, insidiously, it starts saying the opposite.)

This book explores the question of the relationship between the writer's self and literary expression. The work of each of the four writers studied here provides a space for a meditation on the act of literary creation and on the ways in which that act intervenes in the world. Mouloud Feraoun, Assia Djebar, Albert Memmi and Abdelkébir Khatibi were born in three different countries in North Africa (Algeria, Tunisia and Morocco) during the first half of the twentieth century, and have varied origins: Kabyle, Berber, Sephardi Jew, Arab.[2] They share a complex relationship to language, since all of them write in French, a legacy of colonial intervention in those countries, but this relationship varies according to differences in ethnic identity, class and gender. The texts studied here were published over a fifty-year period (the second half of the twentieth century) and they are therefore intimately bound up with the histories of European colonialism, war, decolonisation, and independence. The individuals who wrote them therefore engage not only with their own personal histories, but also with the collective histories of North Africa and of Europe. The notion of 'identity' is necessarily a focus of the readings here, even though, as Amin Maalouf, a Lebanese writer who lives in France, warns us above, this is a term that has been much used and abused. Not only are the origins and identities of these writers different from each other and complex in their own right, but so are those of the geographical region into which they were born.[3] Khatibi has written

1

about what he calls the 'plural' nature of the Maghreb, revealing the diversity of cultures that has at times been celebrated, at other times fought over, challenged, threatened with erasure, and that has nonetheless survived for centuries. North Africa has been, and continues to be, the site of both powerful clashes and mixing – of empires, religions and cultures. The work of the writers here is testament to this history and in many ways can be seen as restoring the complexity of cultural memory denied by both colonial and nationalist discourses.[4]

The corpus here is deliberately limited,[5] focusing on one or two works by each writer, to enable close readings of the writing strategies at work in texts that I have termed 'autobiographical discourses', rather than 'autobiographies'. I explain more fully my reasons for this terminology in the first chapter, which provides a theoretical introduction to the readings that follow. I would add here that the term 'discourses' is also preferred since it further allows this study to function within the broad theoretical framework of postcolonial studies, and again this is discussed more fully in the first chapter, as, indeed, are issues related to the term 'postcolonial' itself. I also use the concepts of 'postcolonial' and 'postcolonial writer' without the additional description 'Francophone', which carries within it, as I also explain further in Chapter 1, a political agenda linked to French colonialism, despite the recent convincing use of the term 'Francophone postcolonial studies' by colleagues in the field.[6] It was, of course, Edward Said who showed in his seminal work *Orientalism* that colonialism operated not only as a form of military rule but also as a discourse of domination, and that language and the forms of knowledge for which it is a vehicle are the sites of cultural assumptions.[7]

The term 'autobiographical discourses' is used not only to widen the debate concerning the definition of autobiography and because of the associations of 'discourse' with critical and postcolonial theory, but also because it indicates the complexity of the texts under analysis. These are texts that engage not only with the question of individual self-expression, but also with social, ideological and historical contexts, and as such they provide a form of political as well as personal discourse. I have accordingly also made use of feminist criticism on autobiographical discourses, particularly in its attention to experimental writing strategies as a form of personal and political (in the widest meaning of the term) resistance to dominant discourses.

From the 1950s onwards several writers in North Africa, among them the four studied here, sought to 'represent' (in both meanings of the word, to portray and to speak for) the experience of the colonised as a collective through the experiences of the individual. The question of 'representation' within the postcolonial context is a complex one, and both terms lend themselves to misunderstanding and to polemic. This has been explored, for example, by the critic Gayatri Spivak, in a seminal article for postcolonial studies in which she argues that the narratives of nationalism continue to 'construct' those she terms the 'genuinely disenfranchised', who therefore remain without voice or agency just as in colonial narratives. Spivak remains ambivalent concerning political representation.[8] This analysis of 'representation' has led to a considerable volume of criticism and counter-criticism concerning the development of nationalism and nationalist discourse and the role of the intellectual elite in countries formerly colonised by European powers. Neil Lazarus counters criticism of intellectuals by Spivak and other postcolonial theorists.[9] He reminds us that Edward Said placed great significance on literature 'as a specific medium of intellectual production' in the cause of anti-imperialism in the second half of the twentieth century and in the 're-establishment of a national and cultural heritage'.[10] Said argues that intellectuals, such as the writers under discussion here, have contributed to the processes of decolonisation by 'writing, thinking, speaking', becoming 'agents of illumination within the realm of the colonised'.[11] Lazarus urges postcolonial theorists to think again about 'the potentialities of intellectualism', potentialities that are clearly apparent to the writers analysed here. Certainly, the individual situation of each of these writers, while pointing up the situation of communities under colonisation and in the postcolonial world, is very particular, and not 'representative' of the wider experience of the majority of the community into which they were born. Nonetheless, in their engagement with questions concerning identity and the relationship between the individual and history, all of the writers studied here have contributed to the analysis of the effects of colonisation and of resistance to oppression on the identity of the individual, of the immediate community and of the nation.

Given these debates around the notion of 'representation', the terms 'individual' and 'collective' also need to be carefully considered, again an issue that I address in the first chapter. I would add a further reason for the necessity of this. The emphasis in critical studies, particularly by French critics, on North African writing in French has been on the 'collective voice' of such writings, often to the detriment of the analysis of very individual writing strategies, and again masking, whether deliberately or not, assumptions inherent in Eurocentric thinking concerning the organ-

isation of societies, and also concerning the 'literary value' of both the
novel and autobiography as genres.

The dangers of a Eurocentric position and thinking with regard to
the cultures and forms of cultural production of non-Western societies
have been debated by numerous postcolonial critics. The broad theoretical framework within which I am working will be developed in the
course of this study. Although readers will find useful a knowledge of the
work of (for example) Edward Said, Gayatri Spivak and Homi Bhabha,
and of the thinking of Foucault and Derrida as used in postcolonial
theory, my readings do not assume such knowledge beyond an appreciation that all of these thinkers address the issue of the power relations at
work between dominant and 'marginal' political, historical, social and
cultural discourses.[12] Such an approach follows the brief of this series,
which seeks to provide studies that are useful to students while incorporating current research in the field.

Each analysis provides a close textual reading that places an emphasis
on the writing strategies used by each of these writers to explore the issue
of identity, and that privileges the use of language and of textual structure. Clearly each one of these works has the potential to yield many
other types of reading, but this is the thread I have chosen to follow, in
order not only to uncover the complex relationship to 'identity' and to
the need for self-expression at work in individual texts, but also to try to
see what unites and/or divides these diverse creative interventions around
these issues. A further aim is to explore what we might learn more generally from these writers concerning both the politics and the poetics of the
autobiographical act, and concerning what may be termed the ethics and
the aesthetics of postcolonial literature.[13]

In the case of each writer I have emphasised the texts under discussion as being part of a larger 'life-writing' project, for an element that
links all of these writers is a meditation on individual experience that
finds multiple and diverse forms of expression, and that opens up the
potential for the understanding of a more universal experience. The question of the 'universal', particularly in a postcolonial Francophone space,
is, however, fraught with difficulties, and I shall return to this in the
conclusion.

In the case of Mouloud Feraoun (with whom I begin, since my readings proceed chronologically), not only is *Le Fils du pauvre* (1950)
analysed, but also his published letters and diaries, which have received
less critical attention. My aim is therefore to follow the construction of
a life story through expression in different narrative forms. Feraoun is

also an important starting point because his life story bears witness not only to a childhood and youth spent under French colonisation, but also to the events leading to independence in Algeria, which stand at one extreme of the experience of colonisation in the Francophone world. Feraoun's writing also sets up many of the themes that will be explored later by other writers, notably the need to understand the past in order to understand the present, the desire to retrieve personal and cultural memory from the erasure with which it has been, and continues to be, threatened, and the ambiguous position of the often isolated and marginalised writer and intellectual when confronting the cultures between which he or she stands in a (post)colonial world.

The work of Albert Memmi, a Tunisian Jew, is explored principally in relation to two texts, *La Statue de sel* (1953) and *Le Scorpion* (1969), although it should be emphasised that of all the writers here, his life's work in particular should be considered as a project based on the individual experience of having belonged to a minority all his life, as he himself has written. In this chapter, in addition to those shared themes indicated above, emphasis is placed on the way in which Memmi develops an experimental textual strategy in *Le Scorpion* in order to grapple more fully with the complexities of the written expression of selfhood and with the broader issues of identity in a colonial and postcolonial context.

Published two years after *Le Scorpion*, the Moroccan Abdelkébir Khatibi's *La Mémoire tatouée* (1971) also develops a multi-layered, multi-voiced textual strategy in order to work through the process of decolonising the self, presenting itself as the *autobiographie d'un décolonisé* in its subtitle and, despite the violence in expression in much of the text, offering finally the potential for a reconciliation of the multiple elements of the writer's identity.

Two texts by Assia Djebar, *L'Amour, la fantasia* (1985) and *Vaste est la prison* (1995), two parts of a larger four-volume project, bring the voice and writing of a woman to this exploration of selfhood. The lack of attention to gender in the founding discourses of postcolonial theory has been criticised by feminist thinkers, and Djebar's work provides a focus for the personal and collective histories of Algerian women under colonialism, during the Algerian War and after independence. Like Khatibi, Djebar is intensely bound up with the issue of writing in French; the consequences of this for her relationship to her oral mother tongue, and therefore to the community of women in her culture, are constantly returned to in her work. Like all the writers here, Assia Djebar commits herself to a quest for the retrieval of historical and cultural memory, for knowledge and self-knowledge, in a complex interweaving between archaic past and collective and personal recent past and present. She also develops experimental writing strategies to express selfhood, as is the case in the work of Memmi and Khatibi. All these writers give narrative form to the issue of identity in the contemporary world and to the need to constantly renegotiate a way of being in the historical situations in which they live or lived.

Finally, with regard to the critical approach adopted here, I have avoided using psychoanalytical criticism in a way that may appear surprising in a study so bound up with the notion of selfhood and literary creativity. Despite the success with which some critics have used psycho-analytical methodologies in reading these types of text, and more fundamentally, despite the ways in which seminal texts by Fanon and Memmi analyse the effects of colonisation on the psyche of both colonised and coloniser, my own engagement is informed by issues of cultural difference and also by the political nature of these texts as defined by Gilles Deleuze and Félix Guattari.

In their study of Kafka, Deleuze and Guattari analyse three charac-teristics of what they term 'minor literature'. While we might want to reconsider that label, they make clear what they mean by this: the liter-ature of a minority expressed in a 'major' language, a situation that describes writers working in French in the North African context. Deleuze and Guattari sum up these three characteristics in the following way: 'la déterritorialisation de la langue, le branchement de l'individuel sur l'immédiat-politique, l'agencement collectif d'énonciation'[14] ('the deterritorialisation of language, the connecting of the individual onto the political-immediate, the collective construction of enunciation'). The first will become evident in the analysis of the writing strategies under discus-sion here, the third I will be questioning during the course of this study, as previously indicated. The second is relevant for this introductory section, since Deleuze and Guattari's analysis of the political raises ques-tions concerning the (non-)viability of classical psychoanalytical approaches to literature when reading a 'minor' literature. In fact Deleuze and Guattari advocate that in 'minor' literature, everything is political ('tout y est politique'):

> Dans les 'grandes' littératures [...] l'affaire individuelle (familiale, conju-gale, etc.) tend à rejoindre d'autres affaires non moins individuelles, le milieu social servant d'environnement et d'arrière-fond; si bien qu'aucune de ces affaires oedipiennes n'est indispensable en particulier, n'est absolument nécessaire, mais que toutes 'font bloc' dans un large espace. La littérature mineure est tout à fait différente: son espace exigu fait que chaque affaire

individuelle est immédiatement branchée sur la politique. L'affaire individuelle devient donc autant plus nécessaire, indispensable, grossie au
microscope, qu'une toute autre histoire agite en elle. C'est en ce sens que le
triangle familial se connecte aux autres triangles, commerciaux,
économiques, bureaucratiques, juridiques, qui en déterminent les valeurs.
Lorsque Kafka indique parmi les buts d'une littérature mineure 'l'épuration
du conflit qui oppose père et fils et la possibilité d'en discuter', il ne s'agit
pas d'un fantasme oedipien, mais d'un programme politique.[15]

(In 'great' literatures [...] individual matters (family matters, conjugal
matters, etc.) tend to join up with others which are no less individual, the
social surroundings serving as environment and back-drop; so that none of
those Oedipal matters is indispensable in particular, nor absolutely necessary, but all 'form a block' in a large space. Minor literature is completely
different: its small space makes it necessary for each individual matter to be
immediately connected onto politics. Therefore the individual matter
becomes all the more necessary, indispensable, enlarged under the microscope, because a completely different story is at work within it. It is in this
sense that the family triangle is connected to the other triangles – commer-
cial, economic, bureaucratic, juridical – which all determine its values.
When Kafka indicates among the goals of minor literature, 'the purge of
the conflict which opposes father and son and the possibility of arguing
about it', he's not talking about an Oedipal fantasy but a political
programme.)

While I wish to remain careful concerning the labelling of these texts as
'political' to avoid an identification with dismissive readings of
Francophone literature by French critics as 'documentary', with little
intrinsic 'literary' value (I shall be arguing the very opposite, with an
emphasis on the texts' poetics as well as their politics), all the works
studied here do privilege a political agenda as well as a personal one.
Albert Memmi's presentation of the father–son conflict in *La Statue de
sel* is an illustration of Deleuze and Guattari's point. Above all Western
psychoanalysis promotes an ego that is self-projecting, and does not take
into account different values of self in other cultural contexts.[16] Edward
Said has also pointed out that, while Freud was certainly deeply interested in what we would now call the 'other' and also in 'universal'
behaviour, his was a Eurocentric view of culture. Indeed, Said doubts
whether Freud thought that he would have non-European readers.[17]

This is, of course, not to say that the texts analysed here are not generated by a psychological situation with far-reaching consequences. Indeed,
the reader must also 'disclose' himself or herself in relation to these life-
writing projects.[18] These writers also force us as readers to engage actively
with the question: 'Who am I?'. The writing strategies of many autobiographical texts, and certainly not exclusively those produced in colonial
and postcolonial contexts, implicate the readers and force them to turn

their gaze on themselves, rather than exhibiting self-obsession on the part of the writer, as might popularly be thought of the autobiographical genre. When we begin reading these texts it is important, therefore, to be aware of our own assumptions, whether cultural, political, gendered, generational, or based on our own personal experiences, and to be aware of our limitations; for example, I am a European, British-educated woman with a limited experience of North African culture. We should also be aware of our potential: we want to engage with these writers and can bring our own reading and life experiences to bear on them in a creative and productive way.

CHAPTER 1

Life/Writing in the Colonial and Postcolonial Contexts

Le portrait de l'artiste par lui-même ne saurait être qu'une composition de marqueterie, un puzzle à pièces multiples, qu'il faut patiemment assembler; mêmes si certaines se sont perdues et demeurent introuvables.

Albert Memmi, *Ce que je crois*[1]

(The portrait of the artist by himself can only be a marquetry-composition, a jigsaw-puzzle with many pieces that have to be patiently put together; even if some have got lost and can never be found.)

AUTOBIOGRAPHY, AUTOBIOGRAPHICAL EXPRESSION, FICTIONS OF IDENTITY

The initial question of defining the status of the texts under analysis here, and therefore of defining some of the aims of this book, is a complex one. The issue of attributing the label 'autobiography' is difficult for a variety of reasons, all interlinked and each worthy of discussion in its own right, even though the writers considered here have all, at some point, made explicit the autobiographical nature of the texts analysed here. First, none of the texts that will be discussed in the course of this book can be called an autobiography in the strictest sense of the term. Certainly none of them is described as such on the front cover, and although the subtitle of Abdelkébir Khatibi's *La Mémoire tatouée* describes the text as the 'autobiographie d'un décolonisé' ('autobiography of a decolonised man') on the inside cover, the term *roman* ('novel') is used on the front cover, as it is for both of the texts by Assia Djebar, *L'Amour, la fantasia* (*Fantasia: An Algerian Cavalcade*) and *Vaste est la prison* (*So Vast the Prison*). One of the texts by Albert Memmi, *Le Scorpion* (*The Scorpion*) takes up the idea of a confession in its subtitle, and the confessional mode is often considered as one of the attributes of autobiography, but it is a 'confession imaginaire' – an imaginary confession. There is use made of the third person, as well as the first person, in all the texts and there is little attempt to make explicit the fact that the narrator and the author are the same person, named as such, although after publication (often

9

long after publication) the authors have given clearer indications that these texts are indeed expressions of their personal experiences. I am of course referring obliquely here to the criteria established by Philippe Lejeune in order to define autobiography as a genre. These criteria have become, particularly in the field of French literary studies, an essential reference point, even though other definitions or other typologies of autobiographical texts have been formulated by other critics. Indeed Lejeune himself went on to refine his early criteria, and yet this is the definition that has come to be seen as 'classic'.[2] Among other notable criteria for defining the autobiographical status of a text are those of Elizabeth Bruss, a critic referred to by Lejeune, who proposes three parameters that give classical autobiography its particular generic value: truth value, act value (i.e. autobiography is a personal performance) and identity value. Bruss also insists on the contextual rather than the formal features of autobiography. All of her points are suggestive for the analysis of autobiographical writing in the colonial and postcolonial situations:

> The generic 'force' of autobiography and the leading features that have distinguished it throughout its history from other kinds of discourse are contextual rather than formal. There is no narrative sequence, no stipulated length, no metrical pattern, and no style that is unique to autobiography or sufficient to set it apart from biography or even fiction. To count as autobiography a text must have a certain implicit situation, a particular relationship to other texts and to the scene of its enactment. Three parameters define this situation and give classical autobiography its peculiar genetic value:
> Truth-value.   An autobiography purports to be consistent with other evidence; we are conventionally invited to compare it with other documents that describe the same events (to determine its veracity) and with anything the author may have said or written on other occasions (to determine its sincerity).
> Act-value.   Autobiography is a personal performance, an action that exemplifies the character of the agent responsible for that action and how it is performed.
> Identity-value.   In autobiography, the logically distinct roles of author, narrator, and protagonist are conjoined, with the same individual occupying a position both in the context, the associated 'scene of writing', and within the text itself.[3]

It is not my purpose here to criticise Lejeune's criteria particularly, as they have proved extremely important in the development of a serious body of criticism around the production of autobiography and autobiographical texts, although it is also important to add that no two specialists on autobiography fully agree on what constitutes autobiography. Of more consequence for the analysis here is the point that these criteria prove to be particularly limiting when we begin to investigate texts outside the male-dominated Western canon. It may seem extraordinary to speak of a 'canon' in a field of study as relatively recent as autobiographical studies, and yet a quick examination of recent books devoted to the subject, especially in France, will turn up the 'usual suspects' – St Augustine, Montaigne, Rousseau, Chateaubriand, Stendhal, Gide, Sartre, Leiris, Perec, with women writers such as George Sand, Simone de Beauvoir, Nathalie Sarraute and Marguerite Duras sometimes included. Very interestingly, however, hardly any of these texts actually fulfil the requirements to qualify for the status of autobiography according to Lejeune's criteria. We begin to see how an approach such as that of Elizabeth Bruss, founded on the notion of truth value, act value and identity value, may contribute fruitfully to an understanding of the processes through which autobiography functions. Indeed the relationship of autobiographical discourse to truth and the consequences of 'truth value' for the writer and the reader seem to be the most constant features of autobiographical texts. The concept of truth is of course also at the heart of Lejeune's 'autobiographical pact'. It is this idea that we believe what we read to be true that makes the relationship between reader and text fundamentally different in the cases of fictional and autobiographical texts.

Michael Sheringham has called autobiography 'an anxious genre', and argues that all autobiographers write in the 'margins of major conceptual systems, existing narratives, or paradigms of selfhood at large in philosophy and psychology'. He also makes the point that the autobiographer necessarily engages not only with the self, but also with the other in various forms, and raises at the same time the question of the heterogeneous, hybrid form of autobiography, an idea to which I will return.[4] If this is true of all autobiography, then the challenges inherent in the autobiographical act have a particular resonance for the colonial and postcolonial subject writing against the dominant discourses of the colonial system.

When we begin to consider the forms and strategies employed by writers of North African origin writing in French in the colonial and postcolonial situations (the use of the term 'postcolonial' will be discussed in the next section) to think about and to express selfhood we are confronted by several prevailing discourses, some of which will be dealt with in due course. First, I wish to return to the question of genre and to a prevalent discourse in the work of French critics who have taken an interest in North African writing in French, the idea that since an autobiographical tradition does not exist in Arabic literature, the genre of autobiography has in some way been 'borrowed' from the European tradition, and that these colonial and postcolonial subjects are 'imitating' a way of constructing the self that is not part of a traditional way of thinking about the individual within their own communities. Yet autobiography has also been called a tool for 'decolonising the mind' within the colonial and postcolonial context, and the autobiographical productions of writers from formerly colonised territories have frequently led to experimental textual practices in which the self becomes a 'place of creative, and by implication, political intervention'.[5] There are then a series of issues that need to be addressed concerning the contribution of texts by North African writers (and, of course, by the wider community of writers in a postcolonial context) to the genre of autobiography, and concerning the development of writing strategies by these writers. This in turn has implications for the elaboration of appropriate reading strategies when we engage with these texts, and the development of what will be termed here acts of 'motivated reading'.[6] The notion of the subject and the ways in which it is constructed are of course central to the strategies employed in any autobiographical discourse. With regard to autobiographies written by a colonised, or previously colonised, subject in the language of the colonising force, in the language of its institutions and its power in the domains of both the political and the imagination, the problem of the identity of the subject is extremely complex and the site of many different and often conflicting theories. The aim here is to analyse the ways in which the 'creative interventions' of such writers help us to understand the implications of the autobiographical act when used by writers who occupy a different space in relation to the dominant discourse of European history and culture.

I want, therefore, to begin with a brief reminder of the development of autobiography in the Western literary tradition in order to contextualise more fully the issue of writers whose origins lie outside this tradition, or who at least occupy, more or less uncomfortably, a space between two or more cultures.

French, British and American critics generally agree on the first appearance of the word 'autobiography' in English around 1800, and in French, taking on board the English term, around 1850.[7] While Jacques Lecarme notes that the term is more widely used in the English-speaking world as a description of texts for which French keeps the term *mémoires*, a general consensus can be found after a survey of a wide variety of commentators that the memoir is generally concerned with the external world of the author in history, while autobiography is concerned with the inner world of the author, the development of his or her personality and a self-reflection on his or her experience of life.[8] This is perhaps as clear-cut a definition as one can achieve, for autobiography is certainly not a 'stable' genre, which is no doubt part of its fascination, and it is why the work of Philippe Lejeune and Elizabeth Bruss on definitions and criteria is so essential, even if other critics may disagree with them endlessly. Otherwise, either nothing or everything can be classified as autobiography. Although Lejeune, as has previously been noted, is best known for his definition of a set of criteria and the notion of the auto-biographical pact made with the reader that centres on the guarantee of truth, another of the essays contained in his seminal *Le Pacte autobi-ographique*, 'Autobiographie et histoire littéraire' ('Autobiography and Literary History'), is equally important for the study being undertaken here. In that essay Lejeune focuses on the issues that need to be borne in mind when attempting to establish the notion of autobiography in its historical development, while keeping his focus on reader expectation:

> Ainsi, dans le domaine français, il est difficile de comprendre l'autobiogra-phie à la Rousseau sans le situer par rapport à la tradition de confessions religieuses, ou sans voir comment, depuis le milieu du XVIIème siècle, un jeu d'échanges entre les mémoires et le roman avait peu à peu transformé le récit à la première personne. Ce genre d'études doit être mené de manière précise, sans qu'on cherche à montrer que tel ou tel aspect est 'déjà' de l'au-tobiographie, ou, en sens inverse, sans vouloir prouver que l'autobiographie 'n'est que' la laïcisation du genre séculaire des confessions religieuses.[9]

> (Thus, in the French domain, it would be hard to understand Rousseau's style of autobiography without situating it in relation to the tradition of religious confessions, or seeing how, from the mid-seventeenth century onwards, frequent exchange between memoir and novel had little by little transformed the first-person narrative. This kind of study should be under-taken in a precise way, without seeking to show that this or that aspect is 'already' autobiographical in character; or, going the other way, trying to prove that autobiography is 'merely' a laicisation of the centuries-old tradi-tion of religious confessions.)

Here Lejeune is not only highlighting a problem with which I will deal in a little more detail, the relationship in the West between religion and autobiography, but he is also challenging those commentators who have attempted to chart the development of autobiography from antiquity to the present.[10] Bearing in mind Lejeune's caveat, it is nonetheless useful to remind ourselves of the ways in which most critics agree that the Western form of autobiography developed from confessional status, and notably the conversion narrative of, most famously, St Augustine (actu-ally born in North Africa, and writing in Latin, the language of the coloniser, as Assia Djebar reminds us in *L'Amour, la fantasia*), through various modes of spiritual autobiography, to a new conception of the individual born of the Enlightenment and a focus on the human rather than the divine, together with the changes in the social order and the rise of the middle class. This is the schema usually invoked together with the same landmark names of French and British and/or American writers depending on which language, or which country, the account of the development of autobiography is written in. Indeed Lejeune himself has noted the chauvinism of autobiographical criticism, and established literary criticism has displayed a rather ambivalent attitude towards autobiography, with attitudes being characterised for a long time by distrust and disdain (although paradoxically, biography was an acceptable genre, especially in England), and then with various critics within the European tradition claiming for their own country the foundations of autobiography.

James Olney provides a well-informed account of the development of autobiographical criticism up until the 1980s and he makes the important point that autobiography has in fact always contained its own criticism, constantly commenting on the form of its medium and the difficulties of self-expression.[11] For all the faults of a linear history of autobiography, the basis of this account of its evolution in the West is important for my object of study here, for it rests upon what Karl Weintraub has called in his seminal work in this area 'the value of the individual'.[12] The idea of the individual so prevalent, and so prized, in the contemporary Western world is actually a late development of Western culture, and this is not the most prevalent concept of the human being when world cultures are considered. When commenting on autobiography, however, most Western critics remain steadfastly Eurocentric, holding up the importance of this measure of individuality for approval, with the subtext that the degree to which the individual is valued is a measure of that society's civilisation. Weintraub charts in a considered and convincing argument the ways in which kinship ties and man's place in the *polis* are evidence of a very different view of the individual in the ancient world, going on to consider Augustine's 'typical story of all Christians' (while noting also that this model was actually very little imitated and stands out as an exception). Weintraub then turns to medieval texts and their adherence again to 'models of being' (the 'devout monk', the 'good knight', etc.), and moves on to individual examples, such as Montaigne 'seeing himself in passage', to show the general cultural conditions he believes were responsible for the emergence of 'individuality as a self-conscious concern'. Inescapably this history is linked to the history of religion in the West, and Weintraub highlights the impact of Protestantism and the importance of self-examination when there is no priest to confess to and the reliance on sacraments for personal salvation is removed, while also noting the importance of the 'inward search' of the Catholic mystics. Jacques Lecarme also notes the prevalence of autobiographers of Protestant upbringing or origins compared to those of Catholic background, at least up until the middle of the twentieth century. Nonetheless Weintraub points out the care needed with such generalisations:

> there is no reason to assume that Protestantism, any more than Catholicism, had a 'natural' or inevitable leaning towards that specific mode of self-conception. Essential elements within Protestantism were as inhospitable to that ideal of selfhood as was Catholicism. In some ways Protestantism may have contributed more to the eventual growth of individualism, which expressed a conception of the ideal relation between individual and society, than to the personality conception of individuality. This is important – since it seems altogether likely that the ideal of individuality needs the social conception of individualism while it is certainly not true that individualism is dependent on the ideal of individuality.[13]

This difference between individualism (the relation between the individual and society) and individuality is crucial, and I shall return to these notions.

There is then, as most observers would agree, a link between religion and the autobiographical model in the West. A further interesting more general point made by Weintraub is that the split in the Christian church provoked by the Protestant Reformation led to ever-multiplying centres of authority rather than one central interpretative authority, and that '[this] step once taken led inevitably to splitting up the Christian community into more and more self-assured sects and sub-sects, until the individual finally claimed a right to his own personal variant. Protestantism thus stimulated a process of differentiation in the direction of individual autonomy'.[14] Weintraub is also careful, however, to point out that Protestantism was not the sole cause of changes is the perception of the relationship between the individual and the community, but a powerful additional factor in a Europe that was changing politically and culturally, and in which the distinction between monastic and secular life was blurring.

Most commentators on North African writing in French continue to insist that autobiography does not exist in Arabic literature and that the model was 'borrowed' by North African writers writing in French, particularly from the 1950s onwards. Jean Déjeux, for example, argues that French is the 'language of the self' ('la langue natale du je') for such writers:

> Cette émergence du 'je' durant les années 1945–1950 dans la littérature maghrébine (algérienne en particulier) de langue française se tient à plusieurs facteurs: changements socio-économiques dans les sociétés, mutations dans les mentalités, entrée à l'école française, voyages, acculturation donc, dans le contexte musulman qui est celui du Maghreb. Les modèles occidentaux faisaient éclater et bouger l'unanimisme des attitudes et comportements traditionnels basés sur les manières islamiques de voir le monde et de l'éprouver.[15]

> (This emergence of 'I' in Maghrebi literature (especially Algerian literature) written in French during the years 1945–1950 is attributable to several different factors: socio-economic changes in societies, changes in mentality, entry into French schools, travel, and thus acculturation, in the Muslim context which is that of the Maghreb. Western models shifted and broke apart the unanimity of traditional attitudes and behaviour based on Islamic ways of seeing and experiencing the world.)

Déjeux goes on to say that the 'I' does exist in Muslim societies, but that this is the 'je de témoignage' (the witness to faith):

> Le témoin dit 'je', de même que le croyant atteste personnellement en proclamant la *chahada*, profession de foi musulmane. Mais il ne s'agit pas là du 'je' intime qui dévoile l'intérieur et par lequel l'homme s'affirme comme sujet en tant qu'homme et pas seulement en croyant.[16]

> (The witness says 'I', just as the believer attests personally by proclaiming the *shahada*, the Muslim profession of faith. But this is not the intimate 'I' which reveals the inner self and by which man affirms himself as subject by reason of being a man and not merely by being a believer.)

For Déjeux, autobiography as we know it and have known it rather vaguely 'for a long time' in the West is unknown in Muslim societies in as much as they are religious societies 'où l'holisme prime l'individualisme' ('where holism takes precedence over individualism').[17] He quotes a diverse selection of North African intellectuals who certainly lend authority to this view, for example the Tunisian historian and thinker Hichem Djaït affirming that the quest of the West has been the self in the sense of the affirmation of the individual, and that Islam 'a ignoré le moi' ('has been unaware of the self'); 'il a ignoré l'humanisme comme support des valeurs civilisatrices' ('it has been unaware of humanism as the basis for civilising values');[18] the Moroccan historian and thinker A. Laroui stating that 'le sujet n'avait aucune base objective dans la société arabe' ('the subject had no objective base in Arab society')[19]; and the Moroccan sociologist Fatima Mernissi writing:

> Notre identité traditionnelle reconnaissait à peine l'individu qu'elle abhorrait, car perturbateur de l'harmonie collective. En Islam, la notion de l'individu à l'état de nature dans le sens philosophique du terme est inexistante. La société traditionnelle fabriquait des musulmans, littéralement des 'soumis' à la volonté du groupe. L'individualité dans un tel contexte est découragée, toute initiative est *bid'a*.[20]

(Our traditional identity barely recognised the individual, abhorring it as a disturber of collective harmony. In Islam the notion of the individual in the natural state (in the philosophical sense of the term) does not exist. Traditional society produced 'Muslims', literally those who 'submitted' to the will of the group. Individuality in that sort of context is discouraged; all initiative is *bid'a*.)

Déjeux then makes further references to writers such as Tahar Ben Jelloun, Mohammed Dib and Rachid Mimmouni to support this view. His main argument in this article (which in many ways builds on an earlier article on which I will comment later) is to show the role of the French school and the French language in the development of the notion of the individual: 'Nous nous arrêtons à l'école et à la maîtrise de la langue française, c'est qu'il y a là, nous semble-t-il, un facteur plus privilégié et plus radicalement bouleversant des mentalités'[21] ('We dwell on the school, and mastery of the French language, because we consider that they constitute a particularly privileged factor, one which changes mentalities more radically'). Déjeux takes the case of Mohammed Kacimi, who seems to him one of the best examples of this expression of 'le passage de l'univers religieux musulman à celui de l'individualisme "laïque, séculier"'[22] ('passing from the Muslim religious universe to that of "lay, secular" individualism').

From a very different perspective, but one that equally has consequences for the consideration of autobiographical expression, North African commentators themselves also contribute to this idea that the autobiographical genre is a 'borrowed' one in North African literature. Abdallah Bounfour goes as far as to say that all Francophone writers in the Maghreb are *étranges* (a word that has multiple meanings in French: foreign, strange, unfamiliar) and that the literature produced by such writers differs not only from European literature, but also from Arab literature, including that produced in Arabic in the Maghreb:

> On croit que la littérature francophone du Maghreb est d'inspiration arabe, qu'elle est une transposition dans la langue française. Tel n'est pas le cas. Elle ignore la littérature arabe jusqu'à une date très récente. Elle ne peut donc être inspirée par elle. En revanche, des schèmes de pensée, des traits narratifs et des images viennent de la culture 'orale' des écrivains. Ils sont arabes, berbères et arabo-berbères. La littérature francophone du Maghreb est travaillée par la culture profondément inconsciente de ses producteurs d'autant plus que cette dernière est performée dans la langue réellement maternelle. On croit que cette littérature est 'orientale' dans son essence. Certes, mais à condition d'entendre cet 'orientalisme' dans le sens d'un regard de plus en plus extérieur. L'écrivain maghrébin francophone est 'étranger' comme l'est le héros de Camus. Du moins l'Orient mis en scène par lui est différent de celui qu'on rencontre dans la littérature arabe y compris celle du Maghreb.[23]

(People believe that Maghrebi literature in French is Arab in inspiration, transposed into the French language. Such is not the case. This literature was unaware of Arabic literature until very recently, and therefore could not be inspired by it. However, modes of thought, narrative traits and images come from the writers' 'oral' culture. They are Arabs, Berbers and Arab-Berbers. Maghrebi literature in French is worked on by the profoundly unconscious culture of its producers, the more so since this culture is formed in their true mother-tongue. People think that this literature is 'oriental' in essence. It is, but only if that 'orientalism' is understood in the sense of a progressively more external view. The Maghrebi writer in French is an 'outsider' like Camus' hero. At least, the Orient he features is different from that found in Arabic literature, including Arabic literature of the Maghreb.)

The impersonal *on* ('people') no doubt refers here to the French public of critics and readers, and the crux of the argument that revolves around the language of expression is an interesting one. For my purposes at this point however, I would like to refer to Bounfour's ideas in this article about the development of autobiography in the Arab world. He makes the common analogy with texts from the Middle East, and notably from Egypt, where from the beginning of the twentieth century a certain number of texts became standard reference points in the development of modern autobiographical expression. Among these are a number of important examples: Tāhā Husayn's *al-Ayyām* (an extremely popular book that appeared in English in three parts, *An Egyptian Childhood*, *The Stream of Days* and *Memoirs (A Passage to France)*); Salāma Mūsā's *Tarbiyyat Salāma Mūsā* ('The Education of Salāma Mūsā'); Ahmed Amin's *Hayātī* (*My Life: The Autobiography of an Egyptian Scholar, Writer, and Cultural Leader*); and Tawfīq al-Hakīm's *Zahrat al-'umr* ('The Flower of Life') and *Sijn al-'umr* (*The Prison of Life: An Autobiographical Essay*). Most critics agree that it is true to say that Arabic literature underwent a major literary and intellectual transformation after Arab societies were opened to the West, and at the beginning of the twentieth century novels and autobiographical writings were produced that differed from the forms and styles of classical Arabic literature. However, as Leila Ahmed has pointed out, forms of autobiographical discourse did exist in classical Arabic literature:

> Autobiography is an anciently known form in Islamic-Arabic letters. Famous early autobiographical works include one by the religious scholar and philosopher Al-Ghazālī *Munqidh min al dalāl* (The Confessions of Al-Ghazzālī), and another by Usāma ibn Munqidh *Kitāb Al-I'tibār* [...] Indeed, there are even distinguishable varieties of Islamic autobiography, including autobiographies of rulers, religious-mystic autobiographies, and the autobiographical accounts of scholars.[24]

And as Amira Hassan Nowaira has written:

> Autobiographical writing has a long and rich history in Arabic letters, and
> it is possible to trace it back to the intensely personal poetry written in pre-
> Islamic and early Islamic times [...] With increased contact between the Arab
> world and the West in the nineteenth century there was a revival of interest
> in the art of autobiography, and writers tried to reconcile the imported
> Western forms and the indigenous classical models drawn from the Arab
> heritage.[25]

She too notes the importance of the work of Al-Ghazālī and of Usāma
ibn Munqidh, and also of Ibn Khaldūn, used by Assia Djebar as one of
her epigraphs in her own autobiographical text:

> There is little doubt that al-Ghazālī's work has a distinct place in the history
> of Arabic autobiographical writing not only because it explores with force-
> fulness and forthrightness the intimate nature of the Sufi (mystic) experience
> but, more importantly, because the personal element in it is given far more
> weight and importance than the public. This is where it diverges from the
> mainstream Arabic autobiographical tradition, in which personal and public
> elements were often fairly well balanced. A prominent example of this
> balance can be found in the autobiography written by the Arab knight
> Usāma ibn Munqidh [...] Usāma recounts his personal experiences and
> adventures side by side with descriptions of the political and social events
> of his time, in a simple, direct style, using the vernacular and moving away
> from the heavily ornate style of literary discourse prevalent during this era
> (the twelfth century). Of great interest to the history of Arabic autobio-
> graphical writing is the book by the philosopher, sociologist, historian,
> traveler and politician Ibn Khaldūn (1332–1406) entitled *al-Ta'rīf bi-Ibn
> Khaldūn* ('Introducing Ibn Khaldūn': French translation published as
> *Voyage d'occident et d'orient*). Its significance stems from the fact that it bril-
> liantly interweaves personal history with accounts of political and historical
> events.[26]

In 1937 Franz Rosenthal wrote a survey article, 'Die Arabische
Autobiographie', in which he discusses what Thomas Philipp has called
'all the major autobiographical materials' compiled by Arab authors
about themselves from the beginning of Islam until the sixteenth
century.[27] The monumental work by Georg Misch on the development
of autobiography from antiquity in different areas of the world contains
a section on Islamic scholars' autobiographies.[28] Thomas Philipp's terminology of 'autobiographical materials' is nonetheless fundamental, and
brings us back to the ever-present question of how to define autobiography. Philipp's careful discussion of types and forms of autobiography
in the Arabic tradition is important and in his analysis he proposes that
the memoir form, even in modern Arabic literature, is much more prevalent than 'actual autobiographies'.[29] He quotes the conclusion Rosenthal
reached in 1937: 'None of these autobiographies arose from an awareness of the value of the uniquely personal aspect of life; those
autobiographies, especially, which are more than just a *vita* are written

for objective purposes.'[30] Philipp also notes, however, Fedwa Malti-Douglas's observation that there is a basic difference between classical and modern Arabic conceptions of literature which becomes most visible in the modern autobiography: 'The literary text ceases to be an expression of collective norms and becomes a personal work'.[31] Philipp is also careful to point out that it is doubtful whether a history of autobiography in modern Arabic literature can be written, since the question of influence between the texts from the Middle East that he analyses and the production of autobiographical discourses in the Maghreb is problematic, and indeed highly questionable, as Bounfour has pointed out. Something that all these Arabic writers do have in common, however, is that they became alienated from their traditional backgrounds and 'needed to make a specific intellectual effort to cope with their alienation'.[32] I shall return to this question of how a text 'ceases to be an expression of collective norms and becomes a personal work'. The issue of alienation from traditional backgrounds is also certainly an element in the work of all the writers discussed here, as I indicated briefly in the introduction. For the moment, I wish to return to this question of the forms of 'autobiographical materials' in Arabic literature. Bounfour in fact evokes the classical Arabic literary tradition with regard to autobiography, pointing out that it is inexact to think of autobiography in this context as 'borrowed' from the European tradition: 'Jusqu'ici j'ai fait comme si l'autobiographie était un emprunt à la littérature européenne et l'on risque de comprendre que ce genre n'existe pas dans la tradition littéraire arabe. Il serait inexact de l'affirmer sans nuance'[33] ('Up to this point I have been speaking as though autobiography was borrowed from European literature and I risk giving the impression that this genre does not exist in Arab literary tradition. It would be incorrect to state this without further precisions').

He goes on to evoke two traditions in medieval and classical Arabic literature – Sufi initiatic or conversion writings and autobiographical fragments by historians and theologians, usually addressed to their descendants:

> L'autobiographie soufie n'est pas d'une grande abondance et elle est trop singulière pour être inspiratrice de l'écriture moderne. Quant à celle des clercs, elle est rarement autonome, c'est-à-dire qu'elle est généralement insérée dans un texte ayant une autre intention que le pur récit autobiographique. Quand il est suffisamment autonome des autres oeuvres, le récit autobiographique tient plus des mémoires et de la chronique que du récit de vie. Tel est le cas de al-Yûsi ou de Ibn Khaldû ou de Usâma ibn Munqid pour ne citer que les plus connus.[34]

(Sufi autobiography is not very plentiful and is too individual to be the inspirer of modern writing. As for that of the clerics, it is seldom autonomous, i.e. it usually forms part of a text whose intention is other than autobiographical. When it is sufficiently autonomous from other works, autobiographical narrative is more in the nature of memoirs or chronicles than an account of the writer's life. This is the case of al-Yūsi or Ibn Khaldūn or Usāma ibn Munqidh, to cite only the most well-known.)

What is striking here to the student of the development of autobiography in the West is not that this is different history, but that it is in fact similar to that which Karl Weintraub has charted in *The Value of the Individual*, previously discussed. As Roger Allen explains, within the intellectual currents in Islamic history,

> [the] extreme emphasis of mystics on the role of the individual conscience in assessing personal conduct towards God and other people led to opposition from traditionalist theologians who were anxious to codify proper behaviour on a more communal level [...] Al-Ghazzālī's achievement in incorporating Sufism into the mainstream of Islamic faith led to a palpable increase in popular interest in the more personal approach to God that the mystical path appeared to offer.[35]

In his discussion of the development of the tradition of a prose discourse in Arabic literature, Allen also notes the importance of the *hadith* (a report of a statement by Muhammad) and the *sirah* (the record of the Prophet's life),[36] and indeed the centrality of biographies of the Prophet in the Islamic faith. He also points out that the links between

> the genres of Arabic literature, the concept of *adab* (usually serving as the equivalent of the English word 'literature' in the modern context, but describing a much broader field of writing in earlier centuries), and the terms used to describe their analogues in Western literary traditions are rarely exact.
>   To cite just a single example: within the realm of narrative, the concept of *adab* admits of categories (travel narratives and biographies, for example) that have not generally attracted the attention of literary critics in the Western world.[37]

The issue of 'comparison' between Arabic and Western genres is therefore a complex one and remains unresolved and open to critical interpretation, with critics often having hidden agendas. Sabry Hafez makes clear that the question of the rise of narrative in modern Arabic culture has been marked by two opposing tendencies: 'those who wanted to emphasise the impact of the West attributed to it significant influence, while those who wanted to deny the West's influence looked for older Arabic narrative forms'.[38] As he points out, neither argument fully explains the emergence of Arabic fiction at the times when it appeared. If its origins stretch back to the medieval *maqamah* (session), he argues, why did it take nine centuries for a form with major modifications to appear? And if the modern Arabic narrative is a direct product of Western influences, why did it take almost a century after the confrontation with Europe to emerge, and 'more importantly, how does one account for its originality and difference from its European counterpart?'.[39] Hafez's own approach is to position the debate in the domains of the sociology of literature and of poststructuralist theory, positing the 'concept of genesis with its sociocultural dimensions versus the old concept of origin, genealogy or mimesis'. He argues that there is a more positive relationship between Arabic and European traditions, and the concept he invokes is one that is productive for the reading of the writers under discussion here: 'The relation of modern Arabic narrative to either Western narrative discourse or classical Arabic archetypal fiction is, therefore, not one of genealogy but of *dynamic intertextuality*' (my emphasis).[40]

Roger Allen further notes that the development of literary genres also depended on a number of geographical and cultural factors, and that as far as modern Arabic fiction is concerned the 'deep penetration' of French culture into the educational system of the countries of the Maghreb has meant that the 'balance between French and Arabic expression remains a hotly debated issue'.[41]

It is therefore essential to understand that the writers under discussion here, although born in North African countries, were all educated within the French school system and are therefore able to take as general literary and cultural reference points the French writers read during their childhood and adolescence, and indeed there are specific references in their work to a number of French writers, as will be seen. However, it seems to me an over-simplification to suggest that as adults (or indeed as children, as Assia Djebar makes clear) they are unaware of types of literary discourse in other cultures, including their own cultural heritage, or that they are simply borrowing a Western form of expression when they engage with the processes of autobiographical discourse. There is also clearly a huge difference between the position of Mouloud Feraoun, writing in the 1940s and 1950s, and that of Assia Djebar or Abdelkébir Khatibi, writing in the 1970s and 1980s. Khatibi clearly takes a great deal of inspiration from Sufi writing, and Assia Djebar makes explicit reference to the autobiography of Ibn Khaldūn in an epigraph in *L'Amour, la fantasia*. These issues are further complicated by the role of religion and the question of selfhood, the issue of gender and the value placed on the individual in the composition and functioning of different societies. Attitudes towards selfhood and society in Christianity (both

Catholicism and Protestantism), in Islam and, in the case of North African Jewish writers, in Judaism need to be taken into account when considering the development of autobiography.

This attention to the place of religion in the development of autobiography in the West, previously discussed, is important when we come to consider autobiographical texts written by authors from non-Western cultures, and it also brings us to another essential debate concerning conceptions of the individual and his or her place in society. Many critics analysing North African literature in French – and the same has been true, for example, concerning Black American autobiographical writing – will maintain that the collective voice is more important than the individual, that every 'I' masks a 'we', that the writer speaks on behalf of a community that has often been deprived of a voice, due to colonialism, or due to slavery in the case of America. In the work of writers active during the 1950s, those most directly linked to independence movements in North Africa, there is certainly the will to 'represent', in both meanings of the word (to portray and to speak on behalf of), the experience of their colonised peoples, while simultaneously forging a process through which an independent subjectivity could come into being after being denied by the colonising forces. In so doing, these writers contributed to the analysis of the effects of colonisation and of resistance to that oppression on the identity of the individual and of the nation. However, as previously discussed in the preface, the issue of a writer, part of an intellectual elite, 'representing' the wider community is problematic.

The almost invariable references to the 'I' that masks a 'we', the *je pluriel* (a plural, multiple, collective self), have become mere commonplaces, at best narrative instances that the critic expects to find and therefore does not question. There are also implications in such an attitude for the (mis)understanding of the place of the individual in Islamic culture. Jean Déjeux, whom I criticised earlier for his very French Republican insistence on the importance of the French school, is rather more interesting in an earlier article:

> Cette question de l'apparition de l'autobiographie est primordiale au regard des écrits maghrébins. De fait, le 'je' et l'exposition du moi, de l'homme-sujet, ne vont pas de soi dans le contexte de la civilisation et de la culture arabo-musulmanes. Or, ce 'je' a bel et bien fait son entrée dans les romans autobiographiques et dans les récits de vie non fictionnels, histoires de vie, journaux intimes et mémoires.
>
> Le 'je' ne va pas de soi, compte tenu du contexte sociologique et culturel. De prime abord, l'impression dominante est, en effet, que c'est le 'nous' qui est d'abord mis en avant dans les romans [...] Le roman maghrébin est né

d'un désir ardent de faire connaître aux étrangers les réalités maghrébines et de donner à voir les Maghrébins, 'la véritable voix narrative de ce roman [...] et n'est ni un "je" égoïste, ni un "il" aussi abstrait qu'impersonnel, mais un "nous" terriblement exigeant et foncièrement ambivalent.' 'Je suis plusieurs, toute une foule de colonisés et de protégés', écrivait Driss Chraïbi en 1962 dans *Succession ouverte*. On peut bien avancer alors que quand le romancier dit 'je', il pense souvent 'nous'. Et pourtant, nous constatons bien une émergence du 'je' dans la narration chez un certain nombre d'auteurs lors de la naissance de cette littérature maghrébine, mais surtout dans les récits de vie. Les romanciers ont voulu mettre en évidence leur moi, ceci dans un contexte d'acculturation française et de modèles venant de l'école moderne occidentale, mais aussi dans une évolution des pays maghrébins eux-mêmes vers la modernité aux prises avec les changements socio-économiques et les mutations dans les mentalités sous la pression de l'étranger colonisateur, hier, et des bouleversements intervenant dans le monde. L'économie du marché, occidentale et capitaliste, a bouleversé les données traditionnelles et les cohérences internes des sociétés vivant sur leur quant-à-soi; les individus ont été bousculés dans leur équilibre et déstabilisés dans leur manière de voir et de sentir le monde. L'émergence du 'je' s'est ainsi faite dans des conditions particulières tenant tant aux structures des sociétés maghrébines hier qu'à l'histoire de leur évolution, stimulées par la présence des étrangers, dans un double désir du Même et de l'Autre. [42]

(This question of the appearance of autobiography is fundamental in regard to Maghrebi writing. In fact, the 'I' and the exposition of the self, of man as subject, are not to be taken for granted in the context of Arab-Muslim civilisation and culture. Now, this 'I' really has entered into the autobiographical novels and non-fiction accounts of the writer's life, life-stories, personal diaries and memoirs.

The 'I' is not to be taken for granted, bearing in mind the sociological and cultural context. In the first place, the dominant impression is, in practice, that it is the 'we' which comes to the fore in novels [...] Since the Maghrebi novel is born of a burning desire to make Maghrebi realities known to others and to make Maghrebi people visible, 'the real narrative voice of this novel [...] is neither a self-centred "I" nor an abstract, impersonal "he", but a terribly demanding and deeply ambivalent "we".' 'I am many, a whole crowd of colonised people and protégés', wrote Driss Chraïbi in 1962, in *Succession ouverte* (Open Succession). So it is perfectly possible to maintain that when the novelist says 'I', he is often thinking 'we'. Nevertheless, we certainly do see the emergence of 'I' in the narratives of a certain number of authors when this Maghrebi literature is developing, most of all in life-stories. The novelists chose to give evidence of the self, and did so in a context of French acculturation, and models drawn from the modern Western school, but also in the context of the development of the Maghreb countries themselves towards a modernity that is trying to cope with socio-economic changes and changes in mentalities under the pressure yesterday of the colonising foreigner, and the transformations taking place in the world today. The market economy of Western capitalism has altered the traditional givens and the internal coherence of societies which lived on their own substance; individuals have been shaken off their balance and destabilised in their way of seeing and feeling the world. The emergence of 'I' has thus taken place in particular conditions which derive both from the structures of Maghrebi societies in the past and from the history of their development, stimulated by foreigners, in a double desire for the Self and for the Other.)

I shall leave aside the complications glossed over here in not making a distinction between the novel and the life story (a form of autobiographical discourse that is important in postcolonial studies) since Déjeux does note at the end of the article that while the communal *nous* behind the *je* continues to dominate in the novel, a *je* is more affirmed in the life story. More disturbingly, the social, political and personal implications of this 'stimulation' by the 'Other' are far from fully dealt with. Nonetheless Déjeux does highlight the importance of trying to understand the particular conditions of the region, and this article is altogether more finely nuanced than the later one to which I referred earlier. He goes on to deal with the Muslim context, and I again wish to quote him at some length, since it seems to me that his observations are important, although they remain resolutely Eurocentric, and have often been taken at face value and over-simplified by subsequent observers:

> Au Maghreb – et plus largement en pays musulman ou encore dans les sociétés agraires – c'est, en effet, l'homme social qui compte avant tout dans les attitudes et les conduites traditionnelles reçues par la communauté. L'individu ne doit pas se singulariser (surtout pas les femmes, qui n'ont pas dans ce contexte à se mettre en valeur dans la vie publique puisque leur domaine est celui de la maison et de l'espace privé). La solidarité et l'éthique du groupe entraînent l'uniformisation et le conformisme, freinant l'affirmation du 'je' et de la personnalité. C'est l'Autre, l'étranger qui débarquant sur la terre du Maghreb a apporté la *fitna*, c'est-à-dire l'épreuve troublante et déstabilisante. Il a obligé les sociétés à bouger, à remettre en question l'unanimisme des comportements traditionnels, à sortir du rang et des normes d'hier dans un double mouvement de résistance au colonisateur et d'attirance devant son savoir-faire et sa maîtrise de l'Histoire, du temps et des techniques. L'étranger a fait circuler ses modèles.[43]

> (In the Maghreb, and more widely in Muslim countries, or in agrarian societies, it is in practice the social man who really counts in the traditional attitudes and behaviour accepted by the community. The individual should not stand out (especially not women, who in this context must never make their presence felt in public life, since their domain is the house and private space). Solidarity and group ethics lead to uniformity and conformity, acting as a brake on the affirmation of 'I' and one's own personality. It was the Other, the foreigner, who, disembarking on Maghreb land, brought the *fitna*, i.e. the troubling, destabilising test. It was he who obliged societies to shift, to question the unanimity of traditional behaviours, to leave the ranks and the norms of yesterday in a double movement of resistance against the coloniser and attraction to his knowledge and mastery of History, times and techniques. The foreigner put his own models into circulation.)

Déjeux goes on to quote Hichem Djaït once again, writing that Islam has been unaware of humanism as a basis for civilising values,[44] but here he is quoted explaining more clearly the Islamic attitude: 'Précisons: l'humanisme en tant que valorisant la personne humaine en tant que telle, car il existe un humanisme musulman de l'homme en tant que croyant, pris dans le religieux' ('To be more precise, humanism in so far as it gives a value to the human person as such, because there does exist a Muslim humanism of man as believer, from the religious aspect'). Déjeux ends again with an interesting but ambivalent attitude:

> L'émergence du 'je' dans la littérature maghrébine de langue française depuis les années 50 n'est certes pas à comprendre comme une réduction purement et simplement à notre personnalisme occidental. Il n'empêche: ce 'je' est bien le signe d'une personnalisation de plus en plus accentuée des sociétés ne faisaient pas suffisament sa place à la personne (autonome et responsable) en tant que telle. La création romanesque dans l'activité scripturale est donc bien ici le lieu privilégié où cette personne peut s'affirmer et donc, par le fait même, entrer en conflit, mais aussi sortir du 'communautarisme' et du conformisme pour être une personne à part entière.[45]

> (The emergence of the 'I' in Maghrebi literature in French from the 1950s onwards is certainly not to be understood purely and simply as a reduction to our Western individualism. Notwithstanding that fact, this 'I' is actually the sign of a more and more pronounced individualism in societies which did not give sufficient weight to the person (autonomous, responsible) as such. The creativity of the fiction writer is thus the most favourable place for the self-affirmation of this person, who therefore, by that very fact, may enter into a situation of conflict, but may also escape from 'communitarism' and conformism in order to be a person in the full sense.)

Here there is none of the worry expressed by Doris Somner concerning the double-edged sword of autobiography, which may be a form that allows the formulation of resistance, but may also undermine conceptions of selfhood different to our Western ideal, which nonetheless carry value within their particular cultural context:

> Is [autobiography] the model for imperialising the consciousness of colonised peoples, replacing their collective potential for resistance with a cult of individuality and even loneliness? Or is it a medium of resistance and counter-discourse, the legitimate space for producing that excess which throws doubt on the coherence and power of an exclusive historiography?[46]

My point is not to deny the different status of the 'I' in Islam, about which numerous commentators, including the writers themselves, speak with authority – and here I will take as an example (in fact, a passage also quoted by Déjeux) the position of Assia Djebar, whose concept of selfhood is indeed further complicated by her status as woman, writing in 1985, the year of the publication of her autobiographical text *L'Amour, la fantasia*: 'Parler hors la chaleur matriarcale, hors de l'antienne de la Tradition, hors de la "fidélité" – ce terme pris au sens religieux – écrire à la première personne du singulier et de la singularité, corps nu et voix à peine déviée par le timbre étranger, rameute tous les dangers symboliques'[47] ('to speak outside matriarchal warmth, outside the antiphon of Tradition, outside "faithfulness" – in the religious sense – to write in the first person of the singular and singularity, naked, one's voice barely inflected by foreign tones, arouses all the symbolic dangers').

I wish, however, to pursue a little further this issue of the different conception of the individual in the Islamic faith, even though the writers under discussion here do not speak from within traditional Islamic culture. Feraoun consistently claims a Kabyle identity for himself that differentiates him from Arabo-Muslim culture; Memmi is obviously quite a different case, being of Jewish origin and growing up in a minority community within the dominant Islamic culture; both Khatibi and Djebar pose challenges to traditional interpretations of Islam.

Andrew Rippin, in his very clear analysis of Muslim beliefs and practices, points out the centrality of the concept of 'identity' in the history of Islam:

> central to the presentation of the emergence and history of Islam is the idea of 'identity': that is, how a religion functions on both a personal and a social level to provide 'that stable niche in a predictable environment'. The role Islam has played, and continues to play, in creating and developing an understanding of the world and of the relationship between individuals is vital; yet this too is not an unchanging mechanism but one which has gradually and subtly changed in response to the realities and pressures of the world.[48]

Rippin notes particularly, for example, what might be termed the politicisation of Islam in diaspora populations as the affirmation of Islamic practices becomes part of an expression of identity:

> Another way of expressing this is as the 'Islamisation of the self', and the use of Islamic symbols to provide identity on a personal level. This tendency is connected not only with the move from a rural to an urban society, but also, one might contend, from a 'Muslim' country to a 'non-Muslim' one [...] This tendency toward personalisation of faith may be the result of the general globalisation of Islam within the world community.[49]

As is generally well known, however, the 'community' of Muslims is essential to the Islamic faith: 'Those who follow (or "submit to", as the word *muslim* suggests in its root meaning) this path of Islam form the *umma*, the community of Muslims whose common bond in religion symbolically reflects the central concept of the unity of the Divine'.[50] The notion of 'community', *umma*, usually seen as originating with the move of the Prophet to Yathrib, later Medina, is a 'defining point of the Islamic sense of identity'.[51] The 'witness to faith' (*shahada*), evoked earlier by Jean Déjeux, consists of the repetition of the two phrases 'There is no god but God' and 'Muhammad is the messenger of God'. These two phrases are found in the Koran, but 'they are not put together as a single statement, nor are they suggested in that book to be some sort of defining notion of what a Muslim is, as is implied within the concept of their ritual use [...] The emergence of the statement as a key part of Muslim identity is witnessed on coins from the first Muslim century and in the Dome of the Rock inscriptions, as well as in the *hadith* literature.'[52] Among the different types of prayer in Islam, there exists the *du'a*, 'a non-ritualised individual address to God. Prayer is not therefore restricted to the daily five prayers alone but may be performed on other occasions as the need and desire arise within the individual Muslim':

> Thus prayer as a phenomenon in Islam does not function simply to bring the community together at regular times of the day and the week; neither is it just a matter of providing structured time periods within the day to Muslim society, nor a way of simply providing a constant reminder of the presence of Islam in the world. Certainly it is all these things, but it also seems to be conceived as a personal communication with God, providing the opportunity for expressions of thankfulness and worship in the full sense of those words.[53]

It is clear therefore that the Muslim is an individual before God, and Islam is thought of 'as the element which provides the grounding for an individual's life, the interpretative core through which life's experiences may be understood'.[54]

Rippin also very interestingly notes the contribution of Muhammed 'Abduh, a significant Modernist figure in nineteenth-century Egypt:

> He argued for the need to make Koran commentary available to the people as a whole. The intellectual efforts of the past had made the text 'illegible'; any sense of a distinction between what was important and what was not had been lost. As well, the efforts of the past did not respond to the needs and questions of his day. 'Abduh thus embarked on a commentary that would be minus the theological speculations, the detailed grammatical discussions, and the obtuse scholarship of the past. The similarities in impulse and direction to those of the Protestant Reformation of Europe may be noted – Luther's Bible translation taking the text out of the hands of the clergy alone and giving it to the common person – along with the impact of the printing press, which became a major factor in the development of Egypt, with the first press established there in the 1820s.[55]

We are returned here to the previous discussion concerning the similarities in the development of autobiographical discourses in the European and Arabic traditions. What I am suggesting is that again the issue comes back to the ways in which autobiography is defined, and the discourse that surrounds both this discussion of individual and collective identity. Indeed the whole debate concerning whether or not autobiography exists outside Western culture except as an imitation of that model is reminiscent of the ways in which generalisations led to the obscuring of women's autobiography until feminist critics began to define the different modes in women's self-expression. Not conforming to the male-dominated discourse of autobiography and its worldview, women's autobiographical texts were dismissed as a type of sub-genre that did not really 'reach the necessary standard', that were somehow not really auto-biographies. The question of whether or not autobiographical discourse exists outside the West is certainly complex, and depends on standpoint, definition and, once again, personal agenda. Here the seminal article by Georges Gusdorf (also much vilified by feminist critics) has had an impact on critical discourse, and it is useful to remind ourselves of this with a selection of statements that make up his definition, in order to understand the 'orthodoxy' reinforced by many (usually male) critics:

> First of all, it is necessary to point out that the genre of autobiography seems limited in time and space: it has not always existed nor does it exist everywhere. If Augustine's *Confessions* offer us a brilliantly successful landmark right at the beginning, one nevertheless recognises immediately that this is a late phenomenon in Western culture, coming at that moment when the Christian contribution was grafted onto classical traditions. Moreover, it would seem that autobiography is not to be found outside our cultural area; one would say that it expresses a concern peculiar to Western man, a concern that has been of good use in his systematic conquest of the universe and that he has communicated to men of other cultures; but those men will thereby have been annexed by a sort of intellectual colonising to a mentality that was not their own [...] It is obvious that autobiography is not possible in a cultural landscape where consciousness of self does not, properly speaking, exist [...] Autobiography becomes possible only under certain metaphysical preconditions. To begin with, at the cost of a cultural revolution humanity must have emerged from the mythic framework of traditional teachings and must have entered the perilous domain of history. The man who takes the trouble to tell of himself knows that the present differs from the past and that it will not be repeated in the future; he has become more aware of differences than of similarities; given the constant change, given the uncertainty of the events and of men, he believes it a useful and valuable thing to fix his own image so that he can be certain it will not disappear like all things in this world [...] Each man matters to the world, each life and each death; the witnessing of each about himself enriches the common cultural heritage [...] Henceforth, man knows himself a responsible agent: gatherer of men, of lands, of power, maker of kingdoms or of empires, inventor of laws or of wisdom, he alone adds consciousness to nature, leaving signs there of his presence.

Nonetheless, like Weintraub, Gusdorf does also note that

> [this] conscious awareness of the singularity of each individual life is the late product of a specific civilisation. Throughout most of human history, the individual does not oppose himself to all others; he does not feel himself to

exist outside others, and still less against others, but very much with others in an interdependent existence that asserts its rhythms everywhere in the community.[56]

Despite the awareness of the risks of an 'intellectual colonising', this remains a clearly Eurocentric and indeed male view, since, as feminists have pointed out, women have not generally been 'gatherers of lands and makers of kingdoms and empires', and one must ask what was the experience of those on the receiving end of this swashbuckling vision of world history. Above all, it is a view that privileges a Western conception of the individual and his (and I stress 'his') place in the world. I previously quoted Jean Déjeux and noted the assumptions that he makes. He does not specify how long the 'long time' actually is that autobiography has been an integral part of Western literature and the Western worldview. In fact, the history of autobiography as we think of it at the beginning of the twenty-first century dates back only to the second half of the nineteenth century. Déjeux crucially does not make the distinction between individualism and individuality that Karl Weintraub has been at such great pains to maintain, and neither does Gusdorf. Indeed, Gusdorf's analysis would suggest that it is from the notion of individuality and not individualism that the autobiographical impulse stems in the male-dominated Western autobiographical canon. Yet as, for example, feminist criticism has shown, there are other attitudes both to the relationship between the individual and society, and to the writing of the personal experience of this. Indeed, just as there seems to be wilful misinterpretation in the West of the notion of the individual in Islam, so conversely there seems to be a similar attitude on the part of some Islamic commentators on the Western notion, as the following discussion of the definition of humanism within Islam makes clear:

> On ne peut que souligner avec force que le noyau de l'humanisme islamique n'est pas l'individu seulement. L'être humain est un être de sociabilité et sa première sociabilité est la famille. Lorsqu'on dit en occident que l'autonome de la raison et le primat de l'individu sont deux fondements de la modernité, cela pose un problème en islam. Il n'y a pas pour l'islam de primat de l'individu en ce sens qu'il serait dégagé de tout lien d'humanité; son premier lien d'humanité est le lien avec la famille. Il y a omniprésence de cette préoccupation: un humanisme au cœur même de la première relation sociale qui est celle de la reconnaissance des père et mère.[57]

> (One can only underline strongly that the kernel of Islamic humanism is not the individual alone. Human beings are social beings, and their first sociability is the family. When it is said in the West that the autonomy of reason and the primacy of the individual are the two foundations of modernity, that poses a problem in Islam. For Islam there is no primacy of the individual in the sense of something detached from every link with mankind; and the indi-

vidual's first link with mankind is the link with the family. This preoccupation is omnipresent: a humanism at the very heart of the first social relation,
that of recognising one's father and mother.)

While there certainly is generally, though not universally, a different
emphasis on the relationship between individual and family in Western
society, it is not the case that the notion of the individual is devoid of any
link between the self and the rest of humanity in whatever form this may
take, nor are the links between the individual and those around him or
her, particularly links in the form of family relationships, denied or not
valued.

The writers under discussion here all consider in different ways the
situation of the individual in an evolving historical and social context
that necessarily generates a tension between various conceptions of selfhood. These texts are not strictly autobiographies, as has previously been
stressed, but they are more than third-person narratives: they are intimately concerned with questions of identity in ways that seem to be more
intense and to exceed the concerns of the vague notion of 'autobiographical novel'. The idea of a 'creative intervention' that was used at
the beginning of this chapter brings us to a rather different aspect of the
definition of autobiography. In attempts to define what autobiography
is, or is not, the comparison is often made with fiction and here the
problem is also complex, not least because, as Jean Starobinski has
pointed out in an article on the style of autobiography, there is no one
generic style or form, a position further complicated by the ways in which
autobiography (or at least classical autobiography) uses the traditional
devices of fiction – characters, family chronicle, narrative.[58] Nevertheless,
the use of these devices does not turn an autobiography into a fiction.[59]
In attempts to define the genre there are, however, two constants. The
first is the question of truth, to which critics return again and again in
different ways, whether in terms of authorial intention ('this happened
to me'), or in terms of reader perception and expectation, or both, and
which clearly defines an autobiographical mode in opposition to the
expectations of fiction. The second defining feature is the genre's
hermeneutic mode. Autobiography is the place of self-interpretation,
usually, and especially in contemporary texts, with an initial emphasis
on childhood and the conditions of the author's origins, leading to an
analysis of events and people who have influenced the developing personality in an attempt to explain actions and motives, or to find a pattern
to that life. In the case of professional writers there is usually also the
expression of the impulse to try to understand what pushed them to begin

writing, as they ask not only 'who am I?', but also 'why do I write?'.[60]
Autobiography, as we have seen, is the place of a great many present-day
assumptions. As one critic puts it, the general approach to autobiography
involves

> assumptions concerning the relationship between literature and autobiog-
> raphy. Assumptions too about what constitutes style in literature and life
> [...] assumptions about the author's own values, moral code, ethics, and
> assumptions about culture, society, religion. Assumptions about life itself,
> about feelings – one's own and others. Assumptions about one's body and
> soul.[61]

The need to understand and move beyond these assumptions is
particularly important for developing reading strategies to deal with
North African texts in the colonial and postcolonial contexts, and in the
following section I shall attempt to define the need for what may be called
'motivated' reading strategies. The assumption most frequently made, or
at least the commonplace most often repeated concerning autobiography
in North Africa, as we have seen, is that the genre of autobiography is
unknown in, or indeed completely alien to, Arabic and Islamic culture,
and that the autobiographies produced from the 1950s onwards therefore 'borrow' in some way a Western genre. I would argue that while it
is possible to agree to some extent with the idea of influence through
access to Western culture via the French language (an access either
imposed or sought), this approach can only limit the status of these works
unless other heritages and other textual practices are also considered, and
unless we ask at the same time what these writings contribute to the
modes of autobiographical expression. Autobiography is a mode of
writing that constantly reinvents itself and whose basic premise is that of
self-questioning, not only of the subjectivity under investigation, but of
the very forms in which that investigation may take place.

POSTCOLONIAL STUDIES, THE POSTCOLONIAL SUBJECT
AND MOTIVATED READING STRATEGIES

> The struggle for the power to name oneself and one's state is enacted funda-
> mentally within words, most especially in colonial situations. So a concern
> with language, far from indicating a retreat, may be an investigation into
> the depths of the political unconscious.[62]

Among the assumptions that have been referred to above is the underlying assumption among many French critics that the French school and
the French language are forces for good, providing the tools that enable

a kind of liberation through language (French as the language of self-hood, as Déjeux declares it). The origins of this assumption lie in the discourse of the French Republican model, which I will discuss further below. The discourse of French critics, even when they are writing positively about literatures in French from outside the *metropole*, is often unsettling to the British, American and Australian critics who choose their vocabulary more carefully in a postcolonial context. An example is the introduction to a collection of papers from a major conference held in France in 1994 dedicated to Francophone autobiography, in which these writings are referred to as 'les littératures francophones de la périphérie'[63] ('Francophone literatures of the periphery'), while their 'problématiques esthétiques toutes contemporaines' ('completely contemporary aesthetic problematics') are nonetheless valued. The French Empire may well be writing back, but the term 'postcolonialism' has made slow progress in its usage in France.[64] Indeed much of the pioneering work on postcolonial texts from countries formerly colonised by France has been done by critics working in the USA, such as Françoise Lionnet and Anne Donadey. This is one reason why some critics, within France and elsewhere, are questioning the value of the 'Francophone' label, and have begun to prefer to talk about the postcolonial historical and political context, and the postcolonial attitude of writers and critics, as I shall explain below, in order to approach the question of the effects of French colonialism both politically and culturally.[65]

The more interesting issue concerning language with regard to texts written in French from outside metropolitan France transcends the incessant debate about the language the authors choose to write in and concerns the relationship between the individual and the language available with which to express selfhood. This in no way suggests that the language choice, or indeed lack of choice, confronting these writers in the colonial and postcolonial situation is not a vital point, and this is an issue that will be addressed in the reading of the texts here. The study of autobiography adds a further dimension to the language debate, since it could be said that in order to write the self, all writers of autobiographical discourse have needed to battle with their mother tongue. The obvious modern example in French literature is Michel Leiris: the opening to *Biffures*, the scene in which the small boy realises for the first time that language does not belong to him, but that he 'belongs' in some way to language, language that is used by everyone else, is an extremely powerful description of the 'entry into language', to use a Lacanian framework that is appropriate in the case of Leiris:

> Il n'est plus maintenant une chose à moi: il participe de cette réalité qu'est
> le langage de mes frères, de ma sœur, et celui de mes parents. De chose propre
> à moi, il devient chose commun et ouverte [...] en quoi le langage articulé,
> tissu arachnéen de mes rapports avec les autres me dépasse, poussant de tous
> côtés ses antennes mystérieuses.[66]

> (Now it is no longer my own: it shares in that reality which is the language
> of my brothers, my sister, and the language of my parents. From being mine,
> it has become something open, common to all [...] in which the many-
> branched language that forms a spider's-web of links between me and other
> people, has gone beyond me, thrusting out its mysterious antennae in all
> directions.)

Indeed, when human beings learn a language 'they imitate others and
they become themselves'.[67] It has been suggested in an analysis of Black
autobiography that all autobiography is minority autobiography, that
every autobiographer is isolated and questions the relationship between
the minority constituted by the individual and the majority, not feeling
any 'kinship with anything outside its own limitations'. Black autobiography is the writing of a minority within a minority, in which each
member of the minority attempts to 'reach an understanding of both
himself and the reality in which he has been placed'.[68] This question of
the forms such discourses of the self might take has been extensively
treated in feminist studies of autobiography and in, for example, Black
Studies, both in Britain and the USA. My approach here will very much
take as a reference point the work done in these areas and the ways in
which autobiographical expression questions dominant ideologies and
discourses, and indeed the form the canon takes. As James Olney points
out with reference to English and American literature,

> Not only have previously excluded groups of writers – women, blacks, other
> minorities – been given entry into the canon, but also various writing modes,
> in particular autobiography, are recognised as having claims equal to those
> of more traditional literary genres. And these two aspects of the redefinition
> of the literary canon are not unrelated since women and Afro-Americans
> especially among previously slighted groups have always been strongly
> drawn to the creation of a distinct identity through autobiographical expres-
> sion.[69]

Of particular relevance for the study here is the analysis of the alternative and diverse autobiographical practices of women writers that call
into question the assumptions made by Western male autobiographers
and by histories of the development of the genre written by male critics
that have promoted the Western ideal of individual identity with a self
that defines itself as complete and separate from the other. Shari
Benstock, for example, poses the following questions: 'What forms are
included under the autobiographical? Where does authority rest for

writing "autobiography"?'[70] 'How do women from differing races, social classes, nationalities, religions, sexual preferences, and historical time periods and places define the terms of autobiographical writing?'[71] Benstock criticises Gusdorf's theory in the essay previously quoted, not only from the perspective that several feminist critics share, that is to say that autobiography is seen as the glorification of a man and his public life, but also in relation to the notion of autobiography as a 'mirror in which the individual reflects his own image' (Gusdorf), since 'certain forms of self-writing [...] have no investment in creating a cohesive self over time. Indeed, they seem to exploit difference and change over sameness and identity. Psychic health is measured in the degree to which "self" is constructed in separateness, the boundaries between "self" and "other" carefully circumscribed'.[72] And Benstock adds: 'This view of the life history is grounded in authority'[73], a point that is essential when considering power relations in the colonial and postcolonial contexts and the challenge posed by the texts under discussion in this book. Susan Stanford Friedman has also noted that 'psychoanalytical models of the autobiographical self remain fundamentally individualistic because the healthy ego is defined in terms of its ability to separate itself from others'.[74] A similar point was made in the introduction here concerning hesitation in applying Western analytical models to non-Western cultures. Indeed some feminist critics establish a link between male autobiographical practice, the cult of individuality and colonialism. This returns us crucially to Weintraub's distinction between individualism as a conception of the ideal relation between the individual and society, and the personality conception of individuality. Women's autobiographical practices, like the postcolonial practices under analysis here, seem to explore the social conception of individualism. The 'I' does not necessarily 'represent' a 'we', but is often a vehicle to explore the relation between the 'I' and that 'we'.

Gusdorf, as we have seen, calls the Western male 'gatherer of men, of lands, of power, maker of kingdoms or of empires'. However, as Susan Stanford Friedman comments, not only are women rather the 'gathered, the colonised, the ruled',[75] but '[a] white man has the luxury of forgetting his skin color and sex. He can think of himself as an "individual". Women and minorities, reminded at every turn in the great cultural hall of mirrors of their sex or color, have no such luxury.'[76] She also argues that there is in women's autobiographical practice a resistance against the 'individualistic concept of the autobiographical' that challenges traditional definitions of autobiography, and that a feature of women's autobiography is collective identity and interdependent identification. Of particular interest for this study is the analogy that Friedman makes between Gusdorf's description of a culture in which autobiography is impossible and what she calls the 'marginalised cultures of women', a type of culture without the elements Gusdorf considers to be the necessary preconditions for autobiography, a culture in which

> the individual does not oppose himself to all others; [in which] he does not feel himself to exist outside of others, and still less against others, but very much with others in an interdependent existence that asserts its rhythms everywhere in the community [...in which] lives are so thoroughly entangled that each of them has its center everywhere and its circumference nowhere. The important unit is thus never the isolated being.[77]

As Friedman goes on to point out,

> The very sense of identification, interdependence, and community that Gusdorf dismisses from autobiographical selves are key elements in the development of a woman's identity according to theorists like Rowbotham and Chodorow. Their models of women's selfhood highlight the unconscious masculine bias in Gusdorf's and other individualistic paradigms.[78]

Indeed the 'maleness' of autobiography has been taken for granted by many critics, and feminist critics have also analysed how the place of women writers in the development of autobiographical writing has been neglected, with the result that 'critical work in the field, for all its insistence on mirroring universals, has presented a distorted reflection of the history of the autobiographical genre'.[79] Brodzki and Schenk reiterate the points made by Benstock concerning the ways in which masculine autobiographies usually incarnate the Western ideal of an essential self, and that female autobiographers are often identified as lacking a sense of individuality.[80]

Furthermore, feminist autobiographical criticism has recognised the interpretative problem for texts in which a marginalised subject speaks a dominant discourse that echoes the complex politics of language in postcolonial contexts.[81] However, the canon has changed far more radically in British, American and Australian universities – necessitating an equally radical shift in critical attitude to these texts – than it has in France, and this point is linked to previous remarks concerning both writing from the Maghreb and the concept of postcolonialism more generally. The texts that will be analysed in this book are not 'autobiographies' in the strict sense, as pointed out before, but it is useful to maintain some kind of definition in order to understand better how all forms of 'autobiographical discourse' function and the particular strategies that these writers make use of. By 'autobiographical discourse' here

I mean texts that we know (or suspect) write the life or parts of the life of the author, but in which the reader is reliant on outside information to substantiate this. Perhaps a more useful way of describing these texts may be to invoke the notion of *la fiction identitaire* ('identity fiction'; fiction concerned with notions of identity) suggested by Laurence Joffrin writing about migrant literature in French Canada.[82] Joffrin believes that the term 'autofiction' that is used in contemporary debate does not sufficiently take into account the 'jeu référentiel sur l'identité de l'auteur' ('the referential game around the author's identity'). The attitude inside Quebec to *la littérature migrante* ('migrant literature), which differs radically from the attitude of metropolitan France to 'Francophone literatures', is also discussed by Joffrin:

> L'écriture migrante constitue une topographie de la porosité identitaire québécoise: minoritaire parmi les minoritaires, l'écrivain migrant vit de façon exacerbée le motif de base de la littérature québécoise. Il renvoie ainsi aux Québécois une image à la fois fascinante et inquiétante de leur identité culturelle. Notons que les éditeurs et les critiques québécois, loin de considérer l'écriture migrante dans sa différence, ce qui reviendrait à lui assigner une position de littérature de ghetto, l'intègrent à la littérature québécoise, non dans une volonté d'assimilation, mais pour sa capacité de déplacer la réflexion sur l'identité culturelle. Il me semble que l'expression la plus représentative de ce courant est la fiction identitaire, dans la mesure où ce type d'écriture ne propose pas une identité circonscrite, mais exhibe, au contraire, les brèches sous-jacentes à toute culture. Si l'on considère que les nouvelles formes de l'autobiographie remettent en question l'unité du sujet postulée par l'autobiographe traditionnel, la fiction identitaire s'inscrit de plain-pied dans cette démarche.[83]

> (Migrant writing represents a topography of Quebec's porous identity: as a minority among minorities, the migrant writer experiences the basic motif of Quebec literature in an accentuated way. And thus he or she mirrors back to Quebec readers an image of their cultural identity which is both fascinating and troubling. Note that Quebec publishers and critics, far from contemplating the difference of migrant writing (which would mean assigning it to the status of ghetto literature) integrate it into Quebec literature, not by way of assimilation, but because of its capacity to displace reflection on cultural identity. It seems to me that the most expressive term for this current is 'identity fiction', since this type of writing does not offer a circumscribed identity, but on the contrary reveals the fissures underlying all cultures. If the new forms of autobiography are considered as calling into question the unity of the subject which is a postulate of traditional autobiography, then identity fiction holds a central place in that questioning.)

In migrant literature the consideration of the individual subject leads to an analysis of the culture in which the individual lives, not only of the community to which he or she belongs, but of the whole of society. Furthermore, the relationship of migrant literature to the literature of the dominant culture ('minor' literature and 'major' literature, in Deleuze and Guattari's terms) and the issues of 'ghettoisation' and 'assimilation' are treated very differently in the French and Francophone contexts when compared to the multicultural model more familiar to the British or American reader.

In order to explore a number of different approaches to the question of the postcolonial subject writing in French, it is therefore useful to begin by moving outside the limits of French and Francophone studies, as previously suggested, and to place the debate more generally within the current discussions in the field of postcolonial studies, notably with reference to work being done in the English-speaking world. Despite the care with which the critic needs to approach the term 'post(-)colonial',[84] it is nonetheless a more appropriate and useful critical term for the reading of these necessarily politicised texts than the 'Francophone' label under which these writers have been previously grouped in French critical terminology, and through the application of which they are accepted or rejected by literary and cultural institutions, and indeed are often categorised in French bookshops, the site of their diffusion in French society (although this has changed noticeably in some places over the last few years).[85] Here I am using the term 'postcolonial' in its broadest sense, as it has been used by literary critics from the late 1970s onwards in what the French term the 'Anglo-Saxon' world to discuss 'the various cultural effects of colonisation'.[86] It is important to stress that the readings here are mainly concerned with these 'cultural effects', although the political, economic and social situation is of course bound up with this. Of the many phenomena that postcolonial studies take as a topic for analysis, the aspect that most concerns us here is the 'subtleties of subject construction in colonial discourse and the resistance of those subjects'.[87] Within the framework of this study, 'postcolonial' remains a more satisfactory concept than the 'Francophone' label in order to designate writers whose origins lie outside metropolitan France, and usually in former colonial territories. Although the term 'Francophone' can be used simply to indicate the ability to speak French, in reality *francophonie* is generally used to designate a political strategy, and even a form of neo-colonialism. The difference between postcolonialism and *francophonie* can be seen as residing in differing political stances:

> Unlike *francophonie*, the political dimensions of which are masked by a term which superficially appears to denote a purely cultural field of reference, the post-colonial highlights a political condition characterising certain forms of cultural production, i.e. the legacy of colonial domination out of or against which cultural practices are seen to emerge. In its own way, the 'post' in post-colonial often connotes a political assertion akin to, or rather in contra-

diction with, that underlying *francophonie*: to speak of a post-colonial condition is to affirm the right to political and cultural self-determination.[88]

This 'masking' of the political dimension of the term 'Francophone' is also objected to by Roger Little:

> The man credited with forging the word '*la francophonie*' in the 1880s, the geographer Onésime Reclus, thereby proposed a division of the world's population not on the traditional basis of 'race', tribe, colour, skull shape, supposed intellectual or real technological superiority, but on that of a shared language. From the outset, therefore, the neologism has socio-political implications, reinforced by the fiercely republican sentiments held by all the Reclus brothers. But increasingly, since the revival of the term in the November 1962 issue of *L'Esprit* devoted to '*Le français dans le monde*' ('French in the world'), its descriptive, etymological sense has been superseded, not to say hi-jacked, by a political one. The latest report on *l'Etat de la Francophonie dans le monde* by the *Haut Conseil de la Francophonie* makes a position statement which is unambiguous (even if surprisingly frank about its concentration on window-dressing): '*En effet, cette institution intergouvernementale se préoccupe de sa promotion politique, afin qu'elle soit plus visible et plus crédible*' (Indeed, this inter-governmental institution is concerned with its own political promotion in order that it may be more visible and credible).[89]

More generally there is a political issue concerning the use of language in former colonised territories. As John Erickson has put it concerning the use of the adjectives 'Anglophone', 'Francophone' and so on to identify countries outside the 'mother' country:

> By their prefixes, these terms put a premium on the language and the culture of the 'mother' country: metropolitan England, France, Spain or Portugal. They valorise the political and economic interests of the 'mother' country and gloss over the significant cultural/linguistic differences existing between the non-metropolitan countries and the Metropole as well as between themselves.[90]

Yet there are problems with the term 'post(-)colonial' also. I do not wish to rehearse here the thorough analysis of the critiques of postcolonial theory, for example, in the introduction to Hargreaves' and McKinney's edited collection *Post-Colonial Cultures in France*, but indicate the usefulness of the discussion for readers here.[91] A number of issues are flagged up, including the danger of postcolonial theory 'replicating what it purportedly critiques' and the charge that by maintaining the post-European colonial periodisation, postcolonial studies remain Eurocentric. Alec Hargreaves and Mark McKinney also discuss the problem of postcolonial theory being simply an addition to the other 'posts' that indicate a crisis in Western theory and as such failing to reflect the real concerns of the cultures it seeks to read and re-read. Nonetheless the term is adopted by them as a 'valuable heuristic device in the study of cultural practices in contemporary France'.[92]

Anne McClintock has argued that the term 'confers on colonialism the prestige of history proper; colonialism is the determining marker of history [...] The world's multitudinous cultures are marked not positively by what distinguishes them but by a subordinate, retrospective relation to linear European time'.[93] She goes on to argue that the term 'postcolonialism' is 'prematurely celebratory and obfuscatory in more ways than one' and especially unstable with respect to the position of women who do not share the same singular or 'postcolonial condition'.[94] Charles Forsdick and David Murphy, in *Francophone Postcolonial Studies*, emphasise the positive contribution of Postcolonial Studies in a further useful discussion of its development. They remark both on the ways in which Postcolonial Studies have led English literature departments to revise the literary canon (a point also made by James Olney, as cited earlier) and on the willingness within the field to 'refine the object of its research in the light of criticisms of earlier definitions', taking as an example the use or non-use of the hyphenated form. Like these critics, Bart Moore-Gilbert remains optimistic, especially in the domain of comparative analysis across cultural contexts, despite a suspicion that the postcolonial 'moment' has been and gone, or at least 'dissipated'. Moore-Gilbert remains aware of the power relationship between the discipline and its objects of study, and argues that the pressing issue is

> how to conceptualise the relationship between these plural kinds of post-colonial identity and the wide variety of cultural forms and modes of cultural analysis to which they give rise. This problem is also bound up with the issue of how to theorise the relationship between complex varieties of postcolonial identity and modes of cultural/critical production on the one hand and, on the other, groupings and cultural/critical forms which are organized in reference to often quite different forms of social and historical experience, more particularly the areas of gender, class and sexuality.[95]

The emphasis on hybridity and plural identity in postcolonial studies has therefore, according to Moore-Gilbert, generated significant problems as well as potential.

Robert Young's analysis provides much-needed precision in the use of the term, and his argument constructs an enabling way of using the concept:

> Postcolonial critique involves the reconsideration of the history of this (the long, violent history of colonialism), particularly from the perspectives of those who suffered its effects, together with the defining of its contemporary social and cultural impact. This is why postcolonial theory always intermingles the past with the present, why it is directed towards the active transformations of the present out of the clutches of the past. The post-colonial does not privilege the colonial. It is concerned with colonial history only to the extent that this history has determined the configurations and power structures of the present [...] The entire world now operates within

the economic system primarily developed and controlled by the west, and it is the continued dominance of the west, in terms of political, economic, military and cultural power, that gives this history a continuing significance.[96]

Very importantly, Young makes a distinction between the terms 'colonial' and 'postcolonial', on the one hand, and 'imperialism' on the other – the world in which we live may be described as postcolonial, but imperialism in its broadest sense continues to operate. Young defines colonialism as a pragmatic need to exploit and settle other territories, while imperialism is driven by ideology, and tellingly he sees this as originally a French political ideology:

> Many of the problems [concerning the term 'postcolonial'] can be resolved if the postcolonial is defined as coming after colonialism and imperialism, in their original meaning of direct-rule domination, but still positioned within imperialism in its later sense of the global system of hegemonic economic power. The postcolonial is a dialectical concept that marks the broad historical facts of decolonisation and the determined achievement of sovereignty – but also the realities of nations and peoples emerging into a new imperialistic context of economic and sometimes political domination.[97]

As for the criticisms levelled against postcolonial theory as yet another Eurocentric theory, Young is clear in his counter-argument. He sees such criticism as engaging in the 'common anti-postcolonial trope',

> the form of which repeats the assumption of cultural inferiority so searchingly analysed by Fanon: anything that has come to be regarded as being of intellectual or political significance in the west could have had nothing to do with the (so-called) Third World, even when it is itself a critique of the west conducted from one of the many locations and positions of the three continents. Postcolonial theory, in other words, 'must' be European, if it has made such an impact in the west [...] Those who reject contemporary postcolonial theory in the name of the 'Third World' on the grounds of it being western, however, are themselves in doing so negating the very input of the Third World, starting with Derrida, disavowing therefore the very non-European work which their critique professes to advocate.[98]

Essentially, Robert Young identifies the postcolonial as a form of knowledge, and it is this that is important for our reading here:

> It is this mixture of material, historical conditions and hybrid discourses, together with analysis of their cultural effects on people's identities and epistemologies, that captures the distinctive, constitutive feature of the postcolonial as a form of knowledge.[99]

As Hargreaves and McKinney point out, the experience of colonialism, decolonisation and its aftermath, particularly with reference to North Africa and specifically in the case of Algeria, is a legacy that has not yet been fully dealt with in contemporary French culture and politics; they argue that 'the very limited presence of an explicitly "post-colonial" discourse in France is in many ways a reflection of lingering neo-colonial reflexes'.[100] I would add here the personal experience of being met with bewilderment in France when speaking of France's 'third major war this century', meaning the Algerian War of Independence (to say nothing of the conflict in Indo-China immediately following the end of the Second World War). Indeed, the 'war with no name' was only acknowledged as a war at the very end of the twentieth century, being more usually referred to until that time as 'the events' (Mouloud Feraoun refers to them as *les événements* in his diary, which will be explored in Chapter 2), in a way reminiscent of British references to 'the Troubles' in Northern Ireland. On 5 October 1999, the National Assembly in France finally adopted a draft law officially recognising the Algerian War. The reluctance to come to terms with the conflict in Algeria needs to be seen in relation to the more general problematic of coming to terms with France's recent history since the Second World War and the Occupation, as has been so powerfully analysed by Henry Rousso, for example. This reluctance in France to address the country's colonial heritage is evident in various forms of cultural production, including cinema and television, as well as in political life.[101] I am in no way suggesting that the British attitude to Britain's colonial history and its legacies is somehow 'better', or has been more successfully dealt with, but these are issues that the non-French reader must be aware of in order to read the work of North African writers in the political context that surrounds them, and especially to understand some of the problems with their reception in France. A further issue is that the multiculturalism that characterises postcolonial society in the English-speaking world is approached very differently in France. In France attitudes towards the postcolonial world are bound up very closely with the sense of French identity, and with citizenship and the ideals of French republicanism, which involve a very different view of the constitution of society, one that does not easily accommodate difference and alternative identities. These fundamental ideas about identity have resulted in a contemporary culture in France in which identity-based politics and multiculturalism, such a feature of cultural and political life in Britain, the USA and Australia, are much less prominent (although the debate is again changing towards what Mireille Rosello terms 'hybrid' or 'tactical' universalism), and in which the notions of ethnic difference and ethnicity are not commonly invoked, particularly since the resurgence of the republican model of integration in the 1980s:

> According to its French defenders, the republican model conceives of integration as a process by which individuals subordinate their particularist origins and accept membership in a unitary nation-state defined by refer-

ence to shared universalist values, in contrast to the multicultural model associated with the United States and Great Britain, which preserves particularist identities and fosters group-based integration into the multicultural nation-state. Whereas multicultural states recognise ethnic communities and preserve cultural differences, republican states only recognise individuals and individual rights, and strive to overcome differences. Under the republican model, ethnic origin is deemed unacceptable as a basis for organisation and mobilisation by political actors, or for the conferring of rights, recognition, or entitlements by public authorities.[102]

This is a manifestation in French contemporary society of the legacy of the universalist values and 'civilising mission' of French colonialist policy, which was at its most powerful under the Third Republic. The French colonial regime promoted the idea of the 'assimilation' of colonised peoples, and the legacy of this was nowhere more apparent than in Algeria, particularly after the imposition of the colonial laws of 1863 and 1865, the latter stipulating that 'the Arabs and Berbers were subjects; it allowed them to apply for French citizenship, with the proviso that they follow the French code and renounce their "personal status", namely their Muslim identity'.[103] Azzedine Haddour goes on to argues that

> [the] *senatus-consulte* of 1865 stipulated that all the colonised indigenous were under French jurisdiction, i.e., French nationals subjected to French laws, but it restricted citizenship only to those who renounced their Muslim religion and culture. There was an obvious split in French legal discourse: a split between nationality and citizenship which established the formal structures of a political apartheid encouraging the existence of 'French subjects' disenfranchised, without any rights to citizenship, treated as objects of French law and not as citizens. Fanon's view of colonialism as a Manichean discourse, as a system of apartheid promoting the politics of compartmentalised spaces, as well as Memmi's critique of the theory of assimilation as a contradictory discourse must be situated in this political context.[104]

Robert Young has also analysed the contradictions at the heart of French assimilationist theories, following his discussion of the term 'imperialism' in its 'original French reference' and of the use made of the concept by Marx to analyse the French nationalism developed by Louis Bonaparte, nephew of Napoleon, after the *coup d'état* of 1851, which looked back to the era of the First Empire and Emperor in France, and which 'increasingly implied a policy of pursuing national prestige through conquest and expansion abroad':

> The *mission civilisatrice* (to bring the benefits of French culture, religion and language to the 'unenlightened races of the earth') was more central to French imperial ideology than any other on account of the French colonial doctrine of assimilation. As the image of the greater France implies, however far away the colonies may have been, they were administratively and concep-

tually treated as part of mainland France. The French colonial system of assimilation was originally derived, via the French Revolution, from an Enlightenment belief in a common liberty, equality and fraternity for humankind [...]

Broadly, the French [...] operated a rational theorised system for their colonies based on the doctrine of assimilation, whereby the colonies were integrated as *Départements d'outre-mer* (overseas counties) and were thus not technically colonies at all. There was a further paradox within the assimilationist doctrine: on the one hand, it was the most progressive of all imperial ideologies, to the extent that it assumed the fundamental equality of all human beings, their common humanity as part of a single species, and considered that however 'natural' or 'backward' their state, all native people could immediately benefit from the uniform imposition of French culture in its most advanced contemporary manifestation. On the other hand, this very assumption meant that the French model had the least respect and sympathy for the culture, language and institutions of the people being colonised – it saw difference, and sought to make it the same – what might be called the paradox of ethnocentric egalitarianism.[105]

Young also notes that it is no accident that many of the major anti-colonial intellectuals, for example Senghor and Césaire as well as Fanon and Memmi, came from the French colonies after paradoxically benefiting from the educational opportunities on offer. He also stresses the importance of understanding the French system (which he describes very much as a system, compared to haphazard and commercially based British colonialism) in order to understand not only the work of a theorist such as Fanon, but much of the origins of postcolonial theory:

Apart from [Edward] Said, postcolonial theory is predominantly based on the work of Frantz Fanon, and it was Fanon who developed the analysis of colonialism as a single formation (in *Towards an African Revolution*). In this he was following Sartre, who insisted on this aspect in his 1952 essay 'Le colonialisme est un système'. Both of them were describing French colonialism, which indeed was comparatively systematic [...] Broadly speaking, it could be said that what has occurred in postcolonial theory is that a theoretical base, derived largely from French anti-colonial theory, has been deployed upon examples drawn from the history of the British Empire which operated on very different principles.[106]

In the multiple aspects of the preceding discussion, we can see therefore a number of reasons for the slow progress made by the perspectives of postcolonialism in France's approaches to its colonial history. There are certainly, however, also multiple manifestations of a diverse culture in opposition to a view of French society inherited from the republican model described above, just one example being the music of popular rap artists in which

the ideological underpinnings of racism in France are also dissected and rejected: there is a vehement anti-nationalism, an explicit rejection of the integrationist 'republican' model of 'race-relations' in France and of colonialist and imperialist attitudes, which shape French education, distort African and Maghrebi history, and reinforce economic domination.[107]

In this book I am therefore using the concept of postcolonialism not to refer to a period or a movement coming after colonialism, but 'more flexibly [to refer to] the contestation of colonial domination and the legacies of colonialism'.[108] The work recently done in the field of postcolonial studies needs of course to be juxtaposed with the fundamental ideas of three of the most influential commentators in French on the question of the postcolonial subject: Aimé Césaire and in particular his discussion of *la chosification* (objectification) of the colonial subject, the writings of Frantz Fanon on the 'split subject', and Albert Memmi's writing on the depersonalisation of the colonised and on the power relations within the 'duo' of coloniser and colonised. All three are influential writers who are frequently referred to and drawn on in postcolonial studies in English, as Robert Young points out especially with regard to Fanon. Nonetheless, it is important to realise that these writers are themselves drawing on French intellectual traditions in order to challenge them, a feature of resistance to colonial rule being the use, and often subversion, of the dominant discourse of the coloniser whereby the discursive processes of the dominant culture are challenged from within:

> anti-colonial movements and individuals often drew upon Western ideas and vocabularies to challenge colonial rule. Indeed they often hybridised what they borrowed by juxtaposing it with their own interpretative lens, and even using it to assert cultural alterity or insist on an unbridgeable difference between coloniser and colonised.[109]

The concept of hybridity, a term used here to mean the ways in which aspects of the dominant colonial discourse were challenged and undermined and then appropriated by the previously colonised peoples, is a positive challenge to the dominant discourse, and I shall be exploring this particularly in the writing strategies employed by the writers under analysis here. It is always essential, however, to be aware of the 'system of representation' operating on postcolonial writers: 'Colonialism […] is an operation of discourse, and as an operation of discourse it interpellates colonial subjects by incorporating them in a system of representation. They are always already written by that system of representation.'[110]

Indeed, many of the writing strategies used by the writers I shall analyse are conscious attempts to write themselves out of the dominant system of representation, and to find another way of being. I would reiterate, therefore, that it is a useful critical strategy to step outside this particular 'system of representation' and the French intellectual framework that informs the work of these writers and the expectations of their readers in French, and to think conceptually using some of the terminology current in postcolonial studies. One point that rapidly becomes clear when we try to think about the identity of the postcolonial subject is how the web of language (to take the image used by Michel Leiris, whom I quoted earlier and who grappled incessantly with the question of his own subjectivity and its creation in language) weaves itself around the writer and the reader. Consequently, the critic needs to make clear his or her own stance in relation to the material to be examined. Just as the writer challenges assumptions concerning the perception of the individual in the colonial and postcolonial situations, so must the reader: 'The post-colonial is especially and pressingly concerned with the power that lies in discourse and textuality; its resistance, then, quite appropriately takes place in – and from – the domain of textuality, in (among other things) motivated acts of reading. The contestation of post-colonialism is a contest of representation.'[111]

This is what I mean by the necessity for an act of 'motivated reading' with regard to texts created in colonial and postcolonial situations. Such a reading is crucial if the tension between competing discourses is to be made clear: 'The theoretical challenge lies in bringing sophisticated skills to the service of a politically informed reading of texts [...] Political and social considerations inform any reading, for all readers are political and social beings. To deny the applicability of political and social considerations is to take a political position.'[112]

Nancy Miller also advocates a political reading. Here the emphasis is on gender, but a more general point is also made about 'reading for difference':

> To read for difference, therefore, is to perform a diacritical gesture, to refuse a politics of reading that depends on the fiction of a neutral (neuter) economy of textual production and reception. This refusal of a fiction of degendered reading is a movement of oscillation which locates difference in the negotiation between writer and reader. The difference of which I speak here, however, is located in the 'I' of the beholder, in the reader's perception. I would propose then, the notion of gender-marked reading: a practice of the text that would recognise the status of the reader as a differentiated subject, a reading subject named by gender and committed in a dialectics of identification to deciphering the inscription of a female subject.[113]

Here my aim is to decipher the inscription of the postcolonial subject. Indeed images and metaphors of deciphering and inscription recur time and time again within the textual production of the writers under analysis as a new relationship to the past is forged. The reader is made an active participant in what becomes a type of archaeological process.

Miller also notes how Lejeune's definition of autobiography changed as he came to see the issue being as much about a mode of *reading* as about a mode of *writing*: 'a contractual genre dependent upon codes of transmission and reception'.[114] This raises an important issue concerning reader identification and audience. Helen Carr has explicitly articulated the problem of the position of the Western reader in relation to postcolonial texts, in a statement that has resonances with my own position, as I noted in the introduction: 'As an Englishwoman writing about Native American women's autobiography, I am at a double remove from my subject; yet I hope that remove may have its advantages. There is a sense in which it is easier – perhaps deceptively so – for the colonising nations to grasp one another's dubious imperial histories rather than their own.'[114]

As an English woman writing about North African texts in French, I am similarly at a double remove, in what I hope to be a productive critical position. There is, however, a need to 'declare oneself' in relation to these texts, since as these writers grapple with the tensions and contradictions within their own identities, they force the reader to examine his or her own conception of self. Postcolonial studies shares with feminist critical theory, therefore, an attention to motivated and self-aware practices of reading. Feminist reading practices have always been concerned with historically constructed discourses of patriarchy and male authority, and with the accompanying 'cultural silencing' of women in these dominant discourses, whether in the public, private or artistic domains. As Brodzki and Schenck have put it, 'to become a feminist reader of autobiography is to become a new kind of subject'.[116] The same can be said of the motivated reader of postcolonial texts, who also becomes a new kind of subject. Indeed Françoise Lionnet points out that modifications in autobiographical discursive practice bear testimony to the pluralities of postcolonial existence, and thus challenge readers 'to become multicultural subjects as well, capable of recognising the different shapes that a post-colonial artist's shadow might cast on the conventions of genre'.[117] Western feminist critical practice has paid particular attention to rereading dominant discourses that present a distorted history of women's identity, subjectivity and self-expression, and to analysing the challenge posed by women's cultural production to the internalisation of the hegemonic Western male worldview. It is clear, then, that for many feminist critics, women share many of the characteristics of the colonised subject (and especially the experience of the fragmentation of the subject and of its culture under the dominant power, together with the removal of agency and ensuing self-denial), to the extent that some commentators have spoken of the need for a 'self-decolonisation' of the female subject. Re-readings of women's writing have always also made clear their relation to allied fields of interest – race, class, religion, history and politics – and as such make feminist theory a useful analytical tool in the reading of colonial and postcolonial texts – not only those produced by women, but all texts produced in a situation where the writer is resisting oppression and challenging the historically imposed image of the self in order to reappropriate the past and to re-evaluate a repressed culture in order to facilitate the construction of a subjectivity previously repressed.[118] In other words, what is involved here is 'reading for difference'. Feminist reading practices necessarily insist on the responsibility and the identification of the reader, and make abundantly clear the political implications of all analytical strategies and principles. Indeed, feminist discourse has made clear the universalising agenda of Western theorising and confronts postmodern theory that has challenged notions of the subject, for in feminist practice the question of 'who is speaking' is essential: 'The discourse of authority, of patriarchy, of morality can be spoken very differently from various vantage points. The discourse may be the same, but it affects people differently, and people affected are likely to think, act, and feel differently.'[119] For the postcolonial writer also it makes a great deal of difference who is speaking. This is not to say that postmodern theories of the subject have no place in feminist reading practice, for postmodern theory poses a challenge to the authority of the prevailing discourse:

> To question the radical deconstruction of the subject, however, is not to ignore the valuable critique of traditional conceptions of the 'self' supplied by these theories. Their authors may have been reacting to mid-twentieth-century revolutionary dogmatism centred on modern versions of a 'humanistic' discourse, but feminists have also found that discourse anti-thetical to a recognition of women's traditional concerns, indeed, to a qualitatively different reorganisation of social structures. Feminists may, therefore, share a certain portion of these critical perspectives.[120]

Linda Hutcheon also points to a similar issue as she underlines the major difference between theories elaborated by postcolonial studies and by feminist criticism, on the one hand, and the theories of the postmodern on the other:

> Feminisms have had similar impacts on both post-modern and post-colonial criticism. They have redirected the 'universalist'-humanist and liberal discourses in which both are debated and circumscribed [...] The current post-structuralist/post-modern challenges to the coherent, autonomous subject have to be put on hold in feminist and post-colonial discourses, for both must work first to assert and affirm a denied or alienated subjectivity:

> those radical post-modern challenges are in many ways the luxury of the dominant order which can afford to challenge that which it securely possesses.[121]

Certain postcolonial critics have also pointed out the danger of post-modern conceptions of the decentred subject, going so far as to make an analogy between postmodernism and neo-colonialism: 'post-structuralist theories of split and agonistic subjectivity came into vogue just at the moment when marginalised subjects were finding a more powerful collective voice. Is the notion of the decentred subject the latest strategy of Western colonialism?'.[122]

Feminist critics seek to analyse and articulate female subjectivity without falling into the trap of essentialism, again a problem that needs to be addressed in postcolonial writing.[123] Frantz Fanon, for example, attacked the Négritude movement for its totalising and essentialist approach to 'Blackness'.[124] Although twentieth-century critical theory has undermined the notion of selfhood in the diverse approaches of Althusser, Foucault and Lacan, 'a feminist agenda cannot include further or repeated marginalisation of female selfhood without betraying its own political program'.[125] This is again an especially important point in the reading of postcolonial texts, when the reader needs to be aware of the authority of universalising, patriarchal, hegemonising discourses, while at the same time seeking to hear the articulation of marginalised discourses.

Postcolonial theory and feminist theory have also raised the particularly difficult issue of 'interpretative colonialism'. As Helen Carr has expressed it,

> Westerners have assumed that they can see and judge the inhabitants of the Third World more clearly than they do themselves, just as women have been traditionally evaluated by the male gaze. But in both cases the gaze has been myopic, selective, reifying. These autobiographies, with all their limitations, remind us of the need for sensitive agnosticism and for the acknowledgement of other subjectivities, other points of view.[126]

Conversely, feminism also highlights the 'central problem we have in reading any women's autobiographies: interpreting a text in which a marginalised subject speaks a dominant discourse'.[127] And as Julia Watson and Sidonie Smith have made clear,

> We do want, however, to call into question Western literary practices and theorising. It does us no good, it does literary practice no good, to take up critical definitions, typologies, reading practices, and thematics forged in the West through the engagement with canonical Western texts and to read texts from various global locations through those lenses. Different texts from different locales require us to develop different theories and practices of

> reading, what we might call 'stand-point' reading practices. Such practices call all of us, positioned specifically in our own locales, both to engage the autobiographical practices of colonial subjects and to critique our own points of observation.[128]

While such caveats need to be observed, we also need however to bear in mind the points raised earlier concerning Robert Young's discussion of the danger of branding postcolonial theory as solely 'Western'.

The reading strategies employed in this book take up the approaches advocated by Françoise Lionnet in her own work, in which she uses a variety of analytical techniques, described by her as involving

> close attention to the language of the texts discussed but also concern for the ways in which this language embodies and reflects the social, historical, and political dynamics of the larger cultural realms that surround it and give it value and power [...] I adhere, however, to what I would call a 'feminist practice of reading', understood as a resistance to reductionist theories or to the territorialising of texts by critics who remain deaf to the 'confusion of tongues' by which these texts are inhabited. I have tried to show how a careful understanding of textual structures and verbal patterns can guide our interpretative strategies and enrich our experience of this diverse body of literature.[129]

There are limits, of course, to the Western critic's ability to succeed in this. What I can aim to provide are readings aware of themselves as an 'enabling limitation', as Gayatri Spivak has described the limited way in which a literary critic can be 'helpful for the study of culture and for the historical study of the aftermath of colonialism and the post-colonial present'.[130]

Finally, a useful definition of the two 'archives' of postcolonialism is provided by Helen Tiffin:

> The first archive here constructs it [the archive] as writing [...] grounded in those societies whose subjectivity has been constituted in part by the subordinating power of European colonialism – that is, as writing from countries and regions which were formerly colonies of Europe. The second archive of post-colonialism is intimately related to the first, though not co-extensive with it. Here the post-colonial is conceived of as a set of discursive practices, prominent among which is resistance to colonialism, colonialist ideologies, and their contemporary forms and subjectificatory legacies. The nature and function of this resistance form a central problematic of this discourse.[131]

It is this second archive of 'resistance' discourses that concerns us here. The act of autobiography is just such an example of a discursive strategy that may challenge colonialist perceptions of the colonised subject. This contestation leads to a consideration of the concept of agency, of 'who or what acts oppositionally when ideology or discourse or psychic processes of some kind construct human subjects'.[132] The writers under consideration here are not 'subaltern', to use the term suggested by Gayatri Spivak and widely used in postcolonial studies to describe 'authentic' native voices silenced by colonialism; they belong to an intellectual elite, as I stressed in the introduction, despite the poverty that Feraoun and Memmi, for example, were born into. However, they all articulate, to differing degrees, resistance to the representation of the colonised, and can be said to share in posing two of the questions raised by Homi Bhabha (whose work has greatly influenced postcolonial studies in English), namely: How do we begin to historicise the dehistoricised? What is the relation of the self to the otherness of the self's own history?[133] These two questions are clearly fundamental to the enterprise of writing autobiography in the colonial and postcolonial situations, and the writers to be analysed here explicitly question the relation of the self to the historical situation of colonialism. The postcolonial writer is a critic of and a commentator on the system of representation in which he or she has been formed, and seeks to construct another system of representation that marks out his or her difference. It is at this point of difference that the reader and the writer meet:

> Post-colonial textual reading and cultural analysis have been grounded in a phenomenology, a heuristics, and a hermeneutics of difference. Like the political process of decolonisation with which it shares much of its ground and motivation, post-colonial studies seek to identify, valorise, and empower what colonialist discourses label the barbarous, the primitive, the provincial. Thus 'difference', which in colonialist discourse connotes a remove from the normative European practice, and hence functions as a marker of subordination, is for post-colonial analysis the correspondent marker of identity, voice, and hence empowerment. Difference is not the measure by which the voiceless alien fails to be European; it is the measure by which the European episteme fails to comprehend the actual self-naming and articulate subject.[134]

Attention paid to the power of difference may help the Western critic to avoid the charge frequently directed against postcolonial studies, that the colonies once again provide the 'raw material' for a Western discourse. And despite the potential of, for example, Robert Young's more positive interpretation of the strategies of postcolonial theory, it is nonetheless important to keep in mind the criticisms with which Ania Loomba ends her survey of the issues surrounding postcolonial studies, which for her

> remain curiously Euro-centric, dependent upon Western philosophies and modes of seeing, taught largely in the Western academy, unable to reject convincingly European frames of reference, and guilty of telescoping the complexity of different parts of the world into the 'colonial question'. This is partly why the question of the postcolonial critic's location and political

affiliations has become a contentious, often bitterly fraught issue in recent years. [135]

This book is open to such a charge. It is written by a Western woman and largely destined for the institutions of the Western education system. In that system it will be read nonetheless by readers from very different cultural, religious, political and social backgrounds. And why should such readings not be valid as long as they are held within the tension produced by the complex relationship between Western and non-Western readings? Or within the differences between readings generated by gender? Or by generation? All these readings can be held side by side so that the hierarchies that still prevail in the assessment of cultural practices continue to break down and other processes come into being. My own position is closer to the way in which Anne Donadey defines post-colonial literature as opposed to earlier anti-colonial literature:

> The main difference, to my mind, lies in the move *from Manichean dualism to multiple technique*. The [postcolonial] literature underscores the fractures in the grand narratives of decolonization; it begins to effect a slippage away from the (former) colonizer as its main target and instead turns to a multiplicity of struggles [...] The mark of the postcolonial, then, is the blurring of neat, dichotomous boundaries – *which does not mean the end of power differentials or the end of oppositionality*.
> Postcolonial literature underscores the impossibility of Manichean resistance as well as the necessity for continued opposition to old and new oppressive structures. [136]

In the work of the four writers analysed in the following chapters, we will read just such a 'multiplicity of struggles' and complex opposition to many types of 'oppressive structures'. The readings seek to work with the 'difference' of the texts under analysis, not to locate them as removed from European 'normative practice'. The aim is rather to read with an awareness of 'difference' while simultaneously seeking to understand what 'difference' brings to our knowledge of ourselves and of the experience of what it is to be human, the fundamental aim of all life-writing.

CHAPTER 2

Mouloud Feraoun:
Life Story, Life-Writing, History

Si le peuple algérien est le peuple maudit de ce siècle, il lui reste à mourir en bloc, le plus tôt sera le mieux. Mais à mourir debout en criant son mépris au bourreau.

Mouloud Feraoun, *Journal*, 16 January 1957

(If the Algerian people are the accursed of this century, the only thing left for them is to die together, and the sooner the better. But to die on their feet, shouting their contempt for the executioner.)

Il est nécessaire que tu me présentes aux lecteurs [...] Avec le premier (*Le Fils du pauvre*), tu parleras de l'œuvre scolaire en Algérie, etc. C'est une quasi-autobiographie, tu parleras de moi, un peu trop, peut-être... Tu parleras des Kabyles, insuffisamment, peut-être.

Mouloud Feraoun, *Lettres à ses amis*, letter to Emmanuel Roblès, 10 July 1952

(You will need to introduce me to the readers [...] With the first ('The Poor Man's Son'), you'll talk about schoolwork in Algeria, etc. It's a sort of auto-biography, so you'll say something about me, perhaps a little too much... You'll say something about the Kabyles, perhaps not enough.)

The publication of Mouloud Feraoun's *Le Fils du pauvre* ('The Poor Man's Son') in 1950 is generally recognised as a founding moment in the literary, cultural and political context of North African writing in French. A claim can be made for this text as the first real expression of the voice and experiences of an indigenous Algerian writer as opposed to the writing concerning North Africa produced by the French themselves during the nineteenth and early twentieth centuries. These texts are often described as 'Orientalist' (for example the work of Eugène Fromentin and Théophile Gautier) and 'exotic' (for example the novels of Pierre Loti and Louis Bertrand), and they were followed in the 1930s by the group of writers usually assembled under the label 'l'Ecole d'Alger', which included, for example, Gabriel Audisio, René-Jean Clot, and the early work of Albert Camus. *Le Fils du pauvre* is also different in its aims from the writing by Algerian writers usually described as 'assimilated' during the same period:

Les romanciers qui commencent à publier récits et romans à partir de 1920 écrivent des œuvres à thèse, avec discours d'idées, manifestant comme un double désir du même et de l'autre: celui du maintien de leur identité ou personnalité algérienne (c'est-à-dire musulmane) et celui, modulé selon chaque auteur, d'assimilation ou d'intégration politique (non religieuse) ou d'alliance politique seulement avec le colonisateur parce qu'il apporte le progrès matériel, l'évolution vers la modernité.[1]

(The novelists who began to publish stories and novels from 1920 onwards wrote works with a message, setting out their ideas, showing a sort of double desire of the same and of the other: the desire to maintain their Algerian (i.e. Muslim) identity or personality; and also, in different ways depending on each author, that of political (not religious) assimilation or integration, or only of political alliance with the colonisers because it was they who brought material progress, and development towards modernity.)

Le Fils de pauvre was first published by Les Cahiers du Nouvel Humanisme and was financed by the author himself. Feraoun had actually begun work on the text in 1939, and continued to work on it until 1944. He gives his own account of the difficulty in finding a publisher in his published correspondence, *Lettres à ses amis*.[2] A note accompanying these published letters by the *pied-noir* writer, intellectual, and long-standing friend of Feraoun, Emmanuel Roblès, is revealing of Feraoun's attitude and of the relationship between a North African writer and a French readership in the colonial situation:

Sans me consulter, Feraoun l'avait publié à compte d'auteur. J'étais allé chez lui, en mai 1950, à Tizi Hibel, et il ne m'en avait soufflé mot. J'en avais reçu à l'automne un exemplaire avec la dédicace: 'A E.R., au risque de lui paraître ridicule'. Je lui fis de véhéments reproches et alertai Le Seuil.[3]

(Without consulting me, Feraoun had had it published at his own expense. I had been to visit him at Tizi Hibel in May 1950 and he had not breathed a word to me about it. I received a copy of it in the autumn, dedicated 'To E.R., at the risk of seeming ridiculous to him.' I reproached him vehemently and notified Le Seuil [the publisher].)

The incident is more than anecdotal since it reveals an attitude on the part of Feraoun that seems to be influenced by genuine modesty concerning this first writing endeavour, a modesty that has in its turn marked the tone of the critical attention paid to *Le Fils du pauvre*. However, close attention to the text itself and to Feraoun's own behaviour in negotiating his way in the colonial context reveals a far more complex situation than appears on the surface. Most critics comment on the simple style employed in *Le Fils du pauvre*, on its description and portraits of Kabyle life, culture and values, and on its directness and its authenticity.[4] The *Encyclopaedia Britannica* reference, to which an average reader wanting to know more about Feraoun might turn, describes Feraoun as 'a gentle man of integrity', and *Le Fils du pauvre* as 'the portrayal of the simple life of the mountains [...] filled with nobility, human compassion, and a love of family and native soil'. Much of the critical attention the text has received focuses on the content as documentary evidence of a lifestyle and a historical period rather than on the literary strategies employed. This approach is common in the consideration given to early North African writing in French, qualifying this type of literature as 'ethnographic', as Jean Déjeux's evaluation illustrates:

> Il parle de la misère dans la montagne kabyle, de la vie simple et dure. L'auteur ne crache pas le feu, son discours n'est pas anticolonialiste. Il veut montrer que ses compatriotes sont des hommes comme les autres.[5]

> (He speaks of the poverty in the Kabyle uplands, the simple, hard life people lead. The writer does not breathe fire and his discourse is not anti-colonial. He wants to show that his compatriots are human beings just like everyone else.)

Le Fils du pauvre achieved publishing success, with the first edition of a thousand copies selling out within a year and the award of the Grand Prix Littéraire de la Ville d'Alger. As previously indicated, it was generally received by the French critics at the time (and often since) as simple and touching, and as portraying a rather positive vision of the French *mission civilisatrice*, given that the protagonist is able to become a school-teacher, despite his poor Kabyle peasant background, thanks to the education provided by the French school system in Algeria. It is therefore a text often criticised as being 'assimilationist' in attitude and tone. Such criticism, however, does not take into consideration the ways in which Feraoun implicitly criticised the conditions in which his community (the poor Berber peasant farmers of the Great Kabylia mountains in Algeria) lived, by bearing witness to the harsh reality of such lives. It also neglects the ways in which the novel foregrounds individual identities within a hitherto anonymous group of the indigenous population, whom the colonialists generally considered an uneducated and primitive people who somehow did not share the feelings and sensibilities of Europeans. In fact, the narrative strategies employed in the text, the ironic distance between the narrator and the main character and the ways in which the narrator secures the reader's sympathy bring into question the notion of this being the work of a largely assimilated colonial subject and suggest that this is, rather, a self-consciously 'naïve' novel, and one that, to some extent knowingly, manipulates the reader of the time. Feraoun does not apparently question the status quo and the power relations between coloniser and colonised, while at the same time he puts forward his own observations on the situation, which can be seen as forming an ideological stance with the aim of reinstating the Kabyles' rights to be considered as an autonomous and civilised society with its own set of values that should be maintained. Jean Déjeux has pointed out that in the 1950s, to speak of Algeria as Feraoun did was already an achievement, although Khatibi is more severe in his analysis:

> Trop de pitié et de bonté écrasent ce livre, c'est l'autobiographie d'un homme de bonne volonté [...] Voilà une différence avec des écrivains comme Kateb, Memmi, Chraïbi qui, quand ils se racontent, ne voient qu'une suite de mutilations, et des enfances blessées et ratées.[6]

> (This book is awash with too much pity, too much kindness. It is the autobiography of a man of good will [...] Here lies the difference between it and writers such as Kateb, Memmi, and Chraïbi, who, in their writings, see only a succession of mutilations, of childhoods that were wounded and ruined.)

More recent critics have developed this criticism, evoking both the 'fatalistic' attitude of the protagonists and the failure to trace colonisation as a cause of Kabyle poverty, both resulting in the text's adherence to the assimilationist ideal.[7] I shall return to this issue in the analysis of the narrative strategies used in the text.

The actual life story of the 'son of a poor man' is more complex than this apparently straightforward itinerary of the peasant farmer's son who became a primary school teacher through his own diligence and the opportunities provided by the French school, thereby achieving a certain status in his own community. The influence of Mouloud Feraoun extended far beyond that.

Feraoun was born in 1913 in Tizi-Hibel, a small village in Upper Kabylia. In 1936, after having successfully obtained a scholarship and a place at the Ecole Normale de Bouzaréa (where he met Emmanuel Roblès), he qualified as a teacher and obtained a post in Taourirt-Aden, near his native village (1936–37). After several posts in the same region (Taboudrist, 1937–45, during which time [in 1938] he married his cousin Dehbia; Aït-Abdel-Moumen, 1945–46; Taourirt-Moussa, 1946–52), he was appointed head teacher of a school in Fort-National in 1952. He asked to be transferred to the suburbs of Algiers due to the harassment he endured, notably from a French administrator and member of the Sections administratives spécialisées (SAS). In 1957 he took up a post as a head teacher there, and the following year he became an inspector of the Centres sociaux, which had been set up by the United Nations Educational, Scientific and Cultural Organisation (UNESCO) in order to look at ways to provide education for the poorest in society. He was assassinated at the age of 49 on 15 March 1962 in El-Biar with five of his colleagues by the French colonial right-wing terrorist group l'Organisation Armée Secrète (OAS), the year that Algerian independence was achieved.

Feraoun's death is one of those 'dramatised' in Assia Djebar's *Le Blanc de l'Algérie*,[8] a book of mourning and remembrance for the writers and intellectuals that Algeria has lost, either through illness, accidents or execution, beginning with Camus, but also including the more anonymous victims, especially women, murdered in Algeria in the 1990s. Djebar's account of the experience of the son of one of the friends executed with Feraoun, Salah Ould Aoudia, a Kabyle who had converted to Christianity, is revealing of the politics of the situation. In the imagined scenario, Jean-Philippe Ould Aoudia is called to the hospital where the dead have been taken and recognises among the six bodies those of his father and of Feraoun:

> Le préposé est déçu par cette identification limitée à deux corps seulement. Il me demande: 'Quel drapeau on leur met?' Comme je ne comprends pas le sens de sa question, il m'explique qu'il faut mettre sur les cercueils soit le drapeau bleu-blanc-rouge de la France, soit le drapeau vert et blanc de l'Algérie pour mettre les corps soit du côté des Français, soit du côté des Arabes, pour éviter des disputes. Tandis que le jeune Ould Aoudia ne peut s'arracher au spectacle du visage paternel qui, deux plaies sur le front, garde encore son masque de souffrance, il entend derrière lui quelqu'un répondre enfin à l'interne qui se préoccupait des drapeaux: 'Docteur, remarque haut l'employé, les balles qui les ont tués, elles sont tricolores, non?'[9]

> (The official is disappointed by this identification of only two of the bodies. He asks me: 'Which flag do we put them under?' Since I don't understand the meaning of his question, he explains that you have to cover the coffins either with the blue, white and red of France or with the green and white flag of Algeria so that you can lay out the bodies either on the side of the French or the side of the Arabs, to avoid arguments. While the young Ould Aoudia can't tear himself away from the sight of his father's face which, with its two wounds in the forehead, still retains its mask of suffering, he hears someone behind him at last make a reply to the attendant worried about the flags: 'Doctor,' he remarks emphatically, 'The bullets that killed them bear the tricolour, no?')

Questions of identity and of belonging, and of the consequences of colonialism on the individual, as well as on the community, therefore infuse Feraoun's death scene as they did his life.

The life story of Feraoun is bound up with the drama of Algeria as it lives the last days of French colonisation, the events of the Second World War, and as it fights to achieve independence. On one level his work goes beyond individual experience to detail the everyday life of a community under colonial rule and then at war, and his writing is also concerned with the politics, in the widest sense of the word, of a specific period in French colonial history and in the history of Algeria. On another level, it raises complex questions concerning the relationship between self and other in such a situation, whether that other is the coloniser or the community to which the individual belongs, and the place the individual may occupy between the two: 'Dans le texte féraounien se répondent, se confortent et se contestent vision du dehors et vision du dedans, image pour soi et image pour l'autre autant qu'image de soi par l'autre'[10] ('In Feraoun's text there is a correspondence, a mutual strengthening and a conflict between the outward gaze and the inward gaze; the image for oneself and the image for the other, and also the image of the self by the other').

Feraoun's intellectual successes had led him into a teaching degree at the Ecole Normale de Bouzaréa, which in turn inspired in him a lifelong commitment to teaching and the administration of education in Algeria, to non-violent support for the independence movement, to friendships and acquaintances among French and Algerian intellectuals, among whom he counted Camus and, of course, Roblès. His writings encompass not only novels, but also published correspondence and a published diary, which will be used here as part of my project of analysing Feraoun's contribution to North African writing in French as a life-writing project, moving beyond the founding text of *Le Fils du pauvre* to consider the other forms of autobiographical discourses that make up this project. In addition to *Le Fils du pauvre*, Feraoun published a second novel with Le Seuil in 1953 entitled *La Terre et le sang*, a love story between a Kabyle and a Frenchwoman, which again offers a depiction of the life of the peasants in the mountains of Kabylia, and which won the Prix Populiste. A further text devoted to everyday Kabyle life, *Jours de Kabylie*, with illustrations by Charles Brouty, was published the same year. A third novel, *Les Chemins qui montent*, appeared in 1957, and a rather different type of text, an essay that presents the life and work of the Kabyle poet Si Mohand Aït-Irathen, was published in 1960 as *Les Poèmes de Si Mohand*, fifty years after the poet's death. This presentation of the poems in French and Kabyle by means of Feraoun's own transcription system, using the French/Latin alphabet, can also be seen as a subtle political statement. Feraoun uses the Kabyle literary heritage to insist on the importance of culture to Kabyle identity, and the publication of this work during the War of Independence had, of course, a special relevance and significance, with regard both to the French coloniser and to the liberation movement.[11] Around the same time Feraoun had been working on a third novel, *L'Anniversaire*, which was unfinished at the time of his assassination. Four chapters were published, with a set of other texts, including the text entitled *Fouroulou Menrad* that originally accompanied what we know as *Le Fils du pauvre*, in a 1972 Le Seuil publication that takes the title of this last unfinished novel. Feraoun's diary, begun in 1955 at the prompting of Roblès, chronicling both the events of the War of Independence and the author's daily life, was published early in 1962, just weeks before his death. A selection of correspondence from 1949 to 1962 was published in 1969 covering many of the same events, although with a distinctively different emphasis. These last two texts will be discussed later in this chapter, my intention being to read the ways in which these different elements of Feraoun's life-writing project come together to construct a life story through the use of different narrative forms.

NAMING THE POOR MAN'S SON: IDENTITY AND THE COLONISED SUBJECT IN *LE FILS DU PAUVRE*

> Vous savez bien que Fouroulou c'était à peu près moi. Un moi enfant tel que je le voyais il y a dix ans. Maintenant il se peut que je le voie autrement.
> Mouloud Feraoun, *Lettres à ses amis*, letter to Mme Landi-Bendos, 4 February 1955

> (As you well know, Fouroulou was more or less me. Myself as a child, the way I saw him ten years ago. Now I might well see him differently.)

The novel's original title was *Le Fils du pauvre, Menrad instituteur kabyle* ('The Poor Man's Son: Menrad, a Kabyle Schoolteacher') and it had four parts: 'La Famille', 'Le Fils aîné', 'Bouzaréa' and 'La Guerre' ('The Family', 'The Eldest Son', 'Bouzaréa', 'The War'). The second edition was published in 1954 by Le Seuil, after Emmanuel Roblès introduced Feraoun's work to the publishing house, and was composed of only the first two parts.[12] As I have previously indicated, the 1972 Le Seuil publication of diverse writings by Feraoun includes these last two parts in a section entitled *Fouroulou Menrad*, and the author's original intention was for these parts to be the continuation of the story of the main character of *Le Fils du pauvre*. The suppression of this second part may have been, as has frequently been recorded, on Roblès's advice that the whole lacked unity. However, it is also clear that criticism of the French is more explicit in this second part. In *Le Fils du pauvre*, Feraoun ostensibly presents a portrayal of the hardships and extreme poverty borne by the Kabyle peasants, in a region where the primary manifestation of French colonialism is in fact the primary school that the main character Fouroulou Menrad attends, and there seems to be no direct criticism of colonial rule. Yet it can be argued that the text implicitly indicates that the very reason that the peasants never break out of their circle of poverty is a direct result of French colonial power and its economic system. In *Fouroulou Menrad*, the Algerians' awareness of their betrayal militarily, economically and politically by the French colonial power during the period of the Second World War is made explicit to the reader.[13] An initial indication of narrative complexity can firstly be identified in the name of the main character, partly an anagram of the author's own. Feraoun was very aware of the impact of the attribution of a name to its bearer, and in the examination of his own name the power relationships under the colonial system are made clear. As he wrote to his friend Pierre Martin in 1949:

> Tu t'imagines aussi que chez nous on m'appelle Feraoun. Erreur. C'est le nom français. On en a collé à chaque famille kabyle vers 1890 et qui ne correspond que très rarement au vrai nom. Peu nous chaut. Nous acceptons tous les grimaces qu'on nous impose tout en sachant qu'elles n'ont pas de sens. Nous y gagnons la simplicité et la tranquillité.[14]
>
> (You also imagine that at home I'm called Feraoun. Wrong. That's the French name. Each Kabyle family got given one around 1890, and it seldom has anything to do with their real name. It doesn't worry us much. We accept all the faces we are made to pull, while knowing full well that they are meaningless. It makes life simpler and more peaceful for us.)

And four years later, after being asked for a biography and a photograph for the press, he writes to Roblès:

> Inutile de dire que je ne m'appelle pas Feraoun et de démolir ma réputation 'd'écrivain et d'éducateur' ou vice versa. On le dira après, pour rire. Nom: F. Prénom: Mouloud. Date officielle de naissance: 8 mars 1913. (En réalité, j'ai dû naître en février, comme Fouroulou du *Fils du pauvre* mais un an après lui, je le tiens de la grand-mère qui reçut effectivement une mémorable averse.)[15]
>
> (There is no need to say that I am not called Feraoun and to demolish my reputation as a 'writer and teacher' or vice versa. We will say it later, for a laugh. Surname: F. First name: Mouloud. Official date of birth: 8 March 1913. (In reality, I must have been born in February, like Fouroulou in *The Poor Man's Son*, but a year later than him; I know that from my grandmother, who did in fact go through quite a storm.))

Roblès adds to this letter, in the Le Seuil edition of the letters edited by him, the following note on the circumstances: Feraoun's family name was given by the officers of the French colonial power (Officiers des Affaires Indigènes, or AI) charged with establishing a list of the population in order to control them:

> Ces officiers AI savaient l'arabe, non le berbère. Ils tournèrent la difficulté en octroyant d'autorité des patronymes. Tous ceux de la karouba des Aït-Chaâbane, les ancêtres de Mouloud, furent voués à la lettre F. Mais à Tizi-Hibel le nom n'est employé par personne et celui d'Aït Chaâbane sert

toujours à designer les membres de cette famille.[16]

(These AI officials knew Arabic but not Berber. They avoided the difficulty by imposing patronymics officially. All the people from the *karouba* of the Aït-Chaâbane, Mouloud's ancestors, were given the letter F. But at Tizi-Hibel that name is not used by anyone, and the name Aït-Chaâbane is always used to designate members of the family.)

In her presentation of the same letters in a different edition, Christiane Achour, commenting on the explicit references that Feraoun makes to the publication of his work, ends by saying:

La correspondance explicite d'autres allusions du texte de création comme celles sur le patronyme de Fouroulou et ne laisse aucun doute sur l'appréciation que Feraoun porte sur la nomination coloniale et situe un peu plus concrètement la question identitaire.[17]

(The correspondence clarifies other allusions in the creative text, such as those on Fouroulou's patronymic, and leaves no doubt about Feraoun's view of the colonial system of imposing names, and puts the question of identity in a clearer setting.)

In full awareness then of the issues around naming and individual identity, Feraoun creates in *Le Fils du pauvre* a whole meaning for the protagonist's first name:

Comme j'étais le premier garçon né viable dans ma famille, ma grand-mère décida péremptoirement de m'appeler Fouroulou (de *effer*: cacher). Ce qui signifie que personne au monde ne pourra me voir, de son œil bon ou mauvais, jusqu'au jour où je franchirai moi-même, sur mes deux pieds, le seuil de notre maison.
　　On serait peut-être étonné si j'ajoutais que ce prénom, tout à fait nouveau chez nous, ne me ridiculisa jamais parmi les bambins de mon âge, tant j'étais doux et aimable.[18]

(As I was the first boy in my family to survive birth, my grandmother decided peremptorily to call me Fouroulou (from *effer*, to hide). Its meaning was that no-one in the world would be able to see me, for better or worse, until the day when I myself crossed the threshold of our house on my own two feet. It may sound surprising if I add that this name, which was completely new to everyone, was never laughed at by the other boys of my age, because I was such a gentle, friendly child.)

In the close anagram of the author's own name, the invented name for his protagonist signifies an ability to hide and to show himself at will, a key to a narrative voice which in turn hides itself until it is ready to speak out. As has previously been noted, much critical attention has focused on the modesty of both the writer and the enterprise of *Le Fils du pauvre* and I have suggested that a closer reading of the style and of narrative construction actually reveals a more complex project. Accepted by a French readership for its apparent simplicity in the depiction of a lifestyle, the novel was criticised by Algerian nationalist intellectuals, who saw it as 'regionalist' and as undermining a unified nationalist cause in its attention on the Kabyles. It was further criticised because it did not openly denounce the colonialist regime. Kabylia had been the main stronghold of the final insurrection against the French in 1871, and despite Arabic influence and the spread of Islam, many traditions remained purely Berber, including the use of Berber dialects. Throughout his writings and his educational work, Feraoun remained committed to his Kabyle identity.[19] A case can also be made for reading Feraoun's work as more challenging than is usually perceived within the historical context of the period, as well as on the narrative level:

> Feraoun expressed his displeasure at the absence of authentic Algerian people in the novels of Roblès, Camus and other Algerian-born French writers, who all reflected an alien reality based on alien experiences. The writing of *Le Fils du pauvre* was an attempt to offer his people a place in fiction, as well as to create a genuinely Algerian novel which differed from the French novel not only in its content but also in its language. Although the novel is written in French, it can hardly be described as a French work, not only because the writer peppers his narrative with Berber words, but also because the writer's imagery and logic differ greatly from those of French writers.[20]

Indeed the texts with Fouroulou Menrad as the protagonist set up many of the themes that were to recur in the work of later North African writers writing in French: poverty and the realities of everyday life in colonial and postcolonial systems; education and difference; the separation from the family and community brought about by education; the impact of the French language on the identity of the colonial subject; the relationship to power, to history, to the other; the politics of self-determination in the colonial context. The mechanisms by which the colonised subject makes himself heard will also be considered through the figure of Fouroulou, who, as I have noted, simultaneously hides and reveals himself.

POVERTY, KNOWLEDGE AND SELF-KNOWLEDGE

Le Fils du pauvre opens with a quotation from Chekhov, an epigraph that seems to set the tone for and indeed presage the life and death of its author, who will not be allowed the luxury of growing old: 'Nous travaillerons pour les autres jusqu'à notre vieillesse et quand notre heure viendra, nous mourrons sans murmure et nous dirons dans l'autre monde que nous avons souffert, que nous avons pleuré, que nous avons vécu de longues années d'amertume, et Dieu aura pitié de nous'[21] ('We will work for others until we are old, and when our time comes we'll die without a murmur, and in the next world we'll say that we have suffered, that we have wept, that we have lived long years of bitterness, and God will have pity on us').

Feraoun uses the established literary device of a preface written by an unknown narrator to introduce and contextualise the third-person narrative that follows, in this case a manuscript that the protagonist, Fouroulou Menrad, keeps in the drawer of his desk in the school where he works.[22] The text therefore opens with two voices: that of the Russian novelist, which heralds the account of the harsh life that is to follow, and another that comments on the text we are to read, a voice encouraging the story of Fouroulou to be told, a voice also encouraging complicity on the part of the reader: 'Tirons du tiroir de gauche le cahier d'écolier. Ouvrons-le. Fouroulou Menrad, nous t'écoutons' ('Let's take the exercise-book out of the left-hand drawer. Let's open it. Fouroulou Menrad, we're listening to you'). Menrad, who keeps a diary, the narrator explains, was inspired to write the story of his life by reading Montaigne, Rousseau, Daudet and Dickens. He does not wish to compare himself to these great writers, but, like them, to leave a kind of self-portrait, 'se peindre' (to sketch himself); and in an impulse typical for an autobiographer, to give order to a life: 'Il considérait que s'il réussissait à faire quelque chose de cohérent, de complet, de lisible, il serait satisfait' (p. 10) ('He felt that if he managed to do something that was coherent, complete, and readable, he would be satisfied'). The enterprise is destined to be a failure, however: 'Devant les innombrables obstacles qui se dressent à chaque tournant de phrase, à chaque fin de paragraphe, devant les mots impropres, les tournures douteuses et les adjectifs insaisissables, il abandonne une entreprise au-dessus de ses forces, après avoir rempli un gros cahier d'écolier. Il abandonne sans esprit de retour, sans colère' (p. 10) ('Faced with the countless obstacles that arose with every turn of phrase and every paragraph-ending, at the unsuitable words, the doubtful structures and the adjectives that never sounded right, he abandoned the effort as being beyond his strength, after he had filled a school exercise-book. He abandoned it without hoping to come back to it, and without any anger'). Here we read not just the problems of any autobiographical enterprise, the struggle to re-create a life in language, but also the struggle with a language that is difficult to manipulate, and here specifically a second language whose rules must be wrestled with. Yet once again, another 'hidden' strategy can be discerned: while stating his inferiority with respect to the European cultural heritage that Fouroulou

acknowledges as universal, the Kabyle heritage is simultaneously celebrated through reference to a folktale, as Naget Khadda points out:

> Quant à la référentialité, qui joue, ici, essentiellement par l'invocation de
> noms illustres et par des citations d'extraits de textes mis en exergue aux
> articulations stratégiques du récit, elle travaille à dérégionaliser l'aventure
> pour lui donner une dimension universelle. Une universalité conçue par
> l'écrivain acculturé comme européenne. Cependant, en sous-main, la narra-
> tique du terroir agit, structurant le développement du récit. En effet, le
> modèle narratif du *Fils du pauvre* est informé, autant que par le roman réal-
> iste ou le récit autobiographique européens, par le conte et, plus
> spécialement, par un conte kabyle intitulé 'Histoire du Myriapode et du Fils
> du Pauvre' dont le titre d'ailleurs est déjà indicatif.[23]

> (As for referentiality, which operates here essentially by invoking illustrious
> names and using extracts from texts to head strategic points of the narra-
> tive, it works to de-regionalise the project so to give it a universal dimension.
> This universality is conceived by the acculturated writer as European.
> However, territorial narrativity works secretly to structure the development
> of the writing. And so the narrative model of *Le Fils du pauvre* is informed
> both by the European realist novel or autobiography, and by the tale, more
> specifically by a Kabyle tale called 'The Story of the Millipede and the Poor
> Man's Son', whose title is, of course, highly indicative in itself.)

In addition to the European and Kabyle traditions, we know from
his letters and articles that Feraoun was also inspired in this first literary
undertaking by the writing of Roblès and Camus:

> La voie a été tracée par ceux qui ont rompu avec un Orient de pacotille pour
> décrire une humanité moins belle et plus vraie, une terre aux couleurs moins
> chatoyantes mais plus riche de sève nourricière; des hommes qui luttent et
> souffrent, et sont les répliques exactes de ceux que nous voyons autour de
> nous.[24]

> (The trail was blazed by those who broke with the cheaply pretty version of
> the Orient to describe a less attractive and truer kind of people, a land of
> less shimmering colours but richer in life-giving sap; men who fight and
> suffer, and are the exact replicas of those we see around us.)

He also mentions Gabriel Audisio, Edmond Brua, Jules Roy, Rosfelder,
Claude de Fréminville, René-Jean Clot, and Marcel Moussy. In his letters,
however, Feraoun explicitly criticises Camus for the lack of indigenous
characters in *La Peste*, but also notes how much he has learnt about
himself and others through this fiction and how this inspires him to write
from his own perspective, as he writes in a letter to Camus:

> Si je parvenais un jour à m'exprimer sereinement, je le devrais à votre livre
> – à vos livres qui m'ont appris à me connaître puis à découvrir les autres et
> à constater qu'il me ressemblent. Ne puis-je donc me payer ce ridicule: tenter
> à mon tour d'expliquer les Kabyles et montrer qu'ils ressemblent à tout le
> monde? A tous les Algériens, par exemple? Ce fossé qui s'élargit, ne faudrait-
> il pas essayer de le combler?[25]

(If ever I managed to express myself serenely, I would owe it to your book – your books, which have taught me to know myself and then to discover other people and realise that they are like me. And so can I not allow myself this fantastic notion: to try in my turn to explain the Kabyles and show that they are just like everybody else? Just like all Algerians, for example? This ever-widening gulf, shouldn't we try to fill it in?)

And to Roblès, Feraoun is even clearer about how the depiction of those living in his country by the *pied-noir* writers aided him in the presentation of his own people, and why he felt the need to do this:

> Je n'avais jamais cru possible de faire véritablement entrer dans un roman un vrai bonhomme kabyle avant d'avoir connu le docteur Rieux et le jeune Smaïl. Vous les premiers vous nous avez dit: voilà ce que nous sommes. Alors nous vous avons répondu: voilà ce que nous sommes de notre côté.[26]

> (I had never believed it possible to bring a real Kabyle man into a novel before meeting Doctor Rieux and young Smaïl. You first said to us, 'This is what we are.' And then we answered, 'And this is what *we* are.')

Feraoun therefore sets out to try in his turn to 'expliquer les Kabyles et montrer qu'ils ressemblent à tout le monde' ('explain the Kabyles and show that they are just like everyone else'). There is, therefore, a clear understanding of the potential power and impact of fiction and of what the creative process can achieve that transcends a critical documentation of the political and social reality. Feraoun is clearly aware of the subtleties of the political dimension of a work of art that may function by omission, rather than by an overtly political stance. There is also an awareness of the question of the subject and the other that lies at the heart of the relationship between the coloniser and the colonised. There seems to be a belief that fiction can bring about an understanding between peoples, because it works on the imagination, in ways that direct political intervention is unable to do. The power of culture, of cultural understanding, of a multi-faceted cultural memory, are the foundations on which Feraoun bases his life-writing project. He certainly acknowledges and respects the French education system and its Enlightenment-inspired values (despite the paradoxes of the forms these take in assimilationist policies), but he writes in order for the Kabyle culture to be acknowledged and valued both within Algeria and outside it.

Le Fils du pauvre opens with a very explicit focus on the other, *le touriste*, and particularly on the gaze of the other, the 'Westerner', and the way he sees Kabylia:[27]

> Le touriste qui ose pénétrer au cœur de la Kabylie admire par conviction ou par devoir, des sites qu'il trouve merveilleux, des paysages qui lui semblent pleins de poésie et éprouve toujours une indulgente sympathie pour les

mœurs des habitants [...] Mille pardons à les touristes. C'est parce que vous passez en touristes que vous découvrez ces merveilles et cette poésie. (p. 11)

(The tourist who dares to penetrate into the heart of Kabylia admires, out of conviction or a sense of duty, sites that he finds marvellous, landscapes that seem to him to be full of poetry, and he always feels an indulgent sympathy for the inhabitants' way of life [...] A thousand apologies to the tourists, but it is because you come as tourists that you discover those marvels and that poetry.)

Misunderstandings and misconceptions on the part of the 'tourist', and a criticism of the realities of life in Kabylia, are interwoven in these opening pages. In the first part of the text, 'La famille', it is the life of the community and an explanation of the values and way of life of the Kabyle peasants that dominate. Critics have frequently commented on the sociological and almost 'documentary' style employed by Feraoun, who also however deploys irony in the descriptions of the comparatively rich in the community:

Quelques habitations prétentieuses ont été construites récemment grâce à l'argent rapporté de France. Ces maisons dressent leurs façades impudiques et leurs tuiles trop rouges parmi la vétusté générale. Mais on sent que ce luxe est déplacé dans un cadre pareil. D'ailleurs nous n'en sommes pas trop fiers. Vues de loin, elles forment comme des taches blanches qui jurent avec l'ensemble, couleur de terre. Nous savons qu'à l'intérieur elles ressemblent à toutes les autres. Elles méritent le dédaigneux dicton qu'on leur applique: 'Ecuries de Menaiel', extérieur rutilant, intérieur plein de crottin et de bêtes de somme. (p. 13)

(Some pretentious dwellings have been built recently with money brought back from France. These houses raise their shameless façades and their too-bright red tiles among the general dilapidation. But this rich display feels out of place in such a setting. Moreover, we are not all that proud of them. Seen from a distance, they are like white spots that clash with the earth-colour of the rest. We know that inside they are just like all the others. They deserve the contemptuous dictum which is applied to them of 'Menaiel stables' – a brilliant exterior, and the interior full of animal droppings and beasts of burden.)

This money, obtained by working in France and therefore a direct consequence of the colonial system, disturbs the harmony of the community. The Kabyles appreciate simplicity, a sense of belonging to a *karouba* (the immediate family environment that unites different generations), to a village and to a community, where there is no real distinction between rich and poor, and where people help each other and share the same fate:

En plus de cette origine commune ou identique, nous sommes de la même condition parce que tous les Kabyles de la montagne vivent uniformément de la même manière. Il n'y a ni pauvres ni riches.
   Certes, il existe deux catégories de gens: ceux qui se suffisent régulièrement et ceux qui passent, au gré de la bonne ou de la mauvaise fortune, de

la misère la plus complète à l'humble aisance des favorisés du ciel. Mais on ne peut ni établir un classement définitif ni constater des différences essentielles dans le genre de vie des habitants. (p. 14)

(As well as this common or shared origin, we are the same because all upland Kabyles live in exactly the same way. There are neither poor people nor rich people. Admittedly, there are two kinds of people: those who live regularly within their means, and those who, depending on good or bad luck, go from the most abject poverty to the humble ease of people blessed by heaven. But it is not possible to divide them into categories or to find any essential differences in the kind of life the inhabitants lead.)

The description of the layout of the village and of its houses is exceptionally meticulous, noting the materials used, how the buildings are decorated, how and where things are stored. The early life of Menrad is therefore contextualised within the physical and social landscape that surrounds him by an apparently objective narrator, who is nonetheless part of the community ('Nous, Kabyles') ('we Kabyles'), while observing the situation.[28] The narration then moves into the first person as the narrator describes his family and the *karouba*: 'Mes parents avaient leur habitation à l'extrême nord du village, dans le quartier d'en bas. Nous sommes de la karouba des Aï Mezouz, de la famille des Aï Moussa. Menrad est notre surnom' (p. 18) ('My parents had their house at the very north end of the village, in the lower quarter. We belong to the *karouba* of Aï Mezouz, and to the Aï Moussa family. Menrad is the name given to us'). He describes Lounis his uncle, his father Ramdane, their authoritarian mother Tassadit, Helima and Fatma chosen by the mother as Lounis's and Ramdane's wives respectively. Later he moves on to Fatma's two sisters Khalti and Nana, whose happiness is undermined by a poor marriage and a still-born child, and whose death leads to Khalti's madness. The young Fouroulou is the only boy in either household, and he bullies his sisters and his girl cousins: 'pénétré de mon importance dès l'âge de cinq ans' (p. 25) ('filled with a sense of my own importance from the age of five'), in a culture where such behaviour by male children is tolerated. Outside the family, he realises that he cannot behave in the same way and adopts a different method, revealing as he does so insights into his own nature, a characteristic of the 'confessional' stance of autobiographical discourse:

J'adoptai donc avec tous mes voisins et toutes mes voisines la seule attitude que je pouvais adopter: je me faisais doux, aimable, patient; je savais flatter le plus audacieux, je donnais ou je prêtais sans trop de difficultés ce qu'on me demandait et mes parents voyaient s'écrouler, peu à peu, leur rêve de faire de moi le lion du quartier, plus tard le lion du village. (p. 26)

(I therefore adopted towards all my neighbours, both boys and girls, the only attitude I could: I became gentle, friendly and patient; I knew when to flatter the boldest, I gave or lent what people asked me for without too much difficulty, and my parents saw their dream of making me into the lion of the quarter, and later the lion of the village, crumble away little by little.)

Fouroulou manages to negotiate the outside world more successfully after his friendship with another boy, Akli, develops, and his uncle is also always ready to take his side against bigger boys. It is clear that it is part of the necessary education of a young boy to be able to function in the largely masculine space outside the house by proving and protecting himself when necessary. There is also a clear division set up between the external masculine space and the feminine space inside the home, represented especially by the two aunts. Much of the first part of the text revolves around a particular incident that takes place in this outside space which has repercussions not only for Menrad, but also for his community. The young boy insists on sitting right next to one of the villagers, Boussad N'amer, as he is making a basket from olive branches. Despite the warning, Fouroulou will not move further away and he is accidentally cut across the forehead with the knife that Boussad uses when one of the branches breaks. The family is outraged, and a fight ensues as his uncle pursues Boussad with the women following. The whole village assembles; the head of the village (the *amin*) and the marabout arrive. Some think that the *roumis* (the term used to refer to the French) should deal with it, others the Caïd, reflecting the diverse opinions concerning the colonial and traditional embodiments of authority. A couscous is prepared for the arrival of the *amin* and other important people at the Menrads' house. Calm is restored through a mixture of traditional law and payment to the Caïd, with the French authorities simply being excluded: 'Il est inutile d'aller à la justice française qui compliquerait tout' (p. 38) ('It would be pointless to go to French justice: that would only complicate everything'), a revealing insight into how the Kabyle community operated its own value system in parallel to French law. But the harmony of the community is broken and the two families no longer speak to each other or help each other. Nonetheless, a Kabyle system of values is upheld, as is the way in which a community continues to function according to its own rules, and the French presence remains shadowy and ineffectual, largely ignored by the indigenous population.

The following chapter moves into the feminine space of the two maternal aunts, who live together in a small house left to them by Fouroulou's grandfather, 'my cherished childhood prison':

> On s'y trouve à l'étroit ainsi que des roitelets dans leur nid rond et obscur. Mais on y sent une douce chaleur d'intimité discrète et tranquille. Les murs qui vous frôlent à chacun de vos mouvements semblent vous caresser et les

objets vous sourient dans le pénombre. Non, elle n'avait rien de triste la chère prison de mon enfance, les moments que j'y passais me paraissent trop courts. (p. 39)

(You're hemmed in like wrens in their round, dark nest. But you feel a gentle warmth, a discreet, tranquil intimacy. The walls which brush against you every time you move seem to caress you, and the objects smile at you in the dimness. No, there was nothing sad about the beloved prison of my child-hood: the times I spent there seemed too short to me.)

The young boy is full of tenderness for these two women: 'Le caractère de Khalti convenait très bien au petit Fouroulou. Nous nous compre-nions à merveille. J'aimais tendrement Nana qui n'avait que des caresses pour moi' (p. 41) ('Khalti's character fitted in very well with young Fouroulou. We understood each other perfectly. I loved Nana tenderly, and she had nothing but caresses for me'). Khalti is someone who treats him as an equal and with whom he enjoys discussion; Nana spoils him. This chapter presents in great detail the activities of the aunts making pots and decorating them, weaving wool, and at the end of the working day, telling stories, all representative of a creative Kabyle culture. It is Khalti who feeds the imagination of the young boy and the power of language becomes apparent through story-telling, setting the story-teller apart:

Je dois dire que ces histoires m'attiraient beaucoup chez mes tantes [...] pendant les récits, nous étions elle [Khalti] et moi des êtres à part. Elle savait créer de toutes pièces un domaine imaginaire sur lequel nous régnions [...] je suis reconnaissant à Khalti de m'avoir appris de bonne heure à rêver, à aimer créer pour moi-même un monde à ma convenance, un pays de chimères où je suis seul à pouvoir pénétrer. (pp. 46–47)

(I have to say that those stories attracted me strongly towards my aunts [...] during the story-telling, she [Khalti] and I were like beings apart. She was able to create a whole imaginary domain over which we reigned together [...] I am grateful to Khalti for having taught me so early to dream, to like creating a world to suit myself, a land of imaginary beings which I alone can enter.)

The young boy learns that the imagination can provide a refuge for the individual.

The following two chapters take up two themes that will be devel-oped with more impact by Albert Memmi, as I shall analyse in the next chapter, but it is clear that the experience of school and the experience of poverty are also key to understanding the development and identity of Feraoun. Feraoun's protagonist's first year at school is inauspicious, as the young Fouroulou has to repeat the year. He is surprised, however, to find that the teacher has noticed him and has spoken to his father about him, and he now takes up the role that he says suits him, 'the good pupil', although he is recognises that this option is attractive to him at least as much because he is less good at fighting and at playing games:

> je devins bon élève, presque sans effort [...] Aux paisibles et aux peureux qui se confondaient forcément, ils restait les plaisirs nobles de l'étude et des meilleures places [...] Avec le consentement de tous mes camarades, je devins donc bon élève [...] Dès le cours élémentaire, je travaillai donc avec un imperturbable sérieux, à l'insu de mes parents qui continuaient à manifester pour mes progrès la plus grande indifférence. (p. 52)

> (I became a good pupil, almost without effort [...] For the peace-lovers and the cowards, who were necessarily mixed together, there remained the noble pleasures of study and coming first [...] With the consent of all my comrades, therefore, I became a good pupil [...] So from the first form onwards I worked with unshakable seriousness, unknown to my parents, who continued to show the greatest indifference towards my progress.)

The indifference of the family to the young boy's education is apparent, and this is a theme that also occurs in, for example, Memmi's work. In fact Fouroulou's father is far more concerned with feeding his family, and education is primarily useful because it means that the boy is at home less often and therefore eats less:

> Je n'outrepasse pas la vérité en disant que la seule utilité visible de ma scolarisation était mon absence prolongée de la maison qui réduisait la quantité de figues et de couscous que je mangeais. (p. 53)

> (I am not exaggerating when I say that the sole use they saw in my education was my prolonged absence from the house, which reduced the quantity of figs and couscous that I ate.)

Education and knowledge, will therefore, as for Albert Memmi, create a gulf between the young boy and his family. The experience of poverty will also bring about another form of knowledge for both writers, and a specific life lesson is learned by Fouroulou when he and two other friends decide to go and see their fathers, currently labouring on building sites. The visit is not innocent. The boys choose to go at the moment when the men stop to have their meal (their boss is an 'educated man' and likes to 'imitate' certain French habits, such as taking meals at set times). Their fathers are clearly unhappy, but the boss allows the boys to eat, and their shame is overcome by the appeasing of their hunger. The scene is re-lived intensely, narrated in the present tense:

> Il nous ordonne de nous asseoir et nous mangeons, la tête basse. Nous mangeons quand même. D'abord une bonne soupe avec des pommes de terre. Et nous recevrons chacun un gros morceau de galette levée; puis du couscous blanc de semoule, avec de la viande. Devant de telles richesses, la joie prend le pas sur la honte du début. C'est la joie animale de nos estomacs vides. Dès que ceux-ci sont pleins, nous nous sauvons, le front ruisselant de sueur, sans remercier personne, emportant dans nos mains ce qui nous reste de viande et de galette. (p. 58)

(He orders us to sit down and we eat, keeping our heads down. We eat all the same. First some good soup with potatoes. And we each receive a big piece of flatbread; then some white couscous, with meat. At such riches joy takes over from our initial shame. It is the animal joy of our empty stomachs. As soon as they are full, we run off, our foreheads dripping with sweat, without thanking anyone, carrying our remaining bread and meat in our hands.)

As Fouroulou expects, his father is not happy about his behaviour and promises to bring home most of the food for his son each night if he does not return to the workplace. The father keeps his promise, the boy does not. The memory of the smell and taste of the food is more than he can bear. Fouroulou and Saïd return, and Fouroulou's father gives up his place for him, saying that he is going home to rest and is not hungry. The boys eat under the disapproving gaze of the other men. When he returns home Fouroulou finds his father eating from the boy's own bowl and realises his mistake: 'Ce jour-là, il retourna au travail le ventre à moitié vide, mais il grava, une fois pour toutes, dans le cœur de son fils, la mesure de sa tendresse' (p. 59) ('That day he went back to work with a half-empty stomach, but he engraved once and for all on his son's heart the measure of his tenderness'). The experience of poverty and hunger and the value system they instil is a powerful image for the realities of peasant existence, and of survival.

The narration then returns to the rest of the family, the rivalries between various members, the unpleasantness of Fouroulou's aunt, Helima, the working lives of the two brothers, the banality of their existence. The description appears to follow a traditional realist narrative form, but the way in which it is constructed also reveals an awareness of the nature of memory and the partial version of a childhood that is restored through it. The distance between the first-person narrator and the main character is also evident in the use of irony:

En somme, mon enfance de petit Menrad, fils de Ramdane et neveu de Lounis s'écoule banale et vide comme celle d'un grand nombre d'enfants kabyles. J'ai gardé de cette âge, pour tout souvenir, un tableau qui me semble uniforme et terne et que j'évoque chaque fois sans y trouver ni charme ni émotion excessive. Je me revois ainsi vêtu d'une vieille gandoura décolorée par les mauvais lavages, coiffé d'une chéchia aux bords effrangés et crasseux, sans chaussures ni pantalon, parce que, dans ma mémoire, c'est toujours l'été. Les pieds sont noirs de poussière, les ongles de crasse, les mains de taches de fruits; la figure est traversée par de longues barres de sueur séchée; les yeux sont rouges, les paupières enflées. Si c'est un jour de toilette, eh bien, c'est le Fouroulou actuel, moins la barbe naturellement. (p. 67)

(To sum up, my childhood as a little Menrad, son of Ramdane and nephew of Lounis, went by as ordinary and empty as the lives of a great number of Kabyle children. All my memory of that age is a tableau which seems to me to be uniform and dull and that I evoke each time without finding in it either charm or excessive emotion. I thus see myself wearing an old tunic, faded by bad washing, a fez with frayed, dirty edges, shoeless and trouserless, because in my memory it is always summer. My feet are black with dust, my nails with dirt, and my hands are stained with fruit-juice; my face is streaked with long stripes of dried sweat, my eyes red, my eyelids swollen. If it is a day for dressing up, then it is the present Fouroulou, without the beard.)

Other family memories are narrated, this time in connection with his aunts, his intimacy with them during Nana's pregnancy, and then her death in childbirth. Each time there is an awareness of the discrepancy between memory and the act of writing, the act of constructing a life story in language: 'Les souvenirs d'enfance manquent de précision et de lien: on garde certaines images frappantes que le cœur peut toujours unir l'une à l'autre lorsqu'il les évoque' (pp. 70–71) ('Childhood memories lack precision and links; you retain a set of striking images, which your heart can always connect together when it recalls them'); 'Dans le fil de mes souvenirs, cette scène est suivie immédiatement de celle-ci' (p. 72) ('In the chain of my memories, the latter scene is always followed immediately by the former'). The death of Nana and the madness of Khalti and her subsequent disappearance bring the first part of the narrative to a close. The family are in a permanent state of mourning, even though death is of course a necessary part of life in such harsh conditions:

> Pour les gens du village, ce qui nous arrivait là ne sortait pas de l'ordinaire. La mort fauche couramment des gens dans la fleur de leur âge. On pleure, on se lamente à s'enrouer la voix pour une semaine, puis on se tâte pour se dire que l'on reste après le disparu et que, malgré tout, le mal est sans remède puisque rien n'influe sur l'inexorable horloge du Destin. Or un mal sans remède est toujours supportable. (p. 74)

> (For the people of the village, what was happening to us there was nothing out of the ordinary. Death very often strikes people down in the prime of life. You cry, you lament until your voice is hoarse for a week, and then you take stock, and tell yourself that you are still there after the person's death and that in any case there is no remedy for the evil, since nothing can influence Destiny's inexorable clock. And an irremediable evil is always bearable.)

The family is at once part of the community, and yet, importantly for Feraoun's project, a particular case. Something has changed forever: the aunts' house and the land on which it stood is sold, and this death provokes a change in the relationship with the mother and father:

> Nous n'eûmes plus alors notre bon refuge, notre cher nid, personne à aimer en dehors de nos parents, personne qui s'intéressât à nous. Nous n'avions plus qu'à nous serrer peureusement autour du père et de la mère. (p. 83)

(Then we no longer had our safe refuge, our beloved nest, nobody to love except our parents, nobody to take an interest in us. All we could do was group fearfully about our father and mother.)

Feraoun therefore makes clear the impact of this personal tragedy and its consequences. The anonymity of poverty, of marginalisation, of death is made individual, and in the colonial situation the challenge to anonymity is itself a political act, part of Feraoun's aim to 'explain' the Kabyles to others and to show that they are 'just like everyone else', as he had expressed it in the letter to Camus.

At this point the narrative in the first person by Fouroulou Menrad ends and the second part, 'Le Fils aîné', is continued by 'un frère curieux et bavard' ('a curious and talkative brother'), another narrator to whom it is entrusted 'par modestie ou par pudeur' (p. 87) ('out of modesty or embarrassment'). A second epigraph opens the text, this time bringing the nineteenth-century French historian Michelet (who was himself born into poverty and who also kept a diary) into the dialogue of voices. The reader's attention is once again therefore drawn to the theme of poverty through the epigraph:

> Aujourd'hui cette indigence, fièrement, noblement supportée par les miens fait ma gloire. Alors, elle me semblait une honte et je la cachais de mon mieux. Terrible respect humain!

> (Today that poverty, proudly, nobly supported by my family, is something I glory in. At the time, I felt it was shameful, and I did my best to hide it. Terrible human respect!)

The narrative construction therefore takes on another voice as Fouroulou hides himself once again, moving here from the first person to the third, promoting a multiplicity of identities as the narrator addresses both the reader and Fouroulou himself:

> Tel est le fragment de confession que chacun peut lire dans le gros cahier rayé de Menrad Fouroulou. Le narrateur qui en a eu connaissance et qui le propose au lecteur prend, de ce fait, l'engagement d'aller jusqu'au bout. Faut-il répéter que Fouroulou se tait par modestie ou par pudeur, qu'il passe la plume à un ami qui ne le trahira pas mais qui n'ignore rien de son histoire, un frère curieux et bavard [...] Tu voudrais que le narrateur se taise. Non, laisse-le faire. Il n'a pas beaucoup d'illusions mais il t'aime bien. Il racontera ta vie qui ressemble à des milliers d'autres vies avec, tout de même, ceci de particulier que tu es ambitieux, Fouroulou, que tu as pu t'élever et que tu serais tenté de mépriser un peu les autres, ceux qui ne l'ont pas pu.
>
> Tu aurais tort, Fouroulou, car tu n'es qu'un cas particulier et la leçon, ce sont ces gens-là qui la donnent. (p. 87)

(Such is the fragment of a confession that everyone can read in Menrad Fouroulou's thick, ruled exercise-book. The narrator, who knows something of it and who offers it to the reader, takes from this fact his commitment to continue to the end. Is it necessary to repeat that Fouroulou stopped speaking out of modesty or embarrassment, and passed the pen to a friend who will not betray him but who knows his whole story; a curious and talkative brother? [...] You would like the narrator to keep quiet. No, leave him alone. He is under no illusions, but he likes you. He will tell the story of your life which resembles thousands of other lives, but which nevertheless has this feature of its own: that you are ambitious, Fouroulou; that you managed to raise yourself and you would be a little tempted to despise others, those who hadn't managed to.

You'd be wrong, Fouroulou, because you are only one particular case, and the lesson you learnt was taught you by those others.)

There is then a complex relationship between Fouroulou and the *narrateur-frère* ('narrator-brother'), who shares in the responsibility for telling Fouroulou's life, and an equally complex sharing of roles within the text, between the place occupied by Fouroulou within the writing of his 'confession', that of the narrator who has read it and then presents this second part, and the place of the reader of the published text who is manipulated into a position of sympathy and of collusion with Fouroulou by this narrator. There is a very acute awareness on the part of Feraoun concerning the complexity of many of the issues surrounding autobiographical and biographical discourses, including, for example, the status of the writer in life, the stance of the narrator of the life around which the text is composed, the place of the protagonist in the life being narrated, and the multiple roles adopted by the readers of that life. There is also a question raised about the relationship between the individual life, which is at the same time ordinary and extraordinary, and the other lives that surround him.[29] There is a celebration of the life of the community, but at the same time the protagonist is marked out, made special, made individual. The relationship between collective and individual identities is complex. The individual is a part of a community whose values he upholds and continues, but which he also sometimes criticises. His education marks him out as different. And education also plays a role in the balance of the power relations between coloniser and colonised; such an individual has the means to make his voice heard, a voice that privileges the individual, for that is the currency that the coloniser values, while at the same time representing a traditional cultural heritage and community-based value system. Feraoun thus constructs a protagonist who forges an identity between the collective and the individual, giving form to the individualism discussed in the introduction.

This second part, 'Le Fils aîné', is marked by the birth of a second son to Fatma and Ramdane and therefore represents Fouroulou's passage from only son to eldest son, as the title suggests. It is less generally descriptive of the general environment than the first part, and focuses more on the daily life and struggles of the family. In particular it focuses on Fouroulou's father's illness, and the subsequent need for him, once recovered, to go to France to look for work, and his accident there, as a result of which he eventually returns to the family. The importance of reading and writing is given its full force in a short chapter that centres on the exchange of letters between the father in Paris and the family. Fouroulou is too unsure of his abilities either to read out loud or to compose the reply to the first letter that arrives written on behalf of his father, but when the second arrives a fortnight later, he manages. The relating of these events reveals several attitudes and values. Firstly, the letter, the written word, is seen as conveying the very presence of the father: 'Tout le monde est content. La famille entière, rassemblée autour des deux écoliers, voit le père à travers la feuille de papier' (p. 94) ('Everyone is happy. The whole family, gathered around the two scholars, sees their father through the sheet of paper'). The presence of the father is therefore conveyed in French, written by a third party, and then translated in order for the family to hear his news. The power of the written word, and the relationship between French and the indigenous oral language, is made evident in a very direct way. Secondly, Fouroulou's teacher has greater confidence in him than he has in himself: 'Le lendemain, il porta la lettre à l'école d'où elle devait être remise au facteur. Le maître s'étonna de ne pas reconnaître l'écriture de son élève et lui qu'il le croyait capable d'écrire à son père' (p. 95) ('The next day he took the letter to school, to be handed over to the postman from there. The teacher was surprised not to recognise his pupil's handwriting, as he believed him capable of writing to his father'). Fouroulou is only ready to send the letter when the teacher gives his approval. In the third letter, the young boy uses the formula learnt in class to tell his father that he has been accepted to sit an exam in Fort-National. Through letter-writing, a complex interplay of status and values comes into play – the formal use of French, learnt in a French institutional context, intervenes in a necessary and emotional way in the lives of a people who have already been disrupted by the presence of the French colonial language, a vehicle of its power. Would the father have been so poverty-stricken as to have to make the journey to France if the colonial regime were not economically exploiting the country? Or would his situation have been worse, since at least he has an opportunity to make money elsewhere? In any case, it is unlikely that he would have been separated from his family, making written communication necessary. The formulaic opening announcing the news of his scholarly opportunity reveals the young boy's own relationship to the French language:

> Cette formule apprise à l'école [...] lui parut belle en elle-même et digne d'être lue à Paris. Comme elle traduisait la réalité, elle lui parut plus belle encore et digne de sortir de la plume d'un nouveau diplômé. Il était fier à l'avance de l'effet qu'elle produirait sur 'l'écrivain' à Paris. (p. 95)

> (This formula which he had learnt at school [...] seemed to him beautiful in itself and worthy to be read in Paris. As it conveyed reality, it seemed to him still more beautiful, and worthy to come from the pen of one who had recently gained his diploma. He was proud in advance of the effect it would produce on 'the writer' in Paris.)

Last, but not least, the written word in French is able to convey the 'reality' of a situation, conferring status on the one who uses it, and creating a new and special relationship of communication, 'writer' to 'writer'. Reading and writing disrupt old forms of communication and the relationships that they support, create new ones, and engender new hierarchies of power. The exam that Fouroulou sits is taken in Fort-National about twenty kilometres away, a place clearly marked by the colonial presence, and which impresses the boy: 'une vraie ville, avec beaucoup de français, de grands bâtiments, de belles rues, de beaux magasins, des voitures roulant toutes seules' (p. 96) ('a real town, with lots of French people, high buildings, beautiful streets, beautiful shops, cars driving around by themselves'). He is confident once in the exam room, where there are 'l'inspecteur, les examinateurs, beaucoup de roumis authentiques' (p. 96) ('the inspector, the examiners, lots of genuine *roumis*'). His own teacher would not recognise him, he thinks, and indeed Fouroulou is about to undergo a change in his identity. His father rewards his success with a packet of books entrusted, together with a letter and money for the family, to a friend returning to Algeria, and this reading material is gently revealed as being inappropriate:

> un grand catalogue d'une maison de chaussures et un roman d'amour: 'Collection Gauloise', entourés d'une ficelle:
>   Alors! Il paraît que tu es instruit, toi? Eh bien, voilà des livres que ton père t'envoie. Il est très content, tu sais. Et Fouroulou prit le paquet. (p. 96)

> (a big catalogue from a shoe company, and a love-story published by 'Collection Gauloise', tied together with a string:
>   'So! Apparently you're educated, are you? Well, here are the books your father sends you. He's very happy, you know.' And Fouroulou took the parcel.)

In a way that foreshadows the itinerary of Memmi, but with less shattering consequences for his relationship with the family, Menrad decides to pursue his scholarly career by preparing for the scholarship exam. He knows he would be more useful at home, and that eventually his choice will provoke a break with his past. The narrative exposes a sense of guilt in the attempt to shift the responsibility for the decision:

> Dans son for intérieur, il savait qu'il serait plus utile à la maison comme berger. Mais ses camarades du certificat n'abandonnant pas l'école, il ne pouvait faire autrement que de les imiter. Et puis les seuls animaux étaient la chèvre et son petit. Cette chèvre n'avait pas besoin d'un gardien spécial. On l'avait intégrée au troupeau du village. (p. 97)

> (In his heart of hearts he knew that he would be more useful at home as a goat-herd. But his Certificate classmates were not giving up school, and he could not do otherwise than imitate them. And then, their only animals were the nanny-goat and her kid. The nanny-goat did not need a special goat-herd. They had put her together with the village flock.)

His sisters help their mother, his father sends money, his uncle sends things from market: 'Il peut aller à l'école sans déranger personne' (p. 97) ('he can go to school without disturbing anyone'). Deprived of and sometimes regretting the freedom of the fields, Fouroulou nonetheless succeeds in passing the exam brilliantly. The subject of the essay question set is revealing of the attitudes of the French school: 'Votre père, ouvrier en France, est ignorant. Il vous parle des difficultés qu'y rencontrent ceux qui ne savent ni lire ni écrire, de ses regrets de n'être pas instruit, de l'utilité de l'instruction' (p. 98) ('Your father, who works as a labourer in France, is uneducated. He speaks to you about the difficulties encountered there by people who cannot read or write, about his regrets that he is not educated, and about the value of education'). It is not a difficult scenario for the young Fouroulou to imagine. The topic again points up the gulf between oral communication and the written word which the examination itself exemplifies.

His enjoyment of his success is cut short by the news of his father's workplace accident in France, but the final assurance of his safety comes, again in writing and in a way revealing of the relationship between coloniser and colonised: 'Lounis alla à Tizi-Ouzou et envoya un télégramme avec réponse payée au patron de l'hôtel où logeait son frère. Le télégramme revint, une lettre le suivait de près. Un Français ne peut mentir. On finit par se rassurer' (p. 100) ('Lounis went to Tizi-Ouzou and sent a reply-paid telegram to the owner of the lodging-house where his brother was living. The reply arrived, soon followed by a letter. A Frenchman could not lie. In the end they were reassured'). On his return, the father recounts the seriousness of the accident and his long hospitalisation, and how he finally managed to get his insurance money. An interjection on the status of life and writing is made with reference to the essay Fouroulou wrote for his exam:

> Si Fouroulou avait pu imaginer cette histoire au concours des bourses, il aurait certainement ajouté un paragraphe à sa rédaction en racontant tous les tracas de son père, ce qui sans doute aurait bien étonné les examinateurs. (p. 104)

> (If Fouroulou had been able to imagine this story in his scholarship exam he would certainly have added a paragraph to his essay describing all his father's troubles, which would undoubtedly have surprised the examiners greatly.)

This is an example of the subtle irony that pervades the apparently simplistic narrative technique, as the actual experience of Fouroulou's father is used to criticise the attitudes of the French towards their colonial subjects.

After a couple of days' rest his father returns to work in the fields. A short time later he reveals to Fouroulou his plans for their land, plans that are very different from those the boy has for himself: 'étudiant pauvre, mais brillant' (p. 105) ('a poor but brilliant student'). His father's opinion is that study is the preserve of the rich and that they are poor. He maps out a future for his son including working in France and returning to marry, a description of a traditional life: 'Telle est la vie que je te propose. C'est la seule qui nous convienne. Ton frère grandira, tu le guideras. Tes sœurs se marieront. Tu me remplaceras en toutes choses et je pourrai mourir tranquillement. Fouroulou écoutait silencieusement et admirait cette sagesse' (p. 106) ('"That is the sort of life I offer you. It's the only life that is right for us. Your brother will grow up, you will guide him. Your sisters will get married. You will take over from me in everything and I will be able to die peacefully." Fouroulou listened in silence and admired this wisdom'). There is none of the revolt against the father that will make Memmi's protagonist's choice so dramatic for his family. However, that evening the news of his success in the scholarship arrives. In contrast to the experience recounted by Memmi, Fouroulou's father supports him by buying the things he needs and, while nonetheless remaining sceptical about his son's likely successes, feels that they may as well take advantage of the money offered by the state:

> Le père Menrad n'était pas dupe. Il savait bien que son fils n'aboutira à rien. Mais, en ville, Fouroulou serait mieux nourri que chez lui, il grandirait loin de la dure existence des adolescents de chez lui. Puisque l'état voulait bien aider à l'élever, Ramdane ne s'y opposait pas. L'essentiel était de voir son fils devenir vite un homme afin qu'il partageât avec lui le soin de nourrir la famille. (p. 107)

> (The Menrad father was no dupe. He knew very well that his son would come to nothing. But in town Fouroulou would be better nourished than at home, and he would grow up away from the hard life of his fellow-adolescents. Since the State wished to help raise him, Ramdane had no objection.

What mattered was to see his son become a man quickly, so that he could share with him in the task of feeding the family.)

Fouroulou intends to continue his education and go on to teacher training college. The first day, in his European suit, Fouroulou feels very out of place: 'Il suffoque, il se dit qu'il n'est pas à sa place. Allons donc, l'ex-gardien de troupeau'; 'Il lui semble être un intrus dans cette nouvelle société qui l'éblouit' (p. 110) ('He felt stifled and told himself he was out of place. Why, he was an ex-goatherd'; 'He felt like an intruder in this new, dazzling society'). However, he soon manages to shake off his feelings of inferiority, this time in a way that foreshadows Camus's experience (detailed in *Le Premier Homme*), and again Memmi's experience, as a poor boy among those from a more advantageous social position than himself, and who can only gain any sort of status through studying hard:

> Menrad ne tarda pas à perdre le complexe d'infériorité qui lui enlevait tous ses moyens. Quand il s'aperçut que ses camarades n'étaient pas des 'phénomènes', il se mit résolument au travail pour acquérir un rang honorable. Il ne tarda pas, tout comme son ami, à passer pour un 'bûcheur'. Ni l'un ni l'autre ne considéraient ce qualificatif comme une injure. Très vite on se le tint pour dit et on les laissa tranquilles. (p. 113)

> (It did not take long for Menrad to lose the inferiority complex which made him feel so helpless. When he realised that his classmates were not 'prodigies', he set himself to work determined to achieve an honourable place. Before long he and his friend were known as 'swots'. Neither of them considered this an insult. Very soon it was taken for granted and they were left in peace.)

A further family drama unfolds, indirectly linked to Fouroulou's studies. His father borrows money to pay for his son's stay in Algiers and for a suit for him to take an exam. He enjoys the ease of the transaction after a life of such hardship and begins to get into debt. The scholarship grant does not come through and Fouroulou has to return to the village, where he is exposed to the jealousy and hostility of the community. He manages to continue his education and he still wants to become a teacher, even though he is aware of the potential for failure. His father supports him emotionally despite all the attendant problems:

> Si tu échoues, tu reviendras à la maison. Dis-toi bien que nous t'aimons. Et puis, ton instruction, on ne te l'enlèvera pas, hein? Maintenant je remonte au village. Ta mère saura que je t'ai parlé. Je dirai que tu n'as pas peur. (p. 120)[30]

> (If you fail, you can come back home. Remember that we love you. Also, nobody can take your education away from you, OK? Now I'm going back to the village. Your mother knows I've spoken to you. I'll tell her you're not afraid.)

The second part of *Le Fils du pauvre* ends therefore with Fouroulou in the cultural and political no-man's-land of the educated colonised subject within a system that reinforces European power, while he is not yet able to challenge that power.

The texts collected under the title *Fouroulou Menrad* included in the 1972 Le Seuil edition of various writings by Feraoun, *L'Anniversaire* ('The Birthday' or 'The Anniversary'; the nature of the event alluded to is not clear in the fragment that remains), fall into three parts: 'Bouzaréa', 'La Guerre' ('The War'), and an 'Epilogue'. The first continues with the third-person narration and details Menrad's time at the Ecole Normale de Bouzaréa.[31] The young man is happy for himself and for his family, seeing this as 'l'aisance assurée de tous' (p. 103) ('assurance of prosperity for all'). The differing fortunes of his classmates, and their resultant attitudes towards him, lead to a rare (up to this point) piece of self-examination, and also to a more general reflection on human nature:

> Il eut honte de son exaltation du début, se replia sur lui-même, méprisa ses camarades qui prenaient sa joie pour de la méchanceté et les élans de son cœur pour de l'hypocrisie. Non! Ils ont bien raison ceux qui nient l'existence du bonheur parfait ici-bas: nos amis, les premiers, se chargent de le troubler. (p. 104)

> (He felt ashamed of his initial exaltation, turned in on himself, and despised his classmates who mistook his joy for malice and his heartfelt elation for hypocrisy. No! People who deny the existence of perfect happiness in this life are right: our friends are the first to destroy it.)

The time spent in the teacher training college is so sacred that Fouroulou feels he does not have the ability, or the right, to put it into words. The text thus reveals a contrast between the lay French teaching system and the sacred aspect that the young Kabyle endows it with:

> Fouroulou entra à l'Ecole Normale et y passa trois ans. Il semble qu'on ne peut pas dire plus. Il accorde une telle importance à ces trois années, elles comptent tant dans sa vie, que c'est presque un sacrilège que d'essayer d'en parler surtout lorsqu'on n'est pas assez habile pour les faire revivre par la plume comme il les a exactement vécues ou comme il aime les revivre par le souvenir. (p. 105)

> (Fouroulou entered the *Ecole Normale* and spent three years there. It seems that nothing more can be said. He accords so much importance to those three years, they count for so much in his life, that it is almost a sacrilege to try and speak of them, especially for someone who is not skilful enough to bring them to life in writing exactly as he lived through them or as he likes to re-live them in his memory.)

This provides further comment on the act of the transcription of a life, and its relationship either to the reality of the way in which that life was lived, or to how the author would like to present it in writing, by a writer aware of the discrepancy between the power of memory and the means available to express it in language.

At this point, the French, who remained largely absent from the first two parts of Fouroulou's story, suddenly erupt into the narrative, not only because of his new environment, but because of experiences not previously recounted, revealing the attitudes of the young Kabyle towards them:

> Menrad est kabyle. Ce n'est pas sa faute. Il connaît les Français depuis son jeune âge. Les premiers furent les gendarmes. Lorsqu'ils apparaissaient, il se sauvait de la djema avec les autres gamins. Puis, ils se rassuraient tous en voyant l'amin, revenaient se poster à une distance respectueuse, prêts à disparaître au moindre danger et admirant, en attendant, ces hommes si blancs, si propres, si bien habillés, si forts, qui parlaient un français presque incompréhensible [...] Plus tard à l'E.P.S., cette crainte, sans disparaître tout à fait, fit place à une sorte de respect. Une espèce de sentiment que l'on éprouve, comme malgré soi, pour des gens d'un autre milieu, apparemment plus riche, plus beaux, plus intelligents, plus heureux, peut-être plus vertueux. (p. 106)

> (Menrad is a Kabyle. It is not his fault. He has known the French from his earliest youth. The first were the gendarmes. When they appeared he would run away from the *djema* with the other little boys. Then, seeing the *amin*, they would regain confidence and come back to stand at a respectful distance, ready to disappear at the first sign of danger, and meanwhile admiring those men who looked so white, so clean, so well-dressed, so strong, who spoke French in a way that was almost unintelligible [...] Later at the E.P.S., that fear, without altogether disappearing, gave way to a sort of respect. The sort of feeling one has, almost despite oneself, for people from another sphere of life, who seem to be richer, handsomer, more intelligent, happier, perhaps more virtuous.)

Feraoun again inserts an ironic distance between the narrator and the young protagonist. There is no affection in Fouroulou's admiration because of the disdain with which the French regard the indigenous population. He becomes 'resigned' to a system in which he is cast as inferior. Yet the simple telling of this 'resignation' highlights the effects of the colonial system. Feraoun does not need to be explicit in his criticism for the criticism to be clear:

> Ils [les Français] méprisent l'indigène, ils veulent à toute force former une caste à part et ne pas voir les autres. Fouroulou, encore jeune, s'est aperçu de ces choses. Il finit par les admettre et par croire qu'une loi naturelle veut qu'il y ait des supérieurs pour détester les inférieurs. Ses professeurs, eux-mêmes, favorisent ouvertement ses camarades français et certains internes. Il se vit obligé d'être inférieur et détestable. Il se résigna. (p. 106)

> (They [the French] despised the natives, wanting at all costs to form a class apart and not see the rest. Fouroulou registered these facts while still young.

> He ended up by admitting them and believing that it was a law of nature that
> there should be superior beings who detested their inferiors. His teachers
> themselves favoured his French classmates and certain of the boarders. He
> felt he was obliged to be inferior and detestable. He resigned himself.)

At the teacher training college, however, Fouroulou experiences a
feeling of equality and meets a wide range of students, including French,
Spaniards, Arabs and Jews. Here the ironic distance of the narration is
abandoned in the homage paid to the teachers there who restore his dignity
and who are contrasted with the values of the rest of the colonial system:

> Le premier et superbe cadeau que lui firent ses maîtres à L'Ecole normale,
> ce fut de lui rendre sa dignité. Comment donc les oubliera-t-il? Là-bas, plus
> de barrières, il n'y trouva ni des Français, ni les indigènes, mais seulement
> des élèves-maîtres et des maîtres qui veillaient à leur formation avec un soin
> jaloux. Fouroulou en voudra à quiconque essayera de travestir, de romancer,
> cette période essentielle de son existence [...] La première tâche des
> professeurs, le directeur en tête, fut d'abolir dans l'esprit de leurs élèves
> indigènes, toute idée de méfiance, de crainte, d'infériorité. Ils les placèrent
> d'emblée, d'un commun accord, sur le même plan que les autres. (p. 106)

> (The first and supreme gift given him by his teachers at the Ecole Normale
> was that they restored his dignity. How could he ever forget them? There,
> there were no more barriers: he did not find either Frenchmen or natives
> there, but only student-teachers and teachers who watched over their
> training with jealous care. Fouroulou would resent anyone who tried to
> ridicule or lie about this essential period in his life [...] The first task which
> the teachers undertook, starting with the principal himself, was to remove
> from the minds of their native students any trace of mistrust, fear or inferi-
> ority. By common accord, right from the start they set them on an equal
> footing with all the others.)

This is the only period when Fouroulou lives in proximity to the
French: 'avant l'Ecole normale, il ne les connaissait guère; les trois années
écoulées, il ne les voit plus que de loin. Il retourne dan son bled avec son
bagage de primaire, une foule de souvenirs et un choix de belles émotions'
(p. 110) ('before the *Ecole Normale* he had not known them at all; after
the three years had passed, he only saw them from a distance. He went
home to his village with his primary-school training, a crowd of memories and a selection of wonderful emotions'). Yet he is finally prepared
to admit that those years were perhaps not quite as perfect as he likes to
think, and he goes on to describe how different groups formed, first by
nationality, and then along lines of rich and poor, of class. Again, the
reality of the education system becomes a major theme, one that will be
treated with much more ferocity by Memmi:

> La race ne réussit pas plus que le clocher à rassembler ses gens. Il reste la
> condition sociale, la coupe du costume, la situation de parents. Fouroulou,
> issu d'un milieu fruste, ne peut pas ressembler à tel Français, fils d'un

directeur d'école, d'une directrice d'école. Ayant un frère professeur. La gentillesse de son camarade et son exquise politesse n'y peuvent rien. Ils se tutoient tout juste. Aucune familiarité. Tel autre, Tlemcenien ou Oranais, fils d'un avocat ou d'un interprète, bon musulman, citadin pur sang, est aussi étranger à Fouroulou que son camarade français. (p. 111)

(Race succeeded no better than religious affinity in uniting people. There was still the question of social status – the cut of one's clothes, the situation of one's parents. Fouroulou, coming from an uncultured background, could not resemble one of the Frenchmen, son of a headmaster or headmistress, and whose brother was a teacher. His classmate's friendliness and exquisite manners could not overcome this fact. They used the *tu* form in speaking to one another, but there was no familiarity. Another classmate coming from Tlemcen or Oran, the son of a lawyer or interpreter, a good Muslim and a pure-blooded city-dweller, was as far removed from Fouroulou as his French comrade.)

Fouroulou has more in common with the Spanish waiter's son, the poor Jew, the poor Arab and above all with the two Kabyles, whose own lives so closely resemble his own, than with the French or with the urban Algerians. Albert Memmi will write of a similar experience with the rich Jewish boys at his school.

The other observation that Fouroulou makes regarding the differences between French and Kabyle culture concerns the notion of love, and the relations between the sexes. As an adolescent he experiences all the usual sexual desire of a young man, but he knows that the girls he sees in Algiers are not for him. He admires the notion of love he has read about, but at the same time he is critical of the way in which the segregation of the sexes in his own culture makes relations between men and women unnatural. There is an open attitude towards sex during childhood:

L'enfant kabyle apprend de bonne heure son origine. Il sait d'où il vient, ses camarades se chargent de le renseigner. Il voit de ses yeux la différence anatomique entre le garçon et la fille, entre l'homme et la femme. Il sait pourquoi son père couche avec sa mère. Le cousin s'exerce avec la cousine lorsqu'ils ont cinq ou six ans. Un peu plus tard, peut-être, il s'exercera avec le cousin parce que dès l'âge de dix ans la fille rentre dans le clan des femmes. (p. 113)

(The Kabyle child soon learns about his origin. He knows where he came from, because his friends tell him. He sees with his own eyes the anatomical difference between a boy and a girl, a man and a woman. He knows why his father sleeps with his mother. A boy practises with his girl-cousin when they are five or six. A little later, perhaps, he will practise with a boy-cousin, because from the age of ten the girl is taken into the women's clan.)

But men and women then move to a situation in which there is no trust.[32] It is around the question of the relationship between the sexes, specifically between himself and his new wife, that Fouroulou finally revolts against his family. His money is indeed helping the family, and he does manage to find a way to manage his father's debts. He marries according to custom, but he has rather different ideas about his wife, influenced no doubt by his education: 'Il croyait, par exemple, qu'il était de son devoir d'aimer son épouse. Elle le lui rendait bien. Ils ne s'en cachaient pas' (p. 120) ('He believed, for example, that it was part of his duty to love his wife. She certainly returned it. They did not hide this from one another'). When he takes his wife's side in an argument against his family, he refuses to repudiate the woman as his father demands, while not condemning 'les gens de chez lui qui ont si peu confiance en l'homme et la femme' (p. 117) ('the people where he came from who have so little confidence in men and women'). The family accepts this; his behaviour is different, but can be tolerated.

The Second World War then breaks out, as indicated by the title of the following section, 'La Guerre'. At first, the war has little effect on daily life. Fouroulou is a committed pacifist and notes his worries in a diary entry that is placed within the text, dated 25 December 1939, an insertion that again renders complex the layers of narrative and the relationship between narrator, protagonist and reader. Fouroulou is unsure of the emotions provoked in him, and he is most concerned for those who depend on his income if he were to be called up. The ambiguity of his position in the community, as shown in the attitudes of those around him, is revealed. He is sometimes called on to give news on the war at the café since he receives the only newspaper in the village, but his French education makes him suspect. Feraoun is aware of all the ambivalence generated by the place he occupies between the coloniser and his own community: 'Tu auras à cœur de parler, de démontrer, de persuader. Mais au bout du compte tes opinions ne convaincront même pas les plus rustres qui savent par avance que tu soutiendras le gouvernement qui te donne à manger' (p. 124) ('You will have a strong mind to speak, demonstrate and persuade. But in the end your opinions won't even convince the most ignorant, because they know beforehand that you will support the government that feeds you'). Fouroulou reads all he can about the 'disaster' in France (the Fall of France in 1940), and about the causes for it given in the newspapers, where he reads that he is even 'held responsible himself', since one opinion has it that France's defeat is the fault of the schoolteachers who have not brought up the young generations as they should have. The opinion of the Kabyle peasants is simple: in a war allegiances change according to the strength of one side or the other, and they are more concerned with their own position:

Les Français battus par leurs ennemis séculaires se donnent un nouveau chef. Ce chef dit beaucoup de mal de ses prédécesseurs – nous sommes d'accord, le perdant au jeu n'a jamais raison – en même temps il dit du bien de ses ennemis. Les anciens amis détruisent les bateaux français à Mers el-Kébir. Nous changeons de çof. Nous sommes hitlériens à présent. C'est permis. Cependant quels avantages en tirons-nous? Et quels inconvénients? (pp. 126–27)

(The French, beaten by their age-old enemies, have got themselves a new leader. This leader says a lot of bad things about his predecessors – we agree, the loser is always wrong – and at the same time he says good things about his enemies. Their former friends destroy French ships at Mers el-Kebir. We change course. At present we are pro-Hitler. It's allowed. However, what advantages do we get out of it? And what disadvantages?)

The disadvantage is that they become even poorer as their lives become bound up with a history in which they are implicated by colonialism. The Kabyles working in France return, as do the soldiers, and the region is plunged into near-famine and then into disease. As Fouroulou continues his diary entries, the narrative becomes less concerned with his own problems (although he does now have fifteen people depending on his income) than with those of the Kabyle people in general: 'L'histoire du dock de Beni Rassi restera dans toutes les mémoires comme une tragique histoire, dit Fouroulou dans son journal, nos enfants en parleront à nos petits-enfants' (p. 129) ('"The story of the Beni Rassi dock will remain in everyone's memory as a tragedy," says Fouroulou in his diary, "our children will tell it to our grandchildren"'). He tells of the abject poverty, the hunger, the petty tyrants that arise from among the people in the distribution of what food there is – the type of man who 'veut se venger sur des pauvres diables toutes ses bassesses devant les riches' (p. 131) ('wants to take revenge on poor wretches for all his self-abasement before the rich'). Fouroulou is precise about details: for a year from 1942 to 1943, for example, he received 320 kilos of barley for five people, about enough to feed a chicken. When Germany is finally defeated the Kabyles' ironic opinion of the French, as understood from their own cultural perspective, is clear: 'Personne ne s'en étonne. Les saints ont intercédé auprès du Prophète. Les Français peuvent prétendre nous avoir sauvés' (pp. 134–35) ('Nobody is surprised. The saints interceded in the presence of the Prophet. The French can claim to have saved us'). The British and Americans are welcomed; the Kabyles believe that the immense wealth of America will help them, although they continue to suffer from the spiralling costs due to economic uncertainty:

Les Américains trompèrent l'espoir insensé de l'un et le désespoir des autres. On demanda beaucoup d'ouvriers. Les Kabyles formèrent des équipes, des compagnies de travailleurs. Ils gagnèrent de l'argent et rapportèrent des habits. Beaucoup de familles furent tirés de la misère. Mais on avait beau gagner, la montée vertigineuse des prix faisait l'existence toujours aussi difficile. (p. 135)

(The Americans disappointed the senseless hope of some and the despair of others. They asked for many workmen. The Kabyles formed teams and companies of workers. They earned money and brought back clothes. Many families were saved from the depths of poverty. But however much they earned, the dizzying price-rises meant that life was always just as hard.)

The ways in which the international crisis impinges on the Kabyles are explicitly criticised. Writing in October 1944, when he signs off, Fouroulou explains that the Kabyles have suffered, but they have pity for those who have been bombed, occupied, deported, tortured. They now think only of being able to return to France, this time revealing the irony in the pragmatism of the Kabyle workers in France, showing the underside of the colonial system; they want to 'aller retrouver leur Normandie ou leur Alsace, leur Saint-Etienne, Lyon ou Paris [...] S'ils ont commis des petits péchés en doutant quelquefois de la France, ils ne s'en souviendront plus. Leur conscience ne leur reprochera jamais rien car le cœur simple n'a jamais varié, même quand leur langue a suivi un autre mode' (p. 136) ('go back once more to their Normandy, or their Alsace, their Saint-Etienne, Lyons or Paris [...] If they ever committed any little sins by doubting France, they will never recall that again. Their conscience will never reproach them for anything, for their simple hearts have never been fickle, even when their tongues have gone in another direction'). Feraoun examines and reveals the hypocrisy of both the coloniser and the colonised, dismantling the binary oppositions that underpin colonialist and nationalist discourses. The epilogue, dated 1948, opens with an epigraph from Camus expressing a simple humanism: 'Il y a dans les hommes plus de choses à admirer que de choses à mépriser'(p. 137) ('There are more things to admire in men than to despise'). According to Fouroulou, a man can only look inside himself and try to understand himself despite deceptive external appearances:

Il n'a qu'à s'en prendre à lui-même, découvrir son mal et se soigner. Il n'est pas jusqu'à Fouroulou qui ne refuse de se reconnaître dans sa confession: trompeuse façade qui fait songer aux sépulcres blanchis dont parle l'Evangile ou encore à l'écurie de Menaiel qu'évoquent les kabyles pour caractériser les dehors attrayants de la vanité et de l'hypocrisie. (p. 138)

(He has only to take the blame on himself, to reveal his disease and apply the treatment. Everyone, even Fouroulou, refuses to recognise himself in his confession: a deceitful façade which recalls the whitened sepulchres referred to in the Gospel, or the Menaiel stables, as Kabyles call the attractive exteriors which hide vanity and hypocrisy.)

There follows an analysis of the problems of true self-examination – Fouroulou wants to re-examine his past life in order to understand the origins of the present troubled period, but the narratorial voice[33] casts doubt on such an enterprise: 'C'est la méthode qu'emploie le docteur pour diagnostiquer un mal. C'est aussi la méthode du charlatan' (p. 138) ('It's the method used by a doctor to diagnose a disease. It's also the method used by a quack'); 'l'intention est louable. Il n'en est pas de même du résultat' (p. 138) ('the intention is praiseworthy. The same can't be said of the result'). The people around him talk about ideas, politics and religion, but he sees no-one who sacrifices his own interests to an ideal; ideas and actions do not coincide. There is little for Fouroulou to do but to try to be true to himself and his family: 'Fais un peu de bien autour de toi si tu peux et sache que c'est la seule chose qu'on ne se reproche jamais' (p. 141) ('Do a little good to those around you if you can, and realise that that's the only thing you'll never have to reproach yourself for'). Fouroulou seems to wish to content himself at the end of the text with caring for his family and being a good teacher. Feraoun's own life-story will continue far beyond that modest wish.

A DIALOGUE WITH SELF AND OTHERS: *LETTRES À SES AMIS*

Feraoun's published correspondence, *Lettres à ses amis*, contains – in addition to details of his own everyday family and professional life – opinions and comments on other people and events, personal feelings, and advice to friends, and these letters are in some ways closer to a 'confessional' literature than the partly autobiographical text ('Fouroulou c'était à peu près moi'; 'Fouroulou was more or less me') I have looked at above. Beginning in Spring 1949, the letters are addressed to a circle of friends that includes other teachers such as Jeannine and René Nouelle, who then lived near Paris (and with whom Feraoun had set up an exchange of correspondence between the Kabyle and French pupils in their respective schools), and Pierre Martin, a mutual friend of Feraoun and the Nouelles who worked for the Service civil international (SCI) in Algeria. The circle of correspondents also includes other writers and critics such as Paul Flamand, Madame Landi-Benos, literary critic for Radio-Alger, Henri Combelles (to whom the final letter is addressed on 14 March 1962, the day before Feraoun was assassinated) and Louis Groisard, with whom Feraoun collaborated on a French textbook for African and North African schoolchildren. There is notably correspondence with Emmanuel Roblès, with whom Feraoun became friends in 1932 at the Ecole Normale de Bouzaréa, and an important series of letters to Camus, with whom the exchange grows increasingly friendly. The body of correspondence to Camus may be enlarged to include two texts on the situation in Algeria included by Le Seuil in *L'Anniversaire*. 'La Source de nos malheurs communs' ('The Source of Our Common Misfortunes') is a letter addressed to Camus after the publication of his *Chroniques algériennes*. 'Le Dernier message' ('The Last Message') is an extract from a 'Hommage à Camus' published in *Preuves*, Paris, April 1960. Feraoun's admiration for Camus is evident not only in this direct communication with him, but in letters to other friends. In an early letter to René Nouelle (16 June 1949), Feraoun talks about the way in which Camus wrote about the suffering of Kabylia, and shows at the same time his own political awareness in a direct way that is rather different to the narrative stance devised for *Le Fils du pauvre*:

> J'ai lu et relu *La Peste*. C'est bien une veine d'entendre Camus. Est-ce que cette chance pourrait m'arriver! Tu sais que je le connais depuis longtemps: en 1937, j'étais encore presque normalien (Promo: 32–35). De vrais démocrates algérois décidèrent de faire paraître un journal libre (actions de 200F majorité instituteurs). Ce journal existe encore quoiqu'à présent franchement communiste – cela lui fait tort, d'ailleurs.
>
> Eh bien Camus était rédacteur en chef *d'Alger républicain*. Et en 1937 il a publié un reportage retentissant sur les Kabyles et la Kabylie. Il a vu pas mal d'instituteurs et ces gens-là ne l'ont pas oublié.
>
> (I have read and re-read *The Plague*. It's a real piece of luck to hear Camus. Could I be so lucky! As you know, I met him a long time ago – in 1937 I was almost still a college student (class of 1932–1935). Some true Algerian democrats decided to bring out an independent newspaper (shares of 200 francs, with schoolteachers as majority shareholders). That newspaper still exists, though now it is frankly Communist – which wrongs him, what's more.
>
> Well, Camus was the chief editor of *Alger républicain*. And in 1937 he published a telling report on the Kabyles and Kabylia. He met a large number of schoolteachers and they have not forgotten him.)

It is not until 27 May 1951 that Feraoun writes to Camus to acknowledge the latter's reaction to reading *Le Fils du pauvre*:

> Je viens de recevoir ici, à Taourirt-Moussa, la visite de mon ami Roblès. Il m'a dit tout le bien que vous pensez de mon petit ouvrage et m'a donné votre adresse que je désirais connaître depuis longtemps. L'hiver dernier j'avais demandé à Pierre Martin du S.C.I. de vous faire parvenir un exemplaire du *Fils du pauvre*. Lui aussi pouvait me communiquer votre adresse mais je n'avais pas osé vous écrire.
>
> (I have just had a visit from my friend Roblès here at Taourirt-Moussa. He told me how much you think of my little book, and gave me your address, which I had been wanting to find out for some time. Last winter I asked

Pierre Martin of the S.C.I. to send you a copy of *Le Fils du pauvre*. He too could have given me your address, but I didn't dare write to you.)

He evokes the same memory of seeing Camus in 1937 at Tizi-Ouzou and recounts his reading of the articles in *Alger républicain* and especially his reading of *La Peste*, which he feels he understood 'better than anything else he had read'. He goes on, however, to provide a forthright analysis of the lack of indigenous characters in the novel and of the gap, 'ce fossé entre nous' ('that gap between us'), between the *pied-noir* experience and that of the Algerian people:

> J'avais regretté que parmi tous ces personnages il n'y eût aucun indigène et qu'Oran ne fût à vos yeux qu'une banale préfecture française. Oh! Ce n'est pas un reproche. J'ai pensé simplement que, s'il n'y avait pas ce fossé entre nous, vous nous auriez mieux connus, vous vous seriez senti capable de parler de nous avec la même générosité dont bénéficient tous les autres. Je regrette toujours, de tout mon cœur, que vous ne nous connaissez pas suffisamment et que nous n'ayons personne pour nous comprendre, nous faire comprendre et nous aider à nous connaître nous-mêmes [...] Je suis un bon maître d'école; j'ai beaucoup d'élèves et je rêve à mon aise. J'ai réussi à attirer sur nous l'attention de Audisiau [sic], Camus et Roblès. Le résultat est magnifique. Vous êtes algériens tous trois et vous n'avez pas à nous ignorer...

> (I regretted the fact that among all the characters there was not a single native Algerian and that in your eyes, Oran was just another French prefecture. Oh, it's not a reproach! I simply thought that if there were not that gap between us you would have got to know us better, you would have felt able to speak of us with the same generosity as you showed to all the others. I always regret with all my heart that you don't know us well enough and that we have no-one to understand us, make others understand us, and help us to know ourselves [...] I'm a good schoolteacher; I have a lot of pupils, and I dream as I choose. I've succeeded in attracting the attention of Audisiau [sic], Camus and Roblès towards us. The result is magnificent. All three of you are Algerian, and you can't be ignorant about us...)

The reading of Camus is insightful and highlights the gulf between the indigenous population and even the community of poor colonisers to whom Camus belongs. It also throws into stark relief the reality of Feraoun's own project in *Le Fils du pauvre*. Importantly also for the reading of Feraoun's project as a whole here, he provides a sort of programme for the kinds of self-knowledge that lead to the better understanding of self and other that life-writing seeks, together with the kind of political programme that both he and Camus would have liked to see in Algeria. This 1951 letter provides an essential framework within which to read Camus's own semi-autobiographical text, *Le Premier Homme*, which was not published until 1994, but was being worked on by Camus during the 1950s and found with him in the car crash in which he was killed.[34]

As Christiane Achour identifies in her presentation of the 1992 edition of the letters, it is through the writing of this correspondence that Feraoun keeps around him a network of other people with whom he can dialogue in confidence and overcome the isolation of his position, an isolation that is not only geographical, but also intellectual.[35] The letters are also a dialogue with the self, and Feraoun offers insights into his thoughts and character in a type of self-examination, an examination of his conscience:

> J'ai retrouvé mes craintes, mes suppositions, ma façon de voir de blédard et j'ai décidé, derechef, d'attendre votre lettre pour écrire [...] Il y a peut-être aussi l'influence du milieu; je veux dire du paysage. D'ici on voit les choses de haut, certainement. Toutefois une colline cache l'autre. La vue plonge jusqu'au fond de la vallée mais il suffit de lever la tête pour voir une muraille qui barre le ciel et vous empêche de voir loin. D'ici on ne domine rien. On se sent enfermé, prisonnier, aux prises avec soi-même, toujours à se poser des questions absurdes lorsqu'on appartient à la catégorie des gens qui se posent des questions. (To Mme Landi-Benos, 15 April 1951)

> (I've rediscovered my fears, my assumptions, my rustic outlook, and I decided once again to wait for your letter before writing [...] There is also perhaps the influence of my surroundings: I mean the countryside. From here you certainly see things from a height. But at the same time one hill hides another. You can see all the way to the bottom of the valley, but you only have to raise your head to see a wall which blocks out the sky and prevents you from seeing very far. From here you can't see the whole of anything. You feel shut in, imprisoned, at odds with yourself, always raising absurd questions if you are the type of person who questions himself.)

The reference to his *bled* is a frequent one ('Je suis kabyle et blédard' ['I'm a Kabyle and a rustic'] he writes in the first of the letters, to René Nouelle, on 12 April 1949), and this fusion of self with landscape, physically and mentally, is a strong image for a writer and intellectual who refused offers to leave a terrain and a solitude that were at once alien to the writer he had become, and inseparable from the Kabyle he remained. Feraoun's place in the world and metaphorical place in the word, and his consciousness of this place and of the ambiguity of his position, are evident in these letters, just as they were in the image of Fouroulou reading out the news of the war to the men around him.

The letters also document his own reading, and therefore both Feraoun's own interests and the influences on him, and the development of his own writing and publications. The letters also present the opportunity for him to reflect on his own behaviour and on that of others towards him as an Algerian. An example is a letter written to Pierre Martin after a trip to Paris:

> Une chose qui s'est imposée à mon esprit c'est précisément la bêtise, l'inutilité de nos grimaces. Pas tant vis-à-vis de Dieu qui s'en moque, mais entre

nous: nos conventions, notre hypocrisie, notre égoïsme. Tout cela ne mène exactement à rien. Vain château de cartes, a dit Bossuet.

Tu imagines que j'ai une arrière-pensée en te racontant tout cela. Tu peux en dire plus et beaucoup mieux, je sais. Ne sois pas tenté de croire que je veux me moquer de toi. C'est de votre faute à tous. Peut-être fûtes-vous hypocrites avec moi: j'arrive à Paris exactement comme si je tombais de la lune. J'y trouve des 'pays' très nombreux et même des parents. Non, c'est vous qui me recevez en frère. Je n'ai rien à te dire contre les gens de chez moi. Mais vous les fîtes oublier à tel point que je ne crois pas avoir ici parmi nous autant de gens auxquels je tienne plus qu'à vous. Il est peut-être malséant de le dire. Tant pis pour moi et pour vous. Je continue mon discours même si nos relations ne doivent pas avoir de lendemain. Ce qui m'a plu en vous tous, c'est précisément votre simplicité et votre franchise devant la vie. Vous essayez de jouer au naturel et vous y réussissez. (18 September 1949)

(One thing that has forced itself on my notice is precisely the stupidity, the pointlessness of the faces we make. Not so much at God, who laughs at them, as at each other: our conventions, our hypocrisy, our selfishness. All that leads to exactly nothing. An empty house of cards, as Bossuet said.

You may imagine that I have something on my mind, to say all that. You could say more, and say it much better, I know. Don't be tempted to believe I want to laugh at you. You're all to blame. Perhaps you were hypocrites towards me: I arrived in Paris exactly as though falling from the moon. There I found many different 'countries' and even relations. No, you were the ones who welcomed me as a brother. I had nothing to tell you against my own people. But you made me forget them to such an extent that I don't think there is anyone here that I'm more strongly attached to than to you. Perhaps it's wrong to say that. So much the worse for me and for you. I'll carry on my exposition even if our relationship has to end now. What I most liked about all of you was precisely your simplicity and frankness towards life. You tried to be utterly natural, and you succeeded.)

A whole philosophy of life becomes apparent, as do the divisions between Feraoun's origins and his education that have become part of his identity. In letters to René and Jeannine Nouelle he moves from such meditations to describe the routine of everyday life, which is in stark contrast to the negotiations he is involved in for the publication of *Le Fils du pauvre*, revealing the preoccupations that are competing for his attention:

Je fais mes provisions pour l'hiver. Je tiens compagnie aux ouvriers qui travaillent dans la cour, je cueille des feuilles de frêne pour la chèvre, je fais travailler un peu les petits, ma femme fait sa lessive et nous attendons la rentrée. (18 September 1949)

(I am making my provisions for the winter. I work together with the workmen in the courtyard, I gather ash-leaves for the goat, I make the children do their little jobs, my wife does the washing, and we wait for school to start again.)

And the following month:

J'attends l'hiver sans souci, tout comme les gens avisés et favorisés. C'est ma femme qui a les plus grosses peines: quatre enfants, plus le ménage, il y a ordinairement un malade dans la maison [...] Nous vivons dans un perpétuel désordre. Mais en somme, tous ces petits tracas font partie de l'existence. J'en parle non pour me plaindre mais pour vous donner une idée de l'insignifiance de notre vie, ici. C'est un peu l'histoire du Colimaçon; on ne peut pas faire autrement. (30 October 1949)

(I'm waiting for winter without concern, just like the wise and favoured of this world. It's my wife who has the greatest troubles: four children and the housework, and there's usually someone ill at home [...] We live in a state of perpetual disorder. But all in all, these little difficulties are part of life. I speak of them not to complain but to give you some idea of the insignificance of our lives here. It's a bit like the story of the Snail: we can't do anything else.)

He also writes of the tribulations with colleagues and pupils in school, especially after moving to Fort-National and a larger school in 1952, where he feels isolated from his colleagues:

Tu vois que je suis au même point que toi qui t'isoles de plus en plus. Non je ne crois pas que ce soit un effet de la fatigue ou de la vieillesse – Sans être vieux ni fatigué on est obligé d'en arriver là parce que c'est une vérité. Et la vérité on finit toujours par la connaître. C'est une affaire entendue, on est seul. Tant pis. Ça ne change rien. Ce n'est ni l'égoïsme ni de la neurasthénie. D'ailleurs quand on vient on vient tout seul, et puis après on s'en va tout seul. Simplement nous l'oublions. (To René and Jeannine Nouelle, 15 December 1952)

(You see that I'm at the same point as you, as you are isolating yourself more and more. No, I don't think it's the result of tiredness or old age. Without being old or tired one is compelled to come to that point, because it's the truth. And one always ends up by realising the truth. It's a well-known fact that one is alone. So much the worse. It doesn't change anything. It's neither selfishness nor fatigue. What is more, when one comes, one comes alone, and afterwards one leaves alone. It's just that we forget it.)

Yet, amid the 'insignificant' life he leads, there is always his writing – and in this same letter he moves from the detail of everyday life to the manuscript (of *Le Fils du pauvre*) which he would like to see published, but about which he remains reserved:

Je reste toujours embarrassé de mon manuscrit. Je me demande si je dois vous embarrasser à votre tour. Je sais que vous voudriez le lire. D'ailleurs je tiens à vous le faire lire mais il est inutile de vous déranger. Vous ne disposez guère de temps pour courir après des éditeurs qui le refuseraient infailliblement. Alors j'écris moi-même, j'ai des adresses et je fais des propositions. Si l'on me répond pour me dire de l'envoyer, je vous l'adresse pour le transmettre. Vous en prendrez connaissance auparavant. Si je renonce à vouloir le publier je vous le confierai sans condition.

(I'm still embarrassed about my manuscript. I wonder if I ought to embarrass you in your turn. I know that you would like to read it. What's more, I'm eager to get you to read it, but there's no point in bothering you. You don't have time to be running after publishers who will certainly refuse it. So I'll write to them myself, I've got some addresses, and offer it to them. If they write back and tell me to send it, I'll send it to you to forward to them. You can have a look at it beforehand. If I decide not to have it published I will let you have it unconditionally.)

In another letter to René and Jeannine Nouelle in December of the same year he tells them he has sent a typescript to the Nouvelles Editions Latines in Paris, since he knew that they had published 'une collection de machins autochtones' ('a collection of native stuff'). Feraoun remains pessimistic: 'Si jamais il passe je t'en aviserai tout de suite. Sinon je ne m'occuperai jamais plus de vouloir être imprimé car je finirai par comprendre que mes histoires n'en valent pas la peine' (20 December 1949) ('if it ever goes through I'll let you know straight away. If not I'll never try and get published again because I'll finally realise that my stories are not worth it'). Pierre Martin had also taken the manuscript to read, and Feraoun writes to him on 25 December 1949 to ask him to return the manuscript, concerned not only about the lack of value of his writing, but also about its conventionality:

> le fameux cahier, il faut me le renvoyer le plus tôt possible après l'avoir fait lire au moins de monde possible – vous deux j'espère et pas plus – Tu trouveras qu'il est trop conformiste et il te décevra. Ça, j'en étais sûr. Mais je suis prêt à en parler avec toi. A t'expliquer ma pensée un jour, si tu veux. Comme on pourra discuter d'autre chose.

> (as for the famous exercise-book, send it back to me as soon as possible, having let as few people read it as possible – you two, I hope, and no-one else. You'll find it too conformist, and it will disappoint you. I was sure of that. But I'm ready to talk to you about it. To explain my thinking to you one day, if you like. As we could talk about anything else.)

Pierre Martin must have read the manuscript and not been overly critical, for in a follow-up letter of 22 January 1950, after suggesting some places where the work that the Frenchman is carrying out would be useful among the most illiterate people of the region, Feraoun returns to the subject of his writing, being more self-critical than his correspondent was critical of him, and, very interestingly, more concerned about the quality of the content of the book than about its form:

> Nous parlerons également de Fouroulou. Mais je te dis à l'avance que je m'attendais à être jugé plus sévèrement. Naturellement les critiques qui s'adressent à la forme ne me disent rien. Je ne dois pas avoir de prétention. Il y a des choses à dire sur le fond. Là, il ne faut pas me laisser passer pour un imbécile.

> (We'll also talk about Fouroulou. But I'll tell you in advance that I was expecting you to be more severe on me. Naturally, criticisms about its form don't interest me. I can't have any ambitions in that direction. There are things to be said about the substance of it. In that sphere I can't allow myself to be taken for an imbecile.)

In the letters to René and Jeannine Nouelle and to Pierre Martin a pattern is therefore set, references to Feraoun's writing interspersed among news of the family and everyday life: 'Voilà du nouveau! L'éditeur dont je te parlais accepte de l'éditer mais il me demande de faire souscrire l'Université et m'impose un préfacier que je ne connais pas. Deux conditions inacceptables [...] Maintenant nous attendons tous les chevreaux. Nous ne buvons plus de lait depuis octobre' (to René and Jeannine Nouelle, 1 February 1950, showing that Feraoun is no dupe in publishing matters) ('Some news! The publisher I mentioned to you before has agreed to publish it, but he asks me to make the University subscribe to it, and is imposing a preface-writer on me whom I don't know. Two unacceptable conditions [...] At present we're waiting for all the goats. We haven't had any milk since October'); 'Nous aussi, depuis cette sacrée neige, nous sommes tous enrhumés et nous toussons en chœur. Mais les amandiers du jardin sont déjà en fleurs. Nous savons que c'en est fini du froid. Entendu, tu m'apporteras le cahier quand tu viendras. Tu auras les dernières nouvelles le concernant' (to Pierre Martin, 6 February 1950) ('We too, since that awful snow, have all got heavy colds and are coughing in unison. But the almond-trees in the garden are already in flower. We know that that's the end of the cold. OK, you can bring me the exercise-book when you come. You'll have the latest news on it'); and by 9 October 1950 he can write to Pierre Martin that the manuscript has been published:

> L'éditeur m'écrit que la chose est en vente. Le service de presse est déjà fait. Il ne manque plus que le succès. C'est pour y aider que je t'envoie d'autres bulletins. Ma dose de naïveté reste entière car tu n'ignores pas que notre région est réputée en Kabylie pour ses navets. Je pourrai toujours me consoler en me disant que je ne faillis pas à la tradition.

> (The publisher writes that the thing's on sale. Press releases have gone out. All that's left is its success. To help with that, I'm sending you some leaflets. I still have my full share of naivety, because as you know, our region has a reputation in Kabylia for its 'turnips' [see below]. I can always console myself by telling myself that I've upheld the tradition.)

In the self-deprecatory tone and the word-play on *navet* (both a turnip and a 'flop' or failure) at his own expense, there is clear self-doubt, just as there is genuine pleasure when the book does receive attention:

> Après une longue lettre juste un mot pour vous dire qu'on m'invite aujourd'hui de Radio-Alger à écouter l'émission littéraire de jeudi prochain 22 février à 19h30 (heure d'Algérie), c'est-à-dire 20h30 de chez vous. Il y aura 5 minutes pour mon bouquin. Et ça fera la 3e fois que Radio-Alger aura parlé du livre – le directeur des émissions arabes est un ancien de Bouzaréa, ami de Roblès, et très chic par-dessus le marché [...] Et il suffira de fermer

les yeux pour vous imaginer ici près de nous pendant ces 5 minutes – c'est beau tout de même, la Civilisation. C'est si beau qu'on en meurt... (To René and Jeannine Nouelle, 15 February 1951)

(After a long letter, just a word to say that I was invited to Radio Algiers today to listen to the literature programme for next Thursday, 22nd February at 7.30 p.m (Algerian time), i.e. 8.30 pm your time. There'll be 5 minutes about my book. And that'll be the 3rd time Radio Algiers has talked about the book – the head of Arabic broadcasting is a Bouzaréa graduate, a friend of Roblès, and very nice into the bargain [...] And you'll only have to shut your eyes to imagine yourselves here with us for those 5 minutes – Civilisation is something wonderful, after all. It's so wonderful it kills you...)

This is a most telling final line and one that presages the price that will be paid in Algeria for upholding values and beliefs on both sides in the coming conflict.

Political references of a general nature concerning the 'civilisation' that the French colonial mission sees itself as incarnating (as above), and of a more specific, local type, are also prevalent in the letters. Feraoun continues, for example, to offer advice and make suggestions to Pierre Martin:

Passons aux choses sérieuses: les instituteurs de Taourirt-Moussa seraient heureux d'avoir la route jusqu'à l'école. Comme cette dernière se trouve près de la mairie, le président à son tour serait heureux d'avoir la même route devant son bureau. Je pense que M. l'administrateur ne verrait cette réalisation que de bon oeil. Le Centre est déjà prêt à voter votre contribution [...] J'ai parlé du Service civil au président. Il trouve l'idée excellente car les propriétaires des champs que traverserait la route seraient impressionnés par les roumis et croiraient que les ordres viennent d'en haut. Comme c'est un travail d'intérêt général évident tout le monde y trouverait son compte, à commencer par lesdits propriétaires qui auront alors toutes sortes de possibilités: magasins, garages, maisons sur la route, etc. (25 April 1950).

(Now for serious matters: the teachers at Taourirt-Moussa would be happy if the road came as far as the school. As the school is close to the town hall, the Mayor in turn would be happy to have the same road in front of his office. I think that the Administrator could not fail to approve of this outcome. The Centre is all set to vote for your contribution [...] I've spoken about the *Service civil* to the Mayor. He thinks it's an excellent idea, because the owners of the fields which the road would go through, would be impressed by the *roumis* and would believe that the orders came from higher up. As it's a project of obvious general advantage everyone would get something out of it, beginning with the aforementioned field-owners, who would then have all sorts of possibilities: shops, garages, houses along the road, etc.)

Such references give a personal insight into the workings of colonial rule and into how the indigenous population worked with and around it. They also indicate again Feraoun's situation as occupying a position between the two sides, and show how clearly he understands the psychology of the colonial situation. Roblès's note to this letter provides a deeper understanding into the disparaging treatment given even to an educated man of local importance such as Feraoun by the representatives of colonial power:

> L'administrateur de Beni-Douala convoque F. un jeudi de Ramadan à midi. F. fit toute la route à pied, sous le soleil et le ventre creux. L'administrateur le fit attendre et puis lui dit: 'J'ai bien reçu votre lettre. C'est non.' F. repartit donc étonné qu'on ne lui eût pas tout bonnement signifié ce refus par lettre. Il refit tous les kilomètres de piste mais parvenu à l'entrée de Taourirt-Moussa, il entendit la voiture de l'administrateur. Celui-ci venait au Centre municipal et cette visite était prévue depuis dix jours! (*Lettres à ses amis*, p. 37)

> (The Administrator of Beni-Douala asked F. to go and see him at mid-day on a Thursday in Ramadan. F. walked all the way there, in the heat of the day, on an empty stomach. The Administrator kept him waiting and then told him: 'I have received your letter. The answer is no.' F. then set off home, astonished that he hadn't simply been told of the refusal by letter. He did all those kilometres home on foot, but just as he got to Taourirt-Moussa, he heard the Administrator's car. The Administrator was coming to the Municipal Centre, on a visit that had been arranged ten days before!)

His own writing projects as well as local affairs continue to preoccupy him and by March 1951, Feraoun is writing to René and Jeannine Nouelle about the manuscript of *La Terre et le sang*, giving an indication of his writing methods:

> Je n'envoie pas de chapitres bien que j'en ai 25 de prêts. Je finis le bouquin à l'état brut, ensuite je découpe, j'arrange l'ensemble, je recopie en corrigeant le détail. Un boulot du diable mais je ne peux pas faire autrement. Je suis sûr qu'à la fin aucun chapitre ne gardera sa physionomie actuelle. Beaucoup changeront de place, d'autres disparaîtront. Je tâtonne comme un aveugle. Il ne faut pas me prendre au sérieux. (11 March 1951)

> (I'm not sending any chapters although I've got 25 of them ready. I finish a rough draft of the book, and then I cut it, re-arrange it, and write it out again, correcting it in detail. It's a horrible lot of work, but it's the only way I can do it. I'm sure that in the end not a single chapter will look the way it does now. Some will be switched round and others will disappear. I feel my way along like a blind man. Don't take me seriously.)

He also writes to them about the research he wishes to do in Northern France on the Kabyle miners there (29 April 1951), and throughout 1951 and 1952 he refers in letters to René and Jeannine Nouelle and to Roblès to various writing projects, and to the programme on Radio-Alger on *Le Fils du pauvre* (for which he was paid, but which he did not enjoy). Here and there, there are astute asides concerning the reception of his work, local politics, and the attitude of others towards Algerians:

> J'ai été invité par le P.E.N. Club à assister à une assemblée générale qui doit se tenir en juin à Nice au titre 'd'écrivain arabe' mais j'ai refusé parce qu'il

y a une conférence à faire et aussi (surtout) pour ne pas me séparer de ma femme à une mauvaise moment. Si toutefois ma présence est exigée au Seuil pour la sortie du bouquin, je vous tomberai dessus je ne sais quand. Je fais des prières pour cela au bon Dieu des 'Arabes'. (To René and Jeannine Nouelle, 15 April 1952)

(I've been invited by the P.E.N. Club to attend an AGM in Nice in June, as an 'Arab writer', but I refused because there's a lecture to be given, and also (especially) so as not to be separated from my wife at a difficult time. If my presence is required anyway at Le Seuil for the book launch, I'll land on you sometime, I don't know when. I shall pray for that to the God of the 'Arabs'.)

He gives domestic excuses, but it is clear that one part of a possible identity in the national context that he does not accept is that of 'Arab'. He is and remains a Kabyle, and this commitment to an identity will become increasingly difficult for Feraoun in the heightened nationalistic climate of the next few years.

Feraoun is also astute about the strengths of his various books, and about asking friends, especially Roblès, for help in promoting them: 'Dommage car une préface de toi au F. du pauvre n'aurait fait de mal ni à toi, ni à moi, ni à l'école. De toute façon, dis-moi ce qu'il faut faire: je suis prêt à parler de moi en 15 lignes comme je l'ai fait en 200 pages' (to Roblès, 24 January 1953) ('It's a pity because a preface by you to "The Poor Man's Son" wouldn't have done any harm to you, me or the school. Anyway, tell me what I need to do: I'm ready to talk about myself in 15 lines as I have done in 200 pages'). The tone to Paul Flamand later that year is rather different:

Il n'y a rien a dire: je vous dois de la reconnaissance mais c'est difficile à expliquer. Vous avez lu *Le Fils du pauvre*. Vous pouvez donc mesurer le chemin parcouru par le petit Kabyle. J'ai dit dans ce livre que mes bons maîtres m'on rendu ma dignité de jeune homme mais, depuis que j'ai quitté l'école et vécu dans le bled, avec les miens, je suis devenu fataliste et j'ai perdu mon assurance. Maintenant, de nouveau, grâce à vous, et pour toujours, cette fois, je me sens redevenir un homme. Un homme, comme tout le monde, qui peut croire à la liberté, à l'amitié, à la bonté. (25 June 1953)

(There's nothing to be said: I owe you a debt of gratitude, but it's hard to explain. You've read *Le Fils du pauvre*. So you can measure the road followed by the little Kabyle. I said in that book that my good teachers restored my dignity as a young man, but after I left school and lived in the village, with my people, I became a fatalist and lost my self-confidence. Now once again, thanks to you, and this time permanently, I feel that I've become a man again. A man like everyone else, who can believe in freedom, friendship, and goodness.)

There is a complexity of feeling here – personal insecurity certainly, but one also reads a feeling of inferiority caused partly by Feraoun's isolation, and a lack of certainty in his own identity. This is made more

complex by feelings of gratitude to those who provided the education
that allowed a possible way out of the harshest realities of peasant life.
The letter continues in what we would now read as an 'assimilated' vein,
and it is clear here why Feraoun has been considered as being quite apart
from the writers who came after him, with their vehement criticism of
the French and of the colonial regime. Yet this would be to underesti-
mate Feraoun's own reading of the situation:

> Je vais vous paraître ridicule et pourtant je vous dis ce que je pense, ce que
> je sens au plus profond de mon être. J'ai toujours eu foi en l'homme, parti-
> culièrement l'homme de France, généreux et instruit qui représentait pour
> moi l'idéal. Puis des doutes me sont venus, des déceptions, des colères. Il a
> fallu lutter pour vivre, se moquer des principes, ne plus être un naïf.

> (You're going to think me ridiculous, and yet I am telling you what I think,
> what I feel in the depths of my being. I have always had faith in man, and
> particularly in the Frenchman, generous, educated, who represented my
> ideal. Then came doubts, disappointment, and anger. I had to struggle to
> survive, laugh at principles, and stop being so naïve.)

The struggle of the colonised subject is evident, and this type of candid
and searing disappointment in the 'generosity' of the French will be
explored later by both Memmi and Khatibi.

Towards the end of 1953, and more so into 1955, national events
begin to intrude into the daily lives of the correspondents:

> Pour l'affaire du Maroc les gens hochent la tête et vous rendent directement
> responsables: vous n'avez plus de crédit. C'est très mauvais. On n'a plus
> confiance en vous. Dans ces conditions je préfère ne pas venir cette année.
> (To René and Jeannine Nouelle, 30 August 1953)

> (About the Morocco affair, people shake their heads and hold you directly
> responsible: your credit is ruined. It's very bad. People don't trust you any
> more. In these conditions, I'd rather not come this year.)

And the warning to Roblès is stark once the War of Independence has begun:

> A Beni-Douala, avant-hier, là où si tu t'en souviens on s'est arrêté un jour
> avec ta femme pour cueillir des brindilles sur un talus, juste là, une bagarre
> a eu lieu entre militaires et 'rebelles'. Les vallées que tu as parcourues sont
> toutes le refuge de gens armés. Ne compte pas sur une visite en Kabylie, ce
> serait un suicide. (12 September 1955)

> (At Beni-Douala the day before yesterday, at the spot where, if you
> remember, we stopped one day with your wife to pick some twigs on a hill-
> side, just there, there was a fight between soldiers and 'rebels'. The valleys
> you travelled through are all hiding-places for people with guns. Don't think
> of coming to Kabylia, it would be suicide.)

The war changes the relationship of Kabyle and *pied-noir* to the place
where they were born.

By the beginning of 1956 home and professional life are disrupted:

> L'école de F. N. [Fort-National] est l'une des rares qui continuent de fonc-
> tionner. Toutes les autres ont été d'abord fermés, puis incendiées (presque
> toutes). Pour nous pas de changements apparents: l'angoisse, la peur, ça se
> dissimule le mieux que l'on peut et l'on occupe de son travail. Je suis devenu
> absolument casanier: la case étant l'enceinte qui m'emprisonne et met à l'abri
> provisoirement l'existence de tes amis. (To René and Jeannine Nouelle, 15
> February1956)
>
> (The F. N. school is one of the few still running. All the others have been
> first closed and then (almost all) burnt down. For us, no apparent changes:
> one covers up the anguish and fear as best one can, and gets on with one's
> work. I've become a complete home-bird: the house being the box which
> imprisons me and provisionally shelters your friends' existence.)

Feraoun continues to be very concerned for Roblès, while feeling that his
own work is being overtaken by events and aware he is seen as a *vendu*
(someone who has sold out) by those struggling for the liberation of
Algeria, as he writes to Paul Flamand:

> Dans mon esprit *Le Fils du pauvre* et *La Terre et le sang* ne sont que des
> chroniques parallèles et très voisines qui doivent avoir leur aboutissement à
> la veille du drame que nous vivons. J'ai été pris de vitesse et mon demi-
> témoignage n'aura servi de rien.
>   C'est un demi-témoignage pour l'un et l'autre de mes livres puisqu'il s'ar-
> rête à l'avant-guerre. Il n'aura servi de rien puisqu'il est cruellement dépassé.
>   Aux yeux de mes compatriotes, aux yeux de ceux qui souffrent et qui
> luttent, j'apparais comme quelqu'un de tiède qui a peur d'atteindre la vérité.
> Aux yeux des agitateurs politiques, je ne suis qu'un vulgaire 'vendu'. Pour
> moi, je suis tout simplement un ambitieux qui a surestimé ses forces [...] Ni
> les Français ni les Musulmans ne trouveraient leur compte dans cet ouvrage
> (*Les Chemins qui montent*). Du moins j'aurais témoigné en toute sincérité
> et j'aurais réglé mes comptes avec moi-même. (31 March 1956)
>
> (To my mind, *Le Fils du pauvre* and *La Terre et le sang* are simply two
> parallel, closely-related accounts which had to end on the eve of the drama
> we are living through. I was overtaken by events, and my semi-testimonial
> will have served no purpose.
>   It's a semi-testimonial, in both the one and the other book, because it
> stops before the war. It will have served no purpose because it has been
> cruelly surpassed.
>   In the eyes of my compatriots, in the eyes of those who are suffering
> and fighting, I am a lukewarm person who is afraid of reaching the truth.
> In the eyes of the political agitators, I'm just another of those who've sold
> themselves. To myself, I am quite simply an ambitious person who overes-
> timated my own strength [...] Neither the French nor the Muslims will find
> anything for them in the book ('The Upward Paths'). At least I will have
> borne witness in all sincerity and I will have settled my accounts with myself.)

Here Feraoun seems to prefer turning in on himself to embracing the
historical moment that has invaded his life. Yet he does go on to engage
with events in Algeria. He chronicles the rapid deterioration of the situ-

ation in Kabylia, especially in letters to Roblès, and is especially worried for his own family in Tizi-Hibel, where the events are particularly violent and uncertain, but where he is determined to go in August 1956. A measure of the very real danger is evident in the fact that Feraoun writes to tell Roblès where he can find the diary ('cinq cahiers manuscrits'; 'five handwritten notebooks') that he began to write in 1955 (which I will explore in the following section) and keeps in the house in Fort-National. In September he writes to René and Jeannine Nouelle and to Roblès to tell them about the situation in the Kabyle villages, giving a depiction of the uncertainty of everyday life for the villagers caught up in the war, making them suspicious of everyone:

> Et lorsque survient l'événement ce n'est jamais celui qu'on attendait, ce n'est jamais la fin de la souffrance mais toujours une menace supplémentaire. C'est toujours un ratissage, un incendie, une pendaison, un mitraillage, ensuite les journaux annoncent une conférence, publient une déclaration, apportent un nouvel espoir... Les villages se replient sur eux-mêmes comme si le monde entier leur était devenu hostile et des cousins, des amis, m'ont accueilli avec une réserve discourtoise à laquelle je ne m'attendais pas. (To Roblès, 8 September 1956)

> (And when it happens it's never what one expected, it's never the end of suffering but always an additional threat. It's always a search, an arson attack, a hanging, a shooting, and then the newspapers announce another conference, publish a declaration, bring a new hope... The villages withdraw into themselves as if the whole world had become their enemy, and cousins, friends, have received me with a discourteous coldness I wasn't expecting.)

In the midst of his own anguish he writes a moving letter to Camus after the award of the Nobel prize, in which Feraoun reaffirms a shared vision for Algeria and his own affection and admiration for the writer:

> N'attachez aucune importance, aucune signification au silence des écrivains musulmans. Quant à moi, j'ai cru devoir vous exprimer ma satisfaction simplement parce que je me place beaucoup plus près de vous que les autres. Lorsque Roblès, notre ami commun, me parle de vous, il me rapporte jusqu'à vos secrètes pensées que vous ne lui celez jamais et j'en suis arrivé à être au courant de vos opinions, de votre angoisse, de votre souffrance. Croyez-vous que vos confrères vous connaissent de la sorte même s'ils vous comprennent et vous apprécient mieux que je ne puis le faire? (30 November 1957)

> (Don't attach any importance, any meaning, to the silence of Muslim writers. As for me, I felt I had to tell you how happy I was, simply because I feel much closer to you than the others. When Roblès, our mutual friend, speaks of you to me, he tells me about your most secret thoughts, which you never hide from him. Do you think that your colleagues know you as well as that, even if they understand and appreciate you better than I can?)

Feraoun writes of how in Algeria people are becoming accustomed to death, and of his own isolation in the suburbs of Algiers, where he moved for the safety of his family, with words that would have a bitter irony given subsequent events: 'Et nous voilà tous ici, au milieu des Arabes des bidonvilles, perdus dans un monde où nous ne pouvons nous adapter mais à l'abri des sollicitations impérieuses et contradictoires qui n'auraient pas manqué de mettre en péril mon irremplaçable existence!' ('And here we all are, in the middle of the Arabs of the shanty-towns, lost in a world we cannot adapt to, but protected from the imperious and contradictory demands which would not have failed to endanger my irreplaceable life!'). Again he speaks of his isolation, but this time it is in a different place and for different reasons. He ends with his belief that his and Camus's vision will triumph:

> J'y voulais mettre surtout mes pensées affectueuses et vous dire qu'en dépit du prix fort et peut-être à cause de cela les hommes de chez nous parviendront à construire ce monde fraternel que vous avez toujours cru possible. J'en ai la conviction profonde. Un monde qui sera le nôtre et où vous serez le meilleur des guides.
>
> (I would like to add my warmest greetings, and tell you that despite the terrible cost, and perhaps because of it, people here will manage to build the world of brotherhood that you have always believed possible. I am deeply convinced of this. A world which will be ours and where you will be the best of guides.)

To Paul Flamand also he writes of the difficulty with which he and his family are adapting to life in Algiers, and of the effects on his writing. As he has written in an earlier letter to Roblès, the only thing he manages to keep working at is the diary: 'Enfin, j'ai tenu un journal qui relate tout dont j'ai été témoin depuis mon dernier voyage à Paris, bientôt trois ans. Un brûlot rageur où chacun en a pour son compte. Que sortira-t-il de valable de toutes ces proses? Pas grand chose probablement' (to Paul Flamand, 23 December 1957) ('Finally, I've kept a diary which tells everything I have witnessed since my last trip to Paris, nearly three years ago. A blistering attack with something for everyone. Will anything of value emerge from all that prose? Not much, probably'). By the summer of 1958, however, he is writing to Roblès, who has been correcting the proofs of *Les Poèmes de Si Mohand*, saying that he has begun a new novel. He has also sent a copy of 'La Source de nos malheurs communs' ('The Source of Our Common Misfortunes') to Camus, whom he had seen earlier that year and with whom his correspondence is increasingly informal. Writing again becomes his only sustenance, as Feraoun comes increasingly under threat, and is often sought after to participate in events:

> Aujourd'hui j'ai reçu trois visiteurs qui tous les trois voulaient me mettre sur une liste de candidats au conseil municipal. Je présume qu'on va essayer

encore toutes sortes de pressions pour m''intégrer'. En vérité je suis en plein
dégoût! Et il ne me reste plus que le désir d'écrire. Rien d'autre ne m'in-
téresse. Je m'accroche à cette planche de salut. Ecrire, seulement écrire. (To
Roblès, 6 April 1959)

(Today I received three visitors who each wanted to put me on a list of candi-
dates for the town council. I expect all sorts of pressures will still be tried
on me so as to 'integrate' me. The truth is that I am utterly revolted by it!
And I've nothing left except the desire to write. Nothing else interests me. I
hang on to that as my last hope. Writing, just writing.)

Yet Feraoun's frustration with the demands of the family and work spill
over into another letter, and the reader can see how and why writing has
become an ideal given the pressures both inside and outside the household. As he writes again to Roblès: 'Pour excuser mon retard voici mon
emploi du temps: 6 heures, lever, 6 à 7, bagarres avec mes enfants. 7h30,
ouverture du portail, préparation de la rentrée, visite des locaux pour
vérifier si le nettoyage est fait correctement. 7h45, ruée de 700 gosses:
avec des dames en *haïk* et des messieurs qui s'installent devant mon
bureau' (15 November 1959) ('As an excuse for the delay, here is my
timetable: 6 o'clock, get up. 6 to 7, fights with my children. 7.30, open
gate, prepare for arrival of schoolchildren, check rooms to make sure
they've been properly cleaned. 7.45, avalanche of 700 kids: with women
in *haïk* and men who plant themselves in front of my office').

By the autumn of 1960, a new post and another house move mean
that Feraoun devotes little time to the diary, but he expresses the wish to
give Roblès what he has written for him to show Paul Flamand so that
he might 'se rende compte de ce que cela représente' ('realise what that
represents'). He is unsure in his new post and the pressure of the family
weighs on him. The network of friends is more important than ever and
consoles him in an uncertain existence as he writes to Roblès: 'Depuis
que je suis à Alger il me semble que ma vie n'a plus de sens et qu'elle
consiste à vieillir, à élever les enfants qui poussent, me poussent, m'élim-
inent peu à peu. Il reste quand même les amis. Ça tu l'as compris et c'est
grâce à toi que je l'ai compris moi aussi' (20 November 1960) ('Since I
came to Algiers it seems to me that my life no longer has any meaning
and that it consists of growing old, raising children who are growing,
outgrowing me, and pushing me aside little by little. However, there are
still my friends. You've understood that and it's thanks to you that I've
understood it too').

At the beginning of 1961 events are taking their toll: 'Pour ma part
je vis de très mauvais moments et ce sera miracle si je sors intact morale-
ment de tout ce qui se passe. Mon remède? J'essaie d'oublier, de me faire

bête, de passer pour tel' (to Roblès, 16 January 1961) ('As for me, I'm going through some very bad times and it will be a miracle if I come out of it all morally intact. My solution? I try to forget, to make myself stupid, to be taken for stupid'); 'Parfois je me mets à souhaiter non pas de crever – remarque que ça me serait égal – mais de devenir fou. Je me dis qu'il y aurait là une espèce de libération' (to Roblès, 8 March 1961) ('Sometimes I start hoping, not to drop dead – mind you, I wouldn't care about that – but to go mad. I tell myself that that would be a sort of liberation'). He is disillusioned by his professional work, which has become meaningless: 'Aux centres sociaux, je fais un travail assommant dont je me fiche éperdument et qui n'intéressera jamais personne. C'est du bla-bla le plus stérile mais aussi je me rends compte que toute l'Académie est du bla-bla. Il n'y a de vrai que le travail de l'instituteur' (to Roblès, 8 April 1961) ('At the social centres I do extremely boring work which I simply couldn't care less about and which nobody will ever be interested in. It's the most fruitless rubbish imaginable, but I also realise that the whole Academy is rubbish. The only real work is that of the teacher'). He explains more about the education programme destined for the rural masses to Paul Flamand, and in so doing pinpoints the effects of the collapse and failures of the colonial education system:

> En principe très grand programme, très intéressant: l'ancien boulot de l'instituteur du bled systématisé, codifié, officiellement encouragé, soutenu… Trois fois hélas! Il fallait faire ça en 50 et maintenant personne n'y croit: ni l'administration, ni les éducateurs, ni les usagers. Peut-être y faudra-t-il revenir plus tard, lorsqu'on aura fini de se tuer ou de se mentir. (6 August 1961)

> (In principle it's a very great programme, and very interesting: the original job of the country school-teacher, systematised, codified, officially encouraged, supported… Alas! It should have been done in 1950 and now nobody believes in it: neither the administration, nor the teachers, nor the pupils. Perhaps it will have to be revived later, when people have stopped killing each other and lying to each other.)

And he goes on to talk about the diary and its value as a record of historical events:

> J'ai relu cette semaine l'ensemble de mes notes prises au jour le jour depuis 55. D'abord très régulièrement jusqu'en 1959. Puis espacées en 1960 et davantage encore en 61. En tout, il y a environ 700 pages de cahier d'écolier. Environ 600 pages dactylographiées. Bien entendu l'impression d'ensemble est très bonne. Si jamais un tel livre voyait le jour, les gens comprendraient que la guerre d'Algérie n'est pas une plaisanterie et tous les guerriers en prennent pour leur grade.

> (This week I re-read the whole collection of notes I made, day by day, from 1955 onwards. Very regularly at first, until 1959. Then more scattered in

> 1960 and still more so in '61. Altogether there are around 700 pages of a
> school exercise-book. Around 600 typed pages. Of course the overall
> impression is very good. If ever a book like that saw the light of day, people
> would understand that the Algerian war is not a joke and all the fighters are
> getting it in the neck.)

By September 1961 the situation was chaotic and increasingly dangerous:
'A présent c'est la pagaille. On mitraille n'importe qui, on fait sauter n'importe quoi. Les journaux eux-mêmes en parlent à peine' (to Roblès, 13
September 1961) ('At present it's chaos. They're shooting anybody at all,
they're blowing up any place at all. The newspapers themselves hardly
even mention it'). On 14 March of the following year Feraoun wrote a
final letter to Henri Combelles; the next day he would be dead. The letters
are therefore a document of this period of Algerian history, but also an
important dialogue in which the writer engages with a circle of friends,
and above all with himself. They are an essential element of the life-
writing project that sustained Feraoun as a writer, teacher and
intellectual, but also as a friend, colleague, husband and father.

WITNESSING HISTORY, THE SELF AS WITNESS:
JOURNAL 1955–1962

Feraoun decided to begin his diary on 1 November 1955, exactly a year
after the outbreak of violence that began the War of Independence and
at a time when events were becoming seriously worse.[36] As I have already
shown, his letters had begun to reflect more and more the events of the
war, which had at first seemed removed from his daily life and the lives
of those around him. The entries for the first week of the diary mark the
change in the language of the personal philosophy of Feraoun and his
understanding of human existence and human needs that recalls some of
the later letters:

> Cependant il y a un fait: l'atmosphère n'est plus ce qu'elle était. Cela se sent,
> cela se voit. Le changement est brutal mais en apparence seulement.
> L'apparence, la voici: lorsque la révolte éclata nous n'avions pas voulu en
> mesurer l'importance. Effectivement ce n'était pas important. Nous nous
> étions installés dans une quiétude sincère, une existence supportable faite de
> petites nécessités, de besoins et de devoirs quotidiens, de maladies qu'on
> soigne, de difficultés qu'on surmonte [...] C'était une quiétude méritée et
> nécessaire, nécessaire pour que chacun puisse se croire utile – à soi-même et
> aux autres – et digne de vivre. Et cette quiétude, il était inconcevable que du
> jour au lendemain on la crût menacée. Et cette dignité de vivre, il nous
> semblait injuste qu'on songeât à la discuter. (*Journal 1955–1962*, 6
> November 1955, p. 13)

(However there is one fact: the atmosphere is no longer what it was. You can see and feel that. The change is brutal but only in appearance. The appearance is this: when the revolt broke out we chose not to measure its importance. It did not in fact matter. We took our stand on a sincere quietude, a bearable existence made up of little necessities, daily needs and duties, sick people we looked after, difficulties we overcame [...] It was a well-merited and necessary quietude, necessary for each individual to be able to think that they are useful – to themselves and to others – and deserve to live. And it was inconceivable for us to believe, from one day to the next, that this quietude could be threatened. And we thought it unjust that anyone could dream of denying the fact that we deserve to live.)

Christiane Achour's analysis highlights the fundamental difference between the letters and the diary, which cover some of the same period:

> D'un côté comme de l'autre sont parfois évoqués les mêmes événements mais la narration en est différente tant dans le style que dans la contextualisation et la sélection des faits: pas de dissonance mais une autre coloration.[37]

> (In the one and the other, the same events are sometimes referred to, but the telling of them is different, both in the style and the contextualisation and selection of facts: no actual discrepancies, but a different colouring.)

The difference in tone is indeed striking. The letters never seem destined for publication (although it may also be said that the letters of writers are also a form of literary enterprise and are therefore necessarily public), while the diary always had a private reader or public readers in view, as Feraoun writes in a letter to Emmanuel Roblès, who had first prompted him to keep the diary: 'Je me suis mis à prendre des notes comme tu me l'avais suggéré. Dès qu'il y en aura assez je te ferai lire le cahier. Cela m'occupe un peu chaque jour' (to Emmanuel Roblès, 12 April 1956) ('I've started to take notes as you suggested. When there are enough of them I'll give you the notebook to read. I spend a little time on it every day').

In his presentation of the published *Journal*, Roblès notes that Feraoun felt a real commitment to its publication, despite the potential danger that it entailed:

> Cette volonté d'agir et de témoigner lui inspira également l'idée de publier son Journal, mais au Seuil on hésitait, dans la crainte qu'une telle publication, à l'heure même ou les passions s'exaspéraient plus que jamais, n'entraînât des représailles contre l'auteur. Comme je partageais ces craintes, Feraoun m'écrivit pour insister: 'S'il ne paraît pas en ce moment, on m'accusera plus tard de lâcheté et alors il vaudra mieux qu'il ne paraisse jamais.' (Preface, p. 9)

> (His determination to act and to bear witness also gave him the idea of publishing his Journal, but Le Seuil hesitated, fearing that a publication of that kind, at the very time when passions were more enflamed than ever, would bring down reprisals on the author. As I shared these fears, Feraoun

wrote to me to insist: 'If it isn't published now, I'll be accused later of cowardice, and then it would be better if it never came out at all.')

The diary documents the hardships, fears and problems endured by ordinary Algerians as well as by Feraoun himself, his family and friends, and adds a further dimension to this life-story project in which the self is simultaneously turned outwards to other and inwards to self, as he is solicited for his opinion:

> A Alger, la grève du tabac avait commencé. Et celle de l'alcool. Il me fallait fumer en cachette, ne pas entrer dans les cafés. Les Indigènes sont très disci-plinés. Un journaliste venu à ma rencontre pour bavarder me signale que des jeunes s'attaquent aux fumeurs. Il voudrait connaître mon point de vue. Je pense qu'après notre rencontre il n'aura rien appris, rien à dire de ma part. Qu'est-ce que je pense de tout ceci? Je n'en pense rien, parbleu! Les collègues français sont tous préoccupés par ce qui se passe et qui promet toutes sortes de complications. Moi j'en suis à me demander: 'Est-ce un bien, est-ce un mal?' Ce qui me préoccupe c'est plutôt l'issue, le résultat. En tirerons-nous bénéfice? Dans ce cas, oui, quel en soit le prix. Tant pis pour moi, c'est-à-dire pour les cas particuliers. (12 November 1955, p. 16)

> (In Algiers the tobacco boycott had started. And the alcohol boycott. I had to smoke secretly, and not go into cafés. The Natives are very self-disci-plined. A journalist who came to see me for a chat informed me that youths were attacking smokers. He wanted to know what I thought of it. I don't think he learnt anything from our meeting, nothing he could say of my view-point. What do I think of all this? Obviously, I don't think anything of it! My French colleagues are all worried by what's happening and all the threat-ened complications. I just ask myself: 'Is it something good, is it something bad?' What concerns me is the outcome, the result. Will we benefit from it? If so, then yes, no matter what it costs. Too bad for myself, i.e. for individual cases.)

In 1955, Feraoun could not yet know how heavy that price would be, nor the cost of individual suffering. On the one hand the diary bears witness to some of the reactions of Algerians to the pressures imposed on them by the differing factions in the war, each one interfering in their daily lives and an equal threat and nuisance:

> J'ai vu des jeunes gens au café, leurs capuchons craquant et tintant de bouteilles de rouge. Ils vitupéraient les '*fellagh* fanatiques' qui voudraient les empêcher de 's'amuser'. Ils sont allés boire leur vin en dehors du village et le soir, je les ai revus braillant à tue-tête qu'ils allaient prendre le maquis et envoyant à tous les diables la France, ses soldats et ses gendarmes. (8 December 1955, p. 24)

> (I saw some young people in the café, with their hoods stuffed with clinking bottles of red wine. They were cursing the 'fanatical *fellagh*' who wanted to stop them 'enjoying themselves'. They went off to drink their wine outside the village, and I saw them again that evening, yelling at the tops of their voices that they were going to join the *maquis*, and consigning France, her soldiers and her gendarmes to hell.)

On the other hand, the questioning of self and others in order to answer the inevitable question 'What do you think?' pervades the diary and leads to a quest for an understanding of the situation. Complacency is shaken by violence that paradoxically has one positive outcome: it leads to self-examination: 'Il est juste cependant de dire que la violence même du terrorisme a fait sortir pas mal d'entre nous de notre quiétude et de notre paresse à réfléchir. Chacun a été obligé de se pencher sur le problème, de faire son examen de conscience' (November–December 1955, p. 47) ('However, it's true that the very violence of terrorism has made quite a few of us come out of our quietude and laziness and start thinking. We have each been obliged to dwell on the problem and examine our own conscience').

On a visit to his native village, Tizi-Hibel, Feraoun wants to know the thoughts of the Kabyles, his compatriots, and this desire provokes a long, and very literary, meditation on the way such a question may lead to the release of long-buried feelings whose very nature is in danger of being deformed:

> Je voulais lire sur leur visage, deviner leurs impressions, savoir ce qu'ils pensent. Ils répondent à mon salut gravement, d'un air entendu comme si nous n'avions rien à nous dire. Il n'y a rien à nous dire en effet. Pourquoi voudrais-je les faire parler alors que moi-même, si j'avais à le faire, ne saurais comment m'y prendre. C'est tellement plus simplement de se taire. Et puis, allons, assez d'hypocrisie! Je ressemble trop à ces gens-là pour avoir besoin de leurs confidences. Ce que je pense, moi? Je ne pense à rien. Ou bien alors il faudrait chercher loin. Au tréfonds de moi-même. Des idées, des jugements, des conclusions monteraient, interminables, que je ne saurais plus discipliner ou arrêter. Elles monteraient de moi qui les ai toujours portées sans m'en rendre compte parce qu'elles ont toujours été en moi. Si elles trouveraient une issue pour s'échapper, elles sortiraient toutes comme ces vapeurs très denses qui, dans les légendes, attendent patiemment qu'une main providentielle vienne desceller le couvercle de la marmite de cuivre où un puissant génie les avait enfermées depuis des siècles. Et de même que ces vapeurs, ce qui est en moi se condenserait hors de sa prison et apparaîtrait, aux yeux ahuris de ceux qui croient me connaître, sous les traits d'un diable boiteux et hilare. Un diable perspicace et méchant dont les ricanements accusateurs ignoreraient la pitié ou la reconnaissance, un personnage effrayant qui réclameraient réparation, qui serait implacable et sourd. Ce que l'on pourra entendre de la bouche du démon, ne sera ce que je pense, ce que pensent mes compatriotes. Pareil à celui de la légende, il serait boiteux pour avoir perdu un peu des ses vapeurs: la partie la plus subtile, la plus généreuse, la seule susceptible d'amitié et de pardon, qui se serait dissipée pour ne laisser en vous que la haine. (13 November 1955, p. 18)

> (I wanted to read their faces, guess their impressions, know what they were thinking. They replied to my greeting gravely, looking as though we understood each other and had nothing to say. We did have nothing to say to each other. Why would I want to make them talk, when I myself, if I had to talk,

wouldn't know how to set about it? It's so much simpler to keep quiet. And what's more, that's enough hypocrisy! I resemble those people too closely to need their confidences. What do I think? I don't think anything. Or if I do, I'd have to go a long way to find it. Right down to the depths of my being. Ideas, judgements, conclusions would rise up non-stop and I'd no longer be able to control them or stop them. They'd rise out of me, when I've always carried them around without realising it because they've always been in me. If they found a way out they'd all escape like those thick vapours which, in legends, wait patiently till a providential hand comes to unseal the lid of the copper pot in which a powerful genie had shut them up centuries before. And like those vapours, what's inside me would condense outside its prison and appear to the horrified eyes of the people who thought they knew me, in the shape of a lame, laughing demon. A perspicacious and malicious demon, sneering, accusing, devoid of pity or gratitude, a fearful character who demanded recompense and was implacable and deaf to all pleas. What would be heard from the mouth of the demon would not be what I think and what my compatriots think. Like the one in the legend, he'd be lame because he'd lost something of his vapours: the finest part, the most generous part, the only part capable of friendship and forgiveness, which would have vanished, leaving only hatred in you.)

On a trip to Paris with his daughter, Feraoun is haunted by the war in Algeria because he is asked again and again about the events there, and also because of seeing Algerians in Paris: 'Comme une obsession m'a suivi l'image de mon pays en révolte, un pays décidé à clamer sa souffrance, sa colère et sa haine. Et j'étais fier d'entendre sa voix, mais effrayé qu'il ne se fasse pas comprendre, que les cris rauques qui sortent de son gosier ne soient pas intelligibles du monde attentif qui l'écoute' (12 December 1955, p. 26) ('The image of my country in revolt followed me obsessively: a country which is resolved to shout out its suffering, anger and hatred. And I was proud to hear its voice, but afraid that it isn't making itself understood, that the hoarse cries that come from its throat are not intelligible to the listening world'). Algeria takes on a new identity for him, an identity born of oppression and the need to make itself heard.

The common image of the 'assimilated' Feraoun is immediately thrown into question by anyone who reads the diary. He is fully aware of the legacy of colonialism as he writes of the injustice evident towards the Algerians he sees in Paris, and he is lucid in his analysis of French–Algerian relations:

> Désormais un infranchissable fossé nous sépare, ce ne sont plus des maîtres, des modèles ou des égaux, mais des ennemis. Ils l'ont toujours été d'ailleurs, avec tant d'aisance dans leurs manières, tant d'assurance dans leurs paroles et leurs actes et tant de naturel que nous avons été conquis non par leur haine mais par leur bonté. Les manifestations de leur bonté à notre égard n'étaient que celles de leur haine. Mais leur haine était si intelligente que nous ne la

comprenions pas. Nous la prenions pour de la bonté. Ils étaient bons, nous étions mauvais. Ils étaient civilisés, nous étions barbares. Ils étaient chrétiens, nous étions musulmans. Ils étaient supérieurs, nous étions inférieurs. Voilà ce qu'ils ont réussi à nous faire croire, voilà pourquoi leurs petites libéralités étaient pour nous les effets de leur bonté. Les plus sincères d'entre nous, les plus intelligents aussi leur manifestaient à l'occasion une reconnaissance infinie et une admiration sans bornes. Et à notre tour nous avons fini par leur faire croire qu'ils étaient sincères avec nous, qu'ils étaient bons et supérieurs. Maintenant il faut qu'ils déchantent. Il faut qu'ils sachent la vérité: ils ne nous tiennent pas et nous ne les aimons plus, Dès lors pourquoi se leurrer? (13 December 1955, p. 27)

(From now on we are separated by an unbridgeable chasm. They are no longer teachers, models or equals, but enemies. They always have been, what's more, but with such ease of manner and such conviction and naturalness in their words and actions that we were conquered not by their hatred but by their kindness. The signs of their kindness towards us were merely signs of their hatred. But their hatred was so intelligent that we didn't understand it. We took it for kindness. They were good, we were bad. They were civilised, we were barbaric. They were Christians, we were Muslims. They were superior, we were inferior. That is what they managed to make us believe, that is why we took their little bits of liberality for the effects of their kindness. The more sincere among us, and the more intelligent, repaid them with infinite gratitude and limitless admiration. And in our turn we ended up by making them believe that they were sincere towards us, that they were good and superior. Now they have to recant. They have to learn the truth: they don't have any hold on us and we no longer love them, so why kid oneself?)

This is an analysis of the relationship of the coloniser and the colonised as complex as the 'duo' theorised by Albert Memmi. The ease, and apparent 'naturalness', with which a series of binary oppositions are constructed between the 'civilised man' and the 'barbarian', between 'superior' and 'inferior', between 'good' and 'evil', is laid bare here. There is also a self-analysis of Feraoun himself concerning his changed attitude to the French, the reasons for his loss of faith in them and his inability to deceive himself any longer. Indeed his thinking is very close to that of Memmi:

La vérité, c'est qu'il n'y a jamais eu mariage. Non. Les Français sont restés à l'écart. Dédaigneusement à l'écart. Les Français sont restés étrangers. Ils croyaient que l'Algérie c'était eux. Maintenant que nous nous estimons forts ou que nous les croyons un peu faibles, nous leur disons: non messieurs, l'Algérie c'est nous. Vous êtes étrangers sur notre terre. (p. 45)

(The truth is that there was never a marriage. No. The French remained apart. Contemptuously apart. The French remained foreigners. They believed that Algeria was themselves. Now that we judge that we are strong, or believe that they are a little weak, we say to them: 'No sirs, Algeria is us. You are foreigners on our land.')

Feraoun is of course also interested in the position and the behaviour of the French schoolteachers. He is under no illusion about the level of commitment of current colleagues compared to the 'pioneers' who previously sought to educate the young Kabyles in harsh and difficult conditions (no doubt thinking of his own teachers): 'mais l'héritage est vraiment trop pesant pour eux. Maintenant qu'ils ont eu les titularisations, les régularisations, les avancements, ils ne pensent qu'à partir. Ils n'ont plus le cœur à l'ouvrage' (18 December 1955, p. 39; part of a very long entry, divided into sections and covering November and December) ('but the legacy is really too heavy for them. Now that they've got their qualifications, their approvals, their advancements, all they think of is leaving. Their heart is no longer in their work'). And again the problem of 'What do you think?' comes to the fore, this time posed by his French colleagues:

> Quelle que soit la pensée du collègue, il y désormais rupture. Une rupture qu'on regrette des deux côtés mais que l'on subit, la sachant inéluctable. Nous évitons de parler politique. Nos collègues français sont pourtant pleins de tact. Lorsqu'il leur arrive de commenter un crime, un sabotage, une attaque, quand ils parlent de leur inquiétudes, ils supposent toujours que nous sommes de leur côté, que notre sort est identique, enfin que nous sommes Français comme eux. Nous admettons le postulat et la vie commune reste supportable. (November–December 1955, pp. 39–40)

> (Whichever way a colleague thinks, there is always a split from now on. A split that both sides regret, but go along with, knowing that it's inevitable. We avoid talking politics. And yet our French colleagues are full of tact. When they find themselves discussing a crime, a piece of sabotage, an attack, or when they speak of their worries, they always assume that we are on their side, that our fate is identical with theirs, all in all that we are French like themselves. We admit the premise and life together remains bearable.)

Real communication has therefore become impossible, and even calmness or indifference on the part of the Algerians leads them to be suspected by the French of playing a double game. At the same time there is the solidarity among the Kabyles, but once again Feraoun shows perspicacity in his analysis of human nature and of how the *maquis* behave towards the local population:

> Les hors-la-loi sont des nôtres. Ils se comportent en Kabyles et ont soin de ne pas nous blesser. Selon le cas ils flattent notre fanatisme, notre orgueil, nos espoirs, ou alors ils partagent nos idées, nos conceptions démocratiques de la société, nos sentiments humanitaires. Ils ont de tout parmi eux. N'importe qui se sentirait à l'aise dans le maquis. A l'aise parce qu'il sait qu'il s'y trouverait avec des frères, qu'il pourrait y discuter, soutenir son point de vue, l'affronter à d'autres points de vue. (November–December 1955, p. 44)

> (The outlaws are our people. They behave like Kabyles and are careful not to wound us. Depending on the case, they flatter our fanaticism, our pride, our hopes, or else share our ideas, our democratic concepts of society, our

humanitarian feelings. They have every kind among them. Anyone would feel at ease in the *maquis*. At ease, because he knows that he'd find himself among brothers, that he'd be able to argue, uphold his own point of view, and set it against other points of view.)

As the violence and dangers escalate, the French and the Algerians shut themselves into their separate universes: 'Eux avec la nostalgie d'un passé pour lequel ils sont décidés à lutter. Nous avec le fol espoir d'un avenir meilleur pour lequel nous acceptons de mourir' (November–December 1955, p. 49) ('They with nostalgia for a past for which they are determined to fight. We with the crazy hope of a better future for which we are ready to die'). The feelings of fraternity Feraoun feels towards the Kabyles do not extend to the behaviour of all his compatriots, and he is aware of the ways in which Islam is being used as a tool of oppression. And the ironic tone is more bitter than that used for the narratorial voice of *Le Fils du pauvre*:

> J'apprends que les cafés maures ont reçu l'ordre d'interdire le jeu: domino, cartes, loto, etc. Oui, d'abord c'est là une pratique contraire à l'Islam. Et puis notoirement le jeu incite à la paresse, la dissipation, l'oubli des devoirs familiaux. Il faut être honnête et travailleur, s'occuper du pain de ses enfants. L'alcool, mauvais. Le tabac, mauvais, le jeu, mauvais. Mauvais! Mauvais! Le temps est à l'austérité. L'obéissance aveugle au décalogue est un devoir impératif. B. m'aborde avec un large sourire et une haute chéchia, tronc de cône écarlate dont le gland égaie ses tresses un peu raides sur le côté. A partir de maintenant, la chéchia sera de rigueur pour nous. Signe visible de ralliement. (5 January 1956, p. 56)

> (I hear that the Arab cafés have been ordered to forbid games: dominoes, cards, lotto, etc. Yes, firstly, that's a practice contrary to Islam. And then, games notoriously induce laziness, dissipation, and forgetfulness of family duties. People have to be honest and hard-working, dedicate themselves to getting bread for their children. Alcohol: bad. Tobacco: bad; games: bad. Bad! Bad! This is a time for austerity. Blind obedience to the commandments is an imperative duty. B. greets me with a big smile and a high fez, a truncated scarlet cone with a tassel spreading its bright, rather stiff strands down one side. From now on the fez will be *de rigueur* for us. A visible sign of alliance.)

And a few days later he describes the fanaticism of some of the Algerian fighters for whom repression and racism have become the norm:

> Les prétensions des rebelles sont exorbitantes, décevantes. Elles comportent des interdits de toutes sortes, uniquement des interdits, dictés par le fanatisme le plus obtus, le racisme le plus intransigeant, la poigne la plus autoritaire. (8 January 1956, p. 58)

> (The rebels' claims are exorbitant, and disappointing. They include prohibitions of all kinds, nothing but prohibitions, dictated by the most obtuse fanaticism, the most intransigent racism, the most authoritarian grip.)

In relation to the complex links between loyalty and betrayal, he observes how the villagers obey the justice provided by the rebels, because despite the danger and the extremism, they are being allowed to recover their dignity. He describes the situation this time with a kind of practical irony:

> Voilà pourquoi les gens de chez nous se soumettent de bonne grâce à la mystique des maquisards; pourquoi ils se remettent sincèrement à découvrir d'exceptionnelles vertus au livre saint de l'Islam et une grande compétence à ceux qui agissent en l'invoquant. Maintenant, me dit Amar, la justice, c'est réglée. Les rebelles arrangent tout le monde, suppriment les désaccords, et fixent les pénalités. Ils ne se trompent jamais d'ailleurs. Ils veulent l'union dans tous les villages, la paix, la fraternité. Toi qui es instruit, si jamais tu les écoutais et discutais avec eux, tu serais conquis. Je ne doute pas que je serais conquis si j'habitais Tizi-Hibel. Ils auraient eu mon adhésion totale, mon admiration sans réserve. Je suis père de famille après tout. Et sur ce point je n'ignore rien de mes lourdes responsabilités. Mais de loin, je ne peux m'empêcher de demeurer circonspect, moi qui précisément instruit, qui connais un peu l'Histoire. (2 January 1956, p. 74)

> (This is why the people at home submit with good grace to the *maquisards'* mystique; why they set themselves sincerely to discover exceptional virtues in the holy book of Islam and great competence in those who invoke it for their actions. 'Now,' Amar told me, 'justice is sorted out. The rebels sort everyone out, suppress quarrels and fix penalties. They're never mistaken, what's more. They want union in all the villages – peace, fraternity. You who are educated, if ever you listened to them and argued with them, you'd be won over.' I don't doubt I'd be won over if I lived in Tizi-Hibel. They'd have my total adherence, my unreserved admiration. I'm the father of a family, after all. And on that point I'm aware of all my heavy responsibilities. But from a distance I can't help remaining cautious, precisely because I am educated, and know a little history.)

Feraoun is clearly aware of how the nationalist discourse necessarily involves the reappropriation and rewriting of history. He does not approve of the behaviour of the French soldiers, who are arrogant and treat the population with arbitrary cruelty and without respect, but he shows compassion for the fact that they are caught up in something they do not understand, risking their lives for a situation that far exceeds them: 'Toutefois ce sont ces garçons naïfs, tous plus ou moins blonds, tous plus ou moins beaux, tous absolument étrangers au mal dont nous voulons plus souffrir, ce sont ces pauvres garçons et surtout leurs parents de Bourgogne ou d'Alsace que nous plaignons. Que sont-ils venus faire ici, bon Dieu? Pourquoi meurent-ils si bêtement?' (23 January 1956, p. 65) ('But anyway it is these naïve boys, all more or less fair-haired, all more or less good-looking, all absolute strangers to the evils that we don't choose to suffer any longer, it's these poor boys and above all their parents from Burgundy or Alsace that we pity. What have they come to do here, in God's name? Why do they die so stupidly?').

The school that Feraoun attended as a child in Tizi-Hibel is burned down. A confrontation with French colleagues concerning the arrest of a Kabyle colleague for rebel activity brings about an outburst of anger in front of his pupils as he remembers his and other Kabyle colleagues' sympathy when a French teacher was kidnapped:

> J'ai lu dans leurs yeux la colère et la haine. Ils étaient là, tous les quatre à me contredire, quatre à m'insulter de leur arrogance, quatre à me cataloguer dans cette catégorie qu'ils n'aiment pas, qu'ils exploitent, qu'ils voudraient massacrer et dont ils ont peur. Une peur folle. Alors j'ai pris le plus raciste d'entre eux et je lui ai crié devant les élèves: – 'M. F., j'en ai assez, j'en ai marre! Je suis aussi Français que vous et je ne voudrais pas avoir à vous le redire!' (30 January 1956, p. 70)

> (I read their anger and hatred in their eyes. There they were, all four of them, contradicting me, four of them insulting me with their arrogance, four of them putting me into the category of people whom they don't like, whom they exploit, whom they'd like to assassinate, and whom they fear. A mad fear. Then I took the most racist of them and shouted to him in front of the students: 'Mr F., I've had enough, I'm fed up with it! I'm as French as you are and I don't want to have to tell you so again!')

The outburst leads to an entry the following day that forces real self-examination and a return to the question of identity and the question of his own 'Frenchness':

> Quand je dis que je suis Français, je me donne une étiquette que tous les Français me refusent; je m'exprime en français, j'ai été formé à l'école française. J'en connais autant qu'un Français moyen. Mais qui suis-je, bon Dieu? Se peut-il que tant qu'il existe des étiquettes, je n'aie pas la mienne? Quelle est la mienne? Qu'on me dise ce que je suis! Ah! Oui, on voudrait peut-être que je fasse semblant d'en avoir une parce qu'on fait semblant de la croire. Non, ce n'est pas suffisant. (1 February 1956, pp. 70–71)

> (When I say that I am French, I am giving myself a label which all Frenchmen refuse me; I express myself in French, I was educated at the French school. I know as much about it as an average Frenchman. But who am I, for God's sake? Is it possible that while labels exist, I don't have my own? Which is mine? Somebody tell me what I am! Oh yes, perhaps people would prefer me to pretend to have one because they pretend to believe it. No: that's not enough.)

This is a clear statement of the types of identity crisis provoked in the educated, colonised subject, and one that North African writers turn to time and time again. Feraoun is aware of inhabiting a space 'in between' two cultures, two histories, two value systems that are now in conflict with each other. He becomes more and more critical of the French administration. He is profoundly upset by the closure of schools, although his own remains open. Feraoun is in a difficult position as a head teacher with regard to the call to resign from such posts and the strikes called by

the Front de Libération Nationale (FLN). On the other hand he is threatened by a young captain from the Sections administratives spécialisées
(SAS) if he does not go back to work. He is admonished by the regional
administrator in a very derogatory manner.[38] The tone he takes towards
the French in his writing changes markedly from then on; he is above all
disappointed by these representatives of what he had believed to be the
humanist culture of France.[39] Feraoun nonetheless continues to believe
in the *pied-noir* community from which Roblès and Camus had come,
and in the Algerians living together, but he will not accept the colonial
system and French oppression and military intervention. He records his
thoughts clearly after a meeting organised with Camus in Algiers on 22
January 1956. If the *pieds-noirs* are Algerians, they should be on the side
of those struggling for the independence of Algeria:[40]

> Je pourrais dire la même chose à Camus et à Roblès. J'ai pour l'un une grande
> admiration et pour l'autre affection fraternelle mais ils ont tort de s'adresser
> à nous qui attendons tout des cœurs généreux s'il en est. Ils ont tort de parler
> puisqu'ils ne sauraient aller au fond de leur pensée. Il vaut cent fois mieux
> qu'ils se taisent. Car enfin, ce pays s'appelle Algérie et ses habitants des
> Algériens. Pourquoi tourner autour de cette évidence? Etes-vous Algériens
> mes amis? Votre place est à côté de ceux qui luttent. Dites aux Français que
> le pays n'est pas à eux, qu'ils s'en sont emparés par la force et entendent y
> demeurer par la force. Tout le reste est mensonge, mauvaise foi. Tout autre
> langage est criminel parce que, depuis des mois, se commettent des crimes
> au nom des mêmes mensonges; depuis des mois meurent des innocents qui
> ont d'ailleurs accepté ces mensonges et ne demandaient qu'à vivre dans ces
> mensonges. Et ces innocents sont surtout des Indigènes. Des gens qui ne font
> rien pour sortir de leur condition et qu'on abat afin que d'autres se taisent.
> Ils se tairont, peut-être, les terroristes. Ce sera le silence de la mort ou du
> désespoir. De nouveau la force reprendra tous ses droits et déplorera
> hypocritement les malheurs que la justice a apportés dans le pays. La force
> pourra ricaner à son aise. Elle aura raison de ricaner: la justice a toujours
> appelé le malheur sans avoir supprimé la force. (3 February 1956, pp. 76–77)

> (I could say the same thing to Camus and Roblès. I feel great admiration for
> the one and brotherly affection for the other, but they are wrong to address
> us, who expect everything from generous hearts if such exist. They are wrong
> to speak because they are unable to get to the bottom of their thinking. It
> would be a hundred times better for them to keep quiet. After all, this
> country is called Algeria and its inhabitants are Algerians. Why fly in the
> face of the facts? Are you Algerians, my friends? Your place is at the side of
> those who fight. Tell the French that the country does not belong to them,
> that they took it over by force and intend to remain by force. All the rest is
> lies and bad faith. Any other language is criminal because, for the past
> months, crimes have been being committed in the name of those same lies;
> for the past months innocent people have been dying, – people, what's more,
> who accepted those lies and asked no more than to live in those lies. And
> those innocent people are mostly native Algerians. People who do nothing
> to change their situation and who are finally butchered to make others keep

quiet. Perhaps the terrorists will keep quiet. It will be the silence of death or of despair. Once again force will regain all its rights and will hypocritically deplore the evils that justice has brought upon the country. Force will be able to grin at ease. It will be right to grin: justice has always called up evil without suppressing force.)

The lies of colonialism become a frequent theme and the word *mensonges* appears time and time again in Feraoun's diary entries: 'Vos mensonges. Un siècle de mensonges!' (14 March 1956, p. 97) ('Your lies. A century of lies!'). He remembers one of the young teachers from France who taught him as a boy, and he is disappointed that such people remained complicit with the colonial system, at the same time describing the way in which the system worked on the hearts and minds of young Algerian schoolchildren:

> Il m'appris très tôt que la France était ma patrie adoptive et que par conséquent j'étais un petit orphelin dont on prenait soin. Cela mit dans mon cœur beaucoup d'humilité et de reconnaissance attendrie et j'aimais la France plus qu'un petit Français. Il m'a expliqué la signification symbolique des trois couleurs ainsi que la devise républicaine à laquelle il croyait avec la candeur des grands enfants, avec la naïveté de sa bonne bouille ronde, rougeaude, toujours souriante [...] Pourtant il était plein de bon sens et de finesse. Je le soupçonne d'avoir compris depuis longtemps. Mais dans son honnêteté foncière, il nous a servi scrupuleusement ce que les programmes lui assignaient de nous servir dans leur lettre et dans leur esprit. Il a compris depuis longtemps et il s'est gardé de nous avertir! Lorsque à notre tour, nous nous sommes mis à poser des questions et à rechercher des réponses la colossale duperie s'est dressée devant nous comme une infranchissable barrière. (15 March 1956, pp. 98–99)

> (He very soon taught me that France was my adoptive country and that therefore I was a little orphan that they were taking care of. That planted in my heart a great deal of humility and tender gratitude, and I loved France more than a little French boy. He explained to me the symbolic meaning of the three colours and the republican emblem which he believed with the simplicity of a grown-up child, with the naivety of his good round face, that was ruddy and always smiling [...] And yet he was full of good sense and perceptiveness. I suspect him of having understood long before. But in his deep honesty, he dished up to us scrupulously what the programmes assigned him to dish up, in the letter and in the spirit. He understood long before, and yet he never warned us! When we in our turn began to ask questions and look for answers, the colossal con-trick rose up before us as an impassable barrier.)

Despite the 'con-trick' of colonialism, Feraoun continues nonetheless to remain open towards the other, and is able to put himself in the place of an ordinary *pied-noir* '*petit colon*' in a way that resonates with Camus's *Le Premier Homme*. He can understand why they want to fight for land to which they also feel they belong, and imagining himself in their place he writes:

Je dois donc supposer que subitement que je me découvre Français d'origine, d'aïeux bourguignons puis petits colons de Beni-Mered. Je suppose aussi que le descendant de ces petits colons n'ait rien pu faire autre qu'instituteur laïque de la IIIe et de la IVe République une et indivisible. Je me nomme Durand, je suis père de famille et j'ai vingt ans de service. Ma caboche d'Algéro-Bourguignon en ce mois de février est aussi tumultueuse que le Plateau des Glières. Mon cœur tourmenté connaît tour à tour l'enthousiasme et le découragement, la haine ou la peur. Je ne sais pas comment tout ceci se terminera. Je sais que je suis menacé, tout comme les miens. Et tout comme les miens je me battrai pour me défendre...

Oui, je me battrai parce que j'ai vécu dans ce pays que je crois être le mien [...] Les tombes des mes aïeux, de mes parents sont là, à Beni-Mered [...] Le pays est à eux, prétendent-ils, nous n'avons qu'à prendre le bateau ou à mourir. Nous en sommes là, à présent. Alors la conquête n'a servi de rien? De quel droit veulent-ils nous chasser? (12 and 15 February 1956, pp. 79–80)

(So I have to imagine that suddenly I discover that I'm of French origin, and my grandparents were Burgundians and then poor colonials at Beni-Mered. I also imagine that the descendant of these poor colonials had no choice but to become a lay teacher in the one and indivisible Third Republic and Fourth Republic. My name is Durand, I'm the father of a family and have twenty years' service. This February my Algerio-Burgundian noddle is as tumultuous as the Plateau des Glières. My tormented heart is swayed in turn by enthusiasm, discouragement, hatred and fear. I don't know how all this will end. I know that I am threatened, just like all my colleagues. And just like my colleagues I'll fight to defend myself...

Yes, I'll fight because I've lived in this country which I thought was my own [...] My grandparents' and parents' graves are there at Beni-Mered [...] They claim that the country belongs to them, and we can either take ship or die. That's where we are at present. So didn't the conquest mean anything? What right do they have to throw us out?)

Feraoun continues to condemn the violence on both sides and often writes about their behaviour in the same way, for the victims are the same, ordinary Algerians, ordinary Frenchmen:

Les militaires sont impitoyables. La chose est presque admise, normale. Les *fellagha* sont impitoyables. La chose est presque admise, normale. Pour les uns et les autres l'ennemi tout désigné, l'homme suspect à menacer ou à malmener, le complice à abattre, à frapper d'amende ou à mener en prison, cet ennemi se trouve au village kabyle. Il arrive cependant que soldats et *fellagha* se rencontrent. Et bien entendu, ce sont toujours, pour les uns et les autres, des rencontres héroïques, d'où l'on sort couvert de gloire quelle que soit l'issue du combat. (6 March 1956, p. 88)

(The soldiers are pitiless. The fact is just about admitted, something normal. The *fellagha* are pitiless. The fact is just about admitted, something normal. For both the former and the latter, the clearly designated enemy, the man who is suspect and must be threatened or ill-treated, the accomplice who must be killed, fined or thrown into prison, that enemy is to be found in the Kabyle village. However, soldiers and *fellagha* do meet sometimes. And of course, for both sides, those encounters are heroic, and they emerge covered with glory, regardless of the outcome of the combat.)

He is afraid for others and he is afraid for himself, and again the question of identity comes to the fore:

> J'ai peur du Français, du Kabyle, du soldat, du *fellagh*. J'ai peur de moi. Il y en moi le Français, le Kabyle. Mais j'ai horreur de ceux qui tuent, non parce qu'ils peuvent me tuer mais parce qu'ils ont le courage de tuer. Ensuite de part et d'autre on légitime le crime, on l'explique. Il devient nécessaire, un acte de foi, une bonne action. (14 March 1956, p. 97)

> (I'm afraid of the Frenchman, the Kabyle, the soldier, and the *fellagh*. I'm afraid of myself. There is in me a Frenchman and a Kabyle. But those who kill horrify me, not because they may kill me but because they have the courage to kill. And immediately, on both sides, the crime is legitimised and explained. It becomes necessary, an act of faith, a good action.)

He writes of the incidents he hears about or is involved in, he records conversations on every side in the conflict, he writes of torture, he writes of death which has become part of everyday life, and the vicious circle engendered by reprisals:

> Maintenant que chaque jour des compatriotes, des connaissances, des amis tombent, je vois que j'avais raison de ne pas me troubler. Non la mort n'est pas impressionnante. Elle n'est ni juste, ni injuste. C'est la mort, voilà tout. Un homme meurt comme une journée passe. Et l'assassin de la veille, le brave gendarme qui a l'habitude de bavarder avec vous vient vous serrer la main pour plaisanter une fois de plus. Jusqu'au jour où vous l'accueillez avec le sourire et où vous lui videz amicalement le chargeur dans le ventre. Alors on l'enterre à son tour et on n'en parle plus. (6 April 1956, pp. 114–15)

> (Now that compatriots, acquaintances and friends are falling every day, I see that I was right not to get upset. No, death is not impressive. It is neither fair, nor unfair. It is death, and that's all. A man dies, just as a day passes. And yesterday's murderer, the splendid gendarme who always chats with you, comes and shakes your hand and jokes once again. Until the day when you greet him with a smile and pleasantly empty your gun into his belly. Then he is buried in his turn, and never mentioned again.)

He writes of newspaper reports and editorials, he writes of actual experience, he writes of hatred, stupidity, injustice, of uncertainty, anguish, terror, he writes of the way in which other events on the international stage overshadow events in Algeria, with the Suez Crisis and especially the invasion of Hungary by the Russians receiving much more scandalised attention, and he notes the bias of the West:

> Je me dis que dans tous ces textes que la presse publie, chaque fois le mot Algérie pourrait remplacer sans exagération le mot Hongrie et ne le remplace jamais. Est-ce, par hasard, que le monde qui nous voit souffrir n'est pas convaincus que nous soyons des humains? Il est vrai que nous ne sommes que musulmans. C'est peut-être là l'impardonnable crime. Voilà une question que je voudrais bien poser à Sartre ou Camus ou Mauriac. Pourquoi? Oui pourquoi? (19 November 1956, p. 167)

> (I tell myself that in all those press articles, the word 'Algeria' could be put in the place of the word 'Hungary' without any exaggeration, and never is. Is it by any chance that the world which sees us suffering is not convinced that we are human beings? It's true that we're only Muslims. Perhaps that is our unforgivable crime. That's the question I'd really like to put to Sartre or Camus or Mauriac. Why? Yes, why?)

One problem is that, given his own ambiguous position, Feraoun sees both sides, and he realises that this is a conflict in which one has to choose and be clearly on one side only. During the visit he makes with his family to Tizi-Hibel in August–September 1956, which he writes about in his letters (as previously referred to), it is made clear that he must share the opinion of the villagers:

> Et ces sentiments étaient ceux de tous sans exceptions, de mes parents, de mes amis, de mes ennemis; il y avait unanimité et il fallait que je pense, que j'agisse, que je parle comme l'unanimité, que je dise et répète ma colère, mon espoir, ma certitude qui étaient exactement les leurs. (9 September 1956, p. 146)

> (And those opinions were held by everyone without exception: my parents, my friends and my enemies; there was complete unanimity and I was obliged to think, act and speak like the consensus, I had to speak of and repeat my anger, my hope, my conviction, which had to be exactly what theirs were.)

Yet Feraoun also feels the pain of Roblès, for they share a position in an in-between space:

> Mais Roblès n'est pas seulement un ami ou un Français. Je ne lui donne aucune patrie car il est de n'importe où, c'est-à-dire exactement de chez moi. Pauvre ami, je crois que tu es encore plus à plaindre que moi et ton désarroi d'Algérien non musulman est plus pathétique que le mien. (2 November 1956, p. 161)

> (But Roblès is not just a friend or a Frenchman. I don't give him any native country because he is from anywhere, i.e. exactly where I'm from. Poor friend, I believe that your case is still more pitiable than mine and your confusion, as a non-Muslim Algerian, is still more pathetic than my own.)

However, fundamental differences between himself and his *pied-noir* friends remain. Roblès returns from Paris, where he has seen Camus, who cannot accept the independence of Algeria and the fact that he would need a passport to enter the country: 'lui qui est Algérien et rien d'autre' ('he who is Algerian and nothing else'). Feraoun's bitter irony shows his awareness of the difference in the relationship between France and the *pied-noir* and that between France and the Algerian, despite the clear compassion he feels for Roblès and Camus:

> Je comprends fort bien l'un et l'autre mais je voudrais qu'ils me comprennent aussi. Qu'ils nous comprennent, nous qui sommes si près d'eux et à la fois si différents, qu'ils se mettent à notre place. Ceux qui m'ont parlé en

langage clair la semaine dernière m'ont dit que je n'étais pas Français. Ceux qui sont chargés de veiller à la souveraineté de la France, dans ce pays, m'ont traité en ennemi, depuis le début des événements. Tout en me traitant en ennemi, ils voudraient que j'agisse en bon patriote français, même pas: ils voudraient que je les serve tel que je suis. Simplement, par reconnaissance, vu que la France a fait de moi un instituteur, un directeur de cours complémentaire, un écrivain, vu qu'elle me verse une grosse mensualité qui me permet d'élever une famille nombreuse [...] J'ai dit tout cela à Roblès qui n'a rien trouvé à répondre, qui était aussi malheureux que moi et qui admet, lui, ce que les autres refusent. J'aimerais dire à Camus qu'il est aussi Algérien que moi et tous les Algériens sont fiers de lui, mais aussi qu'il fut un temps, pas très lointain, où l'Algérien musulman, pour aller en France, avait besoin d'un passeport. C'est vrai que l'Algérien musulman, lui, ne s'est jamais considéré comme Français. Il n'avait pas d'illusions. (18 February 1957, pp. 204–205)

(I understand both of them very well but I would like them to understand me too. I'd like them to understand us who are so close to them and at the same time so different, to put themselves in our place. Those who spoke clearly to me last week told me that I'm not French. Those who are responsible for protecting France's sovereignty in this country have treated me like an enemy ever since the troubles began. And while treating me like an enemy they would still like me to act as a good French patriot, or not even that: they'd like me to serve them just as I am. Simply out of gratitude, since France made me a teacher, a course director, a writer, since France pays me a high monthly wage which enables me to bring up a large family [...] I said all this to Roblès who could find nothing to say in reply, who was as unhappy as I am and who himself admits what the others deny. I'd like to tell Camus that he is as Algerian as I am and that all Algerians are proud of him, but also that there was a time, not very long ago, when a Muslim Algerian needed a passport to go to France. It's true that the Muslim Algerian never considered himself a Frenchman. He was under no illusions.)

The tone becomes simultaneously ever more despairing and angry concerning the attitudes and behaviour on both sides. Feraoun writes despairingly of the FLN, and his forecasting of the repression they will exercise on the population shows an extremely lucid analysis of the situation:

J'ai pu lire d'un bout à l'autre le numéro spécial du *Moudjahid*. J'ai été navré d'y retrouver, pompeusement idiot, le style d'un certain hebdomadaire régional. Il y a dans ces trente pages beaucoup de foi et de désintéressement mais aussi beaucoup de démagogie, de prétention, un peu de naïveté et d'inquiétude. Si c'est là le crème du F.L.N., je ne me fais pas d'illusions, ils tireront les marrons du feu pour quelques gros bourgeois, quelques gros politiciens tapis mystérieusement dans leur courageux mutisme et qui attendent l'heure de la curée. Pauvres montagnards, pauvres étudiants, pauvres jeunes gens, vos ennemis de demain seront pires que ceux d'hier. (12 January 1957, p. 187)

(I was able to read the special issue of *Moudjahid* from end to end. I was upset to find in it the pompously idiotic style of a certain local weekly. In its thirty pages there was a lot of faith and disinterestedness, but also a lot of demagogy and pretentiousness, and a little naivety and worry. If that is the cream of the FLN, I won't have any illusions: they'll reap the benefits for some fat bourgeois, some fat politicians mysteriously hiding in their brave dumbness, as they wait for the time to claim their spoils. Poor moun-tain-dwellers, poor students, poor young people, your enemies of tomorrow will be worse than those of yesterday.)

And a few days later he is no less critical of the French who abuse their own cultural and political heritage and their position of power:

> Des gens raffinés qui prétendent donner au monde des leçons de morale, fusillent sans sourciller des dizaines d'innocents. Des gens délicats et scrupuleux assassinent froidement leurs semblables.
> Des hommes civilisés jouissant de tous les bonheurs, de toutes les facil-ités, de toutes les faveurs de la vie, massacrent et violent un peuple misérable sur lequel semble peser depuis des siècles une inexplicable malédiction.
> Des hommes qui ont tout viennent détruire des hommes qui n'ont rien.
> Est-ce que la parole est capable d'exprimer l'horreur qui nous étreint? (16 January 1957, p. 188)

> (Refined people who claim to give the world lessons in morality, shoot down dozens of innocent people without turning a hair. Delicate, scrupulous people murder people like themselves, in cold blood.
> Civilised men, enjoying all life's good things and facilities and favours, murder and rape a wretched nation on which an inexplicable curse seems to have been weighing for centuries.
> Men who have everything come and destroy men who have nothing. Is language capable of expressing the horror that takes hold of us?)

His despair also relates to the general attitude among his compatriots that the Algerian fighters are always right: 'Le patriotisme intransigeant de chacun se confond, je le crains, avec la lâcheté collective' (24 January 1957, p. 191) ('The stubborn patriotism of the individual is confused, I am afraid, with collective cowardice'). Feraoun's personal indignation is apparent when he recounts in full the confrontation with M. Achard: 'administrateur des Ouadhias, celui qui a ordonné les dizaines d'exécu-tions, les viols, les tortures dans ce malheureux *douar*' ('Administrator of Ouadhias, the man who ordered dozens of executions, rapes and torturings in that wretched *douar*'). His emotion is such he can hardly bring himself to write about the incident, yet at the same time it is evident how essential the act of writing the diary has become for him:

> Voilà six jours que j'ai abandonné ce cahier et le reprendre aujourd'hui est pour moi une séance de torture. Je sais néanmoins que je ne serai pas dérangé. Le reprendre? Par quel bout? Il y a tellement à dire que tout s'entremêle en moi et peut-être l'essentiel se refusera-t-il à sortir pour continuer de m'étouffer. (10 February 1957, p. 198)

> (It's six days since I abandoned this notebook and taking it up again today is a torture-session for me. Nevertheless I know I won't be disturbed. Take it up again? For what purpose? There is so much to say that everything is

mixed up inside me and perhaps what's essential will refuse to come out and will continue to choke me.)

Achard's disdain for Feraoun is evident, and reveals a great deal of the attitudes of those who worked within the institutions of colonialism:

> M. F., là je ne vous suis plus. Les militaires reçoivent des ordres, ils les exécutent. Ainsi, vous, un simple troufion peut vous donner un coup de pied au cul. Le fait que vous émargez aux Editions du Seuil ne change rien. Je trouve plaisants les gens qui regimbent contre notre discipline et suivent ponctuellement celle du F.L.N. Il faut savoir ce qu'on veut. C'est fini, nous n'acceptons plus la passivité. Il faut que vous résistiez aux rebelles de gré ou de force. (10 February 1957, p. 200)

> (Mr. F., there I no longer follow you. Soldiers receive orders and they carry them out. And thus any private soldier can kick you up the backside. The fact that your book has been published by Le Seuil doesn't change anything. People who grumble about our discipline and obey that of the FLN slavishly, I find amusing. You have to make up your mind. It's over: we no longer allow people to be passive. You must resist the rebels willingly or under compulsion.)

At the end of July 1957, with the move to a new school in the suburbs of Algiers, near to where Roblès lived (although he left the city in 1958), Feraoun believes that he and his family will be safer than in Kabylia, but he never feels at home there: 'à la lisière de la grande ville, dans un quartier musulman très populeux, où la misère côtoie l'opulence, et les baraques de tôle, de belles villas bourgeoises. J'ai laissé un pays triste où il n'y a que des vieillards, des femmes et des enfants' (31 July 1957, p. 239) ('on the edge of the big city, in a crowded Muslim quarter where poverty is side-by-side with opulence, and canvas shacks with rich villas. I've left a sad part of the country where there is nobody except old people, women and children'). He constantly hears, and records, news from Kabylia, a catalogue of killings and destruction: 'Tout se passe comme si le maquis tout entier était devenu une jungle avec sa faune et ses lois. Ceux qui ne peuvent pas résister fuient à toute allure avant de succomber. A Alger, au contraire, on a l'impression de vivre dans une humanité organisée. Il y deux clans: le clan des gendarmes et le clan des suspects' (21 August 1957, pp. 244–45) ('Everything goes on as though the whole *maquis* had become a jungle with its wildlife and its laws. Those who cannot resist run away as fast as they can before they succumb. In Algiers, on the contrary, you have the impression of living in organised humanity. There are two clans: the clan of the gendarmes and the clan of the suspects').

Throughout the diary he records the problems faced by Algerian schoolteachers in the French system as their prominence in the community marks them out. On 21 October 1957, he notes the end of the seventeen-month strike by schoolchildren, although the schools in which he had worked had never closed or been burnt as so many had been. Feraoun takes the end of the strike as a good sign that the country has had enough of violence, but by the end of December he is forced to wonder who will tire first, the French or the Algerians. His own decision is made:

> [Le capitaine T.] sait très bien que je peux m'accommoder de l'indépendance de l'Algérie comme je peux opter d'être français, mais que ce choix, je le ferai moi-même, sans équivoque, en dépit de tous les capitaines ou autres coupeurs de gorges. Ce choix que j'ai déjà fait mais qui ne regarde que moi.
>
> Pour moi, personnellement, pour mes enfants, ce qui compte, c'est la paix avant tout, la fin de la misère, des souffrances, des crimes. (30 January 1958, p. 264)

> (He [a French captain who went to see him in Fort-National] knows very well that I can accommodate myself to the independence of Algeria as I can opt to be French, but that this choice is one I will make myself, without equivocation, despite all the captains or other throat-cutters. This choice is one I have already made, but it concerns nobody but myself.
>
> For me personally, for my children, what counts is peace first and foremost, the end of the misery and suffering and crimes.)

By February 1958, Feraoun has been approached by the authorities to play a part in local politics since he is a prominent figure in the community: 'J'ai appris que le préfet recherche des personnalités musulmanes pour constituer la délégation municipale d'Alger. Sur sa liste le capitaine m'a porté avec le numéro un, m'a dit-il. C'est la moindre des choses, a-t-il ajouté' (9 February 1958, p. 265) ('I've learned that the *Préfet* is looking for well-known Muslims to take a place on the municipal delegation. The captain said he had put me down as number one on his list. It's the least he can do, he added'). This incident provokes a personal dilemma that leads to the examination of his conscience: 'Mieux être incorporé au mortier funèbre, comme ça au moins la conscience sera tranquille' (9 February 1958, p. 265) ('Better to be incorporated into the undertaker's, that way at least one would have a tranquil conscience').

In April Feraoun once again takes up the diary that he has neglected for a month – he feels that he has said and indeed repeated everything there is to say, and another month of war is the same as the previous ones. He does note a new phenomenon, the participation of women in the conflict, and he wonders if this will be the beginning of changes for them, but doubts whether it will lead to their liberation – another perspicacious analysis of how the situation would develop after the war. By February 1959, he is recording the treatment meted out to women forced to help the *maquis* when there are no more men: the French prisons and camps start filling up with women, the *fellaghas* cut the throats of any women who betray them, the soldiers shoot, arrest and torture them. Both sides use them for sexual purposes and illegitimate children are born to young girls, widows and married women. For the rest, the multitude of individual dramas continues. On 10 April he sees Camus with Roblès, and again he notes Camus's own compassion and his difficulties in the situation: 'Sa position sur les événements est celle que je supposais: rien de plus humain' (11 April 1958, p. 271) ('His position on the troubles is what I'd imagined: nothing could be more humane').

The ambiguity of his own position is clear. He is praised by the French and is in danger of reprisals by the FLN; the opposite would also be true:

> J'apprends que le capitaine S.A.S. de Béni-Douala a fait à Tizi-Hibel mon panégyrique. Il aurait dit que la France est fière de moi et que mon village serait épargné en dépit de l'attitude hostile des gens.
> Cela m'a valu de mécontenter profondément Kaci, le fameux commissaire politique de l'endroit qui est allé manifester ce mécontentement à mes vieux parents. Mes sœurs, mes vieux parents vivent, paraît-il, dans les affres et s'attendent à ce que le F.L.N. me condamne et m'exécute. Voilà où nous en sommes. (2 November 1958, p. 283)

> (I hear that the SAS captain at Béni-Douala pronounced a panegyric on me at Tizi-Hibel. Apparently he said that France is proud of me and that my village will be spared despite the hostile attitude of the people there.
> That has earned me the profound displeasure of Kaci, the famous local political administrator, who went to see my aged parents to express that displeasure. My sisters and my parents are, it seems, living in fear and are expecting the FLN to condemn me to death and execute me. That is the point we've got to.)

On 9 December he records that his father died on the eve of 1 November, but no-one could telephone him because there was a general strike to commemorate the '"Révolution algérienne"' ('Algerian Revolution'; Feraoun's own inverted commas). The only person who did think to contact him was the same SAS captain, who sent a telegram with his condolences and offered to help if needed. No mere anecdote, but a moving and telling example of the paradoxes of the situation. Feraoun makes the depressing journey home. In December he goes to Paris, 'chargé de mission', where he is offered a post in the Quai d'Orsay, which he refuses, and he records with brevity the company he meets there:

> Envoyé à la présidence du Conseil où j'ai bavardé avec une fille sympathique qui m'a mis à l'aise. C'était G. de Gaulle. Geneviève de Gaulle me fait inviter par Germaine Tillion. Vu quelques minutes Malraux. Bombardé membre du Haut Comité de la Jeunesse où j'ai serré la main à de Gaulle. Rencontré Kadd. Signé avec lui pétition demandant grâce des cent cinquante condamnés à mort. Vu, rue de Lille, Alquier, lieutenant S.A.S. qui a écrit un bouquin dont j'ai parlé dans mes cahiers. Soustelle, m'a-t-il dit, aimerait me

voir. Moi pas. Vu toute l'équipe du Seuil, Roblès, Nouelle. Tous ceux que j'ai rencontrés savaient que je n'étais ni français, ni intégrable. Pour eux il suffisait que je sois moi-même et ils souhaitaient que beaucoup d'Algériens musulmans me ressemblent. (22 December 1958, p. 287)

(Sent to the office of the President of the Council, where I chatted to a very pleasant girl who put me at my ease. It was G. de Gaulle. Genevieve de Gaulle got Germaine Tillion to invite me. Saw Malraux a few minutes. Bombarded a member of the High Committee for Youth where I shook de Gaulle's hand. Met Kadd. Signed petition with him requesting pardon for the hundred and fifty condemned to death. In the Rue de Lille saw Alquier, SAS lieutenant who wrote a book I have spoken of in my notebooks. He told me Soustelle would like to see me. I wouldn't. Saw the whole Seuil team, Roblès, Nouelle. Everyone I met knew that I was neither French nor integratable. For them it was enough that I should be myself, and they wished that many Muslim Algerians were like me.)

By July 1959 Feraoun is thinking of ending this recording of events. It will be for future historians to consider the lessons of the drama he is living, and he subsumes his own situation into that of the collectivity:

Pour ce qui me concerne, je pense pouvoir à présent abandonner ce récit. Un récit sans prologue et qui n'aura pas d'épilogue. Le prologue il fallait le chercher dans un siècle de colonialisme et pour nous de servitude, l'épilogue il faudrait le prévoir dans l'avenir incertain qui me concerne très peu et que mes enfants accepteront quel qu'il soit, tel qu'il sera. Moi, je veux dire ma génération, mes enfants, je veux dire les jeunes générations. (12 July 1959, p. 296)

(For what concerns me, I think I can leave this account aside at present. An account with no prologue and one which will have no epilogue. The prologue must be sought in a century of colonialism and, for us, of servitude; the epilogue will have to be foreseen in the uncertain future which concerns me very little, and which my children will accept just as it is, just as it will be. 'Me' meaning my generation, and 'my children' meaning the young generations.)

Feraoun is optimistic that the young generation, sufficiently educated, will be proud to create a new future for Algeria that will do justice to those who have died for it. And he never gives up hope that relations between Algeria and France will be restored and recognised: 'Mais quand l'Algérie vivra et lèvera la tête, je souhaite qu'elle se souvienne de la France et de tout ce qu'elle lui doit (12 July 1959, p. 298) ('But when Algeria lives and lifts up its head, I hope it will remember France and all it owes France').

In January 1960 he received threatening letters, two in two weeks, one of which portrayed a hanged man, and one of which is published in *Lettres à ses amis*:

Ami Feraoun,
As-tu écrit ton 'apologie de la Rébellion'? Tu devrais te presser, car ton

ami X. et toi-même êtes bien près du grand saut!
     Prépare ton drap, Feraoun
     R.A. (p. 162; RA is the group Résistance-Algérie)

(Friend Feraoun,
     Have you written your 'apologia for the Rebellion'? You will have to
hurry, because your friend X. and yourself are very close to the big jump!
     Prepare your shroud, Feraoun
     RA)

He therefore returns to keeping the diary that he has neglected since the
end of the previous August even though he wonders what value it can
have. Camus has been killed in a car accident; a sense of foreboding
invades the text:

> Il a donc fallu que je reprenne aujourd'hui ce cahier abandonné depuis des
> mois. Non pas qu'il n'y ait rien eu à y noter me concernant ou concernant
> tout le monde, mais l'hiatus sera toujours facile à combler lorsque le détail
> n'a rien de particulier. J'eusse aimé parler longuement de nos souffrances,
> de mes soucis, du malheur qui frappe journellement mes amis, l'un ou l'autre.
> Parler par exemple de Camus mort accidentellement au début du mois;
> des Roblès que j'ai revus en décembre à Paris, de Ak. hospitalisé pour
> déficience nerveuse... Tout cela est triste, vraiment trop triste et je me
> suis dit: à quoi bon? J'en tiendrai, je pense, à la relation objective des
> faits. Tels que je les vois se dérouler sous mes yeux. Cela me permettra plus
> tard de recréer l'atmosphère. Si la vie est longue bien sûr. (25 January 1960,
> p. 300)

> (So today I've had to resume this exercise-book which I left aside some
> months ago. Not that there's been nothing to note concerning myself or
> concerning everyone, but the gap will always be easy to fill in, while there's
> nothing special about the details. I would have liked to speak at length about
> our sufferings and my cares, the misfortune which strikes one or other of
> my friends every day. To speak, for example, of Camus, killed in an acci-
> dent at the beginning of the month; of the Roblès family whom I saw in Paris
> in December; of Ak. who's in hospital with a nervous breakdown... All that
> is sad, quite honestly too sad, and I wondered: what's the good of it? I shall
> restrict it, I think, to an objective narration of the facts. Just as I see them
> unfolding before my eyes. That will enable me to recreate the atmosphere
> later. If my life lasts, of course.)

Feraoun does not find the energy to record anything from the beginning of February until the end of November, when he returns to a page
dated 21 April for which he had written nothing:

> Ce journal abandonné depuis janvier dernier après l'échec des ultra aurait
> pu être tenu plus régulièrement et renfermer des tas de choses intéressantes,
> me concernant, concernant mes compatriotes, la guerre d'Algérie, la France,
> le monde. Je l'ai abandonné par lassitude, beaucoup. Et aussi parce qu'il me
> paraissait puéril de raconter pour mon compte, à ma façon, ce que la presse
> de tous les bords, de tous les pays et touts les radios apportent et jettent en
> pâture quotidiennement. A quoi bon, n'ai-je cessé de me répéter et j'ai aban-
> donné pour cela, un peu.

Ce 21 avril, qu'ai-je voulu écrire? Je n'en sais plus rien. (27 November 1960, pp. 303–304)

(This diary, abandoned since last January after the failure of the extremists, could have been kept more regularly and could have included lots of interesting things concerning me, concerning my compatriots, the Algerian War, France, the whole world. I abandoned it out of weariness, mainly. And also because I thought it seemed childish to tell on my own account, in my own way, what the press on all sides, in every country and on every radio is reporting and feeding people on daily. What's the good of it, I kept telling myself, and I abandoned it for that reason too, partly.

That 21 April, what did I want to write? I have no idea.)

From October 1960 Feraoun is even more vulnerable in his new role as 'Inspecteur des Centres sociaux éducatifs'; his name has appeared on lists of supporters of the FLN[41] and he receives very direct threats, and becomes progressively more despondent for the future of Algeria. During 1960 the situation became more and more tense, and after the referendum on 8 January 1961 approving de Gaulle's Algerian policy (in which he disowned the defenders of *Algérie Française*), the supporters of 'French Algeria' created the Organisation armée secrète (OAS), which was to exacerbate the situation. Feraoun notes the problems brought about by the result of the referendum (which would lead to France's acceptance of Algerian independence in the Evian Agreements the following year):

Le référendum s'est terminé comme d'habitude par la victoire du général de Gaulle. En France naturellement. Une fois de plus, il est chargé de foutre la paix en Algérie. Les musulmans voudraient plutôt qu'il leur foute la paix. Ils se sont abstenus quand ils ont pu ou bien ils ont voté 'oui'. Les roumis ont voté non. Mais les oui l'ont tout de même emporté en Algérie, comme en France. L'atmosphère reste chargé de menaces et on s'attend à tout de la part des activistes. (16 January 1961, p. 317)

(The referendum ended as usual in a victory for General de Gaulle. In France, naturally. Once again, he has been given the task of messing up peace in Algeria. The Muslims would rather he left them alone [play on words here in original]. They abstained when they could, or else voted 'yes'. The Europeans voted 'no'. But the 'yes' votes won anyway in Algeria, as in France. The atmosphere is still full of threats and people are expecting anything at all from the activists.)

While Feraoun worries about the status and the objective value of his testimony ('Certes, il conviendrait de tout revoir, plus tard, de vérifier, de découvrir d'autres aspects d'un même événement pour le cerner de plus près' [20 August 1961, p. 327] ['It's true that it would be necessary to go through the whole lot again later, to verify it and discover different aspects of the same event to be able to see it more clearly']) the activities of the OAS multiply:

Maintenant l'O.A.S. ne prévient plus personne paraît-il, elle abat en voiture, à moto, à la grenade, à la rafale, à l'arme blanche. Elle attaque les caisses des banques, des postes, des sociétés, mise en scène de 'Série noire' avec la complicité des uns, et la lâcheté des autres.

Dernière flambée des terrorismes aveugles des tueurs qui craignent de ne plus pouvoir tuer impunément.

La guerre d'Algérie se termine. Paix à ceux qui sont morts. Paix à ceux qui vont survivre. Cesse la terreur. Vive la liberté! (5 February 1962, pp. 345–46)

(Now the OAS don't give any more warnings, it seems, they kill from cars, from motorbikes, with grenades, with machine-guns, with knives. They attack banks, post-offices, building-societies; they play out scenes from crime thrillers helped by the complicity of some and the cowardice of others.

It's the final blaze of the blind terrorism of killers who are afraid they won't be able to kill with impunity for much longer.

The Algerian War is ending. Peace to those who are dead. Peace to those who will survive. Let terror cease. Long live freedom!)

In March, the OAS assassinated Feraoun and his colleagues, and the final diary entry found in some papers after his death (the manuscript had already been given to his editor the preceding month) seems to contain a premonition:

Bien sûr, je ne veux pas mourir et je ne veux absolument pas que mes enfants meurent mais je ne prends aucune précaution particulière en dehors de celles qui, depuis une quinzaine sont devenues des habitudes: limitation des sorties, courses pour acheter 'en gros', suppression des visites aux amis. Mais chaque fois que l'un d'entre nous sort, il décrit au retour un attentat ou signale une victime. (14 March 1962, p. 347)

To be sure, I don't want to die, and I absolutely don't want my children to die, but I don't take any particular precautions other than those which have become habitual over the past two weeks: limiting the number of times one goes out; buying in bulk; stopping visits from friends. But each time one of us does go out, they come back with news of an attack or the name of a victim.)

But the last word on death should be Feraoun's own, revealing as it does a personal philosophy. In September 1949 he had been marked by the proximity to death he experienced when, shortly after he had got off a bus with his wife, daughter and brother, the bus had plunged down the hillside, killing other passengers.[42] A conversation with a Christian priest had followed concerning the lesson that might be learned from such an incident, with the priest concluding that one must be always ready to meet God. Feraoun's reasoning is different, seeing the priest's opinion as hypocritical:

C'est logique mais mon avis est différent. C'est une suprême hypocrisie que de chercher à se tenir prêt. Pourquoi ne pas vivre simplement, naturellement. Se tenir prêt, n'est-ce pas se composer une attitude? Qui tromperait-on avec

des grimaces? N'est-il pas plus logique de mourir en pleines actions, bonnes
ou mauvaises? (Letter to Pierre Martin, 18 September 1949)

(It is logical, but my opinion is different. It is supremely hypocritical to try
and hold oneself in readiness. Why not live simply and naturally. Doesn't
holding oneself in readiness mean striking an attitude? Whom would one
deceive with one's grimaces? Isn't it more logical to die in the midst of one's
actions, whether good or bad?)

Feraoun's own life is brought to a sudden end, in the midst of action. His
diary, published in September 1962, six months after his assassination
and the end of the war, was much reported in the press.[43] It is an irreplaceable record of the Algerian War in all its facets, and a testimony to
those who suffered and those who died. It is a guard against the forgetting, and indeed the rewriting, of history. It is part of a life-story project
and an expression of selfhood. It is an analysis of the place of the individual within the diverse communities within which he functions: Kabyle
peasant, French-educated student and then schoolteacher, father,
villager, civil servant, intellectual. Feraoun regretted the lost communal
history of France and Algeria and the way in which history is contorted
through the desire for vengeance:

> On se dit aussi que le moment est venu de venger nos aïeux. Ceux qui, il y
> a un siècle, ont été écrasés impitoyablement par un conquérant bien armé
> et avide de colonies. Alors ces jeunes français imberbes n'apparaissent
> plus que comme des continuateurs des premiers zouaves, tandis que les
> jeunes Kabyles qui leur font face ne veulent rien d'autre que venger
> les premiers moudjahidin. Un siècle de vie commune est délibérément
> oublié. Sur ce siècle d'histoire franco-algérienne on jette un pont métallique
> et glacé, pareil au Sirat qui mène au séjour des élus, qui est frêle comme
> une corde, aiguisé comme un glaive et se teinte peu à peu du sang noirâtre
> des pécheurs. Sur ce siècle on dresse une lame flamboyante qui se teint du
> sang des hommes: celui des combattants et des victimes et qui finira par
> ressembler à un trait rouge et justicier barrant une page inutile. (12 June
> 1956, p. 128)

> (People also tell themselves that the time has come to avenge our ancestors.
> Those who a century ago were mercilessly crushed by a well-armed
> conqueror greedy for colonies. So these beardless young Frenchmen no
> longer appear to be anything except the continuers of the first zouaves, while
> the young Kabyles who stand against them want nothing else than to avenge
> the first *moudjahidin*. A century of shared life is deliberately forgotten. On
> that century of Franco-Algerian history an icy, metallic bridge is thrown,
> like the Sirat which leads to the dwelling of the elect, which is as flimsy as
> a piece of string, sharp as a sword, and is stained little by little with the black
> blood of sinners. On that century, they are drawing a flaming blade which
> is stained with the blood of men – that of the fighters and of the victims –
> and which will end up looking like a red line enforcing justice, which is
> drawn across a useless page.)

Feraoun here makes a powerful plea, urging us to struggle against the types of 'forgetting' that those who come to power use to forge their own versions of history, and to continue the difficult work of remembering both collectively and individually. This prefigures the debates that would take place in France from the 1970s onwards as the nation struggled to come to terms with the history of the Second World War and the consequences of decolonisation.[44]

Feraoun's suspicions of both the French and the FLN were well-founded. After the murderous war, with French military losses estimated at 27,000 and Algerian casualties anywhere between 300,000 and 500,000, the promised 'revolution' did not materialise. Post-independence Algeria became a one-party state in 1962 under the FLN's Ben Bella (ousted by a military coup in 1965), Boumedienne and then Chadli Ben Djedid (in 1979), only giving way to multi-party local and national elections in 1990–91. After riots in 1988, Ben Djedid had promised political and economic liberation, including a new multi-party constitution. The FIS (Front Islamique du Salut; Islamic Salvation Front), the original Islamist party in Algeria, legalised in 1989, won the 1990 municipal and communal elections, precursors of the December 1991 general elections. In the first round of these national elections, the FIS won a majority with 47.3 per cent of the vote and 188 seats. The FLN's results were disastrous (23.4 per cent and 16 seats), and the second round of elections (following the French two-rounds voting system) due on 16 January 1992 was cancelled by the Algerian army. A horrific cycle of violence was unleashed. On 11 January, a further military coup took place, and Boudiaf, one of the founding members of the FLN (in March 1954) took power, only to be assassinated in June that year. A decade of civil war ensued, with an estimated 100,000 Algerians massacred, including prominent writers, singers, sports personalities, academics and school-teachers as well as ordinary citizens.[45]

It is here that Assia Djebar, whose writings will be treated in the final chapter, joins her fellow Algerian and Kabyle, Mouloud Feraoun. Feraoun's warnings resonate down the decades, and in *Le Blanc d'Algérie* (*Algerian White*, from which I quoted at the beginning of this chapter the imagined scene of Feraoun's assassination by French right-wing extremists), Assia Djebar picks up the narrative of the violent history of Algeria in the twentieth century where Feraoun left off. She enumerates the long list of the dead, among whom is another Kabyle writer and intellectual, Tahar Djaout, assassinated in Algiers in 1993, at the age of 39, thirty-one years after Feraoun. Because he was uncompromisingly critical of the betrayal of the Algerian revolution, a *fatwa* was issued against the writer by Benhadj, deputy leader of the FIS. The cycle comes full circle with violence instigated in Feraoun's case by French extremists and by Algerian Islamic extremists in the case of Djaout:

> Qui, quels meurtriers sont allés au bout de leur course, de leur mission commandée par l'émir là-haut qui va les féliciter, quels hommes d'armes ont couru, ont marché jusqu'au seuil de la maison de Tahar, pour le héler – lui, leur souriant –, pour lui tirer dans la tête, puis sortir le corps affaissé, l'abandonner au sol, et fuir dans la voiture de la victime?[46]

> (Who, what murderers completed their course, their mission ordered by the emir in the mountains who waits to congratulate them, what armed men ran, walked, to Tahar's house to hail him – he, smiling at them – to shoot him in the head, then leave his collapsed body on the ground, and flee in the victim's car?)

As Assia Djebar writes at the very beginning of *Le Blanc d'Algérie*, she has realised that the writer is a sacrificial victim in an Algeria still struggling with the exercising of power and with its own identity:

> Une nation cherchant son cérémonial, sous diverses formes, mais de cimetière en cimetière, parce que en premier, l'écrivain a été obscurément offert en victime propitiatoire: étrange et désespérante découverte![47]

> (A nation seeking its own ceremonial, in different forms, but from cemetery to cemetery, because, first of all, the writer has been offered as propitiatory victim: strange and despairing discovery!)

The risks, both physical and mental, that the writer runs will be a recurrent preoccupation of all the writers under discussion here.

CHAPTER 3

Albert Memmi: Fictions of Identity
and the Quest for Truth

Chacun de mes livres aura été une étape d'un même itinéraire. J'aurai passé la majeure partie de ma vie à écrire. L'écriture m'a souvent servi de béquille; chacun a la sienne, de sorte que ma vie et mon travail se répondent; de sorte que parlant de l'une je parle de l'autre, et inversement. Toute œuvre est plus ou moins autobiographique; mettons que la mienne l'est plus ouvertement que d'autres. L'autobiographie est, comme toute entreprise humaine, une tentative de dire quelque chose a quelqu'un. J'ai sans doute plus fortement besoin de m'expliquer, de plaider peut-être.

Albert Memmi, Le Nomade immobile[1]

(Each of my books will have been a stage on the same journey. I will have spent the greater part of my life writing. Writing has often served me as a crutch; everyone has their own, so that my life and my work correspond to each other, and in speaking of one I am speaking of the other, and vice versa. All literary work is more or less autobiographical; let's say that mine is more openly than some. Autobiography is, like every human undertaking, an attempt to say something to someone. Unquestionably, I have a stronger need to explain myself, to plead, perhaps.)

L'écrivain dit la vérité avec des mensonges successifs. La formule me paraît heureuse. A force d'ajouter fiction sur fiction, l'écrivain finit par dire presque la vérité.

Albert Memmi, Albert Memmi: Ecrivain et sociologue[2]

(The writer tells the truth through a succession of lies. I think that definition is a happy one. By adding fiction to fiction the writer ends up by telling something like the truth.)

The work of Albert Memmi, a Tunisian writer of Jewish origin, is wide-ranging both in breadth and in time, covering almost half a century of literary production and sociological study. In addition to his creative work – *La Statue de sel*, 1953 (*The Pillar of Salt*); *Agar*, 1955 (*Strangers*); *Le Scorpion*, 1969 (*The Scorpion*); *Le Désert*, 1977 (*The Desert*); *Le Pharaon*, 1988 (*The Pharaoh*) – he has made, in a series of important essays on various forms of oppression, original contributions to political and sociological thinking with concepts such as *le duo* and *la dépendance*, for example in *Portrait du colonisé, précédé de Portrait du colonisateur*, 1957 (*The Colonizer and the Colonized*); *Portrait d'un Juif*, 1962 (*Portrait of a Jew*); *L'Homme dominé*, 1968 ('The Subjugated Man');

131

Juifs et Arabes, 1974 (*Jews and Arabs*); *La Dépendance*, 1979 (*Dependence*); *Le Racisme*, 1982 (*Racism*); and *Le Buveur et l'amoureux*, 1998 ('The Drinker and the Lover'). Memmi began his project by making clear the universal dimension of his own experience and that of the Jews of Tunisia, showing how a particular oppression may reveal the dynamics underlying all systems of subjugation. Of his political and sociological studies *Portrait du colonisé, précédé de Portrait du colonisateur* remains a seminal text for postcolonial studies, and his work on Jewish identity and on racism, for example, places him among the most important ideological and political thinkers in these domains. It is in this first key theoretical text that Memmi presents his concept of the 'duo' (here coloniser and colonised, but later applied to the duos white/black; man/woman; Jew/non-Jew, etc.), whose two members he shows to be inextricably linked as he uncovers the working of the power relationship between them, and indeed he has been referred to as 'le philosophe des duos'[3] ('the philosopher of duos'). His work on dependence is a development of his analysis of the functioning of dominance at work in such relationships, although there are immense differences between the principles ruling dominance and dependence. The latter rests on need and therefore pleasure according to Memmi, and while dominance is unstable, dependence is a force of stability.[4]

The fundamental duo in society is that of the couple, and Memmi has also devoted studies to the relations between men and women, which entail, in his analysis, both dominance and dependence. His work as a whole could be summed up as a 'philosophy of human relationships', studying all forms of domination and oppression.[5] Memmi himself has explained the ways in which his thinking develops from the individual case to a more universal dimension, and how the two are interlinked as he uncovers the mechanisms at work in the power balance of human relationships on both micro- and macro-levels, moving from the relationship in a French–Tunisian marriage, to the relationship between coloniser and colonised, to the relationship between the Jew and the rest of the world:

> Dans *Le Portrait du colonisé*, j'ai cru découvrir, outre ce que je cherchais à propos du mariage mixte et de moi-même, le drame de la colonisation, et son retentissement sur les deux partenaires de la colonie: le colonisateur et le colonisé. Comment leurs vies entières, leurs figures, leurs conduites se trouvent commandées par cette relation fondamentale qui les unit l'un à l'autre, dans un duo inexorable.
>
> Du même coup, je venais d'entrevoir un phénomène infiniment plus vaste, plus terrifiant: la relation de dominance, qui ordonne les rapports de tant d'êtres humains. Je m'avisais que les mêmes mécanismes, qui m'avaient éclairé sur ma vie d'homme colonisé, pouvaient m'aider à comprendre ce

qu'est un Juif. Car j'étais également Juif, et même après la fin de la guerre, de la colonisation, et de tous les bouleversements sociaux, je demeurai séparé, minoritaire, mis en accusation et fréquemment agressé. Il me fallait donc faire l'inventaire de ma vie sous cet autre aspect que fut le *Portrait d'un Juif*.[6]

(In *The Colonizer and the Colonized* I believed that I discovered, in addition to what I was seeking about mixed marriages and myself, the drama of colonisation, and its repercussions on the two partners in the colony: the coloniser and the colonised. How their whole lives, their demeanour, their behaviours are all governed by that fundamental relationship which unites them to one another in an inexorable duo.

At the same time I had just glimpsed an infinitely more vast and more terrifying phenomenon: the relationship of dominance which governs mutual dealings between so many human beings. I realised that the same mechanisms which had enlightened me as to my life as a colonised man could help me to understand what a Jew is. Because I was also a Jew, and even after the end of the war and colonisation, and all the social upheaval, I remained cut off, in a minority, an object of accusation and often attacked. Therefore I had to take stock of my life under that other aspect which was the *Portrait of a Jew*.)

The two texts on which I shall focus here, *La Statue de sel* and *Le Scorpion*, are separated in time by some of this work on the oppression of colonialism and on the status of the Jews, and the extent to which Memmi's fictional and theoretical work inform each other will become clear.[7]

The attention to identity revealed by the frequent use of the term 'portrait' in these sociological studies indicates just how much of a piece Memmi's work is, a point on which he himself has insisted throughout his writing career:

Il s'agit en somme d'une longue entreprise, d'un seul livre constitué par un emboîtement de livres l'un dans l'autre. J'aime cette façon de mettre une œuvre dans une autre et une troisième dans une seconde. Ce n'est pas là un artifice, je crois au contraire que c'est l'expression même de la réalité qui va se creusant, se découvrant de plus en plus profonde.[8]

(It's a long enterprise, it's one single book made up of a linked series of books, one inside the other. I like that way of putting one work inside another and a third inside the second. It isn't an artifice but just the reverse: I think it's the very expression of reality entering more and more deeply into itself, progressively revealing its own depth.)

Memmi has insisted throughout his career that the theoretical aspects of his work are always based on lived experience, as are the fictional texts:

Lorsque, plus tard, je rédigeai mes romans tunisiens, je n'eus qu'à puiser dans mon journal de l'époque. Les portraits du colonisé et du colonisateur, que j'ai tenté de tracer par la suite, reproduisaient des modèles vivants que je côtoyais tous les jours.[9]

(When, later, I wrote my Tunisian novels, I only had to draw on my diary of the time. The portraits of the colonised and of the coloniser which I then tried to paint represented living models whom I came up against every day.)

His *Portrait d'un Juif*, which was published in 1962, has for its subtitle *L'Impasse*, indicating the impossibility of the Jewish position, but the reader of Memmi's other work will recognise a return to the fundamental place of childhood onto which is grafted a conceptual and symbolic meaning that will be worked and reworked in his writing and thinking. Among other recurrent themes, or rather constantly reworked problematics, in Memmi's work are the question of the liberation of the collective and the individual in the face of all forms of oppression, the ensuing search for identity and, bound up inextricably with this, the quest for a 'truth' about human existence and for a set of values, a way of being in the world:

> Dirais-je que toute mon œuvre jusqu'ici aura été un même effort d'inventaire, tantôt grâce à la fiction, tantôt grâce au portrait, à l'essai, ou même à la recherche la plus technique qui me permet la vérification précise, la formulation mathématique de tel ou tel point de cet itinéraire: voilà le sens et la place de tel travail sociologique sur le racisme, d'une étude psychanalytique, ou d'une investigation sur la connaissance d'autrui.[10]

> (I might say that all my output up to the present has been part of the same effort to take stock, sometimes through fiction, sometimes through a portrait or an essay, or even through the most technical kind of research which enables me to make a precise verification, a mathematical formulation of this or that point on the itinerary. That's the meaning and the place of a given social study of racism, or psycho-analytical study, or research into the knowledge of others.)

There are, therefore, multiple interconnections between Memmi's fiction, poetry and psycho-sociological work, beginning with the themes of *La Statue de sel* and radiating out to other fictional works around questions of personal identity, while at the same time he develops aesthetic concerns, and then moves further out to sociological thinking around the questions of colonisation and oppression and Jewishness, and finally towards more abstract and universalist thinking.[11] Memmi showed an awareness of these structures and the forces of interconnectedness at work in his thinking as far back as 1967, and this continues to be apparent.

NEGOTIATING A JEWISH IDENTITY:
THE STATIONARY NOMAD

Je ne me sens pas bien que là où je me trouve, dans des villes que je peux maîtriser de mes pas, avec des maisons qui se chevauchent, des villes qui auraient pu, en somme, s'appeler Carthage. Je suis une espèce de nomade immobile.

Albert Memmi, *Le Nomade immobile*[12]

(I only feel at ease here where I am now, in towns I can encompass on foot, with houses piled on top of each other, towns that could, to sum up, have been called Carthage. I'm a sort of stationary nomad.)

J'ai retrouvé dans mes papiers du lycée, indéfiniment répétée sur les marges de mes cahiers, l'esquisse d'un blason, que j'aurais volontiers arboré si les temps s'y prêtaient. Un bouclier en quatre parties: la première, en haut et à gauche, figurant l'étoile de David; la seconde, en haut et à droite, un islamique croissant de lune; en bas et à gauche, un drapeau tricolore; en bas et à droite, un globe. On voit que presque tout y était, même hésitation entre mes singularités et l'universel. Ce n'était pas encore l'époque de choix politiques, j'exprimais ce que je vivais.

Albert Memmi, *Le Nomade immobile*[13]

(I found among my school papers, repeated indefinitely in the margins of my exercise-books, the sketch of a heraldic device which I would willingly have worn if the times had been right. A shield in four parts: the top left-hand quarter showing the Star of David; the top right-hand, the Islamic crescent; bottom left, a tricolour flag; and bottom right, a globe. You can see that it was almost all there, the same hesitation between what was particular to me, and what was universal. I hadn't yet reached the stage of political choices, I was expressing what I lived.)

Albert Memmi was born in Tunis in 1920, and he spent his early childhood on the edge of the Jewish ghetto, the *hara*, a place that remains a fundamental point in the topology of his work, with more particularly the Impasse Tronja (which becomes the Impasse Tarfoune in *La Statue de sel*) serving as a kind of matrix generating subsequent narratives. Like the hero of *La Statue de sel*, he went first to the *école rabbinique* and then to the *Alliance israélite* before gaining a scholarship to the French *lycée* in Tunis. In *La Statue de sel* he acknowledges the influence of two of the teachers in the *lycée*, 'Poinsot' (in reality Aimé Patri, Memmi's philosophy teacher) and 'Marrou' (the writer Jean Amrouche, his literature teacher):

J'ai eu la bonne fortune de connaître deux hommes qui m'ont aidé à surmonter l'humiliation, et même à l'utiliser [...] On ne s'identifie pas à n'importe qui; si je suis devenu à mon tour professeur de philosophie, abandonnant la médecine à laquelle on m'avait destiné, ce fut pour ressembler à Patri; si j'ai cru trouver mon salut dans l'écriture, c'est parce que

> Amrouche avait tenté d'y trouver le sien. C'est aussi pourquoi parce que le philosophe et l'écrivain, aussi méfiants soient-ils l'un envers l'autre, cohabitent toujours en moi.[14]

> (I had the good luck to meet two men who helped me to overcome humiliation and even to make use of it [...] One doesn't identify oneself with just anyone; if I in my turn became a philosophy teacher, abandoning medicine which had been intended for me, it was in order to be like Patri; if I thought to find my salvation in literature, it is because Amrouche had tried to find his there. It is also why the philosopher and the writer, however mistrustful they may be towards one another, always dwell together within me.)

After school, Memmi went on to study philosophy at the University of Algiers; and again like the protagonist of his first novel, Alexandre Mordekhaï Benillouche, he spent time in the forced labour camps in Tunisia during the Second World War (1943). In *Le Nomade immobile*, he explains the complexity of his situation as an educated Jew in North Africa during the war and the 'historical solitude' of the Jews there in that period, while explaining how his experience in the camp also led to his decision not to go to Israel as a young man:

> J'y avais pris conscience d'un malentendu, que je me jurai de ne plus tolérer en moi. J'avais rejoint les camps a peu près volontairement. Je sais que ce consentement risque de ne pas être compris par mes lecteurs européens. Ils n'ont pas idée de la solitude historique qui était la nôtre, au milieu de français pratiquement tous vichystes, à l'exception de quelques hommes courageux qui rejoindront les Alliés, de Siciliens qui, même pour les plus démunis, étaient tous fascistes et fanfarons, du moins que la victoire de Mussolini semblait acquise, de musulmans qui, à l'exception de quelques esprits avisés, dont Bourguiba, sympathisaient avec les Allemands – parce que les ennemis de nos ennemis sont nos amis.[15]

> (There I had become aware of a misunderstanding which I swore that I would no longer tolerate in myself. I had joined the camps more or less voluntarily. I know there is a risk that my assent will not be understood by my European readers. They have no idea of the historical solitude which was ours, in the midst of Frenchmen who were practically all Vichy supporters except certain courageous men who joined the Allies; Sicilians who, even the poorest, were all Fascists and proud of it, at least as long as Mussolini seemed to be winning; and Muslims who, except for a few shrewd thinkers like Bourguiba, sympathised with the Germans because our enemies' enemies are our friends.)

But the decision made by Benillouche the end of the novel to go to Argentina is a narrative device, while in reality Memmi went to France at the end of the war to continue his studies at the Sorbonne, becoming *agrégé* (qualified as a teacher at university level) in philosophy, and marrying, as in his second novel *Agar*, a Frenchwoman, a blonde, blue-eyed Catholic from Lorraine. Meeting his future wife came at an important moment for Memmi, at a time when he felt in despair in his isolation in Paris, and it is the point at which he turned to writing for support and refuge:

> A Tunis je me battais, et les résistances que je rencontrais nourrissaient la mienne; à Paris c'était le vide, où je me sentais dissoudre. Je fis l'expérience de l'angoisse, que je n'avais jamais connue [...]
>
> Ce fut également la découverte de l'écriture comme recours majeur [...] Dorénavant, dans toutes circonstances difficiles de ma vie, et bientôt quoti-diennement, j'écrirais. Je quittais alors la trop dure réalité, pour un monde façonné selon mes désirs. Les notes prises durant cette période me servirent à rédiger mon premier livre.[16]

> (In Tunis I fought, and the resistance I encountered strengthened my own resistance. In Paris there was a vacuum, in which I felt myself dissolving. I experienced an anguish I had never known before [...]
>
> It was also the discovery of writing as my principal resource. From then on, in all the difficult circumstances of my life (and soon every day) I used to write. Then I would leave harsh reality behind for a world fashioned according to my desires. The notes I took during this period were to be used to make up my first book.)

The potential for a world redesigned according to his own desire and the possibility of a 'salvation' through writing is a theme to which Memmi will return again and again, and as we will see, often in much more powerful terms.

In *Le Nomade immobile*, Memmi is very clear about his disappoint-ment with the philosophy professors at the Sorbonne, and the impact on his initial enthusiasm for philosophy that had begun with his admiration for his teacher, Patri, at the French *lycée* in Tunis. He is also candid about the challenge of his marriage to a woman of such a radically different cultural background (although the tragic failure of such a marriage as presented in *Agar* is not his own experience). The necessity of accom-modating two cultures in the marriage serves, however, as the basis of another of the fundamental challenges that Memmi tries to work out in his writing, and one that again takes on a symbolic dimension that recurs throughout his writing – the question of how to reconcile East and West within his own identity:

> Toute ma vie s'est trouvée dorénavant reprise, orientée, confrontée à elle-même par cet événement. Il a fallu que je me demande qui j'étais, qui j'avais été jusqu'ici et qui je devais devenir pour arriver à vivre dans ce monde nouveau qui s'offrait à moi. Comment concilier en moi l'Orient et l'Occident?[17]

> (My whole life now made a fresh start, guided and brought face to face with itself by this event. I had to ask myself who I was, who I had been up till now and who I wanted to become, so as to live in this new world which was being offered to me. How was I going to reconcile East and West in myself?)

And he writes in *Le Nomade immobile* that a decision to marry into another culture has its own significance:

> On ne se marie non plus par hasard. Mon mariage fut l'aboutissement de ce que je recherchais: la liberté, hors de la minuscule communauté où je suis né, où mes parents avaient repris le relais séculaire, que j'aurais dû reprendre à mon tour, tâche que je refusais. Mais j'allais vérifier également qu'on ne rompt jamais complètement avec une partie de soi. Mon mariage avec une jeune femme d'origine chrétienne – d'une autre civilisation, donc même si elle aussi était en révolte contre les siens et son éducation religieuse – signifiait que j'avais brûlé mes vaisseaux pour ne plus retourner en arrière; affirmait ma détermination d'aller le plus loin possible.[18]

> (One doesn't marry by chance either. My marriage was the culmination of what I had been seeking: freedom, outside the tiny community I'd been born in, where my parents had taken up and passed on the centuries-old tradition which I in turn should have taken up and refused to. But I was also to learn from experience that one never makes a complete break with part of oneself. My marriage to a young woman of Christian origins – of another civilisation, then, even if she too was in revolt against her family and her religious upbringing – meant that I had burnt my boats and could never turn back; showed my determination to journey as far as possible.)

As previously indicated, Memmi began to write seriously in Paris and *La Statue de sel*, dedicated to his father, *le bourrelier* ('the leather-worker'), published in 1953, actually dates from 1950. The second edition had a preface by Camus, which had arrived too late for the first, placing Memmi's work from the beginning in a relationship with the Parisian intellectuals of the period, although his stance remained a very independent one.[19]

The couple returned to Tunis for seven years where Memmi taught and also directed a child psychology clinic (*Laboratoire de psycho-sociologie, Centre de Psychologie de l'enfant*). He was involved in the political activities of this period of Tunisian independence and edited the literature pages of the weekly newspaper *L'Action*, thereby taking a stance with the independence movement rather than with the Zionism with which he had been involved in his youth. Memmi and his wife left Tunisia in 1956 and settled definitively in Paris, where Memmi continued to write both literature and sociological studies, and to teach and research (he was, for example, attached to the CNRS; taught social psychiatry in the *Ecole pratique des Hautes Etudes de la Sorbonne*; and taught for many years at the Université Paris-X Nanterre). Among his work, three anthologies of North African writing in French for which he wrote the introductions should be noted (*Anthologie des écrivains maghrébins d'expression française*, 1964, 1965; *Anthologie des écrivains français du Maghreb*, 1969; *Anthologie des écrivains francophones du Maghreb*,

1985), as well as the *Domaine maghrébin* collection which he edited for the Parisian publishers Maspéro.[20] The titles of these anthologies and their inclusions and exclusions raise interesting issues concerning the corpus of North African writing in French, a question also touched on in the introduction here. Memmi coined the label 'Génération de '52' for the North African writers who came to prominence in the 1950s with the independence movements across the Maghreb, and he occupies a central position for all those writing in French from North Africa. His commitment, in a personal and political sense, to the role of the writer is clear. For Memmi, the writer is necessary to his society and he maintains an ethical position on writing as for other social behaviour: a writer's work should be a kind of testimony to a way of living, a way of being in the world. From the publication of *Portrait du colonisé*, which had a preface by Sartre, Memmi became, as he says (using Sartrean terminology) in *Le Nomade immobile*, 'un écrivain engagé' ('a committed writer'), and this commitment affects the status of the literature he writes:

> Je suis devenu, presque malgré moi, ce que l'on nomme, d'un terme discutable, un écrivain engagé, ce qui implique un certain dédain de la littérature pure. Ce n'est pas complètement inexact dans mon cas, ce qui ne signifie nullement que j'ai le dédain de la forme.[21]

> (I became, almost in spite of myself, what people call a 'committed writer'; a debatable term, implying a certain contempt for pure literature. It is true of me to a certain extent – which absolutely does not mean I have any contempt for form.)

There is, then, commitment to both the political and the aesthetic dimensions of the literary text in Memmi's work. I shall consider this attention to form in a later section, particularly with reference to *Le Scorpion*, although it is of paramount importance to his entire writing project. Memmi is also clear on what the writing of fiction has allowed him to do, while remaining aware of the limits of the literary enterprise:

> Me projetant en des personnages, je tâcherai de me purger de passions nocives; de ruser avec ce que j'ai besoin de dire sans l'oser tout à fait; d'imaginer des fictions qui remplaceront les aventures que je n'aurai pas vécues. Je pourrais rêver à ma guise, sans avoir besoin de croire que mes songes ont quelque réalité […] bref, en devenant écrivain, je pourrais tenter de tout dire, sans tomber dans la crédulité. Utilisant tous les outils de l'établi, l'image autant que l'idée, je pouvais espérer maîtriser et suggérer le réel sans me soumettre à la rigueur que j'attends de la philosophie. La littérature est une espèce de jeu éminemment utile, sinon nécessaire, mais sans illusion sur ses limites et sur les fragilités du joueur; telle est pour moi sa fonction principale.[22]

> (Projecting myself into characters, I will try to purge myself of harmful passions; to find a way round what I need to say without daring to say it

totally; to imagine fictions in place of the adventures which I have not lived through. I will be able to dream at will, without needing to believe that my dreams possess any reality [...] in short, by becoming a writer I would be able to try and say everything without falling into credulity. By using all the established tools, images as well as ideas, I could hope to master and suggest reality without subjecting myself to philosophic rigour. Literature is a kind of eminently useful, if not necessary game, but is under no illusions as to its limits or the weaknesses of the player; that is, for me, its main function.)

Describing writing as a plea following a confession, Memmi also situates his writing fully within the autobiographical quest, and he is aware of the autobiographer's need to seduce the reader to his cause:

> Ma littérature, sinon toute littérature, est un aveu et un plaidoyer. Un aveu donc un plaidoyer: je ne suis pas méchant puisque j'avoue, puisque je sollicite la compréhension du lecteur et la rémission [...] C'est le soulagement de la confession, confession réciproque où l'auteur, se confessant, confesse son lecteur – 'Lecteur, mon semblable, mon frère!' [sic][23]

> (My literature, if not all literature, is a confession and a plea. A confession and therefore a plea: I'm not playing a trick, because I confess, because I beg for the understanding of the reader and for remission [...] It is the solace of confession, reciprocal confession in which the author, by confessing, hears the confession of the reader – '*Reader, my likeness, my brother!*')

Both of these quotations afford insights generally into the relationship between Memmi and literature, and more particularly into the concerns that are worked through in *Le Scorpion*, a text concerned with working out the ethical and aesthetic possibilities of the literary enterprise and at the same time with questioning the status of literature and of 'confession'.

The period of Memmi's early life in Tunisia coincided with the consolidation of the French Protectorate and then the eventual gaining of Tunisia's independence. He is clear in *Le Nomade immobile* concerning the failures of the Marxist analysis of independence and decolonisation due to the lack of a proletariat in the colonial situation. Memmi explains the different type of analysis he undertook himself in *Portrait du colonisé*, insisting on the national, psychological and cultural struggle that had to be undertaken in addition to the economic dimension and the class struggle prioritised by Marxists:

> Cette belle construction avait un défaut grave: le prolétaire n'existait guère aux colonies, en raison de l'absence d'industrialisation. Ce fut l'objet de mon premier écrit sur la colonisation. J'y annonçais que la lutte allait être nationale, psychologique et culturelle, et non seulement économique. La décolonisation sera la reprise en main d'un peuple par lui-même dans toutes ses dimensions.[24]

> (This beautiful construct had one serious fault: there was no proletariat in the colonies, because of the lack of industrialisation. This was the object of

my first written work on colonisation. In it, I announced that the struggle was going to be national, psychological and cultural, and not only economic. Decolonisation would be a nation taking possession of itself in all its dimensions once again.)

Memmi also makes explicit the distinction between his own thinking and the defence of violence propounded by Frantz Fanon. There is a degree of bitterness in his description of Fanon and his politics, and at the same time Memmi includes a certain amount of self-analysis. In fact, history has proved Fanon mistaken in his belief that the 'Revolution' in Algeria would bring the people to power:

> Pour ma part, je m'évertuais à rechercher les moyens de la [la violence] réduire, et n'en faire qu'un recours ultime. Bref, Fanon est un héros du tiers-monde; ce que je ne suis pas. Les héros meurent jeunes, et je n'ai pas pu m'empêcher de vieillir. Le héros choisit la tragédie; je plaide pour le bonheur. Le héros est un passionné en politique comme en amour, je crois la passion mauvaise conseillère. De toutes manières, je me refuse à la démagogie des justes causes.
>
> Je suis embarrassé d'écrire que les événements n'ont pas donné raison au lyrisme fanonien. Il annonçait, suivi par nombre d'intellectuels français, que le 'peuple' algérien prendrait le pouvoir, donnant l'exemple aux colonisés du monde entier. Il me paraissait plus probable que, vu l'état dans lequel se trouvait ce peuple, ce seraient les bourgeoisies nationales qui prendraient le pouvoir. Ce qui se passera presque partout.[25]

> (For my part I endeavoured to find ways to reduce it [violence], and only use it as a last resort. In short, Fanon is a hero of the Third World, which I'm not. Heroes die young, and I have not been able to prevent myself from growing old. The hero chooses tragedy; I plead on behalf of happiness. The hero is as passionate in politics as in love; I believe passion to be a bad adviser. In any case, I reject the demagoguery of just causes.
>
> I am embarrassed to write that events have proved Fanon's lyricism wrong. Followed by numerous French intellectuals, he announced that the Algerian 'people' would take power, setting an example to the colonised peoples of the whole world. It seemed more probable to me, given the state the Algerian people were in, that it would be the national bourgeoisies that would take power. Which is what was to happen almost everywhere.)

The failure of the Algerian War of Independence to bring about the anticipated social revolution, and the violence caused by colonisation, war and civil war, haunt Memmi's work as they do that of Mouloud Feraoun and Assia Djebar, as discussed at the end of the previous chapter.

Memmi's method of working and his relationship to his material were also particular, and, as I have previously indicated, based on personal experience. It was during the period of his return to Tunisia, for example, that Memmi made notes and collected material that would serve as the basis for his work on oppression and racism, and for his later novels.[26]

Memmi's childhood, adolescence and coming to adulthood also coincided with the almost total disappearance of the Jewish community in Tunisia. There is some evidence that the arrival of the French in North Africa may have ameliorated conditions for the Jews to some extent:

> En Algérie, les Juifs seront très tôt naturalisés par les décrètes Crémieux; en Tunisie et au Maroc, ils pourront désormais profiter de 'l'ordre colonial'. Les naturalisations, quoique moins systématiques, s'y multiplient aussi. La communauté s'ouvre à la civilisation et à la culture occidentales. [27]

> (In Algeria, the Jews were very soon naturalised by the Crémieux decrees; in Tunisia and Morocco, they were able to profit from the 'colonial order' from then on. Naturalisation in those countries was less systematic, but there were plenty of instances of it there too. The community opened up to Western civilisation and culture.)

The Crémieux decree of 1870 granted French citizenship to Algerian Jews, for example, and they were not required to renounce their religious practice, as was the case for the Muslim population. However, this citizenship was revoked in 1940 under Vichy. Yet French intervention in the lives of North African Jews was always ambivalent. The execution of Bathan Sfez (usually referred to as the 'Bathan Affair') in June 1857 following a dispute with a Muslim led to the foundation, under French patronage, of the first school set up by the *Alliance Israélite Universelle* in Tunis (referred to by Memmi in *La Statue de sel*). Yet as Guy Dugas has noted,

> Même si les 'judaïcités' tunisiennes auraient souvent été en butte aux catholiques autant qu'aux musulmans, la France, qui venait par le décret Crémieux (1870) de naturaliser collectivement les Juifs algériens, ne pouvait voir d'un mauvais œil cette institution soucieuse de 'faire de ces *Juifs* tunisiens des *israélites*, avec l'espoir d'en faire un jour des *français*'. La communauté juive, de son côté, est déchirée par l'installation du protectorat français, à la suite du traité de Barole (12 mai 1881). Si elle y gagne la liberté et l'occidentalisation dont elle rêvait, l'oubli rapide des trois grands tabous ancestraux, cela ne se fait pas sans mal. Comme en Algérie, les premiers temps de l'occupation, par la suite les moments de plus grande tension, s'accompagnent de violences de la part des troupes ou d'exactions de la part des populations indigènes, et ce sont souvent les h'aras qui en font les frais, sans que la puissance tutélaire intervienne le moins du monde. La France en gardera aux yeux de la minorité judéo-tunisienne, qui représentera toujour moins de 4% de la population de la Régence, l'image double d'une puissance despotique et protectrice à la fois. [28]

> (Even though the Tunisian Jews had often clashed with both Catholics and Muslims, France, which had just naturalised the Algerian Jews collectively by the Crémieux Decree of 1870, could not disapprove of this institution which was concerned to 'make these Tunisian *Jews* into *Israelites*, in the hope of one day making them into *Frenchmen*'. The Jewish community, for its part, was split apart by the installation of the French Protectorate

following the Treaty of Barole (12 May 1881). On the one hand, the Jewish community gained the liberty and Westernisation which it had dreamed of, but the sudden forgetting of the three great ancestral taboos was not achieved painlessly. As in Algeria, the first period of occupation, and afterwards the moments of greater tension, were accompanied by violence on the part of the troops or atrocities on the part of the indigenous population, and it was often the *h'ara* which paid the price, without the occupying authorities intervening in any way. In the eyes of the Tunisian Jewish minority, comprising less than 4% of the population of the French Regency, France would always retain the double image of a power that was both despotic and protective at the same time.)

The Jews in North Africa therefore experienced severe problems, especially with the outbreak of the Second World War and the introduction of anti-Semitic Vichy laws. The Jewish community was caught between the European forces of authority, which were often anti-Semitic, and the Arab majority, who continued to reject them and who, it was felt by many Jews, sought to remove them in the programmes of *arabisation* after independence in 1956. Yet the newly independent Tunisia allowed Jews to vote for the first time and for a very short time there was a Jewish minister in Bourguiba's government, André Barouch. At the height of the nationalist movement in the early 1950s, the majority of the Jewish population was reluctant to take sides. By then the Jewish population consisted of around 80,00 people, approximately 2 per cent of the total population, with another 1 per cent who had taken French nationality.[29] The formative period of Albert Memmi's life therefore coincided with a turbulent period both for the country of his birth and for his own community, caught in a position between Europeans and Arabs, and bound up with the forces of history. These questions of power, of oppression, of identity, of social conformity and non-conformity, and of political allegiance were first worked out in a fictional form in *La Statue de sel*, a novel with a strong autobiographical basis openly acknowledged as such by Memmi. On a surface level, this first novel takes the form of a classic *Bildungsroman*, yet it exceeds such a reading as Memmi's work develops. It provides the founding moment both of the 'coming to writing' that is described there (a fundamental moment in the autobiographical project of any writer) and above all of the sustaining motifs for all Memmi's work: the way in which knowledge about a particular condition of human experience is arrived at, and an analysis of the trigger for the acquisition of that knowledge and the way in which that experience may be used to learn something about the universal human condition. Nonetheless, Memmi has no illusions about the limits of the passage from the individual to universal in its practical application:

En temps qu'un homme moral aspirant à l'universel, le sort de tous les hommes devrait m'être également préoccupant. Mais je ne suis pas un homme universel; je suis d'abord un homme singulier, avec des attaches particulières. Mes liens avec les autres hommes se diluent à mesure que m'en éloignent la culture et la géographie. La fameuse déclaration de Montesquieu sur la préférence qu'il accorde au général sur le singulier, à l'humain sur le familial, est mal interprétée, me semble-t-il: ce n'est pas un constat, c'est un souhait éthique, une décision juridique.[30]

(As a moral being aspiring to the universal, the fate of all men should concern me equally. But I'm not a universal man; I am firstly an individual, with particular attachments. The further I am from other men culturally or geographically, the weaker my links with them grow. Montesquieu's famous declaration about the preference he accords to the general over the individual, the whole of mankind over his own family, is, I think, misinterpreted: it is not an observed fact but an ethical aspiration, a juridical decision.)

I have referred extensively in this introductory section to *Le Nomade immobile*, a recently published text that serves as a kind of *livre bilan* ('book that takes stock') of Memmi's life and work, a book produced by the ageing writer, sociologist and, increasingly, philosopher as a kind of survey of his life and writings, in which he explains and justifies his work, and makes clear his version of certain events in his life. Memmi is often severe about his own conduct and that of others, in keeping with the moralist he felt he had to become since he refused religious faith: 'je suis devenu, surtout, un moraliste: pour expliquer et légitimer ma conduite autrement que par un acte de foi'[31] ('I have become, above all, a moralist, in order to explain and justify my behaviour otherwise than by an act of faith'). I would like to consider a few other elements of this text before moving onto the narrative texts that form the focus of this chapter. The headings of many of the chapters in *Le Nomade immobile* serve to indicate major stages in Memmi's life and thinking: 'La révolte ou le néant'; 'Le prix du savoir'; 'Le pont suspendu'; 'L'apprentissage de la solitude'; 'Retour au pays'; 'Fécondités de l'exil'; 'Les appartenances multiples'; 'La dimension juive'; 'Nous sommes tous dépendants'; 'Le salut par l'écriture'; 'La religion: une fiction commode'; 'Il n'existe pas de société sans morale'; 'La politique: attachement et détachement'; 'La philosophie, bien penser pour bien agir' ('Revolt or Nothingness'; 'The Price of Knowledge'; 'The Suspension Bridge'; 'The Apprenticeship of Loneliness'; 'Return to the Native Country'; 'Fruitfulness of Exile'; 'Multiple Belongings'; 'The Jewish Dimension'; 'We are All Dependants'; 'Salvation through Writing'; 'Religion, a Comfortable Fiction'; 'There is No Society without Morality'; 'Politics: Attachment and Detachment'; 'Philosophy, Thinking Rightly in Order to Act Rightly'). He begins revealingly on the origins of his name, a theme that will return in the two texts I shall be analysing:

Je suis né un 15 décembre pluvieux, à huit heures du matin, 4 impasse Tronja, rue Vieille-Tronja, à Tunis, en Tunisie, de Fradji Memmi et de Maïra Sarfati. Memmi serait un antique patronyme kabyle qui signifie le 'petit homme' ou, autre hypothèse, le vocatif de Memmius, membre de la gens romaine Memmia. Dans le premier cas, mon père serait le descendant d'une vieille souche locale, dans le second, le lointain produit de l'occupation romaine. Du côté maternel, Sarfati, qui signifie le 'Français', est assez courant dans la littérature hébraïque. Plus sûrement que dans les astres, tout se trouve déjà dans cette conjonction.[32]

(I was born one rainy 15 December at eight in the morning at 4, Impasse Tronja, rue Vieille-Tronja, Tunis, Tunisia, to Fradji Memmi and Maïra Sarfati. 'Memmi' may have been an ancient Kabyle patronymic which means the 'little man' or, on another hypothesis, the vocative of 'Memmius', member of the Roman Memmia clan. In the first case, my father would be a descendant of an old local family, and in the second, the distant product of the Roman occupation. On my mother's side, 'Sarfati', which means 'the Frenchman', is quite common in Jewish literature. More surely than in the stars, everything was already present in the conjunction of those two names.)

One of the striking aspects of *Le Nomade immobile* is the pitiless analysis that Memmi exercises on himself and on others around him throughout his life, and the reader begins to understand how the writer forged an individual moral stance for his intellectual life:

Au lycée, j'embarrassais mes professeurs par des questions à contre-courant; je continuais à l'université, contre les doctrines en vogue – le marxisme stalinien et le catholicisme, qui prévalaient alors à la Sorbonne. Plus tard contre l'existentialisme, un certain structuralisme, puis le lacanisme qui leur disputa la place. Non que je fusse toujours sûr de moi, mais là encore la critique – et l'autocritique, bien sûr – était la règle pour mieux diriger ma pensée. Je me méfiais de tout ce qui, devenant une pensée collective, ne laisse pas de place à l'initiative individuelle [...]

Mais aujourd'hui encore je pardonne difficilement, aux intellectuels surtout, la complaisance, sinon la complicité devant l'erreur. Ils ont le droit de se tromper, pas de tromper les autres, même par prudence ou tactique, par solidarité ou par discipline [...] L'intellectuel a d'autant moins le droit de ruser avec la vérité qu'il est plus outillé pour la découvrir, et qu'on l'attend de lui. S'efforcer de voir clair et dire clairement est sa fonction, sinon à quoi sert-il?

C'est durant mes années au lycée que je forgeai ma doctrine à cet égard.[33]

(At the *lycée* I embarrassed my teachers with questions which went against the current; I continued to do this at university, against the doctrines then in vogue: Marxist Stalinism and Catholicism, which were the prevailing trends at the Sorbonne. Later, against Existentialism, a certain Structuralism, and then the Lacanianism which aimed to replace them. Not that I was always sure of myself, but there too criticism – and self-criticism, of course – was my rule for the better guidance of my thinking. I mistrusted everything which, becoming a collective way of thinking, leaves no room for individual initiative [...]

But even today I find it hard to forgive people, especially intellectuals, for complacency towards error, if not actual complicity in it. They have the right to deceive themselves but not to deceive others, even out of prudence or tactics, solidarity or discipline [...] The intellectual has the less right to play about with truth insofar as he is better equipped to discover it, and as people expect it from him. His function is to do his utmost to see clearly and speak clearly – otherwise, what is he there for?

    It was during my years at the *lycée* that I worked out my doctrine on all this.)

The question of truth that I have taken as the fundamental theme to describe Memmi's life project and writing project in the title to this chapter is presented here as fundamental to the way in which he has lived his life:

> Le goût de la vérité est double: besoin de rechercher la vérité, besoin de la faire partager. Si penser juste me paraît toujours une obligation envers moi-même, je suis moins sûr de devoir l'exiger des autres, ni même de faire partager mes conclusions. Pourquoi s'échiner à révéler ce que l'on croit être vrai à des gens qui ne souhaitent pas vous entendre? Pour se rassurer soi-même? Pour vérifier ce que l'on croit avoir découvert? Ou, et c'est plus suspect, pour imposer ses vues et jouir de ce pouvoir? Peut-on et doit-on tout dire? Qui nous le demande vraiment? Horreur! Suis-je loin des prosé-lytes que je dénonce? Je suis pris alors par la tentation du masque, et comprenne qui pourra.[34]

> (The taste for truth is double: the need to seek it out, and the need to share it. But although thinking rightly always seems to me a duty I owe myself, I am less sure that I ought to demand it of others, or even share my conclusions with others. Why wear yourself out trying to explain what you believe to be true, to people who don't want to understand you? To reassure yourself? To verify what you think you have discovered? Or – and this is more suspect – to impose your views on others and enjoy the sense of power? Can we and should we say everything? Who honestly demands this of us? Horrors! Am I, after all, so far from the proselytes I denounce? And then I am seized by the temptation to mask myself, and let anyone understand me who can.)

    As for the wounds Benillouche receives in *La Statue de sel*, Memmi declares that they have healed although the scars remain, and it is partic-ularly revealing for the study here that these scars are the consequence of battles concerned with identity, with the issues of being Jewish, North African, poor:

> Je m'empresse d'ajouter que cette angoisse, si elle n'est pas totalement apprivoisée, me procure aussi le sentiment d'une victoire relative sur le sort et sur moi-même. Lors de la parution de mon premier livre, qui déjà fut un inventaire, on en a quelquefois cité cette phrase: 'Indigène dans un pays de colonisation, juif dans un univers antisémite, Africain dans un monde où triomphe l'Europe...' Il n'y avait pas que cela dans l'ouvrage, mais ce passage en résumait l'un des aspects principaux. Or le temps a passé. Je suis main-tenant de nationalité française, même si je n'ai pas renié ma citoyenneté d'origine et si demeurent en moi des fidélités tenaces. Le racisme est partout

stigmatisé, même s'il n'est toujours pas commode d'être juif. Il n'est plus si infamant d'être d'origine africaine, même si persiste le malheur d'Afrique. Quant à la pauvreté, n'ayant guère de goûts dispendieux, une honnête carrière universitaire a suffi à mes besoins. Bref, mes blessures se sont renfermées, même si les cicatrices sont là, bourrelets gênants qui se rappellent de temps en temps à mon attention.[35]

(I hasten to add that this anguish, although not totally subdued, also provides me with a sense of relative victory over fate and over myself. When my first book, which was already a stock-taking, appeared, there was a passage which was often quoted: 'Native of a colonised country, Jewish in an anti-Semitic universe, African in a world where Europe was triumphing...' There was not only that in the book, but that passage summed up one of its main aspects. Now time has gone by. I now have French nationality, though I have not renounced my original nationality and fiercely retain old loyalties. Racism is condemned everywhere, though it is still not always comfortable to be Jewish. It is no longer so shameful to come from Africa, though Africa's wretchedness still persists. As for poverty, never having had expensive tastes, an honest university career has sufficed for my needs. In short, my wounds have healed, even though the scars are there, painful patches which remind me of their existence from time to time.)

Memmi is also clear about the fundamental paradox in his relationship to his native country, two contradictory convictions that he has never been fully able to reconcile: he is inextricably linked to the climate, smells, light, food, music of Tunisia: 'au point qu'il n'y aura presque aucun de mes livres où tout cela ne sera, d'une manière ou d'une autre, présent' ('to the point where there is not a single one of my books in which all that is not present in one way or another'). But he cannot live there because he would not feel free to express himself:

non seulement parce que je n'appartiens pas à la majorité musulmane – ce qui, tant que les hommes seront ce qu'ils sont, restera un handicap –, mais surtout parce que je n'y disposerai pas de la liberté de pensée et d'expression, qui m'était nécessaire pour vivre et écrire comme je l'entendais. Problème peut-être insoluble; comment ne pas rompre tout en gardant ses distances?[36]

(not only because I do not belong to the Muslim majority – which, for as long as men remain what they are, will remain a handicap – but above all because there I would not have the freedom of thought and expression which were necessary for me to be able to live and write as I intended to. An insoluble problem, perhaps: how to keep one's distance without breaking off completely?)

His 'fate' has been to live his life as part of a minority and it is this that provided him with the source of his thinking on human relationships and on the lack of understanding between minorities and those from the majority community. Memmi's analysis resonates with contemporary debates concerning migration, immigration and integration in Europe:

Les hasards de l'Histoire ont fait de moi un minoritaire, en France comme en Tunisie. Or il existe entre les majoritaires et les minoritaires un malentendu et un fossé. Les majoritaires, lorsqu'ils sont généreux, souhaitent que les minoritaires franchissent ce fossé; les minoritaires le souhaitent aussi, mais, pris de vertige devant ce gouffre, ils s'accrochent à ce qu'ils connaissent, c'est-à-dire à leurs traditions, leurs us et coutumes, ce qui les sépare davantage encore des majoritaires. Si les majoritaires comprenaient mieux l'angoisse de minoritaires devant l'inconnu de l'intégration, et en même temps leur désir éperdu d'intégration – contradiction qui habite la plupart des immigrés –, le problème de l'immigration leur paraîtrait moins opaque et moins redoutable.[37]

(The hazards of History have made me a member of a minority, in France and in Tunisia alike. Now, between members of the majority and members of a minority there exists a misunderstanding and a gulf. Those in the majority, if they are generous, hope that those in the minority will cross that gulf; and the members of the minority hope to do so, but it gives them vertigo and they cling to what they know, i.e. their traditional usages and customs, which separate them still more from the majority. If the majority better understood the minority's fear of the unknown elements of integration, and at the same time their desperate desire for integration – a contradiction which is to be found in most immigrants – the problem of immigration would seem to them less opaque, less formidable.)

Above all, his Jewish identity had an impact on Memmi's thinking and on his conduct, and he insists on the inescapable fact of difference:

Contre ceux qui ne voulaient pas reconnaître la spécificité de la condition juive – qui, après m'avoir applaudi lorsque je dénonçais la condition des colonisés, me suspectaient d'un attachement réactionnaire à la judéité, et, plus généralement, me reprochaient de donner trop d'importance à la notion de la différence, prêtant ainsi flanc à l'agression raciste, et rendant l'intégration plus difficile, etc. [...], j'ai écrit: 'Etre, c'est être différent.' Je continue à le penser, parce que ce n'est pas une revendication mais l'énoncé d'un constat: on n'existe pas comme un être abstrait, mais comme individu singulier, avec des caractéristiques et des attaches particulières[...] La différence est un fait; je n'en fais pas pour cela un drapeau, ni une arme. Il n'y a pas de quoi en être fier, ni s'en affliger. Elle ne légitime en rien une surenchère de soi.[38]

(Against those who did not wish to recognise what is particular about being Jewish – who, after applauding me when I denounced the conditions of the colonised people, then suspected me of a reactionary attachment to Jewishness and, more generally, reproached me for according too much importance to the notion of difference and thus opening up a front to racist aggression, making integration more difficult, etc. [...] I wrote, 'Being means being different.' I still think so, because it is not a claim but a statement of an observed fact: one does not exist as an abstract being but as a specific individual, with particular characteristics and attachments [...] Difference is a fact; which doesn't mean I make it into a flag or a weapon. It's not something to be proud of or to get upset about either. It does not justify over-valuing oneself.)

If 'being means being different', the challenge, as Memmi says, is to reconcile our individual differences. In his attempts to think about how justice could be ensured in the colonial and postcolonial situations, he experienced the impossibility of dissociating oneself from the community of origin, while not wishing to be identified solely with it:

> J'ai ainsi découvert à quel point j'étais dépendant de ma petite communauté d'origine, mais qu'il ne fallait pas lui donner toujours raison. A quel point j'étais proche des autres communautés qui peuplaient le pays, de manières différentes. A quel point les autres vivaient également cette double expérience; les Tunisiens musulmans comme les Européens, plus resserrés sur eux-mêmes qu'en métropole. Mais je découvris en même temps le danger des solidarités excessives, qui rendent injuste et aveugle d'une autre manière. Contre les injustices et les plaidoyers intéressés des colonisateurs, je voulais que justice fût rendue aux colonisés. Mais je me refusais pour cela aux fabulations et à la mauvaise foi des miens et de mes amis. Il fallait tenir compte de cette double nécessité: affirmer ma solidarité avec les victimes de la colonisation, et, cependant, reconsidérer mes liens avec eux pour ne pas fausser jugement. Ce ne fut pas toujours commode, on s'en doute. Il est plus confortable d'approuver son groupe que de le contrer.[39]

> (I thus discovered how dependent I was on the little community I originated from, but that I ought not always to say that that community was in the right. How close I was to the other communities which inhabited the country, in different ways. How those others also lived out that double experience; the Muslim Tunisians and the Europeans too, who were more thrown in upon themselves than in their native land. But at the same time I discovered the danger of excessive solidarity, which makes people unjust and blind in another way. Against the injustices and the self-interested pleas of the colonisers, I wanted justice to be done to the colonised. But for that very reason I rejected the inventions and bad faith of my people and my friends. I had to bear in mind that double need: the need to affirm my solidarity with the victims of colonisation, and nevertheless to reconsider my links with them so as not to judge falsely. It was not always comfortable, you may be sure. It is more comfortable to go along with one's own group than to stand against it.)

Like Mouloud Feraoun, Albert Memmi has inhabited a space that is 'in between' (his own image, used for the title of a chapter in *Le Nomade immobile*, is being on a *pont suspendu*, a suspension bridge) as he has engaged in the same struggle to remain in solidarity with the community from which he came, while being critical of it when necessary within a wider analysis of the effects of colonialism on the identity of the individual and of the collectivity, and on human relationships and behaviour.

POVERTY, SELF-KNOWLEDGE AND POLITICAL KNOWLEDGE IN *LA STATUE DE SEL*

Again like Mouloud Feraoun's *Le Fils du pauvre*, the founding text of Memmi's work can be seen as exemplifying in many ways what can be called a 'typology' of the aims of autobiographical discourses in North African writing in French from the 1950s onwards. Memmi writes as someone from a community that is doubly oppressed and he seeks to affirm its culture, while he simultaneously criticises it. The early childhood spent in the *Impasse* is the matrix that generates all Memmi's subsequent work. In *Le Scorpion* the search for ancestors takes the narrator(s) back into the possibilities of history through the attempt to restore lost origins to the individual and to the Jewish community. The return to childhood is more generally important as part of the quest for origins, which is effected through the memories of others as well as through one's own, as is the quest to restore the identity of the community into which the protagonist was born and which he has since left. Finally, Memmi fluctuates between the use of first and third person in the narratives as he struggles to valorise himself as subject after having been considered an object within the colonial situation. The use of third- and first-person narratives is an important stylistic device in the development of Memmi's fiction-based identity, or identities, and it is by using multiple viewpoints that he believes he comes closest to expressing the 'truth' about himself and his experience:

> Il n'y a pas de vérité absolue. La multiplication des points de vue nous permet de l'approcher. C'est la même chose en littérature. Il n'y a pas de vérité absolue, complète, définitive. La même idée, vous le voyez, court à travers mon œuvre littéraire et mon travail de professeur.[40]

> (There is no absolute truth. We are enabled to approach truth by multiple points of view. It's the same in literature. There is no absolute, complete, definitive truth. The same idea, as you can see, runs through my writings and my teaching work.)

On the surface, *La Statue de sel*, a first novel, is easily identifiable as the work of a young man writing about his childhood and adolescence and his wish to break away from the constraints of the 'tribe' in which he has grown up: 'Au Passage, je découvris et détestai le tribu' (p. 77) ('In the Passage, I discovered and loathed the tribe'). There is at the same time, and seemingly paradoxically, a recovering of the origins of the individual, and a voice and identity given to the hitherto silent and anonymous Jewish community against which the protagonist will rebel, but which he will also champion. However, *La Statue de sel* also makes possible the leaving of the community and the native land, and Benillouche must not look back, or he risks being subjected to the biblical punishment to which the title and the epigraph allude: 'La femme de Loth regarda en arrière et elle devint une statue de sel' ('Lot's wife looked back and was turned into a pillar of salt'). The titles given to the three parts of the novel also indicate this movement. The first part is entitled 'L'Impasse', the name of the alleyway where the family live in the protagonist's earliest childhood, which he evokes with the most nostalgia and which will become a constant reference-point in the topology and conceptual framework of Memmi's work. The second part, 'Alexandre Mordekhaï Benillouche', charts the development of the adolescent, his experience of the *lycée* that provided a French education and the resulting conflict with his family, especially with his father, and the period during which his problematic and ambiguous identity becomes a source of personal anguish. In this part Benillouche also experiences his first love, discovers his sexuality in visits to prostitutes and begins to think of a vocation as a philosophy teacher. Thirdly and finally, 'Le Monde' follows Benillouche as he moves out of the familiar universes of both the family and school and into the harsh realities of wider society and particularly of war, but also begins to make his own choices, as he consciously rejects the middle-class existence promised by his education, to rejoin (although unsuccessfully) other Jews in the labour camps.

There are striking differences in tone between the three parts of the novel. The evocation of childhood and the welcome protection of the family in the first part (for example in the chapter entitled 'Le Sabbat') gradually gives way to a more troubled existence when the family moves. The second part of the novel is characterised by Benillouche's violent reaction against the family and the community, fuelled by an anger and a willpower that permit him to succeed in the new environment of the *lycée*, which offers opportunities, but which is also a place of inequality and struggle. The third part is a more resigned coming to terms with the harshness of a world in which Benillouche feels he has no place. On one level, Memmi's novel charts a revolt against the overwhelming presence of the father, from the opening pages of the text when the small child lies awake listening to the asthmatic breathing of his father (by which the child is curiously comforted), through an adolescent challenge to the authority of the father that takes the form of the refusal of religious practices considered little more than a set of superstitions by the young man, to the final climax concerning the protagonist's education and career. This results in a quarrel with the father in a conflict that has at its centre the question of money and the fact that the eldest son does not contribute a wage to the family, as much as the refusal of religious practice: 'Nous cessâmes de nous parler fort longtemps. Cela ne me causa pas de peine, j'avoue. Comme si cette querelle avait été nécessaire pour clore toute cette partie de ma vie' (p. 253) ('We stopped talking to each other for a long time. That did not cause me pain, I admit. It was as though that quarrel was necessary to close that whole part of my life'). The protagonist seeks self-knowledge against and in spite of the figure of the father, and the ironies that such a revolt entails are also presented, such as in the labour camp at the end of the text when Benillouche has to go through the functions of the Jewish religious ceremony in order to bind together a group of people who it seems have no other ties, ideological or otherwise.

The text is framed by the device of *l'épreuve* (meaning both 'examination' and 'ordeal'), which can be read in terms of the exam that Benillouche is sitting and which gives rise to the situation that engenders the impulse to begin to write his life-story, and the 'testing' which he has endured and which has produced the text we are reading. Underlying this impulse, we can also read a rebellion against the colonial educational system. Benillouche refuses the constraints of the examination and instead examines himself. Presented in italics, this introductory situation forewarns of the failure of the protagonist to make sense of his existence, yet it also hints at the possible salvation through writing which will be more deeply explored in *Le Scorpion*:

> *Soulagement vicieux. Cet oubli par l'écriture, qui seul me procure quelque calme, me distrait du monde; je ne sais plus m'entretenir que de moi-même. Peut-être me faut-il d'abord régler mon propre compte. Quel aveuglement sur ce que je suis, quelle naïveté d'avoir espéré surmonter le déchirement essentiel, la contradiction qui fait le fonds de ma vie! Allons, il faut en convenir; j'ai des bourdonnements d'oreilles et mal à la poitrine. Je n'ai pas voulu y prêter attention. Cela fait maintenant comme une sonnerie de cinéma ininterrompue. La vérité est que je suis ruiné. Il faut déposer mon bilan.* (p. 13)

> (Vicious comfort. This forgetting through writing, which is the only thing that brings me some calmness, distracts me from the world; now I can only speak about myself. Perhaps I have to settle my own account first. What blindness about what I am, what naivety to have hoped to overcome the essential tearing apart, the contradiction that is at the foundation of my life! All right, it has to be admitted: I have buzzing in my ears and chest pains. I didn't want to take any notice of them. Now it's like a constant cinema bell. The truth is that I'm ruined. I have to take stock finally.)

Already, in these first few pages of the novel, a vocabulary is being forged that contains the seeds of recurrent themes in Memmi's work. The blindness with regard to the necessary knowledge of the true nature of the self, a failing that must be combated, and the contradiction that he sees here as the basis for the identity of his protagonist will be played out fully in the use Memmi makes of it as a writing strategy. The constant need to take stock of who he is and what he has achieved will ensure the future generation of different forms of this *bilan*, and will provide the interconnectedness of all of Memmi's work that has been referred to in this first section of this chapter.

The urge for order in a life punctuated by a series of ruptures, either actively sought or brought upon him, is a fundamental dynamic of the text: '*A la fin de l'épuisante séance, j'emportai une cinquantaine de pages. Peut-être, en ordonnant ce récit, arriverai-je à mieux voir dans mes ténèbres et découvrirai-je quelque issue*' (p. 14) ('At the end of the exhausting session I took away about fifty pages. Perhaps, by sorting out that account, I'll manage to see better into my shadows and discover some way out'). And again much later in the text, rupture and the need for order are insisted upon:

> Le souvenir ordonne le passé, lui donne sa signification. Plus tard il m'apparut que ma vie ne fut qu'une suite de ruptures, de plus en plus graves, de plus en plus complètes. Mais j'ai longtemps espéré l'harmonie; j'ai cru que j'arriverais à force de choix et de volonté à mettre de l'ordre en moi et dans mes relations avec le monde. (p. 211).

> (Memory sorts the past into an order, gives it its meaning. Later I thought that my life was only a series of ruptures, progressively more serious and more complete. But I have long hoped for harmony; I have believed that, by dint of choice and will, I would manage to put order into myself and into my relations with the world.)

Such ruptures and the ensuing crises of identity provide the dynamics of the text as the narrator begins to write the story of the boy from the poor family who grows up in an atmosphere that is both tender and violent, in which interaction with the family is both necessary and troubling. The tranquillity of his earliest memories is linked to the geography of the *Impasse* in which the family home is situated: 'De mes premières années, je n'ai pas d'autres souvenirs que celui d'un jeu continuel, en sécurité dans notre Impasse deux fois cachée' (p. 23) ('The only memory I have of my earliest years is that of a continual game, in security within our doubly-hidden *Impasse*'); and the end of this paradise will be his first loss: 'Et comme, peu après, j'allai à l'école, définitivement, je perdis l'Impasse. Mais avant cette catastrophe, depuis ma naissance, le sein de ma mère et la chambre se prolongeaient en un monde irréel et doux comme un vieux chien' (p. 21) ('And as, shortly afterwards, I went to school, definitively, I lost the *Impasse*. But before that catastrophe, from my birth onwards, my mother's breast and the bedroom were prolonged into an unreal world, as gentle as an old dog').

The first major rupture is also linked to going to school for the first time, and significantly takes place in language when the young boy has to learn French, moving out of the maternal patois which marked him

specifically as Jewish because of his accent. It is the first source of the
déchirement (literally, a 'tearing apart') of which Benillouche wrote in
'L'épreuve'. His relationship to French is rather different from that of
Muslim writers in French, who battle with French as a 'tool of oppression'; for the young Jewish boy it will be experienced rather as an
'instrument of liberation' despite the rupture with the maternal world
which it brings, and which is described as a 'catastrophe' here. Benillouche
realises that he is far from unique, but it does not make the rupture of
identity any less troubling just because it happens to so many others:

> des millions d'hommes ont perdu leur unité fondamentale, ils ne se recon-
> naissent plus et se cherchent en vain. Mais je me dis aussi que cette rencontre
> n'a rien de rassurant; que d'autres essayent de recoller leurs membres épars
> sans y parvenir jamais me confirme au contraire dans ce déchirement. (p.
> 44)[41]

> (millions of men have lost their fundamental unity, they no longer recognise
> themselves and seek themselves in vain. But I also tell myself that this meeting
> is not something reassuring; on the contrary, the fact that others try to stick
> their shattered pieces back together without ever managing to, confirms me
> in that sense of being torn apart.)

Further disappointments and intimations of the cruelty of the outside
world begin to puncture the idealised world of the *Impasse*: Benillouche
loses his belief in his father when he does not 'rescue' him from the *colonie
de vacances* (holiday camp) where he is so miserable. Memmi refers to
this incident in *Le Nomade immobile*, and typically draws from it certain
personal and universal lessons:

> J'ai raconté comment, après avoir insisté pour partir en colonie de vacances
> – peut-être, déjà, pour quitter mes parents dans un premier simulacre – , je
> m'étais trouvé enfermé dans un piège mortel: celui de la séparation. De sépa-
> ration en séparation, telle est la vie, jusqu'à la séparation définitive, la mort,
> contre laquelle on a édifié en vain des temples et des pyramides. Je suppliais
> mon père de venir me tirer de là [...] Il finit par venir mais repartit bredouille,
> n'étant pas arrivé, m'expliqua-t-il tristement, à obtenir cette autorisation du
> minable, mais tout-puissant à ses yeux, adjuvant chef du camp [...] Sans que
> j'eusse la moindre preuve d'une forfaiture de sa part, je le sentis complice de
> mon abandon. Mais quel père n'est pas traître? On lui demande tant qu'on
> ne peut qu'être déçu.
>   En revanche, j'y gagnai un enseignement précieux: dorénavant il ne
> fallait compter que sur moi-même. On ne peut compter sur personne, parce
> que rien ne nous est dû.[42]

> (I have told how, after insisting on going to the holiday camp – perhaps,
> already, in a first simulation of leaving my parents – I had found myself shut
> in a deadly trap: that of separation. From separation to separation, that is
> what life is, up to the final, permanent separation of death, against which
> temples and pyramids have been built in vain. I implored my father to come
> and get me out [...] He came in the end but went away again empty-handed,

not having managed, he told me sadly, to obtain authorisation from the petty little adjutant who headed the camp and who was all-powerful in his eyes [...] Without having the slightest proof of any betrayal on his part, I felt that he was an accomplice in my abandonment. But what father is not a traitor? One demands so much of them that one can only be disappointed.

On the other hand, I learnt a valuable lesson from this: from then on I should count on myself alone. We cannot count on anyone else, because nothing is owed to us.)

As in the later series of revolts against the father, this failure is lived as a form of political education, illustrating Deleuze and Guattari's definition of a 'minor literature' as explored in the introduction here. Further political knowledge is gained through lived experience. It is at the holiday camp run by the army that Benillouche also hears for the first time anti-Jewish prejudice from one of the sergeants in charge, who gives his opinion concerning Jews and money when one of the boys, Mimouni, the son of a street-trader (*marchand ambulant*), starts selling his sweets and does not understand why he should not imitate his father. Memmi shows through the use of such incidents how anti-Semitism functions, contaminating Benillouche's own feelings about the Jews:

> pour la première fois je rencontrai l'explication d'une faute ou d'une tare par le judaïsme de son auteur. Le sergent, hurlant, nous révéla pourquoi Mimouni avait eu cette idée ignominieuse: Mimouni était juif et les juifs ont un penchant irrésistible au commerce. Ce fut la première expérience d'une définitive habitude; j'ai appris à associer juiverie et mercantilisme et j'en voulus aux juifs qui osaient négocier. (p. 62)

> (for the first time I found a fault or misdeed attributed to the fact that its perpetrator was Jewish. The sergeant, yelling, told us why Mimouni had had such an ignominious idea: Mimouni was Jewish and the Jews have an irresistible leaning towards commerce. This was my first experience of a definitive habit. I learnt to associate Jewishness with commerce, and I resented the Jews who dared to engage in trading.)

It is therefore through learned behaviour, behaviour that the society around him promotes, condones and approves, that he learns to despise the Jewish trader, to despise his own community. Benillouche's later political awareness will teach him why this is so as he analyses the power systems that govern society.

A further source of Benillouche's contempt will be his own extended family when the family move from the *Impasse* to the *Passage* and live in proximity with his mother's family (p. 77). His first important political lesson comes with the realisation of being poor, after having despised the poor. The way in which the young Benillouche comes to be aware of his family's poverty is told early on in the text in the painful episode of 'Les Vieux vêtements' ('The Old Clothes'). He and his sister despise their cousin to whom their mother gives the clothes they have finished with: 'Nous en voulûmes à Fraji le crasseux qui nous répugnait, à tous ces pauvres qui nous dépossédaient' (p. 37) ('We felt angry with "filthy Fraji" who repelled us, and with all those poor people who dispossessed us'). However, there is a hard lesson to be learned, and his mother finally explains that most of the clothes he wears also originally belonged to someone else, although she reassures him: 'Mais ce n'est pas une honte d'être pauvre et c'est un péché de se moquer des pauvres' (p. 42) ('But there is no shame in being poor, and it is a sin to mock the poor'). This is not a view shared by the young boy, and the awareness of poverty is a fundamental experience:

> Oh si! Il est honteux d'être pauvre! Cela je le savais par les murmures de mes parents [...] Et je méprisais les pauvres. Fraji avait payé de sa honte et si nous étions pauvres, je payerai de la mienne. Dans le désarroi de ma conscience, je fis, ce jour-là, un grand progrès malheureux. (p. 42)

> (Oh yes it is shameful to be poor! I knew that from my parents' whispers [...] And I did despise the poor. Fraji had paid with his shame, and if we were poor I would pay with mine. In my confused awareness, I made great, unhappy progress that day.)

The experience and the knowledge of poverty lead to behaviour that impregnates his very being: 'Depuis, lentement, m'a gagné cette gêne vestimentaire, caractéristique du pauvre honteux' (p. 42) ('Afterwards, slowly, there came over me that embarrassment about my clothes which is characteristic of those who are ashamed of their poverty'). Another hard lesson comes at school when Benillouche lends the meagre money he has to buy lunch to the rich Saül. Again this episode takes place in the first part of the novel, before the experience of the *lycée*, where Benillouche will be confronted by middle-class affluence and values to an even greater extent. Saül is desperate to complete his collection of cards contained in the chocolate bars that the poor Benillouche can hardly ever afford to buy, and that the rich boys squander in the pursuit of a full series of cards. Having already spent twenty-one sous, Saül is still not satisfied and the poor boy is flattered that his money is needed, and is also ashamed to refuse: 'Peut-être aussi aurais-je eu honte de refuser (et c'est de cette honte qu'après je lui en voulus le plus)' (p. 52) ('Perhaps I would also have been ashamed to refuse (and that shame is what I was most angry with him for afterwards)'). He will now be unable to eat at lunch-time and realises that he is the victim of a system:

> J'eus alors l'impression d'avoir été trompé; jusqu'ici je n'avais pas eu la révélation de la jalousie et de l'envie, ou plutôt si j'enviais les beaux vêtements de Saül et son argent de poche, c'était sans animosité, sans amertume

véritable. A l'époque, la puissance des riches m'inspirait encore un certain respect, comme une chance constante et quasi magique. Je ne voyais pas le rapport entre leur richesse et ma pauvreté. L'égoïste inconscience de Saül m'amorça le lien. Il m'enlevait les deux sous de mon déjeuner pour s'acheter un 'Nestlé' superflu, dont il jetterait ce chocolat que je ne pouvais pas me payer. Plus tard j'ai haï les Saül. (p. 53).

(Then I felt I had been cheated; up until then I had not had any revelation of jealousy and envy, or rather, although I had envied Saül's fine clothes and his pocket-money, it was without animosity, without any real bitterness. At that time the power of the rich inspired me with a sort of respect, like a constant, quasi-magical stroke of luck. I did not see the link between their wealth and my poverty. Saül's selfish thoughtlessness made the connection for me. He took the two sous of my dinner-money to buy himself a super-fluous 'Nestlé' bar, and he would throw away the chocolate which I couldn't afford for myself. Later I hated the Saüls of this world.)

I shall return later to the experience of poverty and the development of a political awareness outlined here by Memmi; in *Le Nomade immobile* also he pinpoints poverty as necessary to the understanding of his life.[43]

The young Benillouche begins to withdraw into himself, an intro-spective movement that his studies and intellect will intensify as the distance grows between who he was and who he is becoming:

Constamment, progressivement, dans ces années au passage, je me retirais en moi-même, je me crispais jusqu'à devenir cette silhouette toute en nerfs, insupportable aux autres et à moi-même. Mes études enfin et la transfor-mation profonde de mon matériel d'idées mirent une distance définitive entre la tribu et moi. (p. 78)

(Constantly, progressively, in these years in the *Passage*, I retreated into myself, stiffened, until I became that silhouette covered in nerves, unbear-able to others and to myself. My studies, finally, and the profound transformation of the matter of my ideas, set a definitive distance between the tribe and me.)

In *Le Nomade immobile* Memmi fully acknowledges the importance of his schooling in his ensuing revolt against his background:

Comment la révolte n'aurait-elle pas germé dans ce terreau putride? C'est l'école qui m'en donna la force en m'indiquant l'issue, lointaine mais extra-ordinairement lumineuse comme l'issue d'un tunnel: le savoir! Je devais le recueillir patiemment, pieusement, à l'école primaire puis au lycée où j'eus l'incroyable chance d'entrer.[44]

(How could revolt have failed to germinate in that rotting compost? It was school that gave me the strength for it and pointed to the way out, distant but brilliant, like the end of a tunnel: knowledge! I had to gather it patiently, devoutly, at primary school sand then at the *lycée* which I had the incredible luck to get into.)

This resentment and guilt towards the family is as terrible for the older author who writes *Le Nomade immobile* as it was for the young man who wrote *La Statue de sel*. In *Le Nomade immobile* Memmi acknowledges that he had to distance himself from his family and 'judge' them; resentment finally turned to compassion, but the relationship is no easier:

> Pour faire mon salut, il me fallut également prendre mes distances avec les miens, c'est-à-dire aussi les juger. Et lorsque mon ressentiment se fut transformé en compassion, ce ne fut pas plus commode. Je ressentis la vrille de la culpabilité: j'étais responsable de l'asthme de mon père, coupable des varices de ma mère, du dénuement de tous. Pour leur venir en aide, j'aurais dû travailler au lieu de me consacrer à mes études! Je le payerais cher. En me punissant. En refusant, par exemple, de rendre ces études rentables, financièrement et même socialement. En ne me permettant aucun loisir; je n'ai jamais joué, à rien; je n'avais pas le temps, j'étais toujours occupé à comprendre, afin d'agir plus efficacement. De la pitié ou de la violence, je ne sais pas ce qui est le plus difficile à vivre.[45]

> (To find my own salvation I also had to distance myself from my family, i.e. to judge them as well. And when my resentment had been transformed into compassion, it was no more comfortable. I felt pangs of guilt: I was responsible for my father's asthma, guilty of my mother's varicose veins, of everyone's destitution. To come to their help I should have got a job instead of dedicating my time to my studies. I would pay dearly for this. By punishing myself. By refusing, for example, to make my studies profitable, financially or even socially. By not allowing myself any leisure; I've never played at anything at all; I didn't have the time, I was always busy understanding, so as to act more effectively. Pity and violence: I don't know which of the two is more difficult to live with.)

The writer becomes, therefore, a moralist. In *La Statue de sel* Benillouche begins to undertake an unflinching analysis of himself and his relations to others, making this text a 'confession' in the style of Rousseau, whom Memmi admired, and providing a foundation for the development of his thinking about himself and others.

Despite the obstacles that poverty could be expected to put in his way (the cost of school clothes and books, the need for another salary in the family), Benillouche wins a scholarship to the *lycée* and his studies through school and university are paid for by the *Communauté israélite de Tunis* (Jewish Community of Tunis). The experience of the new world opened up to the boy at school is a profound rupture: learning brings both opportunity and pain, provoking a break with the world of the poor man, bringing knowledge of the world and self-knowledge, and simultaneously offering self-fulfilment and isolation. The *déchirement* ('tearing apart') is experienced both between the child and the world with which he is familiar, and inside a self developing at the cost of an internal conflict between competing forces:

> L'Impasse et l'Alliance appartenaient à une société, le quartier européen et le lycée à une autre. Surtout je commençai l'aventure de la connaissance [...]

Certes la connaissance fut peut-être à l'origine de toutes les impossibilités qui surgissent dans ma vie. Peut-être aurais-je été plus heureux dans le rôle du petit juif du quartier. (p. 88)

(The *Impasse* and the *Alliance* belonged to one society, the European quarter and the *lycée* to another. Above all I embarked on the adventure of knowledge [...] It's true that knowledge was perhaps at the origin of all the impossibilities that arose in my life. Perhaps I would have been happier in the role of the little local Jew.)

In *Le Nomade immobile* Memmi sees the *lycée* as the place where his future destiny was shaped and he is aware also of the moralising attitude he developed as a form of self-protection:

C'est grâce au lycée, beaucoup plus qu'à l'école de la rue Malta-Srira (la petite Malte) que je deviendrais ce que je serais dorénavant. A l'école primaire nous étions entre nous, presque tous de condition modeste. Plus tard, à l'Université, plus rien pouvait vraiment mordre sur moi. Le lycée m'a sorti du ghetto et décrassé l'esprit de ses ténèbres. J'y ai appris à mettre en question tout ce qui m'entourait; le passé où je ne voulais plus vivre, et le futur où je n'étais pas sûr de pouvoir vivre. Je trouvai même au lycée de quoi tenir le lycée à distance. Je méprisais mes camarades, leur futilité satisfaite de bien nourris, leurs passions lilliputiennes, leurs boums du samedi soir, leurs dragues permanentes... (je suis injuste! Encore une mauvaise herbe).[46]

(It was thanks to the *lycée*, much more than the school in Malta-Srira (Little Malta) Street that I became what I was to be from then on. In the primary school we were at home with each other, almost all of us from modest backgrounds. Later, at the University, nothing could really gnaw at me any more. The *lycée* took me out of the ghetto and dispelled its darkness from my mind. At the *lycée* I learnt to question everything around me: the past in which I no longer wanted to live, and the future in which I was not sure of being able to live. I even found in the *lycée* the wherewithal to keep the *lycée* at a distance. I despised my comrades, their futile satisfaction born of their full stomachs, their Lilliputian passions, their Saturday night parties, their permanent flirting... (I'm being unjust! Another bad apple).)

For the moment, however, in Benillouche's life story opportunity dominates regret; the only really sour note remains money. As far as his father is concerned the only positive outcome of this education would be to earn a lot of money. This material consideration conflicts with the boy's own idealised vision of himself as a doctor:

Reprenant à mon compte les rêves parlés de mon père, je désirais ardemment être riche ou plutôt je désirais rompre avec la pauvreté. Mais j'avais étroitement uni l'argent à mon avenir, à ma plus belle image de moi-même. A ma stupéfaction, la pure et désirable lumière se voilait. (p. 102)

(Adopting for myself the dreams which my father expressed, I ardently desired to be rich or rather I desired to break with poverty. But I had linked money closely to my future, to the most beautiful image I had of myself. To my stupefaction, the pure, desirable light was darkened.)

Benillouche develops a destructive feeling of guilt towards his family because he does not bring in money that he knows they need (p. 130). He gives private lessons that just about cover his own needs, and recognises that there will be 'd'autres ruptures et d'autres libérations' ('further ruptures and further liberations') before he can rid himself of a feeling of responsibility to his family (p. 133). His father constantly reminds him of the money brought into their families by other boys of his age (p. 135). Benillouche endures the disapproval of the family by sustaining himself with scholarly success, his source of pride. This is literally the image he prefers of himself, spending long hours with his books at the dressing-table that serves as his desk:

> Chaque fois que je levais la tête de mon cahier, je me rencontrais dans la glace, également brisée, de la table [...] J'aimais assez me regarder, longuement, interrogeant le miroir sur ce que j'étais, sur ce mon visage annonçait. D'avoir travaillé toute mon adolescence devant un miroir, il m'en reste beaucoup certainement. (p. 138)[47]

> (Every time I raised my head from my exercise-book, I saw myself in the dressing-table mirror, which was also broken [...] I quite liked to look at myself, slowly, questioning the mirror on what I was, what my face announced. From having worked in front of a mirror for the whole of my adolescence, unquestionably I retain a good deal.)

This is a striking image of selfhood coming into being.

Benillouche has a type of guardian or mentor, M. Bismuth, the pharmacist whom he has to see once a month to report on his progress at school because he is in receipt of a scholarship. The pharmacist's profession represents for his community the pinnacle of success a boy such as Benillouche could aspire to, when in fact at this stage the young man wants to be a doctor. There is no warmth between them and Benillouche realises later that the older man sees too much of himself in this young boy and that he recognises in Benillouche 'sa pénible bataille personnelle, toujours incertaine' (p. 101) ('his own painful personal battle, whose outcome was still uncertain'). When Bismuth later attacks Benillouche's behaviour, he understands that the man remains insecure in his 'middle-class' status: 'la violence de mon tuteur à défendre les valeurs bourgeoises me démontra son incapacité à devenir un simple bourgeois, serein par inconscience' (p. 104) ('my mentor's violence in defending bourgeois values showed me that he could never become a simple bourgeois, serene in his own unawareness'). Benillouche will also have this experience of never reaching the point of feeling that he truly belongs to the middle-class society that he theoretically enters through his education. As for his studies and his future, for the moment he believes he can 'cheat' by pretending that he is following the plan others have in mind for him. However, his life is about to become much more difficult: 'Parce qu'on me permettait d'aller au lycée, je croyais déjà être victorieux. Je découvrais que la bagarre ne faisait que commencer' (p. 104) ('When I was given permission to go to the *lycée* I thought I had already won. I discovered that the battle had only just started'). The problem of how to behave, how to fit in, how to conceal difference is a constant source of anguish for the protagonist of *La Statue de sel*: 'Toute ma vie, mes amitiés, mes acquisitions furent soumis à une constante réadaptation de ce que j'étais' (p. 44) ('My whole life, my friendships, my gains were subjected to a constant readaptation of what I was'). His accent in French is a source of mockery for the other boys and another source of self-loathing and of his loathing and jealousy of others (pp. 119–20). Encounters with other boys are often problematic. The poor Jewish boy finds his difference accentuated not only by the Europeans with whom he is brought into contact, but also by other richer Jews:

> Ils participaient d'une même civilisation qui restait théorique pour moi parce que je n'en bénéficiais pas. Devant la grille du lycée, ils se serraient cordialement et civilement les mains, puis ils échangeaient les nouvelles d'une planète inconnue. (pp. 120–21).
>
> (They shared in the same civilisation which remained theoretical for me because I could not attain it. In front of the *lycée* gate they would shake hands cordially, politely, and then exchange news of an unknown planet.)

Just as for Feraoun, education reveals more difference, while providing no new forms of solidarity. Benillouche pieces together some of the references to jazz, to sport, to hobbies, but much remains incomprehensible: 'La séparation des classes est aussi profonde que celle des religions et je n'étais pas de leurs' (p. 121) ('The separation of classes is as deep as those of religions, and I was not one of them'). It is the beginning of a self-created identity largely based on the fabrication of moral superiority; not having the money to participate in frivolous activities, Benillouche cultivates a moralistic attitude: 'Moi, je devins intransigeant sur les principes, dogmatique en mes jugements, susceptible, sans pitié pour mes faiblesses et celles d'autrui, ambitieux à crever' (p. 122) ('As for me, I became intransigent about principles, dogmatic in my judgements, touchy, pitiless concerning my weaknesses and those of others, and eaten up with ambition'). This is an attitude that Memmi attributes to himself in *Le Nomade immobile*, as has previously been noted.

Benillouche does try to imitate the boys at school in some ways: by forcing himself to listen to opera, by paying great attention to literature, by participating in youth movements, notably the Scouts; but there is no spontaneity in his behaviour. This is perhaps one of the most real and telling of the experiences of poverty, of education and of the exposure to middle-class values that Memmi describes and is fundamental to his ongoing feeling of isolation from all of those around him, on both sides of the class divide. It is an experience, or rather a way of having to live one's life, that relies on artifice and construct. All is learned behaviour; the pleasure of spontaneity in action and speech is definitively removed; the self is constantly under surveillance from a kind of artificially created middle-class super-ego that is on the lookout for any slip in word or behaviour that will suddenly reveal the true origins behind that careful construct. Here is the origin of the pitiless contemplation that Benillouche exercises on himself: 'Je ne cherche pas à m'embellir ni à me justifier: je me débarrasse ici de ma bouillie de chat, je vomis ce que je ne peux pas digérer par l'oubli' (p. 119–20) ('I don't seek to embellish myself or to justify myself; I get rid of my gibberish at this point, and vomit what I can't digest by forgetting'). This analysis of the self has nothing of the luxury of the self-obsession that autobiographical discourse is sometimes charged with – it is an essential part of what he has become:

> je vis bien que je me coupais inévitablement de mon milieu d'origine, je n'entrais pas dans un autre. A cheval sur deux civilisations, j'allais me trouver également à cheval sur deux classes et à vouloir s'asseoir sur deux chaises, on n'est assis nulle part. (p. 123).

> (I saw clearly that I was cutting myself off inevitably from my home background, and I was not entering into another sphere. Standing astride between two civilisations, I was also going to find myself astride between two classes, and would fall between two stools.)

It is at this precise moment that the young man discovers a 'terrible and marvellous secret' that allows him to bear the burden of this solitude – writing. In putting words on paper he can master a universe over which he usually has no control, while at the same time being aware of how the very act of writing condemns him to even less contact with the society around him:

> Je découvris l'extraordinaire jouissance à maîtriser toute existence en la recréant. Certes ce pouvoir me fut aussi funeste que sauveur: à décrire les êtres, ils me devenaient extérieurs, à contempler le monde je n'en faisais plus partie. Et comme on ne vit pas au spectacle, je ne vivais plus, j'écrivais. Solitude pacifiée mais de plus en plus solitude, car de plus en plus consciente et acceptée. (p. 123)

> (I discovered the extraordinary enjoyment in mastering the whole of life by recreating it. Admittedly, that power did me as much harm as good: when I described beings they became exterior to me, when I contemplated the world I no longer formed part of it. And as one does not live in a perform-

ance one watches, I was no longer living, I was writing. A pacified solitude but more and more solitude, since it was more and more conscious and accepted.)

La Statue de sel is then also the story of a 'coming to writing', a necessary but ambiguous activity that does however permit some shift in power relations with the world that surrounds Benillouche.

The distance between Benillouche and his family grows. He does not want to waste time before an exam participating in the traditional funeral rites for his father's brother, and he refuses to allow his beard to grow as a sign of mourning. It is his cousin who bears the same name who is the legitimate Alexandre Benillouche.[48] Benillouche wants to console his father, but is incapable of the necessary gestures, even in the face of the man's tangible grief. His need to revolt culminates in his defying religious practice and turning off the electric light on the Sabbath, an act recently decreed as being against religious practice, which Benillouche finds ridiculous. This sacrilegious act leads his father to condemn him as no longer being Jewish. Benillouche's intellectual superiority cannot accept the superstition that he sees bound up with such religious practice:

> Ce refus me fit mal. Il déclencha mes tumultes. Je voulais bien partir, mais je n'aurais pas supporté d'être chassé. Etre juif consistait-il en ces rites stupides? Je me sentais plus juif qu'eux, plus conscient de l'être, historiquement et socialement. (p. 164)[49]

> (That rejection hurt me. It unleashed the turmoil within me. I wanted to leave, but could not endure to be driven out. Did being Jewish consist of those stupid rites? I felt more Jewish than they were, more aware of being Jewish, historically and socially.)

In *Le Nomade immobile*, Memmi explains that he believed that his break with his community was also a break with this religion:

> En quittant ma communauté d'origine, j'avais laissé derrière moi, entre autres choses, et définitivement, croyais-je, une religion que l'on ne distinguait guère des croyances et des pratiques magiques, venue souvent de fort loin, de la Carthage punique quelquefois. Les rabbins, issus le plus souvent des milieux populaires, pauvrets dans leur vêtements et dans leur tête. Habillés comme nos grands-parents, chéchias et burnous, ils appartenaient à un passé que nous voulions plus ou moins oublier.[50]

> (By leaving the community I had been born in, I had left behind, among other things, and definitively, as I thought, a religion which was indistinguishable from magic beliefs and practices, often from far away, from Punic Carthage sometimes. The rabbis, more often than not from working-class families, were poor in their clothes and poor in their minds. Dressed like our grandparents, in fez and burnous, they belonged to a past which we more or less wanted to forget.)

Benillouche uses his education and the debating skills he has learned at school to distance himself further and further from this religion, both externally (stopping going to the synagogue) and internally. His withdrawal and his attitude affect the whole family as in order to avoid further conflicts they begin to observe only the major ceremonies. Benillouche has brought his new world to encroach on their traditional one. But that traditional world can also intrude on his: seeing his mother in the ecstasy of a dance as part of rites invoked to save her sister, he feels he cannot recognise her, and is completely shaken by his experience of a spectacle he feels to be 'primitive':

> Ai-je vraiment échappé, arriverai-je jamais à échapper à ces tumultes, à ces rythmes qui vivent au fond de moi, qui maîtrisent aussitôt la cadence de mon sang? Après quinze ans de culture occidentale, dix ans de refus conscient de l'Afrique, peut-être faut-il que j'accepte cette évidence: ces vieilles mesures monocordes me bouleversent davantage que les grandes musiques de l'Europe [...] Ah! Je suis irrémediablement un barbare! (p. 184)

> (Have I really escaped, will I ever manage to escape from this turmoil, these rhythms that live in the depths of me, and instantly dominate the throbbing of my blood? After fifteen years of Western education, ten years of conscious rejection of Africa, perhaps I am forced to accept this proof: those ancient, one-note tunes stir me more than the great European musical compositions [...] Oh, I'm irremediably barbaric.)

The scene of his psychological disturbance is played out in front of his schoolfriend Henry's house as Henry continues to practise his European music, which is perceived as precise and as having the rigour of mathematics in contrast to the rhythms of the music of Benillouche's own culture.[51] The following chapter reiterates the same theme of an Orient that is intrinsically part of his very being as Benillouche remembers his experiences at the *Kouttab*, the school run by the rabbi, which he attended before primary school. One of the games there consisted of a choosing a boy to 'play' circumcision on, and Benillouche recalls his absolute physical fear of and revulsion against the scene. Benillouche has preferred another culture (implicitly one that is more 'civilised') and the choices his intellectual powers afford him.

He believes he has to become part of the middle-class world because his education has taught him to share its aesthetic preoccupations, even though he does not necessarily feel any affinity with the people who make up the middle classes. It is unsurprising, given that this text is charting the development of an adolescent, that one way in which this aspiration is given form is in the shape of Ginou, a young girl from whom Benillouche at first believed himself to be separated because of his poverty (p. 196). She sees in him the future doctor, and deserts him when he decides to pursue philosophy. But prior to this another hard lesson, a lesson as hard as that of dealing with the rich boy Saül, has been learned: he will never truly be middle class. He is adept at disguising his family origins in conversation, his father works 'in leather'. He is quite used to the way in which the rich Jewish boys mock those from the ghetto, but he still wants to participate in some of the things he sees as middle-class social activities. Henry invites him to one such event, a Scout meeting that one of the national leaders is attending. Memmi shows how natural these social groupings are to those born into the middle classes and how the ways in which they retain these links are part of the same social fabric, such as sharing an easy sense of humour:

> Je n'arrivais pas à rire de leurs continuelles blagues, jeux de mots, jeux d'esprit, qu'ils avaient fort aiguisés pour voir le côté comique des choses et des gens. Dès leur naissance, le monde leur était offert, à leur grande satis-faction; pour moi, tout était à conquérir et la lutte ne me donnait pas à rire. (p. 214)

> (I couldn't manage to laugh at their continual jokes, puns, witticisms, which they had sharpened to show up the comic side of things and people. From their birth the world had been offered to them, to their great satisfaction; for me, it was still to be gained, and the fight was no laughing matter.)

When Benillouche arrives at the house where the gathering is to be held he cannot find the light for the stairs, but begins to climb anyway until he is frozen in the darkness, unable to move up or down. It is an extremely painful moment and a highly symbolic image. Physically and mentally vulnerable (childhood fears return), he cannot go higher and he cannot return to where he came from: 'je n'osais ni avancer ni reculer. J'étais trop libre, j'étais prisonnier du vide' (p. 217) ('I didn't dare go forward or go back. I was too free, a prisoner in space'). Someone arrives and he is able to enter. Once inside, he wants to join in, but is unable to, directing his own critical eye on himself once again: 'Je restais étranger, un étranger critique et maussade. Et de rester spectateur dans une fête me donnait le sentiment pénible d'être aussi spectateur de moi-même' (p. 222) ('I remained an outsider, a critical, sullen outsider. And remaining a spectator at a party gave me the painful sensation of being a spectator of myself too').

His behaviour earns the disapproval of Ginou, but he realises he can never belong to that social class and begins to question why he wants to: 'Comment ressembler à Jean-Jean, à Gazelle, à Michel, au commissaire? Polis comme des galets de mer, ils n'ont pas de mémoire' (p. 225) ('How could I be like Jean-Jean, Gazelle, Michel, the Scout-leader? As smooth as pebbles, they have no memory').

I shall return to this question of memory and the issue of shared history. Firstly, it is important to point out that it is again around the issue of poverty and social class that a type of political awareness takes place. Included in the gathering is another young man from a poor background, Pinhas:

> Sans m'expliquer pourquoi, cela me fut désagréable de le rencontrer. Son costume avait certes plus souffert que mon pardessus; ce n'était pas un costume-une-fois-l'an. Mais que faisait-il là, si peu à sa place, si mal habillé? Le Mouvement, pour manifester son intérêt au ghetto, et calmer quelques scrupules, voulait lancer une troupe populaire et avait demandé à Pinhas de s'en occuper. Cette histoire me paraissait odieuse et ridicule. Pouvait-on mêler des gosses de riches, bien habillés, aux poches pleines d'argent, qui emmenaient en sortie de quoi nourrir une famille en fête, à des gamins sous-alimentés, vêtus d'oripeaux. (p. 218)

> (Without realising why, I found it unpleasant to meet him. His suit had undoubtedly suffered more than my overcoat: it was not a once-a-year suit. But what was he doing there, so out of place, so badly dressed? The Scout Movement, to show its interest in the Ghetto and calm certain scruples, wanted to set up a working-class troop and had asked Pinhas to take charge of it. That seemed hateful, ridiculous to me. How could you mix the well-dressed children of rich parents, their pockets full of money, who used to go around with enough on them to feed a whole family on a celebration day, with underfed urchins dressed in rags.)

After this time spent observing the rich at play, and especially witnessing Pinhas's attempt to bring into the discussion some of the difficulties experienced in the poor Scout troops, but not having the courage to insist on this in company where 'tous (étaient) bien d'accord depuis toujours' (p. 221) ('all of them had always been in agreement'), Benillouche finds that on the contrary he *does* have a memory to protect, as opposed to these young people who 'have no memory':

> Pourrais-je jamais oublier tous les Pinhas? Il me fallait les sauver, tous les Pinhas, pour me sauver moi-même. Comment ai-je pensé que je pouvais vivre futile et content de moi? Ce soir-là, peut-être, j'entrevis l'existence des autres. (p. 225)

> (Could I ever forget all the Pinhases? I had to save them, all the Pinhases, if I was to save myself. How could I think that I could live a futile, self-satisfied life? That evening, perhaps, I caught a glimpse of the existence of others.)

These young middle-class people clearly do share a common history, they are 'bien d'accord depuis toujours'; the difference is rather that they are able to voice those opinions in a public arena where they are at ease. Benillouche comes to the realisation that the past of the poor is a burden that passes in silence and although his political awakening is presented as idealistic (and he will be disappointed by the people he thinks he should 'save'), he realises that the collective memory and indeed present situation of the poor must be articulated. The concern for the erasure of the history of the poor is one shared by Camus in *Le Premier Homme*, concerning his own community, the poor *pied-noir petit colons* of Algeria, although Memmi and Camus disagreed over their respective positions in the colonial system, and in their analyses of possible solutions to the situation in Algeria.

Benillouche's own existence changes rapidly at this point in the second section until the end of the text: Bismuth the pharmacist tells him he can no longer support him and as this news coincides with the day of the school prize-giving ceremony (which he misses because Bismuth keeps him waiting), it is the moment when Benillouche must take responsibility for himself. He chooses philosophy and writing over medicine: 'j'ai préféré cette harassante, effrayante recherche de soi qu'est la recherche philosophique, cet essai de maîtrise du monde, jamais achevée, qu'est l'écriture' (p. 234) ('I preferred that harassing, terrifying search for the self which is philosophical research; that attempt to master the world, ever incomplete, which is writing'). In making this choice, two of his teachers are important: Marrou, his French teacher (based on Jean Amrouche), and Poinsot, his philosophy teacher: 'Si Marrou m'a aidé à comprendre qui je suis et m'a fait espérer, Poinsot m'apprit la confiance en moi et la connaissance heureuse' (p. 242) ('Marrou helped me to understand who I am and made me hope, while Poinsot taught me self-confidence and the joy of knowledge').[52] He devises a ruse in order to confront Poinsot with his 'other', poor, self, and takes him home where the teacher meets his mother, but as Benillouche interprets for each of them, he experiences the vertiginous gap in his identity: 'Les deux parties de mon être parlaient chacune une langue différente et jamais ne se comprendraient' (p. 247) ('The two parts of my being were each speaking a different language and would never understand each other'). The experience of *déchirement* returns:

> Aurais-je la force de surmonter mon déchirement? Je commençais à pressentir que malgré toute mon envie de me transformer en Poinsot, je risquais de devenir Marrou. Devant l'impossible union des deux parties de moi-même, je décidai de choisir. Entre l'Orient et l'Occident, entre les croyances africaines et la philosophie, entre le patois et le français, il me fallait choisir; je choisissais Poinsot, ardemment, vigoureusement. (p. 247)

> (Would I have the strength to overcome the tearing apart of myself? I began to foresee that despite all my desire to turn into Poinsot, I risked becoming Marrou. Faced with the impossibility of uniting the two parts of myself, I decided to choose between them. Between the East and the West, between African beliefs and philosophy, between patois and French, I had to make my choice; and I chose Poinsot, ardently, vigorously.)

The full consequences of this choice, made with such willpower, will only become apparent in the experience of the Second World War. For the moment, however, Benillouche returns to his image in the mirror, and this time an identity crisis ensues. He is no longer the conscientious student, an image he created for himself; he is unknown to himself:

> Un jour, entrant dans un café, je me suis vu en face de moi-même; j'eus une peur atroce. J'étais moi et je m'étais étranger. C'était un miroir qui couvrait tout un mur, si net qu'on ne le devinait pas. Je me devenais étranger tous les jours davantage. Il me fallait cesser de me regarder, sortir du miroir. (p. 247)

> (One day, on going into a café, I came face to face with myself: I was hideously afraid. I was me and I was a stranger to myself. It was a mirror that covered the whole wall, so perfectly that you couldn't tell it was one. I became more of a stranger to myself every day. I had to stop looking at myself, to get out of the mirror.)

Despite this crisis, he manages to keep working at his studies and supports himself by working as a *pion* (pupil supervisor) at the *lycée*. It is the period when he begins to keep a diary: 'Il m'est curieux de noter que c'est lorsque je décidai de sortir de moi-même pour aller vers le monde que je commençai cette soigneuse introspection écrite' (p. 251) ('I find it odd to note that it was when I decided to come out of myself and go towards the world, that I began this careful written introspection'). This moment of simultaneous external exploration and introspection is also the moment of the final argument with his father about money.

As has previously been stressed, in the experience of poverty and in the internal conflict brought about by the awareness of being poor there is the development of a *political* awareness. For Albert Memmi, poverty is a form of oppression that must always be seen in relation to wealth, another form of dominating and being dominated which is the subject of a large part of his critical and sociological thinking: 'En somme, oui, je fais de la pauvreté une variété de l'oppression [...] La pauvreté est relative à la richesse, qui l'entretient dans l'obsession de sa misère'[53] ('Altogether, yes, I count poverty as a type of oppression [...] Poverty is relative to riches, which keeps it obsessed with its own wretchedness'). Under the colonial system, the injustices of wealth add to the devalued identity of the colonised and minoritised and must be combated. Poverty is not, however, the only form of oppression which must be fought. In *La Statue de sel* the functioning of different forms of racism is also revealed. As Benillouche crosses the city, for example, he is aware of the different inhabitants of the various neighbourhoods.[54] Benillouche describes the racism practised by the Sicilian workers on the young Jews in the cinema as they sit in the stalls below these workers, who throw lighted cigarette ends into their hair. Racism is an everyday experience in a city which Benillouche perceives as hostile to him and to his community:

> Tu vois bien, ils ne nous aiment pas, disait Bissor avec une conviction désespérée.
> Ils: c'étaient les jeunes Siciliens, l'agent de police arabe, le propriétaire français des journaux, nos camarades de lycée, toute la ville enfin. Et c'était vrai que notre ville natale nous était hostile, comme une mère dénaturée. L'échec était unique et définitif, irréparable. (p. 117)

> ('You see how they don't like us,' said Bissor with hopeless conviction.
> 'They' were the young Sicilians, the Arab police officer, the French newspaper proprietor, our fellow-students at the *lycée*, in short, the whole town. And it was true that our home town was hostile towards us, like an unnatural mother. The defeat was singular, definitive, and irreparable.)

More sinisterly, an apparently trivial incident involving an Arab and a Jew in the street can escalate into riots and the murder of other Jews (p. 289). Benillouche also details the insidious racism of the teachers, especially in the chapter 'Les Autres' ('The Others'), and explains that it was at the *lycée* that he actually began to suffer from experiences concerning his Jewish identity: 'parce qu'on m'obligeait à me demander qui j'étais' (p. 275) ('because I was forced to ask myself who I was'). His personal identity is therefore bound up with that of a community, a people, whether he likes it or not. And it is here that more is revealed of the workings of the mechanics of anti-Semitism, the insidious mechanism that turns Jews against themselves (an idea that will provide the powerful and ambiguous opening image of *Le Scorpion* and that Benillouche had already experienced at the holiday camp):

> Au lycée, par de continuelles remarques, on me suggéra l'image du juif idéal et, pour la découvrir en moi, je m'observais [...] Moi, fils d'artisan et pauvre, je défendais auprès des non-juifs les financiers et les commerçants, tâchant d'expliquer historiquement pourquoi certains juifs se livraient au commerce. Comme si le commerce non juif était plus avouable. Et condamnant le commerce juif, je l'attaquais auprès des juifs, plus violemment car plus ouvertement que les antisémites. (p. 275)

> (At the *lycée*, by continual remarks, the image of the quintessential Jew was suggested to me, and, to find out whether it was within me, I used to observe myself [...] I, son of a workman, and poor, used to defend financiers and traders to non-Jews, trying to explain historically why certain Jews dedicated themselves to trade. As if non-Jewish commerce was more respectable. And, condemning Jewish trade, I attacked it to Jews, more violently, because more openly, than did the anti-Semites.)

This 'racisme insidieux et raisonneur' ('insidious and reasoned racism') was tolerated by middle-class Jews – another source of difference between them and Benillouche. These rich Jews have been exposed to European culture for a generation or more, he explains, they have visited Europe and felt reassured by its proximity. For the Jews of the ghetto, there were certainly benefits, but they remained vulnerable, crowded together and easily identifiable. Benillouche admits that the gulf between the poor Jews and the Arabs was even greater, but differences within the Jewish population remain important (p. 279).[55]

Benillouche had already begun to question the price of his choice of Western philosophy when confronted by bloody reality. War will bring thinking about these personal problems to an abrupt end. The narrative moves towards its conclusion describing the open and murderous racism of Vichy anti-Semitism and German aggression, leading to the rounding up of Jews into camps in Tunisia or Germany. In what Benillouche sees as an ultimate betrayal by the West, young Jews are even refused by the Free French army. He takes up the terms that Camus used when writing about the Liberation and the Purge in France after the success of the Allied landings in 1944, 'victims and executioners', although Camus writes that we should not consent to be either, while at this point Memmi seems to think there is no choice but to be one or the other. Benillouche regrets his naivety and his lack of real political education when confronted by the historical events about to unfold, and feels full of remorse:

> Toute ma conduite a été impulsive. J'ai vécu cette période comme un imbécile moyen, étourdi par les fatigues et la faim, réagissant comme mon entourage immédiat, prêtant foi à n'importe quel racontar. Ou bien, plus simplement, parce que je n'ai pas perdu un bras ou une jambe au camp de travail, parce que je n'ai pas été embarqué pour l'enfer ou parce qu'on n'a pas arraché les ongles, je me sens débiteur envers mon siècle. Victime ou bourreau, l'époque l'exige. Je ne me sens pas assez victime, voilà pourquoi ma conscience reste torturée. (p. 292)

> (All my behaviour has been impulsive. I have lived through this period like an average imbecile, stunned by weariness and hunger, reacting like the people all around me, believing any piece of gossip. Or perhaps, more simply, because I have not lost an arm or a leg in a labour-camp, because I did not embark for hell or because I did not have my finger-nails torn out, I feel that I owe a debt to my era. Victim or executioner, the times demand one or the other. I don't feel I was enough of a victim: that is why my conscience is still tormented.)

When the anti-Semitic laws passed under Vichy are applied in Tunisia, Benillouche perceives this as both political and personal betrayal by the West:

> C'était la douloureuse, l'étonnante trahison, peut-être entrevue mais si brutalement confirmée, d'une civilisation en qui j'avais placé tous mes espoirs, à laquelle j'accordais toute mon ardente admiration. Brusquement,

l'idée complaisante que les Européens d'Europe étaient différents des Européens coloniaux s'effondrait. L'Europe toute entière se révélait injuste. Je fus d'autant plus blessé dans ma dignité que j'avais ouvert mon âme sans précaution, que j'aspirais moi-même à l'Europe. (p. 293)

(It was a painful, astonishing betrayal, perhaps glimpsed before but so brutally confirmed, by a civilisation in which I had placed all my hopes, for which I had felt total, ardent admiration. Suddenly, the comforting assumption that the Europeans of Europe were different from the colonising Europeans collapsed. The whole of Europe was seen to be unjust. I was the more wounded in my dignity, in that I had opened my soul without reserves, in that I myself had aspired to attain Europe.)

As the Germans arrive, the Jewish community is isolated and in serious danger. Benillouche thinks first to save himself through his contacts with the French administration. Not even Poinsot will help him (p. 300), and he abandons that idea, realising that as the rounding-up of the Jews becomes more insistent, saving himself would have only caused him shame. The Germans exempt from the camps those with poor health and the elderly, and Benillouche is confirmed as having a shadow on his lung. Another bitter realisation ensues, however, as the real reason for this diagnosis becomes clear to him, and it is one that once again plays into his non-acceptance of his status as 'honorary' middle-class:

Je compris, dans les bureaux, que si les bourgeois s'étaient attelés à la tâche, c'était d'abord pour se sauver et sauver leurs enfants. Les fils de riches occupaient tous des services auxiliaires: bureaux, ravitaillement, transports, infirmeries, services médicaux. On avait décidé d'épargner certaines catégories, par exemple, les intellectuels. Je bénéficiais de l'injuste fortune d'un groupe; ce n'était pas mon poumon qui m'avait sauvé, mais que je fusse étudiant. Je m'expliquai mieux la visite expéditive du médecin.
– Nous avons voulu sauver l'élite de la communauté, expliquait sans rire un notable. (p. 305)

(I understood, in those offices, that if the bourgeois had buckled down to the task in hand it was in the first place in order to save themselves and their own children. The children of rich parents were all employed in the auxiliary services: offices, food supplies, transport, clinics, medical services. It had been decided to spare certain categories, for example the intellectuals. I was profiting from the unjust luck of a group: it was not my lung that had saved me, but the fact that I was a student. I could understand the providential visit of the doctor better.
    'We chose to save the elite of the community,' a prominent figure explained without a smile.)

With pronounced irony Benillouche remarks that luckily almost all the intellectuals were middle-class; the elite was a mixture of intellectual and financial power: 'Or moi, je n'oubliais pas que j'étais un pauvre et n'acceptais pas l'équivoque' (p. 305) ('Now, for myself, I couldn't forget that I was one of the poor, and I would not accept this equivocation'). He decides to join the workers, the ordinary people in the labour camps. It is the final realisation of the solitude of his position. He goes to the camp willingly, but decides to escape when he realises his presence is useless, and that he is too far removed from the ordinary people:

> C'est au camp, dans cette vie quotidienne avec eux, que je réalisai l'étendue de mon éloignement, combien le lycée et mes études m'avaient rendu impossible une vie commune avec mon peuple. (p. 309)

> (It was in the camp, in that daily life with them, that I realised just how far I was from them, how the *lycée* and my studies had made a shared life with my people impossible for me.)

Memmi is already theorising the problematic of the relationship between the intellectual elite and the masses, aware of an issue that continues to be a source of debate in analysis of the postcolonial situation. Language again becomes an issue when he addresses a meeting in French and realises that he should have used his native *patois*, but his identity has become bound up with the French language. His place in the word, and increasingly his place in the world, is in this other language:

> Je pense en français et mes soliloques intérieurs sont depuis longtemps de langue française. Lorsqu'il m'arrive de me parler en patois, j'ai toujours l'impression bizarre, non d'utiliser une langue étrangère, mais d'entendre une partie obscure de moi-même, trop intime et périmée, oubliée jusqu'à l'étrangeté. Je n'ai pas le même malaise quand je m'adresse aux autres, comme si j'utilisais alors un outil indifférent. Mais je ne possédais pas assez de mots en judéo-arabe pour leur dire tout ce que j'avais préparé. (p. 314)

> (I think in French and my inner soliloquies have been in French for a long time. When I happen to speak to myself in *patois*, I always have the strange impression not of using a foreign language but of hearing a dark part of myself, too intimate, outdated, forgotten till it has become a stranger. I don't feel the same unease when I speak to other people, then it's as if I were using an indifferent tool. But I didn't have enough words in Judaeo-Arabic to say everything I had prepared.)

In stark circumstances Benillouche is brought up against the reality of his own situation concerning language, and that of those less educated than himself, situations that the colonial system has engendered. He can speak about everyday things in *patois*, but he has always used French for ideas and intellectual reasoning; his audience does not have the sophistication in French to understand fully what he wishes to communicate. He feels he is playing a role in the camp, and typically feels guilty, realising later that he went to the camp not only to help others, but to win their esteem and approval for himself (p. 318). It is the moment of the full realisation that he cannot be one of them. He regularly keeps a diary (which he later destroys), but feels he could never fully put down in writing that period;

he remembers certain horrific episodes, but says they have no place in his later life. Benillouche escapes and manages to remain hidden until the Germans are defeated. His health has been undermined and above all he has been thrown back onto himself: 'L'échec de ma naïve aventure, de ma recherche des autres, me ramenait à moi-même' (p. 342) ('The failure of my naïve adventure, my search for others, brought me back to myself'). He is forced to take stock of his life:

> Ainsi je ne pouvais plus détourner ma pensée de moi-même, de ce bilan de ma vie, qui s'imposait à moi, inévitable désormais. Jusqu'ici, toujours une tâche urgente détournait heureusement mon attention, qui ne s'arrêtait que par intermittence sur la signification de ma vie. Me voici emprisonné avec moi-même par la guerre et la maladie, sans diversion possible. Le pire de la maladie, je le découvris, est cette concentration de soi sur soi, cette tyrannie de soi-même. (p. 344)

> (Thus I could no longer turn my thoughts away from myself, from that stock-taking of my life which I was forced to undertake, which had long since become unavoidable. Up till that moment an urgent task had always, fortunately, distracted my attention, which only intermittently dwelt on the meaning of my life. There I was, imprisoned with myself by war and illness, with no possible distraction. The worst part of illness, I found, is that concentration of the self on the self, that tyranny of oneself.)

He returns to keeping his diary, but instead of looking outward to the world, it is turned solely on himself:

> Il avait été comme métaphysique, impersonnel, tournant avec passion autour du monde pour le comprendre. Je devins le seul centre de mes préoccupations. Qui suis-je enfin? Quels sont les résultats de cette longue lutte depuis l'Impasse? (p. 344)

> (It had been rather metaphysical, impersonal, concentrating passionately on the world to understand it. Now I became the one centre of my concerns. Who am I, finally? What are the results of my long fight ever since the *Impasse*?)

A full identity crisis is given form in a nightmare in which his mother forces him to look at another self laid out dead (p. 346), and the consequences of his position are revealed as the true source of his suffering in an image in which the symbol of the mirror returns: 'Je suis devant moi-même comme devant un miroir infidèle; l'étrangeté s'est glissé au cœur de ma vie' (p. 346) ('I stand in front of myself as though in front of a faulty mirror: strangeness has slipped into the heart of my life'). His friend Henry provides a refuge as Benillouche watches him paint, creation serving as an act of solace, and as Henry unveils his plans to go to Argentina, as an uncle of his had done, and make a fortune supplying goods and materials to a Europe devastated by the war. When Benillouche cannot join the Free French army, he feels refused for the second time by Europe; he realises he is only to be allowed to be the victim of that war, he cannot be among the conquerors (p. 352). He had excused Europe's first denial of him since the Vichy government was itself not recognised by much of the West, but this time there can be no doubt. He refuses the West, but he is in an impossible position: 'Je ne serai pas un Occidental. Je refuse l'Occident [...] J'avais refusé l'Orient et l'Occident me refusait' (pp. 352–53) ('I will not be a Westerner. I reject the West [...] I had rejected the East and the West was rejecting me').

The university begins to take back students and he returns to his old form of salvation, studying, but questions whether he can now become a philosophy teacher, a functionary of the system. The narration comes full circle and the reader realises more fully why the student at the beginning was unable to participate in the exam and felt compelled to write his life story instead. Benillouche is not allowed to take up his old post at the *lycée* because he resigned rather than being excluded because he was Jewish. Unable to finish the exam, he is once again brought face to face with himself. He has gone from rupture to rupture, been through illness and contemplated suicide, and he provides a résumé of the trajectory that has brought him to the edge of disaster:

> Cette fois le bilan est fait: rien, enfin, ne me cache à mes yeux. Avec l'Impasse, j'ai rompu, parce que ce n'était qu'un rêve d'enfance, avec mon père et ma mère et j'ai eu honte d'eux, avec les valeurs de la communauté parce qu'elles sont périmées, avec l'ambition et les bourgeois parce qu'ils sont injustes et d'idéal frelaté, avec la ville parce qu'elle vit au moyen âge et ne m'aime pas, avec l'Occident parce qu'il est menteur et égoïste. Et chaque fois s'écroulait une partie de moi. (p. 368)

> (This time the reckoning is made: nothing, finally, hides me from my own eyes. I broke with the *Impasse* because it was only a childhood dream, with my father and my mother, and I felt ashamed of them, with the values of the community because they are outworn, with ambition and the bourgeoisie because they are unjust and their ideals are artificial, with the town because it lives in the Middle Ages and dislikes me, with the West because it is untruthful and selfish. And each time, a part of myself was destroyed.)

The idea of death haunts him and he believes he must undergo the punishment of the novel's title, since he has dared to look back:

> je meurs pour m'être retourné sur moi-même. Il est interdit de se voir et j'ai fini de me connaître. Comme la femme de Loth, que Dieu changea en statue, puis-je encore vivre au-delà de mon regard? (p. 368)

> (I am dying for having turned back on myself. It is forbidden to see oneself, and I have come to know myself completely. Like Lot's wife, whom God turned into a statue, can I still live beyond my own look?)

Benillouche is not, however, condemned to remain fixed for eternity.

He moves on and the narrative moves forward to a 'departure'. He returns to see the family, gives the money he has earned as a worker to them, receiving their gratitude and his father's blessing. Ironically he now knows how easy it is to be an eldest son: 'rapporter de l'argent, endosser l'autorité qu'il confère. Même au prix de toute signification personnelle, de toute existence' (p. 372) ('bring home money, reinforce the authority it confers. Even at the cost of all one's personal significance, of one's very existence'). His relationship with his family is again reduced to a question of money. One final image is presented, proof that he can never totally reinvent himself, never totally escape the culture he grew up in, despite his decision to move on, to leave. Benillouche stays with Henry before they leave for Argentina, and he closes the door on his friend, who is writing in full moonlight. The old superstition of the moon sending men mad emerges automatically and he feels he will never be fully liberated, nor will he fully inhabit a new identity: 'Voilà mes libérations [...] Peut-on vivre avec cette défiance et ce refus de soi-même, ce doute continuel, pourtant si nécessaire?' (p. 373) ('So much for my liberations [...] Can one live with this defiance and rejection of oneself, this continual doubt, which is yet so necessary?'). He tells the family of his departure only the day before, and his final act is to destroy his diary. Benillouche has moved from 'Impasse' to 'Departure' (the title of the final chapter). However, it is *l'épreuve*, the 'testing' of the protagonist, that provides the underlying dynamics of the narrative.

Benillouche's life story endures, however, a testimony to the terrible power, simultaneously enabling and undermining, of his new relationship to the written word. In *Le Nomade immobile* Memmi is clear about the necessity of writing, and explicitly acknowledges the experience narrated in *La Statue de sel* as his own:

> L'épisode qui commence mon récit *La Statue de sel* est rigoureusement exact. C'est en racontant mon échec philosophique que je suis devenu écrivain. Je suis un éclopé de la philosophie, et sans doute l'écriture m'a-t-elle littéralement sauvé.[56]

> (The episode which begins my book *La Statue de sel* is rigorously truthful. It was while describing my failure as a philosopher that I became a writer. I am a casualty of philosophy, and, unquestionably, writing literally saved my life.)

La Statue de sel is a form of autobiographical discourse dealing with multiple experience of rupture and an ensuing identity crisis narrated in a more or less chronological and traditional narrative form, despite the use of *l'épreuve* as a framing device that affects the reading of the narrative, given that the reader is forced to link explicitly the beginning and the end of the text, and to 'back-track' as the protagonist has done. The coming to writing, the status of literature and its relationship to identity and lived experience will be developed in a more complex manner in the next text I wish to consider in detail, *Le Scorpion*.

THE SELF AS WRITER IN *LE SCORPION OU LA CONFESSION IMAGINAIRE*

> Projet approximatif donc, où l'on travaille autant par la bande que directe-
> ment; autant sur les manques que les certitudes. Mais qui n'est pas en vain.
> Je ne peux pas savoir *qui* je suis; par accumulations successives, je pourrais
> savoir *comment* je suis. Le portrait de l'artiste par lui-même ne saurait être
> qu'une composition de marqueterie, un puzzle à pièces multiples, qu'il faut
> patiemment assembler; même si certaines se sont perdues ou demeurent
> introuvables.
>
> Albert Memmi, Ce que je crois[57]

> (An undefined project, then, where one works in a roundabout way as much
> as directly; as much on the lacks as the certainties. But a project which is
> not in vain. I can't know *who* I am; by successive accumulations I could find
> out *how* I am. The portrait of the artist by himself can only be a piece of
> marquetry-work, a jigsaw-puzzle with many pieces which have to be
> patiently put together; even if some have got lost or cannot be found.)

Guy Dugas, among other critics, has already noted the explicit link between *La Statue de sel* and *Le Scorpion*, and also their very different dynamics, with sixteen years separating their publication. In the first a narrative is constructed around a series of ruptures that are then given an order, and in the second a proliferating narrative constructs a synthesis that nonetheless remains open-ended and always potential: 'Si le héros de *La Statue de sel* fait l'expérience d'un morcellement du Moi et de son inadéquation au monde environnant, ceux du *Scorpion* tentent celle de la difficile, mais nécessaire, synthèse'[58] ('If the hero of *La Statue de sel* experiences the breaking-up of the self and its non-adaptation to the surrounding world, those in *Le Scorpion* attempt the difficult but neces-sary experiment of synthesis').

   Le Scorpion ou la confession imaginaire was published in 1969 and although on some levels it does provide an explicit link with *La Statue de sel*, not least in many of its themes – the revolt against the father, the figures of the mother and the sister, the questions of identity and of origins, the aftermath of colonisation and decolonisation – it differs most obviously in structure and style. It has often been considered by critics to be a disconcerting text, one that is difficult to categorise, mixing together, as it does, fiction, essay, philosophical meditation, diary and autobiographical discourse, the latter not least in the inclusion of the name Memmi within the text. It also has explicit links to *Agar*, Memmi's second novel, in the theme of mixed marriage, pushed further here not only in the couple Emile–Marie, but in J.H. (usually identified by critics as signifying *Jeune Homme*, 'Young Man') and the wife he forces to convert. *La Statue de sel* and *Le Scorpion* are separated in time by the publication of four sociological studies: *Portrait du colonisé* (1957), *Portrait d'un Juif* (1962), *La Libération du Juif* (1966), and *L'Homme dominé* (1968). *Le Scorpion* is linked to the work on the question of Jewish identity through the image Memmi takes for its title, a symbol of the Jewish people: 'En vérité, nous voyons toujours resurgir le mythe négatif: la nature diabolique du Juif, comme celle du scorpion, le ferait agir contre lui-même'[59] ('In truth, we always see the negative myth being resurrected: the diabolical nature of the Jew, like that of the scorpion, making him attack himself'). The apparent suicide of the scorpion encircled by fire and by a group of onlookers provides the initial image of the text, suggesting an atmosphere of self-destruction (of the individual and of a people) that is nonetheless undermined by the end of the text in which the common interpretation of the behaviour of the scorpion is debunked as false. As several commentators have observed, the negative image of the beginning of the text is therefore retrieved as a positive one at its close. The initial scenario of self-destruction is overcome, but the question of suicide (also contemplated by the young Benillouche) hovers around the novel, in which Emile has disappeared (has perhaps committed suicide?), and in the course of which the story of another suicide, that of J.H., is recounted.

Whereas the first novel is largely chronological in development (although not wholly so, given the framing effect of the first and penultimate chapter, and the 'extemporality' of some of the chapters), *Le Scorpion* has a more radical open-endedness.[60] The use of multiple typefaces and a polyphonic structure suggest that this book shares many of the preoccupations of the French New Novel (despite Memmi's avowed dislike of its experimental work) – the difficulty of representing a unified subjectivity in language, the endless possibility of telling the same story in different ways, the impossibility of seizing the 'truth' of a situation or of a person, the unknowable aspects of human behaviour and of 'reality', and not least the self-consciousness that accompanies the act of writing. It is clear, however, that Memmi is developing a project that is quite distinct from the preoccupations of the New Novel, and he is conscious of the differences between himself and his French colleagues:

> Mes préoccupations esthétiques sont profondément différentes de celles de mes camarades français... Pour moi, l'histoire est encore à faire, les mots sont touts neufs... Moi, j'ai peur et je suis obligé de me battre sans cesse, et c'est cela ma littérature.[61]

> (My aesthetic concerns are profoundly different from those of my French colleagues... For me, history is still to be made, the words are all new... Myself, I'm afraid and I'm compelled to battle ceaselessly, and that is my literature.)

There is, then, a distinction between Memmi's approach to writing and that of Robbe-Grillet in, for example, his 'Sur quelques notions périmées' (1957), criticising, along with the use of character, form and content in the traditional novel, both *histoire* ('history' and 'story') and political commitment. Memmi does not have the luxury of treating history/story as an outdated concept, since his history, and that of all those excluded from the grand narratives of Western history, is still to be written and the act of writing it is necessarily a political one.

Le Scorpion is presented, through the choice of epigraphs, as being of ambiguous status, posed somewhere between Gide's authenticity ('je n'estime plus que les livres dont l'auteur a failli claquer' ['I no longer have any use for any book unless its author nearly died']) and Valéry's lies ('Qui se confesse ment, et fuit le véritable vrai' ['Whoever confesses lies, and flees the veritable truth']). The novel also resonates with the Sartrean problematic of human existence (already resonating in *La Statue de sel* with its repeated exploration of the relationship between self and other), as expressed in fictional form in *La Nausée*, a fundamental text generally for the post-Second World War generation of French writers, and again especially for the French New Novel. This questioning of the status of literature and its relationship to lived experience that manifests itself in other writers' work during this period as an interest in the technical and theoretical aspects of producing fiction, while undoubtedly retaining a metaphysical interest in human existence, is approached rather differently in Memmi's work. Here this concern with experimentation is a necessary part of his ongoing project of self-analysis and then the application on a wider level of his findings. His project is constructed around the quest for some underlying truth about himself and therefore about human nature and the functioning of human relationships, moving, as we have already seen, from the particular to the universal. It is here that the 'quest for truth' begun in *La Statue de sel* develops its full power. In that text, Benillouche exposes his own character flaws while exposing the systems of power, of money, of racism and of anti-Semitism that have dominated his childhood and adolescence. In *Le Scorpion*, the protagonists – who, it is possible to argue, all represent aspects of the author's self – constantly worry in varying degrees about questions of identity, of how to live with oneself and with others, of how to reconcile oneself with death, and indeed of how and why to write:

> Si un écrivain essayait de dire tout, dans un seul livre, ce livre serait-il celui de sa guérison, de sa réconciliation avec lui-même et avec les autres, avec la vie, ou cet effort lui serait-il funeste? (p. 65)
>
> (If a writer tried to say everything, in a single book, would it heal him, reconcile him to himself and to others, to life, or would the effort be fatal to him?)

The different typefaces used are the visual manifestations of the different types of discourse that make up this complex text: diary in small typeface, fiction larger, sometimes more widely spaced, quotations and poems in capitals, notes in small typeface, Marcel's commentary in italics. Memmi had wanted to use different colours to identify different types of discourse, and such a project is discussed by Emile with Oncle Makhlouf, seen here as the guardian of Jewish tradition, with Emile suggesting that the sacred texts should be demystified by using black for historical truths and other facts, pink for fiction and violet for all commentary. Jacqueline Arnaud is severe in her criticism of Memmi's idea, calling it 'a rather infantile desire'. This is rather missing the point. It is a serious analysis of the ways in which discourses purporting to be 'true', indeed the embodiment of 'truth' in the case of sacred texts, are in fact made up of fragments of many other sorts of text.[62] This analysis of the functioning of apparently 'authoritative' discourses is, of course, a major preoccupation of postcolonial theory, informed as it is by poststructuralist analysis and theories of deconstruction. This attention to discourse is another facet of Memmi's analysis of the functioning of power relations.

A further layer of discourse is introduced into the text by the inclusion of a set of illustrations: a medal or coin of some kind depicting Numidian horsemen, and with the name 'L. Memmi' engraved on it; an extract from the twenty-seventh *sura* of the Koran; a photograph of three women in traditional Bedouin dress whom we learn are the narrator's mother and her sisters, with a further layer of meaning introduced when the reader learns that the mother is actually pregnant with Emile (the photograph is therefore also an image of his own origins); a reproduction of a Hebrew text featuring a fish (a Jewish symbol of luck) and the protective Hand of Fatma (shared by Jewish and Arab traditions in North Africa), and identifiable as a *feuille de l'accouché*, a sheet brought for the birth of a son within the Kabbalistic practices of Jewish folklore, and therefore again a link to the origins of the individual; and finally a photograph of a scorpion, the image that gives its title to the text, and a symbol in the Middle Ages of the Jewish people.[63] Memmi has explained that drawings and photographs are used in his work not for illustrative purposes, but as *correspondances*:

> Heureusement, j'ai pu introduire [...] des dessins et des photographies, qui ne doivent pas jouer le rôle habituel d'illustrations, mais de correspondances. Il ne s'agit pas de reproduire des objets extérieurs, mais de suggérer encore le même état intérieur, comme essaie de le faire une image poétique.[64]

> (Fortunately, I was able to include [...] drawings and photographs, not to perform the usual role of serving as illustrations, but as correspondences. The idea was not to reproduce external objects but to suggest the same inner state once again, just as a poetic image aims to do.)

Memmi seems to be suggesting here that the illustration functions as a *correspondance* in the Baudelairean conception as the form given to a sensation, just as in the creation of a poetic image, an embodiment of an abstract experience. It is therefore as much a part of the 'fabric' of the text as a whole as the written word, not an adjunct, or above all not merely illustrative. These visual images serve also as a material manifestation of cultural memory, a link between past and present, especially the past of a community that has disappeared.

This inclusion of the visual into a verbal discourse raises questions concerning the nature and value of the written word and of the ways in which a text is elaborated. It also raises questions around one of the central themes of the text, the tension between what is 'real' and what is 'fabricated', and this is especially true of the inclusion of photographs. As Guy Dugas writes:

> Au sein de la trame discursive, où le réel est constamment remis en cause, l'illustration peut, par son apparence d'irréfutabilité, apparaître comme un arbitre ou un enjeu: parce qu'elle procède d'une mécanique, la photographie impose l'idée que c'est le réel même qui s'exprime à travers elle, non une quelconque de ses représentations.[65]

> (At the heart of the interweaving of discourse, where what is real is constantly being questioned, an illustration may, because of its air of irrefutable evidence, seem like an arbiter, or one of the issues at stake: because it proceeds from something mechanical, a photograph imposes the idea that it is actual reality which is being expressed through it, and not just any of its representations.)

How do the verbal and the visual interact? And what layers of meaning does the visual add to the textual dimension, especially in a text in which a concern with the visual, through the use of various typefaces, is apparent? The inclusion of a visual dimension alerts the reader to the materiality of the written text, to the fabrication of the object that is the literary text; and it is apparent that one of the aims of Memmi in *Le Scorpion* is to draw the reader's attention to the self-conscious process of writing, once again a perception shared with the French New Novelists.

The first of the 'illustrations' included is the medal or coin that may hold the proof of a Roman origin for the name 'Memmi'. This search for the origins of the name is another explicit link to *La Statue de sel*, with both Benillouche and Emile believing that they have found an ancestor, El Mammi, among the followers of the legendary Berber queen and heroine, Al Kahina, who resisted the Arab invasion of North Africa and united Christians, Jews and Berbers against the enemy, and is often invoked as a symbol of Berber identity. El Mammi will become the hero of Memmi's next novel, *Le Désert*. This question of the name (and we should recall Feraoun's treatment of this here) and the search for confirmation of an identity through the analysis of origins is the first main theme I shall consider here.[66] The second main theme that will be analysed here is that of the status of literature and the possibility or impossibility of salvation through literature (again an issue explored, in a different way, by Feraoun).

The structure of *Le Scorpion* is framed by an established literary device, that of 'found papers' in the writer Imilio's drawer, *la cave* ('the cellar') as it is referred to in a metaphorical image resonating with connotations of that which is 'below', or 'underneath' – a place whose contents have possibly been forgotten; it is material that has been placed out of sight and that may hide secrets; it is also a place of potential lost treasures. The writer of the papers is referred to as both Imilio and Emile, adding another layer of uncertain identities in a text in which these proliferate. The use of 'found papers' is a device that inescapably brings to mind, in the context of modern French literature, the 'found diary' of Roquentin in *La Nausée*, which charts not only the protagonist's identity crisis (and the discovery of the contingent nature of man's presence in the world) but also Roquentin's realisation of the impossibility of telling the life of another (and by implication the impossibility of finding an order in which to narrate one's own life). The device also calls to mind, of course, the text found in Fouroulou Menrad's drawer.

In *Le Scorpion* it is Imilio's (Emile's) brother Marcel who has the task of putting some kind of order into the diverse fragments that Emile continued to throw into the drawer. Marcel begins his task as a sceptic concerning literature, '*lit-té-ra-ture*' (p. 13), and he feels at a loss when confronted with the task: '*moi, je n'en connais pas les règles; je ne sais pas faire les livres'* (p. 13) ('I don't know the rules, I don't know how to make books'). He asks himself a question that immediately alerts the reader to questions concerning the status of different types of written accounts and, by implication, to the possibility and impossibility of knowing self, other and 'reality': '*Comment distinguer quoi que ce soit dans ce fouillis? Qu'est-ce qui appartient au roman, au Journal, et au reste?*' (p. 14) ('How can I make out anything at all in this tangled heap? What belongs to the novel, the Journal, and the rest?').

The reader is therefore placed in an active role with Marcel, who, as the text develops, comments both on the fictions contained there and on the diary, agreeing with or contradicting what he is reading. An author's note at the end of the text explains, as I have previously noted, that Memmi had wanted to have different colours for the type, but has had to make do with different fonts: 'Nous comptons sur le lecteur pour un effort complémentaire d'imagination; ce sera sa part dans cette œuvre commune' ('We rely on the reader to make an additional effort of imagination. That will be his contribution to this joint work'). This insistence on the need for an active and collaborative reader again suggests an analogy with the concerns of the French New Novel. However, Memmi's thinking on the nature of the self of the writer is a primary concern for him from the 1950s onwards, and is especially apparent in the experimental form of *Le Scorpion*, some thirty years before the 'new autobiography' produced in France during the 1980s. This was the point at which several of the New Novelists turned their concerns from the status, function and effects of fiction to thinking about questions of shifting identity, multi-faceted perceptions of reality and the production and reception of the written word in relation to autobiographical discourse.[67]

In the section entitled 'La Cave', the method that will be followed throughout the text is established. Marcel reads Emile's work and then comments on it: in this case, since it is a childhood memory, he remarks that he does not share this same feeling about the periodic clearing out of the cellar in the *Impasse Tarfoune* (named as in *La Statue de sel*) by their father. He remains puzzled by the status of such a piece of writing:

> *Allons, Narcisse, revenons à notre puzzle: ou placer un tel texte? Journal ou roman? Aucun rapport avec le pauvre Scorpion en tout cas. Alors Journal? Mais pourquoi Imilio rappelle-t-il ce souvenir d'enfance? A propos de quoi? Peut-être le mieux est-il d'avancer sans chercher d'abord à comprendre. Des lignes de force finiront bien par apparaître d'elles-mêmes: si elles existent!*
> (p. 18)

> (Come on, Narcissus, let's get back to our puzzle: where does this passage belong? With the Journal, or with the novel? Nothing to do with the poor

Scorpion, in any case. The Journal, then? But why is Imilio bringing up this childhood memory? In connection with what? Maybe the best thing to do at first is just to go ahead without looking for any explanations. After a while the guidelines will begin to stand out: if there are any!)

Emile's first concern does indeed seem to be with childhood and the family; he recounts the move from living by the sea, in *La Goulette*, to the *Impasse*, the place that has developed such importance in the topology of Memmi's work:

> Et me voici de nouveau à l'Impasse, à laquelle décidément je reviens sans cesse. Que pourrais-je en dire encore, que je n'aie pas déjà raconté maintes fois, ouvertement ou sous déguisements divers? Que pourrais-je encore découvrir que je ne sache déjà? Arrêtons donc là; je n'étais pas parti pour me raconter moi-même, une fois de plus, mais pour monter bien au-delà, à L'HISTOIRE DE NOTRE FAMILLE. (p. 24; capitals in the text)

> (And here I am in the *Impasse* again. I certainly keep coming back to it. What can I find to say about it now, that I haven't already told many times, openly or disguised in different ways? What can I find out now that I don't already know? Let's stop here; my intention was not to tell about myself all over again, but to go back much further, to THE HISTORY OF OUR FAMILY.)

There follows a discussion of *la médaille*, the medallion or coin referred to also in *La Statue de sel*, reproduced as an illustration in the original edition of *Le Scorpion* and sent to the narrator by the administrator of the Bibliothèque du souk El-Attarine (as described by Memmi in *Le Nomade immobile* and referred to earlier in this chapter). The name engraved on it is very clearly 'MEMMI' (capitals in the text). On one side is a crowned Numidian horseman, suggesting a prince or a hero; on the other, two horsemen standing by their mounts, with the inscription 'L. MEMMI' (probably Lucius Memmi, Emile concludes, p. 27; see also the earlier remarks on this in *Le Nomade immobile*). In the following section, 'Histoire de notre famille', Emile has researched this possible Judaeo-Berber and Roman ancestry, again as referred to in *La Statue de sel*. Memmi returns to these possibilities in *Le Nomade immobile*, and traces a link between the two. Very importantly, Marcel makes a connection between the history of his family and that of the country in which his family lives:

> Que le lecteur me pardonne tous ces détails et cette rigueur, qui exigent de lui une attention soutenue. Mais l'exactitude est ici la seule garantie de la vérité contre les écarts de l'imagination. Et je ne l'aurais pas ennuyé, si l'histoire et le problème de ma famille ne se confondaient pas avec les avatars de ce malheureux pays; et si cette complexité n'était pas la complexité même de notre histoire commune. (p. 32)

> (I hope the reader will pardon me for all these details and all the exactness,

which require him to pay very close attention. But exactness in this case is the only way of defending truth against flights of imagination. I wouldn't have bothered him with this if it weren't that the history and problem of my family are bound up with the ups and downs of this unhappy country and that this complexity is the complexity of our common history itself.)

In addition to the uncovering of personal origins, the concern for cultural memory and collective past, and for preserving that past from erasure, is again apparent.

As in all of Memmi's work, there is an insistence on the importance of the particular for a more general situation. Marcel's commentary reveals his frustration with Emile's 'method', and he criticises above all the 'truth' both of his description of the family and of this research into their ancestry, objecting that this traces only the paternal line – what, he asks, of the heritage of their mother, whose name was Sarfati, meaning 'Le Français', or perhaps more generally 'the Westerner'? (Again, Memmi also discusses this in *Le Nomade immobile*, as we have previously seen.) For Marcel it is the present that matters, and the fact is that although the Jews may have been in North Africa before the Arabs, the Arabs are now the majority and the Jews must live with them (p. 36). He is also concerned about the use of the family name in a 'novel', less on grounds of indiscretion than for aesthetic reasons:

> *Mais arrêtons-là. Je ne veux pas entrer dans le jeu d'Emile. A quoi rime tout cela! S'agit-il d'une reconstruction d'éléments réels, ou d'une pure rêverie? Et, de toute manière, il n'a tout de même pas l'intention de se servir de notre nom, tel quel dans un roman! Non que cela me scandalise (un peu si) mais cela en diminuerait le caractère fictif. Ce qui serait une erreur, non? Je suppose qu'il avait l'intention de transposer après. A quoi aurait servi alors toute cette érudition, tant de précisions, de références minutieuses? A moins qu'elles ne soient déjà en partie imaginaires, comme pour le Palais? Enfin, où en voulait venir Emile?* (p. 37)

> (Enough. I don't want to get caught up in Emile's game. What's the point of it all? Is it a reconstruction using real elements, or merely daydreaming? Anyhow, he certainly doesn't mean to use our name, just as it is, in a novel! Not that that shocks me (well, it does a little), but it would make the book less fictional, and that would be a mistake, wouldn't it? I suppose he meant to transpose afterwards. Then what would have been the good of all this erudition, so many details, so many careful references? Unless they were partly imaginary, like the Palace? What was Emile getting at, exactly?)

All the questions that could be raised by the experienced reader of fiction are set out here, and they are the questions that haunt both contemporary fiction and autobiographical discourse. What is the role of imagination in reconstructing a life, as both Emile and Marcel are doing here as autobiography, biography and fiction collide? It would seem that

the truth can only be found in the multiplying of possibilities, 'par accu-
mulations successives' (as described by Memmi in the quotation used at
the beginning of this section), and that the (re)construction of a life
without the intervention of the imagination is impossible.

The next section moves, with the 'Histoire de Bina', into another
form, and one that Marcel more readily recognises as fiction and where
he feels more at ease, although his uncertainty persists as he remains
caught between these different types of discourse:

> *Allons bon, qui est ce docteur-là? Qui est Bina? Et son père et Baïsa et
> Ghozala? En un sens pourtant, je préfère ça: sans conteste, nous sommes,
> cette fois, dans la fiction. Mais, le rapport avec* Le Scorpion? *Quelle idée,
> Imilio, de jeter pêle-mêle dans ce même tiroir tout ce que tu écris! [...] En
> tout cas, moi, maintenant, je suis perdu entre les fragments du Journal, les
> chapitres du récit (et j'espère qu'il n'y en ait pas deux!), les notations tech-
> niques, des coupures de journaux soigneusement découpées et datées...* (pp.
> 42–43)

> (All right now, who is this doctor? Who is this Bina? And his father, and
> Baïsa, and Ghozala? But in a way I prefer this because this time, no doubt
> about it, we're dealing with fiction. But, what's the connection with *The
> Scorpion*? Ah, Imilio, whatever made you throw everything you wrote into
> the same drawer pell-mell! [...] Anyhow, I'm lost now, what with the frag-
> ments from his Journal, the chapters from the story (I only hope there aren't
> two stories), the notes, newspaper clippings that are carefully cut out and
> dated...)

The next section is in capital letters, and Marcel recognises it as a
quotation from Rousseau concerning his own existence as an outsider
(*étranger*) and the ways in which 'TOUTE SA CONDUITE, TOUTE
SON ŒUVRE S'EXPLIQUENT PAR CECI' (p. 43, in capitals in the text)
('EVERY ASPECT OF HIS BEHAVIOUR, EVERY PART OF HIS
WORK CAN BE EXPLAINED BY THIS ONE THING'). Marcel knows
that Emile is fascinated by Rousseau, and his next commentary holds all
the keys of Memmi's knowing uses of multiple discourses. In spite of the
fact that Marcel feels at this point that he does not hold the key to the
text, the commentary is in fact setting up a reading strategy and this
reveals the aim of the entire writing project:

> *Bon; aucun rapport avec* Le Scorpion *évidemment: avec le Journal? ce n'est
> même pas sûr; une note de lecture plutôt, une réflexion?*
> *Faire un troisième tas? A moins que (hypothèse farfelue), à moins que
> ces différents textes ne soient tout de même pas indépendants. Je veux dire
> qu'ils soient déjà destinés, sitôt jetés sur le papier, à entrer dans un dessein
> unique, plus général. Sinon, pourquoi cette note ici? Le hasard? Et les
> coupures de journaux? Simple plaisir de collectionner? Soit; mais toute
> collection a un sens, pourquoi ces coupures et pas d'autres?*
> *Hypothèse farfelue, et surtout embarrassante; car, alors, il n'y aurait ni
> fiction, ni Journal, ni document, mais une seule intention complexe. Ce serait*

pire; comment ordonner ces feuilles sans connaître cette intention, sans moyen de se retrouver à l'intérieur même de ces textes? En somme, plus que jamais: sans une clef, indispensable et perdue? (p. 44)

(OK. Nothing to do with *The Scorpion* obviously. The Journal? Not for certain. A reading note then? a meditation?

Make a third pile? Unless – crazy idea – unless all these different pieces are not really independent. By that I mean that they were already intended, as they were put down on paper, to be part of one overall plan. Otherwise, then what would this note be doing here? Just chance? And the clippings? Just for the pleasure of collecting them? Fine; but there's a point to every collection. Why these clippings and not others?

It's a crazy idea, and an awkward one too, because in that case, there'd be neither fiction nor Journal nor document but instead, one complex intention. That would be worse. How can I put these pages in order? I'd have to know what his intention was, so as to move right inside what he's written. In other words, I have to have a key, and the key is lost.)

'One complex intention' could be a summary of the whole of Memmi's project; and if we cannot 'move right inside what he's written', and if we do not also look inside ourselves as we read, we are not fulfilling the implied role of the reader, not only of Memmi's texts, but any of the autobiographical discourses under analysis here.

The following section seems to fuse together both diary and fiction. The father, mother and Marcel are described, as is the beating by the father of the sister, Kalla, for having a lover, and her subsequent descent into madness. However, the narrator of this section gives himself the name of the protagonist of *La Statue de sel*: 'Pauvre Alexandre Mordekhaï Benillouche' (p. 47). Marcel's commentary is a refutation of the description given of him and a different version of the sister's madness (she was beaten by the father, although he himself was not a witness in person, being away at university). The proliferation of names is also bewildering for him, although he is relieved that Emile has given up using the name Memmi here:

Quelle est cette 'scène du hammam'? Et d'ailleurs qui est Kalla? Je ne l'ai pas relevé jusqu'ici parce que je croyais qu'il parlait de Marguerite [...] C'est vexant pour le romantisme amoureux, mais Kalla (qui ne s'appelle pas Kalla, comme A. M. Benillouche n'est pas Imilio – et je note avec plaisir qu'il aban-donne enfin les Memmi), Kalla-Marguerite, donc, s'est soumise, sagement, a été mariée, fort bien, à un garçon très convenable... (p. 54)

(What is this 'scene in the hammam'? For that matter, who is Kalla? I didn't notice it up until now because I thought he was talking about Marguerite [...] It may not please the romantics, but the fact is that Kalla (whose name is not Kalla, just as A. M. Benillouche is not Imilio; and I'm glad to see he's finally given up the Memmis), Kalla-Marguerite, that is, quite obediently agreed to be married, very well, to a perfectly acceptable man...)

There are a complex set of subjectivities present in the text: on one level the writer Imilio/Emile; his brother Marcel and provider of the commentaries; the old, wise Oncle Makhlouf; and J.H., a former student of Emile who will return to challenge his teacher. There are then a further series of characters present in the fragments of fiction whose stories are sometimes told and retold under other names and in different ways, notably in the 'Histoire de Bina' (for example, the beating of Kalla, who Emile says is his sister, called Marguerite by Marcel, is the same story told by the character of Bina, this time about a sister called Noucha). There are various mother figures represented, notably in the section devoted to 'Notre mère' (including the reference to the photograph of the mother in old age that recurs in several of Memmi's texts), and there are other important female characters: Ghozala loved by Bina; Kakoucha, Bina's first fiancée; Kalla/Noucha/Marguerite; Marie/Marie-Suzanne. And finally there is the reappearance of Alexandre Mordekhaï Benillouche, as we have seen. Bina questions the authenticity of his own story-telling as he recounts the story of Kakoucha:

> Oh, ce n'est pas une vraie histoire, Docteur, ce n'est peut-être pas une histoire du tout; seulement, jusqu'aujourd'hui, je ne me souviens pas si cela est arrivé ou non. J'ai raconté, après, cette histoire à Kakoucha, elle m'a dit que j'avais tout inventé [...] Et si j'ai inventé cette histoire, pourquoi l'aurais-je inventé? Peux-tu me l'expliquer, Docteur? (pp. 118–19)

> (Oh, it's not a true story, Doctor. Maybe it's not even a story at all [...] Only I still can't remember even now whether that really happened or not. Afterwards I told Kakoucha this story and she told me I'd made up the whole thing [...] And supposing I did make up this story, why would I do that? Doctor, can you explain that to me?)

However, this complexity and the multiple retelling of dramas continue to be a source of frustration for Marcel, who prefers more scientific forms of analysis:

> *La littérature ne peut-elle donc être une entreprise de santé, au lieu de recenser les drames, y compris les drames imaginaires? Et dans ce cas aussi, l'objectivité scientifique (sans guillemets!) est la seule attitude raisonnable, la seule efficace aussi, je le crois.* (p. 55)

> (Can't literature be a healthy undertaking, instead of wallowing in tragedy, including imaginary ones? In this case as well, scientific objectivity (without quotes around it!) is the only reasonable attitude; the only effective one too, I think.)

After a particularly intricate section that intermingles two sizes of font (small, usually reserved for the diary; larger, used for the fictional parts), Marcel criticises literature for not describing the reality of the world and of human existence as it is lived:

> *A quoi joues-tu maintenant, Imilio? Vas-tu intervenir dans Le Scorpion?*
> *'Qatoussa... je l'ai réellement connu', qui est Je? De quelle réalité s'agit-il?*
>   *Cela dit, j'aime assez. Je me suis toujours demandé pourquoi les*
> *écrivains scotomisaient toute une partie de la vie, la plus importante peut-*
> *être: la salive par exemple, ça existe!* (p. 85)

> (What game are you playing now, Imilio? Are you going to step into *The*
> *Scorpion?* 'I really knew Qatoussa.' Who is I? Which reality is this?
>   Apart from that, I quite like it. I've always wondered why writers turn
> a blind eye to one whole part of life, possibly the most important part at
> that. Take saliva, for instance: it does exist!)

What is interesting here, however, is that Marcel's commentaries become
more than criticism or correction of Emile's writing or version of events.
He begins to reveal his own likes and dislikes, writing more about himself,
bringing into being his own life story, his own 'confession':

> *Les odeurs: je n'ai jamais osé avouer à personne que j'aime les odeurs, oui,*
> *toutes; même celles qu'on qualifie de mauvaises, elles ne me dérangent pas,*
> *au contraire elles m'intéressent; oui c'est cela, elles provoquent ma curiosité.*
> (p. 85)

> (Take smells, now. I've never dared tell that I like smells – yes, all of them,
> even the ones that are called bad; they don't bother me; on the contrary,
> they interest me. Yes, that's it, they arouse my curiosity.)

Despite the fact that he adds that he should be worrying more about
what is happening around him in the 'real world' (*'Bon. Mêlons-nous de
nos affaires. Je ne suis pas un écrivain et nos affaires ne sont pas bril-
lantes'* [p. 86] ['OK, let's mind our own affairs. I'm not a writer and our
own affairs are not so good']), he continues to add to his own written
account. It is in Marcel's 'story' that the context of the aftermath of
Tunisian independence (in 1957) becomes apparent and a more political
agenda is outlined in the text through Marcel's experiences and observations:

> *Niel est donc 'remis à la disposition du gouvernement français'; Dubuisson*
> *a rédigé une pétition qu'il fait circuler. Je la signerai, malgré les conseils de*
> *prudence de certains; je n'en parlerai à Marie-Suzanne. Je trouve cette*
> *mesure absurde et révoltante [...] Il [Niel] est maintenant étranger; c'est*
> *également cela la fin de la colonisation, et je l'ai souhaitée moi aussi [...]*
> *C'est insensé de se détester ainsi de techniciens précieux pour tirer des*
> *conséquences formelles de l'indépendance.* (p. 96)

> (So Niel has been 'placed at the disposition of the French Government'.
> Dubuisson has written a petition and passed it around. I'll sign it, despite
> advice from some people to act prudently. I won't tell Marie-Suzanne about
> it. I find it a ridiculous and revolting measure to have taken, though [...]
> Now he's a foreigner. That's also part of the end of colonisation, and I
> wanted it too [...] It's madness to get rid of valuable technicians that way
> just so as to follow independence strictly to the letter.)

A further insight into the effects of colonisation appears in another aspect of Marcel's story, that of the question of schooling for his son and whether he will be able to get a place in the French *lycée*, or indeed whether he should go along with the education programme of the country and go to an Arabic school (p. 191). His own identification with his country is also put into question when he attends a meeting where everyone else is wearing a *chechia* or fez; he is not, and it is remarked on:

> *D'ailleurs, encore un effort: puisque je veux tout comprendre et tout le monde: la chéchia n'est pas seulement un symbole réligieux, mais plutôt un signe de reconnaissance nationale. Si je veux rester ici et m'intégrer à cette nation, pourquoi ne porterais-je pas une, en effet? Mzali n'y mettait peut-être pas, consciemment au moins, de nuance ironique: il me voyait peut-être encore Chef de Service? Mais comment me verrais-je, moi, avec une chéchia?* (p. 193)

> (In fact, there's another effort to be made, since I do want to understand everything and everyone. The *chechia* is not just a religious symbol; it is more of a sign of national gratitude. If I want to stay here and fit into this nation, why shouldn't I wear one too? Maybe Mzali wasn't being the least bit ironic, at least not deliberately. Maybe he still saw me as head of a department? But then, how could I see myself with a *chechia*?)

Marcel tells more and more of his own story – how he decided to become a doctor, his own relationship with the father (pp. 162–63) – and he begins to understand what writing can do: '*Je me suis encore mépris: l'entreprise d'Imilio est peut-être une entreprise de santé*' (p. 164) ('I've been mistaken again. Perhaps, in the long run, what Imilio is undertaking is an effort to restore health').

Emile's notes reveal another insight, although a troubled one, into the narrative 'method' adopted here and included in the notes for the 'portrait' of Oncle Makhlouf (in a continuation of a quotation previously used):

> Si un écrivain essayait de dire tout, dans un seul livre, ce livre serait-il celui de sa guérison, de sa réconciliation avec lui-même et les autres, avec la vie, ou cet effort serait-il funeste? Insupportable aux autres et à lui-même? Ou trouverait-il enfin la paix? Et alors que vaudrait cette paix?
> SI DE TEMPS EN TEMPS NOUS RENCONTRONS DES PAGES QUI FONT EXPLOSION, DES PAGES QUI DÉCHIRENT ET MEURTRIS-SENT, QUI ARRACHENT DES GÉMISSEMENTS, DES LARMES ET DES MALÉDICTIONS, SACHEZ QU'ELLES VIENNENT D'UN HOMME ACCULÉ AU MUR, UN HOMME DONT LES MOTS CONSTITUENT LA SEULE DÉFENSE. S'IL Y AVAIT UN HOMME AU MONDE QUI OSÂT DIRE TOUT CE QU'IL A PU PENSER DE CE MONDE, IL NE LUI RESTERAIT PAS UN POUCE CARRÉ DE TERRAIN POUR S'Y TENIR. (pp. 65–66; capitals in the text)

> (If a writer tried to say everything, in a single book, would it heal him, reconcile him to himself and to others, to life, or would the effort be fatal to him?

Intolerable to others and to himself? Or would he find peace at last? And if so, what would that peace be worth?

IF NOW AND THEN WE ENCOUNTER PAGES THAT EXPLODE, PAGES THAT WOUND AND SEAR, THAT WRING GROANS AND TEARS AND CURSES, KNOW THAT THEY COME FROM A MAN WITH HIS BACK AGAINST THE WALL, A MAN WHOSE ONLY DEFENSES LEFT ARE HIS WORDS. IF THERE WERE A MAN WHO DARED TO SAY ALL THAT HE THOUGHT OF THIS WORLD, THERE WOULD NOT BE LEFT HIM A SQUARE FOOT OF GROUND TO STAND ON.)

Is writing a healing activity or a life-threatening enterprise? Does it render relations with others better or worse? What, finally, is the status of literature and the role of the writer?

After discussions with Oncle Makhlouf (a sufferer from poor vision – a recurrent feature of Memmi's work – who will not allow himself to be treated[68]), during which Emile first raises the notion of different colours for different types of text, we are told that he has made a series of notes that again pose the problem of truth, and above all the *'degrés de vérité'* ('degrees of truth'; italics in text, p. 69) in different types of discourse: 'Comment exprimer ces degrés et ces différences dans un langage commun? Comment passer d'une sagesse à l'autre? Toujours: nécessité d'une clef' (p. 69) ('How can these degrees and these differences be expressed in a common language? How can we go from one wisdom to another? There is always the need to have a key'). In a further discussion with Oncle Makhlouf, ostensibly on the sacred texts and their commentaries, the question of the value of the commentaries and the problem of contradiction suggests a preoccupation on the part of Emile that has potential consequences for all written texts, as I have already noted, and indeed for all commentary and criticism:

> il arrive tout de même que des auteurs se contredisent, que tel commentaire soit contradictoire avec tel autre!
> – La contradiction est en toi: c'est que tu n'as pas une vue de l'ensemble.
> – Soit: supposons qu'il n'y ait pas de contradiction fondamentale. Tout de même: un commentaire n'a pas la même valeur que le texte premier! Un commentaire de commentaire n'a pas la même valeur que le commentaire lui-même. (p. 127)

> ('But, even so, authors do contradict each other sometimes, one commentary can contradict what another one says!'
> 'The contradiction is within yourself. It comes from your not having a view of the whole.'
> 'All right. Let's say there isn't any fundamental contradiction. Even so, a commentary hasn't the same value as the original text! A commentary on a commentary hasn't the same value as the commentary itself!')

Makhlouf's counter-argument revolves around the notion of a fundamental unity in the sacred texts. It is impossible to reconcile all of this only if unity is forgotten:

> La Parole comprend déjà tout ce que tu développes. C'est dans le développement que les détails semblent étrangers les uns aux autres. Toi, tu te dis: de commentaire en commentaire, de commentaire de commentaire en commentaire de commentaire, où est l'essentiel, où est la broderie? Mauvaise manière de voir, dangereuse même: tu finis par te demander où est le texte, où sont les commentaires. Tu finis par douter du texte. Mauvais. Pernicieux. Rappelle-toi: tout est développement d'un même texte. Où alors veux-tu que je te dise? Même ce texte est un commentaire.
> – Alors là! Si le texte principal lui-même n'est qu'un commentaire, comment être sûr de quoi que ce soit? (p. 127)

> ('The Word already includes everything you develop. It is in the process of development that the details seem strangers to one another. You ask yourself: from commentary to commentary, from commentary on a commentary to commentary on a commentary – which is the essential, which is the embroidery? A bad way of looking at things, a dangerous way even: you end up wondering which is the text and which are the commentaries. You end up doubting the text. Bad. Pernicious. Remember: everything is a development of a single text. And shall I tell you something? Even that text is a commentary.'
> 'Ah, now that won't do! If the principal text itself is only a commentary, then how can you be sure of anything at all?')

The underlying anxiety about attaining truth is revealed. If the original text itself is a commentary, where does the origin of the word, and of truth itself, lie?

The discussions with the uncle continue at intervals, and Emile's notes reveal his problem in distinguishing between chronicle and fiction in reading, this time in the sacred texts of the story of Jonah:

> Ce n'est évidemment pas une *Chronique* puisqu'il s'agit de faits à venir, qui ne sont pas encore vrais. Ce sont si peu, encore, des faits réels que Jonas refuse d'obéir [...] Est-ce alors une fiction? Pas du tout puisque, malgré sa volonté, le prophète sera obligé d'aller à Ninive. (p. 167)

> (Obviously, this is not a Chronicle since these are facts that are yet to come; they're not true yet. In fact they are so far from being true facts as yet that Jonah refuses to obey [...] Is it fiction then? No, not at all, because the prophet will be obliged to go to Nineveh against his will.)

Marcel also perceives a double logic behind Emile's inquiry into distinguishing between different levels of discourse with his colour codes for chronicles (black), the *Haggada*, imagination/fiction (pink), and the *Halakha*, commentary (violet, although different colours would be needed for the nuances of these).[69] Emile is categorising not only these discourses but also his own, and Marcel realises that the system has implications for reading all texts:

> *Comment n'ai-je pas vu cela plus tôt! Comment n'ai-je pas deviné ce qu'Emile cherchait au-delà de cette démonstration à l'oncle? Car, évidemment, il ne s'agit pas de persuader seulement l'oncle, il ne s'agit pas seulement de Haggada et de Halakha. C'est un code, valable aussi pour Emile lui-même.* (p. 169)

> (Why didn't I realize that earlier? Why didn't I guess what Emile was getting at, above and beyond that demonstration to Uncle? Now it's clear that he wasn't just trying to persuade Uncle, and it wasn't just the *Haggadah* and the *Halakha* that were involved. The whole thing is a code that's valid for Emile too.)

The idea had already crossed his mind and he had wondered why Emile changed the colour of his ink so often; now he is sure that the use of different colours has a meaning. Marcel now enjoys the game, and yet there is a further complication – Emile wins the argument with the uncle only in his imagination, therefore in the pink of fiction? He begins to apply the system to Emile's texts – Bina's story is *'rose, naturellement'* ('pink, of course'; p. 177) – and then also to everything he reads, and he realises how complex any text is, composed of many different levels of discourse. It is not merely a game: *'un article de journal, un discours d'homme politique, demanderaient un arc-en-ciel, à l'intérieur d'une même page. Quelle démystification!'* (pp. 177–78) ('a newspaper article, a politician's speech, all on the same page – it would take a rainbow. What a demystification!').[70] It is the same kind of analysis that *Le Scorpion* itself requires, an analysis that is allied to the theories of discourse pursued by Foucault and Derrida, and subsequently by postcolonial theory. In addition to the levels of discourse contained within it, there are many intertextual references to other texts written by Memmi, most explicitly to *Agar*, in the form of the blue-eyed blonde Frenchwoman of whom Emile says: 'J'ai déjà raconté si souvent ma vie avec Marie […] et principalement dans *L'Etrangère*, même si, naturellement, j'ai été amené à mêler le réel et le fictif, afin mieux de suggèrer la vérité au lecteur' (p. 144) ('I have already written about my life with Marie so many times […] chiefly in *The Foreign Woman*, even though I did mix reality and fiction, of course, so as to convey truth better').[71] This is an important introspective section and one in which Memmi implicitly draws himself and Emile together. Emile also uses his personal experience to think more generally about human relationships: 'J'ai même essayé d'en tirer des conclusions philosophiques dans un long chapitre de mon "Traité sur le mariage, la misère du couple et la misère de l'homme seul"' (p. 144) ('I even tried to draw the philosophical conclusions of it in a long chapter in my *Treatise on Marriage, Misfortunes of the Married Couple, and Woes of the Single Man*'). He wishes to dissipate misunderstandings around this question of the couple although he recognises the discretion of critics: 'comme s'ils avaient deviné qu'ils touchaient ici à l'un des centres nerveux de ma vie et de mon œuvre' (p. 144) ('they seem to have guessed that this was one of the nerve-centers of my work and my whole life'). The return to Tunisia with a wife is told again in a different version from that used in *Agar* (pp. 147–48). Emile also hints at a 'revelation' he had the first time he visited his wife's native region, which he will talk about more later, he tells the reader (p. 145). This is a type of self-analysis pursued through the analysis of the relationship with another human being: 'Puisqu'elle représentait l'un des pôles les plus éloignés de moi-même et qu'il me fallait pourtant retenir avec force, sous peine de voir, par rupture d'équilibre, tout l'ensemble se pulvériser' (p. 149) ('since she represented one of the remotest poles of my own being and yet I had to hold onto it by force. Because otherwise the whole edifice would lose its balance and crumble into ruin'). The Frenchwoman of course also represents, as in *Agar*, the culture of the coloniser, which Emile envies not least because he sees the coloniser as belonging to one language, one culture, a culture that is universally admired, as opposed to those who live in 'l'éparpillement, le doute, la détresse historiques' ('historical fragmentation, doubt and distress'). Although his wife is clearly not like other colonisers since by marrying him she becomes 'suspect' in the eyes of her own people (p. 150), he is now aware enough to realise that the origins of his own turmoil are internal: 'Le désordre était en moi. Marie ne faisait que le représenter' (p. 153) ('The disorder was within myself; Marie merely represented it'), even though he claims to detest this type of psychology in literature. Here Emile makes a statement of the type that recurs throughout Memmi's work:

> A la fin de ma vie, toutes les pierres seront mises à leur place, dans leur ordre vrai, et l'on apercevra enfin l'ensemble. L'on verra à quel point il n'y a aucun jeu dans aucune partie de mon œuvre. (p. 154)

> (At the end of my life, all the stones will be put into place, in their true order, and finally the whole edifice will be apparent. Then people will see just how carefully every part of it is fitted into the rest; nothing loose anywhere.)

There is a pun here on the word *jeu*, meaning indeed that nothing is 'loose' in the sense of a construction, but also that there is no *jeu* in the sense of a 'game'.

This note irritates Marcel, who had begun to feel close to his brother as he read his writings, and he wonders why there is this feeling of defensiveness in his statements: '*Pourquoi tant de protestations que tu ne joues pas? Qui te le reproche?*' (p. 154) ('Why do you keep insisting you're not playing? Who's accusing you?). Yet this is also the project of *Le Nomade immobile* as Memmi makes clear the unity and indeed the ethics of his life-project.

There are also less explicit textual references to other works in the fictional universe created by Memmi: in the profession of Bina's, Benillouche's and indeed Memmi's father, the leather artisan; or in the conflict with the father and the departure for Argentina with Henri (Henry in *La Statue de sel*); or in a visit to Marrou in Paris (when Emile also describes his disappointment in the France that had been so bound up with his own identity). There are also precise autobiographical references to which Memmi will return, for example the meeting with Gide, which is also recounted in *Le Nomade immobile*, and which here forms part of Marcel's own commentary, made up of his own memories and of those of Emile:

> Peut-être suis-je injuste avec Imilio, peut-être que je continue à ne rien comprendre à la littérature et aux écrivains. Me revient en mémoire le mot d'André Gide, que m'a rapporté Emile lui-même. Tout content de recevoir à sa table son illustre confrère, il avait fait des prodiges pour lui trouver du raisin en plein hiver. A sa stupéfaction Gide refusa même d'en goûter; il n'aimait pas le raisin. 'Je croyais que vous l'adoriez, vous l'avez décrit si magnifiquement!... – Oui, je l'aime beaucoup: en littérature', répondit Gide. (p. 95)

> (Maybe I'm not being fair to Imilio; maybe I still don't understand anything about writing and writers. I recall the anecdote about André Gide that Emile told me himself. Delighted to welcome his illustrious fellow author at his dinner-table, Emile had gone to an enormous amount of trouble to find him grapes in the middle of winter. To his dismay, Gide refused even to taste them: he didn't like grapes. 'I thought you adored grapes, you've described them so magnificently.' 'Oh, I like them very much – in literature,' answered Gide.)

This is a revelatory anecdote about the relationship of the writer to the world, and to the world he or she creates in language. In *Le Nomade immobile* Memmi is even more explicit about the meaning of this encounter and its implications for the relationship between reality and literature:

> Il ne s'agit pas de réalisme, quelle que soit la part prise dans le réel. L'écrivain (profane ou sacré!) est en partie un fabulateur. Une rencontre avec André Gide m'en a administré une preuve inoubliable. Il avait été retenu à Tunis par l'arrivée inopinée des troupes allemandes. A la fin d'un repas chez les Amrouche, le maître de maison offrit son hôte prestigieux une magnifique grappe de raisin, très difficile à trouver alors parce que les Allemands les raflaient tout. Gide y prit juste un grain.
> – Je croyais, s'étonna Jean Amrouche, que vous aimiez beaucoup le raisin, dans *Les Nourritures terrestres*…
> – Je l'aime beaucoup, en effet, répondit Gide impassible, ses yeux de Mongol à moitié fermés: mais en littérature.[72]

(It's not about realism, whatever part it takes in reality. The writer (profane or sacred!) is partly a story-teller. An encounter with André Gide demonstrated this to me unforgettably. He had been held back in Tunis by the unexpected arrival of the German troops. At the end of a meal with the Amrouches, the master of the house offered his renowned guest a magnificent bunch of grapes, very difficult to find at that time because the Germans were taking everything. Gide took just one grape.

'I thought,' said Jean Amrouche, astonished, 'that you liked grapes very much – in *The Fruits of the Earth*...'

'I like them very much indeed,' replied Gide impassively, his Mongol eyes half-closed; 'but in literature.'

It is the understanding to which Marcel must come concerning the functioning of literature, and the understanding at which we as readers, not only of this complex text but of all Memmi's work, must arrive if we are to become competent readers of such a continuous and involved project. Slowly, Marcel becomes just such a competent reader, more alert to the hidden connections in the text. After reading some more of the 'Histoire de Bina', he writes:

> *Voilà donc l'origine du récit de la folie prétendue de Kalla-Marguerite.*
> *La poire et la poudre: allusion, je suppose, à la 'Poudre Legras' et à la petite poire d'insufflation, utilisée par notre père en effet, et par tous les asthmatiques.*
> *Nulle part, jusqu'ici je n'ai vu que le père de Bina était asthmatique. Notre père, oui.* (p. 143)[73]

(So that's where the story of the so-called madness of Kalla-Marguerite comes from.

The spraying bulb and the powder – I suppose this is an allusion to the Poudre Legras and the little insufflation bulb that our father uses (the way anyone with asthma does.)

Nowhere until now had I noticed that Bina's father had asthma. Our father does.)

Yet each time Marcel thinks he is beginning to see a method in Emile's construction, another possibility presents itself. After reading a section on the mother, he becomes confused:

> *En vérité, je me demande maintenant si tout cela a la moindre importance, si le désordre apparent ne vient pas de ce que j'ignore la règle du jeu – du Jeu! – la règle de vie plutôt, l'effort méthodique, oui méthodique, d'Emile pour ordonner ses pensées, comme si ce désordre était l'ordre même voulu par mon frère.* (p. 183)

(To tell the truth, I'm beginning to wonder if any of that matters at all; maybe what seems to be disorderliness really comes from the fact that I don't know the rules of the game, the Game, rules of life, really – Emile's methodical attempt (yes, I mean methodical) to put his thoughts in order. Maybe this disorder is the order that my brother wanted.)

On the other hand, he believes he is coming to a better understanding of Emile himself, '*par-delà de l'affabulation*' ('beyond the story-telling'); even though the question of how we can ever really know another person remains: '*Je prenais notre mère pour une marionnette, il la prenait pour une sorcière. Qui avait raison? Qui est notre mère?*' (p. 186) ('I took our mother for a puppet, and he took her for a witch. Which of us was right? Who is our mother?').

Marcel is by profession an ophthalmologist and questions of seeing, of blindness, representing the more abstract notions of lucidity and of moral blindness, haunt the text as Emile writes:[74]

> Il m'arrive de me réveiller en sursaut et de chercher dans l'obscurité absolue n'importe quel point lumineux, et comme mes yeux, encore tournés vers l'intérieur, sont inhabiles pour quelques secondes à récolter cette miette de lumière rassurante, je m'affole, me redresse sur mon lit: je suis aveugle! (p. 48)

> (Sometimes I wake up suddenly and look for some source of light, in the total darkness, anywhere, anything, and for a few seconds, my eyes are still gazing inward and unable to gather that reassuring little scrap of light. I panic, I sit bolt upright on my bed: I'm blind!)

The importance of looking and the image of the mirror provide the most recurrent metaphors for this text, and appear in Memmi's other works, as has previously been noted with reference to *La Statue de sel*. Indeed the epigraph to the set of interviews in *La Terre intérieure* cites Koestler's 'Tiens ton miroir propre' ('Keep your mirror clean'). All of this imagery is used in a knowing, almost ironic manner by the writer: when Marcel reads of his brother's thoughts on the symptoms of blindness he says he is experiencing, he questions the use of the terms: '*Emile: qu'est-ce que c'est que ce "brouillard"? Parle-t-il en clair ou symboliquement?*' (p. 73) ('Emile, what's this business about a "slight haze"? Does it really mean just that or is it symbolic?'). The almost blind Oncle Makhlouf provides yet another symbolic slant on the question of physical and spiritual blindness. Marcel sees his duty as curing physical blindness, while the old Jewish man has found an internal wisdom and is at peace with himself despite the loss of his sight.

Emile tackles the fundamental question of his existence in a number of discourses and writing styles, spinning endless possibilities in order to arrive at the truth.[75] Marcel is presented as the man of science who questions Emile's versions of events and who is at first hostile to the work of fiction; he is the representative of scientific analysis, of a different methodology, rather like Memmi the novelist and Memmi the sociologist teasing out the mechanisms of human interactions with different approaches to the same underlying preoccupations. In the end, they come together:

Seules nos réponses ont semblé différer quelque temps. Emile a espéré, tenté une intégration par l'imaginaire, je l'ai crue possible dans l'action; mais nous vivons le même drame. Je relirai tout, une fois de plus, pour mieux dialoguer avec toi, pour mieux me comprendre. (p. 266)

(It was only our ways of responding that seemed to differ for a while. Emile hoped he would integrate through the imagination and tried to do it, while I thought it was possible only through action, but we were both experiencing the same dramatic situation. I am going to reread it all once more so as to converse with you better and understand myself better.)

As Corinne Nolin has observed,

à force de le dérober au regard, le texte ne fait que mieux exhiber ce qu'il prétend masquer: Emile/Imilio, Bina et Marcel ne font qu'un, tout comme Kalla-Noucha-Marguerite ne sont qu'une seule et même personne. Comment expliquer autrement que Bina surgisse dans la 'Confession d'Emile' et y invoque sa sœur [...] Kalla, et non Noucha, sinon parce que Bina est un produit du dédoublement de l'écrivain.[76]

(by dint of hiding it from view the text exhibits all the more clearly what it aims to mask: Emile/Imilio, Bina and Marcel are all one person, just as Kalla-Noucha-Marguerite are just one and the same person. Otherwise how could you explain the fact that Bina comes up in 'Emile's Confession' and there refers to his sister [...] Kalla, and not Noucha, unless Bina doubles for the writer.)

This 'integration' through the power of the writerly imagination is a fundamental question for all autobiographical discourses, and here Memmi gets to grips with some of the most difficult problems of self-hood and of the activity of writing that selfhood. After the anger and disillusionment in the face of the impossibility of the situation in *La Statue de sel*, in which the protagonist notably abandons writing his diary, and for whom the life story recounted in 'L'épreuve' seems to be a one-off exorcism that will allow him to move on, *Le Scorpion* obsessively attempts to find unity through the amassing of fragments and through the open-endedness of the experience of writing. There is no one solution; but a solution may be found in contradiction, in ambiguity, in the sheer proliferation of the possibilities of a life. The 'unknowability' of the self is to be celebrated, not feared, for it is in this that its truth is to be found.[77]

Yet the pitiless, relentlessly logical questioning of J.H. cuts away another level of the enterprise with the precision of a scalpel as he takes his former teacher to task for not following through his own political stance, and he sees the writer's *Ecrits politiques* ('Political Writings') as worthless (a reference no doubt to Memmi's own political texts, such as *Portrait du colonisé*). The relentless stance taken by J.H. also makes Emile question the status of literature: 'OU LA LITTÉRATURE EST

UNE EXPLORATION DES LIMITES, OU ELLE N'A PAS PLUS D'IM-
PORTANCE QUE L'ART FLORAL' (p. 236) ('EITHER LITERATURE
IS AN EXPLORATION OF LIMITS, OR IT IS NO MORE IMPOR-
TANT THAN THE ART OF ARRANGING FLOWERS'). The
subjectivities become ever more complex as J.H. reveals that he had a
'revelation' when visiting his wife's home (p. 202; an experience that
Emile had claimed earlier); and that he has had a crisis in front of the
mirror that has undermined his whole being:

> J'étais devenu un énigme pour moi-même [...] ce qui me stupéfiait main-
> tenant que je me suis réveillé, était comment je n'avais pas vu cela avant,
> comment je n'avais pas vu plus tôt le hasard de ma vie, de ma personne, l'ex-
> traordinaire fragilité de la construction. (p. 205)

> (I had become a riddle to myself [...] What I found unbelievable, now that
> I had awakened, was that I had been able to live that way for such a long
> time and hadn't seen it earlier, hadn't felt what a fluke my life and my person
> were and how extraordinarily flimsy the whole construction was.)

The crisis deepens and Emile sees in J.H. a double: 'Décidément,
c'était mon double; mon double lucide et méchant' (p. 213) ('There was
no denying that he was my double, a cruel and lucid double'). J.H. quotes
his teacher's own teachings back to him:

> Vous vouliez, à chaque instant, je vous cite: AVOIR LA CONSCIENCE LA
> PLUS AIGUË DE SOI-MEME ET SA PLACE DANS LE MONDE [...] Vous,
> vous vouliez un inventaire réel, objectif, contrôlé, sans illusions sur soi et le
> monde. (pp. 214–15)

> (At every instant you wanted, and I quote – TO HAVE THE MOST ACUTE
> AWARENESS OF ONESELF AND OF ONE'S PLACE IN THE WORLD
> [...] What you wanted was a genuine, objective, double-checked stock-
> taking, without illusions about oneself or the world.)

Emile recognises the danger in this double: 'Oui, c'était mon double, le
double de ce que je fus; seulement, ce jeune homme veut aller au bout de
ma pensée, jusqu'au bout de moi-même' (p. 217) ('Yes, this young man
is my double, or the double of what I once was, except that he wants to
get to the very bottom of my line of thought, the very bottom of myself,
in fact'). J.H. accuses his former teacher of not following through his
thinking on colonisation to its ultimate and logical conclusions:

> Vous avez décrit avec un juste lyrisme la colère des victimes. Leur décou-
> verte de la violence, comme une lumière irrésistible et empoisonnée. Vous
> avez affirmé que la violence était alors inévitable et légitime. La colonisa-
> tion, par exemple, appelle la violence, parce qu'elle est elle-même violence
> et que rien ne vient à bout de la violence qu'une violence plus forte. Soit.
>   Mais pourquoi vous êtes-vous arrêté là? Pourquoi n'avez-vous pas dit,
> ce qui est toute votre pensée, déployée, allant jusqu'au bout d'elle-même?
> Que la violence est partout? Parce que l'oppression est partout et parce que

tout pouvoir est oppressif? Celui de victimes comme celui des bourreaux. (pp. 223)

(In a deservedly lyrical way, you have described the anger of the victims and their discovery of violence as an irresistible and poisonous light. You have maintained that at that point, violence was inevitable and legitimate. Colonisation, for instance, stirs violence, because it is violence itself, and nothing but greater violence can put an end to violence. All right.

But why did you stop there? Why didn't you tell us everything you were thinking, the full extent of it, as far as you could go? Why didn't you say, violence is everywhere? Because oppression is everywhere and all power is oppressive? The victims' power and their executioners' power.)

In this analysis of violence, Emile is forced to question himself and his actions and involvement: he was never tortured, nor did he use violence himself, but he has been involved in political action, solicited since publication of his *Ecrits politiques* to add his name to manifestos, petitions and so on, which he has done, and has been flattered by it (p. 227). The predicament of the formerly colonised intellectual is forcefully made apparent.

All Emile's works are part of his attempt to come to terms with himself:

Même pour des actes littéraires, ces textes, qui m'ont valu cette réputation de générosité et d'engagement, n'étaient d'abord que des efforts pour mettre de l'ordre en moi-même, et pour me retrouver dans le monde chaotique et cruel des hommes. (p. 228)

(Even on literary grounds, these passages, which brought me a reputation for generosity and commitment, were originally nothing more than efforts to put things in order within myself and situate myself in the cruel and chaotic world of men.)

We read that he had (naively) thought the results of this research were for himself only, and did not realise why friends told him to be careful, until he realised that copies of his books were seized every day in prisons. J.H. is an even more virulent critic of the events after independence, as those who had struggled against the French found themselves in opposition to the new government, impatient as they were for more and faster reform, and suffering for that opposition. Indeed, like Algeria (although without the violent war), after independence Tunisia became a one-party state, with Bourguiba as president and the Neo-Destour party as sole political party (formed in 1934 by Bourguiba and others and becoming the Destourian Socialist Party in 1964). There were to be outbreaks of civil unrest in the 1970s and 1980s (therefore after *Le Scorpion* was published) in protest at the government's refusal to introduce social reform policies.[78]

To return to the narrative of *Le Scorpion*, Emile had thought he would find salvation in literature:

> C'est vrai que j'avais cru découvrir ma solution dans la littérature, et c'est vrai que j'avais ainsi esquivé les questions les plus terrifiantes. Pourquoi suis-je ce que je suis? Pourquoi ce monde? Pourquoi vivre? Pourquoi cette femme et pas une autre? Pourquoi faire des enfants? (p. 238)

> (It's true that I had thought literature would be my solution and it is also true that that's the way I managed to dodge the most terrifying questions – like, why am I what I am? Why this world? Why live? Why this woman and not another? Why have children?)

What is he to reply to the young man who has come to him because as his former teacher he helped him to formulate those same questions? At this point Emile despairs of his own project:

> Il aurait fallu que je réussisse mon LIVRE NECESSAIRE.
>   *Le Scorpion* était évidemment infaisable, ni fait ni à faire; pour le réussir, ce livre, il aurait fallu que je conduise correctement ma vie. Il aurait fallu que ma vie, elle-même soit réussie, qu'elle comprenne une unité, au moins sous-jacente, qui en relie les morceaux; or quelle est-elle? Quelle en est la leçon? Sinon cet échec total, cette dispersion, et cette constante anxiété? J'entrevois maintenant seulement que toute mon œuvre publiée n'est que l'incessant commentaire d'une œuvre à venir; avec l'espoir insensé que ce commentaire puisse finir par constituer lui-même cette œuvre. (p. 238)

> (I'd have had to succeed in doing my own ESSENTIAL BOOK.
>   Clearly, *The Scorpion* was undo-able, neither done nor yet to be done. In order to do it successfully, I'd have had to make a success of leading my life. My life itself would have to be a success, would have had to comprise at least an underlying unity linking the pieces together. But, in fact, what is my life? What is the lesson it teaches? Total failure, dispersion, and constant anxiety. Only now do I sense that all of my published work is just an unending commentary on a work to come – in the insane hope that in the end the commentary itself would constitute the work.)

Yet Marcel comes to an understanding and appreciation of Emile's project, and he protests that the book *has* been written and that the project of Emile's work and of his life *is* a success. He even doubts whether these conversations ever took place, even though he knows that J.H. was one of Emile's best students and that he did commit suicide: '*Mais si, ton livre est fait! Il a son unité; et ta vie aussi: c'est l'ensemble, c'est à la fois, Le Scorpion, le Journal, les collages, peut-être même, pardonne-moi, mes propres commentaires*' (p. 239) ('But your book is done! and it does have unity, and so does your life – it's the whole, everything all at once, *The Scorpion*, the Journal, the collages, and maybe even (forgive me) my own commentaries'). Marcel also comes to a further understanding of himself and is able to make the decision to leave the country as he becomes more and more disillusioned with the consequences of decolonisation that leave the country without the French and the Jews. Marcel succeeds in coming to know himself better, in keeping his marriage together, and in leaving Tunisia, the act which is arguably the real crisis that generates the text. *Le Scorpion* allows Marcel to move on, away from the country of his birth, and to accept the consequences of his actions. Marcel also writes a section, not as a commentary at the end of a piece by Emile as had been the pattern throughout, but his own narrative of his illness, an abscess in his throat (again an illness recounted by Memmi in *Le Nomade immobile*), and his acceptance of his position, his 'double truth', his double exile:

> *CE PAYS HORS DUQUEL N'IMPORTE OU JE SERAIS EN EXIL. (Ai-je lu ça chez Emile? Ou est-ce de moi? De toute manière, si les papiers d'Emile paraissaient un jour, je serais expliqué du même coup.) CE PAYS DANS LEQUEL JE N'AI JAMAIS CESSE D'ETRE EN EXIL.* (p. 263)

> (THIS COUNTRY OUTSIDE WHICH, NO MATTER WHERE, I WILL BE IN EXILE. (Did I read that in something of Emile's? Or did I say that myself? In all events, if Emile's papers were to be published one day, I would be explained at the same time.) THIS COUNTRY INSIDE WHICH I HAVE NEVER CEASED TO BE IN EXILE.)

In *Le Scorpion*, Memmi seems to be preoccupied with the status of his whole enterprise – literary, sociological, personal, political – and its possible value. On the one hand literature is 'healthy', on the other it is futile, merely decorative; his sociopolitical work reveals the mechanisms of human power relationships, but does not change anything in the real political system. Emile's work is at once necessary and meaningless. His analyses have helped him and others to understand better their place in the world; but he is still unsure of any real changes. In the work of literature, he continually constructs and deconstructs, he can never be still and at ease. Literature and life are indissociable, as Tahar Bekri has noted with reference to Memmi: 'La distance fictive voulue par l'auteur entre son récit, fût-il singulier et stylisé, et l'œuvre autobiographique, serait une volonté déployée pour mieux réussir le regard sur soi'.[79] ('The fictional distance willed by the author between his narrative, however singular and stylised it was, and his autobiographical writing, was a decision he took in order to enable him to see himself better').

This attention to form is essential to the literary enterprise and to the enterprise of living as best one can, since it allows 'controlled confession' and an ordering of the world and of a life:

> Et nous voici devant cette autre exigence du métier d'écrire: le lancinant souci de la forme. Plaidoyer, séduction, jeu ne sont pas possibles que par le respect de certaines règles. La mise en forme est l'ensemble des règles qui, dans tout art, visent à la plus grande efficacité. La littérature est un mélange

> de contrainte et de liberté [...] La littérature n'est pas seulement un docu-
> ment, c'est un document mis en forme [...] La mise en forme a un double
> dessein: elle permet une confession contrôlée et, en même temps, une mise
> en ordre de soi et du monde. Elle permet aussi de rendre compte de l'émer-
> veillement devant les êtres et les choses. [80]

> (And here we come to the other demand of the writer's task: the persistent
> concern for form. Pleas, persuasion, games, are only possible through
> respecting certain rules. Giving writing a form means the whole set of rules
> which, as in all arts, aim at the greatest effectiveness. Literature is a combi-
> nation of constraint and freedom [...] Literature is not just a document, it
> is a document which has been given form [...] The giving of form has a
> double purpose: it enables the writer to make a controlled confession and,
> at the same time, to put himself and the world in order. It also enables a
> realisation of the sense of wonder at beings and things.)

There is another *exigence du métier*, the attempt to live with oneself and
with others, and this raises the literary enterprise above any charges of
'game-playing'. Memmi refers to Michel Leiris's description of the risks
and dangers of writing:

> Pour moi, la littérature n'est pas seulement un jeu – ou alors ce serait un jeu
> dramatique –, c'est une tentative de répondre à la difficulté de vivre avec soi-
> même et avec les autres. L'artiste qui se contente de jouer laisse, me
> semble-t-il, ses lecteurs sur leur faim. Michel Leiris comparait l'écriture à la
> tauromachie; je dirais volontiers que, pour moi, l'écriture est une tauro-
> machie où je suis à la fois matador et taureau.[81]

> (For me, literature is not only a game – or then it would be a dramatic game
> – , it's an attempt to respond to the difficulty of living with oneself and with
> others. The artist who is content merely to play, it seems to me, leaves his
> readers unsatisfied. Michel Leiris compares writing to bull-fighting. I'd
> certainly say that for me, writing is a bull-fight in which I am both bull-
> fighter and bull.)

Literature is more than a game, it is a potentially fatal undertaking.
Memmi has also said that his whole life has been a battle: a battle to be
a writer, to master a language and finally to become a philosopher – yet
another attempt to order the world.[82] Philosophy is for him above all
'une sagesse fondée sur les savoirs: l'art de conduire sa vie le plus
raisonnablement possible'[83] ('a kind of wisdom founded on knowledge;
the art of living one's life as reasonably as possible'). Memmi attempts
to remain constantly on guard against pride and self-obsession,
conscious that he has built a whole body of work on his own experience.
In the epilogue to *Le Nomade immobile*, he gives a description of his
personal working environment and of two images he keeps close to him,
both of which resonate with the concerns of *Le Scorpion*, the redemp-
tive nature of confession (and of publication) and the narcissistic nature
of writing:

> Pour me rappeler en permanence la précarité du savoir et les niaiseries de l'orgueil, qui sont souvent complémentaires, j'ai épinglé au-dessus de mon bureau deux petits tableaux. Le premier est un dessin humoristique, où un candidat au suicide, ayant rédigé une confession, s'avise qu'elle est publiable: laissant là son désespoir, il va la porter à un éditeur. Le second est une gravure plus ancienne, non signée, qui représente un homme de lettres se couronnant lui-même devant un dessin sous-titré 'Moi'.[84]

> (To remind me permanently of the precariousness of knowledge and the stupidity of pride, which are often complementary, I've pinned two little pictures above my desk. The first is a cartoon where a prospective suicide, having written a confession, realises that it is publishable: forgetting about his despair he rushes to a publisher with it. The second is an older, unsigned print showing a man of letters crowning himself before a picture captioned 'Myself'.)

At the end of such a life project, is the writer/philosopher finally able to find satisfaction in his life that raises him above despair and narcissism? Is the exercise of autobiography, a writing project generated from the multiple concerns and experiences of the individual, finally a form of the 'salvation' that it promised?

> Suis-je parvenu enfin à la sérénité, qui est l'antichambre du bonheur? On ne guérit jamais complètement de son enfance, mais j'arrive de mieux en mieux à faire bon ménage avec mes souvenirs […] Ainsi j'ai presque fini par me persuader que j'ai assez payé pour avoir le droit de me réjouir du temps qui reste. Apprendre pour cela à me pardonner […] J'ai suffisamment payé pour n'avoir pas été, comme mes parents, définitivement pauvre, malade chronique, battu en me résignant à l'être. J'ai fini par admettre que toutes les insondables misères du monde n'ont rien à voir avec le droit que j'ai de vivre mon unique vie.[85]

> (Have I finally arrived at a state of serenity, the antechamber of happiness? One is never completely healed of one's childhood, but I am managing progressively better to live with my memories […] So I've almost convinced myself that I have paid enough to have the right to enjoy the time that's left. And hence to learn to forgive myself […] I've paid enough for not having been, like my parents, permanently poor, chronically ill, beaten by resigning myself to be beaten. I've finally admitted that all the unfathomable misfortunes in the world have nothing to do with my own right to live my unique life.)

In this epilogue to a life's work Memmi seems to suggest that the former poor Jew, former colonised subject, uneasy intellectual, part of a minority all his life, has come to an acceptance of all the facets of his identity, even though this state remains tentative and seems more a truce than a reconciliation. Born only seven years after Feraoun, but living a much longer life, Memmi forged a position as an intellectual and an academic in France.[86] Throughout the writing of *Le Scorpion*, Memmi kept a diary (unpublished) that adds another layer to his life-writing

project in general and to the textual elaboration of this narrative in particular. He notes the temptation to revert to the more simple linear narrative
of *La Statue de sel*, but knows that '[avec] cette technique complexe, je
pourrai provoquer des émotions plus complexes, plus fines, plus
nuancées, qu'avec le récit linéaire' (27 August 1967) ('[with] this complex
technique I will be able to provoke more complex, delicate, nuanced
emotions than with a linear narrative'). On 28 September he returns to
the problem of the complexity of the project: 'Le danger dans une
construction aussi complexe, de cette distribution sur plusieurs plans, est
de ne rien creuser, de n'aller pas assez loin dans aucune direction... à
moins que la richesse, la diversité des aperçus y supplée?'[87] ('The danger
of such a complex construction, of this spreading over several layers, is
of not digging deep anywhere, of not going far enough in any direction...
unless the richness, the diversity of the perceptions supplies this need?').

Le Scorpion is indeed a complex construction and yet the 'Essential
Book' is written and a synthesis is given to lived experience. The problems of identity, of belonging and not belonging, of exile and of finding
a place in the postcolonial world appear to find resolution – indeed some
kind of salvation – in the act of writing.

Abdelkébir Khatibi: The Deciphering of Memory and the Potential of Postcolonial Identity

Si nous acceptons l'idée d'une identité qui n'est plus fixité au passé, nous pourrions aboutir à une conception plus juste, celle d'une identité qui est en devenir, c'est-à-dire qu'elle est un héritage de traces, de mots, de traditions, se transformant avec le temps qui nous est donné à vivre, avec les uns et les autres. Car, un homme qui ne survit que grâce à son passé lumineux est comme un mort pétrifié, un mort qui n'aurait jamais en quelque sorte, vécu.

Ainsi l'identité ne se définit pas par une structure éternelle, mais, d'après notre propos, elle est régie par des relations dissymétriques entre le temps, l'espace et la culture structurant la vie d'un groupe, d'une ethnie, d'une société, traduction du mouvement de l'être et de sa flexibilité, de son adaptation aux événements, à sa propre énergie de renouvellement.

Abdelkébir Khatibi, 'Le Métissage culturel', Manifeste[1]

(If we accept the idea of an identity which is no longer rigidly anchored in the past, we might arrive at a more just concept: that of an identity which is in the process of becoming. In other words, it is a legacy of signs, words and traditions, which is being transformed through our own allotted lifespan, through different people. Because a man who only survives thanks to his glorious past is like a petrified dead body, a dead person who had in a way never actually lived.

Thus, according to this notion, identity is not defined by some eternal structure, but is ruled by asymmetrical relationships between the time, the space and the culture which build up the life of a group of people, an ethnic group, or a society, translating the entity's movement, its flexibility, its adaptability to events, into its own energy for renewal.)

Celui qui écrit a à découvrir, à explorer différents lieux de langage et qui lui sont trop voilés par le secret de son métier. L'écriture: *initiation* à un secret illisible.

Abdelkébir Khatibi, 'Une psychanalyse personnelle',
Par-dessus l'épaule[2]

(A person who writes has to discover, to explore different sites of language, sites which are too well hidden from him by the secrets of his craft. Writing is an *initiation* into an unreadable secret.)

Abdelkébir Khatibi was born in El Jadida, Morocco in 1938 and therefore belongs to the generation of writers that followed the founding texts of postcolonial writing in French that I have previously considered by

Mouloud Feraoun and Albert Memmi. In addition to novels and literary criticism, his creative works include plays, *La Mort des artistes* ('The Death of the Artists', 1964) and *Le Prophète voilé* ('The Veiled Prophet', 1979), and poetry, such as *Le Lutteur de classe à la manière taoiste* ('The Class Warrior in the Taoist Way', 1976), *De la mille et troisième nuit* ('The Thousand and Third Night', 1980) and *Dédicace à l'année qui vient* ('Dedication to the Coming Year', 1986). He attended both Koranic and French schools in Morocco, and carried out undergraduate and post-graduate study in Paris in the late 1950s and early 1960s. He worked on his doctorate, 'Le roman maghrébin d'expression arabe et française depuis 1945' ('The North African Novel in Arabic and French since 1945', 1965), under the supervision of Albert Memmi, and this was published in book form in 1968 as *Le Roman maghrébin* ('The Novel in North Africa'). He had also previously been a co-editor of an anthology of Maghrebi literature in French.[3] This early research into Maghrebi literature partly addressed the question of how the work of the politically committed writer is to avoid becoming propaganda, especially in what we would now term a postcolonial context.[4] He participated in Abdellatif Laâbi's seminal journal for North African politics and culture, *Souffles*, founded in 1966 and closed down in 1971. As director of the *Institut Universitaire de la Recherche Scientifique* in Rabat he has been closely involved in education and the dissemination of research across a wide range of disciplines in Morocco. Khatibi is also the author of numerous essays, including *Vomito Blanco – le sionisme et la conscience malheureuse* ('Vomito Blanco: Zionism and the Uneasy Conscience', 1974; this involved him in a polemic with Memmi, who criticised the Arab world for not recognising the meaning of Zionism and that of the Jewish state); *La Blessure du nom propre* ('The Wound of One's Own Name', 1974); *Du Bilinguisme* ('Bilingualism', 1985); *Figures de l'étranger* ('Faces of the Stranger', 1987); *Paradoxes du sionisme* ('Paradoxes of Zionism', 1989); *Penser le Maghreb* ('Thinking the Maghreb', 1993); and of sociological studies such as *Bilan de la sociologie au Maroc* ('Review of Sociology in Morocco', 1968) and *Etudes sociologiques sur le Maroc* ('Sociological Studies on Morocco', 1971). He has also written on the visual arts (often in close collaboration with painters and photographers), on Arabic calligraphy and on Moroccan carpet design. As with Memmi, although in a very different way, this diverse body of work is interconnected: 'Khatibi is convinced that story-telling, proverbs, artisan production, urban space, textiles, mosaics and other forms of decoration are modes of cultural transmission that can offer clues to the understanding of an invisible history'.[5]

In *Maghreb pluriel* ('Plural Maghreb', 1983), Khatibi theorises a literature written in the 'language of the adversary, that will answer in that same language the aspirations and cultural specificity of the North African writer of French'.[6] He offers a reflection on the potential of a 'third route' for the so-called Third World, between 'reason' and 'unreason' as the West has thought them, as a way of 'decolonising ourselves and each other', as he explains it. Khatibi therefore not only attempts to 'undermine the domination of one language or culture by another, [but] has also dedicated himself to an even more revolutionary task, that of founding an "other thought" ['une pensée-autre']'.[7] Winifred Woodhull notes the influence of Derrida on Khatibi's thinking, and despite her criticisms of what she sees as the limitations of his approach, especially his insistence on a 'subversive poetics removed from what is conventionally referred to as the political sphere', and of the way his poetics 'often reinforce a patriarchal law', which is problematic for feminist work on literature, culture and decolonisation, she nonetheless adds: 'What is compelling about Khatibi's work is that, in its best moments, it *does* link manifestations of intractable deciphering in the third world to the prospect of significant social change worldwide, change to which he gives the name "decolonisation"'.[8]

Khatibi's first creative work was published in 1971 with the title *La Mémoire tatouée* ('Tattooed Memory'), and a revealing subtitle, *Autobiographie d'un décolonisé* ('Autobiography of a Decolonised Man'), despite being described as a *roman* ('novel') on the cover. This is the text, one that Khatibi has openly acknowledged as autobiographical, on which I will focus here: 'En 1968 je décidai d'écrire ce récit *autobiographique* qui sera *La Mémoire tatouée*, tout en redoutant l'enjeu redoutable qui s'y engage et s'y agite'[9] ('In 1968 I decided to write the autobiographical account which would be published as *La Mémoire tatouée*, though I was daunted by the prospect of what was at stake in it and all the issues it raised'). Two subsequent texts, *Le Livre du sang* ('The Book of Blood', 1979), which again carries the description *roman* on the cover, and *Amour bilingue* (*Love in Two Languages*, 1983) can be said to have at their heart questions of identity and difference, but in extremely complex and elusive ways that take the author far beyond a primary concern with autobiographical discourse. Nonetheless, the problematics of the subject and the relation to language remain essential to Khatibi's work:

> Khatibi [...] reste un des rares écrivains arabes dont l'attention est portée sur les possibilités intenses de la subjectivité et de la présence dans le réel de

l'écriture. Il est question dans son travail, comme il aime à le dire, de l'association de l'intelligible et du sensible. Il y a chez lui un double support
pour l'écriture où le corps et l'esprit se rejoignent dans le même mouvement;
l'auteur est à la fois rivé sur lui-même et sur les paradigmes de sa pensée [...]
Mieux encore, l'écriture, chez Khatibi, est une mesure de la réalité à partir
des fondements de la personne muée en 'paroles du livre'. L'attention à soi
est corollaire à l'attention au langage sans gratuité, mais dans le sens de la
gravité de l'enjeu passionnel, et comme exigence ultime que se donne
l'écrivain.[10]

(Khatibi [...] remains one of the rare Arabic writers whose attention focuses
on the intense possibilities of subjectivity and presence within the reality of
writing. In his work, as he likes to say, he deals with the connection between
what is understood and what is felt. In his work there is a double support
for writing, where body and spirit meet in the same movement; the author
is riveted to himself and, at the same time, to the paradigms of his thinking
[...] Or rather, with Khatibi, writing is a measure of reality starting off from
the basis of the person transmuted into 'words in a book'. The attention to
self is a corollary of his attention to language and is without gratuitousness,
but in the sense of the seriousness of the passion which is at stake, and the
ultimate demand made on himself as a writer.)

The question of selfhood is therefore ever-present in Khatibi's work
and linked to his very being as a writer and the act of writing, as we have
seen was the case for Feraoun and, very intensely, for Albert Memmi.
Despite the complex and diverse theoretical, sociological, philosophical,
psychoanalytical and mystical discourses that underpin his texts, it is
clear also that Khatibi's whole writing project is one that is concerned
with identity. There are, for example, certain 'preferred' myths (that is
to say myths that are repeatedly used by the writer in different ways in
order to multiply their connotations and personal significance), notably
concerning the name and the origins of the individual, that recur and link
his later creative texts to *La Mémoire tatouée*. Nonetheless, Rachida
Saigh Bousta has called the self at the centre of Khatibi's work a 'moi
refracté' ('refracted self').[11] Following the intense reflection on the self of
La Mémoire tatouée (and even in that text the self is bound up with a
multiplicity of other interests and discourses – sociological, philosophical, psychoanalytical, and so on), it should be noted that although the
question of selfhood is present in the later texts, these other types of
discourse predominate to such an extent that the approach taken here to
Khatibi will focus mainly on one text with less reference to subsequent
projects in the manner employed with Feraoun and Memmi. Before
moving on to the analysis of *La Mémoire tatouée*, I would nonetheless
firstly like to explore briefly the problematic presence of the self in these
later texts. This may seem rather perverse, when the focus of the chapter
is precisely the initial exploration of selfhood in the postcolonial situa-

tion that generates the writing of *La Mémoire tatouée*, but my point is to insist on the differences in the relationship between the focus on the self and on other discourses in these texts, in contrast to *La Mémoire tatouée*, which explicitly declares itself the autobiography of a decolonised subject.

WRITING AND THE MULTIPLE DISCOURSES OF SELFHOOD

Khatibi himself has explained the way in which autobiography, fiction, philosophy and mysticism are bound up together in his second 'novel', *Le Livre du sang* ('The Book of Blood'): 'Dans celui-là, il y a bien sûr une inscription autobiographique qui est, elle-même, réinscrite dans une fiction qui pose la question de l'Eros mystique dans une très vieille tradition arabo-musulman'[12] ('In it, there is of course an autobiographical inscribing which itself is reinscribed within a fiction posing the question of the mystical Eros, in a very old Arabo-Muslim tradition'). And as Marc Gontard has said of the same text,

> Je pense qu'à première vue *Le Livre du sang* n'est pas autobiographique, mais il y a pourtant d'une part la dédicace et d'autre part, au centre du livre, une sorte d'anecdote vécue que l'écriture voudrait voiler, dissimuler et qui devient, en fait, une matrice qui va se développer selon des axes symboliques, paraboliques... L'écriture simule et dissimule, de sorte qu'on s'écarte du roman autobiographique, sans que l'autobiographie soit pourtant absente du texte.[13]

> (I think that at first sight *Le Livre du sang* is not autobiographical, but nevertheless there is on the one hand the book's dedication, and on the other, at the centre of the book, a sort of lived anecdote which the writing would seem to want to veil and dissimulate, but which in fact becomes a matrix which develops along symbolical, parabolic axes... The writing simulates and dissimulates, so that one is distanced from the autobiographical novel, while autobiography is never absent from the text.)

It is in the subtle movement from an identifiable autobiographical discourse to a discourse in which autobiographical concerns do not take precedence but nonetheless remain implicit that Khatibi's multiple concerns with the notion of selfhood are manifested.

In *Le Livre du sang* the figure of Orpheus facilitates a meditation on poetic creation, and the ultimate quest of the text seems to be the construction of the text itself, that is to say not the self-examination of the author, nor the ordering of a life, nor any type of confession, all of these being aims previously identified as defining elements of autobiographical discourse:

> *Le Livre du sang* est l'histoire d'un chant et le manifeste poétique de la créa-
> tion. Le mouvement de l'écriture – description, narration, énonciation
> lyrique, pensées aphoristiques – est secondé par un autre mouvement, celui
> de la création, se confondant avec le premier sans l'annuler. Ainsi le sort de
> mort des personnages-figures de la secte oriente le sort du livre ou du narra-
> teur-créateur: sa propre disparition, son ensommeillement. C'est
> l'aboutissement radical de l'œuvre dans l'œuvre. L'histoire du personnage
> finie, le narrateur décomposé, le livre se ferme sur lui-même comme un
> tombeau.[14]

> (*Le Livre du sang* is the story of a poetic epic and the poetic manifesto of
> creation. The movement of the book – description, narration, lyricism, apho-
> risms – is backed up by another movement, that of creation, combining with
> the first but without annulling it. Thus the fated death of the character-
> figures of the sect guides the fate of the book or of the narrator-creator: his
> own death, his falling into sleep. This is the radical consequence of the book
> within the book. Once the story of the character is finished and the narrator
> is decomposed, the book closes upon itself like a tomb.)

However, we may also compare this to Memmi's *Le Scorpion*; in both
texts the quest to bring the text into being is itself bound up inextricably
with the quest for knowledge of the identity of the individual. Again as
in Memmi's text, there is an interest in the multiplicity of identity and
also in intertextuality. Yet there is a tangible difference in the dual erasure
of the self in Khatibi's text as compared to Memmi's. Rachida Saigh
Bousta presents an interesting analysis of what she terms the 'fables iden-
titaires' ('identity fables') in *Le Livre du sang*,[15] and she notes the
occasional veiled allusion in this text to *La Mémoire tatouée*:

> En effet, à travers certains discours, le Récitant renoue avec le narrateur du
> premier récit khatibien lorsqu'il revient sur le passé et rappelle: 'avant ma
> naissance, je fus immolé pour que je renaisse au-delà de ma généalogie, sous
> le ciel bleu de mon pays' (p. 81). Ce clin d'œil à *La Mémoire tatouée* nous
> renvoie à la fable d'une naissance marquée par le souvenir d'un sacrifice
> mythique.[16]

> (What happens is that through certain discourses the Reciter links up with
> the narrator of Khatibi's first book, when he goes back over the past and
> recalls: 'before my birth I was immolated so that I might be reborn beyond
> my genealogy, under the blue sky of my country' (p. 81). This wink in the
> direction of *La Mémoire tatouée* refers us back to the fable of a birth marked
> by the memory of a mythical sacrifice.)

This 'mythical sacrifice', the near-sacrifice by Abraham of his son, is
fundamental to Islam, an act of supreme faith, and a reference to it opens
La Mémoire tatouée. It is a scene that I will examine in more detail later,
and it is referred to more than once in *Le Livre du sang*: 'La musique
d'Islam bat ainsi [...] captant de très loin, dans l'égorgement du fils
d'Abraham qui est MON NOM INCARNE, un formidable cri, soutenu
de siècle en siècle, de millénaire en millénaire'[17] ('The music of Islam has

a beat like that [...] capturing from far off, in the throat-cutting of the son of Abraham who is MY NAME INCARNATE, a great cry, maintained from century to century, from millennium to millennium').

The self is therefore undoubtedly present in *Le Livre du sang*, but in indirect ways, and the preferred myths, as I have termed them, that make up the multiple identity promoted by Khatibi here as elsewhere underpin the diverse discourses that make up the text, among which is a mysticism inspired by Sufism as elaborated by Khatibi in this text.[18]

In a different approach to the presence of the self in Khatibi's work, Abdallah Memmes shows to what extent the author intervenes in the narration of *Le Livre de sang*, and Memmes puts forward the argument that this authorial voice is in fact as prominent as that of the narrator. Memmes's conclusion makes clear the problematic of identity at the heart of *Le Livre du sang*:

> Sur le plan culturel, en réactualisant les aspects de la culture arabe, avec la part du refoulé que représentent les traditions populaires (identité) et ceux de la culture occidentale (différence), il a exprimé ainsi son identité totale, puisque ce qui est censé être la différence fait partie intégralement de sa formation culturelle, et par conséquent, de son être.[19]

> (On the cultural plane, by reactualising aspects of Arabic culture, including the repressed part as represented by popular traditions (identity) and those of Western culture (difference), he thus expressed his total identity, since what is supposed to be difference forms an integral part of his cultural make-up and hence of his being.)

A third text, *Amour bilingue*, pursues the analysis of language and difference through the love between a Frenchwoman and a North African man, a love that takes place in the French language, the language of the woman and the only language in which he can love her: 'Je t'aime, dit-il, dans ta langue maternelle' (p. 50); 'Elle lui disait [...]; je t'aime pour toujours, et déjà cette phrase était dite par la langue elle-même' (p. 67)[20] (' "I love you," he said, "in your mother tongue"'; 'She told him, "[...] I love you for ever," and already that phrase had been said by the language itself'). *Amour bilingue* is again a diverse and complex text, in which both theoretical and fictional discourses are used, although once again there is the presence of a self that can be associated with the author. Nonetheless the main subject of the text seems again to be the text itself:

> Même si la critique est quasi unanime pour reconnaître *Amour bilingue* comme un récit ou une écriture d'obédience romanesque, il n'en reste pas moins que ce texte présente une configuration singulière. En effet, le discours théorique rivalise avec la fiction et prend parfois les allures d'une réflexion sociologique, anthropologique ou philosophique. L'écriture joue sur un double écran. De toute évidence, nous sommes dans un cadre étrange. Le

Récitant-narrateur ne cesse de multiplier les avertissements à l'adresse du lecteur quant aux déploiements romanesques et discursifs. S'agit-il d'un récit? Dans le contexte présent, les réserves sont de rigueur. Il serait question d'un 'récit sans personnage (nous dit-on), ou s'il y en avait, ce serait le récit lui-même'. (p. 12)[21]

(Even though critics are almost unanimous in recognising *Amour bilingue* as a narrative or type of writing belonging to the genre of fiction, it remains true nevertheless that this book has a singular construction. In it, theoretical discourse rivals fiction and sometimes takes on the appearance of a sociological, anthropological or philosophical study. The writing is played on a double screen. The framework is a strange one by any reckoning. The Reciter-Narrator is continually warning the reader about its fictional and discursive construction. Is it a story? In the present context, certain reservations are in order. This would be a 'story with no characters', we are told, 'or if there was one, it would be the story itself').

This self-conscious status of the text resonates once again with the writing strategies employed in Memmi's *Le Scorpion*, and of course with the preoccupations of the modern European novel and particularly with the French New Novel, as noted in the previous chapter. Abdallah Memmes analyses *Amour bilingue* with the logic he has established of seeing both fictional and autobiographical aspects as kinds of 'pretexts' for another intellectual problem:

Amour bilingue se situe dans la même perspective que *Le Livre du sang*, celle qui consiste à envisager les éléments romanesques et/ou autobiographiques non en eux-mêmes et tant que tels, mais comme de simples matériaux destinés à illustrer une réflexion sur une question donnée – en l'occurrence les problèmes linguistiques.[22]

(*Amour bilingue* is on the same plane as *Le Livre du sang*, consisting of envisaging the fictional and/or autobiographical elements not in themselves as such, but simply as material for illustrating the study of a given question – in this case, problems of language.)

Hassan Wahbi concurs with this view that each of Khatibi's texts develops a fundamental question:

Chaque texte est l'espace d'une interrogation spécifique. Et dans *Amour bilingue*, il est question de la double langue comme histoire d'un sujet. A partir d'un récit à facture relativement autobiographique, il organise une narration autour de cette situation exceptionnelle comme mode d'être, de parler et de penser. L'être double, la parole double, la pensée double forment l'instance du récit. Ces caractéristiques spécifiquement réflexives et conceptuelles se transforment en matière d'écriture [...] Le texte khatibien est un texte double: il raconte la pensée et il 'conceptualise' l'existence.[23]

(Each book is the place for a specific question. In *Amour bilingue* it is the question of double language as the story of a subject. Starting from a relatively autobiographical account it organises the narrative around that exceptional situation as a way of being, speaking and thinking. Double being, double speech, double thought give form to the narrative itself. These specifically reflexive and conceptual characteristics become the writing-matter. [...] Khatibi's writing is a double writing: he gives thought a narrative form and he 'conceptualises' existence.)

There are, however, in *Amour bilingue* certain pronouncements, especially concerning the relationship to language and the situation of the bilingual subject, that it is difficult not to read as self-analysis on the part of the author: 'N'avais-je pas grandi, dans ma langue maternelle, comme un enfant adoptif? D'adoption en adoption, je croyais naître de la langue même'; 'La bi-langue? Ma chance, mon gouffre individuel, et ma belle énergie d'amnésie. Energie que je ne sens pas, c'est bien curieux, comme une déficience, mais elle serait ma troisième oreille' (p. 11) ('Had I not grown up in my native language like an adopted child? From adoption to adoption, I believed I had been born of the language itself'; 'The *bi-langue*? My luck, my individual gulf, and my wonderful energy for amnesia. An energy which, curiously enough, I don't feel as a deficiency but as if it were my third ear'). Abdallah Memmes traces several moments in the text when the identity of the author 'breaks through' the '*il/je/elle*' ('he/I/she') narrative structure, and he summarises the impact of these in this way:

> Ces repères autobiographiques indiscutables sont, dans une certaine mesure, confirmés par la structure même de l'œuvre où le récit proprement dit est encadré d'un 'exergue' et d'un 'épilogue', imprimant à l'ensemble une allure autobiographique. Cette personnalité de l'auteur qui se dégage ainsi de l'ensemble de l'œuvre se vérifie enfin à un autre niveau – celui de sa conception de l'écriture – à travers la remarque suivante, rapportée dans 'l'épilogue': 'Si l'on me demandait: Votre récit est-il un nouveau nouveau roman? [...] Je répondrai que le roman n'a jamais voulu de moi. Nous ne sommes pas de la même histoire' (p. 127).[24]

> (These unquestionably autobiographical notes are in a way confirmed by the very structure of the work, in which the narrative as such is framed by a sort of 'prologue' and 'epilogue', giving the whole work the appearance of an autobiography. This personal appearance of the author as distinct from his work is finally verified at another level – that of his concept of writing – through the following remark, related in the 'epilogue': 'If someone were to ask me, "Is your story a new New Novel?" [...] I would say that the novel has never been for me. We don't share the same history/story [play on words]'.)

What is certain is that there is a reflection on identity here and this takes place in relation to the other in the postcolonial context. This is a text in which the writer presents the full force of the colonial situation on the subject using his concept of the *bi-langue*:

> Oui, la langue maternelle m'a perdu. Perdu? Mais quoi, ne parlais-je pas, n'écrivais-je pas dans ma langue maternelle avec une grande jouissance? Et

la bi-langue n'était-elle pas ma chance d'exorcisme? Je veux dire autre chose. Ma mère était illettrée. Ma tante – ma fausse nourrice – l'était aussi. Diglossie natale qui m'avait voué peut-être à l'écriture, entre le livre de mon Dieu et ma langue étrangère, par de secondes douleurs obstétricales, au-delà de toute mère, une et unique. Enfant, j'appelais la tante à la place de la mère, la mère à la place de l'autre, pour toujours l'autre [...] Fils de la langue, je perdis ma mère; fils de la double langue, je perdis mon père, ma lignée.[25]

(Yes, my mother tongue lost me. Lost? But didn't I speak, didn't I write in my mother tongue with great enjoyment? And wasn't the *bi-langue* my chance of exorcism? I mean something else. My mother was illiterate. My aunt – my false nurse – was too. Native diglossia which had perhaps destined me to write, between the book of my God and my foreign language, through second birth-pangs, beyond any mother, one and unique. As a child, I called my aunt in place of my mother, my mother in place of the other, for ever the other [...] Son of the language, I lost my mother; son of the double language, I lost my father, my lineage.)

And as Marc Gontard has observed,

En fait, avec *Amour bilingue*, quelque chose s'achève, Khatibi l'a lui-même confirmé, non seulement dans sa relation douloureuse au bilinguisme, mais dans la relation amoureuse qui affectait son rapport à la langue et renforçait le clivage du moi bilingue.[26]

(In fact, with *Amour bilingue* something came to an end, as Khatibi himself confirmed, not only in his painful relationship to bilingualism but in the loving relationship which affected his rapport with the language and deepened the split of the bilingual self.)

In later fictional texts such as *Un Eté à Stockholm* ('A Summer in Stockholm', 1990) and *Triptyque de Rabat* ('Rabat Triptych', 1993), there is a greater distance between narrator and author, but questions of identity are still much in evidence. All of these texts might therefore exemplify the notion of *fiction identitaire* discussed in the first chapter here. They are certainly fictions, but fictions that are more than 'imagined' in that they tackle from different angles a subjectivity that has been constantly exposed, studied, theorised, meditated upon from many different perspectives throughout the author's writing project. As Rachida Saigh Bousta, has noted there are several distancing strategies at work to mark out author and protagonist in *Un Eté à Stockholm*.[27] Yet the translator/protagonist, Gérard Namir, experiences linguistic and transcultural problems that are familiar in Khatibi's previous work, and Namir declares himself born around the same time as the narrator of *La Mémoire tatouée*: 'Je suis né au cœur du siècle, dans la guerre et la servitude' (*Un Eté à Stockholm*, p. 129) ('I was born at the heart of the century, in war and servitude'); while the narrator of *La Mémoire tatouée* was born 'avec la deuxième guerre' ('with the second war'; *La Mémoire tatouée*, p. 11). Marc Gontard notes the way in which Khatibi seemingly effaces subjectivity in *Un Eté à Stockholm*, and yet the questions of identity remain insistent, while opening onto otherness, almost to the point of effacing the writer's own origins: 'Opération risquée et voulue comme telle, comme s'il avait cherché à tester en lui la possibilité d'une altérité totale ouverte à l'universel jusqu'à l'effacement de ses propres traces, de sa propre origine'[28] ('A risky operation and deliberately so, as if he had sought to test in himself the possibility of a total otherness open to the universal, to the point of effacing all traces of himself and his own origins'). 'A total otherness open to the universal': a project that seems to share some of the preoccupations of Albert Memmi, but is pursued very differently. The enigma of identity is pursued in *Un Eté à Stockholm*:

> Mais qui suis-je moi qui vous parle maintenant, pour vous conduire au cours de ce voyage initiatique sans me faire connaître? Qui suis-je pour vous recevoir en plein ciel sans décliner mon identité, ma véritable identité. [29]

> (But who am I who am speaking to you now, to lead you through this journey of initiation without making myself known? Who am I to receive you under the open sky without stating my identity, my true identity.)

The narrator eventually declares himself to be Gérard Namir; and Gontard goes on to analyse this name with resonances of both France (the French name Gérard) and the Maghreb (the 'Arabic' sound of the surname that in fact means 'tiger' in classical Arabic and also suggests a hero from Berber folktales, Hammu u Namir):

> Ainsi le nom propre est-il ici porteur d'un trouble, d'une ambivalence, désignant un double espace de manière elliptique tout comme le narrateur s'attache à dire son origine en l'effaçant ou en la recouvrant d'un autre sol culturel, en manière de palimpseste difficilement déchiffrable. Habiter, par le biais de l'acte narratif, le nom propre de Gérard Namir, c'est pour Khatibi explorer une altérité où il tente d'égarer ses propres traces [...]
>   A travers la stratégie narrative du récit, on assiste donc à une tentative extrême de déracinement du moi et d'effacement des origines, avec pour perspective la jouissance de l'altérité sous sa forme ludique et hospitalière.[30]

> (Thus his name is here the bearer of a disturbance, an ambivalence, designating a double space in an elliptical way, just as the narrator insists on speaking of his origin while effacing it, or covering it with another cultural ground, like a barely decipherable palimpsest. To inhabit, through the act of narration, the name of Gérard Namir is for Khatibi to explore an otherness where he attempts to dissimulate any signs of himself [...]
>   Through means of the story's narrative strategy, therefore, we witness an extreme attempt at uprooting the self and effacing one's origins, with the intention of enjoying otherness under its playful, hospitable aspect.)

As the narrator says: 'Je suis successivement moi-même, l'autre, et de nouveau moi-même, l'autre et de nouveau moi-même, entre la vitesse et la parole, la vitesse et le silence'[31] ('I am successively myself, the other and myself again, the other and once more myself, between speed and word, speed and silence').

Whereas the protagonist of *Un Eté à Stockholm* is defined as the 'étranger professionnel' ('professional foreigner/stranger/outsider'), the main character of the *Triptyque de Rabat* is described as a 'sédentaire professionnel' ('professional sedentary') (p. 105), suggesting again an interest in 'opposites' and 'others'. The conception of the *Triptyque*, according to Khatibi, coincided with the 1991 Gulf War, bringing an immediate historical and political dimension to the text, although the main focus is the 'political impasse' of the city of Rabat itself.[32] The notion that Rachida Saigh Bousta brings into her own analysis, that of the 'moi refracté' ('refracted self') in Khatibi's writing, is a useful one to work with, suggesting that this is a way to avoid the retrieval of a memory too focused on the self:

> En jouant sur la dérive d'un moi refracté qui interpelle l'entre-deux, la pensée khatibienne jouit des possibilités de se dédouaner d'une mémoire égocentrique. C'est probablement sa façon d'être dans un ailleurs sans pour autant rompre les amarres avec son ensourcement identitaire. Aussi subjugue-t-elle en même temps les carences et l'excédent de la mémoire; comme elle déplace les tensions pour procurer au discours qu'elle invoque un autre souffle. Elle souscrit à une autre dynamique de la réflexion autour d'une généalogie transculturelle.[33]
>
> (Playing on the wreck of a refracted self which questions the in-between space, Khatibi's thought delights in the possibility of clearing himself of an egocentric memory. It is probably his way of being elsewhere without breaking his mooring-ropes to the sources of his identity. It overcomes at the same time both the lacks and the excesses of memory; just as it postpones tensions in order to gain a breathing-space for the discourse it invokes. It subscribes to another dynamic of reflection around a transcultural genealogy.)

This notion of 'ensourcement identitaire' is also very suggestive. Identity is the dynamic that links all these texts, although critics disagree on the extent to which the self is Khatibi's primary preoccupation. Indeed Abdallah Memmes posits that perhaps even in *La Mémoire tatouée*, the autobiographical discourse is rather more a pretext for a set of philosophical and ideological problems that preoccupy Khatibi and indeed preoccupy his generation; it is in his view 'une œuvre programme' ('a book that has a programme').[34] There is therefore a different aim here to that which we usually associate with an autobiographical project. Memmes quotes Khatibi himself:

> On trouve dans *La Mémoire tatouée* la plupart des thèmes qui m'habitent, en particulier la question si essentielle de l'identité et la différence, les notions

de la différence sauvage et l'identité aveugle, le thème du propre et du nom propre dans la symphonie islamique, le thème de l'être bilingue, la question de la pensée nomade et du désert.[35]

(Most of the themes that dwell in me are to be found in *La Mémoire tatouée*, in particular the essential question of identity and difference, the notions of savage difference and blind identity, the theme of one's self and one's own name in the symphony of Islam, the theme of the bilingual being, the question of nomadic thought and the desert.)

Memmes suggests that Khatibi's whole project is more linked to theory than to life story and that the autobiographical discourse is more 'collective' than 'individual':

Elles [ses véritable motivations] consistent, à notre avis, dans un projet théorique du genre, qui s'appuie sur les expériences individuelles (comme simple illustrations) pour esquisser une sorte d'autobiographie collective – laquelle autobiographie collective se vérifie par ailleurs chez d'autres écrivains, à travers ce qu'on appelle le 'roman autobiographique'.[36]

(They [his real motives] consist, in my opinion, of a theoretical project on *genre* which relies on individual experiences (as simple illustrations) to sketch a sort of collective autobiography – and this collective autobiography can also be seen in other writers, through what is called the 'autobiographical novel.')

I have discussed my own general reservations concerning this notion of the representation of 'collective identity' in the first chapter, and will return to it in the conclusion. Khatibi certainly represents a generation and a historical situation, but as for Memmi, the use of individual experience to explore concerns of the immediate community or concerns that are more universal does not render the meditation on the self any less intense. We are returned rather to the issue of an individualism that remains aware of the relationship of the self to the society in which it acts.

Memmes however reads *La Mémoire tatouée* as being much more about the collective identity of Khatibi's generation and a response to those intellectuals who saw only alienation in the double identity of the colonial subject: 'Il devient clair, par conséquent, que derrière l'expérience particulière de Khatibi, c'est une expérience collective qui est retracée. Et dans cette optique, *La Mémoire tatouée* est porteuse d'une véritable projet culturel qui s'adresse à toute une génération, indiquant une issue possible à un problème historique'[37] ('It becomes clear, consequently, that behind Khatibi's individual experience, it is a collective experience which is being retraced. And from that point of view *La Mémoire tatouée* is the bearer of a genuine cultural project that addresses a whole generation, indicating a possible solution to a historical problem'). He notes the similarities in Khatibi's work of the experiences related by several North African writers: circumcision, the Koranic school, the French school and the issue of language, the difficult relationship with the father and/or the family, the street, childhood games and relations with other children, the struggle to a greater or lesser degree with the colonial power, the coming to political awareness:

> Du fait même de ces similitudes (en dépit des variantes et styles forcément différents des auteurs), ce qui est mis en scène dans les écrits (même si, comme dans *La Mémoire tatouée*, l'intention du départ est le récit d'une vie personnelle), c'est, en définitive, l'histoire d'un 'moi' collectif, objectivé par les conditions historiques, sociales et culturelles particulièrement marquantes. Ce qui s'illustre dans les écrits, c'est ce qu'on pourrait appeler 'l'archéologie' de l'être maghrébin d'une certaine génération – celle à cheval entre la période coloniale et l'indépendance.[38]

> (By the very fact of these likenesses (despite the variants and the necessarily different styles of the authors) what is foregrounded in these writings (even if, as in *La Mémoire tatouée*, the initial intention is the story of a personal life), is, finally, the story of a collective 'I', objectivised by particularly striking historical, social and cultural conditions. What is illustrated in the accounts is what can be called the 'archaeology' of what it was to be Maghrebi for a certain generation – straddling both the colonial period and independence.)

The authors and texts that Memmes notes are Memmi's *La Statue de sel*, Chraïbi's *Le Passé simple* (*The Simple Past*), Sefrioui's *La Boîte à merveilles* ('The Box of Delights'), Boudjedra's *La Répudiation* ('The Repudiation'), Ben Jelloun's *Harrouda*, Laâbi's *L'Oeil et la nuit* ('The Eye and the Night') and Serhane's *Messaouda*, and he considers the aims of these writers as incompatible with the 'personal myth' of traditional autobiography. It will be clear from the first chapter that while I accept some notion of the self seeking a way (even if it is impossible and/or questionable) to speak on behalf of the collective in colonial and postcolonial autobiographical discourses, I also believe that focus on the self in the writers I have chosen to analyse here, Khatibi included, ultimately outweighs any focus on the collective. This issue will be returned to in the conclusion.[39]

Nonetheless, if we compare Khatibi's approach to the development of themes, concepts and ideas in both fictional and theoretical texts with that of Albert Memmi, there is, as previously noted, an almost tangible difference between the ways in which the author's own life intervenes in the work of these two writers. Memmi's life remains almost physically present. His personal experience, and what he has learned from it and how he has applied it to a more universal situation, is constantly referred to. Khatibi's life experience often appears to be theorised into the abstract. Like Memmi, Khatibi has pursued his writing project not only in creative texts, but also in sociological studies, as previously noted. All of Khatibi's work is further characterised by a powerful use of the French language in a quest to oppose the domination of French culture on the postcolonial subject by 'destroying' the language of the cultural and political coloniser. It can be argued that Memmi's relationship to French as a Jewish citizen under French colonial rule is very different from that of an Arab. This strategy to undermine the hegemony of French culture with what Khatibi has called a 'littérature sauvage' (a 'savage literature') attempts to create a new use of language more suitable to the identity of the postcolonial subject. Khatibi can be seen as the most prominent theorist of a postcolonial literature and theory in Morocco, and indeed across North Africa, with his theory of the 'double critique', which brings together decolonisation and deconstruction and in which a new perception of the West is posited, not as the enemy, but as a society in contradiction with that of the former colonies. Khatibi attempts to go beyond the types of postcolonial theory that concern themselves with a re-reading and rewriting of cultural and historical discourses in terms of binary oppositions and otherness. He investigates new notions of alterity and seeks to find new expressions and concepts of identity that celebrate the multiple, the constantly changing and the nomadic:

> Qu'il y ait chez Khatibi un très fort penchant pour l'exploration des formes à partir du sens de sa subjectivité et de sa pensée, cela ne nous achemine pourtant pas vers une synergie totalement autobiographique, mais vers une démarche de raccordement du moi avec le monde. Ses récits sont pris dans un courant qui semble tenir compte de l'essentiel de l'expérience pour construire une œuvre pas à pas en transformant ce qui est senti et pensé en forme littéraire.[40]

> (The fact that there is in Khatibi a very strong tendency to explore forms starting from the meaning of his subjectivity and his thought, does not point us towards a totally autobiographical synergy but towards an approach of linking up the self with the world. His narratives are caught up in a current which seems to take account of the essential elements of experience to construct a body of work step by step, by transforming what has been felt and thought into literary form.)

This notion of a 'raccordement du moi avec le monde', of the ways in which the self and the world are linked, is one that I will take up in the work of Assia Djebar in the following chapter, and again in the conclusion.

Before finally moving on to my main object of study here, I would like to refer briefly to one more text by Khatibi that again has a focus on identity, but that has a different form to those already discussed and therefore represents a self expressed through a very different writing strategy. *Par-dessus l'épaule* ('Over the Shoulder') is composed of diverse types of texts: notes, maxims and aphorisms ('Notes de mémoire pour les femmes' ['Little Reminders for Women']; 'Notes de mémoire pour les hommes' ['Little Reminders for Men']; 'Socio-clips'); the diary of 'Une psychanalyse personnelle' ('A Personal Psychoanalysis'); 'Cendres et réliques' ('Ashes and Relics'), the transcripts of recorded conversations with his mother that contain her memories of him as a child and a meditation on his mourning of her; and four meditative essays: 'Du message prophétique' ('The Prophetic Message'); 'Possession d'Iblis' ('Possession of Iblis'); 'L'Oedipe de la fin' ('The Oedipus at the End'); and 'Au-delà du trauma' ('Beyond Trauma'). Khatibi acknowledges this fragmentation within the text itself and is unsure of how the reader will react: 'Je vois la composition de ces notes, mais je ne vois pas assez leur effet sur le lecteur et la lectrice. Cette indétermination convient à mon regard sur le monde et sur moi-même'[41] ('I can see the composition of these notes, but I can't really see their effect on the reader, whether man or woman. This indetermination is appropriate to my view of the world and myself'). Marc Gontard has commented on this use of the fragment and how it is used to question the concept of the self:

> Dans *Par-dessus l'épaule*, Abdelkébir Khatibi, abandonnant les récits symphoniques comme *Le Livre du sang* et *L'Amour bilingue*, met en résonance le Moi maghrébin et son environnement culturel avec le questionnement occidental sur l'être. Et ceci, à travers une stratégie particulièrement remarquable: l'écriture fragmentaire ou, plus exactement, le *fragmental* (ce dernier terme impliquant le fragment comme unité textuelle, mais non l'incomplétude ou l'inachèvement comme pourrait le suggérer l'adjectif fragmentaire).[42]

> (In *Par-dessus l'épaule*, Abdelkébir Khatibi, abandoning symphonic accounts like *Le Livre du sang* and *L'Amour bilingue*, sets up a resonance between the Maghrebi self with its cultural environment, and Western questioning on the nature of being. And he does this through a particularly noteworthy strategy: fragmentary writing or, to be more precise, the *fragmental* (this word implying the fragment as a textual unit, but not the incompleteness or unfinished state suggested by the adjective fragmentary).)

This use of the 'fragmental' would appear to represent a way to explore many different facets of the self and to undermine any totalising narrative, again in a way reminiscent of the strategies employed by Memmi in *Le Scorpion*.

Khatibi also explores in this text the risk that he undertakes in writing: 'Prendre le risque, c'est cela, amener mes écrits à être publiables – impubliables. Je ne peux échapper à ceux qui me regardent *par-dessus mon épaule*[43] ('To take a risk means leading my writings to be publishable – unpublishable. I can't escape those who look *over my shoulder*'). This notion of risk is also one that recurs in the work of all the writers here, as was noted in the introduction, and this is again an idea to which I will return in the conclusion. Just as a number of links are evident between Feraoun's *Le Fils du pauvre* and Memmi's *La Statue de sel*, so there are between the work of Khatibi and Assia Djebar, with Memmi's *Le Scorpion* serving as a kind of bridge between them.

MEMORY, MYTH AND THE POSTCOLONIAL SUBJECT IN *LA MÉMOIRE TATOUÉE*

> Je suis né le jour d'une fête sacrée, Aïd el Kébir; d'où mon prénom, qui est un des mythes fondateurs de tout ce que j'écris.
> Abdelkébir Khatibi, *Par-dessus l'épaule*[44]
>
> (I was born on the day of a special feast, Eid el Kebir; hence my first name, which is one of the founding myths of everything I write.)

In the second edition to *La Mémoire tatouée*, Khatibi adds an introduction (dated 16 October 1978) that tells us something of his own conception of the project:

> Comment ai-je délimité le champ autobiographique? En démobilisant l'anecdote et le fait divers en soi, tout en dirigeant mon regard vers les thèmes (philosophiques) de ma prédilection [...] Chemin faisant, une rage intempestive a fait tout vaciller; d'où ce texte, image délabrée d'un tombeau vide. (p. 11)
>
> (How did I define the field of autobiography? By not bothering with anecdotes and little things that happened, while turning my attention to the (philosophical) themes which were especially dear to me [...] On the way, an ill-timed rage made everything totter; whence this text, the dilapidated image of an empty tomb.)

Lucy Stone McNeece offers a way into the text by suggesting that this is what she calls an 'alterbiography', rather than an autobiography, as it points up the author as another 'cultural invention' of the colonial imagination:

> *La Mémoire tatouée* is unlike any conventional autobiography. Although written in the first person, it is not confessional, and the author does not provide his readers with either realistic scenes of the past, or a coherent psychological portrait of his narrator. He does not present a logical sequence of events that might serve to explain or to legitimise present attitudes. The absence of such a structure of cause and effect deters us from reading the story as a naturalistic tale. Khatibi's protagonist is a construct, not only

because he is the personal invention of the author, but because he is a cultural invention in an extreme sense, an artefact of the colonial imagination. His novel, in part, is an autobiography of the non-I, or 'alterbiography'. We tend to think of autobiography as a vehicle of individual authenticity, and read it for the vicarious pleasure of gaining access to the intimate world of another's self. Khatibi's novel denies us that seductive illusion, dramatizing instead the impossibility of knowing another person as a subject, and exposing the inauthenticity that often characterizes our relations with ourselves as well as others.[45]

This positing of the colonial subject as an artefact of the colonial imagination is a suggestive one, and offers a further perspective on the practices of writing undertaken to attain the state of being 'decolonised' (as claimed by the subtitle of *La Mémoire tatouée*). I would however take a different view on the motivation of the reader of autobiography as reading for vicarious pleasure, for as Philippe Lejeune has pointed out in his own reading of the autobiographical project of Michel Leiris, to read autobiography is often less a reading of the other than a reading of the self of the reader. Taking up Leiris's own use of word-play to reveal the relationship of the self to language, Lejeune makes clear that to read Leiris is indeed to read oneself: 'Leiris; s'y lire' (literally, 'to read oneself in him'). Nonetheless, there is a great deal in McNeece's analysis that can help us here to approach this difficult text:

> *La Mémoire tatouée* amply testifies to the difficulty of speaking or writing from the point of view of an integrated or grounded subject. The novel is an inquiry into the problem, at once epistemological and ontological, of knowing oneself with respect to the Other. It is a meta-discourse about writing and its subjects, in the sense of being both about authorship and about the objects of its narration within the context of a postcolonial society. The process of writing inevitably raises the issue of position and placement. The changing relation of subject to object, of mind to world, of sign to referent, are aspects of a long-standing problem of Western metaphysics that here finds a new and critical reformulation. Khatibi has understood the particular importance of this issue for the postcolonial sensibility. Acutely aware of the fact that political independence in no way guarantees cultural freedom, Khatibi knows that the writer is the one who must assume the task of exploring the implications of the problem, and must be prepared to sacrifice himself, if need be, for those who cannot or dare not pose the questions that must be asked.[46]

One of the striking features of *La Mémoire tatouée* is the extent to which the self is revealed less by a meditation on the knowledge attained through self-examination (as may be said to be the case in one definition of the autobiographical quest) than in the revelation of self by other: 'Comment transcrire, sans trembler, en une autobiographie singulière, le récit de sa vie et de sa mort? N'est-ce pas toujours l'Autre [...] qui te révèle ton histoire, comme un événement inouï?' (introduction to second edition, p. 10) ('How can one write down without trembling, in a singular autobiography, the account of one's own life and one's own death? Is it not always the Other [...] who reveals your story to you, as an event you had never heard before?').

In a kind of preface that is placed separately from the first of the titles that divide up the first part of the text, there is a meditation on the name of 'Abdelkébir', derived from the holy day of Eid and the commemoration of Abraham's near-sacrifice of his son: 'Né le jour de l'Aïd el Kébir, mon nom suggère un rite millénaire et il m'arrive, à l'occasion, d'imaginer Abraham égorgeant son fils. Rien à faire, même si ne m'obsède pas le chant de l'égorgement, il y a, à la racine, la déchirure nominale' (p. 9, first edition, 1971) ('Born on the day of Eid el Kebir, my name suggests a rite which is thousands of years old, and on occasions I find myself imagining Abraham cutting his son's throat. There's no way out. Even if I am not obsessed by the recounting of the throat-cutting, there is at the very roots the tearing-apart contained in the name'). This story of ultimate sacrifice and profound faith in God, in which an animal is substituted at the last moment for Isaac, the son whose father Abraham was ready to sacrifice, as related in the Old Testament (Genesis 22) is also taken up in the Koran as a fundamental moment. In Khatibi's introduction to *La Mémoire tatouée* previously referred to, this importance of the name is again made clear: 'On le redira, le jour de ma naissance (1938) est le jour même de l'Aïd el Kébir, fête commémorant le sacrifice d'Abraham: de là mon prénom, Abdelkébir, Serf du Grand, Esclave de Dieu' (p. 10, second edition) ('To repeat: the day of my birth (1938) is the very day of Eid el Kebir, the feast commemorating Abraham's sacrifice. Hence my first name, Abdelkébir, Serf of the Great One, Slave of God'). This is an opening, then, concerned with the symbolism of the name, and with the notions of death, of sacrifice, and of *déchirure* ('tearing apart'), a recurrent term in the writing of the self in a postcolonial context, as we have already seen: 'mourir, vivre, mourir, vivre, double à double, suis-je né aveugle contre moi-même?' (p. 9, first edition; all subsequent references are to this edition) ('dying, living, dying, living, double to double, was I born blind against myself?'). Hassan Wahbi analyses at some length the significance of this opening on the name and explains the circle of life and death in Arabic thought:

> Naître, c'est naître de la mort. Mourir, c'est pour re-naître après la mort. Ce double signe qui marque toute naissance est introduit au début de *La Mémoire tatouée* – comme intertexte explicite – parce que c'est le premier dédoublement de l'être, sa première dissémination, sa première indétermination. Ce double sens est associé au signe du sacrifice (géré par le couple

Vie/Mort). Les sens que recèle ce couple dans les deux figures est la rupture, la scission et la discontinuité de l'être. Ce qui est essentiel d'après nous dans ces renvois, c'est l'existence même d'un déplacement: la naissance comme 'biographème' est singularisée en devenant le commencement d'une histoire de l'écriture, le sacré d'un concept qui joue un grand rôle dans l'écriture de Khatibi: la blessure.[47]

(Being born means being born from death. Dying is in order to be re-born after death. This double sign which marks all birth is introduced at the beginning of *La Mémoire tatouée* as an explicit intertext, because it is the first doubling-up of being, its first dissemination, its first indetermination. This double sense is associated with the sign of sacrifice (overseen by the couple 'Life/Death'). The meaning which this couple holds in the two figures is that of rupture, splitting, the discontinuity of being. What is essential in my view in these cross-references is the very existence of a displacement: birth as 'biographeme' is singularised by becoming the beginning of a story of writing, the sacred element of a concept which plays a major role in Khatibi's writing: the wound.)

Indeed, a meditation on the name and on naming is another recurrent feature of the writing concerning both the colonial and the postcolonial subject, as we have seen in the work of Feraoun and Memmi; the name bears both personal history and History and is a way of literally writing the self into the enterprise of writing.[48]

The experience of circumcision is also presented by Khatibi as a kind of mythical event with the same echoes of sacrificial violence, but whose violence engenders a second birth: 'Je m'évanouis une première fois. Le cri de ma mère me réveille. Elle fait semblant de m'accoucher une deuxième fois et elle pleure' (p. 29) ('I faint for the first time. The cries of my mother bring me round. She pretends to be giving birth to me a second time, and she is crying'). It is also linked to a tattooed sign: 'Alors, pour toute mobilité, l'éclosion d'une fleur de sang, tatouée entre les cuisses' (p. 29) ('Then, for all mobility, the blossoming of a flower of blood, tattooed between my thighs'). The sign of the tattoo of course gives its title to the text and I will be analysing this in more detail further on.

The complexity and fragmented structure of *La Mémoire tatouée* has previously been noted, and fragmentation is an integral part of the writing strategy employed in the text: 'Non point le bonheur fêlé, ceci est un miroir dont je bricole les reflets, mais la projection d'un enfant au-delà de ses signes' (p. 24) ('Not a cracked happiness, this is a mirror whose reflections I am making myself, but the projection of a child beyond its signs'). It is a text that constantly questions and even undermines its own status, questioning the functioning and validity of memory: 'Mon enfance, ma vraie enfance, je ne pourrais jamais la raconter' (p. 69) ('My childhood, my real childhood, I could never tell the story of it'). Indeed there is a whole meta-discourse on the possibilities and impossibilities of writing autobiography which comes to inscribe itself on and in the process of composing the actual autobiographical discourse:

> Est-ce possible le portrait d'un enfant? Car le passé que je choisis maintenant comme motif à la tension entre mon être et ses évanescences se dépose au gré de ma célébration incantatoire, elle-même prétexte de ma violence rêvée jusqu'au dérangement ou d'une quelconque idée circulaire. Qui écrira son silence, mémoire à la moindre rature? [...] qui dira mon passé dans l'effacement d'une page? [...] faire une enfance, rien ne fermera l'idée d'une transcription. (p. 18)[49]

> (Is the portrait of a child possible? Because the past which I choose now as the motif of the tension between my being and its evanescences is laid down at the whim of my incantatory celebration, itself a pretext for the violence that I dreamed of to the point of derangement, or for any circular idea. Who will write his own silence, a memoir to the slightest crossing-out? [...] who will say my past in the effacement of a page? [...] to make a childhood, nothing will close the idea of a transcription.)

These theoretical concerns on the status of autobiographical discourse are again written a more than a decade before the French New Novelists pursue the same problems concerning writing about the self in the 'new autobiography'. There is also a comparison here with Memmi's approach to similar questions in *Le Scorpion*, published two years before *La Mémoire tatouée*.

The nature of memory and its distortions are commented on by the narrator: 'Par le jeu de la dissimulation, le souvenir métamorphose la ville de notre passé en une nostalgie blanche' (p. 38) ('By the game of dissimulation, memory metamorphoses the town of our past into a white nostalgia'). It is his 'mémoire nomade' ('nomadic memory'; p. 38) that allows access to this past, but in his situation memory remains painful, difficult to come to terms with: 'l'enfant que j'étais se brisait, à tout hasard, mourir enfin, vivre enfin, mourir enfin, vivre contre soi-même dans l'écartement de la mémoire' (p. 51) ('the child that I was used to break just in case, to die finally, to live finally, to die finally, to live against himself in the separation of memory'). The colonial situation has torn historical memory apart, and in a way reminiscent of Memmi's description of the functioning of the 'duo' of coloniser and colonised, has bound the two together in a bizarre way, as the narrator writes: 'Et il n'y a de plus atroce que la déchirure de la mémoire. Mais déchirure commune au colonisé et au colonial, puisque la médina résistait par son dédale' (p. 46) ('And there is nothing more atrocious than the tearing-apart of memory. But it was a tearing-apart which was common to colonised and coloniser alike, because the *medina* resisted by its tangled maze').

La Mémoire tatouée is a polyphonic text on several levels, the first being in the use of pronouns. The *je* dominates, but the narratorial voice also uses *il* and *tu*, which destabilises the more usual first person of auto-biography, and it also changes the relationship of the subject to the past, promoting instead the present of writing:

> L'écriture autobiographique dans *La Mémoire tatouée*, au lieu de s'enfermer dans le ressassement de soi par la même figure subjective du *je*, crée la démar-cation des contraintes du genre en adoptant d'autres figures de soi dans un même contexte. Au lieu que l'autobiographe utilise la successivité des événe-ments dans leur chronologie et dans la constance de l'identification directe, il insère un espace verbal entre le passé et le présent. L'identité du sujet ne réside pas dans l'accumulation des donnés autobiographiques en tant que matière par l'écriture. L'identité est dans le présent de l'écriture. Ainsi l'émer-gence du *tu* instaure un moyen d'insister sur ce présent et sur cette technique de l'identité fragmentée.[50]

> (The autobiographical writing in *La Mémoire tatouée*, instead of being shut into an endless dwelling on the self by the same subjective figure of 'I', creates the demarcation of the constraints of the genre by adopting other figures of the self in one same context. In the place where autobiography uses the succession of events in their chronological order, given constancy by direct identification, *La Mémoire tatouée* inserts a verbal space between the past and the present. The identity of the subject does not reside in the accumu-lation of autobiographical data as writing-matter. Identity is in the present in the process of writing. Thus the emergence of 'you' instigates a way of insisting on this present and this technique of fragmented identity.)

The dialogue between 'A' and 'B' towards the end of *La Mémoire tatouée* (again over a decade before Nathalie Sarraute would make use of a similar textual device, and again in a certain way reminiscent of *Le Scorpion*, with its narrative voice divided between Emile and Marcel, the latter constantly commenting on the former's project) is based on a discussion about autobiography. 'A' has written the autobiography and explains and defends himself; 'B' is a sort of double who questions and criticises, addressed by 'A' as 'mon ami' ('my friend') and 'frère de mon père' ('my father's brother'). As Hassan Wahbi has pointed out, 'B' also has a place in the writing strategy: 'il est inventé pour les besoins de la démonstration et de la contradiction. Il élève la voix nécessaire à la polémique interne. Son travail accompli, il disparaît dans "la fresque chinoise" comme s'il ne s'agissait que d'un signe, d'un élément abstrait'[51] ('he is invented by the needs of demonstration and contradiction. He raises a voice which is necessary to the internal polemic. Once his work is done he disappears into the "Chinese fresco" as though he were no more than a sign, an abstract element'). There are numerous examples of this critical discourse on the whole enterprise being undertaken in the text in this first part of the final chapter: 'Tu racontes ton enfance, tu fais le tour de ta petite vie qui n'a rien d'exemplaire [...] Mais malin que tu es...' ('You're telling the story of your childhood, making a tour of your little life which is in no way exemplary [...] But in your crafty way...'); 'Quel bricolage d'identité!' ('What a way to throw an identity together!'), and so on.

The point at which the narrator moves from childhood memories to those of his adolescence is explicitly marked and also raises issues about the choices an autobiographer makes:

> On rompt une enfance, par arrêt méditatif, à l'intersection d'une identité qui se dévore elle-même et la fatigue d'une fascination à l'âge successif. Comment dissoudre à l'instant la profusion des reflets et violenter la nostalgie? Très bas, il y a, au terme de la scène, maints souvenirs en crescendo. Se trahir par quel masque, quand une ivresse en vaut une autre, et que s'effiloche le savoir? Une séparation à figurer dans un ensemble mouvant, et je passe, la tête inclinée. (p. 65)

> (One breaks off a childhood, with a meditative halt, at the intersection of an identity which devours itself and which wears itself out with a fascination in the following age. How are the multiple reflections to be dissolved in an instant, doing violence to nostalgia? Very low down, at the end of the scene, there are many memories in crescendo. Which mask to betray oneself by, when one drunkenness is the same as another, and knowledge is unravelling? A separation to be figured in a moving ensemble, and I go by with my head bowed.)

I would like to reiterate Hassan Wahbi's point that the identity of the subject is in the present of writing, and not in the accumulation of autobiographical 'facts'. This is essential to the deciphering of the text and of its importance as a development of the autobiographical genre. As Wahbi concludes of *La Mémoire tatouée*: 'L'autobiographie de Khatibi est alors chargée de signes de spécificité en affichant le désir d'aller au-delà de l'exercice du genre pour combler l'espace subjectif de l'écriture' ('Khatibi's autobiography is then charged with signs of specificity, displaying a desire to go beyond the normal practice of the genre in order to fill the subjective space of writing').[52] Here is a further link to *Le Scorpion* and the writing strategies used in that text.

La Mémoire tatouée is divided into two parts, 'Série hasardeuse (I)' and 'Série hasardeuse (II)' ('Hazardous Series' I and II), with the narrator suggesting a break, and a new narratorial voice being introduced at the end of the first part: 'Je parle de mon passé comme s'il s'agissait chaque fois d'un temps à expulser. Soit! Je donne la parole à un autre double' (p. 145) ('I speak of my past as if each time it were a time to be expelled. All right. I'll hand over to another double'). The titles of the two parts imply a musical organisation, but also have connotations of chance and lack of coherence. These two parts cover four areas of a life story: firstly, the childhood of the narrator in Morocco under colonial rule, spent in two towns, El Jadida and Essaouira; secondly, his adolescence in Marrakesh: 'avoir douze ans et partir pour Marrakech!' (p. 65) ('to be twelve and setting off for Marrakesh!'), and the coming of independence: 'Voici l'époque chaude de l'histoire et de l'action' (p. 94) ('Here comes the hot period of the story and the action'); 'le sabotage de la sécurité de l'Autre' (p. 95) ('the sabotage of the Other's security'); 'L'Indépendance fut l'irrésistible bonheur d'une identité rêvée jusqu'au délire' (p. 102) ('Independence was the irresistible happiness of an identity which had been dreamed of to the point of delirium'); thirdly, the narrator's 'exile' in Paris: 'Je partais à Paris sans autre histoire que celle d'un étudiant ombrageux, à la recherche d'une autre image des autres et de moi-même' (p. 114) ('I left for Paris with no other history than that of a bad-tempered student, in search of another image of other people and of myself'), a journey that he had dreamt of since his childhood: 'Ce vol, rencontrer l'Occident dans le voyage de l'identité et de la différence sauvage' (p. 115) ('That flight, finding the West in the journey of identity and savage difference'), and elsewhere in Europe (London), and his experiences there; and finally a long journey taken in order to return to the country of his birth. This passage from childhood to adulthood follows, as in Feraoun's and Memmi's texts, the various stages of the narrator's education: the Koranic school and the French school in his childhood, an adolescence spent in the *collège des notables*, and his experience of higher education in France. It is also often structured according to a series of binary oppositions: two mothers (his own mother and his aunt); two towns (El Jadida and Essaouira); two environments (the family and the French school); two cultures (North African Arabo-Muslim and French); two languages (Arabic and French); two countries (Morocco and France): 'Séparation d'un adolescent, arraché d'un double exil, deux villes et deux mères' (p. 66) ('Separation of an adolescent, torn from a double exile, two towns and two mothers').[53] However, rather than these being directly described incidents with a fixed chronology, Khatibi presents a series of highly charged 'scenes' that serve to evoke the atmosphere in which the narrator's experience took place.[54] There are, however, other types of structure at work, as suggested by this series of binary oppositions. For example, in the presentation of the narrator's childhood, the scenes are organised within two very different cultural and political spaces: the traditional space of the narrator's own culture that encompasses both the inside space of the home, associated necessarily with the feminine and often highly eroticised, and the outside space of the street and of the wider community: 'Je traverse mon enfance dans ces petites rues tourbillonnantes, maisons de hauteur inégale, et labyrinthe qui se brise au coin d'un quelconque présage' (p. 33) ('I travel through my childhood in those little spiralling streets, houses of uneven heights, and labyrinth which shatters on the corner of any portent'); and the literally 'other' space of the French school and therefore of colonial power and domination.[55] Abdallah Memmes gives a succinct analysis of how these scenes, memories, legends all mesh together:

> Le narrateur commence par décrire le caractère agressif de l'aménagement colonial du territoire auquel 'la médina résistait par son dédale'. Cette idée de résistance rappelle la légende de Aïcha Kendicha, d'abord comme résistante, puis comme ogresse. Ce dernier aspect capte, à son tour, l'idée des 'jnouns' dont l'enfant avait peur; et de là, il en vient à l'évocation d'une pièce de théâtre que l'auteur avait écrite plus tard en France. Au moyen de cette génération, nous passons ainsi d'un épisode historique (la politique coloniale), à une légende (le mythe de Aïcha Kendicha toujours vivace dans la mémoire populaire), à une croyance superstitieuse (celle de ce qu'on pourrait appeler les 'jnouns' domestiques), pour aboutir enfin à la création artistique (les débuts littéraires de l'auteur).[56]
>
> (The narrator begins by describing the aggressive character of the colonial development of the territory, which 'the medina resisted by its tangled maze'. This idea of resistance recalls the legend of Aïcha Kendicha, first as resister, then as ogress. This last aspect captures in its turn the idea of the djinns which the child was afraid of; and from there he goes on to the evocation of a play which the author wrote later in France. By means of this generative process we pass from a historical episode (colonial policy) to a legend (the myth of Aïcha Kendicha, still alive in popular memory), to a superstition (what could be called the domestic djinns), to end up finally with artistic creation (the author's beginnings in literature).

The narrator is addressed by multiple voices, and this use of voices from the community foreshadows the use Assia Djebar will make of the same motif (albeit in a very different way) to such strong poetic and political effect in her work from the 1980s onwards, as I will show in the next chapter.

The way in which language is used is also essential to the understanding of the differences and oppositions set up in the text:

> The language used to express the tribal culture is rife with poetic effects such as alliteration, repetition, pronounced rhythms, and unusual phonetic patterns. The lexical choices include words transliterated from dialect and are rich in sensory and physical references. The language is opalescent, fluid, sensual, and erotic, and its intonations and rhythms have a kinaesthetic impact upon the reader.[57]

This use of language contrasts with the language associated by the narrator with the West:

> The language associated with the colonials translates the rationalistic mentality of the dominant culture: it is dry, transparent, explicit, and cognitive. Its syntax is logical, direct, and often monotonously symmetrical. There are harsh consonants, polysyllabic words, and little sensuality. That Khatibi makes these different attitudes speak in direct, rather than indirect, discourse, allows us to experience some of their seductive force upon the child, and to comprehend his inability to integrate these disparate perspectives.[58]

The colonisers also leave the physical mark of their 'rational' culture on the towns: '"Il faut créer des jardins rationnels, des villes géométriques, une économie en flèche, il faut créer des Paradis sur terre, Dieu est mort, vive le colon." Voici la parole du colon dessinant la ville comme une carte militaire' (p. 45) (' "We need to create rational gardens, geometrical towns, a growth economy, we need to create Paradise on earth, God is dead, long live the coloniser". Those are the words of the colonisers designing a town like a military map'). As a child, the narrator sometimes played in the park created by the French, 'le terrain sacré du conquérant', 'la fraîcheur de l'esprit cartésien' ('the sacred terrain of the conqueror', 'the freshness of the Cartesian spirit'):

> Je me retrouvais perdu dans ce montagne d'images baroques, défilant dans le désordre d'un enfant colonisé. Que pouvions-nous faire, écrasés dans nos corps, sinon, Bel Occident, déflorer ta nature, sauter sur tes zones interdites et attraper les petits poissons rouges frétillant dans ta matrice? (pp. 45–46).
>
> (I found myself again lost in this mountain of baroque images, filing past in the disorder of a colonised child. What could we do, crushed in our bodies, except, Fair West, deflower your nature, jump on the forbidden zones and catch the little red fish wriggling in your womb?)

The transgressions of these childhood games carried out against the physical presence of the West, which is already symbolised by an eroticised body, are symptomatic of a much deeper trauma. Khatibi shows at the same time how the possession of this physical space by the coloniser also brought about the appropriation of the history of the colonised people, leaving the latter few gaps in which to function:

> On connaît l'imagination coloniale: juxtaposer, compartimenter, militariser, découper la villes en zones ethniques, ensabler la culture du peuple dominé. En découvrant son dépaysement, ce peuple errera, hagard, dans l'espace brisé de son histoire. (p. 46)
>
> (We know the colonial imagination: juxtapose, compartmentalise, militarise, cut up the towns into ethnic zones, silt up the culture of the conquered nation. On discovering its own exile, that nation will wander, crazed, in the broken space of its history.)

The place of the colonised subject within the power structures of the colonising force, its language, its institutions, its occupation of physical and mental space, discussed in the first chapter, is powerfully described here.

Another set of 'voices' that address the narrator are, of course, the French writers he discovers at school, and the list of names includes Sartre, Daudet, Prévert, Racine, Corneille, Eluard, Mallarmé, Valéry, Baudelaire, Robbe-Grillet, Vian, Senac and Segalen.[59] There is a parallel here with Feraoun, Memmi and Assia Djebar, who also make explicit their relationship to the French literature (and other literatures) encountered in their childhood and adolescence and write of how they were made to feel inferior to these giants of cultural superiority. The challenge of the projects of such writers to the hegemony of Western culture is thrown into relief as Khatibi explains how a young mind becomes colonised:

> Arbre de mon enfance, le Coran dominait ma parole alors que l'école, c'était une bibliothèque sans le Livre [...] on se sentait des enfants conçus en dehors des livres, dans un imaginaire anonyme. Et de cours en cours, disparaître derrière les mots, en prenant soin d'éliminer toute trace suspecte. Chacun est le flic de ses mots, ainsi tourne la culture. (p. 58)

> (Tree of my childhood, the Koran dominated my speech while school was a library without the Book [...] we felt like children conceived outside books, in an anonymous imagination. And, lesson by lesson, disappearing behind the words, taking care to eliminate every suspicious trace. Each is the policeman of his own words, that is how culture goes round.)

In this process 'l'esprit d'un enfant se colonise' (p. 59) ('a child's mind becomes colonised'), although the young boy's heart remains with what he calls the 'magic' of his own culture: 'le cœur jouait plutôt avec les talismans' (p. 59) ('his heart played readily with talismans'). Nonetheless, in the confrontation of cultures the image presented to the colonised of themselves surprises them, and they end up feeling ashamed, despite their emotional attachment to their own culture and religion. The given image of Morocco is 'un joyeux folklore' ('joyous folklore'), steeped in a meaningless religion: 'la prière, c'était parler au vide' (p. 59) ('prayer was talking to emptiness').

In the struggle against colonial domination in both the domain of the political and that of the imagination, Khatibi explicitly acknowledges his debt to Kateb Yacine, through whose work his own culture was restored to him:

> Ainsi l'intellectuel colonisé luttait, abrégé dans ses racines les plus vivantes. Je fus reconnaissant à Kateb – notre meilleur écrivain – de susciter en moi un encerclement mythique, ce contre quoi toute histoire s'effiloche. *Nedjma*,

merveilleuse incandescence! Avec ce poète errant, j'ai réappris ma rue d'enfance et son énigme, l'égarement des souvenirs quand me harcelait la guerre.
(p. 129)

(Thus the colonised intellectual fought, cut off short in his most vital roots.
I was grateful to Kateb – our best writer – for awakening in me a mystical
encircling, against which all history unravels. *Nedjma*, a marvellous incandescence! With this wandering poet I re-learnt my childhood street and its
enigma, the distraction of memories when I was harassed by war.)

Equally if not more significant than these references to Western
culture and its impact on the colonised subject are the references and
allusions to rewritings and even parodies of texts from Arabo-Muslim
traditions. Compared to the texts of Feraoun and Memmi, Khatibi's text
is dense with such ideas and many of these can only be guessed at intu-
itively, or indeed remain opaque, for the Western reader not familiar with
such writings and practices. I am necessarily reliant on the readings of
these by North African critics, such as Abdallah Memmes, who describes
these procedures in terms used by Gérard Genette:

En effet, partout sont injectés des fragments textuels (hypertextes) qui
imitent de façon ludique un ensemble d'hypotextes, appartenant à différents
registres sacrés et culturels: le Coran, le hadith, les textes mystiques, les
formes du conte, le langage parabolique, etc.[60]

(What happens is that fragments of texts (hypertexts) are inserted everywhere which playfully imitate a collection of hypotexts belonging to
different registers, both religious and cultural: the Koran, the Hadith,
mystical texts, different types of tales, the language of parable, etc.)

Yet each reader finds a way into the text on his or her own level, and a
text of such complexity never stops offering yet another reading or mode
of interpretation. There are many scenes and more explicit references to
events that are less difficult to grasp, enabling any reader to find a way
into the dense texture woven here.

Unsurprisingly, in a text that opens on the scene of the sacrifice of a
son by his father, and in a cultural context in which (as we have already
seen in the work of Feraoun and Memmi) the relationship between father
and son is often difficult,[61] the figure of the father is a recurrent one.
Here, however, the father is described as ineffectual, and is often the
object of irony on the part of the narrator. He is presented, for example,
as unlikely to be able to stop the American forces violating the family
home should they wish to. The image of the father is unflattering, but is
also not without tenderness: 'La seule photographie que j'ai conservée de
lui me renvoie un visage de bagnard, une tête nue, les cheveux coupé ras,
les oreilles en flèche, le regard d'une douceur acide, et en bas de la
photographie des empreintes digitales bien fanées' (p. 16) ('The only

photograph I have kept of him sends me back a convict's face, bare-headed, his hair cut close, ears sticking out, a gentle bitterness in his eyes, and below the photograph a set of very faded fingerprints'); 'Sa pauvre tête suggérait la tristesse de ceux qui se font expulser dans une dépossession de plus en plus mutilante' (p. 17) ('his poor head suggested the sadness of those who are expelled in a progressively more mutilating dispossession').

Other male figures, the aunt's husband and the mother's second husband after the death of the narrator's father, are also presented in critical and indeed often grotesque terms. When the father dies, the strangeness of the relationship between father and son is revealed: 'J'étais parfaitement énigmatique à moi-même, de lui à moi, un amour brûlé' (pp. 27–28) ('I was a perfect enigma to myself, from him to me, a burnt love'). In contrast, the figure of the mother is presented in poetic and mythical terms. As we have seen, it is her cry that brings the narrator to life again in his 'second birth' after circumcision, and even though he feels he does not know her well, she is presented as a victim of this situation, not its perpetrator: 'Ma mère, ma pauvre mère, je l'ai connue à peine, je l'ai côtoyée sur la pointe des pieds. Elle mettait au monde ses enfants, la rue les happait' (p. 28) ('My mother, my poor mother, I hardly knew her, I followed her on tip-toe. She brought her children into the world, and the street snapped them up'). The mother's name, Aïcha, is linked by the narrator to the myth of the ogress Aïcha Kendicha. According to the story told about her, Aïcha Kendicha was originally a beautiful young woman who, during the Portuguese occupation of the town of El Jadida, would go out at night to seduce and kill the foreign soldiers in revenge for the death of one of her family, and therefore came to be seen as a symbol of resistance against the occupier. In the popular imagination only the evil part of this story was kept and the woman became an ogress.[62] The feminine space of Khatibi's text is highly eroticised, from the fantasised rape of the mother to the 'harem de sept fillettes berbères' (p. 32) ('harem of seven little Berber girls') in Essaouira, to the wives of a neighbour, and the female cousins, to the 'cohabitation amoureuse avec une bonne' (p. 33) ('loving cohabitation with a nurse'). The maternal space is an important element of the autobiographical project of Khatibi:

> Dans *La Mémoire tatouée*, tous les passages de l'enfant de l'espace maternel à l'espace patriarcal prennent la forme d'une séparation douloureuse. Il s'agit notamment du sevrage, de la circoncision, de la nomination, du rapt de la mère et de la tante [...] Ces différents rites qui ont signé à jamais le corps de l'enfant jouent le rôle de médiateurs pour l'introduire dans la sphère paternelle. Ainsi les inscriptions de ces signes dans la mémoire du narrateur

sont décrites sous l'emblème de la fêlure, de la blessure et de la scission [...]
Car, si le père est du côté de la loi, de la religion et du sens, la mère quant à
elle baigne dans une ambiance mythique et populaire. L'identité de l'enfant
se redéfinit alors par le retour au cri prénatal et par l'écoute du chant
mythique initial [...] la quête identitaire n'est pas donc à chercher exclusivement dans l'histoire-sens mais aussi dans une prise en charge de la
mémoire collective la plus archaïque.[63]

(In *La Mémoire tatouée*, all the passings of the child from the maternal space
to the patriarchal space take the form of a painful separation. In particular
in the case of the weaning, the circumcision, the naming, the abduction of
the mother and the aunt [...] These different rites, which marked the child's
body for ever, play the role of mediators to introduce him into the paternal
sphere. Thus the inscribing of these signs onto the narrator's memory is
described under the emblem of cracks, wounds, splits [...] Because if the
father is on the side of the law, religion and meaning, the mother, for her
part, bathes in an atmosphere of popular myth. The child's identity then is
redefined by the return to the prenatal cry and the hearing of the initial mythical song [...] the quest for identity is not, therefore, to be sought exclusively
in meaning and history, but also in a taking over of the most archaic collective memory.)

The importance of collective memory within the text, a cultural
memory that is the preserve of women and is set up in opposition to a
dominant version of history, again provides a link with the work of Assia
Djebar, as we will see in the next chapter.

As for Feraoun and Memmi, so here it is the entry into the French
school that marks the rupture in the narrator's experience and identity
as well as the entry into the paternal space of his own culture described
above, a rupture made physical through expression in language:

Mon père m'envoya à l'école franco-musulmane en 1945 [...] A l'école, un
enseignement laïc, imposé à ma religion; je devins triglotte, lisant le français
sans le parler, jouant avec quelques bribes de l'arabe écrit, et parlant le
dialecte comme quotidien. Où, dans ce chassé-croisé, la cohérence et la conti-
nuité? (p. 54)

(My father sent me to the French-Muslim school in 1945 [...] At school,
laicised teaching imposed on my religion; I became trilingual, reading French
but not speaking it, playing with a few snatches of written Arabic, and
speaking dialect in everyday life. Where, in that confusion, were coherence
and continuity?)

The narrator subsequently seeks to repair this rupture through the act of
writing. Writing therefore becomes a sacred act, endowed with the
protective and ancient properties of the tattoo in Khatibi's culture. As is
the case for Albert Memmi in *La Statue de sel*, *La Mémoire tatouée* relates
the story of the coming to writing. The act of writing is again indisso-
ciably linked to an identity that is coming into being, that is created in

and with the written word. As Rachida Saigh Bousta has explained, the process of this coming to writing is fundamental:

> Le récit s'élabore en allant jusqu'aux limites de la formule rimbaldienne: 'je est un autre'. Il varie entre un Moi enfoui, qui n'est plus qu'évanescence de l'être-écrivant, et son déploiement spectaculaire lorsqu'il rapporte l'événement le moins sujet à contestation et souligne son authenticité [...] L'instance qui se dérobe ou se livre à un certain exhibitionnisme révèle elle-même certaines variantes du Moi-narrant/narré. L'autobiographie a peut être moins pour l'objet la reproduction d'un Moi singulier que la réflexion, à rebours, sur un Moi hypothétique et sur le devenir du Moi-écrivant.[64]

> (The narrative is constructed by going to the very limits of Rimbaud's 'I is another'. It varies between a buried 'I', which is no more than the evanescence of the writer-being, and its spectacular deployment when he relates the event which is least subject to contradiction and underlines its authenticity [...] The authorial voice which is concealed or which goes in for a certain exhibitionism, itself reveals certain variants of the narrating/narrated 'I'. The autobiography's object is perhaps less the reproduction of a singular 'I' than the reflection, in reverse, on a hypothetical 'I' and the becoming of the writerly 'I'.)

Writing is necessarily linked to the acquisition of knowledge, as we have previously seen in the examples of Feraoun and Memmi, and once again this is also the case for Assia Djebar, as we will see in the next chapter. Indeed the quest for knowledge is explicitly linked to the legacy in writing the narrator will leave; it is a quest to 'écrire pour les survivants de mon déracinement – ma génération, – rivé à un double langage' (p. 66) ('write for the survivors of my uprooting – my generation – riveted to a double language').

In *La Mémoire tatouée* the young boy becomes a voracious reader and begins writing in a sort of cannibalistic act that empowers him:

> Le lecture me rendait à la vie, à la mort. Le parfum d'un mot me bouleversait. Je tremblais. Quel travail forcené que d'avaler le dictionnaire des rimes et celui des synonymes! D'ailleurs, je prenais le livre à son auteur, le rendant discours de mon propre miroir. En établissant ma tyrannie, je vidais tel livre de sa pourriture, en sauvais, pour le bonheur de l'auteur et du mien, quelques phrases immortalisées par moi, dans un carnet de citations, attribuées d'un trait désinvolte aux écrivains les plus célèbres. (pp. 80–81)

> (Reading returned me to life, to death. The fragrance of a word overpowered me. I trembled. What forced labour, swallowing the rhyming dictionary and the dictionary of synonyms! More than that, I took the book from its author, making it the discourse of my own mirror. In establishing my tyranny I emptied such a book of its rottenness, saved up, for the sake of the author's happiness and my own, some phrases immortalised by me in a notebook of quotations, attributed with one casual pen-stroke to the most famous writers.)

The power of writing knows no bounds and it opens up another space for him to inhabit: 'J'écrivais puisque c'était le seul moyen de disparaître du monde, de me retrancher du chaos, de m'affûter à la solitude' (p. 87) ('I wrote because it was the only way of disappearing from the world, of retreating from the chaos, of sharpening myself in solitude'); 'Je me voulais écrivain sans en mesurer la souffrance et le vertige. Ecrire était une manière de survivre au souvenir, de flotter dans le temps, feuille hasardeuse et trouble' (p. 93) ('I wanted to be a writer without counting the cost of the suffering and vertigo. Writing was a way of surviving memory, of floating in time as a chance, storm-tossed leaf').

Although writing is a space he creates for himself, the narrator's behaviour in the French school becomes inauthentic, divorced from any innate sense of selfhood, and again like Memmi, he proceeds by imitation. In *La Mémoire tatouée*, however, the narrator seems to enjoy the character he creates through the imitation of the West, largely to be attractive to young girls:

> Car ces filles que je désirais profondément me caressaient de loin. Elles disaient que je différais de mes compatriotes. On m'acceptait parce que j'étais semblable, annihilant d'avance toute mon enfance, toute ma culture. Devant un tel plaisir complexe, je me mis des moustaches et une cravate de soie bariolée. Le personnage se donnait un certain air dévergondé. (p. 114)

> (Because the girls whom I desired deeply caressed me from afar. They said I was different from my fellow-countrymen. I was accepted because I was like them, so that all my childhood, all my cultural background was annihilated in advance. Faced with this complex pleasure I wore a moustache and a colourful silk tie. The character gave himself a certain air of licentiousness.)

During his stay in Paris, the narrator again imitates, putting on the clothes and the posture of the Western intellectual, although he knows that 'l'Occident colonial restait un déguisement à franchir' (p. 115) ('the colonial West remained a disguise to be overcome'), and discovers that 'inexorablement, Paris apparaissait comme une inépuisable parole où je devais déchiffrer ma propre énigme' (p. 125) ('inexorably, Paris appeared like an inexhaustible word where I had to decipher my own enigma'). It is to the deciphering of this enigma that I will now turn.

WRITING STRATEGIES AND THE DECIPHERING OF A 'TATTOOED MEMORY'

Séduit par l'Occident, je désirais mon propre déchiffrement
Abdelkébir Khatibi, *La Mémoire tatouée*[65]

(Seduced by the West, I desired my own deciphering.)

The subtitle of *La Mémoire tatouée* describes the book, as we have previously seen, as the autobiography of a *decolonised* subject. It is perhaps truer to say that the subject *becomes decolonised* through the writing strategies utilised and through which the position of the subject in relation to the story of his life and to History becomes clearer to the narrator. These strategies reveal a profound commitment on the part of the author to both a politics and a poetics of writing, as is the case for all the writers considered here. In the use made of language and in the use made particularly of symbols, of myths and of metaphors, there is a challenge to the power of the coloniser's language over the mind and behaviour of the individual, and by extension over the functioning of the society to which he belongs. Khatibi's work is a particularly striking example of these texts that bring together the creative and the political as a single 'site of intervention'.[66] One of the consequences of the writing strategies employed by Khatibi is that the unified 'personal myth' of traditional Western autobiography is exploded, in order to posit a multiple identity, and he writes ironically of the temptations of autobiography in *La Mémoire tatouée*: 'De même à cet âge la tentation d'être utile à tout hasard, d'être nécessaire, de laisser une histoire ou un personnage, de forcer le destin à coups d'idées et d'actes généreux. Il y a de quoi vivre quand des autobiographes astucieux prennent cela pour un goût d'éternité' (p. 27) ('In the same way at that age the temptation to be useful at all costs, to be necessary, to leave a story or character behind one, to force destiny by dint of generous ideas and deeds. There is something to live for when astute autobiographers take that for a taste for eternity').[67] As Lucy Stone McNeece has written,

> [*La Mémoire tatouée*] is both polymorphic and polyphonic, shifting frequently among voices and grammatical subjects [...] The style is consummately self-conscious, yet gains its urgency from the sense it conveys that everything is risked in the process of writing itself. At moments the narration approaches the kind of disintegration associated with schizophrenic discourse, before it regains penetrating lucidity [...] Khatibi's novel invites the reader to become fully aware of what it means to write in a postcolonial context, and how close indeed writing is to one's sense of self and one's desire. He demonstrates that writing in the language of another culture involves no less than the sacrifice and recreation of the self.[68]

One of the ways in which Khatibi subverts the myth of unified self-hood while he simultaneously elaborates a recreation of the self is through the use of metaphors and mythical allusions in order to investigate the mystery of identity and to reconstruct it in all its complexity. An individual identity does come into being, but it remains multiple, put together through the choice of certain privileged, 'preferred' signs and symbols that often take on new meanings and resonances as the whole builds towards the construction of that new identity. Khatibi describes these signs in the following way: 'J'ai dans *La Mémoire tatouée* tenté de suivre à la trace les signes et les événements qui frappent un corps et le marquent définitivement'[69] ('In *La Mémoire tatouée* I tried to follow the traces of the signs and events which strike a body and mark it permanently').

It is possible to read Khatibi's text both as revealing the attitude towards autobiography described by Michel Leiris in *L'Age d'homme*, in which 'se trouvent confrontés souvenirs d'enfance, récits d'événements réels, rêves et impressions effectivement éprouvés'[70] 'childhood memories, accounts of real events, dreams and impressions which were really experienced, find themselves face to face'); and as part of an Arab tradition that mixes different genres and types of discourse in the way discussed in the introduction:

> 'L'Adab' classique fait de l'autobiographie un prétexte pour se livrer à un discours pluriel ouvert sur l'essai, le propos philosophique, le commentaire d'événements divers, les théories de l'écriture. Ce type de littérature est particulièrement cultivé par certains soufis tels que Ibn Arabi dans 'Al-Futuhat al-Makkiyah' et 'Rissalât al-Qûds'. Influence qu'on retrouve chez son disciple Sohrawardî, et plus particulièrement dans son ouvrage 'L'Ange empourpré'. Lorsqu'on sait combien Khatibi exploite certains éléments de mystique à des fins autres que l'objectif initial, on s'étonnera peu d'un tel investissement dans *La Mémoire tatouée*.[71]

> (The classical '*Adab*' makes autobiography a pretext for launching into a plural discourse that opens on to the essay, the philosophical thesis, the commentary on various events, theories of writing. This type of literature is particularly cultivated by certain Sufis like Ibn Arabi in *Al-Futuhat al-Makkiyah* and *Rissalāt al-Qūds*. His influence is seen in his disciple Sohrawardī, and more particularly in his work 'The Empurpled Angel'. When one knows how much Khatibi exploits certain elements of mysticism for other ends than their original purpose, one is not really surprised at this sort of investment in *La Mémoire tatouée*.)

In his own analytical work *La Blessure du nom propre* (1974), Khatibi offers an analysis of the significance of the tattoo that provides the richly suggestive image of the title of *La Mémoire tatouée*, and a definition that can help us as readers to begin the act of deciphering the multiple meanings of this extremely complex and often difficult work:

> le tatouage est une écriture en points (c'est le nom utilisé parfois par les Arabes pour le désigner), dont on suppose qu'elle obéit à un savoir, à un savoir-faire, à un désir, à la circulation des signes tantôt inscrits dans le corps, tantôt migrants dans d'autres espaces, signes dont le symbole originaire est souvent perdu pour nous, mais dont l'inscription encore vivante défie nos théories du signe.[72]

> (Tattooing is a writing with dots (that is what it is sometimes called by Arabs) which one supposes follows a certain knowledge, a skill, a desire, the circulation of signs, now inscribed on the body, now migrating into other spaces, signs whose original symbolism is often lost to us, but whose inscribing still lives, challenging our theories about signs.)

Among the many and diverse metaphors that are to be found throughout the text, it seems to me that a founding metaphor, the matrix of the text itself, is in the tattoo of the title of this 'projet initial – autobiographie et méditation' ('initial project – autobiography and meditation'), as Khatibi calls it in the postface to the first edition. Memory is uncertain, troubling, mentally and physically painful, as described on the first page with the author's birth: 'peu de souvenirs me reviennent de cette époque'; 'longtemps après quand j'essayai de transcrire cette misère, je ne pus le faire que par un désordre aigu de tout le corps, barbelé dans la plus complète incertitude' (p. 11) ('Few memories come back to me of that first era'); ('long afterwards, when I tried to transcribe that misery, I could only do it through a piercing disordering of my whole body, caught in the barbed-wire of the most complete uncertainty'). The past that the narrator is able to write about is a version chosen by him:

> Car le passé que je choisis maintenant comme motif à la tension entre mon être et ses évanescences se dépose au gré de ma célébration incantatoire, elle-même prétexte de ma violence rêvée jusqu'au dérangement ou d'une quelconque idée circulaire. Qui écrira son silence, mémoire à la moindre rature? [...] me revient un lapsus: mère à la place de mémoire, double absence dans un double hasard. (p. 18)

> (Because the past which I choose now as the motif of the tension between my being and its evanescences is laid down at the whim of my incantatory celebration, itself a pretext for the violence that I dreamed of to the point of derangement, or for any circular idea. Who will write his own silence, a memoir to the slightest crossing-out? [...] I recall a slip: mother instead of memory, double absence in a double chance.)

The only dream from his childhood that the narrator remembers with any precision shows him 'enroulé par une grosse vague, puis projeté sur une plage [...] Mer, mère, mémoire, lapsus échappés à cette frileuse nostalgie' (p. 22) ('rolled over by a great wave, and then thrown up on a beach [...] Sea, mother, memory, slips which escaped from this shiv-

ering nostalgia'). Memory is therefore uncertain, vague, open to interpretation. But according to the title, this memory he is working with is
above all 'tattooed'. What is the sign of the tattoo? Just like the games
played by memory itself, the tattoo hides multiple meanings. The author
explains that '[la] mémoire tatouée – le titre du livre – est une dédicace
à la mère' (postface) ('[the] tattooed memory – the title of the book – is
a dedication to the mother'). The first reference in the text to tattooing
places it under the sign of the feminine and of the ancestral, of the erotic,
and of protection against death:

> Me saisit la même fascination devant toute Bédouine tatouée, j'épouse ma
> fixation au mythe. Tout calligraphie éloigne de mon désir, et le tatouage a
> l'exceptionnel privilège de me préserver. Aucun point de chute dans le chaos,
> seulement la force d'une impression dénouée, un graphe prompt comme un
> clin d'œil.[73]

> (I am seized by the same fascination at the sight of every tattooed Bedouin
> woman, I espouse my fixation with the myth. All calligraphy places my
> desire at a remove, and tattooing has the exceptional privilege of preserving
> me. No port of call in the chaos, only the strength of an untied impression,
> a graph as prompt as the blinking of an eye.)

And in the dialogue 'Double contre double' ('Double Against Double'),
almost at the end of the text, the gaze of 'A' is 'brusquement attiré par
l'image d'une femme tatouée sur le fond d'une fresque chinoise, capable
d'engloutir les apparences, y compris les personnages A et B' (p. 180)
('suddenly drawn by the image of a woman tattooed on the background
of a Chinese fresco, capable of swallowing up appearances, including the
characters of A and B'). In this 'double' dialogue, 'A' shares his actual
vision of the present and 'le tatouage – premier signe – m'initie à me
souvenir' (p. 186) ('the tattooing – first sign – initiates me into remembering'). The tattoo is therefore linked inextricably to memory; indeed it
is the very thing that initiates its workings.

Khatibi devotes a large part of *La Blessure du nom propre* to an
analysis of the tattoo in North African culture and to a meditation on its
significance. What attracts his attention is what he terms the 'migration
des signes'. Khatibi writes about this 'migration of signs', the ways in
which the signs of the tattoo circulate, 'migrate' from object to object,
from object to body, and so on: 's'étendant par exemple d'une gravure
rupestre à une calligraphie, en passant par un tapis, un tatouage, une
vannerie ou un foulard dessiné' ('spreading for example from a cave-
drawing to a piece of calligraphy, by way of a carpet, a tattoo,
basketwork or the design on a scarf'). How not to see, then, in such a
questioning of this circulation of signs, a quest to understand the 'migra-

tion of signs' in memory, this tattooed memory, in which the signs of remembered scenes and experiences migrate, circulate, and constantly need to be deciphered? Khatibi continues:

> Or, ce tremblement des signes n'est rien d'autre que le motif productif (lui-même voyageur) de notre interrogation. Déplacement donc des signes en une série hasardeuse [a title that he gives to two parts, I and II, of *La Mémoire tatouée*], et dont la figuration tantôt vibre en décrochant le sens, tantôt fige cette migration en un geste blanc, effaçant en quelque sorte l'espace giratoire qui se réduit ainsi à un point, une pointe.[74]

> (Now, this trembling of signs is nothing other than the productive motif (itself a traveller) of our questioning. A shifting, then, of signs in a hazardous series, whose figuring sometimes vibrates while bringing out the sense, and sometimes fixes that migration in an empty gesture, somehow effacing the giratory space which is thus reduced to a point, a pointing.)

Just as for the Bedouin woman in *La Mémoire tatouée*, the decorated body somehow holds death at bay:

> Témoin d'une écriture maintenant morte, le tatouage agit, selon un tracé presque immuable, dans le champ d'une différence si oubliée et si sommaire que la scène devient libre pour une méditation décorative sur la mort. Accoler ces deux mots (décoration et mort) n'est pas un hasard: nous pensons que la perte absolue du sens et de la lecture est la plus grande violence qu'on puisse apporter au savoir. Se désapproprier ainsi du corps, trahir la hiérarchie de ses valeurs, et noter, par un artifice tourbillonnant, un faux masque de la mort: le tatouage ne s'invoque que dans ce rythme; un corps décoré dont la nudité enlève la mort.[75]

> (Witness of a writing that is now dead, the tattoo works, according to an almost immutable line, in the field of a difference which is so forgotten and so summary that the stage is left free for a decorative meditation on death. The putting together of these two words, decoration and death, is not a mere chance: we think that the absolute loss of meaning and reading is the greatest violence that can be done to knowledge. To be thus dispossessed of the body, to betray one's hierarchy of values, and mark, with a twisting artifice, a false death-mask: the tattoo is only invoked in that rhythm; a decorated body whose nakedness takes away death.)

It is true to say that autobiographical writing implies a meditation on death or at least on that which is threatened with disappearance, but Khatibi's project seems not to be a project to erect a memorial or to challenge death in the way that 'classical' Western autobiography is often considered to do, but is rather a way of contemplating death in order to fabricate a 'tissu' ('fabric' or 'tissue'), as Khatibi calls it, here a decorated body that keeps death at bay. 'How to write this woman?', he asks in *La Blessure du nom propre*. 'How to write this life?' is the question that seems to be posed in and by the elaboration of *La Mémoire tatouée*. The definition of 'tissu' given by Khatibi is revealing:

> Appelons tissu l'ensemble des dessins décorant le corps: dans le mot tissu, il
> y a l'idée d'une composition microphysique de la matière, l'idée d'un espace
> rythmé et, *last but not least*, la notion de l'écriture [...] Appelons signes
> migrateurs les tissus et le formes géométriques qui traversent plusieurs
> systèmes sémiotiques. L'objectif est de dissoudre notre discours dans une
> telle animation.[76]

> (Let us call fabric the whole set of designs decorating the body: in the word
> fabric, there is the idea of a microphysical composition of matter, the idea
> of a rhymed space and, last but not least, the notion of writing [...] Let us
> call migratory signs the fabrics and geometric forms which traverse several
> semiotic systems. The objective is to dissolve our discourse in that kind of
> animation.)

It would seem that the writing strategies in Khatibi's autobiographical
text are just such 'tissus' and 'signes migrateurs', myths and metaphors
that circulate from memory to memory, from scene to scene (real or imagined, lived experience or fantasy), from meditation to meditation, from
commentary to commentary. At one level of meaning, memory is
tattooed because it holds in its depths the mysteries of its own meaning.
The tattoo is writing, but a form of writing that must be deciphered, a
writing that does not give itself up to a simple reading.

The explanation of the use of 'tissu' continues in a way that provides
a theoretical approach to this whole enterprise:

> La production d'un tissu se forme selon deux mouvements:
> – un idiolecte social: quelques signes suffisent à produire un système sémi-
> otique local (tribal, par exemple);
> – un idiolecte personnel, qui est le style de la tatoueuse ou du tatoueur.[77]

> (The production of a fabric is formed according to two movements:
> – a social idiolect: a few signs are enough to produce a local semiotic system
> (tribal for example);
> – a personal idiolect, which is the style of the tattooist, whether woman or
> man.)

I have treated firstly this latter concept, the 'personal idiolect' of the
tattoo-artist/writer. The fundamental meaning of this privileged
metaphor, which gives its image to the title of the text, resides in the
personal meditation of the author on the process and the dynamics of
meaning in the act of writing/tattooing, and in the forms which mark the
tattooed body. Khatibi places as a kind of epigraph to the section 'Le
corps et les mots' ('Body and Words') a dream in which body and
language, or rather words, the 'marks of language', are one: 'J'ai rêvé,
l'autre nuit, que mon corps était des mots' (p. 79) ('I dreamed the other
night that my body was words'). The body as text – the ultimate metaphor
for the writer and his relationship to the written word. As Lucy Stone
McNeece writes:

The work's title indicates the way in which Khatibi concretises the most elusive concepts, affirming the relation of the body and desire to language and writing. The title also establishes the primacy of the sign, or rather of the material signifier, in the formation of personal identity. By the conjunction of *'mémoire'* and *'tatouée'*, Khatibi articulates the degree to which memory is not cognitive but corporeal, sensuous, and indelible.[78]

Among the other myths and legends used by Khatibi in *La Mémoire tatouée*, the story of Calypso and Ulysses is interpreted by the author as a meeting with the West: 'la fraîcheur mythique de cette rencontre avec l'Occident me ramène à la même image ondoyante de l'Autre, contradiction d'agression et d'amour. Adolescent, je voulais me définir dans l'écoute nostalgique du mythe initial' (p. 15) ('the mythical freshness of this meeting with the West recalls me to the same surging image of the Other, contradiction of aggression and love. As an adolescent, I wanted to define myself in the nostalgic listening of the initial myth'). The myth is therefore linked to the origins of his own identity, but also comes to define the relations of dependence in the colonial encounter. Here, though, the expected power relations are subverted as Calypso keeps Ulysses captive in her cave, promising immortality if he stays, and providing an image for the narrator's mother's interpretation of the French as the weak, dependent partner in the colonial relationship as the boy imagines his mother imagining herself as Calypso: 'croyait-elle, ma mère, ma douce mère, être la Nymphe Calypse, la toute-divine au langage ailé qui enferme Ulysse dans sa grotte aux quatre sources' (p. 15) ('did she believe, my mother, my sweet mother, that she was the Nymph Calypso, the all-divine with winged language who imprisoned Ulysses in her cave with its four streams'). This mixture of power, desire and rejection in an eroticised relationship will be further pursued through the image of the tattoo, as I shall discuss further.

This mythical meeting brings me to my second reading of this tattooed memory, since this memory is tattooed not only by a 'personal idiolect', but also by history. Khatibi tells us in *La Blessure du nom propre* that 'l'auteur de ces pages n'a pas oublié que la circulation de ce mot dans ces textes y est déroutante pour ceux qui ne connaissent que le tatouage de l'humiliation (chez les prisonniers ou les déportés)' ('the author of these pages has not forgotten that the circulation of this word in these texts is disconcerting for those who only know of the humiliating kind of tattooing (as on prisoners and deportees)').[79] We should then also consider the second idiolect described by Khatibi, the 'social idiolect', since the subtitle of *La Mémoire tatouée* is of course is *Autobiographie d'un décolonisé* ('Autobiography of a Decolonised

Man'), and therefore of a man caught up in historical and political events. The dedication to the mother in the postface is immediately followed by the question: 'Se décoloniser de quoi?' ('Decolonise oneself from what?'). It is clear in the text that the struggle is to decolonise oneself not only from the colonial imagination, as has previously been described, but also from the ambivalent desire for the West: 'Séduits par l'Occident, nous nous arrachions à la différence et voulions défaire sa mémoire. Fallait-il choisir entre le rêve et l'histoire?' (pp. 83–84) ('Seduced by the West, we tore ourselves from our difference and wanted to destroy the memory of it. Did we have to choose between dream and history?'). There is a comparison here with the revolt of Memmi against his own desire for the West, as portrayed in *La Statue de sel*, and with his account of his betrayal by the West during the Second World War. However, Memmi's position as a Jew with regard to the West is very different from that of the Arab Khatibi, although some experiences are similar. For example, in *La Mémoire tatouée*, the reading of French literature during the narrator's adolescence seemed to be the route to true paradise, the paradise of the other: 'Je voulais plaire au professeur de français, puisque par Corneille je serais entré dans l'éternité de l'Autre' (p. 86) ('I wanted to please the French teacher because through Corneille I would enter into the eternity of the Other'). However, independence arrives: 'Epopée inoubliable de notre adolescence!' (p. 101) ('Unforgettable epic of our adolescence!'); and with independence, the realisation concerning the difference between the narrator's world and that of the French authors he is reading, including even that of Sartre, critic of the French government's colonial policy: 'Le monde sartrien était antichrétien et antibourgeois, le mien magique et épique, superposé de masques, mon esprit, mon corps colonisés' (pp. 106–107) ('The world of Sartre was anti-Christian and anti-bourgeois, mine was magical, epic, masks superimposed on it, my mind and body colonised'). The reference to Sartre underlines the enormous difference between France and the North Africa of Khatibi's youth. Sartre, despite his stance on the Algerian war against the French government, the preface he wrote to Memmi's *Portrait du colonisé*, his articles criticising the colonial system, and his position as a French intellectual militating against French colonialism, is nevertheless far removed from Khatibi's own experience.

This is the period in which the West, or at least Europe, is seen to begin doubting its own power, in the aftermath of the Second World War, and with the rise of the independence movements across the world challenging the system of European colonial power. Paradoxically this uncertainty provokes an uncertainty in the colonial subject also, in the very depths of his being, because he is locked into a relationship with the West (again there is a parallel to be drawn with Albert Memmi from the very different perspective of the Tunisian Jew, but with similar consequences):

> Je reconnaissais de cette culture le bricolage du savoir, la répression, le dépaysement; j'en saisissais la faille dans l'intimité de mon être. Et parce que lié à cette séduction, je me perdais dans la trame du désir. Aimer l'Autre, c'est parler le lieu perdu de la mémoire, et mon insurrection qui, dans un premier temps, n'était qu'une histoire imposée, se perpétue en une ressemblance acceptée, parce que l'Occident est une partie de moi, que je ne peux nier que dans la mesure où je lutte contre tous les occidents et orients qui m'oppriment ou me désenchantent. (pp. 107–108)[80]

> (I recognised in this culture the makeshift knowledge, the repression, the exile; I grasped its failings in the depths of my being. And because I was linked to that seduction, I lost myself in the web of desire. To love the Other is to speak of the lost place of memory, and my revolt which, to begin with, was only a story imposed from outside, is perpetuated in an accepted resemblance, because the West is part of me, a part that I can deny only insofar as I struggle against all the wests and easts which oppress or disenchant me.)

Having been seduced, and even prostituted and symbolically raped by the coloniser, the colonised subject has to revolt in order to preserve something of his own identity:

> Au bout de la parabole, il y avait le même terrain vague de la culture, j'avais les yeux ouverts au cœur de la France idolâtre et je disais: Occident, j'allongerai ton corps d'albâtre, vrai de vrai, rien, néant de rien, rien. Je t'allongerai sur un tronc d'arbre, par l'ondulation de ma main droite, retenue à la déchirure de ta robe. (p. 175)

> (At the end of the parable, there was the same wasteland of culture, I had my eyes opened to the heart of idolatrous France and I said: West, I will stretch out your alabaster body, real and true, nothing, nothingness of nothing, nothing. I will stretch you out on a log by the wave of my right hand, held back by the rip in your dress.)

And finally, the subject of the text who bears the mark of history tattoos the West in a further eroticised encounter filled with desire and violence: 'Je tatoue sur ton sexe, Occident, le graphe de notre infidélité, un feu au bout de chaque doigt. Point nodal, crac!' (p. 175) ('I tattoo on your genitals, West, the graph of our infidelity, a fire at the tip of each finger. Nodal point, bang!'). In *La Blessure du nom propre*, Khatibi explains that the tattooing of the pubis is more common among prostitutes than among other women in North African culture.[81] The West is tattooed in a double gesture of desire and humiliation, in a game of power, of disdain and eroticism mixed together. The West must now give itself; and this body that is now tattooed is very different from the tattooed woman of his dreams: 'C'est à ce moment qu'elle arrive, la femme voilée. Rappelle-toi ses mains tracées au henné, rappelle-toi sa protection, sa douceur, ses mythes, ses contes fantasques. Rappelle-toi aussi le bruit de la mer' (p. 181) ('It is at that moment that she arrives, the veiled woman. Remember her hennaed hands, remember her protection, her gentleness, her myths, her fantastic tales. Remember too the noise of the sea'). In Western culture and history, writes Khatibi, the tattoo is the mark of domination and this tattoo will therefore be experienced as such.[82] In his culture, however, the tattoo protects. And beyond that, all writing is a form of tattoo, as Khatibi writes in *La Blessure du nom propre*:

> Comment devenir tatoueur(se)? La technique est relativement simple. Mais elle relève du discours mythique: rappelons ce rite marocain pour l'apprentie tatoueuse qui procède à des offrandes au marabout protecteur. La nuit, elle rêve: le saint homme lui offre l'aiguille. Nous n'avons pas fait autre chose en écrivant ce texte. Mais qui le saura?[83]

> (How to become a tattooist, man or woman? The technique is relatively simple. But it contains an element of mythical discourse: we should recall that Moroccan rite for the apprentice tattooist who proceeds to make offerings to the protecting marabout. In the night she has a dream: the holy man offers her the needle. We have done nothing different in writing this text. But who will know it?)

Through writing, Khatibi will himself become endowed with the power of the tattoo-artist, and will connect with the mythical discourses of his culture, as he writes in *La Mémoire tatouée*: 'A côté du Coran, il y avait le talisman et la magie des femmes, par le henné et le tatouage. C'est pourquoi, signe des signes, le sexe est la fin de la mémoire désordonnée' (p. 57) ('Besides the Koran, there was the talisman and the magic of women through henna and tattooing. That is why, sign of signs, sex is the end of disordered memory').

For all the violence of much of *La Mémoire tatouée*, Khatibi's narrator eventually comes to terms with the fact that the West is part of his identity, and the autobiographical act becomes his liberation, making him unafraid of contradiction. There is reconciliation between the cultures that form his identity: 'Certes, Occident, je me scinde, mais mon identité est une infinité de jeux, de roses de sables, euphorbe est ma mère, je suis protégé, Occident!' (p. 173) ('All right, West, I am split, but my identity is an infinity of games, sand roses, euphorbia is my mother, I am protected, West!'). The reference to the *roses de sable*, the intricate sandstones, each one unique, formed in the desert landscape of North Africa, provides a striking visual image. This reconciliation of two cultures is, nonetheless, the culmination of a personal struggle. Khatibi's project may be symptomatic of the concerns of a generation, as previously discussed, but, like all the writers here, his coming to terms with his history remains an intensely writerly resolution.[84]

At the end of the text another striking image is introduced, that of the *rosace*, the geometrical figure of the rosette, the stylised figure of the rose: 'Une rosace en mosaïque; je suis fasciné chaque fois que j'y jette un regard. Quelle pensée de pierre me hante' (p. 212) ('A mosaic rosette: I am fascinated every time I glance at it. What a thought of stone haunts me'). Lucy Stone McNeece comments on this image and also on the 'haunting' of the narrator:

> The *'pensée de pierre'* ('thought of stone') suggests ancient inscriptions, perhaps those of the Rosetta Stone. The verb *'hanter'* ('haunt') echoes the words of a man who gave the narrator a talisman as a boy: *'Il dit: tu es divisé de part et d'autre du corps… Il dit: tu es hanté'*. (p. 52) ('He said, "You are divided between the two parts of your body"… He said, "you are haunted"'). *'Hanter'* condenses the theme of doubling, conveying both a shadow outside the self and a level of subconscious experience within. It suggests both the spectre of the Other and the mask of oppression. It recalls the voluptuous tribal voices who, throughout the narration, have reminded the narrator of his origins. Articulating both the way desire is governed by the Other and the way identity is founded upon difference, the verb *'hanter'* effectively sums up the dynamics of the text.[85]

The use of the term 'haunting' has recently become important in the study of cultural memory with, for example, Derrida's notion of 'hauntology', history as traces of a past that both is and, at the same time, is not there in the present.

McNeece very effectively analyses the *rosace* in terms of a heterogeneous sign: 'the very image of the signifier, embedded in various forms in both the Arabic and Christian traditions as a symbol at once mythical and erotic'.[86] I am equally interested in this idea of the 'pensée de pierre' and the implication of writing, identity and 'ancient inscriptions'. Is Khatibi also referring here to an inscription of a lost language, one that would belong absolutely to his traditional culture, and one therefore that would allow a written identity that would belong wholly to him? This allusion to an ancient inscription provides a direct link to the quest of the writer in Assia Djebar's work, as I shall analyse in the following chapter.

CHAPTER 5

Assia Djebar: History, Selfhood and the Possession of Knowledge

L'entre-deux-langues, j'y suis comme écrivain depuis trente ans, dans un tangage-langage (pour reprendre le titre de Michel Leiris) qui détermine jusqu'à mes résidences géographiques. Un aller-retour entre France et Algérie et vice-versa, sans savoir finalement où est l'aller, vers où aller, vers quelle langue, vers quelle source, vers quels arrières, sans non plus savoir où se situerait le retour, retour certes impossible et mythique de l'émigrée, mais aussi vers un passé origine, vers une langue origine d'une mère sourde et muette [...] Ce tangage entre deux langages, s'inscrivant dans mon espace de vie, il me semble en avoir établi un premier bilan dans un premier livre ouvertement autobiographique: *L'Amour, la fantasia.*

Assia Djebar, 'La Langue dans l'espace ou l'espace dans la langue'[1]

(As a writer, I have found myself placed between two languages for the past thirty years, in a 'pitching of language' (to use Michel Leiris's title) which has determined everything, even where I live. Going backwards and forwards between France and Algeria and vice versa, ending up not knowing which way is forward, where to go to, towards which language, which source, which way is backward, and without knowing either where to return to – a return which is anyway impossible, mythical, for all emigrants – but also a return towards one's past, towards one's mother-tongue, the tongue of a deaf and dumb mother [...] This pitching between two languages, inscribed on the very space of my life, is something I think I made a preliminary assessment of in my first openly autobiographical book: *Fantasia: An Algerian Cavalcade.*)

En somme, 'je ne vous ai pas tout dit', un peu comme dans une confession dans la tradition chrétienne. Je n'ai jamais été au confessionnal, mais il y a quelque chose de la confession dans le texte autobiographique. Une fois que dans une confession vous avez avoué quelque chose, cela ne peut pas être repris, c'est trop tard. Le texte autobiographique est irréversible dans ce sens. Ainsi l'autobiographie a un déroulement infini.

Assia Djebar, 'Violence de l'autobiographie'[2]

(To sum it up, 'I haven't told you everything', a bit like in confession in the Christian tradition. I've never been into a confessional, but there is something like confession in an autobiographical text. Once you've said something in confession, you can't take it back, it's too late. In the same way, autobiographical writing is irreversible. And so the unrolling of an autobiography is an endless process.)

The first of the above statements by Assia Djebar, principally concerning her relationship to language, raises several crucial issues that will be

248

treated during the course of this chapter. Coming to terms with writing in the French language is a recurrent source of reflection for many writers in a colonial and postcolonial context, as we have previously seen. In addition, Djebar takes as reference point here Michel Leiris's conception of the relationship of the writer to language, as I also did in the first chapter. This conception is typically conveyed by Leiris in word-play that concerns the way in which the very use of language, of the written word, is necessarily a form of commitment ('ce tangage/t'engage', 'this pitching/commits you' – homophones in the French) by the writer struggling with concepts of selfhood. The very nature of language forces the writer concerned with authentic self-expression to commit to the quest for an identity in language, with the consequent personal, political, social and creative implications.[3] This commitment is for Assia Djebar very much an extended project seeking to express both a poetics and a politics of identity, as it is for the writers previously discussed. In the quotation given above, Djebar declares *L'Amour, la fantasia* to be 'openly' autobiographical, even though the writer's real name, Fatima-Zohra Imalayen, does not appear on the cover, and the title page describes it as a *roman*, a novel (although this description was added by the publisher, not by the author, and it was originally called *Essai d'autobiographie*, an autobiographical essay or an attempt at autobiography).[4] As a Muslim woman intellectual of Arabo-Berber origin educated within the French school system while her country was still under colonial rule, and who witnessed the Algerian War, Djebar encompasses in her work the personal and collective experiences of the colonial and postcolonial cultures of North Africa, like the writers previously considered here. In her work, however, there is clearly the added dimension of gender and the female experience to be considered, although the issue of poverty that is so important in the conception of the self for Feraoun and Memmi is not a part of her struggle. She herself recognises that she comes from a privileged background within her own culture, and her status as a girl sent to school and not veiled at puberty is a particular one.[5] This issue of the North African writer who uses French as the language of written expression, as a linguistic and social 'outsider' in relation to two cultures, is one to which I shall return in the conclusion.

Djebar's work is therefore political as well as intensely literary, particularly concerning the position of women, but also more generally concerning the continued violence in Algeria (during colonisation and then during the Algerian War, after independence and into the 1990s, as

I described at the end of Chapter 2), although this balance shifts from book to book. However, the question of the power of such a literary project and the status of the intellectual within the reality of the political sphere remains, as is the case with Khatibi's work. Nonetheless, such work does challenge many of the assumptions of a postcolonial world and leads to a reconsideration of the place of the intellectual in the face of globalisation, as Mireille Calle-Gruber identifies:

> Travail d'anamnèse singulière et collective ainsi tentative de recomposition d'un sujet multiculturel de l'écriture, les livres d'Assia Djebar sont tous affrontés, explicitement ou non, à cette problématique [la question de la globalisation et de son analytique par le biais de la littérature] et l'œuvre se situe de façon exemplaire au cœur de ce qui s'est noué au XXᵉ siècle de rapports de force autour du colonialisme et puis du 'postcolonialisme'.[6]

> (Works of individual and collective commemoration, attempts at reconstructing the multicultural subject of writing, Assia Djebar's books all confront this problematic [the question of globalisation and the analysis of it through literature] and her work takes its place as a model at the heart of the lines of force traced around colonialism and then 'postcolonialism' in the twentieth century.)

The novels, essays, theoretical work and films of Assia Djebar have brought her to deserved prominence as a writer not only in the field of Francophone literature, but more widely in the debates concerning oppression, liberation and particularly the place of women in the postcolonial world. In this chapter I shall be concentrating on two volumes of her 'Algerian Quartet': *L'Amour, la fantasia* (1985; reprinted 1995; *Fantasia: An Algerian Cavalcade*), which has received much critical attention, mainly focusing on the rewriting of the history of the colonisation of Algeria undertaken by Djebar in the text; and a later text, *Vaste est la prison* (1995; *So Vast the Prison*).[7] The second volume of the quartet, *Ombre sultane*[8] (*A Sister to Scheherazade*) is also concerned with questions of identity; but although the name of Isma, one of the protagonists in this text, returns in *Vaste est la prison* (in which she is identifiable as a facet of Djebar herself, given that she is the director of a film using women from her native region, like Djebar herself), the narrative strategy of identity is rather different in *Ombre sultane*. While it can certainly be said to be of interest for the consideration of the development of a *fiction identitaire*, Djebar does not engage with an autobiographical discourse in *Ombre sultane* in the same way as she does in the first and third volumes of the quartet.

In *L'Amour, la fantasia* and *Vaste est la prison*, the subject of the liberation of the individual and of the collective, and the strategies the writer uses to achieve that liberation, are bound up with the types of knowledge (about history, about language, about cultural and individual identity) and the types of self-knowledge that are necessarily at work in the development of a discourse of identity in the colonial and postcolonial contexts. The exploration, or rather the excavation, of history is undertaken by Djebar in particular in *L'Amour, la fantasia* in order to facilitate a new relationship with the past. This exploration or excavation of history becomes bound up with the quest of the writer for the creation of a new place in the world for herself and for the postcolonial writer more generally. As Djebar made clear a long time before the publication of the quartet: 'La repossession de l'identité ne peut passer que par l'histoire. Il faut rétablir la dialectique passé-présent'[9] ('The repossession of identity can only pass through history. The past-present dialectic has to be restored'). I shall therefore be considering the ways in which Djebar seeks a path to the liberation of the self and of the wider community (notably the community of women, both past and present) through the re-examination of history and the relationship of the individual and of the collective to their histories. This may appear to be a slight shift in my position regarding the 'collective' potential of autobiographical discourse. However, Djebar's own approach towards this mediation of the voices of others (especially, but not exclusively, women's voices,) is a particular one, as we will see, and the singular voice of the writer comes progressively to the fore. The focus will remain on the writing strategies employed in the two texts in order to uncover these other histories, and I shall consider in particular Djebar's own relationship to the task of the writer and to her own particular position – 'fugitive et ne le sachant pas' ('fugitive without knowing it') as she says of herself in *Vaste est la prison* – and then coming to know the meaning of such a way of living.[10] I shall finally suggest that her work charts the way in which the possession of knowledge provides the possibility of resolving conflicts that may allow a different way of being in the postcolonial world – or at least a different way of being for the writer, for although Djebar certainly creates for herself the role of 'medium' through which silenced voices pass (especially for those women, both historically and in the contemporary world, whose voices have not been or are still not heard), and although hers is a very political voice, there is no doubt also that she remains quintessentially interested in what literature, the written, can do.[11]

The role of the written word is made more complex, not only because Djebar is a Muslim woman, but also due to the conflict between her oral 'maternal' Berber language, and the written 'paternal' language, which

for her is not (Modern Standard) Arabic, but French. For by the time
Djebar writes *Vaste est la prison*, French has changed from being the 'stepmother' tongue of *L'Amour, la fantasia* to being identified in her work
with the father (himself a teacher in a French primary school) who
bestowed this ambiguous gift upon her through her schooling, a problematic already being explored towards the end of *L'Amour, la fantasia*.
The conflict between oral and written modes of expression and the
struggle to reappropriate the written word for herself and for other
women remain at the heart of her identity as a writer, her strategy as a
writer, and her very being as a writer.[12] In *L'Amour, la fantasia* Djebar
describes the power and the danger of the act of writing in French, and
the risk of writing about the self in French is made explicit:

> Ecrire la langue adverse, ce n'est plus inscrire sous son nez ce marmonnement
> qui monologue; écrire par cet alphabet devient poser son coude bien loin
> devant soi, par-derrière le remblai – or dans ce retournement, l'écriture fait
> ressac.
>   Langue installée dans l'opacité d'hier, dépouille prise à celui avec lequel
> ne s'échangeait aucune parole d'amour... Le verbe français qui hier était
> clamé, ne l'était trop souvent qu'en prétoire par des juges et des condamnés.
> Mots de revendication, de procédure, de violence, voici la source orale de
> ce français des colonisés.
>   Sur les plages désertées du présent, amené par tout cessez-le-feu
> inévitable, mon écrit cherche encore son lieu d'échange et de fontaines, son
> commerce. Cette langue était autrefois sarcophage des miens; je la porte
> aujourd'hui comme un messager transporterait le pli fermé ordonnant sa
> condamnation au silence, au cachot. Me mettre à nu dans cette langue me
> fait entretenir un danger permanent de déflagration. De l'exercice de l'au-
> tobiographie dans la langue de l'adversaire d'hier... (*L'Amour, la fantasia*,
> p. 241)[13]

> (Writing the enemy's language is more than just a matter of scribbling down
> a muttered monologue under your very nose; to use this alphabet involves
> placing your elbow some distance in front of you to form a bulwark –
> however, in this twisted position, the writing is washed back to you.
>   This language was imported in the murky, obscure past, spoils taken
> from the enemy with whom no fond word was ever exchanged... French –
> formerly the language of the law courts, used alike by judges and convicted.
> Words of accusation, legal procedure, violence – that is the oral source of
> the colonized people's French.
>   As I come to the inevitable ceasefire at the end of every war, my writing
> is washed up on the deserted seashores of the present day and looks for a
> place where a linguistic armistice can be arranged, a patio with fountains
> playing where people come and go. This language was formerly used to
> entomb my people; when I write it today I feel like the messenger of old,
> who bore a sealed missive which might sentence him to death or to the
> dungeon. By laying myself bare in this language I start a fire which may
> consume me. For attempting an autobiography in the former enemy's
> language...)

Yet Djebar continues to undertake the endeavour and to persevere with the act of writing despite, in defiance of, or perhaps because of, the ever-present risk inherent in such an act.

Fatima-Zohra Imalayen was born in 1936 near Cherchell, Algeria. She chose the pen name Assia Djebar for the publication of her first novel *La Soif* (1957):

> The young writer asked her fiancé, an Algerian nationalist who would soon be on the run from the French police, to recite the ninety-nine modes of address to Allah in the hope of finding herself a *nom de plume*. She selected *djebbar*, the phrase that praises 'Allah the intransigent', but in her haste spelled it '*djébar*', unwittingly transforming the classical Arabic into the vernacular term for 'healer'. The accent has since been dropped [...] As for Assia, she has said 'it was just a family first name that everybody liked'. But it has far-reaching symbolic resonances. In standard Arabic, it designates Asia and the mysterious Orient, thus 'orientalising' its bearer. It also happens to be the name of the Egyptian princess who rescued Moses and is so honoured in Algerian lore as a holy woman and called 'Pharaoh's sister'. In the vernacular, it designates the flower variously known as the immortelle or the edelweiss.[14]

Mireille Calle-Gruber also comments on the pen-name of the author, attributing slightly different meanings to the name, although the connotations of healing and of consoling remain: 'ASSIA DJEBAR, qui signifie "intransigeance" (*djebar* en arabe classique c'est l'Intransigeant) et "consolation, réconciliation" (Assia en dialecte c'est "celle qui console, qui accompagne de sa présence")'[15] ('ASSIA DJEBAR, which means "intransigence" (*djebar* in classical Arabic is The Intransigent), and "consolation, reconciliation" (*Assia* is dialect for "she who consoles, who accompanies with her presence")').

Educated in Algiers and Paris, Assia Djebar was the first Algerian woman to be accepted at the Ecole Normale Supérieure de Sèvres in 1955, but she ended her studies there the following year after participating in the strike by Algerian students. During the Algerian War of Independence, she wrote for the newspaper of the FLN (Front National de la Libération), *Moudjahid*, by publishing interviews with Algerian refugees in Morocco and Tunisia. After continuing her studies, she lectured in history at the universities of Rabat, Morocco (1959) and Algiers (1962), where she was also involved in journalism and broadcasting. She had a prolific early career as a writer, publishing four novels by the age of 31: *La Soif* (1957; translated as *The Mischief*), *Les Impatients* ('The Impatient Ones', 1958), *Les Enfants du nouveau monde* ('The Children of the New World', 1962) and *Les Alouettes naïves* ('The Naive Larks', 1967), and in the following two years writing a play (with

Walid Garn, her husband at the time, *Rouge l'aube* ('Red the Dawn'), in 1969, performed at the Third Pan-African Cultural Festival held in Algiers) and publishing a volume of poetry, *Poèmes pour l'Algérie heureuse* ('Poems for Happy Algeria', 1969). In the 1980s she divided her time for a number of years between France and Algeria. She has more recently worked increasingly within academic centres in the United States, at Louisiana State University, Baton Rouge (1997–2001) and as Silver Professor (French and Francophone Studies) at New York University since 2001.

The early novels published in the decade 1957 to 1967 already focused on the couple, on the body, and on the experience of women. Her fiction attracted some criticism inside Algeria for not paying sufficient attention to the country's political situation, although a further theme is in fact the experience of the young generation marked by the struggle for liberation. These are all themes that would be developed in her later work, as would the sensitivity to the issue of language that she was already writing about in 1969:[16] 'Si l'on considère la situation actuelle du Tiers-Monde en ce domaine, le bilinguisme n'est pas vécu comme un enrichissement mais bien davantage comme un déchirement'[17] ('If one considers the present situation of the Third World in this sphere, bilingualism is not experienced as enriching but rather as tearing apart'). As far as writing is concerned, there then followed a long and important silence for the development of her writing, until the publication of the collection of short stories, *Femmes d'Alger dans leur appartement* (*Women of Algiers in their Apartment*), in 1980. During this period, however, she continued working creatively, turning to film-making, and importantly returning to her maternal oral language, with *La Nouba des femmes du Mont Chenoua* ('The Nouba of the Women of Mount Chenoua', 1978; winner of the Critics' Prize at the Venice Biennale, 1979, and in which musical sequences alternate with oral testimonies based on the experiences of peasant woman in the Algerian War), and later *La Zerda ou les chants de l'oubli* ('The Zerda, or Songs of Forgetting', 1982, a documentary juxtaposing newsreels of the First and Second World Wars and Algerian women singing traditional songs). This film work is therefore critical for an understanding of her creative journey.[18] As Assia Djebar herself has said, film gave her writing a vision.[19] *Femmes d'Alger dans leur appartement* takes as its title the famous Orientalist Delacroix painting, and also contains a complex and revealing theoretical essay in the form of a 'postface' entitled 'Regard interdit, son coupé' ('Forbidden Gaze, Severed Sound') that deals with the politics of the gaze and female representation.[20] As in the 1962 and 1967 novels, the War of Independence forms the background to many of these stories, this time especially its aftermath and the effect on the lives of women, but there is a new insistence on the writer as the medium through which the unheard, silenced, oppressed, repressed voices of these women may pass, often presented in italics in this and later texts. In a television interview Assia Djebar has spoken of her ambition to 'passer inaperçue dans mon texte [...] comme si c'était vingt algériennes qui mêleraient leurs voix'[21] ('to go unnoticed in my writing [...] as though it were the mingled voices of twenty Algerian women'), and from the early 1980s onwards Djebar's project encompasses not only the lives, experiences, voices of these women, but a whole history which has been obscured, a quest which will be further fulfilled in *L'Amour, la fantasia*. In many ways, in both content and form, *Femmes d'Alger* heralds the autobiographical work that follows five years later, and it is clear that this text remains central to Djebar's work, with an updated edition being published in 2002 which includes an additional story.

Djebar's own 'silence' between the novels published up to the end of the 1960s and the short stories published in 1980 was essentially a silencing of the written word. The films that she made during this period returned her to her Berber origins, and most especially to her mother tongue, as previously noted. As far as the relationship to language is concerned, this was a reconnection with the oral language and traditions of her ancestors, continued in the lives of contemporary women:

> J'ai pensé que je pouvais devenir un écrivain de langue arabe. Il fallait que je me réapproprie l'oralité, le son arabe [...] Il y a eu le plaisir de travailler avec la langue arabe lors du montage, de réfléchir sur les bruits, les voix, la musique. La littérature ne me donnait pas cela. Sortie de là, je me suis réconciliée avec l'écriture en langue française [...] J'ai fait au cinéma le travail que je n'avais pas pu faire comme poète – comme poète arabe bien sûr.[22]

> (I thought that I could become an Arabic-language writer. I needed to reappropriate the spoken language, the sound of Arabic [...] There was the pleasure of working with the Arabic language during filming, reflecting on the sounds, the voices, the music. Literature did not give me that. Once I'd finished, I was reconciled to the idea of writing in French [...] In my films, I did the work I had not been able to do as a poet – as an Arabic poet, of course.)

This statement concerning a reconciliation with the French language can be compared with that of Khatibi, although in both cases the situation remains complex. In fact French is also used in the voice-over of Djebar's first film, *La Nouba*; as she has put it, French became her camera.[23] Whether there is a complete reconciliation with writing in French remains

open to interpretation. Assia Djebar remains ambiguous about her relation to French in her writing and in interviews, and such a stance, which
is unafraid of contradiction, provides a particularly rich source for the
reader interested in pursuing the question of bilingualism, or multilingualism, and personal identity.[24] What is certain is that in the space
between her oral and written languages that is created 'representation'
can take place:

> Ecrire en langue étrangère, hors de l'oralité des deux langues de ma région
> natale – le berbère des montagnes du Dahra et l'arabe de ma ville –, écrire
> m'a ramenée aux cris des femmes sourdement révoltées de mon enfance, à
> ma seule origine.
>   Ecrire ne tue pas la voix, mais la réveille, surtout pour ressusciter tant
> de sœurs disparues. (*L'Amour, la fantasia*, p. 229)
>
> (Writing in a foreign language, not in either of the tongues of my native
> country – the Berber of the Dahra mountains or the Arabic of the town where
> I was born – writing has brought me to the cries of the women silently
> rebelling in my youth, to my own true origins.
>   Writing does not silence the voice, but awakens it, above all to resur-
> rect so many vanished sisters.)

On a technical level, material from the oral testimonies of Algerian
peasant women during the War of Independence is introduced into 'Voix'
('Voices'), the second part of *L'Amour, la fantasia*, bringing the type of
oral testimonies used in the film-making to the written word, and into
'Un silencieux désir' ('A Silent Desire'), the third part of *Vaste est la
prison*, in which the experience of film-making process is recounted.
However, the need to return to the mother tongue was not just a question of the language of expression, of a return to a source (however
'mythical', as Djebar's own statement used as an epigraph to this chapter
suggests), or indeed of personal identity, but was also a repercussion of
the very act of writing, and of writing in French: 'j'avais une écriture à
la limite de l'autobiographie [...] Ecrire dans cette langue mais écrire très
près de soi, pour ne pas dire de soi-même, avec un arrachement, cela devenait pour moi une entreprise dangereuse'[25] ('my writing went to the limits
of autobiography [...] Writing in this language, but writing very close to
oneself, if not actually about oneself, with such a wrench: that became a
dangerous enterprise for me'). Djebar had already talked about the need
to mask any autobiographical reference in her work very early on in her
writing career:

> J'ai toujours voulu éviter de donner à mes romans un caractère auto-
> biographique par peur de l'indécence et par horreur d'un certain strip-tease
> intellectuel auquel on se livre souvent avec complaisance dans les premières
> œuvres. Ma vie personnelle n'a rien en commun avec mes héroïnes. Je n'ai
> pas de conflit avec ma famille, je n'ai jamais fait de fugue.[26]

(I've always wanted to avoid giving my novels an autobiographical character, for fear of indecency, and horror of a certain intellectual striptease
which people delight to perform in their first books. My personal life has
nothing in common with my heroines. I have no conflict with my family,
and I've never run away.)

Jeanne-Marie Clerc sees the real autobiographical work originating
from 1977 onwards with the making of *La Nouba des femmes du Mont
Chenoua*, and gradually becoming more insistent. However, she also
notes that in fact there are autobiographical elements in Djebar's early
work as she analyses the emergence of the subject in her work:

> Il reste que cette Algérienne occidentalisée [dans *La Soif*] est déjà une forme
> d'image de soi, même si la phrase de Joubert citée en exergue 'la moitié de
> moi se moque de l'autre', incite à se défier de toute identification autobi-
> ographique trop facile [...] Il y a donc, dès ce premier roman, une timide
> émergence du sujet, s'affirmant contre le silence et la claustration, grâce à
> l'apport d'une autre culture, à la fois acceptée dans une mise en scène
> euphorique du personnage, et dénoncée dans l'échec tragique de l'histoire
> contée. Le masque n'est donc pas aussi total que veut l'affirmer l'auteur, qui
> ne reconnaîtra l'amorce d'une affirmation autobiographique que dans son
> troisième roman, *Les Enfants du nouveau monde*, publié à Paris en 1962,
> où, dit-elle, 'j'ai voulu jeter un regard sur les miens. La position de Lila
> (l'héroïne), à côté et, en même temps dedans et témoin, c'est un peu moi'.[27]

> (It remains true that this Westernised Algerian woman [in *The Mischief*] is
> already a form of self-image, even though the phrase from Joubert quoted
> at the beginning, 'half of me laughs at the other half', incites one to mistrust
> any facile autobiographical identification [...] There is then, from this first
> novel onwards, a timid appearance of the subject, affirming herself against
> silence and cloistering, with the help of another culture which is at once
> accepted in a euphoric presentation of the character and denounced in the
> tragic failure of the story that is told. The mask, therefore, is not as total as
> is claimed by the author, who only admits to the beginnings of an autobio-
> graphical statement in her third novel, *Les Enfants du nouveau monde* ('The
> Children of the New World'), published in Paris in 1962, in which, she says,
> 'I wanted to cast an eye over my own family. The position of Lila (the
> heroine), apart, and at the same time inside and a witness, is something like
> me.')

Yet rather than eventually refusing what seems to be an inescapable
urge towards autobiographical expression, Assia Djebar was able in the
1980s, nearly thirty years after the publication of her first novel, to take
this 'dangerous enterprise' to a further limit that would encompass a
reflection on personal memory and on a wider cultural memory, on the
writing and rewriting of individual and of collective history, and on the
analysis of the nature of selfhood in language, necessitating the development of a number of writing strategies, and culminating in what may
truly be called a poetics of identity in the 'Algerian Quartet'. In between
the second and third volumes, two other texts, both fictional and more

theoretical, were published: *Loin de Médine* (1991; *Far from Madina*), a rewriting of the lives of the wives of the Prophet, and *Le Blanc de l'Algérie* (1995; *Algerian White*), a kind of book of mourning for the dead of Algeria, not only writers, but those journalists and schoolteachers executed in the violence that erupted there in the early 1990s in the continuing struggle for power, a text from which I have quoted in the chapter on Mouloud Feraoun. Since the publication of the third volume of the quartet, other texts, both fictional and theoretical, have appeared: *Oran, langue morte* (1997; 'Oran, Dead Language'); *Les Nuits de Strasbourg* (1997; 'Strasbourg Nights'); *Ces voix qui m'assiègent... en marge de ma francophonie* (1999; 'These Voices Which Assail Me... In the Margin of My French Speaking', 1999); *La Femme sans sépulture* (2002; 'The Unburied Woman'); *La Disparition de la langue française* (2003; 'The Disappearance of the French Language'). Although Assia Djebar has moved further away physically from the two sites that have generated her writing, Algeria and France, their presence in these works endures. While taking part in a conference on autobiography and post-colonialism in 1996, Djebar read an extract from what she announced as the fourth volume of the quartet, *La fin du royaume d'Alger* ('The End of the Kingdom of Algiers'): 'Je vais vous lire mon dernier texte, j'espère que c'est le dernier. Il fera partie du quatrième volet du quatuor et il en est le milieu' ('I am going to read you my last piece, I hope it's the last. It will form part of the fourth set of the *Quatuor*, and it's half-way through it'), but at the time of writing, that text has not yet been published.[28] According to Mireille Calle-Gruber, this final volume, 'après celui de la mère (*Vaste est la prison*), devrait composer le "livre du père"' ('while *So Vast the Prison* is the "book of the mother", [this final volume] would be the "book of the father"').[29]

THE (RE-)POSSESSION OF KNOWLEDGE AND THE RELATIONSHIP TO HISTORY IN *L'AMOUR, LA FANTASIA*

> Pélissier, l'intercesseur de cette mort longue, pour mille cinq cents cadavres sous El Kantara, avec leurs troupeaux bêlent indéfiniment au trépas, me tend son rapport et je reçois ce palimpseste pour y inscrire à mon tour la passion calcinée des ancêtres.
>
> Assia Djebar, *L'Amour, la fantasia*, p. 93
>
> (Pélissier, speaking on behalf of this long-drawn-out agony, on behalf of fifteen hundred corpses buried beneath El-Kantara, with their flocks unceasingly bleating at death, hands me his report and I accept this palimpsest on which I now inscribe the charred passion of my ancestors.)

The most obvious of the writing strategies employed in *L'Amour, la fantasia* is the recuperation of a lost history of Algeria, and especially the lost history of the women of Algeria, from between the lines of official history, and then the re-composition of this history as an element of both collective and personal history as it alternates in the text with the childhood experiences of the narrative voice (or at least the main narrative voice).[30]

A quotation from *Une année dans le Sahel* by Eugène Fromentin, the nineteenth-century French painter and writer, serves as an epigraph to the text as a whole. On the surface this is a reference to the 'authority' of the colonial power's language and to the Orientalising interpretation of North African society in the nineteenth century, although when Fromentin's writing is taken up again towards the end of the text the relationship of the author to this nineteenth-century writing is made more complex.[31] There is frequent use made of epigraphs in *L'Amour, la fantasia*, a point to which I will return since few critics, with the exception of Anne Donadey, have paid any attention to the ways in which these function. The text also opens amid noise and clamour, and 'un cri déchirant' ('a piercing cry') which appears to herald the coming violence of 'La Prise de la Ville' ('The Capture of the City'), the title of this first part. The second part of this title, 'ou L'Amour s'écrit' ('or Love Writes Itself') announces the adventure in the written word that will ensue. But as Djebar's English translator, Dorothy Blair, has pointed out, taking up the word-play that Djebar herself explores towards the end of the text, this may also be a homophone of 'l'amour, ses cris' ('love, its cries'), evoking erotic fulfilment and the frequent sensuality of the writing that follows; it is also a near homophone of 'l'amour se crie' ('love declares itself'), suggesting a more ambiguous and anguished emotion as love declares itself in the face of opposition. Djebar's own exploration of these connotations adds that of the act of writing about love: '"L'amour, ses cris" ("s'écrit"): ma main qui écrit le jeu de mots français sur les amours qui s'exhalent' (p. 240) ('"Love, its cries" ("writes itself"): my hand as I write in French makes the pun on love affairs that are aired'). As Blair notes,

> The theme of the love-letter is thus another link between the historical and the autobiographical dimension of the novel as well as a basic part of its structure. The antiphony between the written and the oral elements, between 'l'écrit' and 'les cris', is introduced by the love-letters ('*L'Amour s'écrit*' in the original), but the final response is given to the cries of the *Fantasia*.[32]

This first part has an additional epigraph, with North Africa again seen through French eyes, and indeed ears, those of Barchou de Penhoën in his 1835 text, *Expédition d'Afrique*, five years after the beginning of the French conquest. The first section, 'Fillette arabe allant pour la première fois à l'école' ('A Little Arab Girl's First Day at School'), is given a title but not numbered and presents a personal childhood experience of the narrator:

> Fillette arabe allant pour la première fois à l'école, un matin d'automne, main dans la main du père. Celui-ci, un fez sur la tête, la silhouette haute et droite dans son costume européen, porte un cartable, il est instituteur à l'école française. Fillette arabe dans un village du Sahel algérien. (p. 11)

> (A little Arab girl going to school for the first time, one autumn morning, walking hand-in-hand with her father. A tall, erect figure in a fez and a European suit, carrying a bag of school-books. He is a teacher at the French primary school. A little Arab girl in a village in the Algerian Sahel.)

The second section, numbered 'I' in Roman numerals but not given a title, presents a vision of the French fleet arriving off the coast of Algiers:

> Aube de ce 13 juin 1830, à l'instant précis et bref où éclate au-dessus de la conque profonde. Il est cinq heures du matin. Devant l'imposante flotte qui déchire l'horizon, la Ville Imprenable se dévoile. Blancheur fantômatique, à travers un poudroiement de bleus et de gris mêlés [...] La ville, paysage tout en dentelures et en couleurs délicates, surgit dans un rôle d'Orientale immobilisée dans son mystère. (p. 14)

> (Dawn on this thirteenth day of June 1830, at the exact moment when the sun suddenly blazes forth above the fathomless bowl of the bay. It is five in the morning. As the majestic fleet rends the horizon the Impregnable City sheds her veils and emerges, a wraith-like apparition, through the blue-grey haze [...] The city, a vista of crenellated roofs and pastel hues, makes her first appearance in the rôle of 'Oriental Woman', motionless, mysterious.)

The word 'dawn' links the end of the first chapter and the beginning of the second; and this technique of ending and beginning chapters with the same word is used twice more, between 'La Fille du gendarme français' and the section numbered 'III' ('explosion'); and between 'Mon père écrit à ma mère' and the section numbered 'IV' ('ouvertement'/ 'ouvert'). Not only is there an alternating pattern of autobiographical and historical discourses, of personal and collective history set up, but so also is the metaphor that will pervade the text, that of the body of Algeria as the body of a woman, a body that is highly eroticised under the gaze of the invader. The body and desire are essential elements in the dynamics of the whole text:

> Through the figuring of Algeria itself as an object of desire for the pillaging French troops, Djebar is able to examine the process of colonisation from the novel approach of territorial conquest as a trope of human and cultural relations. With the narrative strategy aimed at evoking the anguish and ambiguity of the colonised subject as desired object, and as desiring subject,

> the dislocation generated by the use of the coloniser's language on the part of the speaking subject, and the historical, cultural, and textual interrelation between desire, the body, and writing, become the means by which Djebar's text eventually inscribes the code of its own affirmation. Crucial here will be the evolving dialectical relationship between writing and desire, in which writing will become inextricably bound to the unveiling and implementation of desire, the obscene imposition of the colonial undertaking, the double quest for recognition, and the integration of a valorised, decolonised self into the historical and cultural continuum.[33]

There is no separation between these autobiographical and historical discourses: the highly personal memory of the summer spent with her cousins and the shared desire and fear of love is followed by Barchou's account of the battle of Staouéli on 19 June 1830, and the history of the conquest of Algeria becomes just as much part of the identity of the narrator. She learns in the Frenchman's text that there were also two Algerian women present, two women driven to terrible acts by the violence that has taken place:

> Ces deux Algériennes – l'une agonisante, à moitié raidie, tenant le cœur d'un cadavre français au creux de sa main ensanglantée, la seconde, dans un sursaut de bravoure désespérée, faisant éclater le crâne de son enfant comme une grenade printanière, avant de mourir, allégée –, ces deux héroïnes entrent dans l'histoire nouvelle.
> Je recueille scrupuleusement l'image, deux guerrières entrevue de dos ou de biais, en plein tumulte, par l'aide de camp à l'œil incisif. Annonce d'une fièvre hallucinatoire, lacérée de folie... Image inaugurant les futures 'mater dolorosa' musulmanes qui, nécrophores du harem, vont enfanter, durant la soumission du siècle suivant, des générations d'orphelins sans visage. (p. 29)

> (These two Algerian women – the one in whom rigor mortis was already setting in, still holding in her bloody hands the heart of a dead Frenchman; the second, in a fit of desperate courage, splitting open the brain of her child, like a pomegranate in spring, before dying with her mind at peace – these two heroines enter into recent history.
> I scrupulously record the image: two warrior women glimpsed from the back or from the side, in the midst of the tumult, by the keen eye of the ADC. A forewarning of the hallucinatory fever that will reign, punctuated with folly... An image that prefigures many a future Muslim 'mater dolorosa' who, carrion beetles of the harem, will give birth to generations of faceless orphans during Algeria's thraldom a century later.)

This 'histoire nouvelle' (new history/story) comes into being, emerging from between the lines of the written account by those men who carried out the military invasion, and above all these women, glimpsed only from behind, come to occupy centre stage, to take their place in a history from which they have been excluded, and of which they have generally been merely victims. And in doing this, the narrator retrieves an identity for the anonymous 'faceless orphans', but equally finds a way in which to express a new identity for herself. This rewriting of the dominant historical discourse concerning the colonisation of Algeria is the aspect of the text that has received most attention by critics up to now. However, as John Erickson has effectively summarised it, this is both a 'plural chronicle' and a 'singular' autobiography.[34]

In the personal story evoked by the narrator there is a range of memories presented, each one analysed for its value and meaning: for example, the place held in the narrator's memory by the French gendarme's daughter whose mother is a friend of her aunt. She reflects on the fascination the woman held for all these young Algerian girls, and indeed the fascination that the whole way of life of the French held for the narrator:

> Car, pour moi, les demeures françaises exhalaient une odeur différente, reflé-taient une lumière secrète – ainsi mon œil reste fasciné par le rivage des 'Autres'. Durant toute mon enfance, peu avant la guerre qui aboutira à l'Indépendance, je ne franchis aucun seuil français, je n'entrai dans aucun intérieur d'une condisciple française... (p. 34)

> (For me, these French homes gave off a different smell, a mysterious light; for me, the French are still 'The Others', and I am still hypnotized by their shores.
>   Throughout my childhood, just before the war which was to bring us independence, I never crossed a single French threshold, I never entered the home of a single French schoolfellow...)

The ridicule which the young girl pours on the terms of affection which she hears expressed in French by Marie-Louise, the gendarme's daughter, when she talks about her fiancé, and the analysis of the later consequences of her reaction for the narrator's relationship to the French language, is also pursued:

> Anodine scène d'enfance: une aridité de l'expression s'installe et la sensi-bilité dans sa période romantique se retrouve aphasique. Malgré le bouillonnement de mes rêves d'adolescence plus tard, un nœud, à cause de ce 'Pilou chéri', résista: la langue française pouvait tout m'offrir de ses trésors inépuisables, mais pas un, pas le moindre de ses mots d'amour ne me serait réservé... Un jour ou l'autre, parce que cet état autistique ferait chape à mes élans de femme, surviendrait à rebours quelque soudaine explosion. (p. 38)

> (An innocuous scene from my childhood: but later, when I reach the time for romance, I can find no words, I cannot express my emotions. Despite the turmoil of my adolescent dreams, this 'darling Pilou' left me with one deep-rooted complex: the French language could offer me all its inex-haustible treasures, but not a single one of its terms of endearment would be destined for my use... One day, because all my spontaneous impulses as a woman would be stifled by this autistic state, one day the pressure would suddenly give and a reaction would set in.)

Another memory evoked is the discovery that her father wrote letters to her mother in French and the general shock of the women around her mother that this act generated, but which for the narrator reveals the love a man and a woman may feel for each other: 'Mon père avait osé "écrire" à ma mère. L'un et l'autre, mon père par l'écrit ma mère dans ses nouvelles conversations où elle citait désormais sans fausse honte son époux, se nommaient réciproquement, autant dire s'aimaient ouvertement' (p. 49) ('My father had dared "to write" to my mother. Both of them referred to each other by name, which was tantamount to declaring openly their love for each other, my father by writing to her, my mother by quoting my father henceforward without false shame in all her conversations'). A criticism of the separation of the sexes within Muslim societies and its consequences for relations between them is a recurrent theme in Assia Djebar's work; here she presents her parents' love using French as a medium as a challenge to this.

Moving from the personal to the historical there is, in the analysis of the accounts of the officers taking part in the colonisation of Algeria from which a 'new history/story' is rescued, a series of terrible and violent encounters between coloniser and colonised that tear apart the silence of the imagined scene of the French fleet arriving: 'Et le silence de cette matinée souveraine précède le cortège de cris et de meurtres, qui vont emplir les décennies suivantes' (p. 17) ('And the silence of this majestic morning is but the prelude to the cavalcade of screams and carnage which will fill the ensuing decades'); firstly the battle at Staouéli in June, recounted by Barchou, previously alluded to; the explosion at Fort l'Empéreur in July that announces the fall of Algiers, recounted by three witnesses, including a civilian, J.T. Merle, 'venu là comme au spectacle' ('for him it is tantamount to a visit to a theatrical performance'); and finally the 'fièvre scriptuaire' ('writing fever') that follows the fall of the city; in all thirty-two accounts in French, inviting a meditation by the narrator on the reasons for the need of so many to write about this conquest. The narrator makes an explicit link between this need of the conquerors to write and to bear witness, and the same need of the clois-tered adolescent girls she shared her holidays with, as personal and collective history intertwine:

> Mes jeunes amies, mes complices du hameau de vacances, écrivaient même langue inutile et opaque parce que cernées, parce que prisonnières; elles estampillaient leur marasme, pour en surmonter plus ou moins le tragique. Les comptes rendus de cette intrusion d'hier décèlent a contrario une nature identique: envahisseurs qui croient prendre la Ville Imprenable, mais qui tournoient dans le buissonnement de leur mal d'être. (pp. 56–57)

> (The girls who were my friends and accomplices during my village holidays wrote in the same futile, cryptic language because they were confined,

because they were prisoners; they mark their marasmus with their own identity in an attempt to rise above their pathetic plight. The accounts of this
past invasion reveal *a contrario* an identical nature: invaders who imagine
they are taking the Impregnable City, but who wander aimlessly in the
undergrowth of their own disquiet.)

The act of writing reveals the problem at the heart of the writing subject:
writing simultaneously reveals and hides. There is a danger that writing
does not enlighten the one who writes, but instead disguises truth. The
task of the writer-narrator is to seek truth (just as in the project of Albert
Memmi) and to restore this truth to writing that may then take on a
different status, and in so doing may liberate the writer, although the way
to this will only be revealed much later in Assia Djebar's writing project.

In the second part of the text, the cries of love become the cries of the
Fantasia of the title, 'Les Cris de la Fantasia', and the epigraph that opens
it this time is from the *Ta'rif*, the autobiography, of Ibn Khaldūn, the
Arab coloniser of the Berbers' land: 'Après avoir pénétré dans leur pays
et vaincu leur résistance, je pris des otages en gage d'obéissance' ('After
I had penetrated into their country and overcome their resistance, I took
hostages to ensure their obedience'). This therefore is an opening text
that yet again begins with a voice of conquest and authority, one with
which the narrator will enter into a dialogue. Importantly it also places
the text under the authority of an Arabic writer of autobiography,[35]
although Anne Donadey has persuasively argued that Djebar's text
becomes a subversive commentary on this epigraph. This reference to an
Arabic text is an important one since the majority of the epigraphs chosen
by Djebar are from European authors, and I shall return to this when
discussing *Vaste est la prison*. In this second part the order of the alternating personal history and collective history is reversed. This time the
historical accounts are placed first and given a title; the personal story
follows, each time identified with a Roman numeral, thus presenting a
mirror image, a symmetry for the two histories. It is particularly in this
section that the image, and indeed extended metaphor, of the body of
Algeria as the body of a woman comes to prominence, as do the roles of
different kinds of women. It is mothers, sisters, wives who are often the
recipients of the accounts of battle in the letters of the French officers,
while the Algerian women are so often their victims. The two captains
whose correspondence is analysed in the first chapter here, 'La Razzia du
Capitaine Bosquet, à partir d'Oran' ('Captain Bosquet Leaves Oran to
Take Part in a *Razzia*'), are Bosquet and Montagnac, both bachelors,
'married to war', and implicitly to the increasingly eroticised Algeria, 'une
Algérie-femme' ('an Algeria-woman') that is in fact impossible to conquer

totally. The officers' clear disquiet troubles the narrator as much as the suffering of those on whom they inflict their violence:

> Ces guerriers qui paradent me deviennent, au milieu des cris que leur style élégant ne peut atténuer, les amants funèbres de mon Algérie. Le viol ou la souffrance des anonymes ainsi rallumés devraient m'émouvoir en premier; mais je suis étrangement hantée par l'émoi même des tueurs, par leur trouble obsessionnel. (p. 69)

> (It is as if these parading warriors, around whom cries rise up which the elegance of their style cannot diminish, are mourning their unrequited love for my Algeria. I should first and foremost be moved by the rape or sufferings of the anonymous victims, which their writings resurrect; but I am strangely haunted by the agitation of the killers, by their obsessive unease.)

The first chapter of the personal story in this part is a highly significant one for the development of the future writer and for her relationship to the French language, tracing as it does the adventure of her first love-letters, letters written in French. The young girl is aware that this exchange takes place in the shadow of the father, who is taken as witness for her to explain her conduct and very importantly to explain why she writes: 'Tu vois, j'écris, et ce n'est pas pour "le mal", pour "l'indécent"! Seulement pour dire que j'existe et en palpiter. Ecrire, n'est-ce pas "me" dire?' (pp. 71–72) ('You see, I'm writing, and there's no harm in it, no impropriety! It's simply a way of saying I exist, pulsating with life! Is not writing a way of telling what "I" am?') (p. 58). She writes in order to express a self, an individual identity. However, this communication also becomes symbolic of the generations of anonymous women who have preceded her and who have never been able to participate in such exchanges. The notion that she is somehow a medium for communication begins to develop. Above all an identity is expressed in the written word to which these women never had access:

> Soudain ces feuilles se mettent à exhaler un pouvoir étrange. Une intercession s'opère: je me dis que cette touffe de râles suspendus s'adresse, pourquoi pas, à toutes les autres femmes que nulle parole n'a atteintes. Celles qui, des générations avant moi, m'ont légué les lieux de leur réclusion, elles qui n'ont jamais rien reçu: aucune voix tendue ainsi en courbe de désir, aucun message que traversait quelque supplication. Elles ne se libéraient que par la psalmodie de leur chant obsidional.
>   La lettre que je rangeai m'est devenue première lettre: pour les attentes anonymes qui m'ont précédée et que je portais sans le savoir. (p. 73)

> (Suddenly these pages begin to emit a strange power. They start to act like a mediator: I tell myself that this cluster of strangled cries is addressed – why not? – to all the other women whom no word has ever reached. Those of past generations who bequeathed me the places of their confinement, those women who never received a letter: no word taut with desire, stretched like a bow, no message run through with supplication. Their only path to freedom was by intoning their obsessive chants.

> The letter that I put away became a first for me: the first expression of
> what those anonymous women who preceded me were waiting for and of
> which I was the unwitting bearer.)

However, there is also the realisation that this written word separates
her from her maternal language, and expression in French becomes a
source of anxiety:

> Préliminaires de la séduction où la lettre d'amour exige non l'effusion du
> cœur ou de l'âme, mais la précision du regard. Une seule angoisse m'habite
> dans cette communication: celle de ne pas assez dire, ou plutôt de ne pas
> dire juste [...] En fait, je recherche, comme un lait dont on m'aurait autre-
> fois écartée, la pléthore amoureuse de la langue de ma mère. Contre la
> ségrégation de mon héritage, le mot plein de l'amour-au-présent me devient
> une parade-hirondelle. (p. 76)

> (As a preliminary to seduction, love-letters do not demand any outpourings
> of the heart or soul, but the precision of a look. When writing, I have but
> one concern: that I should say enough, or rather that I should express myself
> clearly enough [...] And now I too seek out the rich vocabulary of love of
> my mother tongue – milk of which I had been previously deprived. In
> contrast to the segregation I inherited, words expressing love-in-the-present
> become for me like one token swallow heralding summer.)

The following chapter, 'Femmes, enfants, boeufs couchés dans les
grottes' ('Women, Children, Oxen Dying in Caves'), deals with the
account by Pélissier of a terrible moment in the conquest of Algeria in
which the mountain tribe in the Dahra region, the tribe to which the
narrator's ancestors belong, take refuge in caves into which the French
soldiers throw burning logs, burning the people and their animals alive.
The narrator makes clear her own writing strategy, which emerges from
between the lines of the Frenchman's account, and provides a further
enduring metaphor for the whole project here, that of the palimpsest, the
rewriting of another history of Algeria on the parchment of the invader:[36]

> La mémoire exhumée de ce double ossuaire m'habite et m'anime, même s'il
> me semble ouvrir, pour des aveugles, registre obituaire, aux alentours de ces
> cavernes oubliées.
>   Oui, une pulsion me secoue, telle une sourde otalgie: remercier Pélissier
> pour son rapport qui déclencha à Paris une tempête politique, mais aussi me
> renvoie nos morts vers lesquels j'élève aujourd'hui ma trame de mots français
> [...]
>   Pélissier, l'intercesseur de cette mort longue, pour mille cinq cents
> cadavres sous El Kantara, avec leurs troupeaux bêlant indéfiniment au
> trépas, me tend son rapport et je reçois ce palimpseste pour y inscrire à mon
> tour la passion calcinée des ancêtres. (pp. 92–93)

> (I am obsessed by the memories exhumed from this double necropolis, which
> spur me on, even if I feel I am opening a register of the dead, in the region
> of the forgotten caves, for those who will never have eyes to read.
>   Yes, I am moved by an impulse that nags me like an earache: the impulse

> to thank Pélissier for his report which unleashed a political storm in Paris, but which allows me to reach out today to our own dead and weave a pattern of French words around them [...]
>
> Pélissier, speaking on behalf of this long-drawn-out agony, on behalf of fifteen hundred corpses buried beneath El-Kantara, with their flocks bleating unceasingly at death, hands me his report and I accept this palimpsest on which I now inscribe the charred passion of my ancestors.)

The remainder of this part of the text evokes very briefly her brother (with whom the narrator felt no complicity when they were adolescents), the brother who was to join the *maquis* during the War of Independence. It goes on to evoke at greater length, in the historical discourse, the story of the Bride of Mazuna, providing another story of resistance, and the section ends on the personal story of the narrator soon to be married, notably recounted largely in the third person (until the second half), in contrast to the evocation of the brother, expressed in the first person. The cries of the sexual act come to join all the other cries to which a voice has been given in the text: 'Un cri sans la fantasia qui, dans toutes les noces, même en l'absence de chevaux caparaçonnés et de chevaliers rutilants, aurait pu s'envoler. Le cri affiné, allégé en libération hâtive, puis abruptement cassé. Long, infini premier cri du corps vivant' (p. 122) ('A cry which might ring out at every wedding, without the *Fantasia*, even in the absence of caparisoned horses and riders in flaming crimson. The sharp cry of relief and sudden liberation then abruptly checked. Long, infinite first cry of the live body'). This second part ends on the sound of an instrument, the sistrum, and a tumult of voices, above which rises the song of a woman.[37]

The third part of the text has a very different structure, presenting in turn the literally 'buried voices' of its title (or 'Voices from the Past', as the English translation prefers). Following a musical organisation of five movements, it finishes on the *Tzarl-rit*, the Finale, as announced in one of the text's epigraphs, the description given by Beethoven to his Sonatas I and 2 in opus 27: 'Quasi una fantasia...'. The other epigraph is from another 'autobiographer', joining that of the Arab conqueror Ibn Khaldūn; this time it is Saint Augustine meditating on the nature of memory, and in the English translation more of the significant quotation is given: 'And I come to the fields and spreading courts of memory, where there are treasures of unnumbered impressions of things of every kind, stored by the senses'. This is a meditation, then, on the wealth of memories 'stored by the senses', stored in the body, a corporeal and indeed sensual relationship to memory that brings to mind the Proustian revelation of the restoration of lost time through taste, touch and hearing. (I shall return to an analogy with Proust in the discussion of *Vaste est la Prison*.) Augustine will be referred to again towards the end of the text, this time Augustine as another Algerian writing his autobiography under occupation, by the Romans, and writing in Latin, the language of the conqueror: 'La même langue est passée des conquérants aux assimilés; s'est assouplie après que les mots ont enveloppé les cadavres du passé' (p. 242) ('The same language has passed from the conquerors to the assimilated people; has grown more flexible after the corpses of the past have been enshrouded in words').

Within each of the 'movements' of this part of the text, personal memories (each given a title, two to each movement except the fifth) alternate with a series of voices from the past (again two to each movement except the fifth), and interspersed with these voices are a series of short texts in italics, each indicating a different register of the human voice: 'clamour'; 'murmurs'; 'whispers'; 'dialogues'; 'soliloquy', and a series of 'Embraces' ('Corps entrelacés'), as the narrator seeks out the stories of women involved in the War of Independence twenty years later.[38] The first of the personal memories here evokes an unhappy love affair and the narrator's cry of lament in a dark street in Paris, witnessed by a stranger. The power of the voice is revealed in that it can liberate self and affect others:

> Libère en flux toutes les scories du passé. Quelle voix, est-ce ma voix, je la reconnais à peine [...] La voix, ma voix (ou plutôt ce qui sort de ma bouche ouverte, bâillant comme pour vomir ou chanter quelque opéra funèbre) ne peut s'interrompre. Peut-être faut-il lever le bras, mettre la main devant la face, suspendre ainsi la perte de ce sang invisible. (p. 131)

> (It drains off all the scoriae of the past. What voice? Is it my own voice, scarcely recognizable? [...] The voice, my voice (or rather the voice that issues from my open mouth, gaping as if to vomit, or chant some dirge) cannot be suppressed. Perhaps I ought to raise my hand in front of my face to staunch this invisible blood?)

The impact of the voice is therefore powerfully staged, literally setting the scene for the other voices that will follow, mediated by the narrator. These are the voices of women caught up in the War of Independence, the first (who is eventually identified as Chérifa, recounting her story twenty years later to the narrator [p. 141]) telling of her brothers leaving the family to join the *maquis* when '[la] France arriva jusqu'à nous [...] La France est venue et elle nous a brûlés' ('France came right up to our doorsteps [...] France arrived and burnt the whole place down'). The young girl herself is also forced to flee, hiding in the countryside while the fighting continues. The younger brother is killed, and at that point her voice gives way: 'Et ma voix chavira' (pp. 133–38) ('And my voice gave way.') But that voice does not disappear, because through the voice of the narrative it endures; indeed it continues in the following section, a 'clamour', presented in italics, and offering an eternal, poetic evocation continued by the narrator. Contained within the cry of the young girl are the voices of many other women:

> *Elle a entonné un long premier cri, la fillette. Son corps se relève, tache plus claire dans la clarté aveugle; la voix jaillit, hésitante aux premières notes, une voile à peine dépliée qui frémirait, au bas d'un mât de misaine. Puis le vol démarre précautionneusement, la voix prend du corps dans l'espace, quelle voix? Celle de la mère que soldats ont torturée sans qu'elle gémisse, des sœurs trop jeunes, parquées mais porteuses de l'angoisse aux yeux fous, la voix des vieilles du douar qui, bouches béantes, mains décharnées, paumes en avant, font face à l'horreur du glas qui approche? Quel murmure inextinguible, quelle clameur ample, grenelée de stridence?... Est-ce la voix de la fillette aux doigts rougis de henné et de sang fraternel? [...] Voix-cuirasse qui enveloppe le gisant contre la terre, qui lui redonne regard au bord de la fossé.* (pp. 140–41)

> (One prolonged, preliminary cry has escaped her. The child rises, her body an even brighter patch in the transparent air; her voice shrills out, stumbling over the first notes, like the shudder of a sail before it is hoisted on the foremast. Then the voice cautiously takes wing, the voice soars, gaining in strength, what voice? That of the mother who bore the soldiers' torture with never a whimper? That of the little cooped-up sisters, too young to understand, but bearing the message of wild-eyed anguish? The voice of the old women of the *douar* who face the horror of the approaching death-knell, open-mouthed, with palms of fleshless hands turned upwards? What irrepressible keening, what full-throated clamour, strident tremolo? [...] Voice armouring the dead man on the ground, giving him back his eyes on the edge of the grave.)

The second personal memory evoked reveals the distance that her French education has placed between the narrator and her own culture: not only has she not been veiled, but this 'Westernisation' manifests itself in her body and indeed her voice. She is no longer physically comfortable sitting cross-legged with the other women, and she only joins rather uneasily in the traditional songs and cries, preferring to listen to her mother:

> *Ce cri ancestral de déchirement – que la glotte fait vibrer de spasmes allègres – ne sortait du fond de ma gorge que peu harmonieusement. Au lieu de fuser hors de moi, il me déchirait. Je préférais écouter la longue vocifération de ma mère, mi-roucoulement, mi-hululement qui se fondait d'abord dans le chœur profus, puis le terminait en une vocalisme triomphale, en long solos de soprano.* (p. 144)

> (My throat lent itself uneasily, discordantly, to this ancestral plangent cry – which is emitted by spasmodic vibrations of the glottis. Instead of arising spontaneously, it tore me apart. I preferred to listen to my mother giving voice, half cooing, half ululation, blending first with the full-throated chorus then finishing with a triumphant vocalism, a prolonged soprano solo.)

This is arguably a metaphor for Djebar's own strategy and writing practice – the narrative voice is at once singular and plural, weaving in and out of both modes, yet finally becoming strongly and triumphantly singular.

In this evocation she returns also to a very intimate 'confession' concerning the relationship to the French language that has been raised earlier in the text, the fact that she cannot speak words of love in French. Indeed this 'aphasie amoureuse' ('aphasia of love') gives the section its title; she feels subject to an aphasia, the loss of the faculty of speech:[39]

> Cette impossibilité en amour, la mémoire de la conquête la renforça. Lorsque, enfant, je fréquentai l'école, les mots français commençaient à peine à attaquer ce rempart. J'héritais de cette étanchéité; dès mon adolescence, j'expérimentai une sorte d'aphasie amoureuse: les mots écrits, les mots appris, faisaient retrait devant moi, dès que tentait de s'exprimer le moindre élan de mon cœur. (p. 145)

> (The impossibility of this love was reinforced by memory of the conquest. When, as a child, I went to school, the French words scarcely made any impact on this stronghold. I had inherited this imperviousness; from the time of my adolescence I experienced a kind of aphasia in matters of love: the written words, the words I had learned, retreated before me as soon as the slightest heart-felt emotion sought for expression.)

The story of Chérifa then continues with her experience of nursing the wounded, her refusal to marry, joining the *maquisards*, her pursuit and capture by the French, her interrogation and repeated torture. In the first of the 'embraces', the narrator describes Chérifa, twenty years later, at the moment she recounts the story, now married to a widower with five children, ageing herself, and this time her voice liberates memory: 'Sa voix déleste la mémoire [...] Libérant pour moi sa voix, elle se libère à nouveau; de quelle nostalgie son accent fléchira-t-il tout à l'heure?' (pp. 160–61) ('Her voice lifts the burden of memory [...] As she sets her voice free for me, she sets herself free again; what nostalgia will cause her voice to fail presently?'). It is here that the full and terrible contradiction of putting into the written word, and especially into French, the oral history of this woman and of others like her becomes apparent. It exiles the narrator, cutting her off definitively from this community of women bound together in the spoken word, joining the narrator in fact to the officers whose accounts of the colonisation she has read and sought to subvert:

> Je ne m'avance ni en diseuse, ni en scripteuse. Sur l'aire de la dépossession, je voudrais pouvoir chanter.
> Corps nu – puisque je me dépouille des souvenirs d'enfance –, je me veux porteuse d'offrandes, mains tendues vers qui, vers les Seigneurs de la guerre d'hier, ou vers les fillettes rôdeuses qui habitent le silence succédant aux batailles... Et j'offre quoi, sinon nœuds d'écorce de la mémoire griffée,

je cherche quoi, peut-être la douve où se noient les mots de meurtrissure...

Chérifa! Je désirais recréer ta course [...] Ta voix s'est prise au piège; mon parler français la déguise sans l'habiller. A peine si je frôle l'ombre de ton pas!

Les mots que j'ai cru te donner s'enveloppent de la même serge de deuil que ceux de Bosquet ou de Saint-Arnaud. En vérité, ils s'écrivent à travers ma main, puisque je consens à cette bâtardise, au sel métissage que la foi ancestrale ne condamne pas: celui de la langue et non celui du sang.

Mots-torches qui éclairent mes compagnes, mes complices; d'elles, définitivement, ils me séparent. Et sous leur poids, je m'expatrie. (p. 161)

(I do not claim here to be either a story-teller or a scribe. On the territory of dispossession, I would that I could sing.

I would cast off my childhood memories and advance naked, bearing offerings, hands outstretched to whom? – to the Lords of yesterday's war, or to the young girls who lay in hiding and who now inhabit the silence that succeeds the battles... And what are my offerings? Only handfuls of husks, culled from my memory, what do I seek? Maybe the brook where wounding words are drowned...

Cherifa! I wanted to re-create your flight [...] I have captured your voice; disguised it with my French without clothing it. I barely brush the shadow of your footsteps!

The words that I thought to put in your mouth are shrouded in the same mourning garb as those of Bosquet or Saint-Arnaud. Actually, it is they who are writing to each other, using my hand, since I condone this bastardy, the only cross-breeding that the ancestral beliefs do not condemn: that of language, not that of the blood.

Torch-words which light up my women-companions, my accomplices; these words divide me from them once and for all. And weigh me down as I leave my native land.

Just as the act of autobiography in the enemy's language ('la langue adverse') runs the risk of punishment, so the act of transposing the voices of the Algerian women, so necessary to the quest of the construction of an identity, is one which is fraught with danger and potential betrayal, as Patricia Geesey has pointed out:

Djebar is acutely aware of the potential for 'neo-colonisation' of Algerian women's voices and texts as she seeks to relay them to readers in the language of the former colonial power. This dichotomy between oral texts in the mother tongue, transcribed into the Other-tongue is used by Djebar to meditate on the very impossibility of translating Algerian feminine subjectivity into the former 'adversary language'.[40]

The second movement opens on a personal recollection concerning the narrator's grandmother, who used to have female musicians from the city come to play at her house every two or three months, musicians who would play drums and chant while the grandmother danced herself into a frenzy, another way of releasing the voices from the past: 'toutes les voix du passé bondissaient loin d'elle, expulsées hors de la prison de ses

jours' (p. 165) ('all the voices of the past, imprisoned in her present existence, were now set free and leapt far away from her') (p.145). The
narrative then passes to another voice, that of Zohra on whose farm the
maquisards hid until the French burnt it down: 'Ce refuge a servi chez
moi cinq ans. Oui, cinq ans, jusqu'à ce que la "révolution" arrivât à son
terme!' (p. 167) ('They used my farm for five years to hide in. Yes, five
years, until the end of the "revolution"!'). The inverted commas around
'revolution' indicate an ironic use (just as in Feraoun's diary, as noted in
Chapter 2); this was no revolution, especially for women. The narrative
then returns to the narrator's evocation of Jennet, another woman to
whom Zohra fled, having been imprisoned several times and then once
again forced out of her home. The second personal memory of the
narrator returns to the community of women, with a scene in which each
older woman and her daughter-in-law are taking coffee and cakes and
talking about the men in their lives and the problems they bring, talking
about their own dramas, but never using the 'I':

> Quelque fois ses filles reprendront, en commentaires chuchotés mais
> prolixes, le thème autobiographique de la mère [...] Chaque rassemblement,
> au cours des semaines et des mois, transporte son tissu d'impossible révolte;
> chaque parleuse – celle qui clame trop haut ou celle qui chuchote trop vite
> – s'est libérée. Jamais le 'je' de la première personne ne sera utilisé: la voix
> a déposé, en formules stéréotypées, sa charge de rancune et de râles
> échardant la gorge. Chaque femme, écorchées au-dedans, s'est apaisée dans
> l'écoute collective [...] Comment une femme pourrait parler haut, même en
> langue arabe, autrement que dans l'attente du grand âge? Comment dire 'je',
> puisque ce serait dédaigner les formules-couvertures qui maintiennent le
> trajet individuel dans la résignation collective? (pp. 176–77)

> (Sometimes the daughters take up their mother's story, elaborating it with
> their long-winded, whispered exegesis [...] At every one of these gatherings,
> they are trapped in the web of impossible revolt; each woman who tells her
> tale – loud exclamations of the one, rapid whispers of another – gets some-
> thing off her chest. The 'I' of the first person is never used; the time-honoured
> phraseology discharges the burden of rancour and râles that rasp the throat.
> In speaking to the listening group every woman finds relief from her deep
> inner hurt [...]
>   How could a woman speak aloud, even in Arabic, unless on the
> threshold of extreme old age? How could she say 'I', since that would be to
> scorn the blanket-formulae which ensure that each individual journeys
> through life in a collective resignation?

Refusing this 'collective resignation', the narrator herself has been
expelled from this 'theatre of feminine confidences', as she calls it,
and in the following passage 'lays herself bare'. The consequence of
writing about herself and others in the French language is that she is
flayed alive:

Ecrire les plus anodins des souvenirs d'enfance renvoie donc au corps dépouillé de voix. Tenter l'autobiographie par les seuls mots français, c'est, sous le lent scalpel de l'autopsie à vif, montrer plus que sa peau. Sa chair se desquame, semble-t-il, en lambeaux du parler d'enfance qui ne s'écrit plus. Les blessures s'ouvrent, les veines pleurent, coule le sang de soi et des autres, qui n'a jamais séché [...]

Parler de soi-même hors de la langue des aïeules, c'est de dévoiler certes, mais pas seulement pour sortir de l'enfance, pour s'en exiler définitivement. Le dévoilement, aussi contingent, devient comme le souligne mon arabe dialectal du quotidien, vraiment 'se mettre à nu'.

Or cette mise à nu, déployée dans la langue de l'ancien conquérant, lui qui, plus d'un siècle durant, a pu s'emparer de tout, sauf précisément ces corps féminins, cette mise à nu renvoie étrangement à la mise à sac du siècle précédent. (p. 178)

(In writing of my childhood memories I am taken back to those bodies bereft of voices. To attempt an autobiography using French words alone is to lend oneself to the vivisector's scalpel, revealing what lies beneath the skin. The flesh flakes off and with it, seemingly, the last shreds of the unwritten language of my childhood. Wounds are reopened, veins weep, one's own blood flows and that of others, which has never dried [...]

Speaking of oneself in a language other than that of the elders is indeed to unveil oneself, not only to emerge from childhood but to leave it, never to return. Such incidental unveiling is tantamount to stripping oneself naked, as the demotic Arabic dialect emphasizes.

But this stripping naked, when expressed in the language of the former conqueror (who for more than a century could lay his hands on everything save women's bodies), this stripping naked takes us back oddly enough to the plundering of the preceding century.)

The risk of the act of writing has been evoked by all the writers under analysis here; it is lived particularly intensely by the woman writer. Zohra's voice then joins the narrative, all her suffering given expression, her house burnt by the French, the very clothes taken off her and her sister's backs, so many misfortunes that she is eventually considered a madwoman. In the following 'embrace', the narrator goes to see Lla Zohra, now more then eighty years old: 'sa voix creuse dans les braises d'hier' (p. 186) ('her voice stirs the glowing embers of days past'). She tells her tale, and then it is the narrator's turn to tell her a different, older, one: 'Dire à mon tour. Transmettre ce qui a été dit, puis écrit. Propos d'il y a plus d'un siècle, comme ceux que nous échangeons aujourd'hui, nous, femmes de la même tribu' (p. 187) ('It is now my turn to tell a tale. To hand on words that were spoken, then written down. Words from more than a century ago, like those that we, two women from the same tribe, exchange today'). The narrator goes on to tell the tale first recounted by the artist Eugène Fromentin in his book *Un été au Sahara*, after his stay in the oasis of Laghouat in the summer of 1853, a place that had been the site of a terrible siege by the French.[41] His friend, a lieutenant, told

Fromentin the story that he in turn wrote down, of two dancers and prostitutes, bayoneted by the French for their jewellery, one of whom died in the lieutenant's arms still clutching the button ripped off the uniform of her murderer, a button he then gives to the artist. Zohra wants to know who told the narrator the story, and the narrator has to explain that she read it, that an eye-witness told it to his friend who wrote it down. A complex linguistic exchange therefore takes place between oral and written, between French and Arabic, and this exchange has the power to abolish difference and time:

> La main de Mériem agonisante tend encore le bouton d'uniforme: à l'amant, à l'ami de l'amant qui ne peut plus qu'écrire. Et le temps s'annihile. Je traduis la relation dans la langue maternelle et je te la rapporte, moi, ta cousine. Ainsi, je m'essaie, en éphémère diseuse, près de toi, petite mère assise devant ton potager. (p. 189)

> (Meriem's dying hand still holds out the button from the uniform: to the lover, to the friend of the lover who cannot now help but write. And time is abolished. I, your cousin, translate this story into our mother tongue, and tell it now to you, sitting beside you, little mother, in front of your vegetable patch.)

Paradoxically, French has become a vehicle for the restoration of cultural memory, and French representations are the ambiguous records of Algerian history.

The third movement's personal memory revolves around the emotions stirred by music and specifically the 'Ballad of Abraham', which is linked to the narrator's early religious feelings provoked by the telling in song of the story of Abraham and his son.[42] The memory includes how an aunt would recount the life of the Prophet, and the evidence of his love for his wife Khadija made the narrator as a young girl yearn for Islam, revealing an intimate, private relationship to the founding texts of Islamic culture. Another 'voice' then joins the chorus of women with another tale of sons in the *maquis* and shelter given to the *moudjahidin*, as personal and collective memories become more and more intertwined. The 'whispers' this time return to the colonial period and the account of the French general, Saint-Arnaud; but the power of the women's words is such that the old woman's tale and the narrator's writing can abolish all that terrible history; it is women's voices which are finally privileged here: 'Les vergers brûlés par Saint-Arnaud voient enfin leur feu s'éteindre, parce que la vieille aujourd'hui parle et que je m'apprête à transcrire son récit. Faire le décompte des menus objets passés ainsi, de main fiévreuse à main de fugueur!' (pp. 200–201) ('The fires in the orchards gutted by Saint-Arnaud are finally extinguished, because the old lady talks today and I am preparing to transcribe her tale. To draw up the inventory of the tiny objects passed on thus, from febrile hand to fugitive hand!'). For all the restorative power of memory, the issue of its potential danger of memory is also raised, for memory can also chain us to the past: 'Chaîne de souvenirs: n'est-elle pas justement "chaîne" qui entrave autant qu'elle enracine?' (p. 201) ('Chain of memories: is it not indeed a "chain", for do not memories fetter us as well as forming our roots?'). Memory needs to be used to re-establish a lost history and to liberate, not to chain and ensnare. This image of the threat of 'ensnaring' is continued, however. The following personal evocation again concerns the narrator as a young girl still moving around freely as an adolescent among the French girls unaware of the invisible 'snares' around her body, at an age when she should already have been veiled. It is writing that allows this freedom, for her mother's excuse to the shocked women of her community is that her daughter 'is reading':

> 'Elle lit', c'est-à-dire, en langue arabe, elle 'étudie'. Maintenant je me dis que ce verbe 'lire' ne fut pas par hasard l'ordre lancé par l'archange Gabriel, dans la grotte, pour la révélation coranique. 'Elle lit', autant dire que l'écriture à lire, y compris celle des mécréants, est toujours source de révélation: de la mobilité du corps dans mon cas, et donc de ma future liberté. (p. 203)

> ('She reads', that is to say in Arabic, 'she studies'. I think now that this command 'to read' was not just casually included in the Quranic revelation made by the Angel Gabriel in the cave... 'She reads' is tantamount to saying that writing to be read, including that of the unbelievers is always a source of revelation: in my case of the mobility of my body, and so of my future freedom.)

This freedom of the body is very important for her. The narrator describes how women had four languages at their disposal (as men could have four wives, she says): French for secret written communication, Arabic for religious communication, Lybico-Berber to return them to 'the mother-gods of pre-Islamic society', and that of the body which cannot be fully contained despite all attempts. For the narrator, French liberates that body even further:

> Mon corps seul, comme le coureur du pentathlon antique a besoin du starter pour démarrer, mon corps s'est trouvé en mouvement dès la pratique de l'écriture étrangère. Comme si soudain la langue française avait des yeux, et qu'elle me les ait donnés pour voir dans la liberté, comme si la langue française aveuglait les mâles de mon clan et qu'à ce prix, je puisse circuler, dégringoler toutes les rues, annexer le dehors pour mes compagnes cloîtrées, pour mes aïeules mortes bien avant la tombeau. (p. 204)

> (Just as the pentathlon runner of old needed the starter, so, as soon as I learned the foreign script, my body began to move as if by instinct. As if the French language suddenly had eyes, and lent them to me to see into liberty;

as if the French language blinded the peeping-toms of my clan and, at this price, I could move freely, run headlong down every street, annex the outdoors for my cloistered companions, for the matriarchs of my family who endured a living death.)

Between the ages of five and ten, before puberty, the young girl had attended the Koranic school, but then was no longer allowed to go. This form of learning is also linked for her to the body:

> Le savoir retournait aux doigts, aux bras, à l'effort physique. Effacer la tablette, c'était comme si, après coup, l'on ingérait une portion du texte coranique. L'écrit ne pouvait continuer à se dévider devant nous, lui-même copie d'un écrit censé immuable, qu'en s'étayant, pause après pause, sur cette absorption.
>   Quand la main trace l'écriture-liane, la bouche s'ouvre pour la scansion et la répétition, pour la tension mnémonique autant que musculaire… Monte la voix lançinante des enfants qui s'endorment au sein de la mélopée collective. (p. 207)

> (The learning was absorbed by the fingers, the arms through the physical effort. The act of cleaning the tablet seemed like ingesting a portion of the Quranic text. The writing – itself a copy of writing which is considered immutable – could only continue to unfold before us if it relied, clause by clause, on this osmosis…
>   As the hand traces the liana-script, the mouth opens to repeat the words, obedient to their rhythm, partly to memorize, partly to relieve the muscular tension… The shrill voices of the drowsy children rise up in a monotonous, sing-song chorus.)

The two languages, French and Arabic, occupy two different spaces and her body responds accordingly. When she sits curled up to study Arabic her body closes in on itself: 'like the alleyways of the medina' is the image she uses; when she reads and writes French, her body travels in a 'subversive space'. The tension between the two will bring her close to breakdown. This is no easy accommodation of two spaces, two languages, two ways of being. A decision is being made for her, 'light' instead of 'darkness'. That decision, made by her father, will bring contact with the outside, rather than the prison of her companions, but with its own dangers and risks:

> Et mon attention se recroqueville au plus profond de l'ombre, contre les jupes de ma mère qui ne sort pas de l'appartement. Ailleurs se trouve l'aire de l'école; ailleurs s'ancrent ma recherche, mon regard. Je ne m'aperçois pas, nul autour de moi ne s'en aperçoit, que, dans cet écartèlement, s'introduit un début de vertige.[43]

> (My conscious mind is here, huddled against my mother's knees, in the darkest corners of the flat which she never leaves. The ambit of the school is elsewhere; my search, my eyes are fixed on other regions. I do not realize, no-one around me realizes, that in the conflict between these two worlds lies an incipient vertigo.)

The next voice to join those of the community of women is that of a widow whose husband was sentenced to death for working against the French, who managed to escape with some others, but whose village was then constantly burnt and pillaged by the French. The woman in turn ran away and hid for the rest of the war, helping to feed and to clean for the partisans, until she heard that her husband had been killed fighting. A couple of years after his death she went to find the woman who had nursed him, and whose experience she recognised. These stories of ordinary women, very similar in many ways and all stories of resistance, reinforce an understanding of the hardships endured by women in the War of Independence, and bring to attention the everyday lives of thousands of Algerian women. The aim of the narrator, however, is not to 'represent' these women herself, but to allow them to express themselves through the recuperation of their (hi)stories. Djebar gives political expression poetic form, aware of the dangers of being seen as 'speaking on behalf of' women whose experience is so different from her own, as discussed in the first chapter.

The 'embrace' then once again returns to the summer of 1843, and the process of recuperation is manifested intensely in the story of Saint-Arnaud's hostages bound for France by steamship; the narrator has been handed down the story of an unknown woman by the story-tellers and she now takes up her place in the 'circle of listeners': 'Je te ressuscite, au cours de cette traversée que n'évoquera nulle lettre de guerrier français' (p. 214) ('I resurrect you during that crossing that no letter from any French soldier was to describe'). This is the forgotten history of a woman caught up in the conflict for the colonisation of Algeria, emblematic of so many others. The woman gives birth to a still-born child on the voyage, and an old woman helps her to cast it into the sea, reassuring her that this is God's sea, not the Christians' sea, and can be a suitable resting place for the child even if they no longer have a land of their own. It is an act of sisterhood in the face of human tragedy and an example of the powerlessness of the women caught up in a historical drama in which they are the forgotten victims.

The fourth movement evokes the dreams that haunt the narrator connected to the death of her paternal grandmother, leading in turn to the evocation of the maternal grandmother and the differences between the two women and the two sides of the family (her father coming from a poor family and studying to become a teacher and then achieving a more secure life). The difference between them is symbolised by the silence of one grandmother (hence provoking the dream in which the young girl seeks to restore her voice to her), and the voice of the other which enveloped the young girl when the grandmother entered her regular trances. It is the silence rather than the voice that continues to cause pain: 'seul, son silence d'hier continue à m'écorcher aujourd'hui' (p. 221) ('Only her former silence continues to hurt me today'). Silence constantly threatens, and it is against silence that the narrator will continue to struggle. Another widow from the past then adds her voice, a woman who lost her husband, three sons and a brother in the War of Independence. She was given nothing by the people in the city at independence, and even an appeal to a man she had hidden and who was now in charge of allotting empty houses led only to humiliation and refusal. She has to apply to live in a hut, and no longer has any men on whom to depend.[44] The narrator then tells of her conversations with other women she is bound to through her mother's lineage, as she struggles to formulate the difficult question of whether they suffered rape during the war, 'damage' or 'hurt' in the Arabic; such an act was not usually spoken about, the woman living under the mistrustful eyes of the community. How can the narrator speak of that which needs to be expressed, however secret, however painful, however humiliating: 'Vingt ans après, puis-je prétendre habiter ces voix d'asphyxie? Ne vais-je trouver tout au plus de l'eau évaporée? Quels fantômes réveiller, alors que, dans le désert de l'expression d'amour (amour reçu, "amour" imposé), me sont renvoyées ma propre aridité et mon aphasie' (p. 227) ('Can I, twenty years later, claim to revive these stifled voices? And speak for them? Shall I not at best find dried-up streams? What ghosts will be conjured up when in this absence of expressions of love (love received, "love" imposed), I see the reflection of my own barrenness, my own aphasia'). Is there a limit to the project in which she is now engaged, not only in moral terms, but also in terms of what the acts of speaking and writing are capable of? The narrator is caught in both an ethical and an aesthetic dilemma.

The second personal memory of this fourth movement contains a meditation on herself as a woman who uses her voice, in defiance of the silence that constantly threatens, for in her culture the woman who complained out loud was condemned in the community:

> Refuser de voiler sa voix et se mettre 'à crier', là gisait l'indécence, la dissidence. Car le silence de toutes les autres perdait brusquement son charme pour révéler sa vérité: celle d'être une prison irrémédiable.
>
> Ecrire en langue étrangère, hors de l'oralité des deux langues de ma région natale – le berbère des montagnes du Dahra et l'arabe de ma ville –, écrire m'a ramenée aux cris des femmes sourdement révoltées de mon enfance, à ma seule origine.
>
> Ecrire ne tue pas la voix, mais la réveille, surtout pour ressusciter tant de sœurs disparues. (p. 229)

(To refuse to veil one's voice and to start 'shouting', that was really inde-
cent, real dissidence. For the silence of all the others suddenly lost its charm
and revealed itself for what it was: a prison without reprieve.

Writing in a foreign language, not in either of the tongues of my native
country – the Berber of the Dahra mountains or the Arabic of the town where
I was born – writing has brought me to the cries of the women silently
rebelling in my youth, to my own true origins.

Writing does not silence the voice, but awakens it, above all to resurrect so many vanished sisters.)

The use of that voice is now positive, reviving and restoring the stories
of so many lost and forgotten women. For the moment, then, there is a
reconciliation with the written word in French; this is no longer the trap
into which the narrator locked Chérifa's voice, and which threatened the
whole enterprise undertaken here, but a legitimate way of expressing
those other lost, silenced voices. This reflection on the women who voiced
their complaint in turn leads to a complex explanation of the power relationships within the community of women as the narrator unpicks an
aspect of family celebrations: the entrance of the *voyeuses*, the women
who remain veiled even in exclusively female gatherings. These women
have not been invited as part of the gathering, but are allowed to look
on from the vestibule, completely covered except for one eye, and the
narrator begins to understand that they are excluded because they 'shout'
in their daily lives, they are there because the hostess has 'nothing to hide',
and this family can be talked about outside the protection of the family
home without fear. In addition this imposition of the veil on other women
reveals to the narrator the deep resentment of all those women who are
actually cloistered; they take revenge on other women since they are
powerless to take revenge on their men.[45]

A further widow's voice is evoked from the past, a woman who was
part of a group of women left behind to face the French soldiers when
the men take to the hills after they have removed the barbed wire on the
road, as instructed by the *maquis*. The woman's husband was eventually
killed in the public square after being tortured, leaving her with young
children – yet another story of violence and its legacy on the lives of
women. The final 'embrace' returns this time to 1956 with the French
arriving in a deserted mountain village, all the villagers having fled into
the countryside. When they return, the village has been ransacked and
two *maquisards* are captured, interrogated and tortured out in the open
until one of them gives in and tells the French where the arms are hidden.
At this point the narrator intervenes to reveal the written source for the
story: 'Je lis à mon tour, lectrice de hasard, comme si je me retrouvais
enveloppée du voile ancestral; seul mon œil libre allant et venant sur les

pages, où ne s'inscrit pas seulement ce que le témoin voit, ni ce qu'il écoute' (p. 235) ('I come at length upon what he wrote, turn the pages at random, read as if I were shrouded in the ancestral veil; with my one free eye perusing the page, where is written more than the eye-witness sees, more than can be heard'). She then comes across another story, another man's written story, and there is therefore a complex inter-weaving between oral and written, female and male sources for the stories that she brings to light: 'A nouveau, un homme parle, un autre écoute, puis écrit. Je bute moi, contre leurs mots qui circulent; je parle ensuite, je vous parle, à vous, les veuves de cet autre village de montagne, si éloigné ou si proche d'El Aroub!' (p. 236) ('Yet again, one man speaks, another listens, then writes. I stumble against their words which circulate; then I speak, I speak to you, the widows of that other mountain village, so distant or so near to El-Aroub'). This is the story of a certain Bernard who enters a house the night before the French soldiers leave the village, and makes love with the 'pretty Fatma' in the presence of the silent old women hidden in the shadowy background. This story is then offered up by the narrator to these widows twenty years later: 'pour qu'à votre tour, vous vous taisiez' (p. 211) ('so that you in turn can keep silent'). Yet again the circle of silence will not be fully broken, despite the narrator's struggle to write these events, but there is no event that was witnessed that should not now be given some form of expression.

The shorter fifth movement returns the reader to the scene that opens *L'Amour, la fantasia*, the little girl going to school holding her father's hand. Its title, 'La tunique de Nessus' ('The Tunic of Nessus'), provides another fundamental metaphor for the whole of Djebar's writing project and for her relationship to the French language which will be dealt with more fully in the final section of this chapter. For the moment, it is here that all the difficulty of this 'co-habitation', as she calls it, with the French language is presented, this 'langue marâtre' (p. 240; 'stepmother language'), with which she has to take some comfort after having been expelled from the 'langue mère disparue' ('my long-lost mother-tongue'). She likens the conflict between the two languages to the type of rapid offensive and swift retreat that characterised the Spanish attacks along the North African coast long before the arrival of the French, and the narrator is caught in the midst of this conflict with attendant conse-quences for her identity:

> Après plus d'un siècle d'occupation française – qui finit par un écharnement –, un territoire de langue subsiste entre deux peuples, entre deux mémoires; la langue française, corps et voix, s'installe en moi comme un orgueilleux préside, tandis que la langue maternelle, toute en oralité, en hardes dépe-

naillées, résiste et attaque, entre deux essoufflements. Le rythme du 'rebato' en moi s'éperonnant, je suis à la fois l'assiégé étranger et l'autochtone partant à la mort par bravade, illusoire effervescence du dire et de l'écrit [...]

Pour ma part, tandis que j'inscris la plus banale des phrases, aussitôt la guerre ancienne entre deux peuples entrecroise ses signes au creux de mon écriture. Celle-ci, tel un oscillographe, va des images de guerre – conquête ou libération, mais toujours d'hier – à la formulation d'un amour contra-dictoire, équivoque. (pp. 241–42)[46]

(After more than a century of French occupation – which ended not long ago in such butchery – a similar no-man's-land still exists between the French and the indigenous languages, between two national memories: the French tongue, with its body and voice, has established a proud *presidio* within me, while the mother-tongue, all oral tradition, all rags and tatters, resists and attacks between two breathing spaces. In time to the rhythm of the *rebato*, I am alternately the besieged foreigner and the native swaggering off to die, so there is seemingly endless strife between the spoken and written word.

For my part, even where I am composing the most commonplace of sentences, my writing is immediately caught in the snare of the old war between two peoples. So I swing like a pendulum from images of war (war of conquest or of liberation, but always in the past) to the expression of a contradictory, ambiguous love.)

The narrator dates the year of her birth as being 1842, the date of the arrival of Saint-Arnaud to kill the tribe from which she is descended; it is the fires lit by him that have guided her out of the harem, and it is the voices of the long-dead ancestors that encourage her to speak: 'Ils m'interpellent, ils me soutiennent pour qu'au signal donné, mon chant solitaire démarre' (p. 243) ('They summon me, encouraging my faltering steps, so that at the given signal my solitary song takes off'). The last poetic evocation will therefore be a soliloquy, as the section is entitled, a singular voice after making all these other voices heard:

> *On me dit exilée. La différence est plus lourde: je suis expulsée de là-bas pour entendre et ramener à mes parentes la trace de la liberté... Je crois faire le lien, je ne fais que patouiller, dans un marécage qui s'éclaire à peine [...] Ma fiction est cette autobiographie qui s'esquisse, alourdie par l'héritage qui m'encombre. Vais-je succomber?* (p. 244)

> (They call me an exile. It is more than that: I have been banished from my homeland to listen and bring back some traces of liberty to the women of my family... I imagine I constitute the link, but I am only floundering in a murky bog [...] My fiction is this attempt at autobiography, weighed down under the oppressive burden of my heritage. Shall I sink beneath the weight?)

The narrator is not merely exiled, which could carry a connotation of agency on the part of the subject: she has been banished.

The text ends on three short sections that make up the 'finale', the *Tzarl-rit*, a term for which the author gives two French-Arabic dictionary definitions that contradict each other: for one it is the cries of joy uttered by women; for the other, the cries they give when misfortune befalls them. The first section brings yet another woman's voice into the chorus already orchestrated, but this time it is that of a Frenchwoman, Pauline Rolland, exiled from France to Algeria for her role in the 1848 Revolution, arriving in 1852 and kept there for four months. The narrator imagines Pauline Rolland, already ill when she left Algeria, as part of the community of Algerian women, her true heirs being Chérifa and Lla Zohra, for the letters she wrote in those four months show how she shared the existence of the indigenous women. It is with Pauline therefore that the narrator shares a final embrace: 'J'ai rencontré cette femme sur le terrain de son écriture: dans la glaise du glossaire français, elle et moi, nous voici aujourd'hui entrelacées' (p. 250) ('I met this woman on the terrain of her writings: she and I are now clasped in each other's arms, our roots entwined in the rich soil of the French vocabulary'). It is in fact Pauline's words that finally set the narrator free. This is a key moment in the text, as Mary Jean Green has pointed out:

> Yet, in the closing section of the novel, Djebar's narrator discovers a buried text that permits her to come to terms with her own ambivalent relationship to the French language, the language that had made possible her liberation from Islamic sequestration but had never made possible the expression of love, the contact between two beings expressed in the repeated image of the '*corps enlacés*'. The text in question consists of letters written by a Frenchwoman, Pauline Rolland, deported to Algeria in 1852 for revolutionary activity. In the letters she wrote to friends in France, Pauline Rolland speaks of her contact with Algerian women, as she shares their condition of imprisonment, homeless wandering, and menial labour. Djebar comes to see Pauline Rolland as a true ancestor of the women of Algeria whose stories she has herself been telling. By expanding the French documentary resources to include the words of this sister in oppression, Djebar has found a gap in the hegemonic perspective which opens the possibility of real communication.[47]

The *Fantasia* returns the reader to Eugène Fromentin and his travels through Algeria in the same year that Pauline Rolland leaves. He keeps a journal of his stay, and one story he recounts is that of a young woman, Haoua, who comes to watch the *Fantasia* and who is then killed by one of the riders, a lover she has rejected. This is yet another love-story with tragic consequences, but the narrator also sees the young woman as the first Algerian heroine to make her appearance in a story written in French: 'première à respirer en marge et à feindre d'ignorer la transgression' (p. 253) ('the first to murmur a word in the margin, pretending not to realize she is trespassing'). The 'air on the *nay*' (an old type of flute, that gives its name also to the *naylette*, dancer or prostitute, already evoked in the text in Fromentin's story of the button wrenched from the murderer's coat) closes the text, and contains a final image that serves again as a metaphor for the whole writing project. Fromentin offers the narrator an unexpected hand, a hand he never drew, the severed hand of an anonymous Algerian woman he finds in the dust at an oasis which had been the scene of a massacre: 'Plus tard, je me saisis de cette main vivante, main de la mutilation et du souvenir et je tente de lui faire porter le *"qalam"*' (p. 255) ('Later, I seize on this living hand, hand of mutilation and of memory, and I attempt to bring it the *qalam*' [a pen, especially the stylus used to write Koranic verses on tablets in the Koranic school]). Above all, the image of the amputated hand of an anonymous Algerian woman, discarded by Eugène Fromentin, comes to symbolise both the act of writing and Algeria itself:

> mutilated by a history written by the hands of others (French historians, writers, artists) but, perhaps more importantly for Djebar, it also represents Algerian women amputated in their desire to write or express themselves. The dominant images of the novel – abduction and rape – sexualise the representation of Algeria, which becomes in the final analysis, the female body. If it is on this body that the history of the French conquerors has been written, it is from this body that the decolonisation of a people must be written – be they men or women.[48]

Despite the bravery of the endeavour, the intervention of 'la mémoire nomade et la voix coupée' ('nomad memory and intermittent voice'), it is death that the narrator hears in the cries of the *Fantasia*, for the horse will strike again against 'toute femme dressée libre, toute vie surgissant au soleil pour danser!' (p. 256) ('any woman who dares to stand up freely, all life that comes out into the sunlight to dance!'). The writer is just such a woman who has stood up and come out into the sun – the image of light and shade returning once again.

Assia Djebar herself had already insisted, towards the end of the 1970s at the time of her film-making experience, that identity (and here I think we can understand both personal and collective identity) is necessarily linked to history, and that the present needs to be understood in terms of the past. In a later interview with Mildred Mortimer she explained the very specific link between identity and the past in *L'Amour, la fantasia*:

> L'histoire est utilisée dans ce roman comme quête de l'identité [...] J'aborde le passé du dix-neuvième siècle par une recherche sur l'écriture en langue française. S'établit lors pour moi un rapport avec l'histoire du dix-neuvième siècle *écrite* par des officiers français, et un récit *oral* des Algériennes traditionnelles d'aujourd'hui. Deux passés s'alternent donc.[49]

> (History is used in this novel as a quest for identity [...] I tackle the past of the nineteenth century through research into writing in French. Then a link is set up for me between the history of the nineteenth century as *written* by

French army officers, and *oral* accounts by the traditional Algerian women of today. So that two pasts alternate with each other.)

To be precise, these two histories are interlinked, as we have seen in the above analysis of the structure of the text, and take the reader through the colonisation of Algeria from 1830 onwards, based on archival research, and transposed by the writer to the 1954–1962 War of Independence, which is in its turn evoked by the oral testimonies of women from the Chenoua region of her maternal ancestors who participated in the struggle.[50] Assia Djebar, firstly very much the historian, uses the archives of eye-witness accounts written at the time by officers, camp followers and other correspondents in official documents, in private diaries or letters home, in articles for the French readership, and which relate actual events during the often brutal process of colonisation. Is this 'quest for identity' carried out through the retrieval of history successful? Is a coherent identity created for the narrator? Are the voices of the women (detailed above), their stories and histories successfully transmitted? There are conflicting views among critics in the evaluation of these projects. H. Adlai Murdoch has analysed the ambiguity of the relationship to the French language, this time taking another pronouncement in *L'Amour, la fantasia* by the narrator as the starting point: 'ainsi, cette langue que m'a donnée le père me devient entremetteuse et mon initiation, dès lors, se place sous un signe double, contradictoire' (p. 12) ('thus the language that my father had been at pains for me to learn, serves as a go-between, and from now a double, contradictory sign hangs over my initiation'). Murdoch believes that Djebar problematises her own discourse to the point of almost undermining it:

> This duality which the subject must undergo stems directly from the insistence of patriarchal coercion and a falsely constituted desire for alterity through the use of the language of the colonising Other, symbolised through the duality of the paternal inscription; discursive resistance and female subjectivity are thus linked to desire and the subversion of patriarchy, the main issues to which the text addresses itself [...] In other words, if the coloniser's language is read as the mark of colonial desire, then its appropriation by the colonised may undermine the very goal it sets out to achieve, screening the desire of the colonised subject. For, in situating herself as a writer who must come to terms with the history of Algeria and with herself as a postcolonial, Arab, female subject writing in French about Arab women who do not speak French and cannot speak for themselves, Djebar's narrative will inevitably problematise its own discourse to the point where its own tenuous coherence threaten to dissolve.[51]

It is not only the problematising of its own discourse that can be seen to threaten the project. In the same article the plural, fragmented voice of the narrative is analysed ('the narrator proceeds to write, speak, in the names of all those women subjected to oppression, and exiled from their heritage'), as is the oscillation of the narrator between first and third persons, especially in Part III, which Murdoch sees as 'giving vent to the division by which she is figured, and which in turn stems from the presence of an over-determining colonial discourse. This inability to preserve the first person in fact reveals a subject pervaded by ambiguity, as the impossibility of speaking the self as "I" marks an identity-structure at odds with its own integrity.'[52] Yet, Adlai Murdoch also points out, the ambiguity of writing in the 'stepmother tongue' is such that it is possible to read here not only the threatened disintegration of the writing subject under the burden of that language, but also the ways in which it is used as a subversive strategy that attacks this linguistic power from the inside:

> It is equally possible to postulate the thesis that the paradox of having to write in the coloniser's language – since it is, so to speak, imposed from the outside through the dominant forces of assimilation and acculturation – also provides a means for subverting and rewriting the discursive framework of oppression from the very space of its own elaboration.[53]

In some ways this potential 'failure' of the French language to convey the Algerian female subjectivity is reminiscent of the problem of words of love which the narrator cannot express in French. As Djebar's English translator has so perceptively observed, the theme of love is both implicit and explicit in the text, not only in the recounting of her own first love letter and of the extraordinary episode of her father writing to her mother, but in the very act of writing:

> The emancipated woman, who has broken out of the harem, is still reticent in this work about the physical union, whereas her preoccupation with the *physical act* of writing forms one of the original aspects of her work and becomes a metaphor for her dichotomy. She compares the cramped posture she adopts when writing in French with the sensual act of writing in Arabic, when the movements of her body seem to echo the scrolls, the curlicues, the rhythms of the calligraphy. In the very first pages of the novel, she ironically announces the theme of the repercussions of writing: '... there is more danger in love that is committed to paper than love that languishes behind enclosing walls' [...] There is an analogy between love-letters and the correspondence despatched from the encampments by forgotten captains participating in the conquest of Algeria; both are the occasion for self-analysis and result in hindsight into the ambiguity of emotions: '...it is as if these parading warriors, around whom the cries rise up which the elegance of their style cannot diminish, are mourning their unrequited love for Algeria'. The theme of the love-letter is thus another link between the historical and autobiographical dimensions of the novel as well as a basic part of its structure.[54]

This analysis succinctly sums up the intricacy of both the themes and structures of the novel, and shows how difficult it is to read any one of these constituent parts of the text without needing to make reference to other elements. It is for this reason that I earlier carefully followed through the actual composition of the text. However, having made clear how History and individual history are interwoven in the actual structure of the text, I wish to pursue a little further how the rewriting of history functions with regard to gender, before finally going on to some other writing strategies used in the text, and in particular the rich and varied use of metaphor (some of which I have already noted), and of myth.

Patricia Geesey insists that this reinscription of Algerian women into history – women not only obscured in the history written by the colonisers, but also largely effaced from the history of the War of Independence and its aftermath, both expunged from the French and Algerian versions of their country's history – promotes an agenda missing from the analysis and theories of the colonial situation by Fanon and Memmi:

> A great deal has been written about the relationship of colonised peoples to their own history, but to date, little effort has been made to include (de)colonised women in texts that purport to renew the colonised subject's ties with the past. Albert Memmi's and Frantz Fanon's theories about the colonised intellectual and history point out that the first step in 'decolonising the mind' is the construction of a positive historical and cultural heritage in response to the denigration perpetrated against indigenous institutions and attitudes by the coloniser. In their essays, Memmi and Fanon do not enter into a discussion of whether or not the intellectual in question is a male or female subject. They mention the role women have played in revolutionary struggles, but they do not envision the possibility that colonised women have specific concerns in regard to their own relationship to history. At the time when they wrote their seminal studies on colonised psychology, the issue of postcolonial feminine subjectivity had not yet been distinguished from the overall concerns of the decolonised subject [...] [Assia Djebar] brings Algerian women to participate in an analysis of their relationship to the history of their country to point out that they too have a stake in the historical evolution of their nation.[55]

Danielle Marx-Scouras has also raised the point that Assia Djebar's writing allows women's participation in areas from which they have been excluded, specifically in her analysis of the usually masculine public space of war:

> If war is indeed the affair of men, as Hector claimed in the *Iliad*, thereby setting up a literary paradigm that has maintained a hold on us for centuries, then women are exiled from discourse of war. If that is so, why then have a growing number of Francophone women writers from the Maghreb and the Mashreq taken on this essentially masculine problematic? What we have is nothing less than a literary 'event' that raises fundamental rhetorical, economic, political, and sexual questions. We need to ask what happens when women's writing aligns itself with traditionally male fiction on war;

that is to say, what happens to discourse on war if it is linked up to sexuality?[56]

Indeed, as we have seen, the rewriting and reappropriation of the conquest of Algeria becomes highly sexualised in *L'Amour, la fantasia*, and often eroticised, with images of violation dominating the text. Assia Djebar's work therefore goes far beyond the retrieval of a lost history to engage with wider questions concerning gender, colonisation and the impact and aftermath of war more generally.

However, in order to pursue more closely the aim of this study, which is to explore the writing stategies underpinning a life-writing process, I wish to end the analysis of *L'Amour, la fantasia* by looking at the ways in which the exploration of history becomes bound up with the quest of the writer for the creation of a new way of being for the postcolonial subject.

MYTH, METAPHOR AND THE POWER OF LANGUAGE

> C'est un problème peut-être pour toutes les femmes écrivains, mais que moi j'avais un peu plus à cause de cette éducation des femmes de chez moi. On ne doit pas parler de soi, on ne dit jamais je, et plus c'est intime, plus on doit prendre des détours et suggérer la confidence ou le rapport personnel, le suggérer par des métaphores très, très allusives.
>
> Assia Djebar, interview in the documentary film *Femmes d'Alger*[57]
>
> (It is perhaps a problem for all women writers, but one which was a bit more serious for me because of the way the women in my country are brought up. You must never talk about yourself, you never say 'I', and the more intimate the matter is, the more you have to wrap it up, suggest confidence or personal relationships by very, very allusive metaphors.)

In considering the rewriting of historical discourses, it is already clear that part of the writing strategy in *L'Amour, la fantasia* is the production of a metaphorical discourse of great complexity and variety. The act of writing itself as the image of the severed hand, previously discussed, is a metaphor for the past history of Algeria and for the occultation of women from that history. It is equally a metaphor for the literally physical danger the narrator runs in bringing to light this history. Indeed the metaphor of the act of writing is so all-pervasive throughout the text in myriad forms, both as explicit statements and as implicit imagery, that it is often impossible actually to separate the metaphor from the text. It *is* the body of the text. A further bodily metaphor which has previously been discussed in the readings of the rewriting of historical discourses is the body of Algeria itself, at once the body of the nation, the body of the collective of Algerian women and the body of the narrator herself. I wish here to take further the analysis of the use of both metaphor and myth in relation to language in the text. As already indicated, Anne Donadey has analysed the strategy of a palimpsest-like structure in *L'Amour, la fantasia* that is elaborated through the re-reading and rewriting – and indeed the *effacing* – of the French male accounts of the colonisation, and the palimpsest could again be said to be an all-pervasive metaphor for the text as a whole.[58] In 'traditional' autobiography there is of course a necessary 'myth' to be dealt with, the 'personal myth' of the unified identity of the writing subject, as noted in the previous chapter. Through their writing strategies, postcolonial autobiographical discourses can be said to subvert this myth in such a way as to explode the myth of the unified subject. These writing strategies sometimes celebrate the multiplicity of postcolonial identity; they often express a difficult relationship to language. It is in these strategies that the politics of identity truly becomes a poetics, as we have previously seen in the work of Memmi and Khatibi.

In a very suggestive reading of the text, using the idea of what he terms the 'mythomorphoses' of Assia Djebar, Ernstpeter Ruhe analyses the implicit use that Djebar makes of the figure of Prometheus, changed here into a female Promethea.[59] The theme of danger is elaborated on in various forms throughout the text, as we have previously seen, and nowhere more explicitly than towards the end of the text in the analogy drawn with the myth of the Shirt of Nessus. The use of myth and metaphor leads the reader to the heart of Assia Djebar's poetics of identity as she subverts the personal myth by substituting the allusions she describes in the interview quoted from as an epigraph above. These mythical and metaphorical allusions help the reader to see more clearly into the mystery of individual identity and to (re-)construct it in its complexity. As well as the retrieval of a collective identity, there is the elaboration of a particular individual identity in the signs and symbols chosen to 'represent' the self, as I have also discussed with reference to Abdelkébir Khatibi. In a similar way to the rewriting and the reappropriation of history, there is a deconstruction and a rewriting of myth. As Ruhe points out, this deconstruction of mythical figures in order to create 'models of feminine autonomy', as he calls them, is carried out in the knowledge of the potential punishment which may be meted out to the writer – punishments like those visited upon Echo, Prometheus, and in the story of the Shirt of Nessus, on Hercules. As Françoise Lionnet has written, the myth of Nessus is promoted to the level of allegory in *L'Amour, la fantasia*, in which the torment of the Shirt of Nessus is the torment of 'wearing' the French language.[60] This poisoned gift, drenched in the blood of ancestors, and given in love by the father, makes its explicit appearance towards the end of the text: 'La langue encore coagulée des Autres m'a enveloppée, dès l'enfance en tunique de Nessus, don d'amour de mon père qui, chaque matin me tenait par la main sur le chemin de l'école. Fillette arabe, dans un village du Sahel algérien' (p. 243) ('The language of the Others, in which I was enveloped from childhood, the gift my father lovingly bestowed on me, that language has adhered to me ever since like the tunic of Nessus: that gift from my father who, every morning, took me by the hand to accompany me to school. A little Arab girl, in a village of the Algerian Sahel').

This scene of the young girl on her way to school holding her father's hand sends the reader back to the very beginning of the text:

> Fillette arabe allant pour la première fois à l'école, un matin d'automne, main dans la main du père. Celui-ci, un fez sur la tête, la silhouette haute et droite dans son costume européen, porte un cartable, il est instituteur à l'école française. Fillette arabe dans un village du Sahel algérien. (p. 11)

> (A little Arab girl going to school for the first time, one autumn morning, walking hand in hand with her father. A tall erect figure in a fez and a European suit, carrying a bag of school books. He is a teacher at the French primary school. A little Arab girl in a village in the Algerian Sahel.)

The reader is thus invited to reconsider the whole project of *L'Amour, la fantasia* in the light of the allegory. Firstly, we are invited to reconsider the relationship to the father thanks to whom the young Arab girl escapes the fate of her cousins, the father-liberator whose weapon is the French language.[61] But this is also the father who is equally a figure of interdiction in the first love story that she recounts, a love story which takes place in the medium of the written word, and that written word is in French: 'cette langue que m'a donné le père devient entremetteuse et mon initiation, dès lors, se place sous un signe double, contradictoire' (p. 12) ('this language given me by the father becomes a mediator, and my initiation, from then on, has been placed beneath a double, contradictory sign'). As Najiba Regaïeg says: 'la langue française, territoire linguistique où opère la magie de la force et de la puissance paternelle, semble soudain complice de cette figure omniprésente'[62] ('the French language, linguistic territory where the magic of paternal strength and power is at work, suddenly seems to become an accomplice of that omnipresent figure').

The father–daughter relationship certainly does remain troubling and ambiguous, and for Ernstpeter Ruhe, the father is linked to the use of myth: 'le feu de la torche risque de tomber sur Prométhée, car il active par sa chaleur le liquide magique de Nessus, cadeau changé en poison par la jalousie du père-centaure'[63] ('the fire of the torch risks falling on Prometheus, for by its warmth it activates the magic blood of Nessus, the gift turned into poison by the jealousy of the centaur-father'). Nonetheless, the narrator does dare to transgress not only the father's law, by which the use of this language becomes taboo, but also the taboos of ancient and contemporary history. The reader is also therefore forced at the end of the text to recognise and to understand better the dangers that the woman writer runs, not only in the telling of her own story, but equally in the telling of the stories of others. By daring to open the historical and personal chronicles of the conquering soldiers in Algeria in the nineteenth century, in which the anonymous deaths of her ancestors are enclosed, the narrator comes to understand, and makes us understand with her, that the texts composed by the conquerors have become the tomb of these forebears, and that she is consequently condemned to write in a language which is stained with that blood. To refer back to the terminology used by Khatibi, Assia Djebar's project is made up of both a 'personal idiolect' and a 'social idiolect', in which she appropriates for herself and rewrites a myth in order to examine her own relationship to the French language. Khatibi seems to liberate himself from the memory tattooed by colonial history and to come to use the other's language to tattoo in his turn the body of the West with his own sign. In the use made by Assia Djebar of the myth of the Shirt of Nessus, she reminds us that it is not always so easy for North African writers to protect themselves from the dangerous, and even fatal, power of this language that melds with the body, which is part of their very being, and which is part of both an individual and a collective identity. As Françoise Lionnet has written: 'L'écrivain postcolonial est [lui aussi] pris dans les rêts du langage et du savoir occidental: plus il essaie de s'en débarrasser et plus il semble s'y enfermer, puisque ce savoir est partie prenante de son identité'[64] ('The postcolonial writer is also caught in the nets of Western language and knowledge: the more he tries to free himself from them, the more he seems trapped within them, because that knowledge is an active part of his own identity'). To take up again the allegory of Hercules, postcolonial writers are condemned to fight against the seven-headed hydra of language and to equip themselves for the task with a pen-arrow dipped in language-blood, while at the same time attempting to avoid self-hurt: 'une plaie inguérissable, suant les mots tout à côté' (*L'Amour, la fantasia*, p. 245) ('the running sore nearby from which words exude') (p. 219). Each one must find their own way to fight this battle. In her own attempt Djebar, like Khatibi, weaves a poetics of identity in the establishing of 'founding myths' and the creation of 'allusive metaphors'. No wonder then that in the third volume of the Algerian Quartet, *Vaste est la prison*, Assia Djebar will devote a key section to the exploration of the potential of another alphabet, a lost alphabet, one that would allow the formulation of the written word in the mother tongue denied that form of expression, and allow a return from battle, from exile, and access to true liberation and reconciliation.

EXILE, THE HISTORY OF WRITING AND THE QUEST FOR LIBERATION IN *VASTE EST LA PRISON*

> *Ma fiction est cette autobiographie qui s'esquisse, alourdie par l'héritage qui m'encombre. Vais-je succomber?... Mais la légende tribale zigzague dans les béances et c'est dans le silence des mots d'amour, jamais proférés, de la langue maternelle non écrite, transportée comme un bavardage d'une mime inconnue et hagarde, c'est dans cette nuit-là que l'imagination, mendiante des rues, s'accroupit... Le murmure des compagnes cloîtrées redevient mon feuillage. Comment trouver la force de m'arracher le voile, sinon parce qu'il me faut en couvrir la plaie inguérissable, suant les mots tout à côté?*
> Assia Djebar, *L'Amour, la fantasia*, pp. 244–45

(My fiction is this attempt at autobiography, weighed down under the oppressive burden of my heritage. Shall I sink beneath the weight?... But the tribal legend criss-crosses the empty spaces, and the imagination crouches in the silence when loving words of the unwritten mother-tongue remain unspoken – language conveyed like the inaudible babbling of a nameless, haggard mummer – crouches in this dark night like a woman begging in the streets... I shelter again in the green shade of my cloistered companions' whispers. How shall I find the strength to tear off my veil, unless I have to use it to bandage the running sore nearby from which words exude?)

In contrast to this image of the veiling of the autobiographical discourse taken from the end of *L'Amour, la fantasia*, *Vaste est la prison* opens on a singular voice no longer hidden behind the cloistered companions. These companions will return, however, in a different way, and the gaping wound left by expression in the written word at the end of the first volume of the quartet will be inspected unflinchingly in this third volume. Structurally there is a link in the attention to musical forms between these two volumes, the musical forms evident in the title and in other parts of *L'Amour, la fantasia*:

The *Fantasia* (derived from the Arabic *fantaziya* [meaning ostentation]), is in North Africa a set of virtuoso movements on horseback executed at a gallop, accompanied by loud cries and culminating in rifle shots; the *Fantasia*, associated with ceremonial occasions and military triumphs, forms the leitmotif of the novel as well as providing its title. But a *Fantasia* (Italian for 'fantasy' or 'fancy') is also a musical composition in which, according to the definition given in Kennedy's *Concise Oxford Dictionary of Music*, 'form is of secondary importance... in the sixteenth and seventeenth centuries such compositions were usually contrapuntal and in several sections, thus being an early form of variations... Compositions in which the character of the music suggested an improvisational character or the play of free fancy'. The author uses Beethoven's instruction to his Sonatas 1 and 2, '*Quasi una fantasia...*' as the epigraph to Part Three of her novel, so establishing the title unambiguously as a serious word-play on the double character of the work, and highlighting strong musical associations of form and style. Moreover the third part of the novel, in which the musical references are most insistent, is divided into five 'movements', to which is added a coda in the form of a short chapter entitled 'Air on a *Nay*' (an ancient kind of flute), where the strands of sound, episode and imagery are drawn together.[65]

The title of and epigraph to *Vaste est la prison* (*So Vast the Prison*) are taken from a Berber song, a precise reference to which occurs much later within the text at a point of great emotional anguish. The structure of the text is again one that is divided into a series of parts, this time four, with a short, preface-like text to open, 'Le silence de l'écriture' ('The Silence of Writing'), which would suggest a contrast to the cries and voices of the beginning of *Fantasia*. Indeed the theme of silence, and of being unable to speak, will be a recurrent one. The first part, 'L'Effacement dans le cœur' ('Erased in the Heart'), composed of seven short sections, charts an unfulfilled love story experienced by the narrator that nonetheless contributes to an enormous change in her life when she takes the decision to leave her husband; the second part parallels this 'erasing' that takes place in the heart, with the 'erasure' of writing: 'L'Effacement sur la pierre' ('Erased on Stone'), again has seven short sections and then a short italicised section with a place name as its title, 'Abalessa'. The third part, 'Un silencieux désir' ('A Silent Desire'), takes up the idea of the silence of writing that opened the text. It is structured in a way that resonates with *L'Amour, la fantasia*, opening with a short text in italics, 'Fugitive et ne le sachant pas' ('Fugitive Without Knowing It'), followed by the evocation of seven scenes that make up part of 'Femme arable' ('Arable Woman'), which the reader learns is a film made by the narrator in the mountain region of her ancestors (a place already evoked in *L'Amour, la fantasia* and a reference also to Djebar's own film work). These seven scenes are interspersed with seven 'movements' of personal memories, including the memories of the mother and grandmother of the narrator. The fourth and final part, 'Le Sang de l'écriture' ('The Blood of Writing'), again links writing and blood, an image used frequently in *L'Amour, la fantasia*, and contains two short texts, 'Yasmina', which brings the narrator up against the contemporary events in Algeria, and the 'Finale', reiterating 'The Blood of Writing', which mirrors the 'Silence of Writing' on which the text opened.

LOVE AND SELF-KNOWLEDGE

A further link between *L'Amour, la fantasia* and *Vaste est la prison* is the problem of the language of love, as Jeanne-Marie Clerc has identified:

> Mais si l'écriture de la guerre a été trouvée et retrouvée, semble-t-il, au long de ces pages réécrites à partir des mots extraits du silence où ont été immergées les héroïnes de l'Indépendance, il n'en est pas de même pour l'écriture de l'amour qui reste une question posée, et se transmettra intacte au roman suivant, *Vaste est la prison*.
>
> Ce dernier roman semble né, en effet, de la prise de conscience progressive d'une identité à la fois de soi-même et de son écriture, vécue d'abord, implicitement, dans l'écartèlement ressenti entre la langue du père et celle de la mère, puis amenée à la conscience claire par le travail sur l'Histoire. Identité et écriture de '*fugitive ne le sachant pas*', puis '*le sachant désormais*'.[66]

> ('But if war writing has been found again and again, as it seems, throughout these pages re-written on the basis of words extracted from the silence into which the heroines of the War of Independence have been plunged, the same is not true of love writing, which remains an unanswered question, and will be transmitted intact to the following novel, *So Vast the Prison*.
>
> This latter novel seems to have been born of the progressive awareness of the identity both of herself and of her writing, lived out firstly, implicitly, in the distancing she experienced between her father's language and her mother's, and then brought clearly to the fore by her work on History. Identity and writing as a 'fugitive without knowing it' and then later, 'knowing it, henceforth'.)

As I have previously discussed, Assia Djebar does not deny that the language of the oppressor, which in turn became the gift of her father, is also the language of her individual liberation, and is consequently the language of a possible collective liberation through her writings, despite all the problems of 'representation'. Yet the gaping wound left at the end of *L'Amour, la fantasia* remains; the French language is a double-edged sword, but it is the only weapon with which she is equipped in the mortal endeavour in which she is engaged, writing and death being apparently inextricably linked. *Vaste est la prison* opens on the link between death and writing: 'Longtemps, j'ai cru qu'écrire c'était mourir, mourir lentement' ('For a long time I believed that writing meant dying, slowly dying'), and a little later 'Longtemps, j'ai cru qu'écrire c'était s'enfuir...' ('For a long time I believed that writing meant fleeing...'). There is an irresistible analogy here with perhaps the most famous first line in French literature, beginning with 'Longtemps' and using the perfect tense, that of Marcel Proust's *A la recherche du temps perdu*: 'Longtemps, je me suis couché de bonne heure' ('For a long time I went to bed early'), a text that deals with memory, the passage of time, loss, the impossibility of love, and the salvation that may be attained through the work of art. Proust's novel is also concerned with the retrieval of a self through the process of writing, and with the type of knowledge and self-knowledge that may be attained through the suffering of love; the type of suffering with which the whole first part of *Vaste est la prison*, 'L'effacement dans le cœur', is infused.[67]

This first section opens on a scene with other women in the *hammam* which took place about fifteen years previously according to the narrator, when one of her mother-in-law's friends refers to her husband as '*L'e'edou*', 'the enemy', not, as is explained to the narrator, because he necessarily mistreats the woman – he is no worse than any other husband – but because this is the way these women talk about their men among themselves. In the very private first part of this text, the struggle followed through in the process of writing therefore passes from history to the private life of the individual.[68] This word, uttered in the oral dialect, is described as being like an arrow that carries silence within it, that pierces the narrator's heart and leaves her silent in its wake, since it tears apart the warmth of the maternal tongue and reaches the 'source of her writing':

> ce mot d'"ennemi', proféré dans cette chaleur émolliente, entra en moi, torpille étrange; telle une flèche de silence qui transperça le fond de mon cœur trop tendre alors. En vérité, ce simple vocable, acerbe dans sa chair arabe, vrilla indéfiniment le fond de mon âme, et donc source de mon écriture [...]
> Elle sortit dignement, la dame du bain. Nous la suivîmes peu après ma belle-mère et moi. Moi, sans voix, et durant les quelques années qui s'écoulèrent ensuite, dépouillée, noyée dans un deuil de l'inconnu et de l'espoir.
> Par elle, la langue maternelle exhiba ses crocs, inscrivait en moi une fatale amertume... Dès lors, où trouver mes halliers, comment frayer un étroit corridor dans la tendresse noire et chaude [...] Ne me faudrait-il mendier, plongée dans la nuit de la langue perdue et de son cœur durci, comme en ce jour de hammam? (*Vaste est la prison*, pp. 14–15)

> (The word 'enemy', uttered in that moist warmth, entered me, a strange missile like an arrow of silence piercing the depths of my then too tender heart. In truth that simple word, bitter in its Arabic flesh, bored endlessly into the depths of my soul, and thus into the source of my writing [...]

> The lady from the baths left in dignity. My mother-in-law and I followed her shortly afterwards. I was speechless and for the next few years felt stripped bare, drowned in mourning for things unknown and for hope.
> Through her the mother-tongue had shown its teeth, inscribing a deadly bitterness within me... Where was I to find my lair from now on, how was I to open a narrow corridor into the warm, black tenderness [...]?
> Would I not have to beg, plunged into the night of the lost language and its hard heart, as at the *hammam* that day?)

This word that gives expression to the relationship between men and women in her culture throws her own relationship to that maternal language into disarray. It also reveals just how far removed she is herself from that community of women. Both of these problematic relationships will be major themes throughout the text, and the diverse facets of the female condition will be explored in many forms. The epigraphs place the first part of *Vaste est la prison* initially under the auspices of a European literature concerned with the self, with the inner life of the individual, with quotations from Hölderlin and Virginia Woolf. Indeed the majority of Djebar's epigraphs are drawn from European authors (not necessarily French), and this raises questions of how these function and why the author chose to frame her own experience (and that of other women) and to 'dialogue' with these writers in particular. Gérard Genette's analysis of the practice of using such references from 'high literature' is negative, suggesting that an author thereby makes a show of 'intellectual belonging'. The epigraphs do also, however, add a dialogic and autobiographical layer. As Mary Stevens has written,

> Indeed, the epigraphs' echoes reveal *Vaste est la prison* to be a much darker text than its critics have often implied. As it drowns in blood and vomit (pp. 338–348) writing struggles to hold on to any redemptive function. This tension between suffering, pain and loss and potential recuperation is played out in the epigraphs. For example, both the Woolf short story [...] and the Hölderlin poem deal with the passing of time and a lyrically expressed yearning for a lost utopia, a remembered place of serenity.[69]

The Woolf short story deals with two lovers returning to a boarded-up house, haunted by their past selves. They discover that the past is irretrievable,

> whilst at the same time uncovering its legacy [...] This is precisely the movement that operates in the narrator when, after a long absence, she encounters 'L'Aimé' ('the Beloved') on a Paris street corner: 'Ainsi, mon amour silencieux, auparavant si difficilement maîtrisée, changeait de nature, il subsistait en moi, toujours secret. Dépouillé de sa fragilité qui m'avait si longtemps troublé' ('Consequently my silent love, formerly so hard to control, changed in nature; it was still there within me, still secret, but no longer had the fragility that had troubled me for so long'). However the quotation from

> Hölderlin, which also deals with a form of resolution [...], points towards the violence and the distress that has brought us to this place of tranquillity.[70]

These epigraphs therefore highlight forms of self-knowledge gained through loss.

It is in 'La sieste', the first section, that the narrator begins the unfulfilled love story referred to above with, in some senses, its conclusion at the point when she is 'cured' of the infatuation with a younger man which has lasted thirteen months, and she is able to return to the 'banality' of everyday life: 'Comme c'est réconfortant simplement d'exister' (p. 22) ('How comforting it is just to exist'). After all the energy expended in unfulfilled love, the passion has been erased, the image of erasure that dominates the whole text closing this first short section: 'Treize mois donc s'étaient usés dans une lutte étirée, dans le harcèlement d'une passion à la face aveugle, à la vie séchée. Treize mois s'effacèrent dans mon sommeil de ce jour de novembre' (p. 24) ('So thirteen months had been exhausted in a long-drawn-out battle, harried by a blind-faced passion whose life had dried up. Thirteen months were wiped out in my sleep that November day'). The details of her passion, of the shared moments without real fulfilment are painstakingly and painfully described in all their details – the face of the loved one, his voice, the time spent alone or with other friends, the sudden need to see him – and the experience leads to self-exposure (to the other), to self-questioning (an internal quest) and to self-deception: 'Ainsi je me dévoilais. Ainsi je me cherchais. Ainsi, à moi-même, je tentais de me masquer' (p. 32) ('Thus I unveiled myself. Thus I was in search of myself. Thus I attempted to disguise myself from myself').

Some elements of the happiness she feels in the company of the 'Beloved' seem to be partly the return to childhood, as represented for example when they play table-tennis in a nostalgic return to the idealised utopia of childhood:

> 'Comme c'est bon, l'enfance à deux' me suis-je soudain avoué, interloquée de ma découverte, (du coup j'oublie de parer, je perds, fais sembler de le regretter, je suis si loin en arrière). Ma surprise grandit: Vais-je revivre un passé englouti? Me trouver dans l'enfance avec toi? Est-ce cela tout le mystère? (pp. 34–35)

> ('How much fun it is, being children together!' I suddenly confess, taken aback by my discovery (with the result that I forget to parry, I lose, pretend to be sorry, I'm so far behind!). My surprise increases: Am I going to relive a past that has been swallowed up? Find myself in childhood with you? Is that the whole mystery?)

In fact in the third part of the text, a number of scenes from child-hood will become accessible to the narrator, and it is as if this troubling of her heart, this 'étrange maladie' (p. 37; 'strange illness') breaks up the screen of her current life and allows access to the past:

> Tout me revient; rien, vraiment, n'est oublié; pourtant l'effacement fait agir inexorablement son acide. J'avais trente-sept ans alors; depuis l'âge de vingt ans, j'avais connu un amour tranquille, enrichissant, sans doute plein d'am-biguïtés qui ne m'apparaissaient encore; l'histoire, à sa manière, pouvait continuer. Que signifiait cette houle, pourquoi, me demandais-je, ce désir fou d'enfance à revivre, ou plutôt à vivre enfin et pleinement? (pp. 36–37)

> (Everything comes back to me; nothing is actually forgotten; yet the acid of erasure is inexorably at work. I was thirty-seven at the time; ever since the age of twenty I had experienced a calm, enriching love, though full of ambi-guities I did not yet understand; the story, in its own way, could go on. What did this surge of feeling mean? Why, I wondered, did I feel this mad desire to relive childhood, or rather to live through it fully at last?)

The narrator traces the growing complicity between herself and the younger man; working in the same building (where the narrator is carrying out research into traditional music, like one of the protagonists in *Femmes d'Alger dans leur appartement*), they hold hushed telephone conversations, imagine that they are 'cousins' carrying out whispered exchanges, although the relationship remains at the level of friendship. Despite her infatuation, she is aware of social and political differences between them because of their age; he speaks only French and is not inter-ested in Arabic, since he has no desire to 'faire carrière' ('make a career for himself'). She does not rebuke this attitude, but thinks of the polit-ical significance of Arabic during the War of Independence and in doing so reveals a change that has taken place since independence: 'A quinze ans, moi, je vivais dans un pays en guerre! L'arabe était la langue du feu, pas à présent celle du pouvoir! On n'apprenait pas l'arabe, hors des écoles, pour faire carrière, mais pour désirer mourir!' (p. 42) ('When I was fifteen, I lived in a country at war! Arabic was the language of flame – not yet of power! When we learned Arabic, away from school, it was not because of wanting to make a career but because we desired to die!'). Her passion begins to consume her; she imagines going out dancing and drinking with him, spending the night with him, telephoning her husband to say she would not be back that night. She reveals herself in her inti-mate details; she would like to give in to the passion that she is forcing herself to master. She throws herself into her work, leaving the office where she had been working for six months in order to break her daily routine, and going out to meet and interview ordinary people in order to further her research: 'Des enquêtes, des visages, des paroles: une interrogation de sociologue me sollicitait. Engranger une moisson de bruits et de sons; en chercher ensuite l'adéquate utilisation – reportages de radio, tournages de documentaires, récits à publier en deux langues, etc. – après' ('field investigation, faces, words: sociological research was waiting for my attention. I would store up a wealth of noises and sounds, then try to find the best way of using them – radio reports, documentary films, the publication of bilingual accounts, etc. – afterwards'). In this external activity there is the opportunity to lose herself: 'S'oublier dans les autres; les autres qui attendent' (p. 46) ('forgetting oneself in others, the others who are waiting'). But the desire for this man that is somehow coupled to a desire to return to her childhood persists: 'Etait-ce une fièvre que je quêtais en lui, que je savais en moi?' (p. 48) ('Was it a fever I was seeking in him, a fever I knew was within myself?'). She wonders if it stems from the fear of losing her youth. She realises that she and her husband are no longer a couple, but have become two old friends who have little to say to each other. This incomprehensible desire she is experiencing forces self-examination. She is seeking to live out the adolescence she did not allow herself, preferring solitude at that time, despising the little groups of friends who did everything together; she feels a nostalgia for that period: 'Ce n'était pas un besoin de groupe; plutôt une nostalgie, pour moi, de cet âge perdu; de n'avoir pas eu de camarades garçons, des connivences légères, gratuites, avec l'autre sexe' (p. 53) ('it was not the need for a group; for me it was, rather, a nostalgia for that lost age; for not having had boys as friends, for having missed that lighthearted, free conspiring with the opposite sex'). During an evening out with a group of the 'Beloved's' friends, to see a well-known French poet and singer (Léo Ferré) popular in the sixties in Algeria (as in France), she observes a whole generation and the way in which they had lived their lives in the audience there that evening:

> Tous les intellos, ex soixante-huitards du pays, sont là!... Nous le saurons à partir de ce soir: notre 'rive gauche' compte trois mille personnes, sexe mâle pour la majorité, et avec 'petite amie' souvent française. Certes ils présentent quelques variantes: la peau claire ou foncée, le poil raide ou frisé, tous francophiles ce soir. (p. 58)

> (All the intellectuals in the country, the old activists of sixty-eight are here!... From now on, we'll know that our 'left bank' consists of three thousand people, most of them male, and their girlfriends are often French. Of course, there are several variations – light or dark skin, straight or curly hair – but all of them are Francophiles tonight.)

Importantly, the narrator feels herself to be in an 'in-between space' and it is as though a whole era is coming to an end, as she watches these few thousand Algerians engrossed by a French singer despite seven years of bloody conflict with France: 'Moi, je n'étais ni là-bas ni ici; je ne cherchais pas ma place, je ne m'en souciais même pas, toutefois je ne pouvais m'empêcher de sentir approcher les nuages, s'annoncer les tempêtes. Le pays, me semblait-il, devenait un cargo ayant déjà amorcé le début d'une dérive en mer inconnue' (p. 59) ('I myself was neither here nor there, not seeking my own place, nor even concerned about it, but still I could not help feeling there were clouds approaching, storms forecast. The country, it seemed to me, was becoming a freighter that had already begun to be adrift in unknown seas'). Even in the middle of this intimate confession of a personal passion, there are political and social observations concerning the recent history of Algeria, sometimes with an ironic stance, sometimes with a sense of foreboding, as in the two examples above. As she dances alone that night, the narrator remembers the way she used to dance in female family gatherings, refusing the traditional dances that each woman does in turn according to protocol, wanting to be different, refusing the constraint of what was expected of her, and again breaking with the traditional community of women:

> je transformais ainsi cette contrainte en une danse solitaire, fugitive, 'moderne', disaient les dames déçues par ma fantaisie qui semblait trahir... Trahir quoi? L'essentiel était, me semble-t-il sans analyser, ce défi de mon corps englouti qui prétendaient improviser le mouvement, l'essentiel était de m'écarter le plus possible de la frénésie collective de ces femmes, mes parentes – je sentais que la joie quasi funèbre de leurs corps, frôlant un désespoir entravé, ne me convenait pas. (p. 62)

> (thus I would transform this constraint into a solitary dance, fugitive and 'modern' as the women called it, disappointed by my imagination, which seemed to them a betrayal... Betrayal of what? Without analysing it, I think that the important thing was the challenge my enclosed body made by aiming to improvise movement. The important thing was to distance myself as much as possible from the collective frenzy of those women, my relatives – I felt I could not accept for myself the almost funereal joy of their bodies, verging on a fettered despair.)

The dance therefore became symbolic of her difference, of the different space that she occupied. That evening as she danced, she felt that she had been 'seen' properly and fully for the first time by a man, for a man, and, most importantly, become 'visible' for herself also: 'd'être vraiment "visible" pour ce jeune homme [...] Visible pour lui seul? Pour moi donc, par là même' (p. 64) ('being truly "visible" to this young man [...] Visible to him alone? The fact of being visible to him made me visible to myself'). She has appropriated the gaze of the other for herself – a further step on the road to self-knowledge.

After the narrator had finished carrying out the interviews in the countryside, she could have returned to her former office and carried on with research into the sound archives, but the time had come to break with the way she had become: 'Venait le temps des ruptures, de l'amputation sur moi-même par moi-même' (p. 66) ('The time was coming for separations, for the amputation to be performed on myself by myself'). She will end a love story that has not even begun, but she continues to live the torment of her passion, waking up in the night hoping to see the man she is in love with the next day, enduring bad dreams, but continuing the enforced separation, trying to end the 'illness' that possesses her: 'Tous les tourments que, par cette séparation, je m'infligeais ne pouvaient entamer ma lucidité. La maladie qui me possédait depuis au moins la fin de l'été avait fait opérer sa maturation; je n'étais pas dupe de moi-même, il me fallait éviter de glisser dans un état imprévisible' (p. 76) ('All the torments that I inflicted on myself by this separation could not cloud my lucidity. The illness which had possessed me since, at least, the end of summer had caused a maturing in me: I could not fool myself, I had to keep from slipping into some unforeseeable state'). She nonetheless finds ways to make contact with him through his family: she imagines meeting his mother, she visits an aunt who lives near his father's surgery and concocts a way of going there, but flees at the last moment. She needs to talk about her suffering and has no-one to confide in:

> Je sais désormais que le besoin de parler – à un ami et donc, à défaut, à l'époux que je ne crus tout autant un ami, s'il n'était plus un amant – avivait le plaisir âcre de m'entendre, par là de me convaincre de la réalité de ce qui m'habitait, de lui donner du poids et de la chair. Celle des mots donc, sinon celle des caresses; en effet, avant et pendant ces mots du dire, le désir de cet homme, servitude nouvelle, me tenaillait. (p. 82)

> (I knew from then on that the need to speak – to a friend and hence, failing that, to the husband I thought of necessarily as a friend, since he was no longer a lover – intensified the bitter pleasure of hearing myself, and as a result convinced me of the reality of what preoccupied me, giving it weight and flesh. The reality of words, if not the reality of caresses; in fact, before saying the words and while I said them, I was tortured by the desire for that man, a new enslavement.)

She finally tells her husband and a violent domestic quarrel ensues which will lead to him beating her and to her leaving him. The sixth section returns to the 'Beloved' and the memory of a particularly intimate conversation and moment together, a moment before the torment she would experience and before the erasure of him from her heart, when he tells her about a former lover, a Frenchwoman: 'Avant l'effacement, mais aussi avant les tourments de l'absence, il y eut les confidences de l'Aimé' (p. 86) ('Before this was all erased, but also before the torment of the absence, my Beloved once confided in me'). As for her husband, she is reminded that he belongs to the ranks of the 'enemy' and is taking up an age-old role allotted to him:

> Je vois, je revois aussi la face tordue de haine de l'époux – soudain je me rappelle que celui-ci est issu de la ville où les femmes mariées, même mariées dans l'harmonie, ou en tout cas sans heurt apparent, appellent secrètement tout époux 'l'ennemi'. Elles entre elles. L'époux, dans cette ultime scène, rejoignait ainsi le rôle que, depuis des générations, la mémoire de la ville lui assignait. Lui, dans sa fureur renouvelée: comme je coupais volontairement le son, il jouait plus aisément son rôle d'ennemi. 'Mon ennemi', soupirais-je, parce que l'ennemi de l'Aimé. (p. 107)
>
> (I see also, I see again, the face of the husband twisted in hatred – suddenly I remember that he comes from the town where married women, even those in a harmonious marriage or one in any case with no open clashes, secretly call any husband 'the enemy'. Women speaking among women.
>   The husband, in that final scene, thus returned to the role that for generations had been assigned to him by the town's memory. In his renewed rage, and because I was deliberately turning off the sound, he played the role of enemy even more easily. 'My enemy,' I sighed, because he was the enemy of my Beloved.)

She is finally able to say goodbye (we may note a final *adieu* rather than *au revoir*) to the young man. The story accelerates. The narrator remarries, she lives in Paris, she writes. This time her husband leaves her. She has no idea why she has felt the need to tell this intimate story about herself: 'Je reviens à ces jours d'avant la sieste, à ces treize mois: je ne sais pas pourquoi avec tant de circonvolutions, en désordre volontairement non chronologique, j'ai fait égoutter ces fontaines de moi-même, alors qu'il fallait les tarir, ou tout au mois les endiguer' (p. 116) ('I go back to those days before the siesta, to those thirteen months. I do not know why I have drained these springs inside myself, with so many convolutions, in a disorder that is deliberately not chronological, when I should have let them dry up, or at least have restricted their flow'). Yet, in the concluding lines of this final section, it becomes clear to the reader that this need was to know herself better, to be as close to self as possible, the *moi* constantly repeated:

> Et cet homme, ni étranger ni en moi, comme soudain enfanté, quoique adulte, de moi; soudain moi tremblant contre sa poitrine, moi pelotonnée entre sa chemise et sa peau, moi tout entière contre le profil de son visage tanné par le soleil, moi sa voix vibrante dans mon cou, moi ses doigts contre ma joue, moi regardée par lui et aussitôt après, allant me contempler pour me voir par ses yeux dans le miroir, tenter de surprendre le visage qu'il venait de voir, comment il le voyait, ce 'moi' étranger et autre, devenant pour la première fois moi à cet instant même précisément grâce à cette translation de la vision de l'autre... (p. 116)

(And that man, who was neither foreign to me nor someone inside me, as though he had been suddenly born from me, although he was an adult; me suddenly trembling against his chest, me curled up between his shirt and his skin, me, all of me, close against the profile of his face tanned by the sun, me his voice vibrant at my neck, me his fingers on my face, me being looked at by him and immediately afterwards going to look at myself to see me through his eyes in the mirror, trying to catch sight of the face he had just seen, as he saw it, this 'me' a stranger and another, becoming me for the first time at that very moment, precisely because of that transference through the eyes of the other...)

A further analogy with the Proustian text is implicit here. In the love of Swann for Odette or the narrator for Albertine there was the consciousness of the loss of selfhood, of not only wanting the other, but to be the other, to lose oneself entirely, to become whole by fusing with the loved one. The narrator of *A la recherche du temps perdu*, like the narrator here, will eventually come to self-knowledge firstly through the pain of losing self in the love for another, and then will fully inhabit a self that does not need another to make it whole, but that is saved through the act of writing. In this painful and painfully intimate love story that opens *Vaste est la prison*, the process of coming to the full possession of selfhood is recounted, as the narrator steps out of one life and into another. In *L'Amour, la fantasia*, the journey back to childhood needed to be accompanied by an excavation of another Algerian history; in the first part of *Vaste est la prison*, the journey into the very being of the narrator is made unaccompanied, and that journey will lead also to the knowledge of potential salvation in the written word.

THE HISTORY OF WRITING

In the second part of *Vaste est la prison* the narrator embarks on a new quest, a quest that will perhaps allow access to a written form of a truly maternal tongue. And here there is a very precise link once again to *L'Amour, la fantasia*, in a short text 'Biffure...' ('Erasure...') in which the narrator imagines the French and Arabic scripts reflected in each other:

> *Et l'inscription du texte étranger se renverse dans le miroir de la souffrance, me proposant son double évanescent en lettres arabes, de droite à gauche redévidées; elles se délavent ensuite en dessins d'un Hoggar préhistorique...*
> *Pour lire cet écrit, il me faut renverser mon corps, plonger ma face à l'ombre, scruter la voûte de rocailles ou de craie, laisser les chuchotements immémoriaux remonter, géologie sanguinolente. (L'Amour, la fantasia,* p. 58)

(I glimpse the mirror-image of the foreign inscription, reflected in Arabic letters, writ from right to left in the mirror of suffering; then the letters fade into pictures of the mountainous Hoggar in prehistoric times...

To read this writing I must lean over backwards, plunge my face into the shadows, closely examine the vaulted roof of rock or chalk, lend an ear to the whispers that rise up from time out of mind, study this geology stained red with blood.)

Could these inscriptions, which somehow come into being from the reflection of the French and Arabic scripts in each other, be another alphabet, a form of expression which is other and yet hers, that would release her from this distorted embrace of the two languages available to her? Such a question is pursued in a different way in *Vaste est la prison*.

A large part of the second part of the text, 'L'Effacement sur la pierre' ('Erased on Stone'), is Djebar's version of the story of a lost alphabet of the Berber language, the history of a form of written expression no longer accessible. This is not merely a historical quest, but an archaeological one both literally and metaphorically, conducted through the accounts of the ruins at Dugga in Tunisia, as she retraces the discovery of a bilingual inscription on a mausoleum found there by various travellers, and eventually sold to the British Museum by Thomas Reade, the British consul general in Tunis in 1842, where it remains today. It consists of two tablets, squared off but which fit together, with the script on the left identified as Punic, and that on the right as Numidian (see Figure 1).[71] This

Figure 1. The stele from Dugga with bilingual inscription in Punic and Numidian. Reproduced by permission of the British Museum.

second part of *Vaste est la prison* opens with an epigraph that concerns a buried alphabet, and the uncertainty as to the location of that alphabet, an alphabet that would allow a new way of being, a way of passing through borders, through limits: 'Un alphabet que je n'employais ni pour penser ni pour écrire, mais pour passer des frontières' ('An alphabet that I did not use either to think in or to write in, but to cross borders'). The author of the epigraph, Charles Dobzynski, also places the text under the sign of exile, and of the struggle with language and the preservation of its oral forms.[72] The story of the lost alphabet of the Berber language begins with Thomas d'Arcos, who first found the tablets in the seventeenth century after a period as a slave of the Turks in Tunis, and who decided to stay there after being freed and who converted to Islam. In the autumn of 1631 he went to the ruins of Dugga where he found an imposing mausoleum:

> Au milieu de cette plaine, un imposant monument, non pas un simple arc de triomphe, mais un mausolée majestueux, harmonieux, étrange même. Thomas considère les sculptures, les inscriptions [...] il prend la décision qui s'impose: de tout ce mausolée, l'insolite, l'inattendu est bien cette inscription en deux faces parallèles, non semblables: la recopier scrupuleusement. Il étudie longuement les caractères, il rectifie: 'les deux écritures', car la magnifique stèle se compose, il le comprend enfin, d'un texte bilingue. (p. 126)

> (In the middle of this plain, an imposing monument, not a simple triumphal arch but a majestic, harmonious, even strange mausoleum. Thomas contemplates the sculptures, the inscriptions [...] he takes the obvious decision. The most unusual and unexpected thing about this whole mausoleum is certainly this inscription on two parallel but dissimilar faces; he will copy it down meticulously. He studies the letters in detail, and corrects himself: 'Both scripts', because he finally understands that the magnificent stele is made up of a bilingual text.)

Two years later a scholar, Abraham Echellen from Rome, came to Tunis and Thomas showed him the writings he had copied. The scholar promised to study them in Rome and write to him, but they ended up in the Vatican archives and their mystery remained untouched for two centuries. What seems to interest the narrator in Thomas's story is not only this archaeological find, but also his own 'in-betweenness', this man who chose to live in exile, who crossed between Christianity and Islam: 'Thomas, entre deux rives, entre deux croyances, sera le premier transmetteur d'une inscription' (p. 128) ('Thomas, between two shores, between two religious beliefs, will be the first transmitter of an inscription'). This 'being between two states' seems to make him a most appropriate discoverer of the tablets. The story then moves forward to the early nineteenth century. Count Borgia arrived in Tunis in 1815, the year of the Battle of Waterloo, and went to Dugga with a Dutch engineer, Humbert. The Count made several sketches of the mausoleum and its inscriptions, and tried to identify the writing ('"punico e punico-hispanico" dit-il avec erreur' [p. 131] ['mistakenly calling them "Punic and Hispano-Punic"']), but he was more interested in the architecture of the building than in the inscriptions. The Count died suddenly two years later and his papers ended up finally with those of Humbert in a Dutch museum (remaining unpublished until 1959, although some scholars did in the meantime go and copy the inscription from his papers). It was in the summer of 1832 that the English lord and enthusiastic archaeologist Sir Granville Temple went to Dugga and examined the mausoleum: 'Sur la face est, une double inscription l'arrête et le fascine: l'une des écritures est punique, il le reconnaît vite, l'autre présente des caractères inconnus, probablement, se dit-il, "un vieil Africain". Il suppose donc que ce mausolée date des dernières années de Carthage punique' (p. 135) ('On the east face a double inscription catches his eye and he is fascinated by it. One of the scripts is Punic – he quickly recognises it. The other has unknown letters, probably "some form of old African", he says to himself. He supposes therefore that this mausoleum dates from the last years of Punic Carthage'). He published the inscription in a book of his travels in 1835, and several scholars tried to decipher it (Honegger; Etienne Quatremètre; de Saulcy; A.C. Judas). Again, it is not only Temple's interest in the inscription that interests the narrator; with the Dane, Falbe, who had made a topographical map of the ruins of Carthage, Temple witnesses in 1837 the siege of Constantine, the bloody reprisal by the French army for their failure to take it the previous year. Although the two men had come to investigate the region's past, they find themselves caught up in its tragic present, just as *Vaste est la prison* as a whole will slowly move forward to witnessing the present of its writing. Finally, the British consul general, Thomas Reade, who had welcomed Lord Temple in 1833, aware of the interest in the archaeological discoveries at Carthage and the rivalry for such finds in Egypt, decided to take the inscription from Dugga to sell to the British Museum. This involved the destruction of much of the monument, which was to be reconstructed, without the inscription, at the beginning of the twentieth century. The alphabet, taken therefore by destruction, remains in the British Museum, itself an institution of another empire, exhibiting artefacts often appropriated from other cultures by a colonial power. Yet another secret remains concerning the alphabet: in the middle of the twentieth century, a French scholar, Poinsot, studied the papers lying forgotten in Holland, and proved that there was another stele, the writing on which was all but erased: 'Ainsi, autour de Dougga, même si le monument funéraire a retrouvé son élégance hybride – mi-grecque, mi-orientale –, un mystère semble encore planer autour de l'écriture lapidaire, celle qui fut violée et emportée, mais aussi celle qui, victime de l'érosion, s'est presque totalement évanouie' (p. 143) ('Thus, even if the funerary monument has regained its hybrid elegance – half Greek, half oriental – a mystery still seems to hang over Dugga, over the writing in stone; the writing that was desecrated and carried off, but also the writing which has almost entirely vanished, victim of erosion'). The fundamental metaphor of the text, that which has been or is about to be totally or partially erased, returns. The secret of the alphabet continues to fascinate the narrator, as it had scholars throughout the nineteenth century:

> Or le doute pointe: et si ce 'vieil Africain' que, dans le nord de l'Afrique, les autochtones eux-même tiennent pour un dialecte, seulement oral, si ce parler 'barbare', avant d'être reconnu 'berbère', s'écrivait, s'était écrit, ne faisait qu'un avec le libyque dont les ombres se profilent durant les sept siècles de la puissance carthaginoise, oui, si cet alphabet archaïque avait précédé la culture phénicienne et s'était maintenu longtemps après elle?
>
> Si cette écriture étrange s'animait, se chargeait d'une voix au présent, s'épelait à voix haute, se chantait? Si ce supposé 'dialecte' d'hommes qui parlèrent tour à tour punique avec Carthage, latin avec les Romains et les romanisés jusqu'à Augustin, et grec puis arabe treize siècles durant, et qu'ils continuèrent, génération après génération, à garder vivace pour un usage endogamique (avec leur mères, leurs épouses et leurs filles essentiellement), si ce parler remontait jusqu'à plus loin encore? Cette langue, celle de Jugurtha exprimant son énergie indomptable à combattre et à mourir, celle-là même de Masinissa tout au long des ses soixante ans de règne! (p. 145)

> (Now comes a trickle of doubt: What if this 'Old African', which in North Africa the indigenous people themselves consider to be merely an oral dialect – what if this 'barbarous' speech, before it was ever called 'Berber', had once been written? What if it had been a written language, was identical with Libyan, whose shadow looms throughout the seven centuries of Carthaginian power? What if this archaic alphabet had preceded the Phoenician culture and survived long after it?
>
> What if this foreign writing came to life, was voiced in the present, was spoken out loud, was sung? What if this so-called dialect of men who spoke by turn Punic with the Carthaginians, Latin with the Romans and romanised until Augustine's time, Greek, and then Arab for thirteen centuries, had continued, generation after generation, kept alive for endogamic use (mainly with their mothers, their wives, and their daughters)? Suppose this speech went back even further? The language in which Jugurtha expressed his untameable energy to fight and die, the very language Masinissa spoke throughout his sixty-year reign!)

It is here also that the heart of the fascination of the possibilities of such an alphabet is revealed: it would be an alphabet that would be essentially the preserve of women. The other languages of power are used by men in the public space; it would be in the private space of the home, of the feminine, that this language endured: 'Ecriture du soleil, secret fertile du passé!' (p. 146) ('The writing of the sun, fertile secret of the past!').

The history of the attempts to decipher the inscription is continued, through Walter Oudney's discovery of writing in Tuareg, the language of a nomadic Berber tribe and the only Berber language to have an indigenous written form, on rocks in the desert; and very importantly, through the correspondence of Bey Ahmed using what had been believed to be a code, but was in fact the ancient alphabet being used for political and military activities: 'Le chef résistant l'utilise comme écriture du danger, justement pour conjurer le danger!' (p. 148) ('The resistance chief uses it to write of danger, in order to ward off danger!'). After the defeat of Bey Ahmed, the Tuaregs remained free for another seventy years: 'Comme si l'écriture ancestrale conservée hors de la soumission allait de pair avec l'irréductibilité, la mobilité d'un peuple qui, suprême élégance, laisse ses femmes conserver l'écriture, tandis que leurs hommes guerroient au soleil ou dansent devant les brasiers de la nuit' (p. 148) ('As if the ancestral writing, preserved outside submission, went hand in hand with the unconquerableness and mobility of a people who, in supreme elegance, let their women preserve the writing while their men wage war in the sun or dance before the fires of night'). Again, this alphabet was entrusted to women. By 1857, Célestin Judas had discovered that the signs on the Dugga inscription and the signs on the rocks in the desert, sent to Paris by a French officer in Constantine, were the same: 'Ainsi au cours des années 1860, se rétablit le tracé émouvant d'une civilisation si ancienne, sa mémoire ayant certes conservé la langue dans sa rudesse et son âcre douceur, mais de leur exil dans les sables, les lettres reviennent à leur source, cherchent à être réécrites, et par tous!' (p. 150) ('Thus, during the 1860s, the evocative lines of such an ancient civilisation are restored. Though its memory had preserved the language in all its toughness and bitter-sweetness, the letters now return to their source from their exile in sand, they seek to be written again, and by everyone!').[73]

Before a last evocation of the alphabet lost and found, there is, most tellingly for Djebar's quest here, an identification with Polybius, the Greek historian under the Roman Empire (again an exile, therefore, writing under a colonial power) and the chronicler for Scipio Aemilianus of the destruction of Carthage:

> Or moi, l'humble narratrice d'aujourd'hui, je dis, tandis qu'à Dougga Jugurtha finit de lire dans la langue ancestrale, je dis que l'écriture de Polybe, nourrie à tant de chutes concomitantes – lui, le témoin du feu de Carthage,

au bris des statues de Corinthe par milliers abattues ou emportées, lui qui, pour finir, aura bientôt à contempler l'incendie de Numance et les morts espagnols convulsés d'héroïsme grandiose – que cette écriture, inscrite dans une langue certes maternelle, mais épousée par les esprits cultivés de l'Occident d'alors, court sur les tablettes, polygame! (p. 158)[74]

(But I, today's humble female narrator, say, while at Dugga Jugurtha stops reading in the ancestral language, I say that the writing of Polybius, which is fed by all these simultaneous falls (he witnessed first the burning of Carthage, then thousands of statues of Corinth being knocked down or carried away, and, finally, he will soon have to contemplate the burning of Numantia and the dead Spaniards convulsed in their grandiose heroism) – I say that his writing, composed in a language that was, of course, his mother-tongue, but espoused by the cultivated minds of the West at that time, runs freely over the tablets and is polygamous!)

Djebar the writer identifies with Polybius's duty to record the events he witnesses; and furthermore there is again the danger of erasure, as was the case for the lost alphabet, for little survived of Polybius's work:

Est-ce pourquoi son œuvre comme la stèle de Dougga, après avoir alimenté, plusieurs siècles, l'appétit de savoir et la curiosité des successeurs, d'un coup, inopinément, par de larges plaques, s'efface?

Car, du témoignage de Polybe sur Carthage, sur Corinthe, sur Numance, ne restent désormais que des débris épars, que des ombres d'ombres dans les miroirs tendus d'épigones d'une statue moindre, Appien, Diodore de Sicile, quelques autres.

Comme si cette poussée scriptuaire sécrétait un risque, une accélération vers l'inévitable effacement! (pp. 158–59)[75]

(Is that why his work, like the stele at Dugga, after having fed his successors' appetite for knowledge and curiosity for several centuries, is suddenly and unexpectedly erased in large part?

For out of Polybius's accounts of Carthage, of Corinth, and of Numantia, there only remain scattered fragments, only the shadows of shadows in mirrors held up by imitators of lesser stature, Appian, Diodorus of Sicily, and a few others.

As if this urge to write secreted a risk, an inevitable acceleration towards erasure!)

There is also an imagined account of the reading of the bilingual inscriptions by the young Jugurtha (who would become King of Numidia and put up serious resistance to the Roman army):

D'une voix bien distincte, qui résonne dans le silence respectueux établi, il commence par 'la langue des Autres', dit-il, et son punique s'élève pour louanger le grand Masinissa, son ascendance et ses trois fils; de la même façon il épelle les noms de l'équipe d'Atban.

Il respire un instant, bref instant où, dans le chaleur avivée, une stridulation de cigale se fait entendre; il reprend la lecture, cette fois 'dans la langue des Ancêtres', dit-il énergiquement. (p. 154)

(In a clear, distinct voice, which rings out in the respectful silence, he begins with 'the Others' language', as he calls it, and his Punic rises in praise of the great Masinissa, his ancestors, and his three sons. In the same way, he calls out the names of the team from Atban.

He pauses for breath, and in that brief moment the shrill noise of a cicada is heard in the intensifying heat; then he begins to read again, this time, he says emphatically, in 'the language of our ancestors'.)

In this scene, Jugurtha goes on to greet the Roman general Scipio Aemilianus in that language. The lost alphabet would not only be a maternal language, the language preserved by women, but would also be a language of resistance. The meditation on the stone inscription developed in the text reveals the possibility that this lost alphabet could effect the return from exile, not only for the writer herself, but for many others:

> Combien sont-ils encore – combien sommes-nous encore – toutes et tous à chanter, à pleurer, à hululer, mais aussi à aimer, installés plutôt dans l'impossibilité d'aimer –, oui, combien sommes-nous, bien qu'héritiers du bey Ahmad, des Touaregs du siècle dernier et des édiles de Dougga, à nous sentir exilés de leur première écriture? (p. 150)

> (How many of them are there still – how many of us are there still – all, men and women alike, singing, weeping, ululating, but also loving or rather existing in the impossibility of loving – yes, how many of us are there who, although heirs of the Bey Ahmad, the Tuaregs of the last century and the Roman *aediles* at Dugga, feel exiled from their first writing?)

A further meditation closes Part Two, with a text in italics under the title of 'Abalessa', the name of a place concerning the legend of Tin Hinan, an ancient Tuareg queen who fled into the desert and who took with her a lost alphabet, used for the inscriptions found in her tomb; an alphabet that would pre-date even that found at Dugga, and would again be a maternal language, the 'legacy of a woman':

> J'imagine donc la princesse du Hoggar qui, autrefois dans sa fuite, emporta l'alphabet archaïque, puis en confia les caractères à ses amies, juste avant de mourir. Ainsi, plus de quatre siècles après la résistance et le dramatique échec de Yougourtha au Nord, quatre siècles également avant celui, grandiose, de la Kahina – la reine berbère qui résistera à la conquête arabe –, Tin Hinan des sables, presque effacée, nous laisse héritage – et cela, malgré ses os aujourd'hui dérangés –: notre écriture la plus secrète, aussi ancienne que l'étrusque ou que celle des 'runes' mais contrairement à celles-ci, toute bruissante encore de sons et de souffles d'aujourd'hui, est bien legs de femme, au plus profond du désert.
> Tin Hinan ensevelie dans le ventre de l'Afrique! (p. 164)[76]

(And so I imagine the princess of the Hoggar who, when she fled long ago, carried away the archaic alphabet, and then entrusted its characters to her friends just before she died.

Thus, more than four centuries after the resistance and dramatic defeat of Jugurtha in the north, and four centuries before the grandiose defeat of Al-Kahina – the Berber queen who resisted Arab conquest –, Tin Hinan of the sands, almost erased, leaves us her legacy, despite the fact that her bones

have now been scattered. Our most secret writing, as ancient as Etruscan or
the runes, but unlike these a writing still noisy with the sounds and breaths
of today, is indeed the legacy of a woman in the depths of the desert.
    Tin Hinan buried in the womb of Africa!)

This story of the lost alphabet is therefore a complex one. It is a
personal quest for 'un moi archaïque' ('an archaic self')[77] as Mireille
Calle-Gruber has expressed it, within a lost language of expression. It is
also a political quest, concerned not only with a history of writing, but
with the history of the languages of Algeria. As Abdelkébir Khatibi writes,

> In the Maghreb, actual bilingualism or multilingualism did not originate in
> the colonial situation; it pre-existed it. The war between languages, between
> idioms, has always played a role in the formation of nation states. A language
> policy, whether declared or indirect, is always involved in this moment of
> formation.
>   Well before the French and Spanish colonisation of the Maghreb, there
> was a double idiomatic discontinuity between, on the one hand, classical
> Arabic and what is called dialectal Arabic, and on the other, Tamazight
> (Berber) and the Arabic language in all its diglossia.
>   We know that the Tamazight language was preserved orally through its
> popular literature and songs. Although rarely written, it had been set down
> with the help of an ancient sign system, the *tifnagh*, and transcribed into
> Arabic script, but it also appears in Latin characters in French Orientalist
> literature. The fate of *tifnagh* shows the very uncertain status of writing in
> pre-Islamic North Africa. It is Islam that imposed on the Maghreb the idea
> of the unity of language and religion, a notion founded on the principle of
> the unity between language and sacred text. This notion constitutes both a
> politics and an eschatology.[78]

This central section of *Vaste est la prison* is generated therefore by a
writing strategy similar to that of *L'Amour, la fantasia*, whereby a new
history/story is retrieved from between the lines of other accounts. The
focus this time, however, is more fundamental: the excavation of a
language of expression, the embodiment of knowledge.

KNOWLEDGE AND SELFHOOD

The third and longest part of the text, 'Un silencieux désir' ('A Silent
Desire'), alternates private memories and a series of scenes from a film
the narrator is making, its title placing it under the sign of silence once
again. Its epigraph, taken from Hermann Broch, could stand as a key to
the deciphering of the text as a whole: 'La confession n'est rien, la
connaissance est tout' ('Confession is nothing, knowledge is everything').
As I have already suggested, self-examination, through confession in the
first part of the text, is the route to self-knowledge. Self-knowledge is not

the ultimate aim, however, for through that may come greater knowledge of others and of the world. In the second part of the text, knowledge comes through the excavation of the archaic and more recent past. In this third part, knowledge will again come through a type of excavation, this time to uncover key private memories. The first section, 'Fugitive et ne le sachant pas', is presented in italics, which suggests that it is to be read in parallel with the closing text of the second part, also presented in italics. In a now familiar strategy, Djebar takes up a story from the past that has a significance, a resonance, with her own enterprise. This time it is the 'Story of the Captive and Zoraida' from *Don Quixote*, which is read here as the first appearance of an Algerian woman in a great founding text of European literature. This is a tale comprised of five chapters that is part of the short stories inserted in the first part of Cervantes's novel. In order to escape her life of enclosure, Zoraida, through letters she writes, offers herself in marriage to a gentleman who had been taken captive in Algiers, and they flee together. The fact that Zoraida takes her destiny into her own hands through the written word and then becomes a fugitive links her to Tin Hinan, and to the narrator herself, who sees Zoraida as the first Algerian woman to write, although once again it is writing that has been erased:

> Son écriture, devenue illisible, s'avère par là même inutile et s'efface – ainsi, la première Algérienne qui écrit, c'est bien elle, Zoraidé qui rencontre, sinon Don Miguel, du moins le captif de Don Quichotte. Ecriture de fugitive, écriture par essence éphémère [...]
> L'histoire de Zoraidé, rapportée devant celle-ci muette par l'ex-captif aux hôtes d'une auberge de campagne où Don Quichotte et Sancho Pança sont de passage, est bien la métaphore des Algériennes qui écrivent aujourd'hui, parmi lesquelles je me compte. (pp. 168–69)

> (Her writing, now illegible, is therefore useless and erased. Thus the first Algerian woman to write is she, Zoraida, who meets, if not Don Miguel, then at least Don Quixote's captive. It is the writing of a fugitive, writing which is ephemeral in its very essence [...]
> Zoraida's story, told in her silent presence by the former captive to the guests at a country inn where Don Quixote and Sancho Panza are staying, is a metaphor for Algerian women writing today, among whom I include myself.)

This story serves therefore as a parallel concerning the aims and risks for the woman writer, but an identification with Andalusian culture and music also provides a link for the narrator with the town of her ancestors:

> La ville de ma famille, ex-Césarée, fut repeuplé de Morisques, par centaines, de ceux qui, contemporains de Cervantès, sont expulsés en masse, définitive et profonde saignée que s'inflige l'Espagne au début du XVIIe siècle. Ils trouvèrent refuge dans les cités du Nord maghrébin, parmi lesquelles ma petite ville si ancienne, l'ex-capitale romanisée [...]

Ainsi reçus-je, au cours des étés de ma première enfance, au milieu des brodeuses, des chanteuses, odalisques jeunes ou vieillies de cette cité fermée sur elle-même, où seul le luth pouvait se plaindre haut, cette lueur vacillante qui traversa les siècles et perpétua la lumière de l'Andalousie des femmes, encore quelque peu nourricière. (pp. 169–70)

(My family's city, the former Caesarea, was repopulated by hundreds of Moriscos, contemporaries of Cervantes who were expelled en masse in a final and profound bloodletting inflicted by Spain on itself at the beginning of the seventeenth century. They found refuge in the cities of northern Maghreb, one of which was my little city, the ancient romanized ex-capital [...]

Thus I received – throughout the summers of my early childhood, surrounded by women who sang or embroidered, odalisques young and old of a city closed in on itself, where only the lute could complain out loud – this flickering light, which crossed centuries and perpetuated the light of the Andalusia of women, still providing a little nourishment.)

This music provides a link directly to her mother who, as a young girl, had noted down the poetry of the *noubas*, of the Andalusian music; this was a precious link to writing for the mother: 'elle qui n'écrivait pas le français, qui apprit ensuite à le parler sans l'écrire [...] Elle en savait par cœur les couplets, mais relire les vers inscrits en arabe la préservait, dans notre cercle, du statut d'analphabète qui aurait pu être la sienne' (pp. 170–71) ('she could not write French, only later learning to speak but not write it [...] She knew the couplets by heart, but being able to reread the written verses in Arabic kept her from being classified as illiterate, as she otherwise might have been'). But one summer during the War of Independence when the apartment was closed up and her mother visiting her son in prison in France, the French soldiers broke in to requisition anything of use to them that they could find, and in the usual acts of destruction that also took place, they slashed the sheets of music whose mysterious writing they took to be some kind of nationalist messages (there are resonances here with the Tuareg alphabet used as code, as described above). Her mother's writing therefore becomes another woman's writing that has been erased, a writing that held in it all the legacy of her ancestors, and in a slipping in and out of identification with other women, the narrator will tell the story of another captive, this time the brother, the story that the mother cannot tell:

Terme d'une écriture de femme, comme si, son corps se mettant en mouvement et sans le voile des aïeules, sa main scripteuse perdait alors et l'ardeur, et la trace! Zoraidé donc de retour, mais en sens inverse; avec un récit nouveau du Captif qui aurait pu être celui du fils libéré des prisons françaises d'hier, qui devient celui de la fille s'emparant du statut de la mère... (pp. 171–72)

(The end of a woman's writing, as if, as her body began to move and no longer wore her ancestors' veil, her writing hand then lost both its ardour and its track! Zoraida has thus returned, but in the opposite direction; with a new tale of the Captive that could have been about the son freed from the French prisons of yesterday, and becomes the tale of the daughter taking on the mother's status...)

This complex movement between Zoraida, the narrator and the narrator's mother shows Djebar's writing strategy at its most subtle, and the section closes on how and why she writes despite the difficulty of the endeavour, as she links the text in a profound way with the experiences of her mother: 'J'écris dans l'ombre de ma mère revenue de ses voyages en temps de guerre, moi, poursuivant les miens dans cette paix obscure faite de sourde guerre intérieure, de divisions internes, de désordres et de houle de ma terre natale. J'écris pour me frayer mon chemin secret' (p. 172) ('I write in the shadow of my mother, returned from her wartime travels, while I pursue my own travels in this obscure peace composed of silent inner warfare, internal divisions, riots and tumult in my native land. I write to clear a secret path for myself'). And she reiterates that this is in French, 'la langue dite "étrangère"' ('the so-called "foreign" language'), and that like Zoraida she has lost all her 'riches', for the narrator her maternal heritage; she is a fugitive who cannot fully 'know', or at least allow herself to 'know', the status she would have inherited, otherwise she would return to silence.[79]

In contrast to that silence, in the first of the scenes of 'Femme arable' ('Arable Woman') the narrator notes that embarking on the film marked a change in her life, and she is full of emotion as she begins the shoot, at one with the community of women who are empowered with and through her:

> J'ai dit: 'Moteur'. Une émotion m'a saisie. Comme si, avec moi, toutes les femmes de tous les harems avaient chuchoté: 'moteur'. Connivence qui me stimule. D'elles seules dorénavant le regard m'importe. Posé sur ces images que j'organise et que ces présences invisibles derrière mon épaule aident à fermenter.
> Ce regard, je le revendique mien. Je le perçois 'notre'. Unique regard perçant les murs des siècles passés, s'échappant hors des maisons-tombeaux d'aujourd'hui et qui cherche à se poser, concentré [...]
> Nous toutes, du monde des femmes de l'ombre, renversant la démarche: nous enfin qui regardons, nous qui commençons. (pp. 174–75)

(I said: 'Action'. I was gripped by emotion. As if all the women of all the harems had whispered 'Action!' with me. Their complicity stimulates me. The only thing that matters to me from now on is their eyes. Their gaze, resting on these images that I assemble and that their invisible presence behind my back helps me to bring to fruition.

This gaze I claim as my own. I see it as 'ours'. A single gaze piercing the walls of past centuries, escaping from the tomb-houses of today, seeking a place to alight and concentrate on [...]

All of us from the world of the women in the shadows, reversing the process: we are the ones finally who are looking, who are beginning.)

The women (and especially the film-maker herself) have taken control of looking at the world: no longer the objects of the male gaze, they become the subjects of a female look, in a movement that reminds us of the scene of the narrator dancing in the first part of the book, in which she believes she is 'seen' for the first time by the 'Beloved', and most importantly becomes visible to herself. This look will also be the look exercised on the self: 'Un regard intérieur sur moi-même, avant ce dialogue de travail qui s'amorce' (p. 199) ('An internal gaze at myself, before this working dialogue begins'). The series of texts concerned with the scenes of the film are as much about the motivation of the narrator as a description of the film-making process and the everyday incidents during filming. She recalls, for example, that hearing about the death of Pasolini on the radio seemed to shake her to her roots and changed her life: 'un coup de hache dans mon histoire individuelle' (p. 200) ('an axe-stroke upon my personal history'). In the film-making process she seems to find a great freedom, and this activity becomes bound up with her very identity:

> Tout a vraiment commencé ce premier jour de la ferme, tout, c'est-à-dire l'existence non plus théorique de ce film, mais sa présence, tandis que je trouvais mon espace quotidien. Cette liberté, mine de rien. Cet espace, au vrai, me ressemble. Ainsi, me dis-je, commencer une fiction de film, lorsque l'espace qui lui convient est trouvé vraiment. (p. 220)

> (Everything really began that first day on the farm, everything, meaning the film's existence, no longer in theory but actually present, while I was finding my daily space. That freedom, looking like nothing at all. That space, in actual fact, is like me. So, I think, begin a fictional film when the space that suits it is found in reality.)

Through these women, who belong to the tribe from which she is descended, she re-establishes the link with the women of her childhood, and the link between the alternating texts concerning the film and family memories is also therefore established. This is also an intertextual link to the women's stories in *L'Amour, la fantasia*. During the filming the narrator is also aware of political issues. She learns that none of the children from the farm and the surrounding area go to school, despite the fact that there is the opportunity to do so in the nearby commune. These houses are a couple of kilometres outside the commune, and there are no public transport services. A widow with little money cannot pay the two dinars for the bus that goes to the school each day. Some families manage to find the money for the boys, very few for the girls (and not necessarily in the richest families). The narrator questions what she and her team are doing there: 'Allons-nous seulement nous installer, le temps d'impressionner les mètres de pellicule nécessaire?' (p. 250) ('Are we just going to move in for just long enough to expose sufficient film footage?'). The technical team pool money to give to the widow and the situation embarrasses the narrator: 'Cela me gêne soudain: tant d'intentions, d'une générosité collective évidente, ne doivent-elles aboutir qu'à l'assistance sociale?' ('Suddenly this bothers me: so many good intentions, coming from obvious collective generosity: should they end up in mere social assistance?'). The dilemma of an intervention of this type is troubling, raising questions concerning her own project, but also about the relationship more generally between traditional rural life and modern society both within and outside Algeria, and between the educated intellectual elite and the people they 'represent' (however ambiguously) in text and film.

The narrator also reflects on what the process of film-making has taught her, and it becomes clearer how the experience of the film, like the experience of the unhappy love affair at the beginning of the text, is linked to the experience of memory. It is memory that holds the text together:

> J'apprenais que le regard sur le dehors est en même temps retour à la mémoire, à soi-même enfant, aux murmures d'avant, à l'œil intérieur, immobile sur l'histoire jusque-là cachée, un regard nimbé de sons vagues, de mots inaudibles et de musiques mélangées... Ce regard réflexif sur le passé pouvait susciter une dynamique pour une quête sur le présent, sur un avenir à la porte. (p. 298)

> (I learned that looking outwards is at the same time a return to memory, to oneself as a child, to previous whispers, to the inner eye that has not moved from the story which was hidden up until now; a gaze surrounded by vague sounds, inaudible words and a mixture of music... This introspective gaze at the past could give rise to the dynamics for a search into the present, into the future which is already at the door.)

As in the unhappy love relationship, this experience returns her to childhood, and the retrieval of such memories, suffused with sensory experiences, again recalls the Proustian quest in which past and present merge to provide a new sense of self.

The present, therefore, can only be understood if the past has been 'resuscitated'. It is from this lesson about understanding the dynamic link between past and present that a creative vision can be developed:

> Apprendre à voir, je l'ai découvert, c'est se ressouvenir certes, c'est fermer les yeux pour réécouter les chuchotements d'avant, la tendresse murmurante d'avant, c'est rechercher les ombres qu'on croit mortes... Puis, dans la lumière délavée, ouvrir les yeux, interroger ardemment du regard, poser

celui-ci, transparent et discret, devant l'inconnu, c'est-à-dire les autres, que l'on voit enfin bouger pour de bon, vivre, souffrir, ou simplement être, être le plus quotidiennement; oui être. (pp. 298–99)

(Learning to see, I found out, is indeed recalling. It is closing one's eyes to hear again the earlier whispers, the earlier murmuring affection; it is retrieving the shadows one had believed were dead... then, opening one's eyes in the muted light, questioning with ardent eyes, then bringing one's gaze to rest, transparent and discreet, before the unknown, meaning the others, and finally seeing them actually move, live, suffer, or simply be, be in the most daily way, yes, be.)

Here then, in the middle of a description of the film, is a whole programme for a creative 'method', an analysis of what the writer must be able to do in order to 'see', to create. *Vaste est la prison*, like *A la recherche du temps perdu*, tells the story of its own coming into being.

The location of the film also brings the narrator back to her ancestors, found through another inscription on a stele set up a few years before and commemorating the last insurrection against the French in those mountains in 1871, in honour of Malek al'Berkani. She does not tell the film team that she is his direct descendant on her mother's side and she wonders if her ancestor would be insulted that she, a woman dressed in jeans and a cap, has not shown her respect to him, but has preferred to give her attention to the shot and to the landscape around him, although she cannot fully forget him. The gulf between Westernised woman and Berber man is tangible. This is memory incarnated in place, just as Tin Hinan endures in Abalessa. For Djebar as for Khatibi, the present is haunted by the past in the traces that remain.

'De la mère en voyageuse' ('Of the Mother as Traveller') begins the section of the text that deals with private memories, and a musical structure reminiscent of the third part of *L'Amour, la fantasia* returns. In this first 'movement', we also return to the world of private memory, and specifically to the mother (linked of course, as we have already seen, to music), to a journey to another land, and to a captive, all themes already set up in the story of Zoraida, as the narrator's mother decides to visit her only son imprisoned in France. The first trip undertaken with the younger sister is not successful; the son writes to them in France while they are there advising them against going to the prison. The mother goes again the next year and manages to see her son.[80] In her mother's sorrow afterwards, the narrator hints at another tragic incident in her mother's life which will be recounted later in the complex shifting between past and present that provides the text's dynamics: 'Elle ne comprend pas, elle ne veut pas comprendre qu'elle revit seulement un autre chagrin du passé, qu'elle verse d'autres larmes qui ne s'étaient jamais écoulées' (p. 197)

('She doesn't understand, doesn't want to understand that she is only re-living another sorrow from the past, that she is shedding other tears that had never yet fallen').

The next 'movement' concerns the narrator's grandmother, given in marriage at the age of fourteen to a very old man, and, while she is living at her aunt's house having left her husband, the narrator tries to imagine the young bride arriving in the house in Caesarea (modern-day Cherchell) that she herself knows well. Her grandmother also later left a man, her third husband, and the narrator imagines the disapproving traditional female voice: 'ainsi, toi aussi, pareille à ta grand-mère, – mais elle, ce sera pour plus tard, pour le plus jeune, le troisième – tu quittes l'homme, tu fuis, tu lui abandonnes maison ouverte?' (p. 212) ('So you're another one, just like your grandmother – but at least for her it was later, the youngest, her third – you're leaving the man, running away, leaving without closing the door behind you?'). The narrator feels the need to go back through these female family relationships now her first marriage is over: 'je m'abîmai dans les méandres de ma généalogie' (p. 214) ('I plunged into the meanderings of my genealogy'). It is in the third 'movement', 'De la mère en fillette' ('Of the Mother as a Little Girl'), that the narrator names herself: she is Isma, the same name as the protagonist of the second volume of the Algerian Quartet, *Ombre sultane*. She is not only Isma, but 'the descendant' of Fatima, the grandmother; she recognises the strangeness of her enterprise and her obsession with the past as she wonders whether her grandmother loved the two husbands she had after the old man of her first marriage: 'Je suis bien certes la seule à m'interroger ainsi sur des morts!' (p. 228) ('I'm definitely the only person to wonder about the dead like that!'). It is in this section also that the song that gives the text its title appears, sung when Chérifa, one of Fatima's daughters, the beloved sister of the narrator's mother Bahia, dies of typhus in the 1924 epidemic. Another sister, Malika, translates the words from the dialect for the women from the city who do not understand it: 'Vaste est la prison qui m'écrase / D'où me viendras-tu, délivrance' (p. 237) ('So vast the prison that crushes me / Release, where will you come from?'). Bahia is struck silent by the death of her sister, and only repeats to herself the words of the lament; she does not speak for months. The woman who will become the narrator's mother was rendered silent by loss, and silence haunts all of Assia Djebar's writing. Slowly the young girl recovers and eleven years later, at the age of eighteen, she gives birth to the narrator, and thirteen months later to her first son. The baby dies at six months old when the family is on holiday in Caesarea. The sorrow that the mother had never properly given in to after seeing the younger son, Sélim, in prison in France, is revealed. The narrator reflects on why she wishes to dwell on this grief, on the work of mourning that was never fully carried out:

> sans doute parce que, au préalable, elle a enterré, avant et avec le bébé de six mois emporté trop rapidement, comme dans un rapt cruel, elle a enterré surtout la langue, celle qui aurait pu être, pour ce premier fils, une couronne de fleurs d'oranger! A moins que cet oubli, que ce refus, que ce reniement ne soit intervenu une première fois longtemps auparavant lorsque, à six ans, elle est restée sans voix à la disparition de Chérifa la toute-belle, que, dans cet autisme si long […] cette langue dont fillette elle a voulu de détourner, d'un coup s'est évaporée: en elle, autour d'elle. (p. 246)

> (undoubtedly because, beforehand, she buried, before and with the six-month-old baby taken away too soon as by a cruel kidnapping, most of all she buried the language – the language that could have been a crown of orange-blossom for that first son! Unless that forgetting, that refusal, that denial had first come long before, when at the age of six she was left speechless by the death of Chérifa the all-beautiful; unless in that long autism […] the language from which she had chosen to turn away as a girl, suddenly evaporated: in her, around her.)

The narrator does all she can to break the silence of women, to restore a language to them, with the silence of the mother being fundamental to this quest.

The fourth movement, 'De la narratrice dans la nuit française' ('Of the Narrator in the French Night'), evokes a very intimate and particular memory from her childhood, a particular night during the Second World War when North Africa is being bombed by the German airforce. The narrator has previously described the apartment the family lived in until she was ten and the fact that they were 'amongst the French' (p. 243). These are the French schoolteachers among whom her father is the only Algerian teacher: 'Ainsi, dans l'immeuble pour familles d'instituteurs, nous touchions aux franges d'un autre domaine, tout à fait étrange pour les gens de Césarée: "les Français de France". Autant dire que, dans le village, nous frôlions quasiment une autre planète, ma mère et moi' (p. 243) ('Thus, in the building for teachers' families we touched the fringes of another domain, altogether foreign to the people of Caesarea: "The French from France". In other words, in the village, my mother and I were almost touching on another planet'). This particular memory concerns a night whose significance the narrator will only be able to decipher much later, but which will be the source of the troubling of her identity and linked directly to the 'dichotomy' caused by the colonial presence:

> cette nuit que je veux évoquer – non pour commencer mes souvenirs de la toute première enfance, non, cette nuit qui opéra en moi, âgée de trois ans,

> un imperceptible glissement... Comme si d'appartenir irrévocablement à la communauté familiale, dans un pays colonisé, et donc dichotomisé, cette appartenance-là allait connaître, en ma conscience de fillette tout à fait arabe, une sorte d'alarme. Dont je ne perçois l'onde souterraine que des décennies plus tard. (p. 253)

> (that night I want to talk about – not that I'm going to begin my memoirs from my earliest childhood, but that night brought about an imperceptible shift in my three-year-old self... As if, after belonging irrevocably to my family community in a colonised and therefore dichotomised country, that belonging was to perceive, within my awareness as a totally Arab little girl, a sort of alarm-bell, whose underground vibrations would not be felt by me until decades later.)

The narrator's family is the only indigenous family in the building and they take refuge with the French families in the shelter when the bombing raids begin. She remembers the strangeness of these expeditions. It is the first time that her mother begins to speak French and the little girl worries about how her mother, so elegant and well-bred, appears to these other women, revealing from a female angle the question of appearance under the gaze of the coloniser that both Memmi and Khatibi also deal with. The little girl also begins to speak French to these 'others': 'Etrangers dont je commençais à balbutier la langue, à peine moins gauchement que ma mère idéalisée' (p. 257) ('Foreigners whose language I was just beginning to stammer, hardly less awkwardly than my idealised mother'). The 'Français de France' remain unreal beings to her; they come into her house rarely and she never goes into theirs, communication is kept to courteous greeting on the stairs and in the courtyard. But then a dramatic event occurs for the young girl, and it is the first time that some French people do not seem alien to her:

> Je m'approche fort malaisément de ce souvenir premier, cette nuit de mes trois ans, dans la chambre de mes parents: est-ce un nœud que je vais dénouer seulement maintenant, est-ce une zébrure, une fêlure, une coupure définitive que j'ai tenté aussitôt d'effacer, cette nuit donc où ces 'Français de France' ne m'ont pas paru, comme c'est étrange, tout à fait étrangers. (p. 258)

> (I come to this first memory very ill-at-ease: that night when I was three, in my parents' bedroom: is it a knot that I am only now going to untie? is it a streak, a crack, a final and permanent cut which I tried to cover up straight away, the night when those 'French from France' did not, strange though it seemed, seem totally strange to me.)

It is as though the narrator has avoided this defining memory that she has tried to erase (more erasure), through all the meanders into the sorrows and dramas of other women's pasts. The memory concerns waking up with a strange noise, a 'French' noise:

> un bruit 'français', comme si la chambre parentale avait glissé horizontale-ment, s'était entrouverte vers la place du village et que là, moi dormant

toujours et mes parents debout, dressés autour de moi, nous nous retrou-
vions exposés aux quatre vents, devant nous, devant 'les autres'. La France
alors, c'était pour moi simplement le dehors. (p. 260)

(a 'French' sound, as if my parents' room had slid sideways, had partly
opened in the direction of the village square, and that there, with myself still
asleep and my parents standing up, around me, we found ourselves exposed
to the four winds, in front of us, in front of 'the others'. France, then, for
me, was simply what was outside.)

The child is in fact in her parents' room, but although it is apparently the
same it is also entirely 'other' because in the bed are a Frenchwoman and
her son, their closest neighbours whom her parents have taken in because
the woman was frightened by the German bombing: 'c'était pour moi le
comble du bouleversement – "lui", chez moi, dans le plus secret du "chez-
moi", du "chez-nous", et il continue à dormir comme si de rien n'était!'
('For me it was the greatest possible upheaval – "him", in my home, in
the most secret part of "my home", "our home", and he went on sleeping
as if nothing was happening!'). It is as though there has been a substitu-
tion for her parents and the discovery impacts on her sense of self, her
sense of belonging, and the notion of identity suddenly becomes much
less stable and fixed:

Cette nuit où le tumulte n'avait pu me réveiller tout à fait, cette nuit devenait celle d'une transmutation: la mère et son garçon, eux, les 'Français', nos
voisins de palier certes, mais aussi les représentants les plus proches de
'l'autre monde' pour moi, eux, ce couple surgi du noir et s'exposant à moi,
allongés là, à la place même de mes parents! [...] Est-ce que soudain je n'allais pas devenir autre? Est-ce que, dans le lent glissement de cette nuit
surprenante, je n'allais pas rester ainsi: à la fois dans la chambre de mes
parents (peut-être même avaient-ils choisi, eux, d'autres rôles, chez les
autres, dans un autre appartement français?) et me retrouvant dans le camp
d'en face? (pp. 262–63)

(That night when the tumult had not succeeded in waking me up completely,
that night became the night of an exchange: the mother and her boy, they,
'the French', our next-door neighours of course but also the closest representatives of 'the other world' to me; they, this pair who had appeared out
of the blue and were lying there in front of my eyes, in my parents' very
place! [...] Wasn't I suddenly going to become other? In that slow slide
during that night of surprises, wasn't I going to stay like that: in my parents'
room (perhaps they themselves had even chosen other roles, in other people's
flats, in another French flat?) and at the same time in the opposite camp?)

An air of unformulated betrayal pervades a scene that bristles with
anxiety concerning unstable identities and roles, resonating with the
shape-shifting imagery of folklore and fairy-tale. It is her 'réveil autre. Le
seul réveil de ma première enfance, qui me demeure soudain le plus
vivace, mais oblique, dans une mobilité cherchant son fragile équilibre'
(p. 264) ('other awakening. The only awakening of my early childhood,

which suddenly remains to me as the most vivid, but oblique, in a movement which was seeking its own delicate balance').

Another memory concerning the same boy is also recounted, an episode she thinks happened soon after 'la nuit française' ('the French night'), when they are playing together climbing trees and she refuses suddenly to go any higher to the place where he is: 'comme si parvenir à la même branche, m'accroupir à ses côtés, me paraissait le péché suprême' (p. 265) ('as if to get to the same branch, to crouch down beside him, seemed to me the ultimate sin'). She is confused by the boy and by her feelings: he still belongs to another world, he is neither 'proche ni l'étranger' ('relative nor stranger'), and it is in this encounter that the 'silent desire' that gives this third part of the text its title is formed: 'Je ne parlais pas français encore. Et le regard que je levais sur le sommet de l'arbre, sur le visage du garçon aux cheveux châtains, au sourire moqueur, était celui d'un silencieux désir informe, démuni à l'extrême car n'ayant aucune langue, même pas la plus fruste, pour s'y couler' (p. 266) ('I could not yet speak French. And the eyes that I lifted to the top of the tree, to the face of the chestnut-haired boy with the mocking smile, were the eyes of a silent, unformed desire, totally helpless, since it had no language, not even the roughest, in which to flow forth'). The narrator will grow to be the very opposite of this inarticulate girl, but the shock of the 'other' has had a dramatic effect on her sense of self, 'a decisive rupture' begun in the experience of 'the French night'. The undertow of desire for and seduction by the other is apparent, given expression not in the violence of such an encounter, as in the writing of Khatibi, but in confusion and in such unease that it has been 'buried' deep in her memory. As I discussed in the first, introductory chapter, certainly such a scene is infused with repressed memory and sexuality, but in the post-colonial context it is also intensely political. This is more than a personal confession; it is the confession of a cultural betrayal.

Another fundamental childhood memory closes this section, a photograph taken of her with all the boys in the class her father teaches, a class in which she has again been silent, 'observatrice, silencieuse dans cette classe de garçons' (p. 267) ('a silent observer in that class of boys'); boys to whom she never spoke and none of whom she particularly remembers: 'Malgré mon âge si précoce, je dois ressentir l'interdit' (p. 268) ('despite my extreme youth, I must have felt the prohibition'). She does not know that they are intimidated by her, only feeling their respect tinged with distrust and even hostility. In the photograph she is queen: 'Trônant et ne le sachant pas' (p. 271) ('Enthroned and not knowing it'); far from the 'fugitive et ne le sachant pas' that she will become, yet the ambiguities of her position are already caught in the image. Mireille Calle-Gruber sees the photograph as 'primordial' for the whole of Assia Djebar's writing project:

> La force emblématique vient de ce que se trouvent scellées, *instantanément*, les forces contradictoires qui ne cessent de travailler la narration d'Assia Djebar: la langue de France; la langue du père; le lieu, impossible si ce n'est pas le temps d'une scène, de l'entrelangues, de l'entremondes; la place faite à l'implaçable place du féminin dans l'espace masculin islamique [...] la photo est primordiale parce qu'elle est testament du père lequel, comme dans le premier Islam où l'héritière est fille du Prophète, lègue à la fille aînée son héritage intellectuel.
>
> Dès lors, malgré ou plutôt *avec* l'altérité, l'adversité, l'inconvenance qui s'attachent aux circonstances de la nuit coloniale et de la nuit islamique, la narration par Assia Djebar de la scène photographique première rend l'écriture de l'entrelangues indissociable de l'amour. Un amour, qui, non pas faiblesse mais exigence supplémentaire, fait résistance à la résistance.[81]

> (Its emblematic force comes from the fact that in it are sealed, instantly, the contradictory forces which are constantly at work in Assia Djebar's narrative: the language of France; the language of the father; the place, impossible except while the scene lasts, between two languages, between two worlds; the place made for the feminine which has no place there, in the Islamic masculine space [...] The photograph is primordial because it is the testament of the father, who, as in the first Islam where the heir is the daughter of the Prophet, bequeaths his intellectual legacy to his oldest daughter.
>
> From then on, despite or rather *with* the otherness, the adversity, the unsuitability of the circumstances of the colonial night and the Islamic night, the narration by Assia Djebar of the first photograph scene makes writing between two languages inseparable from love. A love which, not as weakness but as an additional demand, resists the resistance.)

These memories clearly show the ambiguity, within her own culture, of the narrator's relationship to the male sex and to the masculine public space due to the very particular upbringing she is receiving. Her father is clearly proud of her, placing her in the centre of the photo. He is also proud of his own achievements that irritate 'la petite société coloniale' ('the small colonial society') around them: 'Il pose pour les autres – tout le village, y compris la petite société coloniale qu'il nargue par sa fierté et ses revendications égalitaires' (p. 271) ('He poses for the others – the whole village, including the small colonial society which he irritates by his pride and his claims to equality'). It is from this school that she returns each day with her father, 'main dans la main du père' (p. 268) ('hand-in-hand with my father'); and this was the first photograph taken of her: 'Un jour de classe au début de la guerre mondiale, dans un village du Sahel algérien' (p. 271) ('A schoolday at the beginning of the world war, in a village in the Algerian Sahel'); phrases that recall in their vocabulary and their rhythm the opening of *L'Amour, la fantasia* – the founding moment of a narrative quest that will lead to self-knowledge – and that explicitly link the two volumes.

The fifth movement revives a memory of adolescence when the narrator wears a revealing dress for a cousin's wedding and dances among some of the older women, women who wonder at the upbringing she is receiving, women who know she will never be one of them, and again the traditional female voice intervenes: 'elle ne comprendra jamais car elle ne sera jamais de nos maisons, de nos prisons, elle sera épargnée de la claustration et, par là, de notre chaleur, de notre compagnie!' (p. 279) ('she will never understand because she will never belong to our houses, our prisons, she will be spared the cloistering, and by that very fact, will not share our warmth, our company'). She is for them 'l'étrangère' ('the outsider'). Her position is becoming more and more ambiguous, she is becoming ever more estranged from traditional culture. Yet one of the women would still choose her for her son, if she were to return to a strict Muslim upbringing. The narrator's mother is proud of her daughter and talks about the incident in the gathering at the house of the Caïd where they often visit. At this point in the text the tension between tradition and modernity is apparent in the whole family. When her father comes to fetch them from this female social event in his car it is the 'heure de l'apéritif' ('time for the apéritif'), a mysterious idea to the narrator, the time when the *pied-noir* men would be outside the cafés, and Kabyle and Arab men were also out in the centre of the village. A detour has to be taken by the driver under the father's instructions to avoid both of these masculine publics: 'Double public exclusivement masculin: Européens rassemblés sur les terrasses pour leur apéritif et ouvriers saisonniers soudés dans leur hostilité à contempler les loisirs des autres. Il était impensable, pour mon père, de laisser défiler, même rapidement, "une dame" de là-bas!' (pp. 281–82) ('A double, exclusively male audience: Europeans gathered on the terraces for their apéritif and seasonal workers bound together by their hostility as they watched the others' leisure. It was unthinkable for my father to let "a lady" from down there go past them, no matter how quickly'). Both the female look in the enclosed female world of the wedding party and the male gaze in the public, outside space are potentially hostile, making the narrator's reappropriation of the gaze all the more powerful. This scene also reveals something more of her father's attitudes to the colonisers, and this is developed further in his resentment of the wealthiest *colon* ('coloniser') in the area. The narrator feels that she was being called as a witness of what is important to her father in the situation in which he finds himself:

> Je me dis maintenant que c'était pour moi qu'il se laissait ainsi aller à sa
> diatribe habituelle contre le potentat local... Comme s'il me prenait, tout au
> début de mon adolescence, à témoin: ta mère, ma femme, a un statut à part,
> au moins égal de 'leur' châtelaine et si tous ces hommes – les 'Autres' et les
> nôtres – ne méritent pas de la voir passer, c'est à juste titre... Et moi (c'est
> le discours paternel que je réinvente a posteriori), moi aussi, à l'instar de
> 'leur' maître, je n'expose pas ma femme – le cœur de moi-même [...] Or je
> ne suis que le maître de classe. Le seul maître de classe indigène pour des
> garçons indigènes. Bien raide moi aussi et la tête hardie sous le fez. Avec
> mon admiration de jeune homme pour Ataturk, car, bien sûr, nous n'au-
> rions pas été colonisés, c'est-à-dire chez nous sans être chez nous... (pp.
> 282–83)

> (I tell myself now that it was for my benefit that he launched into his habitual
> diatribe against the local potentate... As if he were calling me to witness
> right from my earliest adolescence: 'Your mother, my wife, has a place apart,
> at least equal to "their" lady-wife, and all those men – the "Others" and
> ours – are not worthy to see her going by, quite properly... And I' – I'm rein-
> venting my father's speech *a posteriori* – 'I, just like "their" master, do not
> expose my wife, the very heart of myself [...] Now I'm merely a school-
> teacher. The only native schoolteacher for the native boys. I too am stiffened,
> and my head is hard under my fez; and I have a young man's admiration for
> Ataturk, because obviously we wouldn't have been colonised, i.e. at home
> and yet not at home...')

'Chez nous sans être chez nous': all the humiliation and displacement
caused by the colonisation summed up in a simple, everyday phrase. It
is in this section that Djebar talks most about the impact of colonisation
on the everyday lives of her family and contemporaries. This is no longer
the archaeology of the past that has been so important to her project up
until this point. We are gradually moving forward in history; her own
history is no longer alternating with events long past, her history is the
contemporary history that needs to be dealt with, that she needs to find
a way of coming to terms with: 'Or nous vivions en pays colonisé. Sétif,
Tébessa, Guelma, ville d'orages – les milliers de morts puis emprisonnés
du 8 mai 1945, c'était deux ou trois ans auparavant' (p. 283) ('Now we
were living in a colonised country. Sétif, Tébessa, Guelma, the town of
storms – the thousands dead and imprisoned after 8 May 1945, just two
or three years earlier').

Her own drama certainly continues. She is becoming other, 'sortie'
('going out'), outside the family and especially outside the traditional
female community: 'ce terme, appliqué aux femmes, aux filles
"sortantes", est dans le dialecte maternel chargé de menaces' ('that term,
applied to women, to girls who "went out", was filled with threats in the
maternal dialect'). While when applied to men it means they are dissi-

dents, for women it can only mean danger. Even when the narrator was younger she was the object of curiosity for the daughters of the Caïd, themselves brought up and dressed traditionally, who grab her and lift up her skirt to see her French-style underwear: 'elles auraient voulu, à travers moi, à cause de la fréquentation scolaire qui me déguisait en fillette française, caresser, palper le corps entier de ces dames lointaines qui leur paraissaient arrogantes, mais si précieuses' (p. 286) ('they would have liked, through me, because of my schooling which made me look like a little French girl, to caress and feel the whole body of those far-off ladies who to them seemed both arrogant and very precious'). Once again her identity is ambiguous; as in 'la nuit française' the narrator is herself almost 'other'. Her status sets her apart; she no longer fully belongs to her own community, but she is also aware of the danger that awaits in leaving it fully. She is distressed when her mother decides to make her remove the amulets given to her by her grandmother, which she wears under her clothes to go to school: 'ces carrés ou triangles d'écriture magique' (p. 287) ('those squares or triangles of magic writing'), amulets that her grandmother gave her to protect her from the school environment that the older woman imagined to be hostile. The amulets keep her close to her grandmother and she feels protected both when sleeping and at school, but her mother is aware of the ridicule that the young girl would be subjected to if they were seen by the other girls; she would be treated as a pagan: 'l'indigène parmi les Françaises' (p. 288) ('the native girl among the French girls'). It is her first great loss, and it is above all a loss of writing, of inscriptions, the first erasure with which the text is so concerned: 'je dus me soumettre: je fus dépouillée, autant dire dénudée. Et ce fut ma mère qui, prise d'un accès rationaliste, me déposséda de cette première écriture' (p. 288) ('I had to submit: I was stripped, as much as to say, stripped bare. And it was my mother who, in a sudden access of rationalism, dispossessed me of that first writing'). A subtle link is therefore made between these inscriptions and the inscriptions so essential to the second part of *Vaste est la prison*. The young girl is truly 'in between', not belonging fully to either community; but the position of the mother is also a painful one as she is forced to compromise her own beliefs and way of life in the awareness of the gaze of the other. The mother is also 'in between': she continues her everyday life, her relationships with the other women, but she remains aware of the difference of her daughter, she is brought close to the other world through her daughter. A poignant example of this is the recounting of the episode of the mother watching the young girl read a book in French that she has brought back from the library. The mother wants to know how it is that the words on the page have the power to make her daughter cry:

> Explique-moi, ô fille, je crois qu'il y a un mystère: moi, je lis en arabe mes paroles de chansons anciennes, je les chante et je les pleure quelquefois dans mon cœur… Mais je chante! […] Tu comprends, ce n'était pas parce qu'elle chantait tout en pleurant, non: elle ne s'arrêtait pas de lire, et en pleurant ainsi, elle donnait l'impression d'éprouver du plaisir: étrange, n'est-ce pas? (p. 290)

> (Explain, my daughter, I think there is some mystery here. I myself read the words of my ancient songs in Arabic, then I sing them and sometimes cry over them in my heart… But I sing! […] You understand, it wasn't because she was crying as she sang: she didn't stop reading, and although she was crying like that she gave the impression that she was enjoying herself: strange, isn't it?)

The mother confesses that she regrets not being able to read French, because it seems to her that one is then never alone; she seems not to be consoled by the nurse's traditional answer that one is never alone because we are under God's gaze. The mother understands the power of communication in the written word and it has caused change and uncertainty in her own beliefs, in the security of her own world.[82]

At the age of ten the narrator's childhood changes when she goes as a boarder to the school in the next village, making friends with a half-Italian girl with whom she embarks on the adventure of reading in the school's library: the French writers Alain-Fournier, Jacques Rivière, Gide, Claudel, Giraudoux, Rimbaud, Apollinaire, Michaux; but she also finds translations for ancient Arabic and Persian poems for her friend to read. Importantly, the acquisition of culture is a two-way process for her, receiving French culture, but also giving her own. It is around this time that she decides to keep a diary: 'Comme Alain-Fournier, comme Jacques Rivière!' ('Like Alain-Fournier, like Jacques Rivière!'), a declaration reminiscent of that of Feraoun's protagonist. She decides that this will be her 'projet de vie' ('life-project', using a similar term to the one used throughout here), at least until she is thirty, beyond which age she cannot imagine:

> Ainsi, moi si isolée dans l'entre-deux de ce village de colonisation, je ne me croyais pas seule. 'Quel serait mon projet de vie?' me demandais-je emphatiquement. J'écrivis, et je me souviens à présent de ces lignes d'un journal d'ailleurs très tôt interrompu et retrouvé par hasard dans un fatras ancien. J'ai relu ces lignes avec une indulgence amusée, et la scène disons 'de la première écriture' se leva intacte:
>   'Je désire, écrivais-je, et je m'engage à obéir la règle de vie qu'aujourd'hui, à quatorze ans, je me choisis […]'
>   J'ai écrit au début de ce journal qui n'eut pas de suite, hormis les notes de nombreuses lectures d'alors:

'Je m'engage et comme je voudrais rester fidèle à cette règle de vie, parce que je la trouve la plus pure:
A ne jamais souhaiter le bonheur, mais la joie!
A ne jamais rechercher le salut, mais la grâce!' (pp. 292–94)

(And so, though I was so isolated in the in-between in my colonised village, I didn't think I was alone. 'What will my life-project be?' I asked myself emphatically. I wrote, and I can still remember these lines from a diary I kept then but left soon afterwards, which I found by chance in a jumble of old things. I re-read the lines with amused indulgence, and the scene of what we could call 'the first writing' was presented intact:
'I desire,' I wrote, 'and I commit myself to obey the rule of life that I choose for myself today at the age of fourteen [...]'
I wrote at the beginning of that diary which had no sequel, apart from notes about the many books I read then:
'I commit myself, and how I would like to stay faithful to this rule of life, because I find it the purest:
Never to aim for happiness but for joy!
Never to seek salvation but grace!')

The narrator may well look on these adolescent writings with an 'amused indulgence', but she is also aware of this being the classical scene of the first act of writing so often included in writers' autobiographies, for writers are not only seeking an answer to the question 'Who am I?', but also an answer to the question 'Why do I write?'.[83] The notion of this 'commitment' to a way of living one's life is also more than adolescent romanticism in a writer whose work reflects a personal and political commitment on every level. Indeed, all the writers studied here embark on the quest to understand how their first writing came into being.

The sixth movement is constructed rather differently, composed as it is of short sections each with an italicised subheading, and each linking mothers to daughters within the narrator's family: *'Celle qui console'* ('She Who Consoles') (and we should remember here also the meaning of the name 'Assia' given earlier by Mireille Calle-Gruber), evoking the grandmother who is concerned about the little girl being brought up like a boy and her mother's ambiguous attitude; *'Celle qui guide'* ('She Who Guides'), jumping forward in time to the narrator who has taken refuge at the aunt's house after leaving her husband, where her mother comes to see her; *'Celle qui s'en va'* ('She Who Goes Away'), comprising the memory of a young neighbour who died young after giving birth to many children; *'Nubilité'* ('Nubility'), telling of the narrator's lack of menstruation and the discovery that she is sterile; *'Maternité'* ('Maternity'), the story of the adoption of a child, one of the victims of the war, a memory recounted largely in the third person (unlike the preceding sections narrated in the first person), with the name 'Isma' being used several times, until fifteen years later she retells the story of how the daughter was chosen; and '*La jeune fille*' ('The Young Girl'), moving forward in time again to the beginning of the wave of violence that hits Algeria in October 1988, the narrator's fears for her daughter living in Algiers, and her insistence that she comes to France. In doing so she realises that she is making her daughter a fugitive like herself, continuing the movement of the women in her family, the grandmother going to the town, the mother opening herself up to the influence of the French she was brought into contact with: 'je faisais de ma fille, prête alors à s'ancrer dans la terre de son père, une fugitive nouvelle. Passeuses désormais, elle et moi: de quel message furtif, de quel silencieux désir?' (p. 320) ('I was making my daughter, who at that time was ready to take root in her father's country, into a new fugitive. Passing on, from then on, both she and I: passing on what furtive message, what silent desire?'). The silent desire that gives its title to this third part returns once again, and in a moment of dramatic communication the narrator, who has now revealed herself so intimately to the reader, addresses that reader directly, making sure no misunderstandings occur concerning the nature of this silent desire:

> – Désir de liberté, diriez-vous tout naturellement.
> – Oh non, répondrais-je. La liberté est un mot bien trop vaste! Soyons plus modeste, et désireuses seulement d'une respiration à l'air libre. (p. 320)

> ('The desire for freedom', you'll say, quite naturally.
> 'Oh, no,' I'd answer. 'Freedom is a word that is altogether too vast! Let's be more modest, desiring merely to breathe in free air.')

Just as suffering is vast (and vast is the prison) and can never be totally defeated, so the notion of freedom is also too vast ever to be totally assumed. The writer suggests in her reply that freedom is unobtainable, not only for her, but for us all. Nonetheless there are ways of arriving at a compromise that allows us to 'breathe', to negotiate a way of living between these vast monoliths, a mode of being that finds a way between the constraints, the absolutes that threaten us.

The seventh and final movement of this part of the text, 'Ombres de séparation' ('Shadows of Separation') again uses a structure with italicised subheadings: '*La belle-mère*' ('The Mother-in-Law'), once again evoking the summer of 1988 and the experience of seeing her former mother-in-law by chance at the airport and the emotion it raises in her, the narrator always feeling the loss of a woman more keenly than that of any man; '*Sidi*', relating to the death of one of her old aunt's husbands, a man belonging to a generation that had seen all the drama of the oppression of the Algerians in the first half of the century and then that enforced on them by their own people, their 'brothers':

> ils avaient subi la première, avec la distance que leur assurait leur foi. Ils ont contemplé la seconde avec du dédain et un grand retrait; un silence rêche et un étonnement mal dissimulé... Le monde des 'roumis' ne les avait pas étonnés; il leur était totalement autre dans son iniquité comme dans son étrangeté [...] Ainsi, ce n'étaient plus les étrangers installés là en maîtres, dorénavant partis, qui se révélaient étrangers. (pp. 329–30)

> (they had endured the first, with the distancing supplied by their faith. They contemplated the second with disdain and great withdrawal; a harsh silence and ill-disguised astonishment... The world of the *roumis* [Europeans] had not astonished them: it was totally alien to them in its injustice and its strangeness [...] Thus it was no longer the foreigners installed there as masters – they had long been gone – who revealed themselves as strangers.)

The betrayal of the Algerian 'revolution' foreseen by Feraoun in his diary is clear and the suffering of men is therefore not absent from a narrative that has focused so much on female experience. The vicious circle of the history of Algeria also affects men such as Sidi, and their descendants are like strangers to them, 'des espèces hybrides' ('hybrid species'). The narrator has told this story of a 'simple death'; 'Pour simplement ouvrir aux autres, aux "morts qui tirent la terre à eux, comme une couverture", ces temps présents' ('Simply to open to others, to the "dead who pull the earth over them for a covering", these present times').

At this point in the text, the narrator is increasingly unable to shake off the literal spectre of the present and its violence. The present is once again haunted, and this time in a terrible way. The narrator would prefer to describe that previous generation, but she cannot, she must face the present:

> Ce sont eux que je veux écrire – pas les victimes, pas les meurtris! Car derrière chacun de ceux-ci, il y a dix meurtriers et je vois, oh oui, j'entrevois des cascades de sang derrière un seul homme, une seule femme aujourd'hui assassinés.
> Je ne peux pas.
> Je ne veux pas.
> Je veux fuir.
> Je veux m'effacer. Effacer mon écriture. Me bander les yeux, me bâillonner la bouche. Ou alors que le sang des autres, des nôtres, m'engloutisse toute nue! Me dilue. Me fige, statue vermillon, l'une des statues de Césarée pour plus tard, bien plus tard, être fracassée et tomber en ruine... (pp. 330–31)

> (They are the ones I want to write about – not the victims, not the murdered people! Because behind each of these latter, there are ten murderers, and I see, oh yes, I glimpse cascades of blood behind each single man, each single woman murdered today.
> I can't.

> I don't want to.
> I want to run.
> I want to erase myself. To erase my writing. To blindfold my eyes, gag my mouth. Or else for the blood of the others, of our people, to swallow me up naked! To dilute me. To paralyse me into a crimson statue, one of the statues of Caesarea, which much, much later would crumble and fall in ruins...)

If she could abandon the text, writing and self would therefore be erased together. But she cannot, she continues with the narration, wondering whether she will call the narrator Isma again, 'Isma, "le nom"' (p. 331; 'Isma, "the name"'), she glosses for the reader with no knowledge of Arabic and of Arabic names, wishing she could bring her to some form of serenity.[84]

Three more short sections follow. First, '*Jugurtha*' moves forward to 1993 in Copenhagen, as the image of the young Jugurtha returns to the narrator in the scene of him at the stele in Dugga as she described previously, an event which seems like yesterday to her even though it took place in 138 BC. In fact, she hears rather than sees him, and he is singing the song *Vaste est la prison* as he is taken to Rome in chains, again providing a link between the archaic past and the personal present. Jugurtha will never be written about in his own language, the legend will remain an oral one, the preserve of women, returning us to the principal concerns of the second part of the text. It will be the Romans writing about their victory who will in fact celebrate the glory of the man they conquered: 'Ce sont "eux", dans leur alphabet à eux' (p. 335) ('It will be "they", in their own alphabet'), a history once again written in the language of the coloniser. Secondly, '*L'éplorée*' ('The Weeping Woman') evokes a different kind of death, the death of a woman caused through illness, who prefers to stay in Algeria rather than to continue to go to Paris for treatment. Thirdly, '*Lamento*' evokes more and more deaths, those of the previous century and those of the present: 'A force d'écrire sur les morts de ma terre en flammes, le siècle dernier, j'ai cru que le sang des hommes aujourd'hui (le sang de l'Histoire et l'étouffement des femmes) remontait pour maculer mon écriture, et me condamner au silence' (p. 337) ('By dint of writing about the dead people from my land which went up in flames in the last century, I felt that the blood of the men of today (the blood of History and the stifling of women) was rising up again to spatter my writing and condemn me to silence'). The narrator relives her mother's grief at the loss of her sister Chérifa; she becomes Chérifa. And all the time, the dead return to Algeria, while the narrator has nightmares in which she has to cut her own throat: 'il m'a fallu couper au couteau une sorte de muscle inutile qui m'écorche, crachat enserré à mes cordes vocales' ('I had to cut out with a knife a sort of useless muscle which hurt me, spittle that was clinging tightly to my vocal cords'). Covered in blood herself, a long bloody history is vomited out of her. She does not cry out: rather she is the cry of the past and of the present:

> Chaque nuit, l'effort musculaire de cet enfantement par la bouche, de cette mise au silence me lancine. Je vomis quoi, peut-être un long cri ancestral. Ma bouche ouverte expulse indéfiniment la souffrance des autres, des ensevelies avant moi, moi qui croyais apparaître au premier rai de la première lumière.
>   Je ne crie pas, je suis le cri. Tout ce chemin ouvert cerne la débâcle de la fête guerrière d'hier, de l'horreur indicible d'aujourd'hui [...] Je ne crie pas, je suis le cri tendu dans un vol vibrant et aveugle; la procession blanche des aïeules-fantômes derrière moi devient armée qui me propulse, se lèvent les mots de la langue perdue qui vacille, tandis que les mâles au-devant gesticulent dans le champ de la mort, ou de ses masques.

> (Every night the muscular effort of that childbirth via the mouth, of that silencing, obsesses me. I vomit what, perhaps a long ancestral cry. My open mouth expels endlessly the suffering of others, of those buried before me, when I thought that I came forth with the first ray of the first light.
>   I don't cry out: I am the cry. All this open road points to the failure of the warrior's feast of yesterday, of the inexpressible horror of today [...] I don't cry out, I am the cry, drawn forth into vibrant, blind flight; the white procession of the ghost-ancestors behind me becomes an army pushing me on, there arise the words of the lost tongue which hesitates, while the males in front gesticulate in the field of death, or of its masks.)

This is again therefore a fundamental scene for the generation of the narratives of *L'Amour, la fantasia* and *Vaste est la prison*, one where the ancestors join her, where the violence of past and the present collide, where the fragile lost language must find a form of expression, where the narrator achieves a moment of self-knowledge.

The fourth and final part of the text has two sections, 'Yasmina' and 'Le Sang de l'écriture – final' ('The Blood of Writing – Finale'). Two epigraphs open this final part, one from Jeanne Hyvrard (another writer concerned with the struggle for expression in the French language) regarding the potential power of suffering to avoid the entire destruction of the world, and the other from Hafiz describing the transformation of stone into precious stone, into ruby, effected only through an internal bleeding 'avec le sang de son cœur' ('with the heart's blood'). These suggest, therefore, that it is possible to move to another of state of being, achieved through pain certainly, but a state that is nonetheless a transcendence of the present, a possibility of redemption:

> Coming at the start of the final section the quotation from Hyvrard pulls together many of the intertextual threads [...] The quotation used in the epigraph initially seems to continue to point to the possibility of redemp-

tion through writing and this comes as a surprise at a point in her text when Djebar seems to be despairing of this prospect. Nothing she can write can ever reverse the senseless murder of twenty-eight year old Yasmina [...] In fact a return to Hyvrard's text reveals it to posit the same irreconcilable dilemma as that confronted by Djebar; her narrator is dying: '*de ce suintement de mots [...] Je meurs de l'écriture*' ('of that bleeding of words [...] I am dying from writing').[85]

This resonates with the end of *L'Amour, la fantasia* when the narrator is suffering from 'une plaie inguérissable, suant les mots tout à côté' (p. 245) ('the running sore nearby from which words exude'), and yet continues to narrate. 'Yasmina' recounts the murder in 1994 by four men (who cut her throat) of a young teacher who also worked for an independent newspaper, a young woman who insisted on returning to Algeria, 'Algérie-sang' ('Algeria-blood'), refusing exile. This is the death of a woman who wrote every day, 'le kalam à la main' ('*qalam* in hand'), who resisted and defied, and whose death led to her companion, a young foreigner, being freed. The image of the *qalam* has also been used at the end of *L'Amour, la fantasia* as part of the theme of an Arabic woman coming to writing linked to the severed hand found by Fromentin: 'Plus tard, je me saisis de cette main vivante, main de la mutilation et du souvenir et je tente de lui faire porter le "qalam"' (*L'Amour, la fantasia*, p. 255) ('Later, I seize on this living hand, hand of mutilation and of memory, and I attempt to bring it the *qalam*'). Mireille Calle-Gruber sees the story of Yasmina as linked to the legend of Tin Hinan as well as being an evocation of contemporary violence, and in addition it returns the theme of the loss of voice, whether through mental or physical suffering, to the narrative, again obliging the reader at the end of the text, as in *L'Amour, la fantasia* with the scene of the little Arab girl on the way to school holding her father's hand, to return to the very beginning and to follow through all the women's words, lost and found:

> Si l'amour du père est indispensable pour recevoir le don de l'alphabet, c'est la chaîne de la sororité et la puissance cathartique des pleureuses qui soutient l'édifice de l'écriture. Et le pendant moderne de l'ancestrale Tin Hinan n'est autre, au terme de l'ouvrage, que Yasmina qui combat avec le qalam, 'arme de liquidité' non moins. Un ultime récit biographique, fulgurant, nous avertit de l'insensé, et que la fracture du monde est devenue insupportable [...] En un crescendo qui enroule des variantes arabesques jusque-là inouïes de l'aphonie et de la gorge tranchée, la narration dénonce l'assassinat de Yasmina, égorgée par quatre hommes. Et aussitôt, la narration de se faire pleureuse: elle *célèbre* la jeune fille, la chante.[86]

> (If the father's love is indispensable for receiving the gift of the alphabet, it is the chain of sisterhood and the cathartic power of the weepers which sustains the edifice of writing. And the modern sequel of the ancestral Tin Hinan is no other, in terms of the work, than Yasmina who fights with the

qalam, no less a 'weapon of liquidity'. A last, lightning biographical sketch warns us of this senselessness, and that the breaking up of the world has become unbearable [...] In a crescendo which pulls in hitherto unheard-of Arabesque variants on voicelessness and the cut throat, the narrative denounces the murder of Yasmina, whose throat was cut by four men. And straight away the narrative turns into a mourner: it *celebrates* the young girl, sings of her.)

The finale of *Vaste est la prison*, 'Le sang de l'écriture', reminding us also of the finale of *L'Amour, la fantasia*, becomes a poetic incantation as the narrator wonders, is indeed overpowered by, how to write about all the dead of Algeria. Not how to find a language or an alphabet, for indeed the dead themselves wish to write their stories, but what to write about them with, for there is only blood with which to do it, and that blood is fresh, still running. The narrator now *knows* herself to be a fugitive and accepts her state, for she has now 'swallowed up' Algeria. It is within her and the fugitive cannot now escape that which is a part of herself: 'L'Algérie, chasseresse, en moi, avalée' ('Algeria, the huntress, inside me, swallowed up').

Assia Djebar began writing *Vaste est la prison* in the late 1980s and continued through to the mid-1990s, when she feared that the recent history of Algeria would again be erased in the violence engulfing parts of the country. It is a text written in the urgency of the moment, and in the urgency of the self, just as Feraoun's diary was. It is also a text of exile, begun in Algiers and finished in Paris. The writer must occupy a space outside the hostile political climate of her native country, where, during that period, both the fundamentalist FIS (Front Islamique du Salut) and the military government posed threats to the intellectual elite and to women.[87] This is a space that is necessarily 'in-between', a state explored throughout the narrative interweavings of *Vaste est la prison*.

The construction of identity requires that the individual be able to situate himself or herself in time and space; there must be a constant work of affirmation in the past, present and future. Through her excavation and exploration of history, Assia Djebar seeks to provides a time and a space that secure a place for the exiled of history in the here and now.[88] Not 'liberation', for that word is too vast, as the narrator has already told us, but another way of being can be created, through a reinvented relationship to language, to history, to other, to self. Such a way of being must be constantly renegotiated, but it is shown to be possible through a writing project that again bestows an ethics as well as an aesthetics on the discourse of autobiography.[89]

Conclusion:
A Place in the World

> The work of art, too, is first of all genesis; it is never experienced purely as result.
>
> Paul Klee[1]

In the discussion of the texts selected, the emphasis has been on the ways in which each one contributes to a larger life-writing project, and on the ways in which these works explore the relationship of the writer to literary creation and to the world around them. As was suggested in the introduction, in the work of all of these writers there is a meditation on an individual experience and on the relationship of that experience to that of others, leading to diverse forms of creative, and political, intervention. A number of other elements unite these writing projects, which are interventions both in a linguistic space (the word) and in a social and political space (the world). In each of them there is an engagement with the question of identity, particularly concerning the use of language, within an analysis of the effects of colonisation and the legacy of resistance to oppression for the individual, for the immediate community and for the wider community. Despite the schism that they have experienced between oral and written language, and the consequences of being linguistic and social 'outsiders' (the term *étrange* in its multiple meanings in French is a recurrent one), within both their culture of origin and the culture that they acquire through education, all succeed in making a space in which to create, to write, to speak. For all of them there is a commitment to the retrieval of historical memory and of a multifaceted cultural memory, and a quest for knowledge and self-knowledge that takes place in the relationship to an archaic past and to a personal and collective recent past and present.[2] There is increasingly a development of experimental writing strategies in order to achieve this more fully. I have shown how even in *Le Fils du pauvre* and *La Statue de sel*, ostensibly 'traditional' narrative forms, there are complex discourses at work, and the themes that recur throughout postcolonial writing in French are developed in these texts: poverty and exclusion; the realities of everyday life in colonial and postcolonial systems; education and the experience of difference; separation and alienation from family and community; the impact of the French language on the identity of the colonised subject; the relationship of the colonised subject to history, to power, to the other; the struggle for the expression of a politics of self-determination for the individual, the community, the nation; the mechanisms through which colonised subjects make themselves heard. *Le Scorpion* stands as a kind of bridge between these earlier texts and the polyphonic narratives of *La Mémoire tatouée*, *L'Amour, la fantasia* and *Vaste est la prison*, although polyphony is already a feature of *Le Fils du pauvre* and *La Statue de sel*. In the dynamic process of each of these life-writing projects there is a focus on the act of writing, on the act of creation as well on recollection and the retrieval of histories, and for all the proliferation of polyphonic discourses, they are the product of one – and as each narrative progresses, increasingly powerful – narratorial voice. These are not 'collective' auto-biographies, as several critics continue to maintain. Certainly, these writers are interested in the individual's relationship to the community and they are concerned with exploring and making known the identity of community as well as that of the self. But finally, despite the ways in which their writing strategies interweave between self and other in all their manifestations, they are singular writing projects resulting in the production of a singular voice.

These writers also have in common the fact that they became, to varying degrees, alienated from their traditional cultural environment and made an intellectual effort in order to cope with that alienation. At the same time, all of them analyse the predicament of the colonial and postcolonial intellectual, frequently retaining a solidarity with their community while being critical of it (and this is perhaps especially true of Feraoun and Memmi, the latter in revolt against his traditional community and ultimately finding a sort of reconciliation with it). They are also all clear on the need to write themselves out of dominant systems of representation, to remove themselves as inventions of the colonial imagination, while simultaneously decolonising themselves from that colonial imagination and from their own ambivalent desire for the West; to posit themselves as subjects.

Three specific examples serve to indicate the types of narrative work undertaken to reach this new way of being. First, there is an attention to the status of the name, not to indulge in the luxury of self-obsession on the part of the various narrators, but because the name is the bearer of both personal and collective history. This is more true, however, of the male writers than of Assia Djebar, who discloses the name of the narrator discreetly. Nonetheless, in her case also this is a name of symbolic function, and hiding the name resonates as fully as disclosure and meditation on its meaning and origins. Secondly, there is the use of epigraphs, notably in the work of the Algerian writers Feraoun and Djebar, and of other references to the legacy of literature. This practice of dialogue with other, often European, writers is more subtle than it first appears, less a symbol of a continuing colonisation of the imagination than a reappropriation that sets up a new type of literary and cultural exchange. Finally, there is the use by these writers of symbols, recurrent metaphors and what I termed 'preferred' myths in order to inscribe a new identity for themselves into a language that was originally used as part of a system of oppression. One element of the process of writing in these texts is in fact sometimes a rewriting of Western sources; another is often a recuperation of lost meanings in order to create a new form of inscription founded on re-reading. Creation is at once an act of writing and an act of reading, both engaged in the deciphering of old and new systems of representation.

There does remain, however, the difference of the attention paid to gender, or rather the kind of attention paid to gender. The issue of women's place in the traditional community, in the colonial system and then in postcolonial society marks out Assia Djebar's work from that of the male writers. Feraoun certainly considers the place of women during and after the War of Independence in his diary, and the position of women is important to all these male writers, but generally women remain objects of sexual desire and/or bearers of cultural and collective memory. Only Assia Djebar restores the missing women in the analysis of the colonial situation begun by Memmi and Fanon, and she is aware that she is writing within a male-dominated cultural and political framework.[3]

I would like to end, however, on two rather more open-ended issues that have hovered around many of the readings here. The first of these is the challenge that all of these writers pose to the notion of the hegemony of European historical, philosophical and literary discourses; the second concerns their contribution to debates concerning identity, whether of individuals or groups, at various levels of contemporary society, and to the role of the writer and to literature generally.

These four writers, among many others born under French colonial rule, are instrumental in making clear the complex cultural and political exchange between so-called 'centre' and 'periphery', not only in the French context, but in the broader postcolonial context. One aim of this study, outlined in the introduction, was to address the assumptions inherent in Eurocentric critical thinking concerning autobiography. As Doris Ruhe has written,

> Il est caractéristique pour ce qu'on peut appeler avec Danielle Marx Scouras une 'myopie culturelle' que la transformation de l'intérieur d'un genre classique est seulement perçue par la critique métropolitaine au moment où elle se manifeste dans les écrits des auteurs consacrés par le canon littéraire établi. Depuis longtemps pourtant, des écrivains de pays récemment décolonisés avaient fait subir à l'autobiographie, genre préféré des jeunes littératures, des changements essentiels liés à leurs expériences vitales. Les sentiments de rupture, de discontinuité, de forces hétérogènes n'avaient pu se contenter des formes traditionnelles de l'autoreprésentation et avaient ouvert des voies nouvelles.[4]

> (It is characteristic of what we can call, with Danielle Marx Scouras, 'cultural myopia' that the transformation from within of a classical genre is only perceived by critics in metropolitan France at the point where it becomes apparent in the writings of authors who are part of the established literary canon. Nevertheless, for a long time before that, writers from recently decolonised countries had brought about in autobiography, a favoured genre in young literatures, changes to its essence which were linked to their own vital experiences. Their feelings of rupture, discontinuity, heterogeneous forces, had been unable to be content with the traditional forms of self-representation and had opened up new paths.)

In addition to this 'cultural myopia', when critical attention has been paid to works by North African writers, the emphasis on the 'collective' voice has led to double standards in the reading of them, particularly among French critics. The result of this has been a subtle devaluing of these writing projects, too readily dismissed as simply describing a cultural and political environment, as bearing witness to the experience of a people and of some 'documentary' value, but not therefore contributing to and indeed developing a literary genre (whether fiction or autobiography) as far as an aesthetics is concerned.[5]

In fact, as advocated by Khatibi's theory of 'double critique', these writers write in a dynamic relationship with Western literature; their literature is in counterpoint to, not in opposition to, that of the former colonising power. Theirs is what has been called a 'cross-cultural imagination', one that both reveals and celebrates difference, and that highlights prejudice.[6] Their practice has much in common with feminist autobiographical practice, as discussed in the first chapter. The texts analysed here push the boundaries of this 'anxious' and 'hybrid' genre by using a range of writing strategies, serving therefore as examples of the ways in which postcolonial autobiographical discourses subvert the myth of the unified self prevalent in European practice and theory of autobiography. Certainly these texts share some of the characteristics of the experimental writing strategies of writers such as Michel Leiris and Roland Barthes (both necessarily referred to in the course of this study). Yet the political nature of these works, as discussed within the framework of the thinking of Deleuze and Guattari in the introduction, confers on them a rather different status. Like the memoir, they are turned to the outside world, yet they are simultaneously works of self-reflection; they are, as has been insisted on throughout, a meditation on both the politics and the poetics of the creative act. This type of meditation is revealing for the question of identity generally in the postcolonial world. As Neil Lazarus has written,

> From the standpoint of postcolonialism, it is today impossible to think about politics without invoking the category of universality. For in the postcolonial world-system, experience is multiply over-determined, and not least by imperialism itself. Social identity has become world-historical in its constitution. 'To understand just one life, you have to swallow the world', Salman Rushdie has his narrator, Saleem Sinai, observe in *Midnight's Children*. Hence, arguably the specific role of postcolonial intellectualism: to construct a standpoint, nationalitarian, liberationist, internationalist – from which it is possible to assume the burden of speaking for all humanity.[7]

In the light of this, the project here could have been widened to include more extensively the work of other French-speaking writers and intellectuals, born in Algeria, but of *pied-noir* rather than indigenous origin; for example, Albert Camus's *Le Premier Homme* (*The First Man*; begun in the 1950s but not published until 1994) and Marie Cardinal's *Les Mots pour le dire* (*The Words to Say It*, 1975) and *Au pays de mes racines* ('In the Country of My Roots', 1980). Jacques Derrida and Hélène Cixous, born into the Jewish community living in Algeria for centuries, could also have been included; both of these writers have increasingly combined autobiographical, theoretical and creative discourses, and in Cixous's case, loss and separation increasingly become preconditions for writing.[8] In the last decade of the twentieth century, the Moroccan sociologist Fatima Mernissi published an autobiography in English, *Dreams of Trespass* (1994), raising further questions concerning selfhood and the relation to language. Such comparative analysis of writers of a wider range of backgrounds would allow further insights into the problematics underlying the analyses undertaken here.[9]

The second and final issue that has been present in some form throughout this study is the issue of identity and the role of the postcolonial writer with which this book opened. Although I have insisted on the importance of 'identity' in these readings, my readings have finally led to less emphasis on the 'crisis of identity' that has received so much critical attention in postcolonial literary criticism, and I shall end on the potential of the creative process with which these writers engage. Theirs is a constant work of affirmation in the past, present and future, and accepting the charge of critical optimism, I would argue against the criticism often levelled against such enterprises that these remain essentially intellectual projects that finally take little account of and make no impact on the political and economic realities of a postcolonial (but not post-imperialist world). A further shared characteristic of all these writers is the notion of the risk they undertake by writing. This risk takes many forms, and the image of sacrifice provides a pervasive metaphor – and in the case of Feraoun a reality – in all the works studied here. These are undoubtedly intensely 'writerly' solutions, yet they give the writers their 'place in the word' and their 'place in the world', even though they are to a greater or lesser degree in exile from their origins. They finally forge a language for themselves and that language becomes a self-created homeland. These solutions should be celebrated as such, for what these types of writing can do, which other forms of knowledge do less well, is to allow us to share in the writer's experience and in the creative process, inviting the reader to reflect in turn on his or her own experience. They write in full awareness, just like the narrators of *Le Scorpion*, that writing is an act that is at once necessary and potentially meaningless, hence the necessity for the writer to adopt an ethical position towards the creative process so that it becomes a kind of testimony to a way of living, a way of being in the world. Writing then becomes a necessary intervention. The identity of the postcolonial writer is 'becoming', *en devenir* as Khatibi says; a new relationship is opened up with time and space. The self of the writer, I have stressed, is in the *present* of writing, not only in the accumulation of autobiographical 'facts' or in the rewriting of a history either erased or appropriated by others. The myth of the 'unified self' of classical Western autobiography is overturned, and theirs is an identity in what can be termed a state of *errance*, a 'wandering', 'nomadic' identity (the term *nomade* is another that recurs frequently), and their writing exceeds any labels that we may try to apply to it.[10]

Like the painter Paul Klee, a statement by whom on the work of art I have chosen here as an epigraph, these writers emphasise the creative act itself. Central to Klee's thinking was the relationship between clearly defined, recognisable forms – the individual units – and an endlessly open process of creation, which he defined as 'dividual' structure.[11] He identified the 'dividual' and the individual in natural forms and processes; from the 'dividual', organisation becomes truly individual when its parts take on a distinguishable form. This is a statement in artistic terms of the individualism, the relationship between the individual and others around him or her, as opposed to individuality (as I attempted to define carefully in the first chapter), that so aptly describes the projects of the four writers studied here; between individual and 'dividual', they create, 'swallowing the world' to understand one life.

Albert Memmi and Abdelkébir Khatibi recently came together as readers of Assia Djebar's work,[12] and I shall end on the place of the reader. In the case of Assia Djebar, and by extension in the case of other writers of North African origins, the reader is the witness, as Khatibi says, of 'la naissance d'un écrivain dans la langue de l'autre, à l'épreuve de l'histoire' ('the birth of a writer in the other's language, and tested by history'). The reader is also a creator, for in the endlessly open and potential process of creation, it is the reader who, as Memmi says, gives the writer his or her 'physionomie définitive' ('definitive physiognomy'). The aim here has been, if not to give any definitive portrait of selfhood and creativity, then at least to provide a clearer outline.

Notes

Introduction pp. 1–8

All translations in the introduction are by Helena Scott.

1. Amin Maalouf, *Les Identités meurtrières*, Paris, Grasset, 1998, p. 15.

2. The term 'Sephardi Jew' in the strict sense describes a Jew of Spanish or Portuguese descent. The Sephardim lived in those countries from the early Middle Ages until 1492 when they were expelled. Many fled to North Africa and some later settled in Western Europe, the Balkans and Macedonia. However, all Jews of the Middle East and North Africa are also often known as Sephardim as compared to Ashkenazim, Jews of Eastern or Central European descent who make up more than 80 per cent of the current Jewish population (see the *Oxford English Dictionary*). A recent book on Albert Memmi carries the subtitle *Du malheur d'être juif au bonheur sépharade* (literally 'from the unhappiness of being Jewish to Sephardic happiness'), stressing therefore the writer's Sephardi origins: Guy Dugas, *Albert Memmi: Du malheur d'être juif au bonheur sépharade*, Paris, Alliance israélite universelle, 2001.

3. Algeria, Morocco and Tunisia are also known as the Maghreb, an area of North Africa north of the Sahara that can also include Libya and Mauritania; its geographical and cultural 'borders' are therefore not clear-cut. The colonisation of Algeria by the French began in 1830; it was considered by the French government an integral part of France, and was colonised by French settlers as well as subject to French administration. Tunisia and Morocco became French protectorates in 1881 and 1912 respectively, retaining political identity, and gaining independence in 1956. In Algeria, the War of Independence began in 1954, and finally ended, after protracted and violent confrontation with the French forces fighting to keep Algeria 'French', in 1962.

4. See for example the discussion of this aspect of Khatibi's work by Winifred Woodhull, 'Postcolonial Thought and Culture in Francophone North Africa', in Charles Forsdick and David Murphy (eds), *Francophone Postcolonial Studies: A Critical Introduction*, London, Arnold, 2003, pp. 211–20, especially pp. 213–16 discussing *Maghreb pluriel* (Paris, Denoël, 1983). According to Khatibi, Woodhull writes, '[North Africa] could well become a privileged site for the cultivation of cosmopolitan forms of "hospitality" that allow an array of languages, cultures and histories to intermingle and to speak through one another without any of them silencing or effacing the other' (p. 213). Woodhull also makes a case for Assia Djebar's work as a restoration of the polyphonic history of Algeria (p. 215).

5. The problem of defining a corpus of North African writing in French also comes up against the issue of what to include with regard to 'indigenous', *pied noir* and 'French' writing of various origins. It is an issue that anthologies of North African writing (notably that edited by Albert Memmi, for example, and referred to in Chapter 3) have also sought to address, with a number of different, and often unsatisfactory, solutions. The question of defining a 'Maghrebi' author is fraught with problems, particularly concerning the use of language, and many of these have been raised, for example, by critics such as Marc Gontard ('Auteur maghrébin: la défini-

tion introuvable', *Expressions maghrébines*, Revue de la Coordination Internationale des Chercheurs sur les Littératures Maghrébines, 1.1 [Summer 2002], pp. 9–16) and Christiane Chaulet-Achour ('Les Masques de la périphérie : éléments d'un débat', in the same issue, pp. 17–29).

6. The term 'postcolonial' is more frequently used among French researchers in the early years of the twenty-first century than it was at the end of the 1990s when I began this research, as will be apparent from some of my references. At around that time, also, several British and American scholars had begun to use the term 'postcolonial' with reference to the French and Francophone cultural and political contexts precisely to avoid the limiting and politicised connotations of the term 'Francophone'. Charles Forsdick and David Murphy have recently made a convincing case for the use of the terms 'Francophone' and 'postcolonial' together in their edited volume *Francophone Postcolonial Studies: A Critical Introduction*, a development that is reflected in the change of name for the British academic association most involved with this literature, the Society for Francophone Postcolonial Studies.

7. Edward Said, in his turn, was using the notion of discourse developed by Michel Foucault, particularly in *L'Archéologie du savoir* (1969). This is a text on which Foucault worked, as Robert Young has pointed out, during his stay in Tunisia, although John McCleod has taken issue with this 'siting' of the development of theory. See Robert Young, *Postcolonialism: An Historical Introduction*, Oxford, Blackwell, 2001, pp. 383–94 and pp. 395–410; and John McCleod, 'Contesting Contexts: Francophone Thought and Anglophone Postcolonialism', in Forsdick and Murphy (eds), *Francophone Postcolonial Studies*, pp. 192–201, especially p. 199.

8. Gayatri Chakravorty Spivak, 'Can the Subaltern Speak?' (1988), in Patrick Williams and Laura Chrisman (eds), *Colonial Discourse and Post-Colonial Theory: A Reader*, Hemel Hempstead, Harvester Wheatsheaf, 1993, pp. 66–111. In this article Spivak notes that German provides two different words for the meanings of 'representation': *Vertretung* in the political sense and *Darstellung* for the artistic sense.

9. Neil Lazarus, 'National Consciousness and the Specificity of (Post) Colonial Intellectualism', in Francis Barker, Peter Hulme and Margaret Iversen (eds), *Colonial Discourse/Postcolonial Theory*, Manchester and New York, Manchester University Press, 1994, pp. 197–220. Other critics have written about these issues with regard to specific writers and intellectuals; for example, David Murphy's work on Sembene is concerned with the notion of representation and Sembene's challenge to the dominant discourses of his society. Murphy also raises the issue of Sembene trying to address the problems of the masses in his work, when the vast majority of Africans are illiterate. See David Murphy, *Sembene: Imagining Alternatives in Film and Fiction*, Trenton, NJ, First Africa World Press, 2001, for example p. 218 and p. 220. Both Nicholas Harrison and Anne Donadey discuss the concept of 'representation' and the construction of the 'subaltern' with reference to Spivak. Donadey also suggests that Assia Djebar's work shows a concern with the problems of mediating subaltern women's voices while being aware of 'letting the subaltern speak', to take up Spivak's terms. See Nicholas Harrison, *Postcolonial Criticism: History, Theory and the Work of Fiction*, Cambridge, Polity, 2003, for example p. 95, p. 98; Anne Donadey, 'Francophone Women Writers and Postcolonial Theory', in Forsdick and Murphy (eds), *Francophone Postcolonial Studies*, pp. 202–10, particularly pp. 206–19.

10. Lazarus, 'National Consciousness', pp. 218–29. He is quoting from Edward Said, 'Figures, Configurations, Transfigurations', *Race and Class*, 32.1 (1990), pp. 1–16.

11. Cited in Lazarus, 'National Consciousness', p. 219.

12. I have therefore tended to work with specific literary criticism on each of the texts chosen here, rather than with these broader philosophical discourses, in my attention to close reading.

13. I am indebted to Mireille Calle-Gruber and her work on Assia Djebar for the suggestive coupling of the notions of ethics and aesthetics that I have extended here to postcolonial writing more generally, and to all the writers under discussion here in particular.

14. Gilles Deleuze and Félix Guattari, *Kafka: Pour une littérature mineure*, Paris, Minuit, 1975, p. 33. See also, for example, Anne Donadey's analysis of Homi Bhabha's exploration of the different use of the primal scene that Fanon makes in the colonial context, in which: 'sexual articulations of the primal scene [...] are translated into – literally carried across into – racial ones' (Donadey, 'Francophone Women Writers', pp. 203–206). Donadey comments on the ways in which Bhabha, working at the 'intersection of psychoanalysis and literary theory', and commenting on Fanon's work on psychology in the colonial context, fails to deal successfully with gender issues and the female subject. Nonetheless, Laïla Ibnlfassi convincingly analyses the work of, for example, Driss Chraïbi using a psychoanalytical framework, and justifies her approach as follows: 'a psychoanalytical reading of his work enlightens us about his disturbed personality such as we encounter it in the depiction of his characters [...] The core element in such a study will be the ego because of its unstable and conflictual situation'. Laïla Ibnlfassi, 'Chraïbi's *Le Passé simple* and a Theory of Doubles', in Laïla Ibnlfassi and Nicki Hitchcott (eds), *African Francophone Writing: A Critical Introduction*, Oxford and New York, Berg, 1996, pp. 59–67; here p. 60.

15. Deleuze and Guattari, *Kafka*, pp. 30–31.

16. See, for example, Nandy Ashis, *The Savage Freud and Other Essays on Possible and Retrievable Selves*, Princeton, NJ, Princeton University Press, 1995. See also David Murphy's approach to Sembene: he rejects the application of a Western psychoanalytical framework to an 'African situation in which the structure of the family is so different to that of its Western counterpart'. He argues that it is not possible to carry out such analyses 'in the absence of a fully developed, coherent psychoanalytical theory adapted to the realities of African societies'. He notes that Third World critics have preferred an approach combining issues of gender, class and race, such as has already been indicated as informing the readings here. See Murphy, *Sembene*, p. 224.

17. Edward Said, *Freud and the Non-European*, London and New York, Verso, 2003, p. 16. 'Why should Freud's view of culture not be Eurocentric', Said writes: 'His world had not yet been touched by the globalisation, or rapid travel, or decolonisation, that were to make formerly unknown or repressed cultures available to metropolitan Europe. He lived just before the massive population shifts that were to bring Indians, Africans, West Indians, Turks and Kurds into the heart of Europe as guest workers and often unwelcome immigrants'. The focus of this essay (originally a paper delivered at the Freud Museum, London) is Moses and the 'archaeology' of Jewish identity. Said shows that Freud never played down the fact that Moses, the founder of Jewish identity, was a non-European, and his analysis goes on to suggest that this is linked to Freud's own unresolved sense of identity (see for example p. 55). Said also notes (pp. 18–21) that Fanon, in one of the appendices to *The Wretched of the Earth*, 'Colonial Wars and Mental Disorders', rejects the European model entirely when cataloguing and commenting on a series of cases he had dealt with whose origins lay in the colonial battlefield, once again calling into question the application of Western psychological models to non-Western cultures.

18. Several critics within postcolonial studies 'disclose' their own identities in a

way not usual in 'traditional' literary criticism – notably, for example, Anne Donadey in her preface to *Recasting Postcolonialism: Women Writing Between Worlds*, Portsmouth, NH, Heinemann, 2001. David Murphy also raises the issue of the position of the Western reader, criticising the stance of Christopher Miller: 'Miller's basic point that the Western reader must be sensitive to differing cultural values when dealing with African literature is no doubt a useful reminder to all Western critics of the dangers of imposing a Western framework on non-Western societies. However, to posit an "authentic" African world that is totally foreign and incomprehensible to the Western reader is another matter entirely'. Murphy, *Sembene*, p. 20, referring to Christopher Miller, *Theories of Africans: Francophone Literature and Anthropology in Africa*, Chicago and London, Chicago University Press, 1990, p. 1.

Chapter One pp. 9–52

All translations in this chapter are by Helena Scott.

1. Albert Memmi, 'Le Moi, cet inconnu', in *Ce que je crois*, Paris, Grasset, 1985, p. 32.

2. Philippe Lejeune, *Le Pacte autobiographique*, Paris, Seuil, 1975. His categorisation of the genre is as follows: 'DEFINITION: Récit rétrospectif en prose qu'une personne réelle fait de sa propre existence, lorsqu'elle met l'accent sur sa vie individuelle, en particulier sur l'histoire de sa personnalité. La définition met en jeu des éléments appartenant à quatre catégories différentes: 1. Forme du langage: a) récit b) en prose. 2. Sujet traité: vie individuelle, histoire d'une personnalité. 3. Situation de l'auteur: identité de l'auteur (dont le nom renvoie à une personne réelle) et du narrateur. 4. Position du narrateur: a) identité du narrateur et du personnage principal b) perspective rétrospectif du récit. Est une autobiographie toute œuvre qui remplit à la fois les conditions indiquées dans chacune de ces catégories' (p. 14). ('DEFINITION: retrospective prose narrative of his or her own life by a real person, with the accent on the life of the individual and especially the story of his or her personality. The definition involves elements belonging to four different categories: 1. Form of language: a) narrative b) in prose. 2. Subject: life of an individual, story of a personality. 3. Author's situation: identity of the author (whose name refers to a real person) and the narrator. 4. Position of the narrator: a) identity of the narrator and the main character; b) retrospective standpoint of the narrative'.) His other main works on autobiography that established it as a serious literary form for critical analysis include *L'Autobiographie en France*, Paris, Armand Colin, 1971; *Je est un autre: L'autobiographie, de la littérature aux médias*, Paris, Seuil, 1980; and *Moi aussi*, Paris, Seuil, 1986.

3. Elizabeth Bruss, 'I for Eye: Making and Unmaking Autobiography in Film', in James Olney (ed.), *Autobiography: Essays Theoretical and Critical*, Princeton, NJ, Princeton University Press, 1980, pp. 296–320. In this collection William Howarth suggests the categories of autobiography as oratory, as drama and as poetry. Louis Renza suggests three modes: memoir, confessional and narcissistic. See also Bruss's other work: for example, *Autobiographical Acts: The Changing Situation of a Literary Genre*, Baltimore, Johns Hopkins University Press, 1976.

4. Michael Sheringham, *French Autobiography: Devices and Desires*, Oxford, Clarendon Press, 1993, Preface, especially pp. viii, ix. Concerning the other, Sheringham discusses not only the other outside the self, but also the ways in which the self becomes other in the process of writing and the way in which the book that contains the story of a life also becomes other. He also notes history as a facet of otherness. In a later chapter on the place of the reader, he analyses the ways in which

the reader is also other, both a threat and an object of desire for the autobiographer (p. 139).

5. Ngugi wa Thiong'o, *Decolonising the Mind: The Politics of Language in African Literature*, London, James Curry, 1986; Sidonie Smith and Julia Watson (eds), *De/Colonising the Subject: The Politics of Gender in Women's Autobiography*, Minneapolis, University of Minnesota Press, 1992, p. xix. Here the editors are talking about women's autobiography, but the concept is also relevant to the postcolonial context.

6. The concept of a 'motivated act of reading' was developed in feminist discourse and criticism, and has also become prevalent in postcolonial studies.

7. See for example Jacques Lecarme and Eliane Lecarme-Tabone, *L'Autobiographie*, Paris, Armand Colin, 1997, p. 7; they see the word in the first instance as a synonym of *mémoires*, but as gradually coming to describe texts in which historical events are of less importance than the personality of the person recounting them. Michael Sprinker ('Fictions of the Self: The End of Autobiography', in Olney [ed.], *Autobiography*, p. 325) details the 1809 usage (by Robert Southey in the *Quarterly Review*) cited in the *OED* and notes that until the end of the eighteenth century works that are today labelled 'autobiography' would have been called 'confessions' or 'memoirs'. An interesting detail about how the use of the word became accepted is explained by James Cox ('Recovering Literature's Lost Ground through Autobiography', in James Olney [ed.], *Studies in Autobiography*, Oxford, Oxford University Press, 1988, p. 123) with reference to Thomas Jefferson's autobiography: when it was first published in 1830 it was entitled a 'Memoir', but in its modern reprinting it is presented as the 'Autobiography' of Thomas Jefferson.

8. Lecarme and Lecarme-Tabone, *L'Autobiographie*, p. 13.

9. Lejeune, *Le Pacte autobiographique*, p. 316.

10. For example, Georg Misch, *Geschichte der Autobiographie*, Frankfurt, Verlag G. Schulte-Bulmke, 1962.

11. Olney (ed.), *Autobiography*, p. 23.

12. Karl Weintraub, *The Value of the Individual: Self and Circumstance in Autobiography*, Chicago, University of Chicago Press, 1978.

13. Weintraub, *The Value of the Individual*, p. 229. He adds that the experiences of both Catholic mysticism and Protestant Puritanism 'accented the convictions through which Christianity had a lasting effect on the Western personality – the high valuation of each human soul, its transcendent yearning, its inwardness and its search for inner coherence and harmony, its pervasive sense that life was a dramatic process and not simply a state of being, and its double commitment to care for oneself and one's brother' (p. 258).

14. Weintraub, *The Value of the Individual*, pp. 228–29.

15. Jean Déjeux, 'Au Maghreb, la langue française "langue natale du je"', in Martine Mathieu (ed.), *Littératures autobiographiques de la Francophonie*, Paris, L'Harmattan, 1996, p. 180. This is a late article, published after Déjeux's death. He takes the idea in his title from the writer Mohammed Kacimi, in an article in which he juxtaposes the 'divine language' of the Koranic School with French as the 'language of the self' ('Langue de Dieu et langue du Je', *Autrement*, série Monde, 60 [March 1992], hors série 'Algérie 30 ans').

16. Déjeux, 'Au Maghreb', p. 119.

17. Déjeux, 'Au Maghreb', p. 182.

18. Hichem Djaït, *L'Europe et L'Islam*, Paris, Le Seuil, 1978, p. 67.

19. Abdallah Laroui, *L'Idéologie arabe contemporaine*, Paris, Maspero, 1967, p. 203.

20. Fatima Mernissi, *Le Harem politique*, Paris, Albin Michel, 1987, p. 32.

21. Déjeux, 'Au Maghreb', p. 188.

22. Déjeux, 'Au Maghreb', p. 188. I would point out here that I have previously worked with these ideas myself in an earlier article on Camus and Memmi, following Déjeux's position of authority in the literary criticism of North African writing in French, but I now believe that there is a more complex set of arguments to be discussed and I have revised my opinion.

23. Abdallah Bounfour, 'Forme littéraire et représentation de soi: l'autobiographie francophone du Maghreb et l'autobiographie arabe du début du siècle', in Charles Bonn and Arnold Rothe (eds), *Littérature maghrébine et littérature mondiale*, Würzburg, Königshausen & Neumann, 1995, pp. 71–79, here p. 71. For a very clear account of Sufism, see Andrew Rippin, *Muslims: Their Religious Beliefs and Practices*, London and New York, Routledge, 2001, pp. 127–39.

24. Leila Ahmed, 'Between Two Worlds: The Formation of a Turn-of-the-Century Egyptian Feminist', in Bella Brodzki and Celeste Schenck (eds), *Life/Lines: Theorising Women's Autobiography*, Ithaca, NY, Cornell University Press, 1988, p. 154.

25. Amira Hassan Nowaira, 'Arabic Autobiography', in Margaretta Jolly (ed.), *Encyclopaedia of Life Writing*, Chicago and London, Fitzroy Dearborn, 2001, pp. 45–47.

26. Nowaira, 'Arabic Autobiography', p. 45.

27. Franz Rosenthal, 'Die arabische Autobiographie', in *Studia Arabica*, Rome, Pontificium Institutum Biblicum, 1937, pp. 1–40; reprinted in Franz Rosenthal, *Muslim Intellectual and Social Life: A Collection of essays*, Aldershot, Variorum, 1990.

28. Misch, *Geschichte der Autobiographie*, pp. 962–1006.

29. Thomas Philipp, 'The Autobiography in Modern Arab Literature and Culture', *Poetics Today*, 14.3 (Fall 1993), pp. 573–604.

30. Rosenthal, 'Die arabische Autobiographie' (1990 edn), p. 40.

31. Fedwa Malti-Douglas, *Blindness and Autobiography*, Princeton, NJ, Princeton University Press, 1988, p. 10.

32. Malti-Douglas, *Blindness and Autobiography*, p. 602.

33. Bounfour, 'Forme littéraire et représentation du soi', p. 74.

34. Bounfour, 'Forme littéraire et représentation du soi', p. 74.

35. Roger Allen, *An Introduction to Arabic Literature*, Cambridge, Cambridge University Press, 2000, p. 42. Allen provides a clear discussion of the interest in genealogy and the compilation of biographical records in Arabic historical scholarship, by writers including those referred to by Leila Ahmed and Amira Hassan Nowaira, especially, for example, Ibn Khaldūn, al-Ghazzālī and Usāma ibn Munqidh. Allen notes that '[w]hile the bulk of the information provided in these works is biographical, the compilers occasionally include autobiographical accounts which tend to record incidents that reflect well on the subject involved rather than provide insights into aspects of personality. However, some individual works do stand out because of the glimpses they afford of the personae of their authors' (p. 156). As far as modern Arabic literature is concerned, he discusses the case of Tāhā Husayn (p. 185), as well as considering modern Arabic novels concerned with the Algerian War of Independence, and novels by North African writers in Arabic (pp. 189–90). Andrew Rippin also analyses the importance of the biographies of Muhammad in *Muslims*, pp. 189–90.

36. Allen, *Introduction to Arabic Literature*, p. 137.

37. Allen, *Introduction to Arabic Literature*, p. 5.

38. Sabry Hafez, *The Genesis of Arabic Narrative Discourse: A Study in the Sociology of Modern Arabic Discourse*, London, Saqi Books, 1993, p. 10.

39. Hafez, *Genesis of Arabic Narrative Discourse*, p. 19.

40. Hafez, *Genesis of Arabic Narrative Discourse*, p. 27.

41. Allen, *Introduction to Arabic Literature*, p. 184.

42. Jean Déjeux, 'L'Emergence du "je" dans la littérature maghrébine de langue française', *Itinéraires et Contacts de Cultures*, 13 (1991), special issue, *Autobiographies et récits de vie en Afrique*, pp. 23–24. His references are to a Canadian thesis, 'Evolution et structures du roman maghrébin de langue française', Université de Sherbrooke (Québec), 1977, vol. II, p. 398.

43. Déjeux, 'L'Emergence du "je"', p. 24.

44. Djaït, *L'Europe et L'Islam*, p. 67.

45. Déjeux, 'L'Emergence du "je"', p. 29.

46. Doris Somner, 'Not Just a Personal Story: Women's Testimonies and the Plural Self', in Brodzki and Schenck (eds), *Life/Lines*, p.111.

47. Assia Djebar, 'Du français comme butin', *La Quinzaine littéraire* (Paris), no. 436 (March 1985).

48. Rippin, *Muslims*, p. 3. His reference is to Hans Mol, *Identity and the Sacred: A Sketch for a New Social-Scientific Theory of Religion*, New York, The Free Press, 1976, p. 55.

49. Rippin, *Muslims*, p. 247.

50. Rippin, *Muslims*, p. 4.

51. Rippin, *Muslims*, p. 42.

52. Rippin, *Muslims*, pp. 98–99.

53. Rippin, *Muslims*, pp. 101–102.

54. Rippin, *Muslims*, p. 177.

55. Rippin, *Muslims*, p. 122.

56. Georges Gusdorf, 'Conditions and Limits of Autobiography', trans. James Olney, in Olney (ed.), *Autobiography*, pp. 28–30; it originally appeared as 'Conditions et limites de l'autobiographie', in Günther Reichenkron and Erich Haase (eds), *Formen der Selbstdarstellung: Analekten zu einer Geschichte des literarischen Selbstportraits*, Berlin, Duncker and Humblot, 1956.

57. Tariq Ramadan, 'Quel humanisme pour l'islam?', talk given at the Eglise Réformée d'Auteuil, 10 March 2001 and available at http://www.erf-auteuil.org/conferences/quel-humanisme-pour-l-islam.html (consulted November 2002).

58. Jean Starobinski, 'Le Style de l'autobiographie', *Poétique*, no. 3 (1970).

59. For a discussion of this, see Barret Mandell, 'Full of Life Now', in Olney (ed.), *Autobiography*, p. 53.

60. Striking examples of this in French literature are the 1980s autobiographies of the 'new novelists', Alain Robbe-Grillet, Nathalie Sarraute and Marguerite Duras. See Chapter 3 n. 67 for more details.

61. Mandell, 'Full of Life Now', p. 67. Or as another critic stresses in the particular case of 'collaborative' Indian autobiography in America (i.e. where an editor has collected the life story of an Indian and presented it as a written text): 'But the assumption of a division between public and private selves, the assumption that the Indian autobiography will be confessional, and the genre can offer the best insight into tribal culture – all these are disturbing preconceptions'. G. Thomas Couser, 'Black Elk Speaks with Forked Tongue', in Olney (ed.), *Studies in Autobiography*, p. 77.

62. Declan Kiberd, *Inventing Ireland*, London, Jonathan Cape, 1995, p. 615.

63. See Mathieu (ed.), *Littératures autobiographiques de la Francophonie*, p. 6. The problem of the 'periphery' is not in fact confined to writers outside France: the so-called 'regional novels', works not published in Paris, suffer from prejudice in the French national press where they are little (if at all) reviewed.

64. This did begin to change towards the end of the twentieth century, and we can note for example the publication of *Postcolonialisme et Autobiographie*, edited by Ernstpeter Ruhe and Alfred Hornung, published in French although the conference was held in Würzburg and the book published in the Netherlands. The work of the researchers involved in ACHAC (Association Connaissance de l'Histoire de l'Afrique Contemporaine) makes explicit use of the framework of postcolonial studies, as does the work of Jean-Marc Moura in, for example, *Littératures francophones et théorie postcoloniale*, Paris, PUF, 1999, in an attempt to 'renew' the study of Francophone literatures 'à la lumière du vaste ensemble de recherches connu, dans le monde anglo-saxon, sous le nom de Postcolonial Studies' (back cover: 'in the light of the vast amount of research known in the English-speaking world as Postcolonial Studies'); and that of Jacqueline Bardolph, *Etudes postcoloniales et littérature*, Paris, Champion, 2001.

65. See for example the work of Roger Little, 'La Francographie: A New Model for "La *Francophonie*"', in Christine O'Dowd-Smyth (ed.), *Littératures francophones: la problématique de l'altérité*, Waterford, WIT School of Humanities Publications, 2001. Note also, however, the convincing case made for the coupling of 'Francophone' and 'postcolonial' by Forsdick and Murphy in their attempt to 'decolonise' the term, emphasising that 'Francophone' refers to all cultures where French is spoken, including, of course, France itself. See 'Introduction: The Case for Francophone Postcolonial Studies', in Forsdick and Murphy (eds), *Francophone Postcolonial Studies*, p. 7.

66. Michel Leiris, '...Reusement!', in *Biffures, La Règle du jeu I*, Paris, Gallimard, 1948, p. 12. Rousseau also talks about the need to invent something completely new for his project.

67. Geoffrey Galt Harpham, 'Conversion and the Language of Autobiography', in Olney (ed.), *Studies in Autobiography*, p. 48.

68. Roger Rosenblatt, 'Black Autobiography: Life as the Death Weapon', in Olney (ed.), *Autobiography*, p. 169, p. 171.

69. Olney (ed.), *Autobiography*, p. xv.

70. Shari Benstock (ed.), *The Private Self: Theory and Practice of Women's Autobiographical Writings*, London and New York, Routledge, 1988, p. 7 in the introduction to Part 1, 'Theories of the Autobiographical', on the question of the definition of autobiographical discourse.

71. Benstock (ed.), *The Private Self*, p. 7.

72. Benstock (ed.), *The Private Self*, p. 15.

73. Benstock (ed.), *The Private Self*, p. 19.

74. Susan Stanford Friedman, 'Women's Autobiographical Selves: Theory and Practice', in Benstock (ed.), *The Private Self*, p. 38. See also her references in n. 3, pp. 56–57 on the valuable studies of autobiography that assume an individualistic model of the self. The whole of this essay is useful.

75. Friedman, 'Women's Autobiographical Selves', p. 55.

76. Friedman, 'Women's Autobiographical Selves', p. 39.

77. Friedman, 'Women's Autobiographical Selves', pp. 29–30.

78. Friedman, 'Women's Autobiographical Selves', p. 38.

79. Brodzki and Schenk (eds), *Life/Lines*, p. 2.

80. They also present a useful summary of how criticism in women's autobiography developed through the work of Estelle Jelinek, who first postulated the existence of a distinct female tradition in autobiography, and then Domna Stanton's work on the challenging of the generic boundaries of autobiography. Schenck herself continues this theoretical challenge to the definition of the genre in 'All of a Piece: Women's Poetry and Autobiography', in Brodzki and Schenck (eds), *Life/Lines*, pp.

281–305. Susan Stanford Friedman ('Women's Autobiographical Selves', p. 56 n. 3) also points out that Gusdorf ignores the early autobiographical writings of women: Hildegard's *Vita* (1160s); Margery Kempe's *The Book of Margery Kempe* (early 1400s); Sor Juana's *La Respuesta* (1691); Gluckel's *The Memoirs of Gluckel of Hameln* (1689–1719); Alice Thorton's *The Autobiography of Mrs Alice Thorton* (late seventeenth century). Kempe's is the first extant autobiography in English. See also Mary G. Mason, 'The Other Voice: Autobiographies of Women Writers', in Brodzki and Schenck (eds), *Life/Lines*, pp. 21–44 on the models of the works of Julian of Norwich, Margery Kempe, Margaret Cavendish and Anne Bradstreet.

81. See for example *This Bridge Called My Back*, as commented on by Biddy Martin, 'Lesbian Identity and Autobiographical Difference(s)', in Brodzki and Schenck (eds), *Life/Lines*, p. 95.

82. Laurence Joffrin, 'La Fiction Identitaire dans l'écriture migrante au Québec: Présentation liminaire', in Mathieu (ed.), *Littératures autobiographiques de la Francophonie*, pp. 223–33.

83. Joffrin, 'La Fiction Identitaire', p. 233.

84. 'Postcolonial studies' remains somewhat controversial, not least because of its interdisciplinarity, and because of what is often seen as its confused political and economic knowledge. See, for example, Ania Loomba, *Colonialism/Postcolonialism*, London, Routledge, 1998, Introduction, p. xi, and for criticism of its political stance, pp. 16–17. For a history and a discussion of the use of the term 'post(-)colonial', with or without the hyphen, see Bill Ashcroft, Gareth Griffiths and Helen Tiffin (eds), *Key Concepts in Post-Colonial Studies*, London, Routledge, 1998, pp. 186–92.

85. On the vagaries of how Francophone writers are categorised in bookshops, see Nicki Hitchcott, 'Calixthe Beyala and the Post-Colonial Woman', in Alec Hargreaves and Mark McKinney (eds), *Post-Colonial Cultures in France*, London, Routledge, 1997, pp. 214–15 on the prize awarded to Beyala by the Académie Française. As Hitchcott points out, this 'demarginalisation' can either be seen positively as an indication of a 'more global definition of literature in French', or negatively as linked to the old colonial policy of assimilation, and as suggesting a neo-colonisation of postcolonial writing.

86. Ashcroft et al. (eds), *Key Concepts in Post-Colonial Studies*, p. 186.

87. Ashcroft et al. (eds), *Key Concepts in Post-Colonial Studies*, p. 187.

88. Hargreaves and McKinney (eds), *Post-Colonial Cultures in France*, p. 4. See also the discussion by Nicholas Harrison in his introduction to *Postcolonial Criticism*, pp. 1–10. See further Alec Hargreaves, 'The Contribution of North and Sub-Saharan African Immigrant Minorities to the Redefinition of Contemporary French Culture', in Forsdick and Murphy (eds), *Francophone Postcolonial Studies*, pp. 145–54.

89. Little, 'La Francographie', p. 102, with reference to Pierre Cassan (ed.), *Etat de la Francophonie dans le monde: données 1995–1996 et cinq études inédites*, Paris, La Documentation Française, 1997, p. 17. Little criticises heavily the unequal economic relationships among the countries that share the French language to some extent, the 'gap between the Francophone label and the non-Francophone speaking reality', and the way in which France maintains its political links for economic reasons. See also Gabrielle Parker's analysis: '"Francophonie" and "Universalité": Evolution of Two Notions Conjoined', in Forsdick and Murphy (eds), *Francophone Postcolonial Studies*, pp. 91–101.

90. John Erickson, *Islam and Postcolonial Narrative*, Cambridge, Cambridge University Press, 1998, p. 3.

91. Hargreaves and McKinney (eds), *Post-Colonial Cultures in France*, pp. 14–17.

92. Hargreaves and McKinney (eds), *Post-Colonial Cultures in France*, p. 17.

93. Anne McClintock, 'The Angel of Progress: The Pitfalls of the Term "Postcolonialism"', in Barker, Hulme and Iversen (eds), *Colonial Discourse/Postcolonial Theory*, p. 255.

94. McClintock, 'The Angel of Progress', p. 260. She analyses what she terms the 'feminisation of poverty'.

95. Forsdick and Murphy (eds), *Francophone Postcolonial Studies*, p. 5. Bart Moore-Gilbert, *Postcolonial Theory: Contexts, Practices, Politics*, London and New York, Verso, 1997, p. 188. This text provides insightful analysis of the work of the major theorists of postcolonial studies and the debates within the field. Finally, Moore-Gilbert argues that 'strategic essentialism' may offer a way of avoiding the danger that different kinds of histories and oppression may be collapsed together artificially (p. 202). His anxiety concerning the passing of the postcolonial 'moment' is a reference to Stuart Hall's 'When was the "Post-Colonial"?', in Iain Chambers and Lidia Curtis (eds), *The Postcolonial Question: Common Skies, Divided Horizons*, London and New York: Routledge, 1996, p. 258.

96. Young, *Postcolonialism*, pp. 4–5. In the early chapters he presents a very clear account and definition of the terms 'colonialism', 'imperialism', 'neocolonialism' and 'postcolonialism'. Also notable in this study is the very personal preface in which Young explains the effect two photographs from the Algerian War of Independence have had on him.

97. Young, *Postcolonialism*, p. 57. Both Young and McClintock note the effects of continuing colonialism as neighbouring countries often invaded countries once the European colonising power left. Young also makes clear that he prefers the term 'tricontinentalism' to postcolonialism.

98. Young, *Postcolonialism*, p. 413.

99. Young, *Postcolonialism*, p. 56.

100. Hargreaves and McKinney continue: 'If Algerians, the largest minority ethnic group in France, are also the most distrusted and disliked by the majority population, this is in no small measure due to the images of racial inferiority and enmity inherited from over a century of colonisation and almost eight years of guerilla warfare that brought France to the brink of civil war [...] In their everyday dealings with the majority population, Maghrebis as a whole (whether of Algerian, Moroccan, or Tunisian origin) cannot escape the generally unstated and often unconscious but nonetheless potent legacy of the colonial era' (*Post-Colonial Cultures in France*, p. 18). Charles Forsdick and David Murphy provide the telling example of Pierre Nora's monumental *Les Lieux de Mémoire* (Paris, Gallimard, 1997) and its 'fleeting recognition of the role played by colonial expansion in the formation of national and Republican identity' (Forsdick and Murphy [eds], *Francophone Postcolonial Studies*, p. 2).

101. See, for example, Hargreaves' and McKinney's introduction (*Post-Colonial Cultures in France*, p. 21) and various chapters in *Post-Colonial Cultures in France*, especially Carrie Tarr, 'French Cinema and Post-Colonial Minorities', pp. 59–83, and Hargreaves, 'Gatekeepers and Gateways: Post-Colonial Minorities and French Television', pp. 84–98. See also Henry Rousso's analysis of France's failure to come to terms with its position in the Second World War in *Le Syndrome de Vichy de 1944 à nos jours*, Paris, Editions du Seuil, rev. edn, 1990 (1987). Anne Donadey has referred to this and to France's 'Algerian syndrome' in *Recasting Postcolonialism*, pp. 5–11.

102. David Blatt, 'Immigrant Politics in a Republican Nation', in Hargreaves and McKinney (eds), *Post-Colonial Cultures in France*, p. 46. See this chapter for a discussion of the history and the consequences of the republican consensus in France,

which renders ethnic politics incompatible with the French political process. The most famous recent example of this policy in action is the attitude towards the wearing of the Islamic headscarf by young girls in French schools (in line with the prohibition of all signs of religious identity in the Republican national school system). Malcolm Cook and Grace Davie make similar points in their introduction to *Modern France: Society in Transition*, London and New York, Routledge, 1999, and see especially the chapter by Cathie Lloyd, 'Race and Ethnicity', pp. 34–52, and her discussion of assimilation, p. 39. Mireille Rosello provides an interesting analysis of the ways in which cultural identity has recently been mobilised in France by Blacks, gays, women, Muslims and Jews towards what she terms a 'hybrid universalism'. See 'Tactical Universalism and New Multiculturalist Claims in Postcolonial France', in Forsdick and Murphy (eds), *Francophone Postcolonial Studies*, pp. 136–44. Once again, the introduction to this book provides a useful discussion, this time on the problems of multiculturalism and the French republican model (pp. 8–9).

103. Azzedine Haddour, *Colonial Myths: History and Narrative*, Manchester, Manchester University Press, 2000, p. 5. See the whole of chapter 1 for his discussion of the effects of assimilation in Algeria. He also points out very importantly the different treatment of the Jews under the policies of assimilation: they did not have to renounce their religion to obtain legal citizenship, making their status different after the 1870 Crémieux Decree until this was revoked under Vichy.

104. Haddour, *Colonial Myths*, p. 18.

105. Young, *Postcolonialism*, p. 29 and p. 32. He also notes the very different attitude of the British: 'The British system of relative non-interference with local cultures, which today appears more liberal in spirit, was in fact also based on the racist assumptions that the native was incapable of education up to the level of the European – and therefore by implication required perpetual colonial rule. Association (the British practice of loose association rather than the French doctrine of centralised assimilation) neatly offered the possibility of autonomy (for some), while at the same time incorporating a notion of hierarchy for the supposedly less-capable races' (p. 33).

106. Young, *Postcolonialism*, p. 18. John McCleod, however, urges caution with the thrust of Young's argument ('Contesting Contexts', p.199), calling it 'a remarkably deterministic narrative that is made concerning a thinker's identity or the location of their work'.

107. Steve Cannon, 'Paname City Rapping: B-Boys in the Banlieues and Beyond', in Hargreaves and McKinney (eds), *Post-Colonial Cultures in France*, p. 162. For a discussion of the history of the French education system and the republican tradition, see Ted Neather, 'Education and Training', in Cook and Davie (eds), *Modern France*, p. 173, and on the concept of *laïcité* which is integral to the French education system see Grace Davie, 'Religion and Laïcité', pp. 201–207.

108. Loomba, *Colonialism/Postcolonialism*, p. 12, with reference to the work of Jorge de Alva, a critic of the lack of a real political stance in postcolonial studies.

109. Loomba, *Colonialism/Postcolonialism*, p. 174.

110. Chris Tiffin and Alan Lawson (eds), *De-Scribing Empire: Post-Colonialism and Textuality*, London and New York, Routledge, 1994, introduction, p. 3.

111. Tiffin and Lawson (eds), *De-Scribing Empire*, p. 10.

112. Elizabeth Fox-Genovese, 'My Statue, My Self: Autobiographical Writings of Afro-American Women', in Benstock (ed.), *The Private Self*, p. 67.

113. Nancy K. Miller, 'Writing Fictions: Women's Autobiography in France', in Brodzki and Schenck (eds), *Life/Lines*, p. 56. This practice is what she calls elsewhere 'overreading': 'Arachnologies: The Woman, the Text, and the Critic', in *Subject to Change: Reading Feminist Writing*, New York, Columbia University Press, 1988.

114. Miller, 'Writing Fictions', pp. 60–61. For another stance on the importance of identification between reader and autobiographical subject, this time in lesbian writing, see Martin, 'Lesbian Identity', p. 84, where the reader is explicitly committed to just such reading strategies for the creation of identity, community and political solidarity.

115. Helen Carr, 'In Other Words: Native American Women's Autobiography', in Brodzki and Schenck (eds), *Life/Lines*, p. 131.

116. Brodzki and Schenck (eds), *Life/Lines*, Introduction, p. 15.

117. Françoise Lionnet, 'Of Mangoes and Maroons: Language, History and the Multicultural Subject of Michelle Cliff's *Abeng*', in Smith and Watson (eds), *De/Colonising the Subject*, p. 341.

118. See, for example, the introduction in Benstock (ed.), *The Private Self*, p. 1 on allied interests to gender and p. 7 on the question of subjectivity under patriarchy.

119. Katherine R. Goodman, 'Elisabeth to Meta: Epistolary Autobiography and the Postulation of the Self', in Brodzki and Schenck (eds), *Life/Lines*, p. 308.

120. Goodman, 'Elisabeth to Meta', p. 309.

121. Linda Hutcheon, 'Circling the Downspout of Empire', in Ian Adam and Helen Tiffin (eds), *Past the Last Post: Theorising Post-Colonialism and Post-Modernism*, Hemel Hempstead, Harvester Wheatsheaf, 1991, p. 168.

122. Loomba, *Colonialism/Postcolonialism*, pp. 247–48, highlighting the views of Nancy Hartsock and Denis Epko, for example.

123. See Brodzki and Schenk's introduction (*Life/Lines*, p. 14) on the essentialism that has plagued both American feminist criticism and *écriture féminine* in France. See, however, my earlier reference to Bart Moore-Gilbert's advocacy of 'strategic essentialism' (note 95 above).

124. See Françoise Lionnet, *Autobiographical Voices: Race, Gender, Self-Portraiture*, Ithaca, NY, Cornell University Press, 1989, p. 72.

125. Brodzki and Schenck (eds), *Life/Lines*, introduction, p. 14.

126. Carr, 'In Other Words', p. 152.

127. Carr, 'In Other Words', p. 139. This is another way of articulating Deleuze and Guattari's 'minor/major' distinction.

128. Smith and Watson (eds), *De/Colonising the Subject*, introduction, p. xxviii.

129. Lionnet, *Autobiographical Voices*, pp. 247–48.

130. Gayatri Chakravorty Spivak, 'How to Read a "Culturally Different" Book', in Barker, Hulme and Iversen, *Colonial Discourse/Postcolonial Theory*, p. 131. Spivak specifically takes a pedagogical standpoint in her reading of an Indian story with American teachers and students in mind.

131. Helen Tiffin, 'Introduction', in Adam and Tiffin (eds), *Past the Last Post*, p. vii.

132. Stephen Slemon, 'The Scramble for Post-Colonialism', in Tiffin and Lawson (eds), *De-Scribing Empire*, p. 22.

133. Quoted by Fiona Giles, '"The Softest Disorder": Representing Cultural Indeterminacy', in Tiffin and Lawson (eds), *De-Scribing Empire*, pp. 141–42.

134. Tiffin, 'Introduction', in Adam and Tiffin (eds), *Past the Last Post*, p. viii.

135. Loomba, *Colonialism/Postcolonialism*, p. 256.

136. Donadey, *Recasting Postcolonialism*, p. xxv, italics in original.

Chapter Two pp. 53–130

All translations in this chapter are by Helena Scott.

1. Jean Déjeux, *Maghreb Littératures de Langue Française*, Paris, Arcantère,

1993, pp. 31–32. In the bibliographic presentation in this book, Déjeux lists five texts in the section 'romans, récits, recueils de nouvelles et de contes' published before *Le Fils du pauvre* (in 1945, 1947 and 1948) by Algerians (including two by women, Marie-Louise Amrouche's *Jacinthe noir* and Djamila Debèche's *Leïla, jeune fille d'Algérie*), but it is Feraoun's text that achieved prominence. For an analysis of Orientalist and exotic writings, and of 'l'Ecole d'Alger', see Peter Dunwoodie, *Writing French Algeria*, Oxford, Clarendon Press, 1998. Peter Dunwoodie has also challenged the generalised reading of Algerian writers in this period as solely 'assimilated'. I have discussed the importance of the policy of assimilation in the French colonial system in the introduction.

2. Mouloud Feraoun, *Lettres à ses amis*, Paris, Le Seuil, 1969, edited with notes by Emmanuel Roblès for the Collection Méditerranée for which he was series editor. I shall discuss this collection of letters later in the chapter.

3. *Lettres à ses amis*, p. 39. For an analysis of the writing of Roblès and his importance in Algeria during this period, see Dunwoodie, *Writing French Algeria*, p. 284: 'Less well-known than his near contemporary Camus, Roblès occupies a unique position in cultural developments in colonial Algeria after 1938, not least because his work engages directly with the limiting and stereotypical depiction of interracial relations dominant in Algerianist discourse and, as yet, only indirectly challenged by the Ecole d'Alger, in so far as their novels were not adequately dealing with the Muslim Algerian dimension'. Le Seuil, the leading Parisian publishing house for which Roblès worked, would continue to support Feraoun's work, publishing a second novel *La Terre et le sang* ('Earth and Blood') in 1953, republishing *Le Fils du pauvre* in 1954 and continuing thereafter to publish his novels and essays: *Les Chemins qui montent* ('The Paths that Lead Upwards', 1957); *Les Poèmes de Si Mohand* ('The Poems of Si Mohand', 1960); *Journal 1955–1962* ('Diary 1955–1962', 1962); *Jours de Kabylie* ('Kabylia Days', 1968; first published in 1954 in Algiers); *Lettres à ses amis* ('Letters to his Friends', 1969); *L'Anniversaire* ('The Birthday' or 'The Anniversary', 1972); see also Déjeux, *Maghreb Littératures*, p. 37.

4. See for example the choice of quotations by Marie-Hélène Chèze in *Mouloud Feraoun: La voix et le silence*, Paris, Le Seuil, 1982, pp. 51–55.

5. Déjeux, *Maghreb Littératures*, p. 37. In an a earlier book, *Littérature maghrébine de langue française*, Déjeux uses this 'ethnographic' label: 'L'œuvre romanesque de Mouloud Feraoun se situe dans ce courant que nous appelons "ethnographique", écrite en général en fonction du lecteur européen. Feraoun s'y révèle témoin de sa société et témoin de son temps' (Sherbrooke, Quebec, Editions Namaan, 1980 [1973], p. 118) ('Mouloud Feraoun's fiction falls within the category which we call "ethnographical", generally written for the benefit of European readers. In it Feraoun reveals himself as a witness of his society and of his time').

6. Abdelkébir Khatibi, *Le Roman maghrébin*, Paris, Maspéro, 1968, pp. 49–52 (also quoted by Déjeux, *Littérature maghrébine*, p. 141). Peter Dunwoodie also notes Khatibi's evaluation of the primary schoolteachers and public sector middle-management writers whom he calls the first valid Algerian novelists, while criticising the writing for being too careful and often aspiring to assimilation (*Writing French Algeria*, p. 23). For an interesting analysis of the stylistic aspects of the novel from a translator's point of view, see Saskia Hepher, 'The Son of a Poor Man – A Translation Project on Mouloud Feraoun's *Le Fils du pauvre*', MA dissertation, Technical and Specialised Translation, University of Westminster, 1998, pp. 4–5 and 6–7; also Naget Khadda, 'Autobiographie et structuration du sujet acculturé dans *Le Fils du pauvre* de Mouloud Feraoun', *Itinéraires et Contacts de Cultures*, 13 (1991), special issue, *Autobiographies et récits de vie en Afrique*, pp. 79–85.

7. Christiane Achour's view is that even the epigraph to *Le Fils du pauvre* makes

it 'assimilationist': 'ce présupposé qui inscrit ce roman dans la lignée des romans adhérant à l'idéal assimilationniste lui donne ce ton misérabiliste et fataliste' ('Formation scolaire et écriture littéraire', in *Réflexions sur la culture*, Algiers, OPU, 1984, p. 50; quoted by Haddour, *Colonial Myths*, p. 153) ('this presupposition, which places this novel among those adhering to the assimilationist ideal, gives it its tone of wretchedness and fatalism'). Haddour himself argues that the text is undermined by being assimilationist and failing to trace colonisation as an origin of Kabyle poverty, although he reads the later *Les Chemins qui montent* as more challenging to colonialist discourse.

8. Assia Djebar, *Le Blanc de l'Algérie*, Paris, Albin Michel, 1995.

9. Djebar, *Le Blanc de l'Algérie*, pp. 116–17.

10. Khadda, 'Autobiographie et structuration du sujet acculturé', p. 80.

11. See Jack Gleyze, *Mouloud Feraoun*, Paris, L'Harmattan, 1990, pp. 77–78, where he points out both the fact that a Kabyle language exists which it is possible to transpose into the Latin alphabet, and that a whole oral culture has been obscured by the imposition of French language and culture through the education system. I shall be returning to this question of an alphabet for the Kabyle and Berber languages in the chapter on Assia Djebar. See the same text for a synopsis of Feraoun's early life, to which I am grateful for the details used here. Feraoun also provides his own summary in a letter to Emmanuel Roblès on 5 January 1953 in *Lettres à ses amis*.

12. This followed the success of Feraoun's second novel, *La Terre et le sang* (1953).

13. Saskia Hepher has also commented on the removal of these last two parts, noting that although it is often argued that this was done to give the novel 'greater unity', 'it cannot be denied that, by removing descriptions of sexual awakening, images of Arab prostitutes and foremostly criticisms of the harsh effects of the Second World War, *Le Fils du pauvre* becomes a seemingly ingenuous work, not a unified whole in terms of the narrative, but in terms of its superficial ideological innocence' ('The Son of a Poor Man', p. 8).

14. Letter to Pierre Martin, member of the Service civil international (SCI) in Algeria, dated 8 September 1949, in Feraoun, *Lettres à ses amis*, p. 14. Feraoun's real family name, Aït Chaâbanne, is provided in the accompanying note by Roblès; see also the letter dated 5 January 1953 to Roblès himself (p. 90).

15. *Lettres à ses amis*, letter to Emmanuel Roblès, 5 January 1953, p. 90.

16. *Lettres à ses amis*, note by Emmanuel Roblès, p. 90; the differences in the spelling of 'Chaâban(n)e' in these notes have been reproduced as in this edition of the letters. The family is therefore known as 'les fils de Chabane': 'comme ceux de Fouroulou dans *Le Fils du pauvre*' (Chèze, *Mouloud Feraoun*, pp. 9–10).

17. Mouloud Feraoun, *Lettres à ses amis, ouvrage présenté par Christiane Achour*, Algiers, ENAG/EDITIONS, 1992, p. xiv.

18. Mouloud Feraoun, *Le Fils du pauvre*, Paris, Le Seuil, 1950, p. 24. The importance of the status of the name and its connotations is a recurrent feature of autobiographical discourses under consideration here, and I shall discuss this in relation to both Albert Memmi and Abdelkébir Khatibi in the following chapters. In a later chapter, Fouroulou gives a further interesting perspective on the use of names within the family: 'Je ne sus le nom de chacune de mes tantes qu'après les avoir bien connues elles-mêmes. Le nom ne signifiait rien. C'était comme pour mes parents. Je me rappelle avoir appris avec une surprise amusée, de la bouche de ma petite cousine, que son père s'appelle Lounis, le mien Ramdane, ma mère Fatma, la sienne Helima. Je compris tout de suite, cependant, que c'étaient les autres qui les désignaient ainsi et que dans la famille nous avions des mots plus doux qui n'appartenaient qu'à nous. Pour moi, mes tantes s'appelaient Khalti et Nana' (p. 39) ('I only learnt the name of

each of my aunts after I had come to know the aunts themselves very well. I remember hearing with amused surprise, from the mouth of my little cousin, that her father was called Lounis, mine Ramdane, my mother Fatma, and hers Helima. I understood straight away, however, that it was other people who called them by those names and that in the family we had sweeter names that only belonged to us. For me, my aunts were called Khalti and Nana').

19. See Zahia Smail Salhi, *Politics, Poetics and the Algerian Novel*, Lampeter, Edwin Mellen, 1999, pp. 114–24 on the polemic around the text. Both Feraoun and Mouloud Mammeri were seen unfavourably by nationalists in the 1950s, especially in comparison to Mohammed Dib's *La Grande Maison*, which was openly critical of colonialism and was committed to the nationalist cause.

20. Salhi, *Politics, Poetics and the Algerian Novel*, pp. 114–15.

21. I have previously noted Achour's reading of the epigraph to *Le Fils du pauvre*. I shall be considering further the use made of epigraphs by all the writers under discussion here.

22. This is a device that was often used in the eighteenth century, when the novel was considered a less 'respectable' literary form than poetry and drama and the idea of 'found' papers provided a conceit in order to 'protect' the author's identity. An intriguing contemporaneous comparison is Sartre's *La Nausée* (1938), in which the novel charting Roquentin's growing existential crisis purports to be made up of the papers found in Roquentin's desk, as indicated in the 'avertissement des éditeurs' with which the text opens.

23. Khadda, 'Autobiographie et structuration du sujet acculturé', p. 81.

24. Mouloud Feraoun, 'La Littérature algérienne', in *L'Anniversaire*, Paris, Le Seuil, 1972, p. 54.

25. *Lettres à ses amis*, letter to Camus, 27 May 1951, p. 204. See the direct criticism of Camus's lack of indigenous characters, quoted and commented on in my later section 'A Dialogue with Self and Others: *Lettres à ses amis*'.

26. *Lettres à ses amis*, letter to Roblès, 6 April 1959, p. 154. Rieux is a main character in Camus's *La Peste* (1947); Smaïl, the hero of Roblès's *Hauteurs de la ville*, is an indigenous Kabyle sentenced to death under the Vichy regime.

27. The gaze of the other has become a central concept in both postcolonial and feminist theory.

28. These descriptions can be compared with Camus's own descriptions in *Actuelles III, Essais, Misère de la Kabylie*, Paris, Gallimard, 1977.

29. Again, see Khadda, 'Autobiographie et structuration du sujet acculturé', on these points.

30. The father's underlying message here differs little from that frequently found within the working classes in Britain after the Second World War towards those who took up educational opportunities – a grudging admiration coupled with the scarcely concealed belief that education was of suspect use, but at least 'they can't take it away from you'.

31. Peter Dunwoodie's description of the central role of the Ecole Normale de Bouzaréa in the wider strategy of using education as 'an effective, and less coercive, means of regulating the indigenous population' is very revealing. Schooling was an essential strategy in the relations between coloniser and colonised: 'as a promise of eventual integration and an instrument of deculturation it could be used to counteract both the increasing politicisation of Algerian migrant workers in mainland France and the growing wave of Pan-Arab feeling'. The teacher training college gave a type of education that aimed to produce students who had fully internalised the humanist ideology of the French education system, yet 'despite its moralising republican ethos, the institution maintained clear racial distinctions, some major, such as

different syllabuses (until about 1924), many minor, such as dormitory, benches, and metal plates for native pupils, chairs and crockery for the Europeans. Similarly, the informal *tutoiement* (addressing them by the familiar form *"tu"* instead of the polite *"vous"*) was the standard form of address to all native pupils who, for instance, could never become *surveillants* (supervisors, or minor school officials). The aim, obviously, was to educate, that is to introduce the Muslim pupils into French culture, while retaining a significant number of distinctions in order to constantly reinforce the notion of difference, inferiority, and dependence which assimilation was officially working against' (*Writing French Algeria*, pp. 23–24). In fact, many of these students took up roles that the French authorities had not intended. Marginalised both by their own community and by the French community, they found a new space: 'in gaining the tools to transmit and so reinforce bourgeois European hegemony, they also acquired a platform from which to challenge the inbuilt subordination in which the system was grounded' (p. 24). Feraoun, however, retained a constant affection for the teachers there, giving the example of the teacher who, when the young student gives in a very poor piece of maths homework because he is worrying about a letter from his family, gives him six hundred francs: 'Si le cœur vous en dit, vous me payerez quand vous serez instituteur' (*Le Fils du pauvre*, pp. 108–109) ('If your heart tells you to, you can repay me when you're a teacher'). The teacher died the following year in the Pyrenees. Assia Djebar's father, who also became a teacher in a French primary school and was the instigator of her own education, also attended the Ecole Normale de Bouzaréa.

32. Assia Djebar analyses more fully the separation of the sexes in Islamic culture and its consequences for relationships, and especially for attitudes towards women, throughout her work.

33. I use the term 'narratorial voice' in contrast to Blanchot's 'narrative voice' as defined in 'The Narrative Voice' (the "He", the "Neutral")' in Maurice Blanchot, *L'Entretien infini*, Paris, Gallimard, 1969 (translated by Susan Hanson, *The Infinite Conversation*, Minneapolis and London, University of Minnesota Press, 1992). Here Blanchot defines the narrative voice as neutral: 'that speaks the work from out of this place without a place, where the work is silent [...] To speak in the neutral is to speak at a distance, preserving this distance without *mediation* and without *community*' (pp. 385–86; italics in original). The project of the writers under discussion here is the very opposite of neutral.

34. Albert Camus, *Le Premier Homme*, Paris, Gallimard, 1994.

35. *Lettres à ses amis*, ed. Achour, pp. viii–ix.

36. Published as Mouloud Feraoun, *Journal 1955–1962*, Paris, Le Seuil, 1962.

37. *Lettres à ses amis*, ed. Achour, pp. viii–ix.

38. *Journal*, 10 February 1957; this administrator's name, M. Achard, appears repeatedly in the novel Feraoun was writing at the time of his death, *L'Anniversaire*; see also the details of these events in Chèze, *Mouloud Feraoun*, pp. 86–87.

39. The criticism of the colonial system is also explicit in the novel published at the beginning of 1957, *Les Chemins qui montent*: 'Ils [les colons] occupent les meilleures places, toutes les places et finissent toujours par s'enrichir [...] Chez nous, il ne reste rien pour nous [...] Notre pays n'est pas plus pauvre qu'un autre, mais à qui est-il notre pays? Pas à ceux qui y crèvent de faim, tout de même' (*Les Chemins qui montent*, Paris, Le Seuil, 1957, pp. 208–209) ('They [the colonisers] occupy all the best places, all the places, and always end up getting rich [...] Our country is no poorer than any other, but to whom is it "our country"? Not those who are dying of starvation in it, anyway'). The hero of the novel, Amer, experiences some of the identity crisis that Feraoun was enduring himself: 'Que suis-je, se demande-t-il... je ne renonce à rien... Suis-je Kabyle, moi, ou Français?' (pp. 211–12) ('"Who am I,"

he asked himself, "... I don't renounce anything. Am I Kabyle, myself, or French?"').
It should also be noted that the narrative of the novel is concerned with the inner life
of its characters, and in the second part, the reader is presented with Amer's diary in
which his internal struggle is made manifest.

40. The text of Camus's communication appears in *Actuelles III*.

41. See Gleyze, *Mouloud Feraoun*, p. 110.

42. Feraoun also recounts the episode more fully in a letter to René and Jeannine
Nouelle written on the same day, 18 September 1949: 'Naturellement cette histoire
m'a secoué au plus haut point. Ça me devient une espèce d'obsession' ('Naturally the
story shook me to the maximum. That becomes a sort of obsession with me').

43. See, for example, the account of this in Chèze, *Mouloud Feraoun*, p. 125.

44. I am referring to the issues raised in, for example, Henry Rousso's *Le
Syndrome de Vichy de 1944 à nos jours*, and the subsequent debates on *devoir de
mémoire*, the duty of remembering, especially concerning the deportation of the Jews
from France. There is, however, also a case to be made for the need for nations to
undergo a 'necessary forgetting' in order to be able to move on. For a clear account
of the development of the Algerian War and especially a useful discussion of France's
attitude to war up to the present see Donadey, *Recasting Postcolonialism*, pp. 5–11,
'Historical Amnesia and the Construction of National Identity'.

45. For short, useful synopses of events in Algeria in the second part of the twentieth century see, for example, entries in Margaret Majumdar (ed.), *Francophone
Studies: The Essential Glossary*, London, Arnold, 2002.

46. Djebar, *Le Blanc de l'Algérie*, p. 230.

47. Djebar, *Le Blanc de l'Algérie*, p. 12.

Chapter Three pp. 131–204

All translations of *La Statue de sel* and of works of criticism are by Helena Scott. All
translations of *Le Scorpion* are taken from Eleanor Levieux (trans.), *The Scorpion*,
New York, Grossman, 1971.

1. Albert Memmi, *Le Nomade immobile*, Paris, Arléa, 2000, 'Prologue', p. 10.

2. Albert Memmi in Jeanyves Guérin (ed.), *Albert Memmi: Ecrivain et sociologue*, Paris, L'Harmattan, 1990, p. 164.

3. *Le Magazine Littéraire*, no. 188, Octobrer 1982; and see for example Guy
Dugas, *Albert Memmi: Ecrivain de la déchirure*, Québec, Editions Naaman, 1984,
p. 31 for an analysis of the duo in his work. Robert Young also notes that Memmi
was 'the first to protest against the strict dichotomy between coloniser and colonised
laid down by Sartre and Fanon, arguing for an understanding of the mutual mental
relations between coloniser and colonised [...] while at the same time undoing the
dialectic by emphasising the spectral presence of all those liminal figures who slipped
between these two categories' (*Postcolonialism*, pp. 422–23).

4. See, for example, Albert Memmi, *La Dépendance*, Paris, Gallimard, 1993
(1979), p. 166.

5. Guy Dugas, 'une philosophie des relations humaines', in *Albert Memmi:
Ecrivain de la déchirure*, p. 28.

6. Albert Memmi, 'Autoportrait', *Souffles*, no. 6, 1967, p. 9; here Memmi names
his 'mixed marriage' to a French Catholic, evoked in *Agar* as holding at that time 'la
clef de mon existence actuelle' ('the key to my present life').

7. A full consideration of the autobiographical elements of Memmi's work would
necessitate a full-length study and would include the other fictional texts (*Agar*, *Le
Désert*, *Le Pharaon*) as well as published full-length interviews (*Entretien*, with

Robert Davies, 1975; *La Terre Intérieure (entretiens avec Victor Malka)*, 1976; *Le Juif et l'autre (propos recueillis par M. Chavardès et F. Kasbi)*, 1995) and texts such as those on happiness (*Bonheurs*, 1992; *Ah, quel bonheur!*, 1995; *L'Exercice du bonheur*, 1998), in addition to the earlier sociological works. Here I have chosen two texts that show a development in the author's writing strategy. Memmi's work on Jewish identity should also be read against the background of the first lengthy study of French Jewish identity by Jean-Paul Sartre, *Réflexions sur la question juive* (1946). Sartre's work is an important reference point for Memmi, as will be seen in the course of this chapter. For a discussion of Sartre and Memmi on Jewish identity see Joyce Block Lazarus, *Strangers and Sojourners: Jewish Identity in Contemporary Francophone Fiction*, New York, Peter Lang, 1999, p. 129. She writes that '[what] is at stake in *La Statue de sel* is whether Jewishness (*"la judéité"*) as a way of life and sense of peoplehood can survive in an overwhelmingly racist world' (p. 18). She also analyses the ways in which Memmi uses 'sensory descriptions and spatial imagery to convey Mordekhai's Jewish perspective on life as seen through his physical encoun- ters with his world' (p. 18), noting how in the movement from the 'The Impasse' to the third section entitled 'The World', chronological, geographical and psycholog- ical evolution is suggested by 'the transformation of spatial images and sensory notations associated with warmth and coldness, darkness and light, enclosures and openness, noises and silence, and pleasant and disagreeable aromas. Spatial and sensory imagery convey the tension of Mordekhai's outsider status through their changing, ambivalent connections' (p. 18). Her reading partly focuses on the way that Benillouche presents his complex relationship with his society and 'portrays his Jewish identity in terms of a visceral attachment to his Jewish roots and community' (p. 18). She very suggestively writes that 'Mordekhai reinvents Judaism based on the notion of *tikkur olam* (repair of the world) and social justice. Mordekhai's concept of Judaism resembles that of a twentieth century theologian, Mordecai Kaplan (1881–1983) who defined Judaism as a civilization and a peoplehood as well as a religion, and who considered "moral responsibility in action" to be the highest purpose of religion' (pp. 24–25). Her reference is to Mordecai M. Kaplan, *Dynamic Judaism*, New York, Fordham University Press, 1985.

8. *Portrait d'un Juif*, p. 21, preface, also quoted by Jacqueline Arnaud, *La Littérature maghrébine de langue française*, vol. I: *Origines et perspectives*, Paris, Publisud, 1986, p. 312.

9. *Le Nomade immobile*, p. 199

10. *Souffles*, no. 6, 1965, 'Fiche', p. 5.

11. See the diagram illustrating this in Dugas, *Albert Memmi: Ecrivain de la déchirure*, p. 46.

12. *Le Nomade immobile*, p. 110.

13. *Le Nomade immobile*, pp. 97–98. He goes on in this section, 'Les Fécondités de l'exil' (pp. 102–104), to reiterate his multiple sites of belonging through language, culture, education and profession: 'je soutiens que si j'omettais une de mes dimen- sions, une de mes appartenances, je fausserais le sens de l'ensemble. Mieux: c'est cette complexité reconnue et acceptée par moi qui sera ma meilleure leçon. Mon exem- plarité, si exemplarité il y a, tient dans cette diversité affirmée, sans orgueil mais sans humilité' ('I maintain that if I omitted one of my dimensions, one of my loyalties, I would falsify the meaning of the whole. Or rather, it is this complexity, recognised and accepted by me, which will be my best lesson. My example, if it exists, consists of that diversity, affirmed without pride but without humility'). And he asserts the necessity today of the acknowledgement of the diversity of identity of so many people. Later in the text, in 'La Dimension juive', he goes on to state that although the four parts of his existence represented in the *blason* previously referred to are essential to

him, there is a hierarchy, and that the fact of being Jewish has had the most impact on him, both negatively and positively (p. 121).

14. *Le Nomade immobile*, pp. 57–59. The respect and affection for his teachers resonates with that of Feraoun, but is tempered by Memmi's own experience.

15. *Le Nomade immobile*, pp. 62–63.

16. *Le Nomade immobile*, p. 70.

17. 'Autoportrait', p. 8; quoted by Déjeux, *Littérature maghrébine*, p. 305.

18. *Le Nomade immobile*, p. 60.

19. The preface also tells us much about Camus during this period as Algeria engages in the war for its independence. See also *Le Nomade immobile*, pp. 72–73 for Memmi's version of the publication of *La Statue de sel* and its preface.

20. For further information on this, see Déjeux, *Littérature maghrébine*, pp. 303–304. The first two anthologies were published by Présence Africaine, the third by Seghers. It should also be noted that, although Memmi goes to France definitively a decade after the end of the Second World War, his move there is characteristic of a much greater influx of Sephardi Jews into France following the conflict. See also n. 49 below.

21. *Le Nomade immobile*, p. 74.

22. *Le Nomade immobile*, p. 145.

23.*Le Nomade immobile*, p. 149, p. 152. The reference is to the first poem in Baudelaire's *Les Fleurs du mal*, 'Au lecteur'. Memmi has notably omitted the word 'hypocrite' from Baudelaire's own address to the reader.

24. *Le Nomade immobile*, p. 85.

25. *Le Nomade immobile*, pp. 87–88. He also clears up in this section, 'Retour au pays', the misconception that he knew Frantz Fanon or his work well. It is rather that their books were appearing at the same time: 'Si nous avions fait connaissance, il n'est pas sûr que nous nous fussions entendus; entier comme il l'était et comme je l'étais à l'époque [...] Mais je ne l'avais pas lu, et je ne sais pas s'il m'avait lu; notre parenté venait de l'air du temps. Nous avions découvert l'un et l'autre le scandale de la colonisation et la nécessité d'y mettre fin; mais, à partir de là, nos interprétations et nos propositions différaient notablement' (p. 86) ('If we had met, it is not certain that we would have understood each other, despite his and my own integrity at the time [...] But I hadn't read him and I don't know if he had read me; our similarity came from the atmosphere of the times. Each of us had discovered the scandal of colonisation and the need to put a stop to it; but from that point on our interpretations and proposals differed widely').

26. See *Le Nomade immobile*, pp. 92–93; and he notes that 'sauf quelques personnages secondaires et les détails de l'histoire sentimentale, tout est exact' ('except for a few minor characters and the details of the love-story, it is all true'). A recent book by Guy Dugas, *Albert Memmi: Du malheur d'être juif au bonheur sépharade*, details events of Memmi's life which can be compared with their fictional transposition.

27. Dugas, *Albert Memmi: Du malheur d'être juif au bonheur sépharade*, p. 12. See also Robert Young on the problem of the acculturation of the Jews in North Africa, who were, in his opinion, 'strangers to their own culture and even to cultural memory, strangers to Arab or Berber culture, and yet strangers also to the French culture and language which they have acquired' (*Postcolonialism*, p. 422).

28. Dugas, *Albert Memmi: Du malheur d'être juif au bonheur sépharade*, pp. 22–23. Dugas notes that in a 1906 report for the French administration in Tunisia there were 1,700,000 Muslims, 64,170 Jews and 130,000 Europeans (81,156 Italians; 34,610 French).

29. See Arnaud, *La Littérature maghrébine*, p. 314.

30. *Le Nomade immobile*, p. 109.

31. *Le Nomade immobile*, pp. 188–89. Memmi has often had to defend his work. As far back as 1953 when he presented *La Statue de sel*, he caused controversy in Tunisia. Memmi had been back in Tunisia since 1949. Four lengthy extracts had been published before the novel appeared, from October–November 1952 to February 1953 in *Les Temps Modernes*, and had already been reviewed in *La Presse de Tunisie*, on 6 February 1953: 'En mars 1953, il présente son roman dans une salle de fêtes du lycée Carnot pleine à craquer, et devant son père presque aveugle. Face à un public déchaîné, il doit se défendre, justifier son choix, récuser les clefs que ses proches croient trouver au roman, affronter leurs attaques et mêmes leurs insultes. A la manière du jeune Chraïbi reniant son premier roman, il culpabilise et éprouve, en public, la tentation de renoncer à l'écriture!' ('In March 1953, he presented his novel in a public hall at the Lycée Carnot which was filled to bursting with people, in the presence of his father who was almost blind. Confronted with a furious audience, he had to defend himself, justify his choice, rebut the clues which those close to him thought they could detect in the novel, and face up to their attacks and even insults. Rather like the young Chraïbi denying his first novel, he felt guilty and experienced in public the temptation to renounce writing!') (Dugas, *Albert Memmi: Du Malheur d'être juif au bonheur sépharade*, p. 40). One of the scenes that would most scandalise the Jewish community was the presentation of the narrator's mother's dance, in which she is surrounded by black musicians and a live white cockerel is sacrificed to save her sister (*La Statue du sel*, p. 31). It is a scene that affects Benillouche profoundly as he questions both the Oriental and the Western values which he feels are part of him.

32. *Le Nomade immobile*, p. 12. He also details later in this text how Jean Rousset, curator at the 'Bibliothèque du Souk-et-Attarine, l'équivalent de la Bibliothèque nationale' sent him the coin with the Memmi name on it that appears in *Le Scorpion*: 'la fameuse petite "monnaie romaine de Byzacène frappée au nom de Memmi, famille consulaire…", m'écrivait-il. Il l'avait trouvé lui-même dans les ruines de Carthage. Je la montre souvent à mes visiteurs à Paris – sa reproduction, car la vraie est dans mon coffre à la banque – qui en sont éblouis; pas autant que moi cependant' (p. 96) ('the famous little "Roman coin from Byzacene struck in the name of Memmi, a consular family…" he wrote to me. He had found it himself in the ruins of Carthage. I often show it to my visitors in Paris – a copy of it, because the original is in my safe at the bank – and they are stunned by it; but not as much as I am'). A reference to and reproduction of the coin appear in *Le Scorpion*.

33. *Le Nomade immobile*, pp. 48–50.

34. *Le Nomade immobile*, p. 52. See Seán Hand's analysis of the 'real truth value' of Memmi's work in 'Don't Look Back: Albert Memmi's *La Statue de sel*' in Ibnlfassi and Hitchcott (eds), *African Francophone Writing*, p. 94.

35. *Le Nomade immobile*, p. 55.

36. *Le Nomade immobile*, p. 95.

37. *Le Nomade immobile*, p. 115.

38. *Le Nomade immobile*, pp. 130–31.

39. *Le Nomade immobile*, p. 203.

40. Memmi in Guérin (ed.), *Albert Memmi: Ecrivain et sociologue*, p. 165.

41. For the writer Memmi will become, a further reflection in this chapter on language is interesting, revealing his belief in the power and magic of language for good and evil, so much so that language for him has the 'density' of the things it describes (p. 45). See Block Lazarus, *Strangers and Sojourners*, p. 26 on Memmi's relationship to the French language as an 'instrument of liberation'. See also Hand's analysis of language as the key to self-liberation in 'Don't Look Back', p. 97.

42. *Le Nomade immobile*, pp. 36–37.

43. *Le Nomade immobile*, p. 13.

44. *Le Nomade immobile*, p. 27.

45. *Le Nomade immobile*, pp. 25–26.

46. *Le Nomade immobile*, p. 42.

47. At this stage the looking in the mirror does not provoke the kind of identity crisis experienced in fiction by Roquentin in Sartre's *La Nausée*, or in life famously by the young Jean Tardieu. The identity crisis experienced later by Benillouche in the mirror of a café irresistibly recalls the existential crisis of Roquentin.

48. This cousin is the first in a series of possible doubles, the men Memmi (and his protagonists) could have been if he had not taken the route of education; compare, for example, Bina in *Le Scorpion*.

49. Memmi would dedicate some of his writing to working through a notion of being Jewish that was not based simply on religious observance, and he developed the concept of *judéité* in addition to *judaïsme* and *judaïcité* to describe a cultural, but not necessarily religious, belonging to a Jewish identity and community. See the discussion of these concepts in Block Lazarus, *Strangers and Sojourners*, p. 4, and Leon I. Yudkin, *Jewish Writing and Identity in the Twentieth Century*, London, Croom Helm, 1982, p. 106. Yudkin analyses French Jewish literature against the background of the Revolution, Dreyfus, the Occupation, and the influx of Sephardi Jews into France after the Second World War.

50. *Le Nomade immobile*, p. 169. He goes on to say that this image contrasted with what he saw at the time as the enlightened Christian priests who had as their model Saint Augustine, for example. This idealised notion of the religion of the colonisers would be destroyed when he had the chance to observe it in practice in France.

51. Henry provides an interesting counterpoint to the troubled Benillouche: 'Fils d'une Française et d'un Juif italien, de nationalité maltaise, sujet britannique, il ne se sentait de nulle part. Trop divers, il n'avait pas de problème particulier à résoudre. La dispute puis la séparation de ses parents portait au point sublime sa vie aérienne, libre comme un fil de la vierge' (p. 213) ('The son of a Frenchwoman and an Italian Jew, with Maltese nationality, a British subject, he did not feel he belonged anywhere. Being so diverse he had no particular problem to resolve. His parents' quarrel and subsequent separation took this detached, floating existence to extremes, leaving him as free as a gossamer-thread').

52. It is only later that he realises that 'Marrou' never overcame his own identity problems. See, for example, Dugas on Amrouche's (Marrou's) position in *Albert Memmi: Du malheur d'être juif au bonheur sépharade*. Born in 1905 in Petite Kabylie (Lesser Kabylia) to parents who converted to Christianity, the writer was 'constamment écartelé entre ses origines et son acculturation, la religion musulmane et le christianisme, la France "esprit de mon âme" et l'Algérie "âme de mon esprit"' ('constantly torn between his origins and his acculturation, the Muslim religion and Christianity, France "the spirit of my soul" and Algeria "soul of my spirit"') (pp. 87–88). He died in April 1962, according to Memmi 'exhausted' by Algeria, a month after the assassination of Mouloud Feraoun.

53. Albert Memmi, 'Les Pauvres', in *Ce que je crois*, p. 58.

54. In 'Autoportrait', Memmi also notes this feeling: 'comme la ville était divisée en quartiers hostiles et méfiants, j'évitais de m'aventurer longtemps ailleurs que dans la nôtre. Ainsi, chacun vivait pour soi, dans ses traditions, ses préjugés, ses peurs et ses haines, Arabes, Juifs, Français, Italiens, Maltais, Grecs, Russes' (p. 8) ('as the town was divided into mutually hostile and mistrustful neighbourhoods, I avoided spending much time in any other district than our own. And so they each lived their

own life, amidst their own traditions, prejudices, fears and hatreds: Arabs, Jews, French, Italians, Maltese, Greeks, Russians').

55. Benillouche does explore the possibility of Jews and Arabs working together in the Nationalist movement, encouraged by Ben Smaan, an Arab in his class, whom he had joined in taunting one teacher's negative appraisal of the French Revolution.

56. *Le Nomade immobile*, p. 211. See also Hand on the move from the 'Impasse' to the 'Départ' and the 'remarkable formal effect' of 'L'Epreuve': 'This moment of realisation is then itself formally exploited in a further instance of looking back/looking forward, for the scene is repeated but transposed to the penultimate chapter [...] A comparison of these two versions (which obliges the reader to look back and look forward) shows how the later one is both dramatically more concise [...] and more politically adumbrated by clear views on Vichy, Western culture and academic and administrative hierarchies' ('Don't Look Back', pp. 99–100).

57. Memmi, *Ce que je crois*, p. 32.

58. Dugas, *Albert Memmi: Ecrivain de la déchirure*, p. 20.

59. Memmi, *Portrait d'un Juif*, p. 198; also quoted by Arnaud, *La Littérature maghrébine*, p. 345; note also the figures of Uncle Khaïlou in *Portrait d'un Juif* and Uncle Makhlouf in *Le Scorpion*.

60. See Arnaud, *La Littérature maghrébine*, on the 'extemporality' of some of the chapters in *La Statue de sel*.

61. Memmi, 'Autoportrait', *Souffles*, no. 6, 1967, p. 6. If there are analogies to be made, I would see Memmi's concerns here as having more in common with the work of Robert Pinget, especially in his use of repetition and contradiction, than with that of Robbe-Grillet and Butor, from whom he explicitly distanced himself. See for example the theories of Robbe-Grillet in *Pour un nouveau roman*, Paris, Minuit, 1963.

62. Jacqueline Arnaud is also very severe about how Memmi 'exaggerates' in *La Statue de sel* the ruptures with his family, and takes him to task for the importance given to the self in his writing without 'the humour', as she calls it, of a Michel Leiris or a Henri Michaux (*La Littérature maghrébine*, p. 332). This is a telling example of the Eurocentric attitudes of the French critic. The ruptures with the family are part of Memmi's political education as colonised subject.

63. These are unfortunately not all published in the later paperback editions of *Le Scorpion* and therefore not readily accessible to readers. This suppression of visual images removes a layer of the text's multiple discourses. For a much fuller, and revealing, discussion of their status and meaning in the text, see Doris Ruhe, 'Le Scorpion en phénix: L'écriture autobiographique d'Albert Memmi', in Ruhe and Hornung (eds), *Postcolonialisme et Autobiographie*, pp. 53–67. The question of the scorpion as symbol of the Jewish people is also discussed, with reference to Marc Brulard's *Le Scorpion, symbole du peuple juif dans l'art religieux des XIVᵉ, XVᵉ, XVIᵉ siècles*, Paris, E. de Broccard, 1935. In the discussion included at the end of Ruhe's article, originally a conference paper, Memmi notes that critics have not paid sufficient attention to the use of illustrations in his work and adds that 'l'utilisation des illustrations chez moi ce n'est pas de l'illustration, c'est une autre dimension du texte' (p. 69) ('the use of illustrations in my work is not illustration, it's another dimension of the text'). It should be noted that the 1986 Gallimard Folio reprint of *Le Scorpion* (used here) also omits the final section 'Chronique du Royaume du Dedans' which is included in the 2001 reprint. Memmi comments on this in Guérin (ed.), *Albert Memmi, écrivain et sociologue*, p. 164: 'Les lecteurs des éditions Gallimard n'avaient pas perçu la correspondance', and they suggested publishing the section separately, which was not done. Also quoted by Ruhe, 'Le Scorpion en phénix', pp. 54–55.

64. Memmi, *La Terre intérieure*, p. 163. Also quoted by Guy Dugas,

'L'Iconotexte dans l'œuvre de fiction d'Albert Memmi', in Guérin (ed.), *Albert Memmi: Ecrivain et sociologue*, p. 71. *La Terre intérieure* contains illustrations (particularly photographs of Memmi's family and the Tunisian Jewish community), as does *Le Désert*, for example. Dugas also notes that this is 'une pratique icono-graphique assez répandue [...] parmi les écrivains juifs du Maghreb' (p. 72) ('an iconographic practice which is fairly widespread [...] among Jewish writers of the Maghreb'). It seems, therefore, as Dugas suggests, that the illustrations provide a link between past and present.

65. Dugas, 'L'Iconotexte dans l'œuvre de fiction d'Albert Memmi', p. 74.

66. For a discussion of genealogy in Memmi, see Corinne Nolin, 'Nomadisme et généalogie: Albert Memmi ou la condition impossible', in Ruhe and Hornung (eds), *Postcolonialisme et Autobiographie*, pp. 35–51. See also Dugas, *Albert Memmi: Du Malheur d'être juif au bonheur sépharade*, pp. 55–57. He also notes, as does Marcel in the text, that the maternal origins are not considered. Albert Memmi's brother Georges Memmi, in an autobiographical text, seeks to rehabilitate the figure of the mother: *Qui se souvient du Café Rubens?*, Paris, Lattès, 1984.

67. These writers include Robbe-Grillet in his 'Romanesques' trilogy (*Le Miroir qui revient*, Paris, Minuit, 1985; *Angélique, ou l'enchantement*, Paris, Minuit, 1988; *Les Derniers Jours de Corinthe*, Paris, Minuit, 1994) questioning the ordering of a life and the relationship between autobiography and fiction; Nathalie Sarraute's device of the 'alter ego' policing the account of her childhood in *Enfance* (Paris, Gallimard, 1983); Marguerite Duras rewriting versions of her early life in *L'Amant* (Paris, Minuit, 1984) and *L'Amant de la Chine du Nord* (Paris, Gallimard, 1991). I am also thinking again of Pinget's 'carnets de Monsieur Songe', where the fictional character apparently publishes his own notebooks (*Monsieur Songe*, Paris, Minuit, 1982; and the notebooks *Le Harnais*, 1984; *Charrue*, 1985; *Du Nerf*, 1990). In a note at the end of *Le Scorpion*, the author announces his intention to publish sepa-rately other texts found in 'la cave'.

68. See Memmi's account of his own detached retina and his fears for his eyesight (in 1970) in *Le Nomade immobile*: 'Ces angoisses transparaissent dans un roman, écrit juste avant, dont le héros rêve qu'il risque la cécité' (pp. 133–34) ('These torments come out in a novel written shortly before, whose hero dreams that he is in danger of going blind').

69. See the table on p. 174 of the novel.

70. There is also an analogy to be made here with the kind of demystifying, decoding reading of apparently 'natural' cultural productions exercised by Roland Barthes in *Mythologies*, Paris, Seuil, 1957.

71. It is interesting that the title of *Agar* becomes *L'Etrangère* ('The Foreign Woman'): in the American translation the title becomes *Strangers*.

72. *Le Nomade immobile*, pp. 145–46; a further reflection on this incident is more revealing still of the relation between truth, literature and memory. Memmi adds that he is unsure whether in fact this was recounted to him by Amrouche and that he was only invited for dessert at that dinner with Gide: 'Preuve supplémentaire que la littérature est bien un mélange de vérité et de fiction, involontaire quelquefois' ('Additional proof that literature really is a mixture of truth and fiction, sometimes involuntary').

73. The father in *La Statue de sel* is also asthmatic, of course.

74. We might also note here the importance of the doctor figure – the profession that the hero of *La Statue de sel* refuses; furthermore Bina constantly interpolates into his story the address 'Docteur' (for example, pp. 117, 120, 121). In the diary that Memmi kept while working on *Le Scorpion*, he notes that the 'E' of Emile's name = *écrivain*, writer, and the 'M' of Marcel's = *médecin*, doctor. See Dugas, *Albert*

Memmi. Du Malheur d'être juif au bonheur sépharade, p. 101.

75. Again compare the textual strategy of Robert Pinget in a text such as *Quelqu'un*, Paris, Minuit, 1965.

76. Nolin, 'Nomadisme et généalogie', p. 41.

77. Compare Pinget's use of contradiction in a text such as *Baga*, Paris, Minuit, 1958; and again in *Quelqu'un*.

78. Bourguiba was not removed from power until 1988 after Ben Ali had restyled Neo-Destour as the Constitutional Democratic Rally (RCD). Ben Ali established rights for women, and took a hard line against Islamic fundamentalism. He continued to be accused of violations of human rights, although Tunisia is generally viewed favourably by the West in this respect compared with many other Arab countries.

79. Tahar Bekri, 'Une lecture de *La Statue de sel*', in Guérin (ed.), *Albert Memmi: Ecrivain et sociologue*, p. 27.

80. *Le Nomade immobile*, pp. 150–51.

81. *Le Nomade immobile*, p. 150.

82. *Le Nomade immobile*, p. 25.

83. *Le Nomade immobile*, p. 25.

84. *Le Nomade immobile*, p. 267.

85. *Le Nomade immobile*, p. 274.

86. As Guy Dugas notes, any influences or exchanges with Feraoun are less evident than those between Memmi and Jean Amrouche, but the two men certainly corresponded (*Albert Memmi: Du Malheur d'être juif au bonheur sépharade*, pp. 88–89).

87. See the extracts of the unpublished diary reproduced by Dugas in *Albert Memmi: Du Malheur d'être juif au bonheur sépharade*. He also notes the analogy to be made with Gide (who of course features in *Le Scorpion*) and his (published) diary, kept while writing *Les Faux-Monnayeurs* (1925) (*The Counterfeiters*): *Journal des faux-monnayeurs*, Paris, Gallimard, 1927.

Chapter Four pp. 205–247

All translations are by Helena Scott.

1. Abdelkébir Khatibi, 'Le Métissage culturel', 'Manifeste', *Abdelkébir Khatibi*, Casablanca, Al Asa-Okad, 1990, p. 149. See also *Francophonie et idiomes littéraires*, Rabat, Al Kalam, 1989. Also quoted by Marc Gontard, *Le Moi étrange: Littérature marocaine de langue française*, Paris, L'Harmattan, 1993, pp. 202–203.

2. Abdelkébir Khatibi, *Par-dessus l'épaule* ('Over the Shoulder'), Paris, Aubier, 1988, p. 69.

3. Abdelkébir Khatibi (with J. Arnaud, J. Déjeux and R. Arlette Roth), *Anthologie des écrivains maghrébins d'expression française*, Paris, Présence Africaine, 1964.

4. 1968 is obviously a key moment in post-war French politics and society, and the question of the role of the committed writer is very much a Sartrean problematic linked to the period of the Second World War and its aftermath in France, although Khatibi's focus remains, of course, North Africa. I have previously indicated the importance of some of Sartre's thinking for Memmi.

5. Lucy Stone McNeece, 'Rescripting Modernity: Abdelkébir Khatibi and the Archaeology of Signs', in Mildred Mortimer (ed.), *Maghrebian Mosaic: A Literature in Transition*, London, Lynne Rienner, 2001, pp. 96–97. This is a clear, concise account of the breadth of Khatibi's concerns.

6. John Erickson, '"At the Threshold of the Untranslatable": *Love in Two*

Languages of Abdelkébir Khatibi', in *Islam and Postcolonial Narrative*, p. 96.

7. Réda Bensmaia, 'Multilingualism and National "Character": On Abdelkébir Khatibi's "Bilangage"', in Anne-Emmanuelle Berger (ed.), *Algeria in Others' Languages*, Ithaca, NY, Cornell University Press, 2002, p. 181.

8. Winifred Woodhull, *Transfigurations of the Maghreb: Feminism, Decolonisation and Liberation*, Minneapolis, University of Minnesota Press, 1993, introduction, p. x and p. xvii. As previously noted with reference to Fanon and Memmi, for example, gender issues are often paid little attention or are absent from the work of male postcolonial writers, as Anne Donadey has also pointed out.

9. *La Mémoire tatouée*, Paris, Denoël, 1971, p. 10; Khatibi's own emphasis.

10. Hassan Wahbi, *Les Mots du monde: Khatibi et le récit*, Agadir, Université Ibnou Zohr, Publications de la Faculté des Lettres et Sciences Humaines, Série thèses et mémoires, no. 3, 1995, pp. 14–16.

11. Rachida Saigh Bousta, *Lecture des récits de Abdelkébir Khatibi: Ecriture, Mémoire, Imaginaire...*, Casablanca, Afrique Orient, 1996, p. 9.

12. Abdelkébir Khatibi, *Al Assa* (Rabat), no.17 (February 1980); also quoted by Abdallah Memmes, *Abdelkébir Khatibi: L'écriture de la dualité*, Paris, L'Harmattan, 1994, p. 4.

13. Marc Gontard, 'Eros mystique', *Al Assa*, no. 17 (Febraury 1980), p. 58, quoted by Bousta, *Lecture des récits de Abdelkébir Khatibi*, p. 138, n. 48; the author intervenes in the text to express his love of 'la Dédicataire – Marie-Charlotte'.

14. Hassan Wahbi, *Les Mots du monde*, p. 72. This concern with the actual process of writing and the 'coming into being' of the literary text is a preoccupation which, again as for Memmi, we may compare with that of the French New Novelists.

15. Bousta, *Lecture des récits de Abdelkébir Khatibi*, pp. 38–41; an interesting concept given the concept of *fiction identitaire* that I discussed in the introduction.

16. Bousta, *Lecture des récits de Abdelkébir Khatibi*, p. 39.

17. *La Mémoire tatouée*, p. 64. See also Rippin, *Muslims*, pp. 16–18 and pp. 23–24 on the place of Abraham in the establishing of Islamic belief.

18. Sufism is the mystical system of the Sufis (Muslim ascetics and mystics), the inner way or spiritual path to mystical union with God. Its followers may be ascetics who isolate themselves from society, or more usually members of a Sufi order. There are many orders, each founded by a devout individual and each having different devotional practices. The movement seems to have started in the seventh century as a reaction against the strict formality of orthodox teaching and reached its peak in the thirteenth century. Sufism has been responsible for worldwide missionary activity. In the nineteenth and twentieth centuries Sufic orders sometimes took on overtly political roles, notably in the Libyan resistance to Italian colonial occupation. Adapted from *The Oxford English Reference Dictionary*, 1996; see also, for example, Eva de Vitray-Meyerovitch, *Anthologie du soufisme*, Paris, Albin Michel, 1995 (1978), p. 15: 'Sur ce chemin spirituel, nous avons indiqué de notre mieux quelques points de repère: une certaine notion du temps, des prescriptions d'ascèse, le saint, la mort, la joie, la mise au diapason de la beauté dans un cosmos sacralisé, une psychologie transcendantale; et, embrassant le tout, l'unité de Dieu, l'unicité de l'existence, et donc l'universalisme essentiel de l'Islam' ('On this spiritual path, we have done our best to indicate some sign-posts: a certain notion of time, prescriptions of asceticism, the saint, death, joy, the falling into line of beauty in a sacralised cosmos, a transcendental psychology; and, embracing everything, the unity of God, the unicity of existence, and hence the essential universality of Islam'). See also Rippin, *Muslims*, especially pp. 127–39, to which I have also referred in the introduction.

19. Memmes, *Abdelkébir Khatibi*, p. 88. See this analysis especially for a clear presentation of the 'plot/story' and the 'characters' (*Le Maître* ['The Master']; *Le Disciple* ['The Disciple']; *L'Echanson* ['The Cupbearer']; *Muthna*) in the text, and of

the use made of Sufi mysticism, especially Ibn' Arabi. Marc Gontard has also written penetrating analyses of this extremely complex text in *La Violence du texte: La Littérature marocaine de langue française*, Paris, L'Harmattan; Rabat, Smer, 1981, which Memmes also discusses and extends, trying to bring together the discussion of ideas presented by Gontard with an attention to the actual processes of writing in the text.

20. The recurrence of this theme of the love between a Frenchwoman and a North African man in, for example, Feraoun's unfinished novel *L'Anniversaire* and in Memmi's *Agar* (referred to in previous chapters), in which the confrontation between the two societies is essentially sexualised, is indicative of the ways in which such relations are played out in writing in the postcolonial context.

21. Bousta, *Lecture des récits de Abdelkébir Khatibi*, pp. 79–80.

22. Memmes, *Abdelkébir Khatibi*, p. 99.

23. Wahbi, *Les Mots du monde*, pp. 113–14.

24. Memmes, *Abdelkébir Khatibi*, pp. 19–20.

25. *Amour bilingue*, p. 75. There are several interesting analyses of Khatibi's concept of the *bi-langue*, for example those of Réda Bensmaia ('Multilingualism and National "Character"'; Bensmaia also provides a very suggestive analysis of the use of the proper name in this respect) and of John Erickson (in *Islam and Postcolonial Narrative*).

26. Gontard, *Le Moi étrange*, p. 53.

27. Bousta, *Lecture des récits de Abdelkébir Khatibi*, p. 97.

28. Gontard, *Le Moi étrange*, p. 61.

29. *Un Eté à Stockholm*, p. 12.

30. Gontard, *Le Moi étrange*, pp. 66–67; p. 72.

31. *Un Eté à Stockholm*, p. 27.

32. Wahbi, *Les Mots du monde*, p. 160. Rabat is the city in which Khatibi lives.

33. Bousta, *Lecture des récits de Abdelkébir Khatibi*, p. 134.

34. Memmes, *Abdelkébir Khatibi*, p. 22.

35. Abdelkébir Khatibi, *Lamatif* (Casablanca), no. 25 (January 1977).

36. Memmes, *Abdelkébir Khatibi*, p. 33.

37. Memmes, *Abdelkébir Khatibi*, p. 33.

38. Memmes, *Abdelkébir Khatibi*, p. 36.

39. This insistence on the 'collective' is compounded by double standards in reading, especially by French critics.

40. Wahbi, *Les Mots du monde*, p. 165.

41. *Par-dessus l'épaule*, p. 40.

42. Gontard, *Le Moi étrange*, p. 49. The use of the 'fragment' also recalls the use made of it by Roland Barthes in his own subversive autobiographical text *Roland Barthes par Roland Barthes* (Paris, Seuil, 1975), and in *Fragments d'un discours amoureux* (1977). See for example 'Le Fragment comme illusion' ('The Fragment as Illusion'): 'J'ai l'illusion de croire qu'en brisant mon discours, je cesse de discourir imaginairement sur moi-même' ('I have the illusion of believing that by breaking my discourse I cease to discourse imaginatively about myself'); 'Du fragment au journal' ('From Fragment to Diary'): 'Sous l'alibi de la dissertation détruite, on en vient à la pratique régulière du fragment; puis du fragment, on glisse au "journal"' ('Under the alibi of a destroyed dissertation, one arrives at the regular practice of the fragment; then from the fragment one slips to the "diary"' (*Roland Barthes*, p. 99). Note also the section 'Le Livre du Moi' ('The Book of Myself'): 'Quoiqu'il soit fait apparemment d'une suite d'"idées", ce livre n'est pas le livre de ces idées; il est le livre du Moi, le livre de mes résistances à mes propres idées [...] La substance de ce livre est donc totalement romanesque' ('Although it is apparently made up of a sequence of "ideas",

this book is not the book of those ideas; it is the book of Myself, the book of my resistances to my own ideas [...] The substance of this book is therefore totally fictional') (*Roland Barthes*, pp. 123–24).

43. *Par-dessus l'épaule*, p. 56.

44. *Par-dessus l'épaule*, p. 89.

45. Lucy Stone McNeece, 'Decolonizing the Sign: Language and Identity in Abdelkébir Khatibi's *La Mémoire tatouée*', *Yale French Studies*, 83 (1993), *Post/Colonial Conditions*, ed. F. Lionnet and R. Scharfman, p. 17.

46. McNeece, 'Decolonizing the Sign', p. 18.

47. Wahbi, *Les Mots du monde*, p. 23; see the whole of this subtle and revealing analysis of the name in the first chapter 'Sur les traces du nom propre', pp. 19–34.

48. Wahbi, *Les Mots du monde*, p. 31.

49. Also again see the analysis of Wahbi, *Les Mots du monde*, Chapter 4, 'L'Autobiographie et son meta-texte', pp. 55–68.

50. Wahbi, *Les Mots du monde*, p. 49; the analysis of the pronominal movement is subtle and rewarding: 'Les voix de la personne, ces hôtes du moi, esquissent à leur manière le travail de la différence sur l'identité, du différent sur le même. Ce travail fait intervenir, dans l'espace de l'écriture autobiographique, une variante de la multiplicité. Aux différences pronominales se surimprime la différence du sujet comme personnage autobiographique' (p. 54) ('The voices of the person, those guests of myself, sketch in their own way the work of difference on identity, what is different on what is the same. Into the space of autobiographical writing, that work brings a variant of multiplicity into play. Upon pronominal differences is superimposed the difference of the subject as autobiographical character').

51. Wahbi, *Les Mots du monde*, pp. 64–65.

52. Wahbi, *Les Mots du monde*, p. 68.

53. See also Memmes, *Abdelkébir Khatibi*, p. 35.

54. See the very useful table produced by Memmes (*Abdelkébir Khatibi*, p. 25), which shows how events are presented in a way that disrupts the typical chronological sequence of a life story.

55. See also McNeece, 'Decolonizing the Sign', p. 19 on this point. Assia Djebar also pays close attention to inside/outside spaces in North African cultural, social and political life, with particular reference to the movement of women in those spaces.

56. Memmes, *Abdelkébir Khatibi*, p. 29.

57. McNeece, 'Decolonizing the Sign', p. 20; much of this description would again be valid for Assia Djebar's use of ancestral and contemporary women's voices in her work.

58. McNeece, 'Decolonizing the Sign'; see also McNeece's very useful analysis of the different use and status of signs in the two cultures: the dense, mystical, erotic signs linked to the sacred in Khatibi's own culture, and the use of religious signs in Western religion that has become 'rational' and virtually secularised.

59. See also Bousta, *Lecture des récits de Abdelkébir Khatibi*, p. 29 on this point. The allusion to Robbe-Grillet does not contradict the points made about the French New Novel. It would not be until 1984 with *Le Miroir qui revient* (Paris, Minuit) that Robbe-Grillet would explicitly address the problems of autobiographical discourse, although it is true to say that his earlier texts are partly concerned with subjectivity and identity.

60. Memmes, *Abdelkébir Khatibi*, p. 29; reference to Gérard Genette, *Palimpsestes: la littérature au second degré*, Paris, Seuil, 1982. Again see Rippin, *Muslims*, for a clear explanation of the importance of commentaries on the Koran in Islamic culture.

61. The most obvious example of the violence of such a relationship is of course

that described by Khatibi's compatriot Driss Chraïbi in *Le Passé simple* (Paris, Denoël, 1954). He published his autobiography, *Le Monde à côté*, in 2000.

62. See, for example, Memmes, *Abdelkébir Khatibi*, p. 41, n. 41.

63. Lahsen Bougdal, 'De la modernité à l'historie: le traitement de l'espace maternel dans *La Mémoire tatouée* d'Abdelkébir Khatibi', *Le Maghreb Littéraire*, 3.6 (1999), pp. 23, 25, 26. There is an interesting comparison to the way in which Nabile Farès recuperates the voice of the feminine in a similar retracing of an archaic history that would come to replace the violence of Algerian colonial history.

64. Bousta, *Lecture des récits de Abdelkébir Khatibi*, pp. 18–19.

65. *La Mémoire tatouée*, p. 119.

66. See Smith and Watson (eds), *De/Colonising the Subject*, again as discussed in the first chapter. Although this is also true of a text such as *Le Scorpion*, it is more explicit and indeed more violent in Khatibi's work.

67. The idea of 'l'élaboration du mythe personnel' is analysed in Philippe Lejeune's *Le Pacte autobiographique*, p. 14.

68. McNeece, 'Decolonizing the Sign', p. 13.

69. Abdelkébir Khatibi, interview in *Pro-Culture* (Rabat), no. 12 (1976).

70. Michel Leiris, *L'Age d'homme*, Paris, Gallimard, 1939, p. 17.

71. Bousta, *Lecture des récits de Abdelkébir Khatibi*, p. 12. Her references are to Abdelfattah Kilito in *Les Séances: Récits et codes culturels chez Hamadhani et Hariri*, Paris, Sinbad, 1983, and Henry Corbin, *Imagination créatrice dans le soufisme d'Ibn Arabi*, Paris, Aubier, 1993. The term 'l'Adab' is usually used to refer to classical Arabic literature, as I have described in the introduction.

72. Abdelkébir Khatibi, *La Blessure du nom propre*, Paris, Denoël, 1974, p. 64.

73. *La Blessure du nom propre*, pp. 13–14.

74. *La Blessure du nom propre*, p. 61.

75. *La Blessure du nom propre*, p. 76.

76. *La Blessure du nom propre*, pp. 80–86.

77. *La Blessure du nom propre*, p. 83.

78. McNeece, 'Decolonizing the Sign', p. 13.

79. *La Blessure du nom propre*, p. 73.

80. Here we can also compare Memmi's theories on the 'duo' and on 'dependence' with reference to the relationship between the coloniser and the colonised.

81. *La Blessure du nom propre*, p. 104.

82. We clearly need to make a distinction between the period when Khatibi is writing and his perception of the historical use of the tattoo, and the use of the tattoo in the West for self-expression and self-adornment, which became increasingly popular in the latter part of the twentieth century.

83. *La Blessure du nom propre*, p. 106, n. 1.

84. It is interesting to note the frequent use Khatibi makes of the word 'identity' in this text, dating from the 1970s, when the concept of identity did not have the popular currency it gained in the 1990s with the rise of 'identity politics'. See for example John R. Gillis, 'Memory and Identity: The History of a Relationship', in *idem* (ed.), *Commemoration: The Politics of National Identity*, Princeton, NJ, Princeton University Press, 1994.

85. McNeece, 'Decolonizing the Sign', pp. 28–29. The notion of 'haunting' is explored by critics such as Avery F. Gordon in *Ghostly Matters: Haunting and the Sociological Imagination*, Minneapolis, University of Minnesota Press, 1997, and Fredric Jameson, 'Marx's Purloined Letter', in Michael Sprinker (ed.), *Ghostly Demarcations: A Symposium on Jacques Derrida's 'Specters of Marx'*, London, Verso, 1999, pp. 26–67.

86. McNeece, 'Decolonizing the Sign', p. 29. I am also reminded of the use made

of the *rosace* in the visual poetry of Pierre Albert-Birot, where it is linked to identity and the creation of the self in writing.

Chapter Five pp. 248–333

Translations of *L'Amour, la fantasia* are by Dorothy Blair, *Fantasia: An Algerian Cavalcade*, London and New York, Quartet, 1985. All translations of *Vaste est la prison* and critical texts are by Helena Scott.

1. Assia Djebar, 'La Langue dans l'espace ou l'espace dans la langue', in Dominique Johnson and Sylvie Ouzilleau (eds), *Mise en Scène d'Ecrivains: Assia Djebar, Nicole Brossard, Madeleine Gagnon et France Théoret*, Quebec, Le Griffon d'argile, 1993, p. 15.

2. Assia Djebar, 'Violence de l'autobiographie', in Ruhe and Hornung (eds), *Postcolonialisme et Autobiographie*, p. 93.

3. 'Langage – bagage lent, langues de l'esprit' as Michel Leiris defines it in 'Glossaire, j'y serre mes gloses' (1939), in *Mots sans mémoire*, Paris, Gallimard, 1969, p. 96. There is a further possible reference to Leiris in the title of one of the sections of *Vaste est la prison* ('Biffure...'), *Biffures* being the title of the first volume of Leiris's extended autobiographical project *La Règle du jeu*. I discussed in Chapter 1 the ways in which all writers concerned with the nature of selfhood struggle with a language with which to express their individual identity given that language predates the individual, who in the Lacanian analysis is 'born into it', and I cited the very powerful image of this with which Leiris opens this first volume. I also noted in the chapter on Khatibi the critic Philippe Lejeune's own play on words concerning the place of the reader in relation to Leiris's work: 'Leiris: s'y lire'.

4. See Clarisse Zimra, 'Autobiographie et Je/Jeux d'espace: Architecture de l'imaginaire dans le *Quatuor* d'Assia Djebar', in Ruhe and Hornung (eds), *Postcolonialisme et Autobiographie*, p. 125. In the same collection of papers, Assia Djebar talks (as she does in several interviews) about one of the 'triggers' for *L'Amour, la fantasia*: she wanted to know why she could not speak any words of love in French. This 'inability' clearly goes to the very core of her double culture and double identity, the dynamic that powers the autobiographical quest in her writing. We should also note that Khatibi's reflection on the use of French also concerns the expression of love in *Amour bilingue*.

5. See, for example, the work of the Moroccan sociologist Fatima Mernissi on women's situations in Islamic culture. See also Erickson, *Islam and Postcolonial Narrative*, pp. 40–46 for a succinct overview of the position of women in North African society.

6. Mireille Calle-Gruber, *Assia Djebar ou la résistance de l'écriture: Regards d'un écrivain d'Algérie*, Paris, Maisonneuve & Larose, 2001, p. 14.

7. Both of these texts have been translated into English and Djebar's work has received a considerable amount of attention in the United States. *L'Amour, la fantasia* (Paris, Albin Michel, 1995 [J.-C. Lattès, 1985]) is translated by Dorothy S. Blair as *Fantasia: An Algerian Cavalcade*, London and New York, Quartet Books, 1985. *Vaste est la prison* (Paris, Albin Michel, 1995) is translated by Betsy Wing as *So Vast the Prison*, New York, Seven Stories Press, 1999.

8. Translated by Dorothy S. Blair as *A Sister to Scheherazade*, London and New York, Quartet, 1987. For interesting analyses of this text, which has received less critical attention than the other two volumes of the quartet I am discussing here, see Calle-Gruber, *Assia Djebar ou la résistance de l'écriture*, pp. 53–67; and Donadey, *Recasting Postcolonialism*, Chapter 4, 'Inter/textual Subversions' (pp. 79–87), in

which she discusses the *Arabian Nights* as 'Narrative of the Frame', and Chapter 5, 'Refiguring French/Orientalist Painting' (pp. 96–102), in which she discusses the text in the light of Pierre Bonnard's work.

9. Assia Djebar, 'Une femme, un film, un regard', *Demain l'Afrique*, no. 1 (September 1977).

10. *Vaste est la prison*, pp. 167–72; see also the end of the book, pp. 347–48, where she becomes finally 'fugitive et le sachant, désormais' ('fugitive and knowing it, henceforth').

11. In the 'ouverture' to *Femmes d'Alger dans leur appartement*, Djebar is very careful to make clear that she does not 'speak for' other Arab women: 'Ne pas prétendre "parler pour", ou pire, "parler sur", à peine parler *près de*, et si possible *tout contre*: première des solidarités à assumer pour les quelques femmes arabes qui obtiennent ou acquièrent la liberté de mouvement, du corps et de l'esprit' ('Not to aim to "speak for" or, still worse, "to speak about", hardly even to speak *close to*, and if possible *right up against*: that is the first of the solidarities to assume towards the few Arabic women who obtain or acquire freedom of movement, both of body and of spirit') (Paris, Des Femmes, 1980, p. 8).

12. Several critics note the ways in which Djebar reappropriates writing; for example, Jeanne-Marie Clerc, *Assia Djebar: Ecrire, Transgresser, Résister*, Paris, L'Harmattan, 1997, p. 67; Hafid Gafaïti, 'L'Autobiographie plurielle: Assia Djebar, les femmes et l'histoire', in Ruhe and Hornung (eds), *Postcolonialisme et Autobiographie*, p. 151.

13. The analogy should also be noted with the imagined biblical punishment for the narrator of *La Statue de sel* threatened with being transformed into a pillar of salt for daring to look back. In 'Violence de l'autobiographie', Djebar speaks very movingly of her shock when she realised that there would actually be readers of this text; it had been as though she had worked on *L'Amour, la fantasia* for two years without realising this. She recounts her 'shame', and how she suffered from tendonitis in her arm for six months after publication, a price she felt she paid for writing and publishing the book.

14. Clarisse Zimra, 'Afterword', in Assia Djebar, *Women of Algiers in their Apartment*, trans. Marjolijn de Jager, Charlottesville, VA, and London, University of Virginia Press (Caraf Books), 1992, p. 160. This is the American translation of *Femmes d'Alger dans leur appartement*.

15. Mireille Calle-Gruber, *Assia Djebar ou la résistance de l'écriture*, p. 11.

16. See, for example, Déjeux, *Littérature maghrébine*, p. 249 and p. 251 on the criticism levelled at the early novels on their publication for their 'egocentrism', the lack of attention to the situation of Algerian women and to the political situation of the period. Nicholas Harrison suggests that this may be one of the reasons why Djebar stopped publishing in the 1970s (*Postcolonial Criticism*, Chapter 1, 'Writing and Voice: Women, Nationalism and the Literary Self', pp. 112–35).

17. Assia Djebar, 'Poésie et bilinguisme', *Algérie-Actualité*, nos. 182 and 183, 20 April 1969; also quoted by Déjeux, *Littérature maghrébine*, p. 272. The term *déchirement*, a tearing apart, is a recurrent one in the work of Albert Memmi, as has been seen in Chapter 3.

18. For an analysis of the ways in which the experience of the film-making led Assia Djebar back to literature, see Clerc, *Assia Djebar*. This analysis is particularly good on the overall structure of Djebar's work, the links between the texts, and especially the links between the films and her written work. Other critics to note the importance of the film work include Valérie Orlando, *Nomadic Voices of Exile: Feminine Identity in Francophone Literature of the Maghreb*, Athens, OH: Ohio University Press, 1999, p. 148; Anne Donadey, in her analysis of *La Nouba* in '"Elle

a rallumé le vif du passé": l'écriture-palimpseste d'Assia Djebar', in Ruhe and Hornung (eds), *Postcolonialisme et Autobiographie*, pp. 101–15, and in *Recasting Postcolonialism*, Chapter 3, 'Re-Membering Colonial History', especially the section 'Mediated Dialogues? Women's Voices', pp. 51–60; and Mireille Calle-Gruber, in two chapters in *Assia Djebar ou la résistance de l'écriture*, in which she calls it 'une expérience refondatrice' (p. 13; 'a re-foundational experience') and emphasises the importance of this ten years of 'silence' in writing (p. 8): 'Faire une scène au féminin' (pp. 199–222) and 'L'Image-son ou la Pharmacie du cinématographe' (pp. 223–44).

19. Assia Djebar in the interview with Clarisse Zimra that accompanies the translation *Women of Algiers in their Apartment*, p. 174.

20. This essay contains a very interesting meditation on the Delacroix painting and on the series of paintings made by Picasso 'after Delacroix' in the early 1950s as the Algerian War was beginning, in which Djebar sees a liberation of the women from the harem and from their passivity under the gaze of the spectator. The notions of the gaze and of the voice that is silenced will be important recurrent themes in her subsequent work. Again see Anne Donadey's analysis of the ways in which Djebar 'refigures' Orientalist painting, in *Recasting Postcolonialism*, pp. 96–102.

21. *Femmes d'Alger*, directed by Kamal Dehane: le Centre de l'Audiovisuel à Bruxelles; l'Entreprise Nationale de Production Audiovisuelle (Alger); l'Unité Documentaire 'Traces' Zeaux Productions (Paris), 1992 (RTBF).

22. Assia Djebar, interview with Philippe Gardenal, *Libération*, 6 May 1987.

23. Assia Djebar in the interview with Clarisse Zimra that accompanies the translation *Women of Algiers in their Apartment*, p. 174. Jeanne-Marie Clerc also reads this as a reconciliation with the French language (*Assia Djebar*, p. 69).

24. This is much more the case with Djebar than with a number of other contemporary Francophone writers, who often take up a single, often defensive position, refusing to engage more openly with the ambiguity of their situation, especially with regard to the publication and distribution of their work. See, for example, Nicholas Harrison's discussion of Djebar's use of French (*Postcolonial Criticism*, pp. 119–22). He also discusses the taboo in North African culture, especially for women, of saying 'I' (pp. 130–31).

25. Assia Djebar, interview with Marguerite Le Clézio, 'Assia Djebar: Ecrire dans la langue adverse', *Contemporary French Civilisation*, 19.2 (Summer 1985), pp. 230–44; here p. 238.

26. Assia Djebar, interview, *L'Action*, 8 September 1958; quoted also by Déjeux, *Littérature maghrébine*, p. 252.

27. Clerc, *Assia Djebar*, pp. 55–56.

28. Assia Djebar, 'Les Yeux de la langue', in Ruhe and Hornung (eds), *Postcolonialisme et Autobiographie*, pp. 97–99.

29. Calle-Gruber, *Assia Djebar ou la résistance de l'écriture*, p. 15.

30. To take a somewhat dated concept of feminist discourse, 'history' literally becomes 'herstory' in *L'Amour, la fantasia*.

31. Eugène Fromentin, *Une année dans le Sahel*, Paris, Flammarion, 1991 (1874). For a discussion within the framework of colonialism of Fromentin's work, see Dunwoodie, *Writing French Algeria*, pp. 50–56. Jeanne-Marie Clerc (*Assia Djebar*) provides an interesting analysis of the use made of the references to Fromentin, seeing him as another 'father' to the text. Anne Donadey has also analysed the use of epigraphs in *L'Amour, la fantasia*, using the categories established by Gérard Genette, in 'Assia Djebar's Poetics of Subversion', *L'Esprit créateur*, 33.2 (Summer 1993), pp. 107–17 (see Gérard Genette, *Seuils*, Paris, Le Seuil, 1987), and in *Recasting Postcolonialism*, Chapter 4, 'Inter/textual Subversions', especially the section 'Eugène Fromentin and Djebar's Algerian Mimicry', pp. 87–92, with reference to *Ombre*

sultane.

32. Blair, *Fantasia: An Algerian Cavalcade*, introduction, n.p.

33. H. Adlai Murdoch, 'Rewriting Writing: Identity, Exile and Renewal in Assia Djebar's *L'Amour, la fantasia*', *Yale French Studies*, 83 (1993), *Post/Colonial Conditions*, ed. F. Lionnet and R. Scharfman, p. 75.

34. See Erickson, *Islam and Postcolonial Narrative*, p. 61.

35. As referred to in Chapter 1. See Anne Donadey's in-depth analysis of this epigraph in *Recasting Postcolonialism*, Chapter 4, 'Inter/textual Subversions', especially the section 'Writing Autobiography and History: Ibn Khaldūn', pp. 70–79. Donadey analyses how Djebar uses Ibn Khaldūn's work subversively, and is critical of his actions.

36. I have previously referred to Anne Donadey's work that explores in more detail this metaphor of the palimpsest, '"Elle a rallumé le vif du passé"'. She also gives her analysis in *Recasting Postcolonialism*, Chapter 3, 'Re-Membering Colonial History', especially the section 'Overwriting the Palimpsest of Algerian History', pp. 45–51. She shows how Djebar 'overreads' the colonial archives, 'reading Algerian women and men back into history', and then '*overwrites* their presence by writing over colonial documents, making her fictional text into a palimpsest' (p. 46). Donadey is using Nancy Miller's concept of the feminist strategy of 'overreading' or 'reading woman back in'; compare the use made of Miller's concept of 'motivated acts of reading' in the first chapter here.

37. The *Oxford English Dictionary* gives the following definition of the sistrum: 'a jingling metal instrument used by the ancient Egyptians especially in the worship of Isis'. Isis was a nature goddess whose worship became the focus of one of the major mystery religions involving the enactment of the myth of the death and resurrection of her husband, the god Osiris.

38. Djebar has spoken of how she wrote and rewrote this third part, which she needed in order to write herself out of the 'double structure' of the first two parts ('Violence de l'autobiographie', p. 93).

39. In medical terms as a result of brain damage.

40. Patricia Geesey, 'Collective Autobiography: Algerian Women and History in Assia Djebar's *L'Amour, la fantasia*', *Dalhousie French Studies*, 35 (1996), p. 155.

41. Eugène Fromentin, *Un été au Sahara*, Paris, Le Sycomore, 1982 (1857).

42. We should recall here the prominence of this same story for Khatibi at the beginning of *La Mémoire tatouée*.

43. The image of being between light and shadow is often used by Djebar and is taken up in the title for the Kamal Dehane film about her, *Assia Djebar: Entre ombre et soleil*, Algiers, November 1991–January 1992. The 'excuse' 'she's reading', adopted by her mother (referred to earlier), is also evoked by Djebar in the interview with her in Dehane's other film, *Femmes d'Alger*; see note 21.

44. It is clear that Djebar is critical of the social policies adopted in Algeria after independence and of the treatment of women who had contributed to the struggle against the French. See Anne Donadey's clear account of the Algerian War and the position of women in *Recasting Postcolonialism*, Chapter 1, 'Historical Amnesia and the Construction of "National Identity"', pp. 1–18.

45. This continued humiliation by women of other women, since no other power is available to them, and who thereby perpetuate the power relations of that society without the men having to enforce them, is used by Fatima Gallaire to devastating and tragic effect in her play *Princesses*, Paris, Editions des Quatre Vents, 1990. The underlying message is of course that women must break out of the vicious circle that men have set up for them, and refuse a type of power that only allows them to dominate other women.

46. It may also be noted that this image of being besieged is taken up by Djebar, although from a different perspective, in a later collection of essays whose title provides another image for her writing project: *Ces voix qui m'assiègent*, Paris, Albin Michel, 1999.

47. Mary Jean Green, 'Dismantling the Colonising Text: Anne Hébert's *Kamouraska* and Assia Djebar's *L'Amour, la fantasia*', *French Review*, 66.6 (May 1993), pp. 964–65.

48. Danielle Marx-Scouras, 'Muffled Screams/Stifled Voices', *Yale French Studies*, 83 (1993), *Post/Colonial Conditions*, ed. F. Lionnet and R. Scharfman, p. 176.

49. Interview with Mildred Mortimer, 'Entretien avec Assia Djebar, écrivain algérien', *Research in African Literature*, 19.2 (Summer 1988), pp. 192–205; here p. 203. This is also made very clear in the film *Assia Djebar: Entre ombre et soleil*, directed by Kamal Dehane.

50. See Geesey, 'Collective Autobiography', p. 153.

51. Murdoch, 'Rewriting Writing', p. 78.

52. Murdoch, 'Rewriting Writing', p. 84 and p. 86 respectively.

53. Murdoch, 'Rewriting Writing', p. 89.

54. Blair, introduction to *Fantasia: An Algerian Cavalcade*, n.p.

55. Geesey, 'Collective Autobiography', pp. 159–60; see also Green, 'Dismantling the Colonising Text', p. 959: 'Women, too, have participated in this historical project, but their task has not been easy. Even within their own culture, women have been largely excluded from history (that is, *written* history) and political life (that which is susceptible of becoming history). The situation of women is also accurately described by Memmi's *Portrait du colonisé*, and women in colonised groups may be said to experience a double colonisation. Since they are, in addition, doubly barred from access to writing, these colonised women seem, as Memmi suggests, condemned to a progressive loss of memory'. This article also provides a good analysis of how Djebar uses French sources 'as an archaeological site for unearthing the buried voices of Algerian women' (p. 963). See also the work of Winifred Woodhull (*Transfigurations of the Maghreb*) and Anne Donaday (*Recasting Postcolonialism*) on feminism and decolonisation.

56. Marx-Scouras, 'Muffled Screams/Stifled Voices', pp. 174–75. She also gives the example of the Lebanese writer Evelyne Accad in *L'Excisée* (1982) and *Coquelicot du massacre* (1988), and notes that in a book of literary criticism by the same author, *Sexuality and War: Literary Masks of the Middle East* (New York, New York University Press, 1990), Accad goes on to ask why it is that male Lebanese writers such as Elias Khouras choose to present war-torn Beirut as a prostitute, whereas a female writer such as Etel Adnan uses the image of the city as a victim of rape: 'Is [Khouras] revealing his attitude towards war, or towards women? Or is war about women? How does his metaphor of the city as a prostitute relate to a centuries old "tradition" whereby war seemingly authorises the raiding of women along with the land and its possessions? The war-torn land and the female body are as one. It is therefore not surprising that the "coming to writing" for women of the Maghreb and the Mashreq is bound up with the question of war, nor that they inscribe the ordeal of their country on their bodies. Unlike their male counterparts, they do not merely personify their homeland as a woman, they depict the devastation of revolutionary and civil war on their writing bodies; the "body in pain" becomes, so to speak, the textual signifier.' The reference is to Elaine Scarry, *The Body in Pain* (New York and Oxford, Oxford University Press, 1985), in which she argues that discourse on war evacuates the human body, the 'body in pain'.

57. Assia Djebar, interview in the film directed by Kamal Dehane, *Femmes d'Alger*.

58. See Donadey, ' "Elle a rallumé le vif du passé"', pp. 101–15, and *Recasting Postcolonialism*, pp. 45–51. Note also Ernstpeter Ruhe, in the discussion following Donadey's paper, insisting on the violent nature of the palimpsest that effaces, and the analogy he makes with the colonial powers, which also attempted to efface the culture of those they oppressed.

59. Ernstpeter Ruhe, 'Les Mots, l'amour, la mort: les mythomorphoses d'Assia Djebar', in Ruhe and Hornung (eds), *Postcolonialisme et Autobiographie*, pp. 161–77.

60. Françoise Lionnet, 'Questions de méthode: itinéraires ourlés de l'autoportrait et de la critique', in Ruhe and Hornung (eds), *Postcolonialisme et Autobiographie*, p. 14. In Greek mythology, the Shirt of Nessus was a poisoned garment that the centaur Nessus gave to Deianira, the wife of Hercules. Nessus had carried her off after falling in love with her. Hercules pursued and mortally wounded the centaur with an arrow dipped in the blood of the nine-headed Hydra, a dragon sacred to Hera that Hercules had managed to slay despite the fact that each head grew again when cut off. As he lay dying, Nessus gave the garment he was wearing to Deianira, assuring her that it would keep Hercules faithful to her. But this supposed love-token caused the hero such terrible pain that, unable to take it off, he immolated himself on Mount Oeta.

61. See Djebar talking about this difference in her life compared to her cousins in the film by Kamal Dehane, *Femmes d'Alger*.

62. Najiba Regaïeg, 'L'Amour, la fantasia d'Assia Djebar: de l'autobiographie à la fiction', *Itinéraires et contacts de cultures, Nouvelles Approches des textes littéraires maghrébins ou migrants*, 27 (1999), p. 134.

63. Ruhe, 'Les Mots, l'amour, la mort', p. 169.

64. Lionnet, 'Questions de méthode', p. 14.

65. Blair, *Fantasia: An Algerian Cavalcade*, introduction. Jeanne-Marie Clerc has analysed the use made of music made by Djebar in her film work: 'Or le film, *La Nouba*, réussit précisément à entrelacer ces deux structures en épousant la "forme" de la "nouba", que le prologue définit à la fois comme "l'histoire quotidienne des femmes" et "aussi une sorte de symphonie, en musique classique dite andalouse, avec des mouvements rythmiques déterminés". *Nouba*, en arabe dialectal désigne également les tours de prises de parole qui se succèdent l'un après l'autre. Ainsi le motif musical suggère les rythmes alternés sur lesquels se calque l'histoire contée par les femmes alternativement visitées par la narratrice, et réveillant tour à tour les souvenirs d'un passé qui se lève en elle, comme les échos de la musique perdue des ancêtres, au fur et à mesure qu'elle entre dans les patios [...] De la sorte, alternent les rythmes des récits entendus et les arabesques des trajets parcourus, selon un schéma explicitement figuré par des cartons reprenant les divers mouvements de la musique andalouse' (*Assia Djebar*, p. 126) ('Now the film *La Nouba* succeeds precisely in interlacing these two structures by espousing the "form" of the "Nouba", which is defined in the prologue as at once "the daily history of women" and "also a sort of symphony, in the classical music known as Andalusian, with certain rhythmical movements". *Nouba*, in the Arabic dialect, also means taking it in turns to speak one after the other. Thus the musical motif suggests the alternate rhythms on which is traced the history told by the women visited by the narrator, and revealing one after the other the memories of a past which rises in her, like the echoes of the lost music of the ancestors, as she penetrates the patios [...] So that the rhythms of the oral histories alternate with the arabesques of the paths followed, in a pattern explicitly mapped out by epigraphs using the various movements of Andalusian music'). Clerc then goes on to analyse the musical structure in a number of Djebar's novels, showing a further link between the cinematic experience and the writing of these texts. Several other

critics have also noted the musical structure of the texts; see, for example, Zimra, 'Autobiographie et Je/Jeux d'espace', p. 119; and Mireille Calle-Gruber, 'Résistances de l'écriture ou l'ombilic de l'œuvre. A propos de *Vaste est la prison* d'Assia Djebar', in Ruhe and Hornung (eds), *Postcolonialisme et Autobiographie*, p. 141, and also in *Assia Djebar ou la résistance de l'écriture*. Calle-Gruber also provides useful stills from the films in this book.

66. Clerc, *Assia Djebar*, pp. 27–28. The narrator thinks in Arabic her word of endearment for the younger man she is infatuated with in the first section of the text: 'Je me rappelle à nouveau comment, mise brusquement en présence de l'Aimé (est-ce que je me trahis moi-même, pensant ce dernier mot en langue arabe?), je concentrais toutes mes forces à ne pas le dévisager' (p. 28) ('I remember again how, suddenly finding myself in the presence of the Beloved (do I betray myself by thinking that word in Arabic?), I concentrated all my strength on not staring at him'). In her analysis, Clerc also notes how French cuts Assia Djebar off from her native soil, but how the film experience provides a counterbalance. See for example her analysis on p. 29 and p. 104.

67. Both Swann and (to a much greater extent) the narrator achieve knowledge about human nature and about themselves through the experience of jealousy in particular. Swann fails to achieve any kind of personal salvation although he comes to recognise his own lack of self-knowledge, while the narrator goes beyond suffering through loss to find a form of salvation through writing. See Malcolm Bowie, *Proust, Freud and Lacan*, Cambridge, Cambridge University Press, 1987 for an analysis of the functioning of jealousy and knowledge in *A la recherche du temps perdu*.

68. See also Calle-Gruber, 'Résistances de l'écriture ou l'ombilic de l'œuvre', p. 145 for an analysis of the way in which resistance moves from an attention to history to private life in *Vaste est la prison*.

69. Mary Stevens, 'Assia Djebar's Buried Treasure: The Relationship between Cultural Capital and Cultural Memory in *L'Amour, la fantasia* (1985) and *Vaste est la prison* (1995) as Explored in the Use of Epigraphs' (unpublished, unpaginated). See Genette, *Seuils*, p. 148. Anne Donadey has analysed how Djebar's use of epigraphs provides a means of 'legitimisation' and insertion into a pre-existing tradition (*Recasting Postcolonialism*, p. 66).

70. Stevens, 'Assia Djebar's Buried Treasure'.

71. It is kept in the Ancient Near East Study Collection. The left-hand side measures 70 cm high and 116 cm wide; the right, 70 cm high, 93 cm wide; they are both about 10 cm in thickness. The tablets are not on general display (although they have been in the past), but can be seen on request to the study collection. References: Dugga (or Thugga) Inscription LH 125226 / RH 125225. For a further analysis of the lost alphabet, see Calle-Gruber, 'Résistance de l'écriture ou l'ombilic de l'œuvre', p. 147, and *Assia Djebar ou la résistance de l'écriture*, pp. 75–81.

72. Stevens, 'Assia Djebar's Buried Treasure'.

73. It is difficult to describe with accuracy the historical and contemporary use of the different languages in North Africa; the situation continues to be highly political and each commentator has an agenda. Even in informal conversation with Algerians, I have received a wide variety of answers depending on the personal situation of the speaker (as Gayatri Spivak warns, there is a need to be wary even of 'native informants'; see 'How to Read a "Culturally Different" Book', p. 135). It can be noted that 'Berber, the oldest language in Algeria, is attested in Lybic inscriptions dating from the Neolithic period. It is the native language of one-fifth of the population. An alphabet using the *tifnagh* alphabet is still in use today amongst the Tuareg; elsewhere, exchanges in Berber are exclusively oral [...] Today the term "Tamazight" which refers to a number of regional variations of Berber throughout the country, is

preferred. In the North speakers of Chenoui, Chouaia and Kabyle are the most numerous. In the Sahara, three other dialects predominate: Mozabite, Zenete, and Tamachek' (Djamila Saadi-Mokrane, 'The Algerian Linguicide', in Berger [ed.], *Algeria in Others' Languages*, p. 48). 'In Algeria, the Berbers have continued to speak their own language to a certain extent over the centuries and under different colonial rules. In Algeria, the Berbers of Kabylia, an Arabic name designating the tribal people [this sentence is slightly confusing, since it is the term 'Kabyle' that usually designates the 'tribes'] still speak Tamazight, the indigenous name for their language, which belongs to the Hamidic, as opposed to the Semitic, family of languages. Tamazight is the language of the "Amazigh", a term that means "free men", a generic name often used by protonations to celebrate their awareness of themselves as an autonomous entity. To this day, about 20 percent of the population of Algeria still use Tamazight, either as their principal language, or as the language spoken at home, hence, indeed, their first language. This population is concentrated in Kabylia, a mountainous region whose isolation explains in part the incomplete penetration of Arabic. Tamazight remains an essentially oral language, even though various written transcriptions were attempted, first in an old Lybic alphabet called *tifnagh*, still in use by the Tuareg, and now in either Arabic or Roman script. The competition between these transcriptions has political and ideological implications: the Arabic script is a way of tying Tamazight to Arabic culture; the Western Roman script ties the language to a genealogical line stretching from the Roman empire to the French conquest' (Anne-Emmanelle Berger, 'The Impossible Wedding: Nationalism, Languages and the Mother Tongue in Postcolonial Algeria', in *idem* [ed.], *Algeria in Others' Languages*, p. 66). Hafid Gafaïti notes that the Berbers are in fact made up of at least five different groups. Within this the Chaouis have traditionally held political, economic and military power, generally embracing the Arabic language and Arabic-Muslim culture. The Francophone elite tended to be Kabyles (as we have seen with Mouloud Feraoun), favoured under colonial rule because they were seen as ethnically linked to Europe rather than to Africa and/or the Middle East. See Hafid Gafaïti, 'Monotheism of the Other: Language and De/Construction of National Identity in Postcolonial Algeria', in Berger (ed.), *Algeria in Others' Languages*, pp. 19–43 for a highly political review of the situation particularly concerning the different discourses and positions of Arabic and French speakers; also for the useful clarification that what is often referred to as 'classical' Arabic, inside the Maghreb, should be more properly termed 'Modern Standard Arabic' when referring to the language taught in schools as part of the programme of Arabisation. See also Berger ('The Impossible Wedding', p. 67) on this 'distancing' of standard Arabic by the use of the terms 'literary Arabic', 'classical Arabic' and 'oriental Arabic'.

74. Carthage is an ancient city on the coast of North Africa, near the present-day city of Tunis, Tunisia. It was founded by the Phoenicians, traditionally in 814 BC, and became a major force in the Mediterranean, bringing it into conflict with Greece in the third century BC and with Rome in the Punic Wars, until it was finally destroyed by the Romans in 146 BC.

75. Only five of the original books by Polybius survive. He spent 18 years (168–150 BC) as a political hostage in Rome. For a further analysis of Djebar's use of Polybius, see Calle-Gruber, 'Résistances de l'écriture ou l'ombilic de l'œuvre', p. 143.

76. Tin Hinan was so revered that the gold in her tomb was never looted. Al-Kahina was a Berber high priestess who claimed conversion to Judaism and opposed the Arab conquest in the seventh century AD, but who eventually surrendered to Umayyad Khalif. She is frequently evoked as a symbol of resistance to conquest by

North African writers of both Berber and Jewish descent, as we have seen in the chapter on Albert Memmi.

77. Calle-Gruber, *Assia Djebar ou la résistance de l'écriture*, p. 71

78. Abdelkébir Khatibi, 'Diglossia', trans. Whitney Stanford, in Berger (ed.), *Algeria in Others' Languages*, p. 157.

79. For an interesting analysis of this section, see Sonia Assa, 'De l'auteure en lectrice: fonction de "L'Histoire du captif" dans *Vaste est la prison*', *Le Maghreb Littéraire*, 4.8 (2000), pp. 31–49. An original speculation is contained in the article firstly on what Djebar actually leaves out in her version and use of Zoraida's story (Zoraida's passion for the Virgin Mary), and secondly on the parallel between Zoraida and the narrator, who both betray their fathers through writing: 'Si Djebar se reconnaît en Zoraidé, l'Obsédée de Marie, c'est bien d'une part parce que, comme elle favorite de son père, elle le trahira justement par l'écriture, et de l'autre parce que c'est son héritage maternel qu'elle se trouvera exalter à travers cette écriture. Comme Zoraidé, elle aura fui à la recherche de la mère' (p. 47) ('If Djebar recognises herself in Zoraida, the woman obsessed by Mary, it is partly because, being the favourite daughter of her father like her, she will betray him by her writing; and partly because it is her maternal inheritance which she will find herself exalting through that writing. Like Zoraida, she also fled in search of her mother').

80. Assia Djebar has confirmed this part of her mother's story; see 'Violence de l'autobiographie'.

81. See the reproduction of the photograph in Calle-Gruber, *Assia Djebar ou la résistance de l'écriture*, opposite p. 254. This text also contains very useful stills from Djebar's film (see also n. 65) and theatre work.

82. There is some apparent contradiction here with the mother's ability to read French. In the section 'Mon père écrit à ma mère' in *L'Amour, la fantasia*, the mother can read some French (certainly the postcard her husband writes to her in her name, seen as a scandalous act by the other women, but as proof of their love by the narrator) and the narrator describes her progress with spoken French.

83. An interesting comparison here is with Nathalie Sarraute's *Enfance* (see Chapter 3 n. 67), in which she describes the scene of the first writing, a school essay. Sarraute also writes about the experience of being divided between two languages, cultures and languages (in her case between France and Russia).

84. The name is also glossed in *Ombre sultane*, pp. 20–21. In Anne Donadey's very interesting analysis of the use of Arabic words by Djebar, she suggests that the interpretation of Isma's name is 'somewhat stretched: The name means "high" or "lofty" and comes from the root s-m-u, whereas the word *ism* (name) comes from the root s-m-y'. Anne Donadey, 'The Multilingual Strategies of Postcolonial Literature: Assia Djebar's Algerian Palimpsest', *World Literature Today*, 74.1 (Winter 2000), p. 27. She also considers whether Isma in *Ombre sultane* and the unnamed narrator of *L'Amour, la fantasia* are the same; see *Recasting Postcolonialism*, pp. 84–85.

85. Stevens, 'Assia Djebar's Buried Treasure'; Jeanne Hyvrard, *La Meurtritude*, Paris, Minuit, 1977, p. 146.

86. Calle-Gruber, *Assia Djebar ou la résistance de l'écriture*, p. 101. In the account of the murder, there is also a clear link to this text's contemporary, *Le Blanc de l'Algérie*.

87. See, for example, Orlando, *Nomadic Voices of Exile* on this question of exile and the political situation in Algeria in the early 1990s. Amnesty International reported on the difficulty of knowing which side in the conflict between the government and the fundamentalist Islamic forces had carried out attacks and murders.

88. In her analysis of *L'Amour, la fantasia* Valérie Orlando suggests an inter-

esting use of Paul Ricœur's concepts of 'time of narration', 'narrated time' and 'fictive experience of time' as developed in *Time and Narrative*, II, Chicago, University of Chicago Press, 1985, p. 77.

89. See Calle-Gruber on this question of the aesthetics and ethics of literature in Assia Djebar's work: 'Résistances de l'écriture ou l'ombilic de l'œuvre', pp. 137–48, especially p. 142 where she discusses *Vaste est la prison* as an autobiographical writing of resistance: 'une œuvre qui ne s'en tient pas aux seuls "effets" de style' ('a work which does not take its stand merely on "stylistic effects"'), and in *Assia Djebar ou la résistance de l'écriture*: 'Où l'on voit que l'autobiographie est un différentiel de forces – Histoire(s), Langues, Différence sexuelle – nouées au nombril de l'œuvre qui est mère des résistances. Relève du genitif. Est la résistance des résistances' (p. 81) ('Where it may be seen that the autobiography is a differential of forces – History/Histories, Languages, Sexual differences – knotted around the central point of the work which is the mother of resistances. The changing-over of the genitive. The resistance of resistances').

Notes to Conclusion
pp. 334–40

All translations are by Helena Scott

1. Paul Klee quoted in Suzanne Colter, guide text to *Paul Klee: The Nature of Creation*, exhibition at the Hayward Gallery, London, 17 January–1 April 2002; adapted from Robert Kudielka, *Paul Klee: The Nature of Creation*, London, Hayward Gallery, 2002.

2. In a similar way, Robert Young defines the postcolonial as a form of knowledge (*Postcolonialism*, p. 56).

3. See also Anne Donadey on this in *Recasting Postcolonialism*, p. xxxii.

4. Doris Ruhe, 'Le Scorpion en phénix', p. 54. Her reference is to Danielle Marx-Scouras, 'The Poetics of Maghrebine Illegitimacy', *L'Esprit créateur*, 26 (1986), pp. 3–10; p. 6.

5. There is a telling parallel here with the attitudes of the French critical establishment with the poetry of the First and Second World Wars, referred to as 'littérature de circonstance', and criticised as being of little aesthetic value. See the analysis of this by Ian Higgins in the introduction to his *Anthology of First World War French Poetry*, Glasgow, University of Glasgow French and German Publications, 1996.

6. See Moore-Gilbert, *Postcolonial Theory*, p. 184. He is discussing Wilson Harris on what he calls the 'void' that allows cultures to come together.

7. Lazarus, 'National Consciousness', pp. 219–20.

8. Robert Young treats extensively the question not only of indigenous writers, but also of French intellectuals who spent time in North Africa at critical moments for the formulation of their thinking; see *Postcolonialism*, especially in the chapters 'Foucault in Tunisia', pp. 395–410 and 'Subjectivity and History: Derrida in Algeria', pp. 411–25. Poststructuralism, Young argues (p. 414), could be better characterised as Franco-Maghrebian theory. Both he and John Erickson (*Islam and Postcolonial Narrative*, p. 33) note the implications for this of 'Western' theory that has in fact grown in part out of the conditions of colonialism. Roland Barthes, who also spent time in North Africa, wrote a postface to Khatibi's *La Mémoire tatouée*, 'Ce que je dois à Khatibi' ('What I Owe to Khatibi'), in which he elaborates how Khatibi's thinking helped him to move outside the framework of taking Western thinking as

universal, particularly concerning notions of identity. Khatibi's work, he says, provides 'de quoi nous permettre de saisir *l'autre* à partir de nous-même' ('something that allows us to grasp *the other* taking ourselves as the starting-point'). Young and Erickson argue therefore that 'French' theories of poststructuralism and deconstruction, which in turn have links to the development of postcolonial discourse, have more complex origins. John McCleod has criticised Young's ideas on the location of thought as deterministic, as discussed in the first chapter here.

9. Anne Donadey discusses the potential of an analysis of several other autobiographical projects from the wider Francophone geographical area in the conclusion to *Recasting Postcolonialism*, pp. 144–51.

10. This 'nomadic' identity is especially apparent in Khatibi's writing and he himself uses this term, as we saw in Chapter 4. A sustained analysis of this concept in the postcolonial literary, cultural and political context would also make an important study. Deleuze and Guattari's analysis of 'minor literature' (*Kafka*, p. 35) is again suggestive for this: 'comment devenir le nomade et l'immigré et le tzigane de sa propre langue?' ('how does one become the nomad and the immigrant and the gypsy of one's own language?').

11. The Swiss-born painter Paul Klee travelled to Tunisia in April 1914, and the journey had a strong impact on his use of colour and abstract forms.

12. During the conference 'Assia Djebar, nomade entre les murs. Pour une poétique transfrontalière', 27–29 November 2003, Maison des Ecrivains, Paris. Organised by Mireille Calle-Gruber.

Bibliography

PRIMARY SOURCES

Djebar, Assia, *L'Amour, la fantasia*, Paris, Albin Michel, 1995 (J.-C. Lattès, 1985). Trans. Dorothy S. Blair, *Fantasia: An Algerian Cavalcade*, London and New York, Quartet, 1985.
— *Vaste est la prison*, Paris, Albin Michel, 1995.
Feraoun, Mouloud, *Le Fils du pauvre*, Paris, Le Seuil, 1950.
— *Journal 1955–1962*, Paris, Le Seuil, 1962.
— *Lettres à ses amis*, Paris, Le Seuil, 1969.
Khatibi, Abdelkébir, *La Mémoire tatouée*, Paris, Denoël, 1971.
Memmi, Albert, *La Statue de sel*, Paris, Gallimard, 1953.
— *Le Scorpion*, Paris, Gallimard, 1969. Trans. Eleanor Levieux, *The Scorpion*, New York, Grossman, 1971.

SECONDARY SOURCES

Accad, Evelyne, *L'Excisée*, Paris, L'Harmattan, 1982.
— *Coquelicot du massacre*, Paris, L'Harmattan, 1988.
— *Sexuality and War: Literary Masks of the Middle East*, New York, New York University Press, 1990.
Adam, Ian, and Helen Tiffin (eds), *Past the Last Post: Theorising Post-Colonialism and Post-Modernism*, Hemel Hempstead, Harvester Wheatsheaf, 1991.
Ahmed, Leila, 'Between Two Worlds: The Formation of a Turn-of-the-Century Egyptian Feminist', in Brodzki and Schenck (eds), *Life/Lines: Theorising Women's Autobiography*.
Allen, Roger, *The Arabic Literary Heritage: The Development of its Genre and Criticism*, Cambridge, Cambridge University Press, 1998.
— *An Introduction to Arabic Literature*, Cambridge, Cambridge University Press, 2000.
Arnaud, Jacqueline, *La Littérature maghrébine de langue française*, vol. I: *Origines et perspectives*, Paris, Publisud, 1986.
Ashcroft, Bill, Gareth Griffiths and Helen Tiffin (eds), *Key Concepts in Post-Colonial Studies*, London, Routledge, 1998.
Ashis, Nandy, *The Savage Freud and Other Essays on Possible and Retrievable Selves*, Princeton, NJ, Princeton University Press, 1995.
Assa, Sonia, 'De l'auteure en lectrice: fonction de "L'Histoire du captif" dans *Vaste est la prison*', *Le Maghreb Littéraire*, 4.8 (2000), pp. 31–49.
Bardolph, Jacqueline, *Etudes postcoloniales et littérature*, Paris, Champion, 2001.
Barker, Francis, Peter Hulme and Margaret Iversen (eds), *Colonial Discourse/Postcolonial Theory*, Manchester, Manchester University Press, 1994.
Barthes, Roland, *Mythologies*, Paris, Seuil, 1957.
— *Roland Barthes par Roland Barthes*, Paris, Seuil, 1975.
Baudelaire, Charles, *Les Fleurs du mal*, Paris, Poulet-Malassis et De Broise, 1857.
Bekri, Tahar, 'Une lecture de *La Statue de sel*', in Guérin (ed.), *Albert Memmi*:

Ecrivain et sociologue.

Bensmaia, Réda, 'Multilingualism and National "Character": On Abdelkébir Khatibi's "Bilangage"', in Berger (ed.), *Algeria in Others' Languages.*

Benstock, Shari (ed.), *The Private Self: Theory and Practice of Women's Autobiographical Writings*, London and New York, Routledge, 1988.

Berger, Anne-Emmanuelle, 'The Impossible Wedding: Nationalism, Languages and the Mother Tongue in Postcolonial Algeria', in *idem* (ed.), *Algeria in Others' Languages.*

Berger, Anne-Emmanuelle (ed.), *Algeria in Others' Languages*, Ithaca, NY, Cornell University Press, 2002.

Betts, Raymond, *Assimilation and Association in French Colonial Theory and Practice*, New York, Columbia University Press, 1961.

Blanchot, Maurice, *L'Entretien infini*, Paris, Gallimard, 1969. Trans. Susan Hanson, *The Infinite Conversation*, Minneapolis and London, University of Minnesota Press, 1992.

Blatt, David, 'Immigrant Politics in a Republican Nation', in Hargreaves and McKinney (eds), *Post-Colonial Cultures in France.*

Block Lazarus, Joyce, *Strangers and Sojourners: Jewish Identity in Contemporary Francophone Fiction*, New York, Peter Lang, 1999.

Boehmer, Elleke, *Colonial and Postcolonial Literature*, Oxford, Oxford University Press, 1995.

Bonn, Charles, and Arnold Rothe (eds), *Littérature maghrébine et littérature mondiale*, Würzburg, Königshausen & Neumann, 1995.

Bougdal, Lahsen, 'De la modernité à l'historie: le traitement de l'espace maternel dans La Mémoire tatouée d'Abdelkébir Khatibi', *Le Maghreb Littéraire*, 3.6 (1999), pp. 17–31.

Bounfour, Abdallah, 'Forme littéraire et représentation de soi: l'autobiographie francophone du Maghreb et l'autobiographie arabe du début du siècle', in Bonn and Rothe (eds), *Littérature maghrébine et littérature mondiale.*

Bousta, Rachida Saigh, *Lecture des récits de Abdelkébir Khatibi: Ecriture, Mémoire, Imaginaire...*, Casablanca, Afrique Orient, 1996.

Bowie, Malcolm, *Proust, Freud and Lacan*, Cambridge, Cambridge University Press, 1987.

Brodzki, Bella, and Celeste Schenck (eds), *Life/Lines: Theorising Women's Autobiography*, Ithaca, NY, Cornell University Press, 1988.

Bruss, Elizabeth, *Autobiographical Acts: The Changing Situation of a Literary Genre*, Baltimore, Johns Hopkins University Press, 1976.

— 'I for Eye: Making and Unmaking Autobiography in Film', in Olney (ed.), *Autobiography: Essays Theoretical and Critical.*

Calle-Gruber, Mireille, 'Résistances de l'écriture ou l'ombilic de l'œuvre: A propos de *Vaste est la prison* d'Assia Djebar', in Ruhe and Hornung (eds), *Postcolonialisme et Autobiographie.*

— *Assia Djebar ou la résistance de l'écriture: Regards d'un écrivain d'Algérie*, Paris, Maisonneuve & Larose, 2001.

Camus, Albert, *La Peste*, Paris, Gallimard, 1947.

— *Actuelles III, Essais, Misère de la Kabylie*, Paris, Gallimard, 1977.

— *Le Premier Homme*, Paris, Gallimard, 1994.

Cannon, Steve, '*Paname* City Rapping: B-Boys in the Banlieues and Beyond', in Hargreaves and McKinney (eds), *Post-Colonial Cultures in France.*

Carr, Helen, 'In Other Words: Native American Women's Autobiography', in Brodzki and Schenck (eds), *Life/Lines: Theorising Women's Autobiography.*

Cassan, Pierre (ed.), *Etat de la Francophonie dans le monde: données 1995–1996 et cinq études inédites*, Paris, La Documentation Française, 1997.

Chambers, Iain, and Lidia Curtis (eds), *The Postcolonial Question: Common Skies, Divided Horizons*, New York and London, Routledge, 1996.

Chaulet-Achour, Christiane, 'Les Masques de la périphérie: éléments d'un débat', *Expressions maghrébines*, Revue de la Coordination Internationale des Chercheurs sur Les Littératures Maghrébines, 1.1 (Summer 2002), pp. 17–29.

Chèze, Marie-Hélène, *Mouloud Feraoun: La voix et le silence*, Paris, Le Seuil, 1982.

Chraïbi, Driss, *Le Passé simple*, Paris, Denoël, 1954.

Clerc, Jeanne-Marie, *Assia ̃ Djebar: Ecrire, Transgresser, Résister*, Paris, L'Harmattan, 1997.

Clifford, James, and George E. Marcus (eds), *Writing Culture: The Poetics and Politics of Ethnography*, Berkeley, University of California Press, 1988.

Cook, Malcolm, and Grace Davie (eds), *Modern France: Society in Transition*, London and New York, Routledge, 1999.

Corbin, Henry, *Imagination créatrice dans le soufisme d'Ibn Arabi*, Paris, Aubier, 1993.

Cox, James, 'Recovering Literature's Lost Ground through Autobiography', in Olney (ed.), *Studies in Autobiography*.

Couser, G. Thomas, 'Black Elk Speaks with Forked Tongue', in Olney (ed.), *Studies in Autobiography*.

Davie, Grace, 'Religion and Laïcité', in Cook and Davie (eds), *Modern France: Society in Transition*.

Déjeux, Jean, *Littérature maghrébine de langue française*, Sherbrooke, Quebec, Editions Namaan, 1980 (1973).

— 'L'Emergence du "je" dans la littérature maghrébine de langue française', *Itinéraires et Contacts de Cultures*, 13 (1991), special issue, *Autobiographies et récits de vie en Afrique*, pp. 23–29.

— *Maghreb Littératures de Langue Française*, Paris, Arcantère, 1993.

— 'Au Maghreb, la langue française "langue natale du je"', in Mathieu (ed.), *Littératures autobiographiques de la Francophonie*.

Deleuze, Gilles, and Félix Guattari, *Kafka: Pour une littérature mineure*, Paris, Minuit, 1975.

— *Capitalisme et schizophrénie: L'anti-oedipe*, Paris, Minuit, 1980.

Djaït, Hichem, *L'Europe et L'Islam*, Paris, Le Seuil, 1978.

Djebar, Assia, *La Soif*, Paris, Julliard, 1957.

— *Les Impatients*, Paris, Julliard, 1958.

— interview, *L'Action*, 8 September 1958.

— *Les Enfants du nouveau monde*, Paris, Julliard, 1962.

— *Les Alouettes naïves*, Paris, Julliard, 1967.

— (with Walid Garn), *Rouge l'aube*, Algiers, SNED, 1969.

— *Poèmes pour l'Algérie heureuse*, Algiers, SNED, 1969.

— 'Poésie et bilinguisme', *Algérie-Actualité*, nos. 182 and 183, 20 April 1969.

— 'Une femme, un film, un regard', *Demain l'Afrique*, no. 1 (September 1977).

— *Femmes d'Alger dans leur appartement*, Paris, Des Femmes, 1980.

— 'Du français comme butin', *La Quinzaine littéraire* (Paris), no. 436 (March 1985).

— interview with Marguerite Le Clézio, 'Assia Djebar: Ecrire dans la langue adverse', *Contemporary French Civilisation*, 19.2 (Summer 1985), pp. 230–44.

— interview with Philippe Gardenal, *Libération*, 6 May 1987.

— *Ombre sultane*, Paris, Lattès, 1987. Trans. Dorothy S. Blair, *A Sister to Scheherazade*, London and New York, Quartet, 1987.

— interview with Mildred Mortimer, 'Entretien avec Assia Djebar, écrivain algérien', *Research in African Literature*, 19.2 (Summer 1988).

— *Loin de Médine*, Paris, Albin Michel, 1991.
— 'La Langue dans l'espace ou l'espace dans la langue', in Dominique Johnson and Sylvie Ouzilleau (eds), *Mise en Scène d'Ecrivains: Assia Djebar, Nicole Brossard, Madeleine Gagnon and France Théoret*, Quebec, Le Griffon d'argile, 1993.
— *Le Blanc de l'Algérie*, Paris, Albin Michel, 1995.
— *Oran, langue morte*, Arles, Actes Sud, 1997.
— *Les Nuits de Strasbourg*, Arles, Actes Sud, 1997.
— 'Les Yeux de la langue' and 'Violence de l'autobiographie', in Ruhe and Hornung (eds), *Postcolonialisme et Autobiographie*.
— *Ces voix qui m'assiègent*, Paris, Albin Michel, 1999.
Donadey, Anne, 'Assia Djebar's Poetics of Subversion', *L'Esprit créateur*, 33.2 (Summer 1993).
— '"Elle a rallumé le vif du passé": l'écriture-palimpseste d'Assia Djebar', in Ruhe and Hornung, *Postcolonialisme et Autobiographie*.
— 'The Multilingual Strategies of Postcolonial Literature: Assia Djebar's Algerian Palimpsest', *World Literature Today*, 74.1 (Winter 2000), pp. 27–39.
— *Recasting Postcolonialism: Women Writing Between Worlds*, Portsmouth, NH, Heinemann, 2001.
— 'Francophone Women Writers and Postcolonial Theory', in Forsdick and Murphy (eds), *Francophone Postcolonial Studies: A Critical Introduction*.
Dugas, Guy, *Albert Memmi: Ecrivain de la déchirure*, Québec, Editions Naaman, 1984.
— 'L'Iconotexte dans l'œuvre de fiction d'Albert Memmi', in Guérin (ed.), *Albert Memmi: Ecrivain et sociologue*.
— *Albert Memmi: Du malheur d'etre juif au bonheur sépharade*, Paris, Alliance israélite universelle, 2001.
Dunwoodie, Peter, *Writing French Algeria*, Oxford, Clarendon Press, 1998.
Erickson, John, *Islam and Postcolonial Narrative*, Cambridge, Cambridge University Press, 1998.
Feraoun, Mouloud, *Les Chemins qui montent*, Paris, Le Seuil, 1957.
— 'La Littérature algérienne', in *L'Anniversaire*, Paris, Le Seuil, 1972.
— *Lettres à ses amis, ouvrage présenté par Christiane Achour*, Algiers, ENAG/EDITIONS, 1992.
Forsdick, Charles, and David Murphy (eds), *Francophone Postcolonial Studies: A Critical Introduction*, London, Arnold, 2003.
Fox-Genovese, Elizabeth, 'My Statue, My Self: Autobiographical Writings of Afro-American Women', in Benstock (ed.), *The Private Self: Theory and Practice of Women's Autobiographical Writings*.
Friedman, Susan Stanford, 'Women's Autobiographical Selves: Theory and Practice', in Benstock (ed.), *The Private Self: Theory and Practice of Women's Autobiographical Writings*.
Fromentin, Eugène, *Un été au Sahara*, Paris, Le Sycomore, 1982 (1857).
— *Une année dans le Sahel*, Paris, Flammarion, 1991 (1874).
Gafaïti, Hafid, 'L'Autobiographie plurielle: Assia Djebar, les femmes et l'histoire', in Ruhe and Hornung (eds), *Postcolonialisme et Autobiographie*.
— 'Monotheism of the Other: Language and De/Construction of National Identity in Postcolonial Algeria', in Berger (ed.), *Algeria in Others' Languages*.
Gallaire, Fatima, *Princesses*, Paris, Editions des Quatre Vents, 1990.
Geesey, Patricia, 'Collective Autobiography: Algerian Women and History in Assia Djebar's *L'Amour, la fantasia*', *Dalhousie French Studies*, 35 (1996).
Genette Gérard, *Palimpsestes: la littérature au second degré*, Paris, Seuil, 1982.
— *Seuils*, Paris, Le Seuil, 1987.

Giles, Fiona, '"The Softest Disorder": Representing Cultural Indeterminacy', in Tiffin and Lawson (eds), *De-Scribing Empire: Post-Colonialism and Textuality*.

Gillis, John R., 'Memory and Identity: The History of a Relationship', in *idem* (ed.), *Commemoration: The Politics of National Identity*, Princeton, NJ, Princeton University Press, 1994.

Gleyze, Jack, *Mouloud Feraoun*, Paris, L'Harmattan, 1990.

Gontard, Marc, 'Eros mystique', *Al Assa*, no. 17 (February 1980).

— *La Violence du texte: La Littérature marocaine de langue française*, Paris, L'Harmattan; Rabat, Smer, 1981.

— *Le Moi étrange: Littérature marocaine de langue française*, Paris, L'Harmattan, 1993.

— 'Auteur maghrébin: la définition introuvable', *Expressions maghrébines*, Revue de la Coordination Internationale des Chercheurs sur Les Littératures Maghrébines, 1.1 (Summer 2002), pp. 9–16.

Goodman, Katherine R., 'Elisabeth to Meta: Epistolary Autobiography and the Postulation of the Self', in Brodzki and Schenck (eds), *Life/Lines: Theorising Women's Autobiography*.

Gordon, Avery F., *Ghostly Matters: Haunting and the Sociological Imagination*, Minneapolis, University of Minnesota Press, 1997.

Green, Mary Jean, 'Dismantling the Colonising Text: Anne Hébert's *Kamouraska* and Assia Djebar's *L'Amour, la fantasia*', *French Review*, 66.6 (May 1993).

Guérin, Jeanyves (ed.), *Albert Memmi: Ecrivain et sociologue*, Paris, L'Harmattan, 1990.

Gusdorf, Georges, 'Conditions and Limits of Autobiography' trans. James Olney, in Olney (ed.), *Autobiography: Essays Theoretical and Critical*; it originally appeared as 'Conditions et limites de l'autobiographie', in Günther Reichenkron and Erich Haase (eds), *Formen der Selbstdarstellung: Analekten zu einer Geschichte des literarischen Selbstportraits* ed., Berlin, Duncker and Humblot, 1956.

Haddour, Azzedine, *Colonial Myths: History and Narrative*, Manchester, Manchester University Press, 2000.

Hafez, Sabry, *The Genesis of Arabic Narrative Discourse: A Study in the Sociology of Modern Arabic Discourse*, London, Saqi Books, 1993.

Hall, Stuart, 'When was the "Post-Colonial"?', in Chambers and Curtis (eds), *The Postcolonial Question*.

Hand, Seán, 'Don't Look Back: Albert Memmi's *La Statue de sel*', in Ibnlfassi and Hitchcott (eds), *African Francophone Writing: A Critical Introduction*.

Hanley, John, *The Postcolonial Crescent: Islam's Impact on Contemporary Literature*, Oxford and New York, Peter Lang, 1998.

Hargreaves, Alec, 'The Contribution of North and Sub-Saharan African Immigrant Minorities to the Redefinition of Contemporary French Culture', in Forsdick and Murphy (eds), *Francophone Postcolonial Studies*.

Hargreaves, Alec, and Mark McKinney (eds), *Post-Colonial Cultures in France*, London, Routledge, 1997.

Harlow, Barbara, *Resistance Literature*, New York and London, Methuen, 1987.

Harpham, Geoffrey Galt, 'Conversion and the Language of Autobiography', in Olney (ed.), *Studies in Autobiography*.

Harrison, Nicholas, *Postcolonial Criticism: History, Theory and the Work of Fiction*, Cambridge, Polity, 2003.

Hawley, John, *Writing the Nation: Self and Country in the Postcolonial Imagination*, Amsterdam, Rodopi, 1996.

Heelas, Paul, and Andrew Lock (eds), *Indigenous Psychologies: The Anthropology of the Self*, London, Academic Press, 1981.

Hepher, Saskia, 'The Son of a Poor Man – A Translation Project on Mouloud Feraoun's *Le Fils du pauvre*', MA dissertation, Technical and Specialised Translation, University of Westminster, 1998.

Higgins, Ian (ed.), *Anthology of First World War Poetry*, Glasgow, University of Glasgow French and German Publications, 1996.

Hitchcott, Nicki, 'Calixthe Beyala and the Post-Colonial Woman', in Hargreaves and McKinney (eds), *Post-Colonial Cultures in France*.

Hutcheon, Linda, 'Circling the Downspout of Empire', in Adam and Tiffin (eds), *Past the Last Post: Theorising Post-Colonialism and Post-Modernism*.

Hyvrard, Jeanne, *La Meurtritude*, Paris, Minuit, 1977.

Ibnlfassi, Laïla, 'Chraïbi's *Le Passé simple* and a Theory of Doubles', in Ibnlfassi and Hitchcott (eds), *African Francophone Writing: A Critical Introduction*.

Ibnlfassi, Laïla, and Nicki Hitchcott (eds), *African Francophone Writing A Critical Introduction*, Oxford and New York, Berg, 1996.

Jameson, Fredric, 'Marx's Purloined Letter', in Michael Sprinker (ed.), *Ghostly Demarcations: A Symposium on Jacques Derrida's 'Specters of Marx'*, London, Verso, 1999.

Joffrin, Laurence, 'La Fiction Identitaire dans l'écriture migrante au Québec: Présentation liminaire', in Mathieu (ed.), *Littératures autobiographiques de la francophonie*.

Jolly, Margaretta (ed.), *Encyclopaedia of Life Writing*, Chicago and London, Fitzroy Dearborn, 2001.

Kacimi, Mohammed, 'Langue de Dieu et langue du Je', *Autrement*, 'World' series, 60 (March 1992), special issue 'Algérie 30 ans'.

Kaplan, Mordecai M., *Dynamic Judaism*, New York, Fordham University Press, 1985.

Khadda, Naget, 'Autobiographie et structuration du sujet acculturé dans *Le Fils du pauvre* de Mouloud Feraoun', *Itinéraires et Contacts de Cultures*, 13 (1991), special issue, *Autobiographies et récits de vie en Afrique*, pp. 79–85.

Khatibi, Abdelkébir (with J. Arnaud, J. Déjeux and R. Arlette Roth), *Anthologie des écrivains maghrébins d'expression française*, Paris, Présence Africaine, 1964.

Khatibi, Adbelkébir, *Le Roman maghrébin*, Paris, Maspéro, 1968.

— *La Blessure du nom propre*, Paris, Denoël, 1974.

— interview, *Pro-Culture* (Rabat), no. 12 (1976).

— *Lamatif* (Casablanca), no. 25 (January 1977).

— *Le Livre du sang*, Paris, Gallimard (1979), 1986.

— *Al Assa* (Rabat), no. 17 (February 1980).

— *Amour bilangue*, Montpellier, Fata Morgana, 1983.

— *Maghreb pluriel*, Paris, Denoël, 1983.

— *Par-dessus l'épaule*, Paris, Aubier, 1988.

— *Francophonie et idiomes littéraires*, Rabat, Al Kalam, 1989.

— *Un Eté à Stockholm*, Paris, Flammarion, 1990.

— 'Le Métissage culturel', Manifeste, *Abdelkébir Khatibi*, Casablanca, Al Asa-Okad, 1990.

— 'Diglossia', trans. Whitney Stanford, in Berger (ed.), *Algeria in Others' Languages*.

Kiberd, Declan, *Inventing Ireland*, London, Jonathan Cape, 1995.

Kilito, Abdelfattah, *Les Séances: Récits et codes culturels chez Hamadhani et Hariri*, Paris, Sinbad, 1983.

Kilpatrick, Hilary, 'Autobiography and Classical Arabic Literature', *Journal of Arabic Literature*, 22.1 (1991).

Laroui, Abdallah, *L'Idéologie arabe contemporaine*, Paris, Maspero, 1967.

Lazarus, Neil, 'National Consciousness and the Specificity of (Post) Colonial Intellectualism', in Barker, Hulme and Iversen (eds), *Colonial Discourse/Postcolonial Theory*.

Lecarme, Jacques, and Eliane Lecarme-Tabone, *L'Autobiographie*, Paris, Armand Colin, 1997.

Leiris, Michel, *L'Age d'homme*, Paris, Gallimard, 1939.

— '...Reusement!', in *Biffures, La Règle du jeu I*, Paris, Gallimard, 1948.

— 'Glossaire, j'y serre mes gloses' (1939), in *Mots sans mémoire*, Paris, Gallimard, 1969.

Lejeune, Philippe, *L'Autobiographie en France*, Paris, Armand Colin, 1971.

— *Le Pacte autobiographique*, Paris, Seuil, 1975.

— *Je est un autre: L'autobiographie, de la littérature aux médias*, Paris, Seuil, 1980.

— *Moi aussi*, Paris, Seuil, 1986.

Lionnet, Françoise, *Autobiographical Voices: Race, Gender, Self-Portraiture*, Ithaca, NY, Cornell University Press, 1989.

— 'Of Mangoes and Maroons: Language, History and the Multicultural Subject of Michelle Cliff's *Abeng*', in Smith and Watson (eds), *De/Colonising the Subject: The Politics of Gender in Women's Autobiography*.

— 'Questions de méthode: itinéraires ourlés de l'autoportrait et de la critique', in Ruhe and Hornung (eds), *Postcolonialisme et Autobiographie*.

Little, Roger, 'La Francographie: A New Model for "La *Francophonie*"', in Christine O'Dowd-Smyth (ed.), *Littératures francophones: la problématique de l'altérité*, Waterford, WIT School of Humanities Publications, 2001.

Lloyd, Cathie, 'Race and Ethnicity', in Cook and Davie (eds), *Modern France: Society in Transition*.

Loomba, Ania, *Colonialism/Postcolonialism*, London, Routledge, 1998.

Maalouf, Amin, *Les Identités meurtrières*, Paris, Grasset, 1998.

Majumdar, Margaret (ed.), *Francophone Studies: The Essential Glossary*, London, Arnold, 2002.

Malti-Douglas, Fedwa, *Blindness and Autobiography*, Princeton, NJ, Princeton University Press, 1988.

Mandell, Barret, 'Full of Life Now', in Olney (ed.), *Autobiography: Essays Theoretical and Critical*.

Martin, Biddy, 'Lesbian Identity and Autobiographical Difference(s)', in Brodzki and Schenck (eds), *Life/Lines: Theorising Women's Autobiography*.

Marx-Scouras, Danielle, 'Muffled Screams/Stifled Voices', *Yale French Studies*, 83 (1993), *Post/Colonial Conditions*, ed. F. Lionnet and R. Scharfman, pp. 172–82.

Mason, Mary G., 'The Other Voice: Autobiographies of Women Writers', in Brodzki and Schenck (eds), *Life/Lines: Theorising Women's Autobiography*.

Mathieu, Martine (ed.), *Littératures autobiographiques de la Francophonie*, Paris, L'Harmattan, 1996.

McCleod, John, 'Contesting Contexts: Francophone Thought and Anglophone Postcolonialism' in Forsdick and Murphy (eds), *Francophone Postcolonial Studies*.

McClintock, Anne, 'The Angel of Progress: The Pitfalls of the Term "Postcolonialism"', in Barker, Hulme and Iversen (eds), *Colonial Discourse/Postcolonial Theory*.

McNeece, Lucy Stone, 'Decolonizing the Sign: Language and Identity in Abdelkébir Khatibi's *La Mémoire tatouée*', *Yale French Studies*, 83 (1993), *Post/Colonial Conditions*, ed. F. Lionnet and R. Scharfman, pp. 17–29.

— 'Rescripting Modernity: Abdelkébir Khatibi and the Archaeology of Signs', in Mildred Mortimer (ed.), *Maghrebian Mosaic: A Literature in Transition*,

London, Lynne Rienner, 2001.

Mdarhri-Alaoui, Abdallah, 'Abdelkébir Khatibi: Writing a Dynamic Identity', *Research in African Literatures*, 23.2 (Summer 1992), pp. 55–64.

Memmes, Abdallah, *Abdelkébir Khatibi: L'écriture de la dualité*, Paris, L'Harmattan, 1994.

Memmi, Albert, *Agar*, Paris, Buchet-Chastel, 1955.

— *Portrait du colonisé*, précédé de *Portrait du colonisateur* (1957), Paris, Gallimard, 1985.

— *Portrait d'un juif*, Paris, Gallimard (1962), 1969.

— 'Autoportrait', *Souffles*, no. 6 (1967).

— *Entretiens (avec Robert Davies)*, Montréal, L'Etincelle, 1975.

— *La Terre Intérieure (entretiens avec Victor Malka)*, Paris, Gallimard, 1976.

— *Le Désert*, Paris, Gallimard, 1977.

— *La Dépendance*, Paris, Gallimard, 1993 (1979).

— *Ce que je crois*, Paris, Grasset, 1985.

— *Le Pharaon*, Paris, Julliard, 1988.

— *Bonheurs*, Paris, Arléa, 1992.

— *Ah, quel bonheur!*, Paris, Arléa, 1995.

— *Le Juif et l'autre (propos recueillis par M. Chavardès et F. Kasbi)*, Paris, Christian de Bartillat, 1995.

— *L'Exercice du bonheur*, Paris, Arléa, 1998.

— *Le Nomade immobile*, Paris, Arléa, 2000.

Memmi, Georges, *Qui se souvient du café Reubens?*, Paris, Lattès, 1984.

Mernissi, Fatima, *Le Harem politique*, Paris, Albin Michel, 1987.

Middleton, Peter, and Tim Woods, *Literatures of Memory: History, Time and Space in Postwar Writing*, Manchester, Manchester University Press, 2000.

Miller, Christopher, *Theories of Africans: Francophone Literature and Anthropology in Africa*, Chicago and London, University of Chicago Press, 1990.

Miller, Nancy K., 'Writing Fictions: Women's Autobiography in France', in Brodzki and Schenck (eds), *Life/Lines: Theorising Women's Autobiography*.

— 'Arachnologies: The Woman, the Text, and the Critic', in *Subject to Change: Reading Feminist Writing*, New York, Columbia University Press, 1988.

Misch, Georg, *Geschichte der Autobiographie*, Frankfurt, Verlag G. Schulte-Bulmke, 1962.

Mol, Hans, *Identity and the Sacred: A Sketch for a New Social-Scientific Theory of Religion*, New York, The Free Press, 1976.

Moore-Gilbert, Bart, *Postcolonial Theory: Contexts, Practices, Politics*, London and New York, Verso, 1997.

Moura, Jean-Marc, *Littératures francophones et théorie postcoloniale*, Paris, PUF, 1999.

Murdoch, H. Adlai, 'Rewriting Writing: Identity, Exile and Renewal in Assia Djebar's *L'Amour, la fantasia*', *Yale French Studies*, 83 (1993), *Post/Colonial Conditions*, ed. F. Lionnet and R. Scharfman, pp. 71–92.

Murphy, David, *Sembene: Imagining Alternatives in Film and Fiction*, Trenton, NJ, First Africa World Press, 2001.

Neather, Ted, 'Education and Training', in Cook and Davie (eds), *Modern France: Society in Transition*.

Nolin, Corinne, 'Nomadisme et généalogie: Albert Memmi ou la condition impossible', in Ruhe and Hornung (eds), *Postcolonialisme et Autobiographie*.

Nowaira, Amira Hassan, 'Arabic Autobiography', in Jolly (ed.), *Encyclopaedia of Life Writing*.

Offord, Malcolm, Laïla Ibnlfassi, Nicki Hitchcott, Sam Haigh and Rosemary

Chapman (eds), *Francophone Literatures: A Literary and Linguistic Companion*, London and New York, Routledge, 2001.

Olney, James (ed.), *Autobiography: Essays Theoretical and Critical*, Princeton, NJ, Princeton University Press, 1980.

— *Studies in Autobiography*, Oxford, Oxford University Press, 1988.

Orlando, Valérie, *Nomadic Voices of Exile: Feminine Identity in Francophone Literature of the Maghreb*, Athens, OH, Ohio University Press, 1999.

Ostle, Robin, Ed de Moor and Stefan Wild (eds), *Writing the Self: Autobiographical Writing in Modern Arabic Literature*, London, Saqi Books, 1998.

Parker, Gabrielle, '"Francophonie" and "Universalité": Evolution of Two Notions Conjoined', in Forsdick and Murphy (eds), *Francophone Postcolonial Studies*.

Philipp, Thomas, 'The Autobiography in Modern Arab Literature and Culture', *Poetics Today*, 14.3 (Fall 1993).

Phillips, Ruth B., and Christopher B. Steiner (eds), *Unpacking Culture: Art and Commodity in Colonial and Postcolonial Worlds*, Berkeley, University of California Press, 1999.

Proust, Marcel, *A la recherche du temps perdu*, Paris, Gallimard, 1927.

Ramadan, Tariq, 'Quel humanisme pour l'islam?', talk given at the Eglise Réformée d'Auteuil, 10 March 2001 and available at http://www.erf-auteuil.org/conferences/quel-humanisme-pour-l-islam.html

Regaïeg, Najiba, 'L'Amour, la fantasia d'Assia Djebar: de l'autobiographie à la fiction', *Itinéraires et contacts de cultures, Nouvelles Approches des textes littéraires maghrébins ou migrants*, 27 (1999), pp. 129–35.

Revue CELFAN/CELFAN Review, Special Issue on Abdelkébir Khatibi, 8.1–2 (Nov. 1988–Feb. 1989).

Reynolds, Dwight (ed.), *Interpreting the Self: Autobiography in the Arabic Literary Tradition*, Berkeley, University of California Press, 2000.

Ricœur, Paul, *Time and Narrative*, II, Chicago, University of Chicago Press, 1985.

— *La Mémoire, l'histoire, l'oubli*, Paris, Le Seuil, 2000.

Rippin, Andrew, *Muslims: Their Religious Beliefs and Practices*, London and New York, Routledge, 2001.

Robbe-Grillet, Alain, *Pour un nouveau roman*, Paris, Minuit, 1963.

Roblès, Emmanuel, *Les Hauteurs de la ville*, Paris, Le Seuil, 1948.

Rooke, Tetz, *In My Childhood: A Study of Arabic Autobiography*, Stockholm, Stockholm University, 1997.

Rosello, Mireille, 'Tactical Universalism and New Multiculturalist Claims in Postcolonial France', in Forsdick and Murphy (eds), *Francophone Postcolonial Studies*.

Rosenblatt, Roger, 'Black Autobiography: Life as the Death Weapon', in Olney (ed.), *Autobiography: Essays Theoretical and Critical*.

Rosenthal, Franz, 'Die arabische Autobiographie', *Studia Arabica*, Rome, Pontificium Institutum Biblicum, 1937, reprinted in Rosenthal, *Muslim Intellectual and Social Life*.

— *Muslim Intellectual and Social Life: A Collection of Essays*, Aldershot, Variorum, 1990.

Rousso, Henry, *Le Syndrome de Vichy de 1944 à nos jours*, Paris, Editions du Seuil, rev. edn, 1990 (1987).

Ruhe, Doris, 'Le Scorpion en phénix: l'écriture autobiographique d'Albert Memmi', in Ruhe and Hornung (eds), *Postcolonialisme et Autobiographie*.

Ruhe, Ernstpeter, 'Les Mots, l'amour, la mort: les mythomorphoses d'Assia Djebar', in Ruhe and Hornung (eds), *Postcolonialisme et Autobiographie*.

Ruhe, Ernstpeter, and Alfred Hornung (eds), *Postcolonialisme et Autobiographie*,

Amsterdam, Rodopi, 1998.
Saadi-Mokrane, Djamila, 'The Algerian Linguicide', in Berger (ed.), *Algeria in Others' Languages.*
Said, Edward, 'Figures, Configurations, Transfigurations', *Race and Class*, 32.1 (1990), pp. 1–16.
— *Freud and the Non-European*, London and New York, Verso, 2003.
Salhi, Zahia Smail, *Politics, Poetics and the Algerian Novel*, Lampeter, Edwin Mellen, 1999.
Sartre, Jean-Paul, *La Nausée*, Paris, Gallimard, 1938.
Scarry, Elaine, *The Body in Pain*, New York and Oxford, Oxford University Press, 1985.
Sheringham, Michael, *French Autobiography: Devices and Desires*, Oxford, Clarendon Press, 1993.
Silverman, Max, *Deconstructing the Nation: Immigration, Racism and Citizenship in France*, London and New York, Routledge, 1992.
Slemon, Stephen, 'The Scramble for Post-Colonialism', in Tiffin and Lawson (eds), *De-Scribing Empire: Post-Colonialism and Textuality.*
Smith, Sidonie, and Julia Watson (eds), *De/Colonising the Subject: The Politics of Gender in Women's Autobiography*, Minneapolis, University of Minnesota Press, 1992.
Somner, Doris, 'Not Just a Personal Story: Women's Testimonies and the Plural Self', in Brodzki and Schenck (eds), *Life/Lines: Theorising Women's Autobiography.*
Spivak, Gayatri Chakravorty, 'Can the Subaltern Speak?', in Williams and Chrisman (eds), *Colonial Discourse and Post-Colonial Theory: A Reader.*
— 'How to Read a "Culturally Different" Book', in Barker, Hulme and Iversen (eds), *Colonial Discourse/Postcolonial Theory.*
Sprinker, Michael, 'Fictions of the Self: The End of Autobiography', in Olney (ed.), *Autobiography: Essays Theoretical and Critical.*
Starobinski, Jean, 'Le Style de l'autobiographie', *Poétique*, no. 3. (1970).
Stevens, Mary, 'Assia Djebar's Buried Treasure: The Relationship between Cultural Capital and Cultural Memory in *L'Amour, la fantasia* and *Vaste est la prison* as Explored in the Use of Epigraphs' (unpublished MS).
Tarr, Carrie, 'French Cinema and Post-Colonial Minorities', in Hargreaves and McKinney (eds), *Post-Colonial Cultures in France.*
Thiong'o, Ngugi wa, *Decolonising the Mind: The Politics of Language in African Literature*, London, James Curry, 1986.
Tiffin, Chris, and Alan Lawson (eds), *De-Scribing Empire: Post-Colonialism and Textuality*, London and New York, Routledge, 1994.
Vitray-Meyerovitch, Eva de, *Anthologie du soufisme*, Paris, Albin Michel, 1995 (1978).
Wahbi, Hassan, *Les Mots du monde: Khatibi et le récit*, Agadir, Université Ibnou Zohr, Publications de la Faculté des Lettres et Sciences Humaines, Série thèses et mémoires, no. 3, 1995.
Weintraub, Karl, *The Value of the Individual: Self and Circumstance in Autobiography*, Chicago, University of Chicago Press, 1978.
Williams, Patrick, and Laura Chrisman (eds), *Colonial Discourse and Post-Colonial Theory: A Reader*, Hemel Hempstead, Harvester Wheatsheaf, 1993.
Woodhull, Winifred, *Transfigurations of the Maghreb: Feminism, Decolonisation and Liberation*, Minneapolis, University of Minnesota Press, 1993.
— 'Postcolonial Thought and Culture in Francophone North Africa', in Forsdick and Murphy (eds), *Francophone Postcolonial Studies.*
Young, Robert, *White Mythologies: Writing History and the West*, London and New

York, Routledge, 1990.
— *Colonial Desire: Hybridity in Theory, Culture and Race*, London and New York, Routledge, 1995.
— *Postcolonialism: An Historical Introduction*, Oxford, Blackwell, 2001.
Yudkin, Leon I., *Jewish Writing and Identity in the Twentieth Century*, London, Croom Helm, 1982.
Zimra, Clarisse, 'Autobiographie et Je/Jeux d'espace: Architecture de l'imaginaire dans le *Quatuor* d'Assia Djebar', in Ruhe and Hornung (eds), *Postcolonialisme et Autobiographie*.
— 'Afterword', in Assia Djebar, *Women of Algiers in their Apartment*, trans. Marjolijn de Jager, Charlottesville, VA, and London, University of Virginia Press (Caraf Books), 1992. American translation of *Femmes d'Alger dans leur appartement*.

FILMS

Dehane, Kamal, director: *Femmes d'Alger*, le Centre de l'Audiovisuel à Bruxelles; l'Entreprise Nationale de Production Audiovisuelle (Alger); l'Unité Documentaire 'Traces' Zeaux Productions (Paris), 1992 (RTBF).
— *Assia Djebar: Entre ombre et soleil*, le Centre de l'Audiovisuel à Bruxelles; l'Entreprise Nationale de Production Audiovisuelle (Alger); l'Unité Documentaire 'Traces' Zeaux Productions (Paris), 1992 (RTBF).

Index